D1613832

SHADERX⁷:
ADVANCED RENDERING TECHNIQUES

WOLFGANG ENGEL

Charles River Media
A part of Course Technology, Cengage Learning

COURSE TECHNOLOGY
CENGAGE Learning™

Australia, Brazil, Japan, Korea, Mexico, Singapore, Spain, United Kingdom, United States

COURSE TECHNOLOGY
CENGAGE Learning™

ShaderX7: Advanced Rendering Techniques
Wolfgang Engel

Publisher and General Manager,
Course Technology PTR: Stacy L. Hiquet

Associate Director of Marketing: Sarah Panella

Content Project Manager: Jessica McNavich

Marketing Manager: Jordan Casey

Senior Acquisitions Editor: Emi Smith

Project Editor: Kate Shoup

Editorial Services Coordinator: Jen Blaney

Copy Editor: Ruth Saavedra

Interior Layout: Shawn Morningstar

Cover Designer: Mike Tanamachi

DVD-ROM Producer: Brandon Penticuff

Indexer: Broccoli Information Management

Proofreader: Mike Beady, Dan Foster

Printed in the United States of America
1 2 3 4 5 6 7 11 10 09

For product information and technology assistance, contact us at
Cengage Learning Customer and Sales Support,
1-800-354-9706.

For permission to use material from this text or product, submit all requests online at
cengage.com/permissions.

Further permissions questions can be e-mailed to
permissionrequest@cengage.com.

All trademarks are the property of their respective owners.

Library of Congress Control Number: 2008932485
ISBN-13: 978-1-58450-598-3
ISBN-10: 1-58450-598-2

Course Technology, a part of Cengage Learning
20 Channel Center Street
Boston, MA 02210
USA

Cengage Learning is a leading provider of customized learning solutions with office locations around the globe, including Singapore, the United Kingdom, Australia, Mexico, Brazil, and Japan. Locate your local office at:
international.cengage.com/region.

Cengage Learning products are represented in Canada by Nelson Education, Ltd.

For your lifelong learning solutions, visit **courseptr.com.**
Visit our corporate Web site at **cengage.com.**

To my wife Katja and my daughters Anna, Emma, and Lena

—Wolfgang

Acknowledgments

The talented editors and contributors of this book spent eight months writing, selecting, editing, and finalizing the articles for the newest volume of the best-selling *ShaderX* series. We hope you find these state-of-the-art graphics-programming articles useful in your own work. As with all the other *ShaderX* books, the topics here cover ready-to-use ideas and procedures that can solve many of your daily graphics-programming challenges.

I would like to thank the section editors for the fantastic job they did. The work of Kenneth Hurley, Wessam Bahnassi, Sebastien St. Laurent, Natalya Tatarchuk, Carsten Dachsbacher, Matthias Wloka, Christopher Oat, and Sam Martin ensures that the quality of the series stands up to the expectations of our readers.

The great cover screenshots were taken from GTA IV. I want to thank Sam Hauser for allowing us to use those shots. I am especially proud of those shots because this is the second game from Rockstar that I contributed to. Those shots are also used to illustrate a shadowing technique covered in the article "Facetted Shadow Mapping for Large Dynamic Game Environments" by Ray Tran.

The team at Charles River Media made the whole project happen. I want to thank Emi Smith, Jennifer Blaney, and the whole production team, who took the articles and made them into a book.

Special thanks go out to our families and friends, who spent many evenings and weekends during the long book production cycle without us.

I hope you have as much fun reading the book as we had creating it.

Wolfgang Engel

P.S: Plans for an upcoming *ShaderX⁸* are already in progress. Any comments, proposals, and suggestions are highly welcome (wolf@shaderx.com).

About the Section Editors

Wessam Bahnassi's professional career began about eight years ago, when he started the development of the DirectSkeleton real-time 3D engine and its pipeline tools for In|Framez. He led the development team for several games and real-time demos based on the same engine, in addition to his many contributions and publications in graphics and programming in general. Wessam has been a Microsoft Most Valuable Professional (MVP) for DirectX technologies for four years. Currently, he works at Electronic Arts in Montreal, doing console and PC graphics and game programming for some of EA's great titles.

Carsten Dachsbacher is a postdoctoral fellow at REVES/INRIA in Sophia-Antipolis, France. His research focuses on interactive and hardware-assisted computer graphics. In particular, he is working on interactive global illumination techniques, procedural models, and point-based rendering. He worked as a freelancer for various (game) companies, programming mainly real-time 3D graphics, and has published some of his work at conferences and in books and magazines.

Wolfgang Engel works in Rockstar's core technology group as the lead graphics programmer. He is the editor of the *ShaderX* books, is the author of several other books, and loves to talk about graphics programming. He has been an MVP DirectX since July 2006 and is active in several advisory boards in the industry.

Kenneth Hurley has worked for game and technology companies such as Electronic Arts and Intel, and most recently was a senior engineer at NVIDIA Corporation. While there, he participated in the areas of Xbox hardware and numerous video games including *Tiger Woods Golf*. Kenneth has been a consultant for several Silicon Valley companies and has worked with the United States government on military equipment, including the highly acclaimed Land Warrior. Kenneth's passion for and more than 20 years of experience in the gaming industry is what has brought him to the helm of Signature Devices, his second start-up as an independent developer. He has contributed to best-selling computer books on 3D graphics and is a requested speaker at conventions and workshops around the country. Kenneth received his BS degree in computer science from the University of Maryland.

Sam Martin is the lead programmer of Enlighten at Geomerics. There, he fell in love with lighting as he nurtured their real-time radiosity SDK from its conception. In a previous relationship with computational geometry, he developed the navigation system behind Lionhead's *Black & White 2*, a tale he may put on paper someday. There was also a fling with Lionhead's early core tech team, and he hasn't forgotten the good times he had with Intrepid and Kuju London. His relationship with patterns and algorithms is going strong, but the temptations of drumming in samba bands and Cambridge beers have been known to lead him astray.

Christopher Oat is a member of AMD's game computing applications group, where he is a technical lead working on state-of-the art demos. In this role, he focuses on the development of cutting-edge rendering techniques for the latest graphics platforms. Christopher has published his work in various books and journals and has presented work at graphics and game developer conferences around the world. Many of the projects Christopher has worked on may be found at www.chrisoat.com.

Sebastien St-Laurent holds a degree in computer engineering from Sherbrooke University in Quebec (Canada), where he graduated at the top of his class in 1999. Since then, he has worked on many video-game titles, including *Space Invaders*, *Dave Mira Freestyle BMX*, *Dave Mira Freestyle BMX2*, *Aggressive Inline*, and *BMX XXX*. Sebastien is now employed by Microsoft Corporation, where he is a graphics developer for the Microsoft Game Studios. Sebastien is a published author whose works include *Shaders for Game Programmers and Artists* and *The COMPLETE Effect and HLSL Guide*.

Natalya Tatarchuk is a graphics software architect and a project lead in the game computing application group at AMD GPG Office of the CTO. Her passion lies in pushing hardware boundaries, investigating innovative graphics techniques, and creating striking interactive renderings. In the past, she was the lead for the tools group at ATI Research, worked on 3D modeling software, and worked on scientific visualization libraries, among other projects. She has published papers in various computer graphics conferences and articles in technical book series such as *ShaderX* and *Game Programming Gems*, and has presented talks at SIGGRAPH and at Game Developers Conferences worldwide. Natalya holds BAs in computer science and mathematics from Boston University and an MS in computer science from Harvard University.

Matthias Wloka is a senior graphics engineer in the technology group at Visual Concepts, where he contributes to the *2K Sports* series of games. His primary responsibility is to enhance a game's look via advanced shading techniques, such as the unique players' sweat technology featured in the national TV commercial "Sweat" for *NBA 2K6*. Prior to working at Visual Concepts, Matthias was a member of NVIDIA's technical developer relations team, a chief technologist at GameFX/THQ, Inc., and a computer scientist at Fraunhofer CRCG. He received an MS in computer science from Brown University and a BS from Christian Albrechts University in Kiel, Germany. Matthias has presented at multiple conferences such as GDC, Microsoft's Meltdown events, and Eurographics, and is the author of multiple articles about real-time 3D graphics.

About the Authors

Marcos Avilés holds his telecommunication engineering and M.Phil. degrees from the Universidad Politécnica de Madrid, where he currently works as a research engineer. His main interests include (GPU-assisted) geometry processing and global illumination algorithms.

Louis Bavoil received his education in Computer Graphics from University of Utah. He is now a developer technology engineer at NVIDIA.

Kristof Beets is business development manager for POWERVR Graphics in the business development group at Imagination Technologies. In this role, he leads the overall graphics business promotion and marketing efforts, as well as leading the in-house demo development team. Previously, he managed the POWERVR Insider ecosystem and started work as a development engineer on SDKs and tools for both PC and mobile products as a member of the POWERVR Developer Relations Team. Kristof has a first degree in electrical engineering and a master's degree in artificial intelligence, both from the University of Leuven, Belgium. Previous articles and tutorials have been published in *ShaderX²*, ShaderX⁵, and ShaderX⁶, *ARM IQ Magazine*, and online by the Khronos Group, Beyond3D, and 3Dfx Interactive.

Bedřich Beneš is an assistant professor in the department of computer graphics technology at Purdue University. His research interests include procedural modeling, artificial life, real-time rendering, and global illumination. Dr. Beneš received his Ph.D. from the Czech Technical University. He is a member of ACM SIGGRAPH, Eurographics, and IEEE.

Allan Bentham caught the programming bug from an Acorn Electron and since then has had a passion for game development. His professional career in games development began over a decade ago. He now works as a senior renderer programmer at Ubisoft, specializing in cross-platform architecture for the PC and major consoles. His hobby is reliving the past by creating home-brew remakes of old games using the cutting-edge technology of today's powerful GPUs.

Jiří Bittner is a researcher at the department of computer science and engineering at the Czech Technical University in Prague. He received his Ph.D. in 2003 at the same institute. He has participated in commercial projects dealing with real-time rendering of complex scenes. His research interests include visibility computations, real-time rendering, spatial data structures, and global illumination.

Charlie Birtwistle started programming in the mid 1990s on the BBC Micro and Acorn Archimedes. He is currently a graphics programmer at Bizarre Creations, Liverpool. As a member of Bizarre's core technology team, he has worked on particle systems, post processing, and various specialist effects across a variety of projects since the Xbox 360 launch title, *Project Gotham Racing 3*. He received a first-class honors degree in computing (visualisation) from Sheffield Hallam University in 2005.

Dave Bookout received his BA from Purdue University and his MS from the Oregon Graduate Institute with a focus on adaptive systems. Currently, he is a graphics software engineer in Intel Corporation's visual computing software division.

Emmanuel Briney began assembly in 1988 on an Amiga 500. He received a Ph.D. in electromagnetism in 2002. He worked at Eko System (2005–2007) as the main next-gen 3D engine and R&D programmer. He has focused his research on ambient occlusion, shadows, and HDR. Since mid-2007, he has worked at MKO Games and develops more general solutions to integrate real-time global illumination and next-gen effects for PC, Xbox360, and PS3.

Ken Catterall graduated from the University of Toronto in 2005 as a specialist in software engineering, where he developed an interest in computer graphics. Subsequently he has been working at Imagination Technologies as a business development engineer. Ken has worked on a wide range of 3D demos for Imagination's POWERVR Insider ecosystem program as well as supporting Imagination's network of developer partners.

Victor Ceitelis started programming on the Atari 520 STF in the late 1980s, coding in a demo-maker group. In the game industry since 2000, he has completed one PlayStation game for Infogrammes and one PC game for Cyanide Studio. He joined Mko Games in 2006, and started working in the R&D department in 2007. His main interests are real-time computer graphics, pipeline production, and optimization. In his spare time, he enjoys playing loud guitar with his band and spending time with his children, Stellio and Leïana.

Mark Colbert is currently a research and development engineer for ImageMovers Digital. He holds a Ph.D. in computer science from the University of Central Florida and his research interests include real-time rendering and interfaces for lighting and material design.

Stephen Coy has been working in computer graphics for more than 20 years. He received an MS (1991) and BS (1985) in computer science from Pacific Lutheran University. Currently, Stephen works for Microsoft Research on a project designed to provide children with a gentle introduction to programming concepts in a game environment. Previous projects at Microsoft include writing screensavers for Vista, 3D UI prototyping, 3D graphics and lighting for Office, Xbox and PC game development, porting the first version of Softimage 3D for NT, and being part of the Direct3D team (DX5 and DX6). In a previous life he was employed by Boeing, where he worked on a large-scale CAD visualization tool, image processing for a kinetic kill vehicle and a flight simulator. While there, he co-authored *Photorealism and Ray Tracing in C,* based on his shareware ray tracer Vivid.

Just after getting his computer science and graphic research masters, **David Crémoux** was the main research and development engineer in a two-year project on physical and realistic rendering between the graphic computer science laboratory SIC-SP2MI in Poitiers, France and Agfa Gevaert Physics and Analytics Department in Antwerp, Belgium. Then he oriented himself on video games, beginning with mobile phone games development at Vivendi Games. He's currently working in the 3D department at Mko Games as a 3D engineer on next-gen effects on PC, Xbox360, and PlayStation 3.

João Luiz Dihl Comba received a BS degree in computer science from the Federal University of Rio Grande do Sul, Brazil, an MS degree in computer science from the Federal University of Rio de Janeiro, Brazil, and a Ph.D. degree in computer science from Stanford University. He is an associate professor of computer science at the Federal University of Rio Grande do Sul, Brazil. His main research interests are in graphics, visualization, spatial data structures, and applied computational geometry. His current projects include the development of algorithms for large-scale scientific visualization, data structures for point-based modeling and rendering, and general-purpose computing using graphics hardware. He is a member of the ACM Siggraph.

Carlos Augusto Dietrich received a BS degree in computer science from the Federal University of Santa Maria, Brazil, and an MS degree in computer science from the Federal University of Rio Grande do Sul, Brazil. His research interests include graphics, visualization, and the use of GPUs as general-purpose processors. He is currently a third-year Ph.D. student working in the computer graphics group at the Federal University of Rio Grande do Sul, Brazil.

Lukas Gruber's enthusiasm for 3D graphics arose in 2003, when he implemented a real-time program based on Pure-Data that is targeted toward live performances. In 2006, he received his BS degree in telematics at the University of Technology of Graz (TUG). For three years he has been software developer at Bongfish Interactive Entertainment, working in various fields of game development. In 2008 he joined the augmented reality mobile group at the Institute for Computer Graphics and Vision (TUG) in Graz.

Takahiro Harada works for Havok. Before moving to Ireland, he was an assistant professor at the University of Tokyo. He received an MS in engineering from the University of Tokyo in 2006. His research interests include physically based simulation, real-time simulation, and general-purpose GPU computation.

Jaroslav Křivánek is a visiting researcher at the Cornell University Program of Computer Graphics. Prior to this appointment, he worked as assistant professor at the Czech Technical University in Prague. He received his Ph.D. from IRISA/INRIA Rennes and the Czech Technical University (joint degree) in 2005. In 2003 and 2004 he was a research associate at the University of Central Florida. He received a masters in computer science from the Czech Technical University in Prague in 2001. Jaroslav's research focuses mainly on realistic rendering and global illumination.

Chi-Sing Leung has been working on image-based rendering for more than 10 years. He was a GDC 2007 speaker. He proposed a two-level compression method for illumination adjustable images and the corresponding real-time rendering methods (published in IEEE Trans. CSVT 2003, IEEE Trans. Multimedia 2002, and IEEE Trans. Image Processing).

He contributed several game-development–related articles to *ShaderX³* and *ShaderX⁴*. He received the IEEE Transactions on Multimedia 2005 Prize Paper Award for his paper titled "The Plenoptic Illumination Function" (published in IEEE Trans. on Multimedia, Vol. 4, Issue 3, September, 2002). Since 2000, he has provided programming consultancy services to Development Bank of Singapore (Hong Kong).

Xiaopei Liu is a Ph.D. student in the department of computer science and engineering at the Chinese University of Hong Kong. He has been programming for all his graphics-related research projects as well as some software. His research interests include real-time rendering, surface modeling, and image-manipulation techniques.

Oliver Mattausch is a Ph.D. candidate at the Institute of Computer Graphics and Algorithms of the Vienna University of Technology. He received an MS in 2004. He coauthored several papers in the fields of real-time rendering and scientific visualization. His current research interests are real-time rendering, visibility computations, shadow algorithms, and real-time global illumination.

Stephen McAuley is a graphics programmer at Bizarre Creations, where he has worked on titles such as *Project Gotham Racing 4*, *The Club*, and *Boom Boom Rocket*. He graduated with a first-class honors degree in mathematics from Queens' College, University of Cambridge, in 2005 and undertook Part III of the Mathematical Tripos before starting work in the games industry. He also enjoys participating in the demo scene, which originally sparked his interest in real-time computer graphics.

Francisco Morán received his telecommunication engineering and Ph.D. degrees from the Universidad Politécnica de Madrid, where he is now a full-time associate professor. He has worked as a researcher in its Grupo de Tratamiento de Imágenes (Image Processing Group) since 1992, and is interested in the modeling, coding, transmission, and visualization of 3D objects. Since the mid 1990s, he has participated actively in European research projects and in the standardization activities from ISO's Moving Picture Experts Group, where he has (co-)edited several specifications related to 3D graphics coding within MPEG-4.

Luciana Porcher Nedel received a Ph.D. in computer science from Swiss Federal Institute of Technology, Lausanne, Switzerland, under the supervision of Prof. Daniel Thalmann in 1998. She received an MS degree in computer science from the Federal University of Rio Grande do Sul, Brazil and a BS degree in computer science from the Pontifical Catholic University, Brazil. In 2005, during a sabbatical year, she spent two months at Université Paul Sabatier in Toulouse, France, and two months at Université Catholique de Louvain in Louvain-la-Neuve, Belgium doing research on interaction. She is an assistant professor at the Federal University of Rio Grande do Sul, Brazil. Since 1991 she has been involved in computer animation research and since 1996 she has done research in virtual reality. Her current projects include deformation methods, virtual humans simulation, interactive animation, and 3D interaction using virtual reality devices.

Elvis Enmanuel Castillo Nuñez's professional career began 10 years ago in the Spanish game industry doing arcade-machine-to-PC conversions at Hammer Technologies. In 1999 he made exporting tools for PyroStudio's *Heart of Stone* PC game. After that, he worked in three gambling-related companies, where he did openGL and DirectX 3D programming and some PlayStation games. He also worked developing newer techniques for LOD, ambient occlusion, and ray-traced shadows for visualization of high detailed architectural scenes in real-time for M2Group. Presently, he works for Indra, a Spanish consulting company, developing tactical simulators for the defense sector.

Ben Padget has been in the games industry since 1999 in a career spanning two millennia. He is currently a senior graphics programmer at Rockstar San Diego, where he works on the *Midnight Club* game series.

David Pangerl's addiction to computers and games started early in life and the vision to create virtual worlds continues to be the strong driver. David is CEO of ActaLogic, a new game development company he founded in 2008. Currently he is working on the new next-gen game engine (http://www.evilm3.com/insomnia/devdiary.php).

Shaun Ramsey is an assistant professor at Washington College, located in Chestertown, MD, in the department of mathematics and computer science. His research interests include ray-tracing, real-time rendering, and realistic materials. He is an advocate for undergraduate research and has directed and co-founded undergraduate research programs. For more information, visit http://ramsey.washcoll.edu.

Paul Rohleder has been interested in computer graphics and game programming since he was young. He is very keen on knowing how all things (algorithms) work, then trying to improve them and develop new solutions. Paul started programming simple 3D games and casual games professionally in 2002. He received a masters degree in computer science at Wroclaw University of Technology in 2004. Since 2006, he has worked at Techland as a 3D graphics/engine programmer. Paul is also a Ph.D. student in computer graphics at Wroclaw University of Technology, researching real-time global illumination techniques and natural phenomena effects.

Gilberto Rosado is a graduate of DigiPen Institute of Technology, where he studied video-game programming for four years. While at DigiPen, Gil was the graphics programmer on the 2005 Independent Games Festival finalist, *Kisses*. Gil is currently at Rainbow Studios, where he works as a graphics and technology programmer on the *MX vs. ATV* series. He has also been published in *ShaderX⁴* and *GPU Gems 3*. When not playing the latest games, you might find Gil at the gym working out or at the local dance studio practicing his salsa moves.

Dieter Schmalstieg is full professor of virtual reality and computer graphics at Graz University of Technology, Austria, where he directs the Studierstube research project on augmented reality. His current research interests are augmented reality, virtual reality, distributed graphics, 3D user interfaces, and ubiquitous computing. He is author and co-author of more than 140 reviewed scientific publications, member of the editorial advisory board, member of computers and graphics, and member of the steering committee of the IEEE International Symposium on Mixed and Augmented Reality.

Andrew Senior graduated from the University of Teesside in 2007, where he received a BS in Visualisation. After graduation, he started work for Imagination Technologies, where he is now developing shader-based demos for embedded devices using OpenGL ES.

Ondřej Šťava is a Ph.D. student at Purdue University in the department of computer graphics technology. He received his masters degree at Czech Technical University in Prague in 2007. His main interests include GPU programming, applied mathematics, and good beer.

Nicolas Thibieroz is part of the European developer relations team for graphics products at AMD Corporation. He started programming on a Commodore 64 and an Amstrad CPC before moving on to the PC world, where he realized the potential of real-time 3D graphics while playing *Ultima Underworld*. After obtaining a BS in electronic engineering in 1996, he joined PowerVR Technologies, where he occupied the role of developer relations manager, supporting game developers on a variety of platforms and contributing to SDK content. His current position at AMD involves helping developers optimize the performance of their games and educating them about the advanced features found in cutting-edge graphics hardware.

Ray Tran works as a senior graphics programmer at Rockstar North, where he most recently worked on *Grand Theft Auto IV*. Prior to joining Rockstar North, Ray worked at Core Design on the *Tomb Raider* series of games.

Damian Trebilco works for THQ on graphics and shader-based systems for game engines. He has a first-class honours degree in software engineering from Queensland University of Technology, with his dissertation covering simulating emotion in virtual characters. Previously, Damian worked for Auran, where he wrote the special effects for the *Bridge-IT* NVIDIA demo for the NV30 launch. In his spare time, he works on the OpenGL debugging tool GLIntercept (glintercept.nutty.org)

Daniel Wagner is a Ph.D. researcher at Graz University of Technology. During his studies, he worked as a contract programmer and joined Reality2, developing VR software. After finishing his computer science studies, Daniel was hired as a lead developer by BinaryBee, working on high-quality single- and multi-user Web games. Next, he worked as a developer for Tisc Media, doing 3D engine development. Later, Daniel was hired as a consultant by Greentube for the development of *Ski Challenge '05*. Daniel is currently working on truly mobile augmented reality. His research interests are real-time graphics and massively multi-user augmented reality on mobile devices. He is the head of the Studierstube Handheld AR project.

Liang Wan has been programming for all her research projects, including graphics and computer-vision–related topics. She was a GDC 2007 speaker. She has written several game technology articles, including for *ShaderX⁴* and *ShaderX⁶*, and developed the publicly available demo codes.

Jian Liang Wang received a BE degree in electrical engineering from Beijing Institute of Technology, China, in 1982. He received MSE and Ph.D. degrees in electrical engineering from Johns Hopkins University in 1985 and 1988, respectively. From 1988 to 1990, he was a lecturer with the Department of Automatic Control at Beijing University of Aeronautics and Astronautics, China. Since 1990, he has been with the School of Electrical and Electronic Engineering at Nanyang Technological University, Singapore, where he is currently an associate professor. His current research interests include control of graphics rendering as well as fault-tolerant control, fault detection, and diagnosis, and their application to flight-control-system design. He has published more than 60 international journal papers and more than 100 conference papers. He is a senior member of IEEE and chairman of IEEE (Singapore) Control Systems Chapter. He served as general chair of the sixth IEEE International Conference on Control and Automation in Guangzhou, China, in 2007.

Pat Wilson has been a developer at GarageGames since 2004, where he has worked on engine technology and games. His research interests focus around game-engine design and graphics programming.

Michael Wimmer is an associate professor at the Institute of Computer Graphics and Algorithms of the Vienna University of Technology, where he received an MS in 1997 and a Ph.D. in 2001. His current research interests are real-time rendering, computer games, real-time visualization of urban environments, point-based rendering, and procedural modeling. He has coauthored several scientific papers in these fields. He also teaches courses on 3D computer games and real-time rendering.

Gabriyel Wong heads EON Experience Lab, the research and development arm of EON Reality, a global leader in virtual-reality technology and solutions. Prior to his role as technical director at EON Reality, Gabriyel co-founded Singapore's first and leading game technology R&D lab, gameLAB, at Nanyang Technological University (NTU). He was responsible for building gameLAB's multi-million R&D portfolio spanning several leading game studios around the world. Gabriyel has a wealth of experience in interactive digital media technology from visual simulation to computer games and virtual reality. As a former technical manager with Singapore Technologies, Gabriyel led the pioneering effort to adopt state-of-the-art game technology for military training. A keen believer of innovation, Gabriyel actively contributes, as author and reviewer, to conferences and journals and has lectured on computer game programming at NTU.

Tien-Tsin Wong is a professor in the department of computer science and engineering at the Chinese University of Hong Kong (CUHK). He has been programming for the last 19 years, including writing publicly available codes, libraries, demos, and toolkits, and codes for all his graphics research. He works on GPU techniques, rendering, image-based relighting, natural phenomenon modeling, computerized manga, and multimedia data compression. He is a SIGGRAPH author. He proposed a method to simulate dust accumulation (IEEE CGA 1995) and other surface imperfections (SIGGRAPH 2005). In SIGGRAPH 2006, he proposed a technique on manga colorization. He also proposed the apparent BRDF, one of the earliest techniques for relighting (precomputed lighting) in 1997. Besides academic papers, he has written game-development–related articles in *Graphics Gems V, Graphics Programming Methods,* and *ShaderX³* to *ShaderX⁶*. Recently, he has worked on projects for general-purpose usage of GPU such as evolutionary computing (such as genetic algorithms) and discrete wavelet transform. He has been the recipient of the IEEE Transaction on Multimedia Prize Paper Award (2005) and the CUHK Young Researcher Award (2004).

Chris Wyman is an assistant professor in the department of computer science at the University of Iowa. His interests include real-time rendering, interactive global illumination, interactive rendering of specular materials, visualization, and human perception of graphics renderings. He has a Ph.D. from the University of Utah and a BS from the University of Minnesota, both in computer science. More information is available at his Web page: http://www.cs.uiowa.edu/~cwyman.

Xuemiao Xu is a Ph.D. student at the Chinese University of Hong Kong. Her research interests include real-time rendering, geometry compression, pre-computed radiance transfer, and image-based modeling.

Alexander Zaprjagaev is a co-founder and CTO of Unigine Corp., developer of the cross-platform Unigine engine, which stands on the bleeding edge of the technology. He is also known for his work on http://frustum.org/, a very popular site where programmers have found his state-of-the-art tech demos with free sources since 2002. His sphere of competence includes almost everything related to real-time virtual worlds: 3D graphics (his main passion), physics simulation, GUI, scripting systems, sound, and much more. He holds an MS degree in radiophysics from Tomsk State University, Russia.

Fan Zhang received his Ph.D. from the department of computer science and engineering at the Chinese University of Hong Kong in 2007. His main research interests include image-based rendering, especially real-time shadow rendering and novel rendering techniques for real-time global illumination.

Contents

Part I	**Geometry Manipulation**	**1**

1.1	**Scalar to Polygonal: Extracting Isosurfaces Using Geometry Shaders**	3
	Scalar Fields Versus Polygonal Representation	3
	Isosurface Extraction Using Marching Methods	6
	Hybrid Cubes/Tetrahedra Extraction	7
	Isosurface Extraction Results and Analysis	29

1.2	**Fast High-Quality Rendering with Real-Time Tessellation on GPUs**	33
	GPU Tessellation Pipeline	37
	Programming for GPU Tessellation	41
	Continuous Tessellation Mode	45
	Adaptive Tessellation Mode	48
	Rendering Characters with Tessellation	51
	Designing a Vertex Evaluation Shader for GPU Tessellation	53
	Accessing Per-Vertex Data Beyond Input Structure Declaration	59
	Tessellation API in Direct3D 10	60
	Lighting with Tessellation and Displacement Mapping	60
	Rendering Animated, Tessellated Characters	61
	Displacement Map Tips and Reducing Surface Cracks	68

1.3	**Dynamic Terrain Rendering on GPUs Using Real-Time Tessellation**	73
	Programming for Adaptive GPU Tessellation	76
	Transforming Mesh Using R2VB	79
	Computing Per-Edge Tessellation Factors	83
	Rendering Tessellated Mesh with Per-Edge Tessellation Factors	89
	Shading Tessellated Displaced Surfaces	93
	Performance Analysis	103

1.4	**Adaptive Re-Meshing for Displacement Mapping**	107
	Introduction	107
	Displacement Map	108
	Adaptive Re-Meshing for Displacement Mapping	109
	LOD	112
	Results	114

Implementation   114
Demo   116
Conclusion   116
Endnotes   116

1.5   **Fast Tessellation of Quadrilateral Patches for Dynamic
       Levels of Detail**   **119**
Introduction   119
The Method   120
How Many Strips Will Be Needed?   123
Where Will Each Strip Be Located?   124
How Do We Tessellate Each Strip?   124
A 3D Interpolation to Place Triangle Strips   124
A 2D Interpolation to Tessellate Strips   126
Results   127
Discussion   128

Part II   Rendering Techniques   **131**

2.1   **Quick Noise for GPUs**   **133**
Introduction   133
Background   133
Math to the Rescue   134
Applying It in the Real World   135
And Now the Bad News   137
Implementation, the Sequel   138
Results   140
Future Work   140

2.2   **Efficient Soft Particles**   **143**
Introduction   143
Hard Particles vs. Soft Particles   144
Implementing Soft Particles the Standard Way   145
Optimizing Soft Particles   145
Results   146
Conclusion   147

2.3   **Simplified High-Quality Anti-Aliased Lines**   **149**
Abstract   149
Introduction   149
Method   150

Texture Creation   150
Vertex Setup   152
Variations on the Theme   154
Conclusion   155
Appendix A: The Shader Code   155

2.4   Fast Skin Shading   **161**
Introduction   161
Background and Existing Art   162
Specular and Diffuse   163
Data Preparation   171
Conclusion   172

2.5   An Efficient and Physically Plausible Real-Time Shading Model   **175**
Introduction   175
Review: Blinn-Phong and Cook-Torrance   176
Some Physics of Light-Surface Interaction   178
Toward an Improved Shading Model   179
Mathematical Formulation   180
Appendix   185

2.6   Graphics Techniques in Crackdown   **189**
Introduction   189
Sky   190
Implementation Notes   192
Clutter   193
Outlines   198
Deferred Rendering   201
Vehicle Reflections   205
Implementation Notes   208
Texture Map Setup   209
Conclusion   214
Endnotes   214

2.7   Deferred Rendering Transparency   **217**
Introduction   217
Transparency   218
Overview   219
Rendering   221
Results Discussion   223
Summary and Future Work   224

2.8   Deferred Shading with Multisampling Anti-Aliasing in DirectX 10   **225**
Introduction   225
Deferred Shading Principles   226
MSAA Requirements for Deferred Shading   227
Implementation   231
Assessment of Alternative Implementation   240
Conclusion   242

2.9   Light-Indexed Deferred Rendering   **243**
Introduction   243
Rendering Concept   243
Light-Indexed Deferred Rendering   244
Combining with Other Rendering Techniques   250
Multi-Sample Anti-Aliasing   250
Transparency   252
Shadows   252
Constraining Lights to Surfaces   253
Multi-Light Type Support   254
Lighting Technique Comparison   254
Future Work   255
Conclusion   255

Part III   Image Space   257

3.1   Efficient Post-Processing with Importance Sampling   **259**
Introduction   259
Problem Statement   259
The Approach of Importance Sampling   260
Tone Mapping with Glow   263
Depth of Field   266
Comparisons to Uniform Sampling   275
Conclusion   276

3.2   Efficient Real-Time Motion Blur for Multiple Rigid Objects   **277**
Introduction   277
Overview   278
CPU-Side Work   278
GPU-Side Work   278
Blurring and Halo Fixing   279
Integration with a Post-Processing Pipeline   282
Coping with Hardware Limitations   282
Conclusion   282

3.3   Real-Time Image Abstraction by Directed Filtering   285
       Introduction   285
       Color Space Conversion   287
       Flow Field Construction   287
       Orientation-Aligned Bilateral Filter   291
       Separable Flow-Based Difference-of-Gaussians   295
       Color Quantization   301
       Conclusions   302

Part IV   Shadows   303

4.1   Practical Cascaded Shadow Maps   305
       Introduction   305
       Flickering of Shadow Quality   307
       Exact Solution   309
       Approximated Solution   311
       Storage Strategy   313
       Non-Optimized Split Selection   315
       Correct Computation of Texture Coordinates   317
       Filtering Across Splits   321
       Method Used in PSVSMs   324
       Analytic Method   325
       Conclusion   328

4.2   A Hybrid Method for Interactive Shadows in Homogeneous Media 331
       Introduction   331
       Participating Media Review   332
       Hybrid Approach   335
       Adding Textured Light Sources   336
       Implementation Details   338
       Results   342
       Conclusions   342

4.3   Real-Time Dynamic Shadows for Image-Based Lighting   345
       Introduction   345
       Related Work   346
       Algorithm Overview   346
       Environment Map Importance Sampling   346
       Visibility Map Generation   349
       Rendering Shadows on Diffuse Surfaces   357
       Rendering Shadows on Glossy Surfaces   358
       Results   359

Conclusion   361
Endnotes   361

4.4   Facetted Shadow Mapping for Large Dynamic Game Environments   363
Introduction   363
The Challenges   363
Existing Shadow Map Approaches   364
Facetted Shadow Map Approach   365
Creating and Using Facetted Shadow Maps   367
Results   370
Conclusion   370

Part V   Environmental Effects   373

5.1   Dynamic Weather Effects   375
Introduction   375
Particle Simulation and Rendering   376
Rendering Motion-Blurred Particles   378
Occlusion   382
Dynamic, Artist-Controlled Weather   384
Additional Effects   385
Conclusion   386

5.2   Interactive Hydraulic Erosion on the GPU   389
Introduction   389
Data Structures   390
Water Movement   392
Erosion   394
Boundaries   400
Rendering   401
Results and Conclusion   402

5.3   Advanced Geometry for Complex Sky Representation   405
Introduction   405
Geometry Generation   406
Conclusion   408

Part VI   **Global Illumination Effects**   **411**

   6.1   Screen-Space Ambient Occlusion   413
            Introduction   413
            The Problems   414
            Previous Work   414
            Overview of the Approach   415
            Implementation   420
            Future Improvements   423
            Results and Conclusion   423

   6.2   Image-Space Horizon-Based Ambient Occlusion   425
            Introduction   425
            Input Buffers for Image Space Ambient Occlusion   429
            Image Space Ambient Occlusion with Ray Marching   429
            Our Algorithm   431
            Reformulating the Ambient Occlusion Integral   431
            Implementation Considerations   435
            Results   440

   6.3   Deferred Occlusion from Analytic Surfaces   445
            Introduction   445
            Method   446
            Analytic Occlusion from other Surfaces   451
            Optimization   451
            Conclusion   453

   6.4   Fast Fake Global Illumination   455
            Introduction   455
            Ambient Occlusion Probes   455
            Screen-Space Ambient Occlusion   458
            Screen-Space Radiosity   462
            Fake Radiosity   462
            Conclusion   466

   6.5   Real-Time Subsurface Scattering Using Shadow Maps   467
            Introduction   467
            Related Work   468
            Theory   469
            Algorithm   471
            Results   476
            Conclusion   477

6.6 **Instant Radiosity with GPU Photon Tracing and Approximate Indirect Shadows** 479
Introduction 479
Techniques We Build On 480
Algorithm Overview 481
Scene Representation for Ray Tracing 483
Ray-Triangle Intersection 484
BIH Traversal 487
Light Source Sampling 489
Photon Shooting 489
VPL Management 490
Rendering the Distance Impostor Cube Map 490
Rendering Deferring Textures 490
Building Pyramidal Occlusion Maps 490
Lighting 491
Adaptive Geometry-Sensitive Box Filtering 493
Performance 493
Conclusion 494

6.7 **Variance Methods for Screen-Space Ambient Occlusion** 495
Ambient Lighting 495
Ambient Occlusion 496

6.8 **Per-Pixel Ambient Occlusion Using Geometry Shaders** 501
Introduction 501
Background 502
Our Approach 502
Results 506
Conclusion 509

Part VII   Handheld Devices 511

7.1 **Optimizing Your First OpenGL ES Application** 513
Introduction 513
Mobile Development 514
Graphics Development Guidelines 518
A Developer's Experience: Insight from
Jadestone into KODO Evolved 539
Conclusion 541

7.2   **Optimized Shaders for Advanced Graphical User Interfaces**   **543**
        Introduction   543
        Handheld GUI Requirements   543
        Optimizing for Power Consumption   544
        Optimizing Blurs   546
        Optimizing Other Popular Effects   549
        Background and Post-Processing   552
        Transitions   555
        Conclusion   560

7.3   **Facial Animation for Mobile GPUs**   **561**
        Introduction   561
        Facial Animation Components   561
        Current Approaches and Efficiency   562
        Mobile Approach: Maximal Efficiency Is Critical   563
        Conclusion   569

7.4   **Augmented Reality on Mobile Phones**   **571**
        Introduction   571
        Developing Augmented Reality Applications   572
        Platform Considerations   581
        Application Initialization   583
        Graphics API Abstraction   586
        Hardware vs. Software Rendering   596
        Scene-Graph Rendering   599
        Video and Image Processing   601
        Fixed Point vs. Floating Point   603
        Conclusion   604

Part VIII   **3D Engine Design Overview**   **605**

8.1   **Cross-Platform Rendering Thread: Design and Implementation**   **607**
        Motivation   607
        Overview   607
        Implementation   612
        Results   617
        Going Further: Add-Ons and Features   618
        Conclusion   620

8.2	**Advanced GUI System for Games**	**621**
	Introduction	621
	Architecture	622
	Rendering	624
	Conclusion	625
8.3	**Automatic Load-Balancing Shader Framework**	**627**
	Introduction	627
	The Problems	627
	User Inconvenience	628
	Performance	629
	The Approach	629
	Workflow	632
	Discussion of Results	632
	GPU Requirements	633
	Conclusion	633
8.4	**Game-Engine-Friendly Occlusion Culling**	**637**
	Introduction	637
	Coherent Hierarchical Culling	638
	Reducing State Changes	641
	Game Engine Integration	643
	Skipping Tests for Visible Nodes	645
	Further Optimizations	646
	Multiqueries	647
	Putting It All Together	650
	Conclusion	653
8.5	**Designing a Renderer for Multiple Lights: The Light Pre-Pass Renderer**	**655**
	Z Pre-Pass Renderer	655
	Deferred Renderer	657
	Light Pre-Pass Renderer	660
	Storing an Additional Diffuse Term	662
	Converting the Diffuse Term to Luminance	663
	Bending the Specular Reflection Rules	663
	Comparison and Conclusion	664
	Appendix: Applying Different Materials with a Light Pre-Pass Renderer	665

8.6   **Light Pre-Pass Renderer: Using the CIE Luv Color Space**   **667**

Introduction   667
Why CIE Luv?   668
Working with Luv Colors   668
Luv Light Buffer Format   671
Grouping and Rendering Lights   672
Integrating Luv into Light Accumulation   675
Conclusion   676

8.7   **Elemental Engine II**   **679**

Part IX   **Beyond Pixels and Triangles**   **683**

9.1   **Sliced Grid: A Memory and Computationally Efficient Data Structure for Particle-Based Simulation on the GPU**   **685**

Introduction   685
Sliced Grid   686
Implementing a Sliced Grid on the GPU   689
Results   693
Conclusion   697

9.2   **Free-Viewpoint Video on the GPU**   **699**

Introduction   699
Background Subtraction   700
Shape from Silhouette   703
Surface Extraction   705
Texture Mapping   709
Conclusion   713

9.3   **A Volume Shader for Quantum Voronoi Diagrams Inside the 3D Bloch Ball**   **715**

Introduction and Preliminaries   715
Von Neumann Quantum Entropy and Its Relative Entropy Divergence   716
Quantum Voronoi Diagrams   717
Quantum Voronoi Diagrams for Pure States   719
Quantum Voronoi Diagrams for Mixed States   723
Quantum Channel and Holevo's Capacity   728
Concluding Remarks   729

9.4   **Packing Arbitrary Bit Fields into 16-Bit Floating-Point
       Render Targets in DirectX 10**   731
       Introduction   731
       16-Bit and 32-Bit Floating-Point Formats   732
       Writing a Valid 32-Bit Floating-Point Output   733
       Converting Between Single- and Half-Precision   733
       Packing and Unpacking Code   736
       Performance Considerations   741
       Conclusion   741

9.5   **Interactive Image Morphing Using Thin-Plate Spline**   743
       Introduction   743
       Thin-Plate Spline-Based Warping   744
       GPU Implementation of TPS Warping   747
       Interactive Image Morphing   750
       Conclusion   752

       Index   **753**

Part I

Geometry Manipulation

NATALYA TATARCHUK

In recent years we've seen tremendous jumps in massively parallel processing for geometry using GPUs. The latest architectures include unified shader architecture, improved load balancing for vertex-heavy graphics workloads, as well as additional stages in the programmable pipeline. These architectures also include improvements in overall load balancing, as well as an increased number of SIMD processing units. These, and other changes, have allowed researchers and developers to come with a slew of novel algorithms to produce interesting and complex geometric manipulations directly using the GPU.

Direct3D 10 has brought us the ability to execute programs on entire primitives via the geometry shader functionality. We can also use the output of such programs to dynamically cull primitives or generate entirely new data. This functionality opens up a number of new algorithms, previously unavailable for development using the GPU pipeline. One of these novel algorithms is described in the first article in this section, "Scalar to Polygonal: Extracting Isosurfaces Using Geometry Shaders," by Natalya Tatarchuk, Jeremy Shopf, and Chris DeCoro. The authors present a hybrid method for extracting polygonal surfaces using the new programmable pipeline available with the Direct3D 10 API, while optimally balancing parallel workloads on the GPU architecture. The dynamically extracted surfaces can be generated from volumetric datasets, either static or time-varying, and can be rendered multiple times once extracted from a variety of algorithms.

With the most recent commodity GPUs, such as the ATI Radeon HD 4800 series, not only are we able to generate new geometry using geometry shaders, but we can also take advantage of new hardware functionality for GPU tessellation. The next article in this section, "Fast High-Quality Rendering with Real-Time Tessellation on GPU," by Natalya Tatarchuk and Joshua Barczak, provides analysis of this new feature and practical guidelines for development. The authors describe how interpolating subdivision evaluation implemented on GPUs, combined with displacement mapping, can be used for efficient and highly detailed character rendering and animation.

1

In the next article in this section, "Dynamic Terrain Rendering on GPU Using Real-Time Tessellation," by Natalya Tatarchuk, the author describes an adaptive method to tessellate geometry using view-dependent screen–space metrics for terrain rendering with smooth and intuitive LODs. The author also describes a displacement-map–based lighting method for high-quality lighting of dynamic surfaces rendered from height fields.

An article by Rafael P. Torchelsen, Carlos A. Dietrich, Luís Fernando, M. S. Silva, Rui Bastos, and João L. D. Comba, titled "Adaptive Re-Meshing for Displacement Mapping" describes a novel multi-resolution mesh subdivision method to adaptively tessellate the mesh for displacement map rendering. The technique presented by the authors provide close to a one-to-one relationship between the features in the displacement map and the mesh vertices. Using this technique, the polygons are subdivided according to the corresponding area in the displacement map, thus providing more uniform subdivision with respect to the features of the displacement map.

In the last article of this section, "Fast Tessellation of Quadrilateral Patches for Dynamic Level of Details," by Carlos A. Dietrich, Luciana P. Nedel, and João L. D. Comba, the authors describe a technique for generating water-tight quad surfaces with differing LODs between neighboring patches. The issues of crack avoidance are thoroughly explored in the article, where the authors describe a fast and robust method for computing new patch tessellations. The tessellation is perfomed using geometry shaders as well as on CPUs (separate implementations are described).

1.1

Scalar to Polygonal: Extracting Isosurfaces Using Geometry Shaders

NATALYA TATARCHUK, JEREMY SHOPF, AND CHRIS DECORO

FIGURE 1.1.1   Example of extracting a series of highly detailed isosurfaces at interactive rates. Our system implements a hybrid cube-tetrahedra method, which leverages the strengths of each as applicable to the unique architecture of the GPU. The left pair of images (wireframe and shaded, extracted using a base cube grid of 64^3) shows only an extracted isosurface, while the right pair displays an alternate isosurface overlaid with a volume rendering.

SCALAR FIELDS VERSUS POLYGONAL REPRESENTATION

The ability to dynamically extract surfaces on demand is highly desirable for many rendering scenarios. The surface can be generated as a result of time-varying dataset visualization or simulations—for example, while rendering fluids or explosions in games. These simulations can take advantage of the massively parallel processing available on the latest commodity GPUs, such as the ATI Radeon HD 4800 series. Furthermore, with the huge amounts of video RAM currently available and increased graphics memory bandwidth, we can visualize extensive datasets in real time.

An implicit surface representation, as opposed to an explicit representation with a polygon mesh or parametric surface, can be a very convenient form for many simulation and modeling tasks. The high computational expense of extracting explicit isosurfaces from implicit functions, however, has made such operations an excellent candidate for GPU acceleration. In this article, we present an intuitive extraction algorithm that can be implemented efficiently using a hybrid marching cubes/marching tetrahedra (MC/MT) approach. We can leverage the strengths of each method as applied to the unique computational environment of the GPU and, in doing so, achieve real-time extraction of detailed isosurfaces from high-resolution volume datasets. We can also perform adaptive surface refinement directly on the GPU without lowering the parallelism of our algorithm. Implicit functions are a powerful mechanism for modeling and editing geometry.

Rather than the geometry of a surface given explicitly by a triangle mesh, parametric surface, or other boundary representation, it is defined implicitly by an arbitrary continuous function, $f(x), x \in \mathbb{R}^3$. By defining an arbitrary constant, (referred to as an *isovalue*, and frequently set to zero), we can define our surface as the set of all points (isosurface) for which $f(x) = c$. For simplicity, we will frequently make the substitution $F(x) = f(x) - c = 0$; without loss of generality. A great variety of simulations are executed on a volumetric dataset, often represented as a scalar or multi-dimensional field. These data fields may be static or time-varying—the latter being a far more interesting case for real-time isosurface extraction. While the convenience and benefits of volumetric representation is undeniable for simulation purposes, the familiar polygonal form of extracted isosurfaces provides a number of advantages.

Though it's feasible to render such surfaces with volume rendering techniques, the polygonal form is beneficial for computing surface-to-surface collisions or other physics-based interactions (such as deformations, for example). Performing these computations on a volume is more computation-intensive and time-consuming. Furthermore, when we wish to render the isosurface multiple times (as is frequently needed in complex environments with shadows, reflections, or refraction-based effects), having a polygonal representation is very convenient. Additionally, with the unified shader architecture of recent gaming consoles such as Microsoft Xbox 360 and the latest consumer GPUs, geometry throughput has increased tremendously. Once extracted, isosurfaces can be drawn multiple times very quickly. Finally, we can use surface extraction to interact with the simulated system or the dataset. Isosurface extraction, at its heart, is a computation-intensive method.

Fast and parallel algorithms for isosurface extraction have been a topic of extensive research for the last several years. Much work has been done to generate highly efficient renderings at high frame rates. Prior to the DirectX 10 generation of GPUs, the programming model lacked support for programmable primitive processing and the ability to output geometric quantities for later re-use. Thus, previous work lacked the ability to generate a polygonal surface directly on the GPU and reuse it for subsequent computation, such as collision detection or optimization of volumetric rendering for surrounding organs. Much of the extraction work was redundantly performed regardless of whether or not the isovalue was dynamically changing, resulting in wasted computation. Nonetheless, a number of researchers succeeded at fast, interactive isosurface rendering. We refer the reader to an overview of recent work in this domain in [Tatarchuk08]. Pascucci [Pascucci04] rendered tetrahedra to the GPU, using the MT algorithm in the vertex shader to re-map vertices to surface positions. Subsequently, Klein *et al.* [Klein04] demonstrated a similar tetrahedral method using pixel shaders, which—at the time—provided greater throughput. Other researchers instead implemented the MC algorithm [Goetz05] [Johansson06]. For a broad overview of direct rendering and extraction methods, see the survey by Silva *et al.* [Silva05]. All of these methods, however, were forced to use contrived programming techniques to escape the limitations of the previously restrictive GPU architecture.

We base our approach on extracting polygonal surfaces from the scalar dataset, a method derived from the MC [Lorensen87] and MT [Shirley90] algorithms. Our hybrid algorithm leverages the strengths of each method as applicable to the unique constraints and benefits of the GPU architecture. Using the geometry shader stage, executing on primitives after the vertex shader and before the rasterizer processing, we generate and cull geometry directly on the GPU. This provides a more natural implementation of marching methods. With our approach, the isosurface is dynamically extracted directly on the GPU and constructed in polygonal form, and can be directly used post-extraction for collision detection or rendering and optimization. The resulting polygonal surface can also be analyzed for geometric properties, such as feature area, volume, and size deviation, which is crucial, for example, for semi-automatic tumor analysis as used in a colonoscopy. Our pipeline provides a direct method to reuse the result of geometry processing in the form of a *stream out* option, which stores output triangles in a GPU buffer after the geometry shader stage. This buffer may be reused arbitrarily in later rendering stages, or even read back to the host CPU.

Our isosurface extraction pipeline (Figure 1.1.2) proceeds as follows: We start by dynamically generating the voxel grid to cover our entire volume, or a section of it. Using a geometry shader and the stream-out feature, we tessellate the volume into tetrahedra on the fly. This allows us to adaptively generate and sample the grid

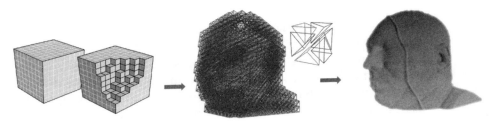

FIGURE 1.1.2   Isosurface extraction pipeline.

based on the demands of the application. Each input voxel position is computed dynamically in the vertex shader. The geometry shader then computes six tetrahedra spanning the voxel cube. As an optimization, we generate tetrahedra only for voxels containing the isosurface, saving memory. Once we have the tetrahedra, we then use the MT algorithm to dynamically extract polygonal surfaces from our scalar volume consisting of material densities. In both passes, for tetrahedral mesh generation and isosurface extraction, we use the geometry amplification feature of the geometry shader stage directly on the GPU.

We utilize the efficiency of parallel processing units on the GPU more effectively by separating isosurface extraction into two passes. Given a set of input vertices, a geometry shader program will execute in parallel on each vertex. Note that each individual instance of this program executes serially on *a given single-instruction, multiple-data (SIMD) unit.* Therefore, to maximize each effective SIMD utilization, we separate extraction into two phases—fast cube tetrahedralization and an MT pass. This reduces the serialization of each individual geometry shader execution instance. We first execute on all vertices in our grid in parallel, generating tetrahedra, and then execute on each tetrahedra in parallel, generating polygons. This also allows us the optimal balance between parallelization of polygonal surface extraction with efficient memory bandwidth utilization (the tetrahedra, exported by the first pass, consist of just three four-component floating-point values).

ISOSURFACE EXTRACTION USING MARCHING METHODS

Our method is based on both the *marching cubes* and the *marching tetrahedra* algorithms for isosurface extraction. The domain in $\Re^3$ over which F is defined is tessellated into a grid at an arbitrary sampling density. In both methods, for each edge $e = (x_0, x_1)$ in the tessellation, we will evaluate $F(x_0)$ and $F(x_1)$; by the intermediate value theorem, if the signs of $F(x_0)$ and $F(x_1)$ differ, an isosurface vertex must intersect *e*. Considering all edges, we can connect vertices to form triangles. Each possible assignment of signs to grid cells can be assigned a unique number. This is subsequently used to index into a lookup table, which will indicate the number and connectivity of isosurface triangles contained in the cell. In the MC method, each cell has eight vertices, so there exist 28 possible assignments of the sign of $F(x)$. Each cube typically produces up to six triangles [Lorensen87]. Therefore, a straightforward lookup table holds $2^8 \times 6 \times 3 = 4,608$ entries. The size of this table presents an important consideration for parallel implementations on the GPU. The edge lookup tables are typically stored in SIMD-specific memory for efficient and coherent access by each shader program instance. However, constructing large tables may result in additional register pressure. This would significantly lower the amount of parallel threads simultaneously running on the GPU. Smaller lookup tables ensure a higher order of parallelization because the GPUs are able to schedule more threads due to a larger number of available registers. Furthermore, Ning and Bloomenthal [Ning93] have demonstrated that MC can generate incorrect connectivity even if the inherent ambiguities are avoided by careful table construction. Therefore, straight MC polygonization would need to handle the undesirable topology in a special-case manner for each geometry shader invocation, increasing serialization for each instance of the program and impairing performance of the resulting algorithm.

The MT method, by its use of a simpler cell primitive, avoids these problems. There exist only 16 possible combinations, emitting at most two triangles, and no ambiguous cases exist. This tiny lookup table allows effective use of the fast-access SIMD registers and, therefore, results in much higher utilization of the parallel units on the GPU. One additional consideration for the related class of applications is that the cube is more intuitive for grid representation and adaptive sampling, with stronger correspondence to the original sampling. We note that the tetrahedron is an irregular shape and does not share these advantages. Straightforward tetrahedralization of a cube requires between four and six tetrahedra per cube, requiring a corresponding factor of increase in the number of function evaluations required for the resulting mesh (if no sharing is done between primitives). To deal with this consideration, we introduce our hybrid method.

HYBRID CUBES/TETRAHEDRA EXTRACTION

The GPU architecture excels at large-scale parallelism; however, we must remember that the programmable units perform in *lock step*, so we must carefully parallelize our computations for maximum performance.

The general strategy is to use MC to exploit the additional information present in cubes, as opposed to tetrahedra. As we mentioned earlier, straightforward tetrahedralization is a relatively complex program in GPU terms, and thus would reduce thread parallelization. Rather than perform triangulation directly, it is preferable to adaptively tetrahedralize the input cubes. We perform final triangulation of the output surface using the simpler extraction operation on the tetrahedral grid. Our method uses the following steps:

Pass 1: Domain voxelization

- Dynamically voxelize the domain
- Tessellate cubes into tetrahedra near the surface
- Output tetrahedra as points to stream-out buffer

Pass 2: Marching tetrahedra

- Perform MT on generated tetrahedra
- Identify edges intersecting surface
- Output each isosurface triangle to a stream-out buffer for later re-use and rendering, or straight to rasterization for immediate results

VOXELIZE INPUT DOMAIN

In many cases (for example, with volumetric data generated by medical imaging tools or physical simulations) the input data itself is specified on a regular (cubic) grid. Therefore, from the perspective of reducing function evaluations (corresponding to texture reads on the GPU), it is most practical to evaluate the function exactly at those points and generate output triangles accordingly. Although tetrahedral meshes provide a straightforward and efficient method for generating watertight isosurfaces, most preprocessing pipelines do not include support for generating tetrahedral meshes directly. Furthermore, we would like to support isosurface extraction on dynamic meshes and, thus, wish to generate tetrahedral directly on the GPU (for particle or fluid simulations, for example). We start by rendering a vertex buffer containing n^3 vertices, where n is the grid size. Using a primitive ID (automatically provided to the SM 4.0 shader as a system-generated value in DirectX 10), we generate the voxel corner locations directly in the vertex shader. Subsequent geometry shaders compute the locations of the voxel cube corners. We can then evaluate isosurface at each voxel corner.

CUBE TETRAHEDRALIZATION

In the geometry shader from the first pass, we tessellate each cube voxel containing the surface into at most six tetrahedra. We can either reuse already computed isosurface values, or, to reduce the stream-out memory footprint, simply repeat evaluation of tetrahedra corners in the next pass. Prior to tetrahedralization, we perform a test to determine whether the isosurface passes through this voxel by comparing the signs of the voxel corners. Using the geometry shader *amplification* feature, we dynamically generate tetrahedra for only those voxels that contain the isosurface. We output tetrahedra as point primitives into stream-out buffers, typically storing only the (x, y, z) components of tetrahedra corner vertices for efficient use of stream-out functionality.

In DirectX 10, we perform both voxelization of the cube domain and tetrahedralization as a single pass. The vertex shader performs domain voxelization, and the geometry shader performs cube tetrahedralization. For the first part, we can conveniently take advantage of the system-generated vertex ID and use point primitives to render this draw call with a tiny vertex buffer (see Listing 1.1.1 for more details). This allows us to save memory by not needing any allocation for the storage of the cube grid.

Listing 1.1.1 Sample code using a Lua front-end rendering engine functionality to perform domain voxelization and tetrahedralization. In this case, we use a grid size of 643.

```
myDummyBuffer  = CreateStreamOutBuffer{ Name = "sDummy", VertexSize = 4,
VertexCount = 1 }


nNumVoxelsXConservative = 64;

nNumVoxelsYConservative = 64;

nNumVoxelsZConservative = 64;


nVoxels           = nNumVoxelsXConservative * nNumVoxelsYConservative *
nNumVoxelsZConservative;

nNumTetraPerCube  = 6;

nNumTetraVertx    = nVoxels * nNumTetraPerCube;

nTetraVertexSize  = 48;


mySOBuffer = CreateStreamOutBuffer{ Name       = "sPointSamples",
```

```
                                      VertexSize   = nTetraVertexSize,
                                      VertexCount = nNumTetraVertx }


//- - - - - - - - - - - - - - - - - - - - - - - -
// Generates tetrahedra from the input points (voxels) (prep for isosurface
// extraction)
//- - - - - - - - - - - - - - - - - - - - - - - -
function ConvertVoxelsToTetrahedra()

   effect = nil
   effect = LoadEffect( "Isosurface.sufx" ):get()

   // Get the volume texture from the object manager and manually bind it
   local volumeModel = IsoVolumes[nCurVolume]:GetModel();
   local volumeTexture = nil
   volumeTexture = volumeModel:GetTextureByName("phong1.tVolume"):get()

   effect:Begin( "GenerateTetraFromVoxels", 1 )

      // Bind the volume texture for sampling
      effect:BindTexture( "tVolume", volumeTexture:GetDefaultSamplingView() );

      // Bind the stream out buffer which will hold the resulting tetrahedra
      effect:BindVertexBuffer( "sDummy", myDummyBuffer );
      effect:BindVertexBuffer( "sPointSamples", mySOBuffer );

      effect:BeginPass(0);

      // Draw some number of points = the number of voxels
      RM:DrawNonIndexed( POINT_LIST, nVoxels, 0 );

      effect:EndPass();

   effect:End()

end    // End of function ConvertVoxelsToTetrahedra()
```

Listing 1.1.2 A D3DX FX-like technique for the first pass of tetrahedralization of the domain

```
//.............................................................
// NULL stream map for generating points. See Code Listing 1 for details on
// creation of this buffer and usage during this draw-call.
//.............................................................
Stream sDummy <  BindDynamicBuffer = "sDummy" >
{
    float PlaceHolder
}
StreamMap smDummy { sDummy }


//.............................................................
// Stream for storing and rendering the tetrahedra:
//.............................................................
// Primary stream, which will be used in MarchingTetras to emit triangles
// Each value xyz contains the tetrahedra vertex coordinates
// The w value contains the evalutation of the scalar field function at
that point
//.............................................................
Stream sPointSamples <  BindDynamicBuffer = "sPointSamples" >
{
    float4 ValueA, // xyz - float3 for corner0, w - x for corner3
    float4 ValueB, // xyz - float3 for corner1, w - y for corner3
    float4 ValueC  // xyz - float3 for corner2, w - z for corner3
}
StreamMap smPointSamples { sPointSamples }


struct Tetrahedra      // To be used in HLSL
{
    float4 vVtx0 : ValueA; // xyz - float3 for corner0, w - x for corner3
    float4 vVtx1 : ValueB; // xyz - float3 for corner1, w - y for corner3
    float4 vVtx2 : ValueC; // xyz - float3 for corner2, w - z for corner3
```

```
};


sampler            sVolume;
Texture3D<float4> tVolume;


float  fIsosurfaceValue;


float EvaluateIsosurfaceBiased( float3 vPos )
{
    // Note that we are applying a bias to move the data to the right range
from the values
    // stored in the texture. In our case the isosurface voxel grid up the
space centered around
    // the origin and in the range of [-0.5; 0.5] on each dimension.
    return tVolume.SampleLevel( sVolume, vPos + float3( 0.5, 0.5, 0.5 ), 0
).w - fIsosurfaceValue;
}


//.............................................................
// TECHNIQUE: Takes input voxel grid and subdivides each voxel cube into
voxel-spanning tetrahedra
// The cube voxel is taken by the lower-left corner of the voxel
//.............................................................
Technique GenerateTetraFromVoxels
{
    Pass P0
    {
        // State setup
        StreamMap    = smDummy
        StreamOutMap = smPointSamples
        CullMode     = NONE
        ZEnable      = false


        // Vertex shader generates voxel cube domain
        //
```

```
VertexShader( HLSL, EntryPoint = "main" )

    int nNumVoxelsX;
    int nNumVoxelsY;
    int nNumVoxelsZ;

    float fVoxelEdgeX;
    float fVoxelEdgeY;
    float fVoxelEdgeZ;

    float fVolumeSize;

    struct VsInput
    {
        float Position : PlaceHolder;
    };

    struct VsOutput
    {
        float4 vPos: SV_Position;
    };

    // Here we use system-generated vertex IDs to generate our
implicit cube domain / grid:
    VsOutput main( VsInput input, uint nVertexID: SV_VertexID )
    {
        VsOutput o;

        // Convert vertex ID to a position in the voxel grid using
given resolution:

        // Determine the index of the voxel we're trying to create:
        int nVoxelIndexZ = nVertexID / (nNumVoxelsX * nNumVoxelsY);
        int nVoxelIndexY =
```

```
                ( nVertexID - nVoxelIndexZ * nNumVoxelsX * nNumVoxelsY ) /
nNumVoxelsX;
            int nVoxelIndexX =
                nVertexID - nVoxelIndexZ * nNumVoxelsX * nNumVoxelsY -
nVoxelIndexY * nNumVoxelsX;


            // Compute actual position of the voxel corner:
            float3 vPosition = float3( nVoxelIndexX * fVoxelEdgeX,
                                       nVoxelIndexY * fVoxelEdgeY,
                                       nVoxelIndexZ * fVoxelEdgeZ );


            // In our case the isosurface voxel grid up the space centered
around the origin and
            // in the range of [-0.5; 0.5] on each dimension so adjust the
position accordingly:
            o.vPos = float4( vPosition - float3( 0.5, 0.5, 0.5 ), 1 );


            return o;
        }
    EndVertexShader


    // Now given a vertex (point) representing a given voxel cube, we
can expand it into
    // tetrahedra. Thus geometry shader computes cube tetrahedralization.
    GeometryShader(HLSL)


        float fVoxelEdgeX;
        float fVoxelEdgeY;
        float fVoxelEdgeZ;


        struct GsInput
        {
            float4 vPosition: SV_Position;
        };
```

```
        // For a given center pt ('vPos') and size in param space
('fCubeSize'),
        // compute the positions of the cube corners and initialize the
isosurface field.
        void ComputeCubeCorners( float3 vPos, float fCubeSize, out float3
vCorners[8] )
        {
            // Compute each cube corner position
            float fCellSize = fCubeSize / 2;
            vCorners[0].xyz = vPos + float3( -fCellSize, -fCellSize, -
fCellSize ); // 1 swap
            vCorners[1].xyz = vPos + float3( +fCellSize, -fCellSize, -
fCellSize ); // diag start
            vCorners[2].xyz = vPos + float3( +fCellSize, +fCellSize, -
fCellSize ); // 1 swap
            vCorners[3].xyz = vPos + float3( -fCellSize, +fCellSize, -
fCellSize ); // 2 swap


            vCorners[4].xyz = vPos + float3( -fCellSize, -fCellSize,
+fCellSize ); // 2 swap
            vCorners[5].xyz = vPos + float3( +fCellSize, -fCellSize,
+fCellSize ); // 1 swap
            vCorners[6].xyz = vPos + float3( +fCellSize, +fCellSize,
+fCellSize ); // 2 swap
            vCorners[7].xyz = vPos + float3( -fCellSize, +fCellSize,
+fCellSize ); // diag end
        }   // End of void ComputeCubeCorners(..)


        // EmitTetra: helper function to emit tetra with given vertices
        void EmitTetra( float3 v0, float3 v1, float3 v2, float3 v3,
                        inout PointStream<Tetrahedra> stream )
        {
          Tetrahedra tetra;

          tetra.vVtx0.xyz = v0.xyz;
          tetra.vVtx1.xyz = v1.xyz;
          tetra.vVtx2.xyz = v2.xyz;
```

```
        tetra.vVtx0.w = v3.x;

        tetra.vVtx1.w = v3.y;

        tetra.vVtx2.w = v3.z;


        stream.Append( tetra );


    }   // End of void EmitTetra(..)


    // Given cube voxel corners (end-points), geometry shader
generates
    // tetrahedra objects spanning each voxel
    //
    [ maxvertexcount(6) ]
    void main( point GsInput input[1], inout PointStream< Tetrahedra
> stream )
    {
        // The input position for the
        float3 vPos = input[0].vPosition.xyz;


        float  fCubeSize = fVoxelEdgeX;


        float3 vCorners[8];


        // First, compute and evaluate the corners of the cube using
the specified isofunction
        ComputeCubeCorners( vPos, fCubeSize, vCorners );


        float vCornersIso[8];
        for ( int i = 0; i < 8; i++ )
        {
            vCornersIso[i] = EvaluateIsosurfaceBiased( vCorners[i] );
        }
```

```
// Do not generate tetrahedra for cubes
// which do not have isosurface passing through them:
if ( sign( vCornersIso[0] ) == sign( vCornersIso[1] ) &&
       sign( vCornersIso[1] ) == sign( vCornersIso[2] ) &&
       sign( vCornersIso[2] ) == sign( vCornersIso[3] ) &&
       sign( vCornersIso[3] ) == sign( vCornersIso[4] ) &&
       sign( vCornersIso[4] ) == sign( vCornersIso[5] ) &&
       sign( vCornersIso[5] ) == sign( vCornersIso[6] ) &&
       sign( vCornersIso[6] ) == sign( vCornersIso[7] ) )

{
    // Don't generate tetra:
    return;
}


        // Then emit the correct tetras (v0, v1, v2, v3), where (v0,
v1) is the longest edge,
        // and (v0, v2) is the second longest edge.  This allows us to
follow subdivision
        // scheme presented in [Gerstner and Pajarola]
        EmitTetra( vCorners[1], vCorners[7], vCorners[4], vCorners[5],
stream );

        EmitTetra( vCorners[1], vCorners[7], vCorners[6], vCorners[5],
stream );

        EmitTetra( vCorners[1], vCorners[7], vCorners[6], vCorners[2],
stream );


        EmitTetra( vCorners[1], vCorners[7], vCorners[4], vCorners[0],
stream );

        EmitTetra( vCorners[1], vCorners[7], vCorners[3], vCorners[0],
stream );

        EmitTetra( vCorners[1], vCorners[7], vCorners[3], vCorners[2],
stream );


        }  // End of void main( triangle GsInput input[3], inout
PointStream<Tetrahedra> stream )
```

```
        EndGeometryShader


        PixelShader(NULL)
    }
} // End of 'GenerateTetraFromVoxels' technique
```

ADAPTIVE ISOSURFACE REFINEMENT

We have a number of options for adaptive polygonization of the input domain. We can perform an adaptive subdivision of the input grid during the first pass of domain voxelization. While sampling the isosurface, we can select to further subdivide the voxel, refining the sampling grid to detect new isosurface parts missed by the original sampling grid. This uses straightforward octree subdivision of the input 3D grid and, if the original voxel missed the isosurface, will generate smaller-scale tetrahedra for the new grid cells on the finer scale. We can additionally add adaptive tetrahedra refinement in the subsequent pass during cube tetrahedralization at very little cost. This allows us to generate new sampling points inside the existing grid cells where the isosurface has already been detected by the previous pass. In the six-tetrahedra tessellation used, each tetrahedron shares a common longest edge along the diagonal of the cube. At the cost of one function evaluation at the edge midpoint, we can perform a longest-edge subdivision for each of the six tetrahedra. We emit only those of the resulting 12 tetrahedra that contain the surface, which are a subset of those previously discarded, the signs of which differ from the sign of the center point. By performing one additional evaluation and at most six comparisons, we can perform a two-level adaptive simplification. Note that, as the subdivision is always to the center shared edge, the tetrahedra of this cell will be consistent with those of neighboring cells and avoid cracks in the output surface.

MARCHING TETRAHEDRA

Using the *DrawAuto* functionality of DirectX 10, we render the stream-out buffer as point primitives in the next pass, performing the MT algorithm in the geometry shader stage. We identify the edges of the current tetrahedron, which contain the output surface. As stated, MT is preferable for GPU implementation due to the significantly reduced lookup table sizes and output complexity. However, by the use of our hybrid method, which reuses function evaluations from the initial cube grid, we can avoid redundancy and, by our adaptive subdivision step, we significantly reduce the number of primitives generated. Thus, our hybrid method is able to utilize the strengths of both methods as adapted to the GPU pipeline.

Listing 1.1.3 A D3DX FX-like technique for the isosurface extraction pass, extracting the surface to an intermediate stream-out buffer prior to rendering

```
// Note that some of the data structures and methods are already defined
in Code Listing 2.


//....................................................................
.......................TECHNIQUE: Takes tetrahedra mesh as input and
performs marching tetrahedra
//....................................................................
.......................Technique ExtractIsosurface
{
    Pass PO
    {
        StreamMap      = smPointSamples
        StreamOutMap = smIsosurfaceTris
        CullMode      = NONE
        ZEnable       = true
        FillMode      = SOLID


        // Passes the tetra through to the GS
        VertexShader(HLSL)
            Tetrahedra main( Tetrahedra input )
            {
                return input;
            }
        EndVertexShader


        // Uses the tetrahedra to perform isosurface extraction
        GeometryShader(HLSL)
            //State matrices
            float4x4 mWVP;
            float4x4 mWV;
```

```
      // Draws a triangle based on input vertices (used in
DrawTetrahedra)
      void EmitTriangle( float4 v0, float4 v1, float4 v2,
                         inout TriangleStream< IsosurfaceData > stream
)
      {
         IsosurfaceData output[3];

         output[0].vPosWS = v0;
         output[1].vPosWS = v1;
         output[2].vPosWS = v2;


         stream.RestartStrip();

      }  // End of void EmitTriangle(..)


      // Given vertices and function values, computes the intersection
point and normal
      //  This function is rather coarse-grained
      IsosurfaceData CalcIntersection( float3 vVertices[4], float4
vfIsovalues,

                                       int iIdx1, int iIdx2 )
      {
         IsosurfaceData output;

         float3 vVtx1 = vVertices[iIdx1];
         float3 vVtx2 = vVertices[iIdx2];

         float fIso1 = vfIsovalues[iIdx1];
         float fIso2 = vfIsovalues[iIdx2];

         // Solve for the best linear solution to the zero-surface
         float t = (- fIso1) / max( fIso2 - fIso1, 0.00001 );
         float3 vPos = lerp( vVtx1, vVtx2, t );
```

```
            // Transform the position into clipspace
            output.vPosWS  = float4( vPos, 1 );

            return output;
        }
int ComputeCase( float4 vfIsovalues  )
{
   int iCase = 0;
   if( vfIsovalues[0] < 0 )
   {
      iCase += 8;
   }
   if( vfIsovalues[1] < 0 )
   {
      iCase += 4;
   }
   if( vfIsovalues[2] < 0 )
   {
      iCase += 2;
   }
   if( vfIsovalues[3] < 0 )
   {
      iCase += 1;
   }
   return iCase;
}    // Function isNullCase: returns true if case will not generate triangles

int IsNullCase( int iCase )
{
   return iCase == 0 || iCase == 15;
}

         [maxvertexcount(12)]
```

```
void main( point Tetrahedra input[1], inout TriangleStream<
IsosurfaceData > stream )
{
    const int EdgeTable[][8] =
    {
        { 0, 0, 0, 0, 0, 0, 0, 1 }, // all vertices out
        { 3, 0, 3, 1, 3, 2, 0, 0 }, // 0001
        { 2, 1, 2, 0, 2, 3, 0, 0 }, // 0010
        { 2, 0, 3, 0, 2, 1, 3, 1 }, // 0011 -2 triangles
        { 1, 2, 1, 3, 1, 0, 0, 0 }, // 0100
        { 1, 0, 1, 2, 3, 0, 3, 2 }, // 0101 -2 triangles
        { 1, 0, 2, 0, 1, 3, 2, 3 }, // 0110 -2 triangles
        { 3, 0, 1, 0, 2, 0, 0, 0 }, // 0111
        { 0, 2, 0, 1, 0, 3, 0, 0 }, // 1000
        { 0, 1, 3, 1, 0, 2, 3, 2 }, // 1001 -2 triangles
        { 0, 1, 0, 3, 2, 1, 2, 3 }, // 1010 -2 triangles
        { 3, 1, 2, 1, 0, 1, 0, 0 }, // 1011
        { 0, 2, 1, 2, 0, 3, 1, 3 }, // 1100 -2 triangles
        { 1, 2, 3, 2, 0, 2, 0, 0 }, // 1101
        { 0, 3, 2, 3, 1, 3, 0, 0 }, // 1110
        { 0, 0, 0, 0, 0, 0, 0, 1 }  // all vertices out
    };

    IsosurfaceData output[4];

    float3 vVertices[4] = { input[0].vVtx0.xyz,
                            input[0].vVtx1.xyz,
                            input[0].vVtx2.xyz,
                            float3( input[0].vVtx0.w,
input[0].vVtx1.w, input[0].vVtx2.w )
                          };
    float4  vfIsovalues;

    vfIsovalues[0] = EvaluateIsosurfaceBiased( vVertices[0] );
```

```
        vfIsovalues[1] = EvaluateIsosurfaceBiased( vVertices[1] );
        vfIsovalues[2] = EvaluateIsosurfaceBiased( vVertices[2] );
        vfIsovalues[3] = EvaluateIsosurfaceBiased( vVertices[3] );

        output[0].vPosWS.xyz = vVertices[0];
        output[1].vPosWS.xyz = vVertices[1];
        output[2].vPosWS.xyz = vVertices[2];
        output[3].vPosWS.xyz = vVertices[3];

        // Compute case and output the triangles from the lookup table
        int iCase = ComputeCase( vfIsovalues );

        // Don't generate any triangles if this tetrahedron does not
contain the isosurface:
        if ( IsNullCase( iCase ) )
        {
            return;
        }

        // Generate triangles for the isosurface:
        int nNumOutputs = 3;
        output[0] = CalcIntersection( vVertices, vfIsovalues,
                                       EdgeTable[iCase][0],
EdgeTable[iCase][1] );
        output[1] = CalcIntersection( vVertices, vfIsovalues,
                                       EdgeTable[iCase][2],
EdgeTable[iCase][3] );
        output[2] = CalcIntersection( vVertices, vfIsovalues,
                                       EdgeTable[iCase][4],
EdgeTable[iCase][5] );

        if ( EdgeTable[iCase][6] != 0 )
        {
            output[3] = CalcIntersection( vVertices, vfIsovalues,
```

```
                                                   EdgeTable[iCase][6],
EdgeTable[iCase][7] );

            nNumOutputs++;

        }


        // Output the triangle(s)
        [unroll] for ( int i = 0; i < nNumOutputs; i++ )
        {
            stream.Append( output[i] );
        }


        return;


    }

    EndGeometryShader


    PixelShader(NULL)


  }  // End of Pass P0
}  // End of technique 'ExtractIsosurface'
```

Listing 1.1.4 A D3DX FX-like technique for rendering the extracted isosurface with Gooch-like shading

```
//..................................................................
.......................//TECHNIQUE: Given the extracted isosurface
triangles, render on screen:
//..................................................................
......................Technique RenderIsosurface
{
  Pass P0
   {
      StreamMap = smIsosurfaceTris
      CullMode  = NONE
```

```
ZEnable    = true
FillMode   = SOLID

// Passes the tetra through to the GS
VertexShader( HLSL )
    $include "FragmentData"

    float4x4 mWVP;
    float3   vScaling;
    float    fOffsetZ;

    struct VSOutput
    {
        float4 vPos    : SV_POSITION;
        float3 vPosWS  : TEXCOORD0;
        float3 vPosTS  : TEXCOORD1;
        float4 vPosVS  : TEXCOORD2;
    };


    VSOutput main( IsosurfaceData i )
    {
        VSOutput o;

        o.vPosWS = ( i.vPosWS.xyz + float3( 0, 0, fOffsetZ )) * vScaling;

        // In our case the isosurface voxel grid up the space centered
around the origin and
        // in the range of [-0.5; 0.5] on each dimension so adjust the
position accordingly:
        o.vPosTS = i.vPosWS.xyz + float3( 0.5, 0.5, 0.5 );

        o.vPos   = mul( mWVP, float4( o.vPosWS, 1.0 ) );
        o.vPosVS = o.vPos;
```

```
            return o;
        }


    EndVertexShader


    PixelShader( HLSL )
        sampler           sVolume;
        Texture3D<float4> tVolume;


        float3 vCameraPosition;
        float4 vIsosurfaceColor;


        float3 vMaxClipping;
        float3 vMinClipping;


        float3 vLightPos;
        float3 vWarmColor;
        float3 vCoolColor;


        struct PixelInput
        {
            float4 vPos   : SV_POSITION;
            float3 vPosWS : TEXCOORD0_centroid;
            float3 vPosTS : TEXCOORD1_centroid;
            float4 vPosVS : TEXCOORD2_centroid;
        };


        float4 main( PixelInput i ) : SV_TARGET
        {
            // Use clip planes settings specified by the user (or the script)
            // to clip isosurface against that. In our case the isosurface
voxel grid
            // takes up the space centered around the origin and in the
range of [-0.5; 0.5]
```

```
// on each dimension.

// X-axis clip plane:
float fCurrX = i.vPosWS.x + 0.5;
if ( fCurrX < vMinClipping.x || fCurrX > vMaxClipping.x )
{
   clip(-1);
}

// Y-axis clip plane:
float fCurrY = i.vPosWS.y + 0.5;
if ( fCurrY < vMinClipping.y || fCurrY > vMaxClipping.y )
{
   clip(-1);
}

// Z-axis clip plane:
float fCurrZ = i.vPosWS.z + 0.5;
if ( fCurrZ < vMinClipping.z || fCurrZ > vMaxClipping.z )
{
   clip(-1);
}

// Compute the light direction vector: (matching volume caster):
float3 vLightWS   =  normalize( -vLightPos.xyz );
          vLightWS.y = -vLightWS.y;

// Compute the view vector:
float3 vViewWS = normalize( vCameraPosition - i.vPosWS );

// Half vector for specular lighting
float3 vHalfWS = ( vLightWS - float3( -vViewWS.x, vViewWS.y, -
vViewWS.z ) );
```

```
            vHalfWS = normalize( vHalfWS );


    // Compute the normal and the density for the given input point
    // by sampling the volume:
    float3 cNormalWS;
    float  fDensity;
    float4( cNormalWS, fDensity ) = tVolume.SampleLevel( sVolume,
i.vPosTS, 0 );


    // Convert the normal to proper range:
    float3 vNormalWS = ( cNormalWS  - float3( 0.5, 0.5, 0.5 )) * 2.0;


    // Compute the normal length:
    float fGradientMag = length( vNormalWS ) + 0.00001;


    // Now normalize the normal:
    vNormalWS = normalize( vNormalWS );


    // Material properties (again to match volume caster):
    float fKAmbient  = 0.2;
    float fKDiffuse  = 0.5;
    float fKSpecular = 0.5;


    // Lighting:
    float fBaseDiffuse = dot( vNormalWS, vLightWS ) * 0.5 + 0.5;
    float fBaseSpec    = saturate( dot( vHalfWS, vNormalWS ) );


    float fSpec    = pow( fBaseSpec, 100.0 ) * fKSpecular;
    float fDiffuse = fKAmbient + (1.0 - fKAmbient) * fBaseDiffuse;


    float4 cColor = float4( lerp( vWarmColor, vCoolColor,
fBaseDiffuse ), 1 );
```

```
                  return float4( cColor.rgb, i.vPosVS.z/i.vPosVS.w ) ;


               }
         EndPixelShader

      }
}  // End of Technique 'RenderIsosurface'
```

Storing Extraction Results for Subsequent Re-Use

We can intelligently generate isosurface on demand, either as a function of the implicit domain changes or when the user modifies the isovalue dynamically. After computing MT, we can output isosurface triangles into a GPU stream-out buffer for re-use in the later passes or even for storage on disk. This capability is a critical feature of our method that is enabled by the latest GPU pipeline. While the extraction already runs at real-time rates, the actual frame rate perceived by the user will be dramatically faster, because most frames are able to reuse the geometry from the stream-out buffer. This frees up GPU resources for additional computation such as, for example, combining high-quality direct volume rendering with isosurface rendering for better context guidance during medical training simulations (as seen in Figure 1.1.1). Furthermore, we utilize the extracted polygonal surface to improve the rendering speed of our volumetric renderer. In our overall system, we combine isosurface extraction and rendering with a volumetric ray caster. We render the isosurface faces as the starting positions for ray casting in the direct volume-rendering algorithm (an optimization for ray casting). The isosurface can also be rendered directly into a shadow buffer for shadow generation on the surrounding organs.

Isosurface Extraction Results and Analysis

We collected results for continuous isosurface extraction and volume rendering for all seven sections of the Visible Human Project dataset. Each section contains 256^3 samples on a regular grid. Previous methods for GPU-based isosurface extraction have been forced to use contrived implementations to escape the limitations of the earlier programmable graphics pipelines. Such methods, while often performant, are complex to re-implement and modify, and typically do not support re-use without significant effort.

Table 1.1.1 Timing results for continuous isosurface extraction including CPU/GPU timing comparisons. All timing results include resulting polygonal surface rendering cost and were collected on a Microsoft Windows Vista SP1 PC with a 2.4 GHz dual-core AMD AthlonTM 64×2 processor with 2 GB RAM and an ATI RadeonTM HD 4870 graphics card

Dataset	Grid		Time	Faces	FPS	Face/sec	GPU:CPU
Head	64^3	GPU	6.3ms	122K	158fps	19.2M	9.9 : 1
		CPU	66.8ms	130K	15fps	1.95M	
	32^3	GPU	2ms	26K	489fps	13M	4.5 : 1
		CPU	9.3ms	27K	107fps	2.91M	
Thorax	64^3	GPU	8.07ms	192K	124fps	24M	9.9 : 1
		CPU	81ms	197K	12.4fps	2.43M	
	32^3	GPU	2.5ms	40K	400fps	16M	5.3 : 1
		CPU	12.3ms	37.2K	81.5fps	3.04M	
Abdomen	64^3	GPU	8.5ms	192K	116fps	22.3M	9.4 : 1
		CPU	79.9ms	189K	12.5fps	2.37M	
	32^3	GPU	3ms	42K	337fps	14.1M	4.3 : 1
		CPU	12.4ms	40.1K	81fps	3.27M	

We have shown that, with the availability of latest generation GPU architectures, flexible and reasonable implementations of marching methods are possible to implement, taking advantage of the massive parallelism available on the GPU maintaining optimal performance characteristics. We found that our hybrid method of dynamic domain voxelization followed by a tetrahedralization pass results in high-performance and high-quality results. In our development of this system, we have explored various types of methods, including using standard MC or MT directly. We settled on the final hybrid algorithm presented here after extensive testing and analysis of performance bottlenecks. The direct implementation of marching tetrahedral requires large amounts of redundant isofunction computations, reducing parallelization. The MC performance was strongly reduced by the large lookup table sizes, as well as extraneous computations for incorrect topology fix-ups. Therefore, this hybrid approach proved to be an excellent tradeoff between the two. An earlier implementation performed the tetrahedral tessellation and surface extraction in a single pass. However, this severely limited parallelism. The difference in running time between a cube that is culled and one that is both tetrahedralized and used for isosurface extraction in a single pass creates a significant bottleneck for GPU resources. Instead, by moving the MT computation into another pass, we fully utilize GPU programmable units parallelization for voxelizing the domain and generating tetrahedra near the surface. Similarly, the MT pass exhibits the same advantages.

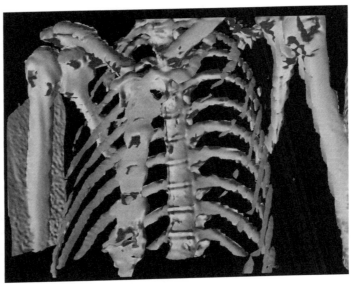

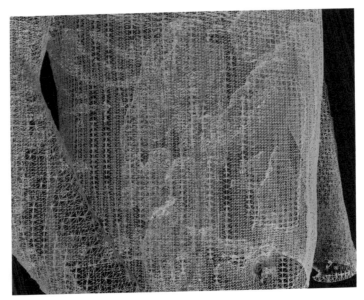

FIGURE 1.1.3   These images show examples of isosurface extraction on two volumetric datasets from the Visible Human Project, each containing 256^3 slices of density data, extracted on a 64^3 grid.

REFERENCES

[Goetz05] F. Goetz, T. Junklewitz, and G. Domik, "Real-time marching cubes on the vertex shader." Proceedings of Eurographics 2005, 2005.

[Johansson06] G. Johansson and H. Carr, "Accelerating marching cubes with graphics hardware." CASCON '06: Proceedings of the 2006 conference of the Center for Advanced Studies on Collaborative research, ACM Press, New York, NY, USA, 2006, p. 39.

[Klein04] T. Klein, S. Stegmaier, and T. Ertl, "Hardware-accelerated reconstruction of polygonal isosurface representations on unstructured grids." (2004). pp. 186–195.

[Lorensen87] W. E. Lorensen and H. E. Cline, "Marching cubes: A high resolution 3D surface construction algorithm." *Computer Graphics* (Proceedings of SIGGRAPH 87), Vol. 21, Anaheim, California, 1987, pp. 163–169.

[Ning93] P. Ning and J. Bloomenthal, "An evaluation of implicit surface tilers." *IEEE Comput. Graph. Appl.* 13 (6) (1993) 33–41.

[Pastucci04]. V. Pascucci, "Isosurface computation made simple: Hardware acceleration, adaptive refinement and tetrahedral stripping." Proceedings of VisSym 2004, 2004.

[Shirley90] P. Shirley and A. Tuchman, "A polygonal approximation to direct scalar volume rendering." *SIGGRAPH Comput. Graph.* 24 (5) (1990) 63–70.

[Silva05] C. Silva, J. Comba, S. Callahan, and F. Bernardon, "A survey of GPU-based volume rendering of unstructured grids." *17ᵗʰ Journal of Theoretic and Applied Computing* (RITA), 12(2):9–29, 2005.

[Tatarchuk08] N. Tatarchuk, J. Shopf, and C. DeCoro, "Advanced Interactive Medical Visualization on the GPU." *Journal of Parallel Distributed Computing*, Elsevier (2008), doi:10.1016/j.jpdc.2008.06.011.

1.2 Fast High-Quality Rendering with Real-Time Tessellation on GPUs

NATALYA TATARCHUK AND JOSHUA BARCZAK

GAME COMPUTING APPLICATIONS GROUP

AMD, INC.

(a) An untessellated character

(b) Character rendered with GPU tessellation

(c) An untessellated character close-up

(d) Tessellated character close-up

FIGURE 1.2.1 An example of using tessellation to render extremely detailed characters in close-up (b and d). On the left, the same character is rendered without the use of tessellation using identical pixel shaders and textures as the images on the right. While using the same geometry memory footprint, we are able to add high levels of detail for the tessellated character.

R eal-time shading has significantly increased in quality and complexity during the past decade. We have seen great strides in our ability to express lighting and shadowing details via pixel shaders. Normal mapping is a de-facto standard for any recently shipped game, regardless of the genre. Advanced titles such as *Crytek's Crysis* create complex surface effects for accurate representation of small-scale surface features and high-quality lighting via techniques such as parallax occlusion mapping [Tatarchuk06]. Nevertheless, realistic shading itself is not enough to create convincing representations of rich worlds on the screen. The need for true geometric detail has not completely gone away, even though we can express surface subtlety with a variety of per-pixel effects. The typical tell-tale signs giving away current games' low-resolution geometric representations are coarse silhouettes.

A simple solution springs to mind—why don't we just increase the polygon count of the objects in the game? Many distinct costs are associated with explicit geometric representation, such as polygonal surfaces encoded in typical meshes. Meshes are an inherently expensive representation. We need to store a fair amount of data per vertex (positions, texture coordinates, and animation data such as skinning weights and indices, for example). This is directly related to the associated memory footprint for the mesh objects—and thus to increasing the pressure on already-scarce memory (as every game developer dearly knows). Furthermore, large meshes display poor utilization of GPU vertex caches, and put a strain on vertex fetch and general memory bandwidth. Also, consider the expense of artist time; animating and texturing extremely large meshes (>1 million vertices) is a tedious and time-intensive process.

It is quite clear that the brute force solution of increasing polygon count for pre-authored objects is not a reasonable solution.

An alternative solution is suggested by the latest advances in GPU architecture. Recent generations of commodity GPUs such as the Microsoft Xbox 360 and ATI Radeon HD 2000, 3000, and 4000 series have shown tremendous improvements in geometry processing. These include unified shader architecture (introduced with the Xbox 360), more dedicated shader units, and hardware tessellation pipelines. The latest graphics APIs (such as Microsoft Direct3D 10 [Blythe06]) provide a convenient programmable model for data recirculation between different passes. These methods can also be accessible via extensions in Direct3D 9 or by using the XDK API. Furthermore, with the introduction of upcoming graphics APIs such as Microsoft Direct3D 11 [Klein08, Gee08], tessellation and displacement mapping will be universally supported across all hardware platforms designed for that generation and, thus, solidify tessellation as a first-class citizen in the real-time domain.

The upcoming generation of games, including those authored for the Xbox 360, will use tessellation for extreme visual impact, high-quality rendering, and stable performance. A thorough understanding of how this technology works is the key to quick and successful adoption.

Hardware tessellation provides several key benefits that are crucial for interactive systems such as video games.

- **Compression:** Using tessellation allows us to reduce our memory footprint and bandwidth consumption. This is true both for on-disk storage and for system and video memory usage, thus reducing the overall game distribution size and improving loading time. The memory savings are especially relevant to console developers with scarce memory resources. When using tessellation, we specify the surface topology, parameterization, and animation data for the coarse control mesh. This mesh is authored to have a low amount of detail, and to capture just the overall shape of the desired object (Figure 1.2.2, left). High-frequency details such as wrinkles, bumps, and dents are only modeled for the super-high-resolution mesh (Figure 1.2.2, right) and are captured by the displacement map for the in-game assets. We can then combine rendering of this control cage with GPU tessellation and displacement mapping to greatly increase the overall amount of detail for the rendered asset (as shown in Figure 1.2.3). Figure 1.2.1 shows an example of this for a character from the AMD demo "Froblins" [Froblins08]. Table 1.2.1 demonstrates memory savings for the Froblin character used in a practical scenario in a complex, game-like, interactive system. Note that animation data is only stored for the control cage. This means that tessellation allows us to increase animation quality by storing more animation data (morph targets or bones) for each control cage vertex.

- **Bandwidth:** Bandwidth is improved because, instead of transferring all of the vertex data for a high-polygon mesh over the PCI-E bus, we only supply the coarse mesh to the GPU. At render time, the GPU needs to fetch only this mesh data, yielding higher utilization of vertex cache and fetch performance. The tessellator directly generates new data that is immediately consumed by the GPU, without additional storage in memory.

- **Scalability:** Because of its recursive nature, subdivision naturally accommodates LOD rendering and adaptive approximation with a variety of metrics. Hardware tessellation allows game developers to implement a simple, flexible LOD management scheme, with no significant runtime cost and little impact on existing content pipelines.

FIGURE 1.2.2   Comparison of low-resolution model (left, 5.1K triangles) and high-resolution model (right, 15M triangles) for the Froblin character.

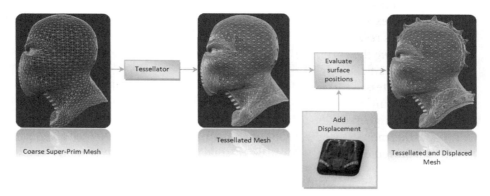

FIGURE 1.2.3   A simplified overview of the tessellation process. We start by rendering a coarse, low-resolution mesh (also referred to as the "control cage" or the "superprimitive mesh"). The tessellation unit generates new vertices, thus amplifying the input mesh. The vertex shader is used to evaluate surface positions and add displacement, obtaining the final tessellated and displaced high-resolution mesh seen on the right.

Table 1.2.1 Comparison of memory footprint for high- and low-resolution models for the Froblin character model.

	Polygons	**Total Memory**
Froblin control cage, low-resolution model	5,160 faces	Vertex and index buffers: 100KB 2K × 2K 16-bit displacement map: 10MB
Zbrush high-resolution Froblin model	15M+ faces	Vertex buffer: ~270MB Index buffer: 180 MB

GPU TESSELLATION PIPELINE

Starting with the ATI Radeon HD 2000 series of graphics cards, PC developers can implement tessellation using dedicated hardware and a programmable pipeline. We designed an extension API for a GPU tessellation pipeline taking advantage of the hardware fixed-function tessellator unit available on recent consumer GPUs to access this functionality in Direct3D 9 and Direct3D 10/10.1 APIs. This tessellator is now available as a stage of the graphics pipeline across multiple APIs (Direct3D 9 through Direct3D 11 and the Xbox 360) (Figures 1.2.4–1.2.6). We can compare how the graphics pipeline has changed with the addition of the tessellator by looking at the current graphics pipeline used by Direct3D applications.

The tessellation hardware is inserted before the vertex shader stage (Figure 1.2.4). The tessellator unit itself does not calculate the new vertex positions explicitly, nor does it store them in memory directly. Instead, this method calculates parametric or barycentric *domain* coordinates for new vertices that are passed to the vertex shader along with indices for the base primitive's vertices. The vertex shader is responsible for calculating the position of the new tessellated vertices, thus *evaluating* the surface. This allows extremely fast generation of new surface points, as well as flexibility in the types of surfaces that we can evaluate. Despite the fact that the tessellator unit is a fixed-function unit, using GPU tessellation we can evaluate a number of different surface types ranging from first-order linear interpolation to higher-order surfaces such as Bezier or Catmull-Clark subdivision surfaces. Furthermore, the newly generated surface positions and their vertex attributes are not stored explicitly in video memory, which improves the overall performance.

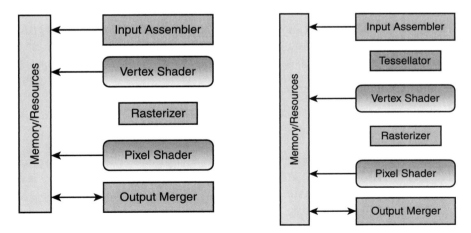

FIGURE 1.2.4 Comparison between the standard DirectX 9 graphics pipeline (left) and corresponding graphics pipeline with tessellation support (right, also representing the Xbox 360 graphics pipeline). Note that sharp-corner boxes represent fixed-function units, and round corner boxes represent programmable stages.

Going through the process for the input polygonal mesh, as shown in Figure 1.2.3, we have the following: The hardware tessellator unit takes an input primitive (which we refer to as a *superprimitive*), and amplifies it (up to 411 triangles, or 15X for the Xbox 360 or ATI Radeon HD 2000–4000 GPU generations, or 64X for the Direct3D 11 generation of graphics cards). We refer to the input primitives as "superprimitives" or "superprims" because each superprim expands into many smaller triangle primitives when run through the tessellator. The API supports a number of primitive types such as lines, triangles, quads, and patches, which is useful for different tessellation-based effects, such as rendering hair with polygonal splines, and so forth. A vertex shader (which we refer to as an *evaluation shader*) is invoked for each tessellated vertex. This vertex shader receives the vertex indices of the superprimitive vertices and the parametric coordinates of the vertex being processed by this shader. For triangles, these parametric coordinates are the barycentric coordinates, and for all other primitive types, the shader receives the parametric *uv* coordinates on the surface domain. The evaluation shader uses this information to calculate the position of the tessellated vertex, using any number of applicable techniques. This means that the vertex shader typically needs to convert from barycentric or parametric coordinates to world space coordinates before it does the usual world space-to-clip space transformation. We can use the following equations to convert from barycentric to world space coordinates for triangle superprims:

$$x = x_1 v_x + x_2 v_y + x_3 v_z$$
$$y = y_1 v_x + y_2 v_y + y_3 v_z$$
$$z = z_1 v_x + z_2 v_y + z_3 v_z$$

where (v_x, v_y, v_z) are the barycentric coordinates of the new vertex generated by the tessellator, (x_1, y_1, z_1), (x_2, y_2, z_2), and (x_3, y_3, z_3) are the triangle superprim vertices, and (x, y, z) is the resulting world space coordinate. For quads, use these equations to convert from parametric space to world space:

$$x = x_1 v_x + x_2 v_y + x_3 v_z + x_4 v_w$$
$$y = y_1 v_x + y_2 v_y + y_3 v_z + y_4 v_w$$
$$z = z_1 v_x + z_2 v_y + z_3 v_z + z_4 v_w$$

where (v_x, v_y, v_z, v_w) is the new vertex generated by the tessellator, (x_1, y_1, z_1), (x_2, y_2, z_2), (x_3, y_3, z_3), and (x_4, y_4, z_4) are the quad superprim vertices, and (x, y, z) is the resulting world space coordinate.

The level of tessellation can be controlled either by a per-draw call tessellation factor (for continuous tessellation, as described below) or by providing per-edge tessellation factors in a vertex buffer for each triangle edge in the input mesh (for adaptive tessellation). For the latter, we can compute the edge factors using the Direct3D 9 API by using the ATI R2VB extension [Persson06].

With the Direct3D 10 API and beyond, we can combine tessellation with several additional features, such as geometry shaders, stream out, and instancing (Figure 1.2.5). This lets us compute per-edge tessellation factors with geometry shaders and stream out. We can also use these features for an animation and transformation pass for the low-resolution control cage. Additionally, should we want to use the geometry shader post-tessellation (perhaps to compute per-face quantities or to output to multiple render targets for cube-map rendering or reflections), the new pipeline supports this functionality.

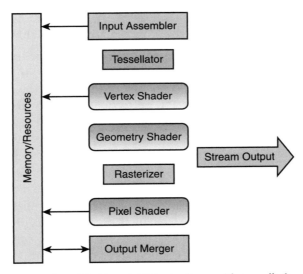

FIGURE 1.2.5   Direct3D 10 and 10.1 pipelines with tessellation support.

The Direct3D 11 pipeline adds three new programmable stages to support tessellation plus, a new compute shader (Figure 1.2.6). We can easily map the methods described in this article to this pipeline, as our current tessellation API along with data recirculation (using appropriate mechanisms in Direct3D 9 or 10) is a close subset of the full Direct3D 11 tessellation support. Therefore, game developers can use the cross-section of features to implement tessellation support across multiple APIs and operating systems.

With this programmable model, we start by rendering our mesh and executing the vertex shader. In the Direct3D 11 pipeline, the vertex shader is used to operate on the original control mesh vertices, performing control cage transformation and animation for the original mesh. Note that, at this point, the control cage mesh can be specified using any primitive format (be it patches or polygons).

In Direct3D 11, the *hull* shader is executed once per control primitive (the input primitive from the coarse control mesh). This can be used to implement per-patch operations. The hull shader can efficiently fetch all per-patch data and can be used to compute patch tessellation factors. Note that we can access the data for the entire primitive in the original mesh. We can also perform domain conversion in the hull shader. This is useful when we want to convert some source mesh stored using one representation (for example, Catmull-Clark patches) to another representation that is better suited for fast hardware evaluation (such as approximating those Catmull-Clark patches with Bezier patches; in this case, the hull shader can transform the control cage into the Bezier domain [LoopSchaefer08]). We can also do per-patch transformations, such as projecting patches into screen-space.

Next, the data is directed to the fixed-function tessellation unit. As in the Direct3D 9 and 10 pipelines, with tessellation support, this fixed-function unit generates *texture coordinates* and connectivity information for the domain primitive and amplifies the original data, up to 64X in Direct3D 11 and up to 15X in the DirectX 9 and 10/10.1 APIs. The amplification rate is important because it provides guidelines for the coarse control mesh polygon budget with respect to the desired features in the super-high-resolution mesh (also referred to as the "limit surface"). If we want to represent high-frequency features in our high-resolution surface (such as small bumps, warts, wrinkles, and bevels), we need to make sure the coarse mesh has enough polygons to generate positions for these features. Therefore, the higher the amplification rate, the lower the polygon count for our control cage can be. Finally, the *domain* shader evaluates and outputs each surface point's position, given patch ID, and the generated *uv* coordinates. At this point, patch data is stored in on-chip storage.

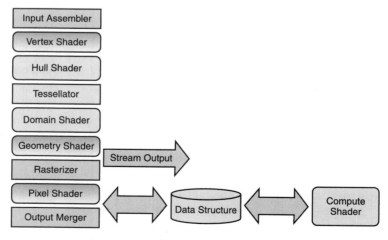

FIGURE 1.2.6 Direct3D 11 rendering pipeline.

PROGRAMMING FOR GPU TESSELLATION

While the Xbox 360 and Direct3D 11 on the PC explicitly support tessellation in their API models, we extended the Direct3D 9 through Direct3D 10.1 APIs to provide access to the tessellation functionality via a wrapper API, known as the ATI GPU tessellation library. This library provides a lean and flexible interface to the tessellator hardware available on ATI Radeon GPUs. We have provided a number of samples implementing tessellation on the media accompanying this book. The library itself, as well as its programming guides, are available at [AMD09]. We are including several SDK samples for rendering characters using this framework on the DVD-ROM accompanying this book. In this article, we'll focus on the details of accessing the GPU tessellation functionality through the ATI GPU tessellation library. We will describe the details of accessing the interface for Direct3D 9 API, but the interested reader can read more details on how to program Direct3D 10 API at [AMD09].

ON THE DVD

The application starts by creating an instance of the `IATITessellationD3D9` interface via the factory creation method, provided an existing D3D9 object and a D3D9 device, as shown in Listing 1.2.1.

Listing 1.2.1 Creating a D3D9 tessellation interface instance using the ATI GPU tessellation library

```
IATITessellationD3D9* Create( IDirect3D9* pD3D, IDirect3DDevice9*
pD3D9Device );


IATITessellationD3D9* sg_pTessInterface =
IATITessellationD3D9::Create( sg_pD3D, sg_pD3DDevice );
```

This interface will be the means that the application uses to access the tessellation extension, so the application should create the instance on start-up and maintain it for the duration of the lifespan of the associated D3D device. If the device is lost or reset, the application needs to delete the associated instance of the tessellation interface (by using the usual C++ constructs) and re-create it using the creation method just described. That method performs the query for GPU tessellation support as well as the necessary interface initialization methods. If the function returns a valid interface object, this means that the extension interface as well as GPU tessellation is supported on the given device. A NULL return would signify that GPU tessellation is not supported on the provided device and cannot be used.

There are also additional methods for querying for tessellation support of specific modes and features using the `IATITessellationD3D9` interface, as shown in Listing 1.2.2.

Listing 1.2.2 Methods for checking support for specific tessellation features

```
//=======================================================================
/// Check tessellation support and query particular features. Once the
query has been completed
/// simply returns the result for subsequent requests for a faster result.
/// \return True if tessellation is supported, false otherwise
//=======================================================================
bool IsTessellationSupported();


/// Queries for support for a specific tessellation mode. Returns true if
the mode is supported,
/// false otherwise
//=======================================================================
bool CheckTessellationModeSupport( TSMode eMode );


//=======================================================================
/// Queries for support for a specific primitive type with tessellation
for a given tessellation
/// mode and indexing mode for the draw call.
///
///     \param eMode
///             Tessellation mode
///     \param ePrimType
///             Primitive type we're querying support for
///     \param bIndexed
///             Specifies whether we're querying for an indexed (=true) or a
non-indexed (=false) draw call.
///
```

```
/// Returns true if the primitive type is supported for the given
tessellation mode for the specified
/// indexing method.
//=======================================================================
bool CheckPrimitiveTypeSupport( TSMode eMode, TSPrimitiveType ePrimType,
bool bIndexed );


//=======================================================================
/// Queries whether unlimited vertex fetch feature combined with indices
retrieval is supported
/// in the given tessellation mode.
///
///      \param eMode
///             Tessellation mode
///
/// Returns true if supported and false otherwise.
//=======================================================================
bool CheckUnlimitedFetchSupport( TSMode eMode );
```

Once a tessellation interface instance has been created, we can use it to set up a related rendering state and issue draw calls. There are two supported tessellation-rendering modes: continuous and adaptive. These modes define how new vertices will be created during tessellation for each domain primitive. We can set the rendering mode for a given draw call by calling the `IATITessellationD3D9::SetMode(..)` method, as shown in Listing 1.2.3.

Listing 1.2.3 A method for setting tessellation mode during rendering

```
//=======================================================================
/// Enable tessellation and set active tessellation mode for subsequent
draw-calls.
///      \param eMode
///             Tessellation mode parameter, specifies what type of
tessellation mode to enable
///             or whether tessellation is disabled
```

```
///     \param dwTessFactorVBSourceIndex

///             Optional parameter. This parameter specifies the index of
the stream source containing

///             tessellation factors during adaptive tessellation draw call.
This parameter is ignored

///             when enabling continuous tessellation or disabling
tessellation.

///             Default value is 1, where stream 0 will contain the regular
vertex information.

///

/// \return true if tessellation is supported and the set call is
successful, false otherwise
//=======================================================================
bool SetMode( TSMode eTessMode, DWORD dwTessFactorVBSourceIndex = 1 ) = 0;
```

Use the following mode values: `TSMD_ENABLE_CONTINUOUS`, `TSMD_ENABLE_ADAPTIVE`, and `TSMD_DISABLE`. A typical sequence for rendering with tessellation will be:

- Enable tessellation by setting up a specific tessellation mode via `IATITessellationD3D9::SetMode(..)`.

- Set up tessellation levels (min/max) as appropriate via `IATITessellationD3D9::SetMaxLevel(..)` and `IATITessellationD3D9::SetMinLevel(..)`.

- Set up all rendering states (shaders, textures, parameters).

- The associated vertex shader needs to be a correct evaluation shader (see following details).

- Issue draw calls through the tessellation interface by calling any of the methods below.

- Disable tessellation by calling `IATITessellationD3D9::SetMode(TSMD_DISABLE)`.

ON THE DVD

The tessellation library supports a number of draw calls, closely matching the Direct3D API. Note that the accompanying DVD-ROM also includes the headers from the library with detailed documentation on the use of parameters for these methods, as shown in Listing 1.2.4.

Listing 1.2.4 Methods for issuing draw calls for rendering tessellated characters

```
HRESULT DrawIndexed( TSPrimitiveType    ePrimType, uint32 nBaseVertexIndex,
uint32 nMinVertex,
                     uint32 nNumVertices, uint32 nStartIndex, uint32
nNumPrimitives );


HRESULT DrawNonIndexed( TSPrimitiveType   ePrimType,
                        uint32            nStartVertex,
                        uint32            nNumPrimitives );


HRESULT DrawMeshSubset( ID3DXMesh* pMesh, uint32 nSubset );
```

The tessellation library supports more primitive types than Direct3D 9 (such as quads). Therefore, to render objects using the `DrawIndexed()` or `DrawNonIndexed()` methods, we need to specify the associated primitive type (for example, `TSPT_TRIANGLELIST`, `TSPT_TRIANGLESTRIP`, or `TSPT_QUAD`).

CONTINUOUS TESSELLATION MODE

Continuous tessellation is used to specify a single tessellation level per draw call. The tessellation level is a floating-point value in the range of [1.0; 14.99] in the Direct3D 9 and 10 APIs. The tessellation level is the amplification factor for the tessellated mesh.

Continuous tessellation allows a smooth change to the LOD depending on the object's position in the scene or other criteria. By using a floating-point number for the tessellation level, we can gradually change the number of vertices and their positions to avoid popping artifacts. New vertices are only added immediately after each odd tessellation level. Notice how, in Figure 1.2.7, when the tessellation level is increased from 1.0 to 1.5, pairs of vertices are added near the center vertex of each edge, creating thin triangles close to existing edges. When we change from level 1.5 to level 3.0, we are not adding new vertices or triangles; we are just spreading the positions of the new vertices away from the center vertices along the edges. The effect of this fractional increase in the tessellation level is that the shape of the object changes gradually, instead of abruptly changing from a low level of detail to high level of detail, which would cause popping. With continuous tessellation, vertices and triangles are created in such a way as to ensure watertight tessellation. Notice that when we use continuous tessellation, the entire object is tessellated uniformly. While this can easily create an extraordinary amount of additional polygons, combining continuous tessellation with different object-based LOD schemes provides excellent tradeoff for fast, high-quality rendering. We can use a number of LOD heuristics to control the tessellation level based on an object's proximity to the camera, the object type, and so on. The SDK sample on the accompanying DVD-ROM named "CharacterRendering" in the directory for this chapter provides an example of computing the tessellation level based on an object's distance from the camera.

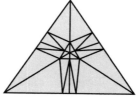

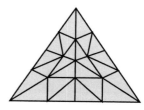

Tessellation Level 1.0   Tessellation Level 1.5   Tessellation Level 3.0

FIGURE 1.2.7 Continuous tessellation of a triangle superprimitive with increasing tessellation levels.

To set up continuous tessellation for a given draw call, we need to enable this mode (by calling `IATITessellationD3D9::SetMode(..)`). We also need to specify the *maximum* tessellation level by calling the `IATITessellationD3D9::SetMaxLevel(..)` method. This is the tessellation level that will be used for rendering the object. Listing 1.2.5 shows an example.

Listing 1.2.5 Example of a draw call for rendering an object with continuous tessellation

```
// Enable tessellation:
sg_pTessInterface->SetMode( TSMD_ENABLE_CONTINUOUS );

// Set tessellation level:
sg_pTessInterface->SetMaxLevel( 7.8f );
```

We then need to make sure that the shaders used for the draw calls are the appropriate evaluation shaders (see details in Listing 1.2.6). For example, we may want to render our object with displacement mapping and with or without wireframe display. This code snippet from the included "CharacterRendering" SDK sample shows just that.

Listing 1.2.6 Example of a render path for rendering a character with continuous tessellation using the ATI GPU tessellation library and D3D9 FX framework

```
// Select appropriate technique to render our tessellated objects:
  if ( sg_bDisplaced )
    if ( sg_bWireframe )
      sg_pEffect->SetTechnique( "RenderTessellatedDisplacedSceneWireframe" );
    else
      sg_pEffect->SetTechnique( "RenderTessellatedDisplacedScene" );
  else
    if ( sg_bWireframe )
      sg_pEffect->SetTechnique( "RenderTessellatedSceneWireframe" );
    else
      sg_pEffect->SetTechnique( "RenderTessellatedScene" );


  UINT iPass;
  UINT cPasses;


  V( sg_pEffect->Begin( &cPasses, 0 ) );
  for ( iPass = 0; iPass < cPasses; iPass++ )
  {
    V( sg_pEffect->BeginPass( iPass ) );
    if ( sg_pTessInterface )
    {
      V( sg_pTessInterface->DrawMeshSubset( sg_pMesh, 0 ) );
    }
    V( sg_pEffect->EndPass() );
  }
  V( sg_pEffect->End() );


  // Compute the number of faces drawn per-frame for the tessellated
object post-tessellation:
  sg_nNumTessellatedPrims =
```

```
    sg_pTessInterface->ComputeNumTessellatedPrimitives( TSPT_TRIANGLELIST,
sg_pMesh->GetNumFaces() );


    // Disable tessellation:
    sg_pTessInterface->SetMode( TSMD_DISABLE );
```

ADAPTIVE TESSELLATION MODE

By using the adaptive tessellation mode, we can specify a tessellation level for each individual edge of the control mesh primitives (superprims). This allows us to *modify* the level of detail for the mesh at render time, using any number of metrics, in a non-uniform fashion. For example, one LOD metric can target a specific screen-space edge length to maintain a reasonable triangle size independent of the object's position with respect to the camera. Thus, we wouldn't waste performance on details that would be unnoticed in the final rendering. The actual resolution of the screen would be automatically accounted for with this LOD technique as well. Alternatively, we can use a vertex-to-camera distance metric or a silhouette-based metric to adaptively subdivide the mesh (in the latter case we would subdivide more at silhouettes to preserve them). This mode provides stable performance by allowing the triangle density to be adjusted locally, so that triangles are created only where needed.

One important consideration when assigning tessellation levels per edge is that we must use the exact same floating-point value for the tessellation level for edges shared between adjacent superprimitives. Failing to do this may result in T-junctions and cracks, especially when combining tessellation with displacement mapping. See the article on dynamic terrain rendering [Tatarchuk09] for more details on how to avoid this with adaptive tessellation.

Figure 1.2.8 shows some examples of superprimitive tessellation using adaptive tessellation. With adaptive tessellation we can also specify a maximum and a minimum tessellation level per draw call. These will serve as range clamps for the individual edge levels. With Direct3D 9 and the Xbox 360, we specify the per-edge tessellation levels via a separate vertex stream along with the regular mesh data (the original vertex stream). All adaptive draw calls in Direct3D 9 and the Xbox 360 must be rendered with nonindexed draw calls. With Direct3D 10/10.1, the tessellation factors are specified directly via the tessellation library interface. Note that to implement dynamic adaptive tessellation, we need to be able to compute per-edge tessellation factors per frame. This is typically done in a pass prior to the tessellation pass at render time.

One immediate concern with using nonindexed rendering for adaptive tessellation draw calls is that typically we render with indexed meshes to optimize for post-transform cache coherence. However, since the tessellator does not generate duplicate vertices, and the original control cage meshes are rather small to start with, using nonindexed meshes does not impose significant performance penalties.

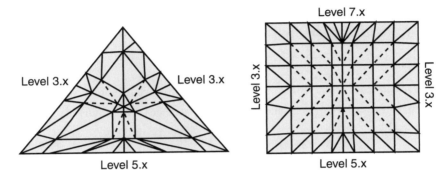

FIGURE 1.2.8 Examples of adaptive tessellation for triangle and quad primitives.

To render with adaptive tessellation, we first need to compute the tessellation factors for all edges in the original mesh. Then we can render our mesh with the associated tessellation factors. In Direct3D 9 we can compute the tessellation factors by using the R2VB extension, which allows us to recirculate vertex data as render targets and vertex buffers as needed. The article on terrain rendering goes into deeper details for computing tessellation factors. Once the per-edge factors are computed and stored in a vertex buffer (an R2VB buffer), we can issue our adaptively tessellated draw call, as shown in Listing 1.2.7.

Listing 1.2.7 Example of a code path for rendering an object with adaptive tessellation using the ATI GPU tessellation library and the D3D9 FX framework

```
// Enable adaptive tessellation (tessellation factors are given in vertex
stream 1 - 3rd parameter):

sg_pTessInterface->SetMode( TSMD_ENABLE_ADAPTIVE, 1 );


// Set min tessellation level:

sg_pTessInterface->SetMinLevel(
IATITessellationD3D9::ATI_TESS_MIN_TESSELLATION_LEVEL );
```

```
// Set tessellation level (this is used for both continuous and adaptive:
sg_pTessInterface->SetMaxLevel( sg_fMaxTessellationLevel );

// Set the vertex declaration and stream source for adaptively tessellated
mesh:
V( pd3dDevice->SetVertexDeclaration( sg_pAdaptiveVBDecl ));
V( pd3dDevice->SetStreamSource( 0, sg_pNonIndexedMeshVB, 0, nVertexSize
));

// Map the tessellation factors R2VB to stream source 1:
V( r2vbSetStreamTexSource( sg_hR2VBTessFactors, 1, 0, sg_pTessFactors, 0,
4 ));

// Select the appropriate technique to render our tessellated objects:
//
if ( sg_bDisplaced )
   if ( sg_bWireframe )
      sg_pEffect->SetTechnique( "RenderTessellatedDisplacedSceneWireframe"
);
   else
      sg_pEffect->SetTechnique( "RenderTessellatedDisplacedScene" );
else
   if ( sg_bWireframe )
      sg_pEffect->SetTechnique( "RenderTessellatedSceneWireframe" );
   else
      sg_pEffect->SetTechnique( "RenderTessellatedScene" );

V( sg_pEffect->Begin( &cPasses, 0 ));
for ( iPass = 0; iPass < cPasses; iPass++ )
{
   V( sg_pEffect->BeginPass( iPass ));
   V( sg_pTessInterface->DrawNonIndexed( TSPT_TRIANGLELIST, 0,
sg_nNumVerts / 3 ));
   V( sg_pEffect->EndPass( ));
}
```

```
V( sg_pEffect->End( ));


// Disengage R2VB tessellation factors:

r2vbDisTexSource( sg_hR2VBTessFactors, 0 );


// Disable tessellation:

sg_pTessInterface->SetMode( TSMD_DISABLE );
```

RENDERING CHARACTERS WITH TESSELLATION

We can render characters using a number of different surface formulations, ranging from linear interpolative subdivision through higher-order surfaces. There exist
a number of different subdivision methods, such as cubic Bezier patches; approximation via N-Patches [VPBM01]; B-splines and NURBs [PieglTiller96]; often
rendered with quads, a Loop midpoint subdivision scheme used with triangles
[Loop87]; and Catmull-Clark subdivision surfaces [CatmullClark78, Stam98].
These schemes differ in the type of refinement rule (face or vertex split), the type of
supported mesh (triangular or quadrilateral or mixed), whether the scheme is
approximating or interpolating, and, finally, the smoothness of the limit surfaces
(C^1, C^2, and so forth). A comprehensive overview of the various approaches can be
found in [ZorinSchröeder00].

In this chapter we describe how to render characters using *interpolating* subdivision. The key idea with this method is that the original mesh vertices remain
undisturbed while the new points are inserted. Therefore, all vertices in the coarser
LODs are maintained, and are also vertices of the refined meshes. With approximating subdivision, the coarse mesh approximates the final, subdivided surface. As
we subdivide the mesh, we approach the final surface with each subdivision level
(which is why it's often referred as the *limit* surface).

The interpolating scheme has several advantages. First, the original control points
defining the low-resolution mesh are also the points on the limit (high-resolution)
surface. This lets us control the limit surface in an intuitive manner. With approximating schemes (such as Catmull-Clark or Bezier patches), the quality of the
resulting surface is typically higher, and the approximating schemes converge to
the limit surface faster than the approximating schemes. However, the evaluation
cost for an approximating scheme, such as Catmull-Clark subdivision, is significantly higher (more than 100X) than that of a planar interpolating subdivision.

Traditionally, the vast majority of game titles support a wide range of graphics hardware platforms. This typically also implies a range of API support, frequently ranging from fairly low specification versions (such as DirectX 8) all the way to DirectX 10.1. At the same time, game production budgets have exploded in recent years, primarily due to the cost of authoring art assets. Therefore, art asset reuse and consistency is very important for game developers, especially those targeting multiple platforms. With interpolating subdivision, the art assets for the coarse control cage can be used to render the object on platforms that do not have support for GPU tessellation. Therefore, the artists would only need to author one set of meshes, animation data, and textures. These assets would have to be authored with tessellation and displacement mapping in mind, but they would successfully render on lower-end platforms. With the updated tool support for displacement map generation and tessellation preview (as in AMD GPUMeshMapper), artists have convenient methods for authoring or interpolating subdivision rendering. However, unless a game is designed to render entirely with subdivision surfaces, to include both subdivision surfaces and triangular meshes, the artists would need to generate two sets of art asserts. Subdivision surfaces are well supported in digital content creation (DCC) tools such as Autodesk Maya, or 3DStudioMax.

To reduce some of the burden of authoring dual art assets (animated triangular meshes for traditional rendering and animated control cages for subdivision surface rendering), artists can maintain some level of association from the original triangular meshes used to generate subdivision surface control cages throughout the creation process for game assets using these tools. At the same time, one would need to be sure to maintain this association, especially when, for example, generating extreme displacement details by using an additional tool, such as Pixologic Zbrush or Autodesk Mudbox. We found that, at this time, the association between the low-resolution model and super-high-resolution model can easily be broken with the existing art authoring pipelines. However, a game wanting to support GPU subdivision surface rendering as well as traditional rendering would need to ship with both sets of art assets; therefore, this association needs to be factored into the art creation process early on.

Given the simplicity of implementation, fast evaluation, and the convenience of authoring art resources, we find that interpolative planar subdivision combined with displacement mapping is an excellent approach for increasing surface quality for rendering highly detailed characters.

In our case, we render our characters using continuous tessellation. We specify the tessellation level per draw call for a given LOD. Therefore, we can use tessellation to control how finely we are going to subdivide a character's mesh. We can use the information about character location on the screen or other factors to control the desired amount of detail. Furthermore, we use the same art assets for rendering the tessellated character as for the regular, conventional rendering used in current games.

Combining tessellation with instancing allows us to render diverse crowds of characters with minimal memory footprint and bandwidth utilization. In the Froblins demo, we render our characters by storing only a low-resolution model (5.2K triangles) and applying a displacement map in the evaluation shader. This lets us render a detail-rich, 1.6 million–triangle character using very little memory. Listing 1.2.9 provides an example of the vertex shader similar to the one used for evaluating the resulting surface positions. In our implementation, we combined Direct3D 10 instancing with GPU tessellation to render large crowds of highly detailed characters. The interested reader can find the exact shader used to render our Froblin characters in [SBCT08].

Designing a Vertex Evaluation Shader for GPU Tessellation

To compute the surface position in the evaluation shader, the subdivision algorithms require access to the vertex data of the entire superprimitive (its control points). This is needed so we can combine the original primitive's vertex data (positions, etc.) using the selected evaluation method (via a control points stencil or by using barycentric interpolation, for example). In Direct3D 11, there are explicit API constructs in the hull and domain shaders to get access to the vertex data for the entire superprimitive (be it control points for a patch or the vertices for a triangle). On the Xbox 360, we can use explicit vertex fetches to retrieve the data as needed.

In Direct3D 9 through 10.1, we need to author the vertex shader using a specific input structure format. This allows the tessellation interface to provide the superprimitive data correctly for the evaluation shader at runtime. There are several ways to access the superprimitive data in the evaluation vertex shader. We can start by using the vertex shader input data (either by declaring vertex shader input semantics in Direct3D 9 or by defining a vertex shader input structure in Direct3D 10/10.1). A regular vertex shader is set up to receive data for the single vertex that is being computed by this vertex shader. However, if, for example, we render the tessellated mesh consisting of triangles, our vertex evaluation shader will need to access vertex data for all three vertices of the original mesh triangles.

The tessellation interface will provide the generated surface position coordinates as well as the superprimitive data to the evaluation shader whenever the tessellation is enabled by setting up either the continuous or the adaptive tessellation mode, and an associated tessellation library draw call is used. However, unlike the typical vertex shader input declaration, we do not explicitly supply the data for superprimitives in the corresponding vertex streams' channels (which would require allocating additional storage in the vertex buffer). Instead, we render the tessellated mesh with the regular vertex buffer set up as we would for traditional rendering (for example, with a vertex and an index buffer set up for indexed rendering). Then, during the tessellated draw call, the additional superprimitive vertex data is automatically inserted into the vertex shader input slots as declared in the evaluation vertex shader.

This is accomplished via explicit input mappings for specifying which superprimitive vertex data needs to be placed into which vertex shader input slots (or DECLs, using Direct3D 9 terminology).

Let's look at an example of modifying an existing Direct3D 9 vertex shader for traditional rendering to be used with tessellation.

Listing 1.2.8 Simple Direct3D 9 vertex shader for rendering with displacement mapping

```
float4x4 mWVP;

float4x4 mMW;


sampler2D sDisplacement;


uniform float  fDisplacementScale;

uniform float  fDisplacementBias;



struct VsInput

{

    float4 vPosition : POSITION0;

    float2 vTexCoord : TEXCOORD0;

    float3 vNormal   : NORMAL0;

};


struct VsOutput

{
```

```
    float4 vPosCS      : POSITION;
    float2 vTexCoord   : TEXCOORD0;
    float3 vPositionWS : TEXCOORD1;
    float3 vNormal     : TEXCOORD2;
};

VsOutput VS( VsInput i )
{
    VsOutput o;

    o.vTexCoord = i.vTexCoord;
    o.vNormal   = i.vNormal;

    // Sample displacement map:
    float fDisplacement = tex2Dlod( sDisplacement, float4( i.vTexCoord, 0,
0 )).r;
        fDisplacement = (fDisplacement * fDisplacementScale) +
fDisplacementBias;

    o.vPositionWS = i.vPosition + (fDisplacement * i.vNormal);

    // Transform position to clip-space
    o.vPosCS = mul( mWVP, float4( o.vPositionWS, 1.0 ) );
    return o;
}
```

Listing 1.2.9 Example of a simple Direct3D 9 evaluation shader for rendering tessellated characters with displacement mapping

```
float4x4 mWVP;
float4x4 mMW;


sampler2D sDisplacement;
```

```
uniform float  fDisplacementScale;
uniform float  fDisplacementBias;


struct VsInput
{
   float3 vBarycentric: BLENDWEIGHT0;

   // Superprim vertex 0:
   float4 vPositionVert0 : POSITION0;
   float2 vTexCoordVert0 : TEXCOORD0;
   float3 vNormalVert0   : NORMAL0;

   // Superprim vertex 1:
   float4 vPositionVert1 : POSITION4;
   float2 vTexCoordVert1 : TEXCOORD4;
   float3 vNormalVert1   : NORMAL4;

   // Superprim vertex 2:
   float4 vPositionVert2 : POSITION8;
   float2 vTexCoordVert2 : TEXCOORD8;
   float3 vNormalVert2   : NORMAL8;
};

struct VsOutput
{
   float4 vPosCS      : POSITION;
   float2 vTexCoord   : TEXCOORD0;
   float3 vPositionWS : TEXCOORD1;
   float3 vNormal     : TEXCOORD2;
};

VsOutput VS( VsInput i )
{
```

```
VsOutput o;

// Compute new position based on the barycentric coordinates:
float3 vPosTessOS = i.vPositionVert0.xyz * i.vBarycentric.x +
                    i.vPositionVert1.xyz * i.vBarycentric.y +
                    i.vPositionVert2.xyz * i.vBarycentric.z;


// Compute new texture coordinates based on the barycentric coordinates:
o.vTexCoord = i.vTexCoordVert0.xy * i.vBarycentric.x +
              i.vTexCoordVert1.xy * i.vBarycentric.y +
              i.vTexCoordVert2.xy * i.vBarycentric.z;


// Compute new normal based on the barycentric coordinates:
o.vNormal = i.vNormalVert0.xyz * i.vBarycentric.x +
            i.vNormalVert1.xyz * i.vBarycentric.y +
            i.vNormalVert2.xyz * i.vBarycentric.z;


// Sample displacement map:
float fDisplacement = tex2Dlod( sDisplacement, float4( o.vTexCoord, 0,
0 )).r;
        fDisplacement = (fDisplacement * fDisplacementScale) +
fDisplacementBias;


o.vPositionWS = vPosTessOS + ( fDisplacement * o.vNormal);


// Transform position to clip-space
o.vPosCS = mul( mWVP, float4( o.vPositionWS, 1.0 ) );
return o;
}
```

Notice the difference in the input structure declaration in the two listings (Listing 1.2.8 and Listing 1.2.9). The evaluation shader in Listing 1.2.9 has seven additional channels (which are not provided explicitly by the vertex buffer data). The programmer just needs to specify the expected data for each superprimitive vertex, and the tessellation interface inserts this data during the draw call directly.

So, to convert a regular vertex shader into a GPU tessellation evaluation shader, we need to provide additional declarations for all of the input channels we want to use for the input mesh's vertices. When designing an evaluation shader, we need to specify enough additional channels for the primitive type we will be using for tessellated draw calls. In the example in Listing 1.2.9, since we are rendering the mesh as a triangle list, we specify three sets of vertex input data. If we wanted to render with quads, we would specify four sets. Note that we can only use usage types that have several usage indices for the per-vertex superprimitive data. For example, position usage can be indexed 0..8 in Direct3D 9 (POSITION0..POSITION7), as with texture coordinates and so on. We can map each stream channel in the input declaration to the superprimitive vertex declaration as follows regardless of the input primitive type:

$$input\_usage\_index + superprimitive\_vertex\_index * 4$$

The default mechanism uses the vertex shader DECL mapping to pass the superprim vertex data to the vertex shader using the USAGE index values 0, 4, 8, and 12. In other words, we can map the data for vertex v_0 to data channels with usage 0, the data for vertex v_1 to data channels with usage 4, and so on (as shown in the code listings above).

The parametric surface coordinates are provided to the evaluation shader in the BLENDWEIGHT0 channel, which should be mapped to floating-point values as you saw in the example above. If we want to access the indices of the superprimitive vertices (which can be useful for accessing additional vertex data or for tessellation edge factor computation), we can access them in the evaluation shader via the BLENDINDICES0 channel (note that the data will be typed as uint).

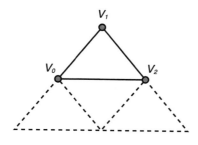

Evaluation Vertex Shader Inputs

SUPERPRIM VERTEX V₀ → **USAGE INDEX 0**
Position 0
TEXCOORD0
TEXCOORD1
NORMAL0

SUPERPRIM VERTEX V₁	**SUPERPRIM VERTEX V₂**
→ **USAGE INDEX 4**	→ **USAGE INDEX 8**
POSITION 4	POSITION 8
TEXCOORD4	TEXCOORD8
TEXCOORD5	TEXCOORD9
NORMAL0	NORMAL8

FIGURE 1.2.9 Rules for mapping from superprimitive vertex data to vertex shader inputs.

ACCESSING PER-VERTEX DATA BEYOND INPUT STRUCTURE DECLARATION

One limitation of the Direct3D 9 and 10 APIs is that we can only access a total of sixteen float4 vertex inputs in the evaluation vertex shader. Since one of these is dedicated to the parametric coordinates, we only have fifteen float4 components to use for loading superprimitive vertex data in these APIs. This means that, as application developers, we must be mindful of data packing in order to bring in sufficient data. If we are rendering with tessellated triangles, this means we can bring in, at most, five float4 components per superprimitive vertex. For quads, we can only bring in three float4 components. This can be insufficient for some applications. This limitation is relaxed for Direct3D 10.1, where we can fetch up to 32 vertex inputs directly.

We can work around these limitations by fetching the superprimitive data directly in the evaluation shader. In Direct3D 9, we can store the vertex buffer in an R2VB resource or a vertex texture and then fetch the data directly in the shader. In Direct3D 10, we can simply reuse the existing vertex buffer, mapping it as a shader resource for loading data in the shader. However, to load the per-vertex superprimitive data in the evaluation shader manually, we need to know the indices of the superprimitive vertices. The tessellation library provides this data to the evaluation shader whenever index retrieval mode in enabled via the following method of IATITessellationD3D9:

```
bool ToggleIndicesRetrieval( bool bEnable )
```

Note that this needs to be toggled per draw call or just enabled for the duration of all rendering. Whenever index retrieval is enabled, the indices of the superprimitive vertices will be passed to the evaluation vertex shader into the BLENDINDICES semantic register. This allows the vertex shader to retrieve additional vertex elements by explicitly fetching them from the associated textures. The texture coordinates for these fetches can be computed from the superprimitive vertex indices, and the textures themselves can easily be generated during asset preprocessing. Using this approach, it is possible to retrieve an arbitrary amount of data for each superprimitive vertex (though one must obviously be mindful of the performance implications of using too many fetches). We have included on the DVD-ROM a Direct3D 9 tessellation SDK tutorial sample created by Nicolas Thibieroz that demonstrates the use of this mode.

ON THE DVD

TESSELLATION API IN DIRECT3D 10

There are a number of improvements when using tessellation with DirectX3D 10 and 10.1 APIs due to increased API flexibility. While we will leave the details of the ATI tessellation library in Direct3D 10 to a later time, here are some important details:

- We can combine tessellation draw calls with instancing in Direct3D 10. This means we can specify the tessellation level per instanced draw call and render an army of characters with a single mesh. We can combine this with texture arrays and other Direct3D 10 methods for creating a varied, interesting array of characters. We can also combine this method with the use of geometry shaders to perform LOD selection dynamically. For more details on this technique used in a practical scenario, see [SBCT08].

- In Direct3D 10, we can simply specify that the mesh's vertex buffer can be used as a texture for sampling data, and bind it as both for the tessellation draw-call; therefore, we don't need to explicitly copy the vertex buffer contents into a separate texture.

- We can use a stream-out post-vertex shader to compute per-edge tessellation factors and to perform control cage animation and transformation. We can also use geometry shader post-tessellation to either stream out the data for later use, to compute per-face quantities, or to perform further amplification (fur fins, render to cubemaps for reflections, etc.).

- In Direct3D 10.1, we also have an increased number of vertex inputs (32). This eliminates some of the pressure to use explicit vertex fetches.

- We have access to system-generated vertex IDs in these API versions' vertex shaders. This eliminates the need to generate this data channel during preprocessing and manually specify it to the shader.

LIGHTING WITH TESSELLATION AND DISPLACEMENT MAPPING

Traditionally, animated characters are rendered and lit using tangent-space normal maps (TSNMs). However, when we are rendering our characters with displacement mapping, to benefit from the additional details provided by the displacement maps, it is necessary to compute the lighting using the normal at the displaced surface position (Figure 1.2.10). This necessitates that the normal stored in the TSNM is computed using the same art assets and tangent space computation as were used to compute the displacement map, ideally at the same time, to ensure that they match identically. This consistency is crucial for accurate lighting. In fact, the ideal authoring pipeline would generate the two maps at the same time, using a single tool. By using the publicly available AMD GPUMeshMapper [AMDGMM08] tool, which provides source code for tangent-space generation, we can ensure these requirements are met, and we can shade our characters using any lighting techniques that utilize TSNM. This is very important, as it allows us to use normal maps for animated character rendering (since world-space normal maps would be problematic for that purpose).

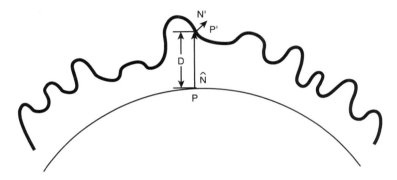

FIGURE 1.2.10   Displacement of the vertex modifies the normal used for rendering.
P is the original point displaced in the direction of the geometric normal
$\widehat{N}$ displacement amount D. The resulting point P′
needs to be shaded using the normal N′.

RENDERING ANIMATED, TESSELLATED CHARACTERS

When we render animated characters with subdivision, we need to perform animation calculations on the control mesh (the superprimitives), and then interpolate between the animated superprimitive vertices. A brute force approach of transforming and animating the superprimitive vertices in the evaluation shader wastes performance and bandwidth due to redundant computations; all newly generated tessellated vertices would perform the same computations as on the original vertices. Because hardware tessellation can generate millions of additional triangles, it is essential to minimize the amount of per-vertex computations post-tessellation, and to perform animation calculations only once per control vertex. In the Direct3D 11 tessellation pipeline, this can be easily expressed in a single rendering pass using various shader types as described in [Gee08]. In the DirectX 9, Xbox 360, and DirectX10/10.1 APIs, a two-pass rendering approach is needed.

In the first pass, we perform all animation calculations for the control cage vertices, and store the results in video memory. This can be implemented using stream output from vertex shaders (DirectX 10) or R2VB and pixel shaders (DirectX 9). In the second pass, tessellation is enabled, and the animated vertices can be directly used by the evaluation shader. In DirectX 10, the multi-pass technique can also be applied to instanced characters, by rendering an instanced point set during the first pass and using the instance and vertex IDs to fetch from a buffer resource during the second pass. Note that using this multi-pass method for control cage rendering is beneficial not only for rendering tessellated characters, but for any rendering pipeline in which we want to reuse results of expensive vertex operations multiple times. For example, we can use the results of the first pass for our animated and transformed characters for rendering into shadow maps and cube maps for reflections.

Although it is helpful to stream and reuse the animation calculations, this alone is not fully effective. The vertex data will be streamed at full precision, and the evaluation shader must still pay a large cost in memory bandwidth and fetch instructions to retrieve it. To improve performance, we use a compression scheme to pack the transformed vertices into a compact 128-bit format to remove this bottleneck and to reduce the associated memory footprint. This allows the tessellation pass to load a full set of transformed vertex data using a single fetch per superprimitive vertex. Although the compression scheme requires additional ALU cycles for both compression and decompression, this is more than paid for by the reduction in memory bandwidth and fetch operations in the evaluation shader.

We compress vertex positions by expressing them as fixed-point values that are used to interpolate the corners of a sufficiently large bounding box that is local to each character. The number of bits needed depends on the size of the model and the desired quality level, but it does not need to be extremely large. For example, in the AMD "Froblins" demo, the dynamic range of our vertex data is roughly 600 cm. A 16-bit coordinate on this scale gives a resolution of about 90 microns, which is slightly larger than the diameter of a human hair.

We can compress the tangent frame by converting the basis vectors to spherical coordinates and quantizing them. Spherical coordinates are well suited to compressing unit length vectors, since every compressed value in the spherical domain corresponds to a unique unit-length vector. In a Cartesian representation (such as the widely used `DEC3N` format), a large fraction of the space of compressed values goes unused. What this means in practice is that a much smaller bit count can be used to represent spherical coordinates at a reasonable level of accuracy. We have found that using an 8-bit spherical coordinate pair for tangent space basis vectors results in rendered images that are comparable in quality to a 32-bit Cartesian format. The main drawback of using spherical coordinates is that a number of expensive trigonometric functions must be used for compression and decompression.

Texture coordinates are compressed by converting the *uv* coordinates into a pair of fixed-point values, using whatever bits are left. To ensure acceptable precision, this requires that the *uv* coordinates in the model be in the 0–1 range, with no explicit tiling of textures by the artist. For small textures, a smaller bit count could be used for the *uv* coordinates, provided that the *uv*s are snapped to the texel centers.

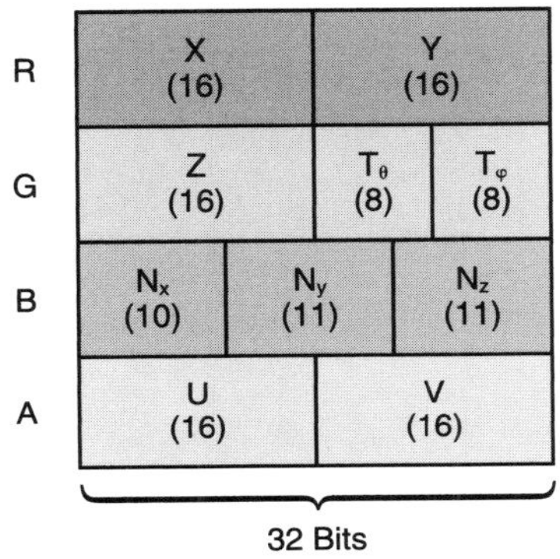

FIGURE 1.2.11   Data format used for compressed, animated vertices.

Our bit layout for the compressed vertices is shown in Figure 1.2.11, and corresponding compression and decompression code is shown in Listings 1.2.10 and 1.2.11. We use 16 bits for each component of the position, two 8-bit spherical coordinates for the tangent, 32 bits for the normal, and 16 for each *uv* coordinate. Since our tangent frames are orthogonal, we refrain from storing the binormal, and instead recompute it based on the decompressed normal and tangent. Since a full 32-bit field is available, we use DEC3N-like compression for the normal, which requires fewer ALU operations than spherical coordinates. If additional data fields are needed, we have also found that 8-bit spherical coordinates can be used for the normal, at a quality level comparable to DEC3N. We experimented with all of these alternatives on the ATI Radeon HD 4870 GPU, but found little practical difference in performance or quality between any of them.

This compressed format would also make an excellent storage format for static geometry. In this case (and for the case of noninstanced characters), the decompression could be accelerated by leveraging the vertex fetch hardware to perform some of the integer-to-float conversions. We cannot do this for instanced characters, because we must explicitly fetch vertex data with buffer loads, using the instance ID of the character, instead of using the fixed-function vertex fetch. On average, we obtained a 25% performance improvement via our multi-pass technique with compression (compared to a single-pass method that animates each tessellated vertex).

Listing 1.2.10 Compression code for vertex format given in Figure 1.2.11

```
// Quantizes a floating point value (0-1) to a certain number of bits
uint Quantize( float v, uint nBits )
{
   float fMax = ((float) (1 << nBits))-1.0f;
   return uint( round(v*fMax) );
}


uint PackShorts( uint nHigh, uint nLow )
{
   return (nHigh << 16) | (nLow);
}


uint PackBytes( uint nHigh, uint nLow )
{
   return (nHigh << 8) | (nLow);
}


/// Converts a vector to spherical coordinates.
/// Theta (x) is in the 0-PI range.  Phi (y) is in the -PI,PI range
float2 CartesianToSpherical( float3 cartesian )
{
   cartesian = clamp( normalize( cartesian ), -1,1 ); // beware of
rounding error
   float theta = acos( cartesian.z );
   float s     = sqrt( cartesian.x * cartesian.x + cartesian.y *
cartesian.y );
   float phi   = atan2( cartesian.x / s, cartesian.y / s );
   if( s == 0 )
     phi = 0; // prevent singularity if normal points straight up

   return float2( theta, phi );
}
```

```
// Converts a normal vector to quantized spherical coordinates
uint2 CompressVectorQSC( float3 v, uint nBits )
{
    float2 vSpherical = CartesianToSpherical( v );

    return uint2( Quantize(  vSphericalNorm.x / PI, nBits ),
                  Quantize( (vSphericalNorm.y + PI ) / ( 2*PI ), nBits ) );
}


// Encodes position as fixed-point lerp factors between AABB corners
uint3 CompressPosition( float3 vPos, float3 vBBMin, float3 vBBMax, uint
nBits )
{
    float3 vPosNorm = saturate( (vPos - vBBMin) / (vBBMax-vBBMin) ):
    return uint3( Quantize( vPosNorm.x, nBits ),
                  Quantize( vPosNorm.y, nBits ),
                  Quantize( vPosNorm.z, nBits ) );
}


uint PackCartesian( float3 v )
{
    float3 vUnsigned = saturate( (v.xyz * 0.5) + 0.5 );
    uint nX = Quantize( vUnsigned.x, 10 );
    uint nY = Quantize( vUnsigned.y, 11 );
    uint nZ = Quantize( vUnsigned.z, 11 );
    return ( nX << 22 ) | ( nY << 11 ) | nZ;
}


uint4 PackVertex( CompressedVertex v, float3 vBBoxMin, float3 vBBoxMax )
{
    uint3 nPosition  = CompressPosition( v.vPosition, vBBoxMin, vBBoxMax,
16 );
    uint2 nTangent   = CompressVectorQSC( v.vTangent, 8 );
```

```
    uint4 nOutput;

    nOutput.x = PackShorts( nPosition.x, nPosition.y );

    nOutput.y = PackShorts( nPosition.z, PackBytes( nTangent.x,
nTangent.y ) );

    nOutput.z = PackCartesian ( v.vNormal );

    nOutput.w = PackShorts( Quantize( vUV.x, 16 ), Quantize( vUV.y, 16 ) );

    return nOutput;

}
```

Listing 1.2.11 Decompression code for vertex format given in Figure 1.2.11

```
float DeQuantize( uint n, uint nBits )
{
    float fMax = ((float) (1 << nBits)) - 1.0f;
    return float(n)/fMax;
}


float3 DecompressVectorQSC( uint2 nCompressed, uint nBitCount )
{
    float2 vSph = float2( DeQuantize( nCompressed.x, nBitCount ),
                          DeQuantize( nCompressed.y, nBitCount ) );
    vSph.x = vSph.x * PI;
    vSph.y = (2 * PI * vSph.y) - PI
    float fSinTheta = sin( vSph.x );
    float fCosTheta = cos( vSph.x );
    float fSinPhi   = sin( vSph.y );
    float fCosPhi   = cos( vSph.y );
    return float3(  fSinPhi * fSinTheta, fCosPhi * fSinTheta, fCosTheta );
}


  float3 DecompressPosition( uint3 nBits, float3 vBBMin, float3 vBBMax,
uint nCount )
    {
```

```
   float3 vPosN = float3( DeQuantize( nBits.x, nCount),
                          DeQuantize( nBits.y, nCount),
                          DeQuantize( nBits.z, nCount) );
   return lerp( vBBMin.xyz, vBBMax.xyz, vPosN );
}


float3 UnpackPosition( uint4 nPacked, float3 vBBoxMin, float3 vBBoxMax )
{
   uint3 nPos;
   nPos.xy = uint2( nPacked.x >> 16, nPacked.x & 0x0000ffff );
   nPos.z  = nPacked.y >> 16;
   return DecompressPosition( nPos, vBBoxMin, vBBoxMax, 16 );
}


float2 UnpackUV( uint4 nPacked )
{
   uint2 nUV  = uint2( nPacked.w >> 16, nPacked.w & 0x0000ffff );
   float2 vUV = float2( DeQuantize( nUV.x, 16 ), DeQuantize( nUV.y, 16 ) );
   return vUV;
}


float3 UnpackTangent( uint4 nPacked )
{
   uint2 nTan = uint2( (nPacked.y >> 8) & 0xff, nPacked.y & 0xff );
   return DecompressVectorQSC( nTan, 8 );
}


float3 UnpackCartesian( uint n )
{
   uint  nX = (n >> 22) & 0x3FF;
   uint  nY = (n >> 11) & 0x7FF;
   uint  nZ = n         & 0x7FF;
   float fX = (2.0f * DeQuantize( nX, 10 )) - 1.0f;
```

```
    float fY = (2.0f * DeQuantize( nY, 11 )) - 1.0f;
    float fZ = (2.0f * DeQuantize( nZ, 11 )) - 1.0f;
    return  float3( fX, fY, fZ );
}


CompressedVertex UnpackVertex( uint4 nPacked, float3 vBBoxMin, float3
vBBoxMax )
{
    CompressedVertex vVert;
    vVert.vPosition = UnpackPosition( nPacked, vBBoxMin, vBBoxMax );
    vVert.vNormal   = UnpackCartesian( nPacked.z );
    vVert.vTangent  = UnpackTangent( nPacked );
    vVert.vBinormal = normalize( cross( vVert.vTangent, vVert.vNormal ) );
    vVert.vUV       = UnpackUV( nPacked );
    return vVert;
}
```

DISPLACEMENT MAP TIPS AND REDUCING SURFACE CRACKS

In this section, we share several practical tips for the generation and use of displacement maps that we have collected throughout our process.

The method used for generation of displacement maps must match the method for evaluating the subdivided surface. This naturally correlates with the absolute need to know the process used by the modeling tool used for map generations. Many DCC tools (for example, Autodesk Maya) first use an approximating subdivision process, such as the Catmull-Clark subdivision method, on the control mesh (the low-resolution, or superprimitive, mesh). Once the mesh has been smoothed, the fine-scale details are captured into a scalar or vector displacement map. If we want to capture the displacement map with this method, and use it during rendering, we must render the final surface using Catmull-Clark subdivision methods during surface evaluation. Combining displacement maps generated with a different surface evaluation method than that used for rendering can lead to unpredictable results. Additionally, a number of concerns arise with topology choices and the treatment of extraordinary points, as well as patch reordering to ensure watertightness during displacement. Some interesting solutions have been described in [Castaño08].

In our case, we used the AMD GPUMeshMapper tool [AMDGMM08], designed specifically for robust generation of displacement maps for interpolative planar subdivision. Given a pair of low- and high-resolution meshes, this tool provides a number of options for controlling the envelopes for ray casting between the low- and high-resolution models to capture displacement and normal information. Furthermore, to achieve controllable results at runtime, we must know the exact floating-point values for displacement scale and bias for the generated displacement map. This tool provides this information, collected during the generation process, in the form of parameters that can be used directly in the shader.

Particular care needs to be taken during displacement mapping to generate watertight, or simply visibly crack-free, surfaces. This is true regardless of the subdivision method used for evaluation. One challenge with rendering complex characters with displacement maps that contain texture uv borders is the introduction of texture uv seams (see Figure 1.2.12, left, for an example of such a displacement map). When sampling across the uv seams, bilinear discontinuities, along with potentially varying floating-point precision of the uv values, may introduce geometry cracks (Figure 1.2.12, center) across these uv borders. One solution to resolve this issue is to lay out the neighboring uv borders with the exact sample orientations and lengths. However, this is very difficult to achieve in practice for character modeling or complex objects. Another approach is to utilize continuous seamless (chartless) parameterization, which is extremely difficult or even impossible to generate.

We solve this problem during the map-generation process, rather than at runtime, via additional features implemented as part of the GPUMeshMapper tool. We postprocess our displacement maps by correcting all the texture uv borders during the displacement map generation, by identifying the border triangle edges and performing filtering across edges (with additional fix-ups) to alleviate displacement seams.

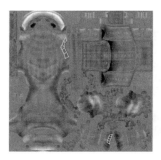  

Displacement Map   *Rendered character using the*   *Zoomed-in view shows*
    displacement map with a seam   *a crack in the surface*

FIGURE 1.2.12 Example of a visible crack generated due to inconsistent values across the edges of the displacement map for this character. On the left we highlighted the specific edges along the seam. Note that the adjacent edges for this seam do not have uniform parameterization.

Acknowledgments

We're grateful to Bill Bilodeau of the AMD ISV engineering team for his help with some of the figures in this article discussing ideas during implementation. We would also like to thank the members of AMD's Game Computing application for their work on the "Froblins" demo, specifically Jeremy Shopf, Christopher Oat, and Abe Wiley (whose art was used for all images in this article). Additionally, we greatly appreciate the fruitful discussions and suggestions from Nicolas Thibieroz, who also constributed the tessellation tutorial SDK sample on the DVD-ROM. Finally, we would like to thank Peter Lohrmann, Budirijanto Purnomo, and Dan Ginsburg for their hard work on the AMD GPUMeshMapper tool.

ON THE DVD

References

[AMD09] AMD Radeon SDK and Documents. 2009.
http://developer.amd.com/gpu/radeon/pages/RadeonSDKSamplesDocuments.aspx

[AMDGMM08] AMD GPU MeshMapper Tool. 2008.
http://ati.amd.com/developer/gpumeshmapper.html

[Blythe06] Blythe, D. 2006. The Direct3D 10 System. *ACM Transactions on Graphics*, 25, 3, pp. 724–734.

[Castaño08] Castaño, I. Water-Tight, Textured, Displaced Subdivision Surface Tessellation Using Direct3D 11. Presentation. Gamefest 2008, Seattle, Wash., July 2008.

[CatmullClark78] Catmull, E. and Clark, J. 1978. Recursively generated B-spline surfaces on arbitrary topological meshes. *Comput. Aid. Des.* 10, 6, 350–355

[Froblins08] AMD ATI Radeon HD 4870 demo, Froblins. 2008.
http://ati.amd.com/developer/demos.html

[Gee08] Gee, K. 2008. Direct3D 11 Tessellation. Presentation. Gamefest 2008, Seattle, Wash., July 2008.

[Klein08] Klein, A. 2008. Introduction to the Direct3D 11 Graphics Pipeline. Presentation. Gamefest 2008, Seattle, Wash., July 2008.

[Loop87]. Loop, C.T. 1987. Smooth subdivision surfaces based on triangles, 1987. Master's Thesis, Department of Mathematics, University of Utah.

[LoopSchaefer08] Loop, C. and Schaefer, S. 2008. Approximating Catmull-Clark Subdivision Surfaces with Bicubic Patches. *ACM Transactions on Graphics* (TOG), V. 27, I. 1.

[PieglTiller96] Piegl, L.A. and Tiller, W. 1996. *The NURBS Book (Monographs in Visual Communication)*, 2nd ed. Springer.

[Persson06] Persson, E. 2006. Render to Vertex Buffer Programming. ATI Technologies Technical Report, March 2006. http://developer.amd.com/media/gpu_assets/R2VB_programming.pdf

[SBCT08] Shopf, J., Barczak, J., Oat, C., and Tatarchuk, N. 2008. March of the Froblins: Simulation and Rendering Massive Crowds of Intelligent and Detailed Creatures on GPU. ACM SIGGRAPH 2008: Proceedings of the conference course notes, *Advances in Real-Time Rendering in 3D Graphics and Games*, Chapter 3, pp. 52–101, Los Angeles, August 2008. PDF

[Stam98] Stam, J. 1998. Exact evaluation of Catmull-Clark subdivision surfaces at arbitrary parameter values. *Proceedings of the 25th Annual Conference on Computer Graphics and Interactive Techniques*, pp. 395–404, July 1998.

[Tatarchuk06] Tatarchuk, N. 2006. Dynamic Parallax Occlusion Mapping with Approximate Soft Shadows. In *Proceedings of ACM SIGGRAPH Symposium on Interactive 3D Graphics and Games* (SI3D '06), pp. 63–69. PDF

[Tatarchuk08] Tatarchuk, N. 2008. Advanced Topics in GPU Tessellation: Algorithms and Lessons Learned. Presentation. Gamefest 2008, Seattle, Wash., July 2008.

[Tatarchuk09] Tatarchuk, N. 2009. Dynamic Terrain Rendering on GPU Using Real-Time Tessellation. In *ShaderX⁷: Advanced Rendering*. Engel, W., Ed. Charles River Media, Cambridge, Mass.

[VPBM01] Vlachos, A., Peters, J., Boyd, C., and Mitchell, J.L. 2001. Curved PN triangles, *Proceedings of the 2001 Symposium on Interactive 3D Graphics*, pp. 159–166, March 2001.

[ZorinSchröeder00] Zorin, D. and Schröder, P. 2000. Subdivision for Modeling and Animation. ACM Siggraph 2000 course.

1.3 Dynamic Terrain Rendering on GPUs Using Real-Time Tessellation

NATALYA TATARCHUK
GAME COMPUTING APPLICATIONS GROUP
AMD, INC.

FIGURE 1.3.1 Real-time rendering of terrain with displacement-map-based lighting and procedurally generated snow placement.

Terrain rendering systems can be found at the heart of many video games and other interactive applications. This vital research topic has been widely explored in the computer graphics literature [LKR*96, DWS*97, Blow00, AsirvathamHoppe05, to name just a few]. Rendering high-quality terrain with robust frame rates poses many challenges. Many terrain systems encompass large spans of space representing various landscape types (such that a player can explore the levels for at least several hours). These continuous spans are often rendered simultaneously at vastly different levels of detail (LODs). Terrain rendering systems frequently need to handle extreme LOD changes, allowing the player to see details at various scales. In many outdoor scenarios, the terrain may take up a great deal of screen-space; therefore, detailed and efficient shading techniques are absolutely crucial. And, of course, we must be mindful of the overarching goal of optimizing the overall application memory footprint.

In short, a high-quality terrain-rendering system requires a good view-dependent, LOD management system.

A number of different approaches for terrain rendering have been developed in recent years. An oft-implemented method is a CPU-managed LOD system, where different sections of terrain are loaded on demand based on the player's or camera's movements. The meshes representing different LODs for terrain are typically pre-tessellated offline using performance or quality heuristics. Frequently, additional heuristics are needed to ensure seamless stitching for the neighboring patches with different LODs. Instanced rendering provides an efficient method for simultaneously rendering multiple terrain patches, as it allows the overall reduction of draw calls and lowers the associated memory footprint. With this approach, each distinct LOD is rendered as an instanced draw call. In the case of an extreme close-up, the associated polygonal patches frequently contain a very large number of polygons (on the order of multiple millions of triangles).

Thus, in many cases, terrain systems that implement this approach may need to render many millions of polygons per frame and can, therefore, become the rendering bottleneck for the system. The polygonal patches representing the closest LOD need to be stored in video memory, as a combination of vertex and indexed buffers, and require a significant memory footprint for polygonal surfaces and the corresponding textures. Rendering these polygonal patches consumes additional memory bandwidth.

An alternative approach for rendering high-quality terrain is to combine displacement mapping with interpolative subdivision using a GPU tessellation pipeline. The GPU tessellation pipeline is described in detail in [TatarchukBarczak09]. With our system, we will render our terrain as a low-resolution input mesh representing a single low-resolution flat quad (Figure 1.3.2a). During rendering, we will dynamically subdivide this quad using the GPU tessellation pipeline and apply displacement mapping post-tessellation (Figure 1.3.2c).

(a) Start with a low-resolution quad.

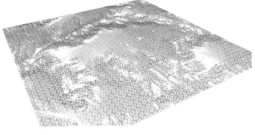

(b) Apply GPU tessellation to the input quad to capture fine details in the resulting mesh.

(c) Finally, apply displacement post-tessellation.

FIGURE 1.3.2   An outline of the process of rendering adaptive terrain using our system. We can take advantage of adaptive tessellation to implement a terrain system that dynamically manages the LOD on the fly in a single draw call. By simply converting the terrain system to use continuous subdivision (as described in [TatarchukBarczak09]) for rendering, we can achieve a tremendous savings in memory and disk storage and improved performance by using tessellation to render the terrain in real-time. Table 1.3.1 compares the memory footprint as well as performance for rendering terrain using explicit LOD management and the GPU tessellation pipeline.

Table 1.3.1 Memory Footprint Comparison for Rendering a Terrain Patch with GPU Tessellation and Without (Using Traditional Rendering Pipeline)

	Rendering low-resolution object with GPU tessellation	Rendering high-resolution mesh using traditional rendering
Input mesh polygon count	840 triangles	1,280,038 triangles
Polygon count for rendered mesh	1,008,038 triangles (post-tessellation)	1,280,038 triangles
VRAM vertex buffer size	70 KB	31 MB
VRAM index buffer size	23 KB	14 MB

Terrains rendered with this approach can be shaded using a combination of artist-authored terrain textures (including normal maps). We also can derive the normal dynamically from the height map(s) and use this normal vector to shade the surface. In our example in this chapter we only use a single height map representing the main landscape formation and a pair of additional normal maps for snow and small rock textures to render and shade the terrain. The terrain material system can support a number of texture maps (height, normal, color) to allow for interesting landscape variations.

In the rest of this chapter, we will describe how to use adaptive tessellation using the GPU tessellation pipeline in Microsoft DirectX 9, and then describe a method for computing per-edge tessellation factors for seamless terrain rendering. We will then provide an example of how to shade this terrain using the normal derived from the height map and procedural snow placement. The techniques described in this chapter are illustrated in a code sample provided on this book's DVD-ROM, "TerrainRendering." This application is implemented using the ATI GPU tessellation library [AMD09].

ON THE DVD

PROGRAMMING FOR ADAPTIVE GPU TESSELLATION

In this article, we implement our approach using the AMD GPU tessellation library [AMD09], which provides a lean and flexible interface to the tessellator hardware available on ATI Radeon GPUs in Direct3D 9.

By using the adaptive tessellation mode, we can specify a tessellation level for each individual edge of the control mesh primitives (super-primitives, or super-prims). This allows us to *modify* the LOD for the mesh at render time. Once the tessellation factors are computed, we can supply them to the terrain render pass with an adaptive tessellation draw call.

Figure 1.3.3 shows some examples of super-primitive tessellation using adaptive tessellation. With adaptive tessellation, we can also specify a maximum and a minimum tessellation level per draw call. The minimum and maximum will serve as range clamps for the individual edge levels. With Direct3D 9 and the Xbox 360, we specify the per-edge tessellation levels via a separate vertex stream along with the regular mesh data (the original vertex stream). All adaptive draw calls in Direct3D 9 and Xbox 360 must be rendered with non-indexed draw calls. Note that to implement dynamic adaptive tessellation, we need to be able to compute per-edge tessellation factors per frame. This is typically done in a pass prior to the tessellation pass at render time.

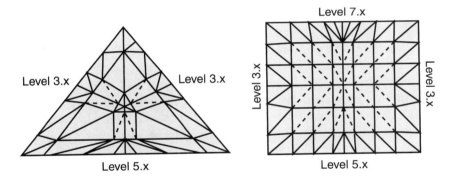

FIGURE 1.3.3   Examples of adaptive tessellation for triangle and quad primitives.

One immediate concern with using non-indexed rendering for adaptive tessellation draw calls is that we typically render with indexed meshes to optimize for post-transform cache coherence. However, since the tessellator does not generate duplicate vertices, and the original control cage meshes are rather small to start with, using non-indexed meshes does not impose significant performance penalties.

We can use a number of LOD metrics to control the quality of rendered terrain and adaptively subdivide to select the right amount of detail as needed. One approach is to dynamically compute tessellation factors in a pre-pass to determine how finely to tessellate each polygon in the terrain. We can calculate the dynamic level of detail per primitive edge on the GPU using a metric for maintaining near-constant screen-space edge length. In this case, the LOD metric can target a specific screen-space edge length to maintain a reasonable triangle size independent of the object's position with respect to the camera; thus, we would not waste performance on details that would go unnoticed in the final rendering. The actual resolution of the screen would be automatically accounted for with this LOD technique as well. Alternatively (or in addition to this metric), we can also account for the details in the displacement map and tessellate more finely around the areas of high displacement. We can also use a vertex-to-camera distance metric or a silhouette-based metric to adaptively subdivide the mesh (in the latter case, we would subdivide more at silhouettes to preserve them). This mode provides stable performance by allowing local adjustment of the triangle density, thus creating triangles only where needed.

One important consideration when assigning tessellation levels per edge is that we must use the exact same floating-point value for the tessellation level for edges shared between adjacent super-primitives. Failing to do this may result in T-junctions and cracks, especially when combining tessellation with displacement mapping. See the article on dynamic terrain rendering [Tatarchuk09] for more details on how to avoid this with adaptive tessellation.

Figure 1.3.4 provides an overview of the passes for rendering with adaptive tessellation. We start by transforming and animating the input (super-primitive mesh). Since we render with non-indexed meshes, we do not want to perform redundant computations when computing the per-edge tessellation factors. Therefore our vertices must be already transformed and animated (though animation is not typical for terrain rendering, if we wanted to render an earthquake, this would be the place to do that) prior to computation of the per-edge tessellation factors.

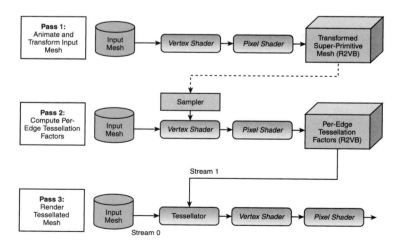

FIGURE 1.3.4   Visual representation of adaptive tessellation rendering passes.

In DirectX 9, we take advantage of the R2VB extension [Persson06] to perform the computations for the first two passes. We can compute the tessellation factors by using the R2VB extension in pass 2, which allows us to recirculate vertex data as render targets and vertex buffers as needed. Once the per-edge factors are computed and stored in a vertex buffer (an R2VB buffer), we can issue our adaptively tessellated draw call using the input super-primitive mesh and the tessellation factors as inputs.

TRANSFORMING MESH USING R2VB

In the first pass, we need to render our input mesh to compute its transformed and animated version. This, in essence, emulates the data recirculation functionality of flexible buffer support available in Direct3D 10.

In this pass, we render our input mesh as point list primitives. The vertex shader transforms the primitives and outputs them to a 2D buffer. We transform the vertices in this pass to screen-space, because our LOD metric for computing the per-edge tessellation factors is based on maintaining near-constant screen-space edge length for the triangles in the rendered mesh. Note that since we are using displacement mapping for our terrain, all displacement mapping and animation must happen prior to transforming the vertices into screen-space. The vertex shader computes the 2D coordinates, and the pixel shader renders the results into the appropriate render target. In our case, this render target is created as an R2VB resource used to store the transformed mesh. Listing 1.3.1 shows an example.

Listing 1.3.1 Example of Direct3D code for setting up the first pass for rendering transformed vertices into an R2VB render target

```
IDirect3DTexture9* sg_pTransformedVerts = NULL;
// Create the texture for the transformed super-prim texture
V( pd3dDevice->CreateTexture( cg_nR2VBTextureWidth, sg_nR2VBTextureHeight, 1,
                    D3DUSAGE_RENDERTARGET, D3DFMT_A32B32G32R32F,
                    D3DPOOL_DEFAULT, &sg_pTransformedVerts, NULL ));


// Create the R2VB handle for the tessellation factors
V( r2vbInit( pd3dDevice, nBufferSize *  sizeof(float), &sg_hR2VBTessFactors ));
```

```
    ...
    IDirect3DSurface9* pCurrentRT = NULL;  // the backbuffer or currently
    rendered to surface
    IDirect3DSurface9* pNewRT     = NULL;


    // Get a pointer to the backbuffer:
    V( pd3dDevice->GetRenderTarget( 0, &pCurrentRT ));


    // Select whether we're applying displacement or not:
    if ( sg_bDisplaced )
      sg_pEffect->SetTechnique( "RenderTransformedDisplacedVerts" );
    else
      sg_pEffect->SetTechnique( "RenderTransformedVerts" );


    // Set the vertex declaration and stream source to the original low-res
    input mesh:
    V( pd3dDevice->SetVertexDeclaration( sg_pVertexIDDecl ));
    V( pd3dDevice->SetStreamSource( 0, sg_pNonIndexedMeshVB, 0, nVertexSize ));


    // Output transformed vertices for the input low-res mesh to a render
    target for use in // the next pass:
    V( sg_pTransformedVerts->GetSurfaceLevel( 0, &pNewRT ));
    V( pd3dDevice->SetRenderTarget( 0, pNewRT ));


    // Render the passes to transform the vertices:
    V( sg_pEffect->Begin( &cPasses, 0  ));
    for ( iPass = 0; iPass < cPasses; iPass++ )
    {
      V( sg_pEffect->BeginPass( iPass  ));


      // Render as points and draw to an R2VB buffer:
      V( pd3dDevice->DrawPrimitive( D3DPT_POINTLIST, 0, sg_nNumVerts  ));


      V( sg_pEffect->EndPass( ));
```

```
}
V( sg_pEffect->End( ));


SAFE_RELEASE( pNewRT );
```

One important detail we need to include for a Direct3D 9 implementation is the need to precompute vertex IDs and store them in the input super-primitive mesh. Unfortunately, vertex IDs are not provided by the runtime in Direct3D 9 (unlike Direct3D 10 and beyond). We need to use these vertex IDs to compute the correct 2D texture coordinate to output the transformed vertex to the render target (the R2VB buffer for the transformed mesh). We also need to propagate that value to the next pass because the vertex IDs are also needed to accurately compute per-edge tessellation factors. Therefore, we simply precompute these values at mesh preprocessing time and store them as the fourth component of the input mesh's position element, as shown in Listing 1.3.2. Note that some methods (such as `DisplaceVertex(..)`) are omitted here for brevity, but are included in the accom-panying sample on the DVD-ROM.

ON THE DVD

Listing 1.3.2 Example of D3DX FX shader for rendering transformed vertices as points into an R2VB render target

```
struct VsTfmInput
{
    float4 vPosOS   : POSITION0;   // (x,y,z) — 3D position, w — vertex ID
(precomputed)
    float2 vTexCoord: TEXCOORD0;
    float3 vNormal  : NORMAL0;
};
struct VsTfmOutput
{
  float4 vPos       : POSITION;
  float  fVertexID  : TEXCOORD0;
  float3 vPosCS     : TEXCOORD1;
};


VsTfmOutput VSRenderTransformedDisplaced( VsTfmInput i )
```

```
{
    VsTfmOutput o;
    int nVertexID    = floor( i.vPosOS.w );
    int nTextureWidth = g_vTformVertsMapSize.x;


    // Compute row and column of the position in 2D texture
    float2 vPos   = float2( nVertexID % nTextureWidth, nVertexID /
nTextureWidth );
            vPos   /= g_vTformVertsMapSize.xy;
            vPos.y = 1.0 - vPos.y;
            vPos   = vPos * 2 - 1.0; // Move to [-1; 1] range


    o.vPos =  float4( vPos.xy, 0, 1 );


    // Propagate the vertex ID to the pixel shader
    o.fVertexID = i.vPosOS.w;


    // Displace input vertex:
    float4 vPositionCS = float4( DisplaceVertex( i.vPosOS, i.vTexCoord,
i.vNormal ), 1 );


    // Transform vertex position to screen-space
    vPositionCS  = mul( vPositionCS, g_mWorldView );
    vPositionCS /= vPositionCS.w;


    o.vPosCS = vPositionCS.xyz;


    return o;


}   // End of VsTfmOutput VSRenderTransformedDisplaced(..)


//--------------------------------------struct PsTfmInput
{
    float4 vPos          : POSITION;
```

```
    float   fVertexID    : TEXCOORD0;
    float3 vPosCS        : TEXCOORD1;
};


float4 PSRenderTransformed( PsTfmInput i ): COLOR0
{
    return float4( i.vPosCS, i.fVertexID );
}


//----------------------------------------technique
RenderTransformedDisplacedVerts
{
    pass P0
    {
        CullMode      = NONE;
        ZEnable       = false;
        ZWriteEnable = false;

        VertexShader = compile vs_3_0 VSRenderTransformedDisplaced();
        PixelShader  = compile ps_3_0 PSRenderTransformed();
    }

} // End of technique RenderTransformedVerts
```

COMPUTING PER-EDGE TESSELLATION FACTORS

In the next pass, we compute the factors that determine how finely each edge of a given primitive will be tessellated during the tessellated mesh draw call. This is the heart of adaptive subdivision and LOD management for terrain rendering. There are many different ways to compute these per-edge factors using a number of metrics, as we have mentioned. The important consideration is smoothness of LOD transition (as the vertices change their relationship to the viewer, we should not see sudden pops in lighting and vertex positions). This is particularly important given that because we are using displacement mapping, sudden changes in terrain silhouettes can be very apparent.

For this pass, we also render our input mesh as a point list. We will use the previously computed transformed vertices R2VB resource and bind it as a vertex sampler to this pass. The vertex shader will rely on the provided vertex ID to compute tessellation factors for each edge and to sample the R2VB resource to fetch the transformed vertex data. Since we are rendering with a non-indexed mesh, we can compute one tessellation edge factor per input vertex and output it to a 2D R2VB render target. Note that the setup in Direct3D 9 is very similar to pass 1, and we refer the reader to the sample SDK application on the DVD-ROM for details.

ON THE DVD

We need to ensure that our resulting surface does not display cracks when applying displacement during rendering. Hence, the adjacent edges must have precision-identical tessellation factors; otherwise, we will instantly notice cracks in the terrain once displacement is applied (Figure 1.3.5). Furthermore, extra care during tessellation factor computation needs to be taken to ensure identical edge direction when evaluating the surface. We use vertex ID for this purpose. See Listing 1.3.3 for details of our approach.

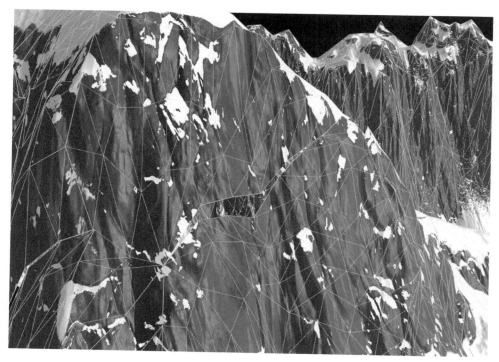

FIGURE 1.3.5 Example of cracks in the terrain surface when computing tessellation factors for edges without aligning edge direction.

Listing 1.3.3 Example of high-level shader language code for computing per-edge tessellation factors based on screen-space edge length

```
struct VsTFInput
{
   float4 vPositionOS : POSITION0;   // (xyz) - camera-space position, w -
vertex ID
};


struct VsTFOutput
{
   float4 vPositionCS : POSITION;
   float  fTessFactor : TEXCOORD0;
};


//-------------------------------------------------
VsTFOutput VSCalculateTFs( VsTFInput i )
{
   VsTFOutput o;

   // Current vertex ID:
   int nCurrentVertID = (int)( i.vPositionOS.w );


   // Determine the ID of the edge neighbor's vertex (remember that this
is done with
   // non-indexed primitives, so basically if the current vertex is v0,
then we have
   // edges: v0->v1, v1->v2, v2->v0


   int nCurrentVertEdgeID = nCurrentVertID - 3 * floor(
(float)nCurrentVertID /
                                          (float) 3);


   int nEdgeVert0ID = nCurrentVertID;      // this works if current vertex
is v0 or v1
```

```
    int nEdgeVert1ID = nCurrentVertID + 1;


if ( nCurrentVertEdgeID == 0 )
{
    nEdgeVert0ID = nCurrentVertID + 1;
}
else if ( nCurrentVertEdgeID == 1 )
{
    nEdgeVert0ID = nCurrentVertID + 1;
}
else if ( nCurrentVertEdgeID == 2 )  // In case of v2 we need to wrap
around to v0
{
    nEdgeVert0ID = nCurrentVertID - 2;
}


// Compute the fetch coordinates to fetch transformed positions
// for these two vertices to compute their edge statistics:
int    nTextureWidth     = g_vTformVertsMapSize.x;


// Vertex0: nCurrentVertID, compute row and column of the position in
2D texture:
float2 vVert0Coords   = float2( nCurrentVertID % nTextureWidth,
                                nCurrentVertID / nTextureWidth );
        vVert0Coords   /= g_vTformVertsMapSize.xy;


// Vertex1: nEdgeVert0ID, compute row and column of the position in 2D
texture:
float2 vVert1Coords   = float2( nEdgeVert0ID % nTextureWidth,
                                nEdgeVert0ID / nTextureWidth );
        vVert1Coords   /= g_vTformVertsMapSize.xy;


// Fetch transformed positions for these IDs:
float4 vVert0Pos = tex2Dlod( sTformVerts, float4( vVert0Coords, 0, 0 ));
float4 vVert1Pos = tex2Dlod( sTformVerts, float4( vVert1Coords, 0, 0 ));
```

```
// Swap vertices to make sure that we have the same edge direction
// regardless of their triangle order (based on vertex ID):
if ( vVert0Pos.w > vVert1Pos.w )
{
    float4 vTmpVert = vVert0Pos;
    vVert0Pos = vVert1Pos;
    vVert1Pos = vTmpVert;
}


// Use the distance from the camera to determine the tessellation factor:
float fEdgeDepth = 0.5 * ( ( vVert1Pos.z) + ( vVert0Pos.z ) );

float fTessFactor = clamp( fEdgeDepth / g_fMaxCameraDistance,
                          0, 1 );            // Map to 0-1 range
        fTessFactor = (1 - fTessFactor ) * 15;  // map to 0-15 range and
invert it
                                            // (higher to lower)


    const float fMinTessFactor = 1.0;
    const float fMaxTessFactor = 14.99999;


    // Clamp to the correct range
    o.fTessFactor = clamp( fTessFactor, fMinTessFactor, fMaxTessFactor );


    // Compute output position for rendering into a tessellation factors
texture
    int nVertexID = floor( i.vPositionOS.w );


    // Compute row and column of the position in 2D texture
    float2 vOutputPos   = float2( nVertexID % nTextureWidth, nVertexID /
nTextureWidth );
            vOutputPos   /= g_vTformVertsMapSize.xy;
            vOutputPos.y = 1.0 - vOutputPos.y;
            vOutputPos   = vOutputPos * 2 - 1.0;   // Move to [-1; 1] range
```

```
    o.vPositionCS = float4( vOutputPos.xy, 0, 1 );


    return o;


}    // End of VsTfmOutput VSCalculateTFs(..)


// Pixel shader for rendering the tessellation factor into an R2VB buffer.
struct PsTFInput
{
    float  fTessFactor : TEXCOORD0;
};


//---------------------------------float4 PSCalculateTFs( PsTFInput i ):
COLOR0
{
    return i.fTessFactor.xxxx;
}


//..............................................................
technique CalculateTessellationFactors
{
    pass P0
    {
        CullMode     = NONE;
        ZEnable      = false;
        ZWriteEnable = false;

        VertexShader = compile vs_3_0 VSCalculateTFs();
        PixelShader  = compile ps_3_0 PSCalculateTFs();
    }

}  // End of technique CalculateTessellationFactors
```

RENDERING TESSELLATED MESH WITH PER-EDGE TESSELLATION FACTORS

In the next pass, we will use the transformed input super-primitive mesh and the newly computed tessellation factors to render the tessellated and displaced mesh. For this draw call, we will use the ATI GPU tessellation library [Tatarchuk Barczak09]. We will bind the transformed mesh R2VB buffer as an input vertex stream 0 and will bind the tessellation factors as stream 1 (see Listing 1.3.4). The underlying driver and hardware platform will automatically use these tessellation factors to generate new surface locations and propagate them to the tessellation evaluation vertex shader (see [TatarchukBarczak09] for details on how to implement evaluation vertex shaders for GPU tessellation).

Listing 1.3.4 Example of Direct3D 9 and ATI GPU tessellation library calls for rendering adaptively tessellated terrain

```
// Enable adaptive tessellation (specifying that tessellation factors are
given in vertex
// stream 1 - 3rd parameter):
sg_pTessInterface->SetMode( TSMD_ENABLE_ADAPTIVE, 1 );


// Set min tessellation level:
sg_pTessInterface->SetMinLevel(
IATITessellationD3D9::ATI_TESS_MIN_TESSELLATION_LEVEL );


// Set tessellation level (this is used for both continuous and adaptive:
sg_pTessInterface->SetMaxLevel( sg_fMaxTessellationLevel );


// Set the vertex declaration and stream source for adaptively tessellated
mesh:
V( pd3dDevice->SetVertexDeclaration( sg_pAdaptiveVBDecl ));
V( pd3dDevice->SetStreamSource( 0, sg_pNonIndexedMeshVB, 0, nVertexSize ));


// Map the tessellation factors R2VB to stream source 1:
V( r2vbSetStreamTexSource( sg_hR2VBTessFactors, 1, 0, sg_pTessFactors, 0, 4 ));


// Select the appropriate technique to render our tessellated objects:
```

```
//
if ( sg_bDisplaced )
  if ( sg_bWireframe )
    sg_pEffect->SetTechnique( "RenderTessellatedDisplacedSceneWireframe" );
  else
    sg_pEffect->SetTechnique( "RenderTessellatedDisplacedScene" );
else
  if ( sg_bWireframe )
    sg_pEffect->SetTechnique( "RenderTessellatedSceneWireframe" );
  else
    sg_pEffect->SetTechnique( "RenderTessellatedScene" );

V( sg_pEffect->Begin( &cPasses, 0  ));
for ( iPass = 0; iPass < cPasses; iPass++ )
{
  V( sg_pEffect->BeginPass( iPass  ));
  V( sg_pTessInterface->DrawNonIndexed( TSPT_TRIANGLELIST, 0, sg_nNumVerts
/ 3  ));
  V( sg_pEffect->EndPass( ));
}
V( sg_pEffect->End( ));

// Disengage R2VB tessellation factors:
r2vbDisTexSource( sg_hR2VBTessFactors, 0 );

// Disable tessellation:
sg_pTessInterface->SetMode( TSMD_DISABLE );
```

Listing 1.3.5 Example of vertex shader for rendering adaptively tessellated terrain

```
//-------------------------------struct VsInputTessellated
{
```

```
    // Barycentric weights for tessellated vertex from the super-primitive
(low-resolution
    // input) mesh (i.e., each tessellated vertex quantity is computed via
barycentric
    // interpolation from the three super-primitive input vertices)
    float3 vBarycentric: BLENDWEIGHT0;

    // Data from super-prim vertex 0:
    float4 vPositionVert0 : POSITION0;
    float2 vTexCoordVert0 : TEXCOORD0;
    float3 vNormalVert0   : NORMAL0;

    // Data from super-prim vertex 1:
    float4 vPositionVert1 : POSITION4;
    float2 vTexCoordVert1 : TEXCOORD4;
    float3 vNormalVert1   : NORMAL4;

    // Data from super-prim vertex 2:
    float4 vPositionVert2 : POSITION8;
    float2 vTexCoordVert2 : TEXCOORD8;
    float3 vNormalVert2   : NORMAL8;
};


struct VsOutputTessellated
{
    float4 vPosCS      : POSITION;
    float2 vTexCoord   : TEXCOORD0;
    float3 vNormalWS   : TEXCOORD1;
    float3 vPositionWS : TEXCOORD2;
};
//--------------------------------
// Render tessellated mesh with displacement
//--------------------------------
```

```
VsOutputTessellated VSRenderTessellatedDisplaced( VsInputTessellated i )
{
    VsOutputTessellated o;

    // Compute new position based on the barycentric coordinates:
    float3 vPosTessOS = i.vPositionVert0.xyz * i.vBarycentric.x +
                        i.vPositionVert1.xyz * i.vBarycentric.y +
                        i.vPositionVert2.xyz * i.vBarycentric.z;

    // Output world-space position:
    o.vPositionWS = vPosTessOS;

    // Compute new tangent space basis vectors for the tessellated vertex:
    o.vNormalWS   = i.vNormalVert0.xyz * i.vBarycentric.x +
                    i.vNormalVert1.xyz * i.vBarycentric.y +
                    i.vNormalVert2.xyz * i.vBarycentric.z;

    // Compute new texture coordinates based on the barycentric
coordinates:
    o.vTexCoord = i.vTexCoordVert0.xy * i.vBarycentric.x +
                  i.vTexCoordVert1.xy * i.vBarycentric.y +
                  i.vTexCoordVert2.xy * i.vBarycentric.z;

    // Displace the tessellated vertex:
    o.vPositionWS = DisplaceVertex( vPosTessOS, o.vTexCoord, o.vNormalWS );

    // Transform position to screen-space:
    o.vPosCS = mul( float4( o.vPositionWS, 1.0 ), g_mWorldViewProjection );

    return o;

}  // End of VsOutputTessellated VSRenderTessellatedDisplaced(..)
```

SHADING TESSELLATED DISPLACED SURFACES

We shade the terrain object using the height map for lighting information (Figure 1.3.6) without relying on terrain normal maps. This allows us to reduce the overall memory footprint for this subsystem. The height map was designed using World-Machine terrain modeling software [WorldMachine08], which can generate very large and complex terrain maps. We use a 2K × 2K height map for our terrain object, and this can be extended to higher spans by combining multiple patches or by using larger map sizes (for example, by converting to Direct3D 10).

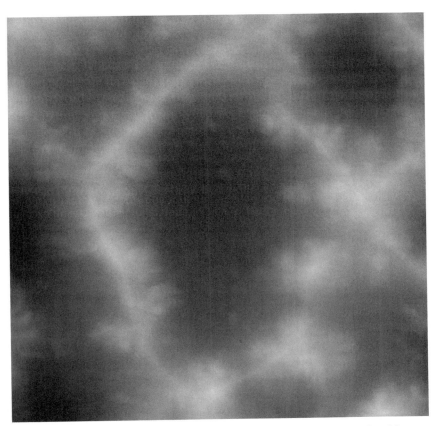

FIGURE 1.3.6   An example height map used to render our terrain object.

We dynamically derive the normal for each rendered pixel from the height map itself (see Listing 1.3.6) using central differences approximation on the height field. There are a number of ways to implement this, and our approach is simply one such method. Another method is outlined in [AnderssonTatarchuk07].

Listing 1.3.6 Example of method for computing the normal from the height map using central differences approach

```
texture  sMap;        // Displacement map
float    fScale;      // Displacement scale
float    fBias;       // Displacement bias


//-------------------------------float DisplacementTapMipped(
float2 vUV, sampler2D sMap, float fScale, float fBias )
{
   float fDisplacement = tex2D( sMap, float4( vUV, 0, 0 )).r;
   fDisplacement = fDisplacement * fScale + fBias;


   return fDisplacement;
}


//-------------------------------float3
CalculateNormalFourTap( float fDisplacement, float2 vUV,
                        sampler2D sMap, float fScale, float fBias,
                        float2 vMapSize  // This parameter is
displacement map

                                         // dimensions
                 )
{
   // Calculate new normal based on gradients of height map:
   float fDeltaU    = 1.0f / vMapSize.x;
   float fDeltaV    = 1.0f / vMapSize.y;

   float fNeighborU = DisplacementTapMipped( vUV + float2( fDeltaU, 0 ),
                                             sMap, fScale, fBias );
   float fNeighborV = DisplacementTapMipped( vUV + float2( 0, fDeltaV ),
                                             sMap, fScale, fBias );
   float fNeighborU2 = DisplacementTapMipped( vUV - float2( fDeltaU, 0 ),
                                             sMap, fScale, fBias );
```

```
    float fNeighborV2 = DisplacementTapMipped( vUV - float2( 0, fDeltaV ),
                                        sMap, fScale, fBias );


    float fDistanceU = fDeltaU;
    float fDistanceV = fDeltaV;


    // Average normals for neighboring quads:
    //
    //        V2
    //    U2  X   U
    //        V

    float3 vUX  = float3(  fDistanceU, fNeighborU  - fDisplacement, 0 ) ;
    float3 vVX  = float3(          0, fNeighborV  - fDisplacement, -
fDistanceV ) ;
    float3 vU2X = float3( -fDistanceU, fNeighborU2 - fDisplacement, 0 ) ;
    float3 vV2X = float3(          0, fNeighborV2 - fDisplacement,
fDistanceV ) ;


    return normalize( normalize( cross(  vUX,  vVX ) ) +
                      normalize( cross(  vVX, vU2X ) ) +
                      normalize( cross( vU2X, vV2X ) ) +
                      normalize( cross( vV2X,  vUX ) ) );


} // End of CalculateNormalFourTap(..)
```

Aside from reducing the associated memory footprint, this method provides easy support for dynamically combining multiple displacement maps. This can be very beneficial for interactive modifications of terrain via destruction or other means. For example, if we were to try to represent a terrain that is affected by a meteorite shower (such as in Figure 1.3.7), we could represent the terrain height field as a dynamic render target and render (splat) the meteorite crater height fields in the regions of impact on top of the main terrain height field. Then we would simply tessellate our terrain quad using this height field and shade by deriving the normal from this combined height field.

FIGURE 1.3.7   Moltke Crater, seven kilometers in diameter, is an excellent example of a simple crater with a bowl-shaped interior and smooth walls. (Apollo 10 photograph AS10-29-4324) (Image courtesy of Walter S. Kiefer, Lunar and Planetary Institute)

We allow combining the lighting from the height map with lighting derived from extra normal maps (such as small rocks or snow) to support diverse terrain materials on the same object. We can control the combining of rocks and snow by the geometric normal of the terrain, thus allowing us to procedurally place snow in the horizontal (flat) areas, and ensure that the steep areas consist of exposed rock. Listing 1.3.7 provides an example of the final pixel shader used to render our terrain.

Listing 1.3.7 Example of method for computing the normal from the height map using a central differences approach

```
// Constant parameters
float c_fRockDetailScale              = 1.0f;
float c_fRockDetailRepeatRate         = 15.0f;
float c_fRockDetailRepeatMultiplier   = 5.0;    // Repeat rate for
rock normal map
```

```
float c_fRockColorDetailRepeatMultiplier = 15.0;   // Repeat rate for
rock base map

float c_fSnowDetailRepeatRate = 100.0f;
float c_fSnowDetailScale       = 0.8;

float c_fSnowMin       = 0.6;
float c_fSnowRockMin   = 0.05;
float c_fSnowFade      = 0.1;
float c_fSnowRockFade  = 0.7;

float2 c_vDisplacementMapSize = float2( 2048, 2048 );

// Since we are rendering a terrain quad, we know its tangent frame is
// constant for all of the vertices (since it's a planar quad)
//   Tangent = <1,0,0>   Normal = <0,1,0>, Binormal = <0,0,-1>
// We can use shader literals for these to avoid having to store them per
vertex
#define QUAD_NORMAL     float3(0,1,0)
#define QUAD_TANGENT    float3(1,0,0)
#define QUAD_BINORMAL   float3(0,0,-1)

struct PsInput
{
    float4 vPosCS       : POSITION;
    float2 vTexCoord    : TEXCOORD0;
    float3 vNormalWS    : TEXCOORD1_centroid;
    float3 vPositionWS  : TEXCOORD2_centroid;
};

//--------------------------------float3
ComputeHemisphericLighting( float3 cDiffuse, float3 cSpec, float3 vViewWS,
                            float3 vBumpNormalWS )

{
```

```
    static const float3 cSkyApexColor     = float3( 0.498, 0.604, 0.8 );
    static const float3 cSkyHorizonColor   = float3( 0.637, 0.761, 0.8 );
    static const float3 cSkyOccludedColor  = float3( 0.2, 0.2, 0.25 );
    static const float3 cSunColor          = float3( 1.0, 0.85, 0.65 );
    static const float3 vSunDirection      = normalize( float3( 0.17, 0.15,
-0.98 ) );


    // Reflection vector
    float3 vReflectWS = Reflect( vViewWS, vBumpNormalWS );


    float3 cSkyLight = cDiffuse * lerp( lerp( cSkyHorizonColor,
cSkyOccludedColor,

                                              saturate( -vBumpNormalWS.y ) ),
                                  lerp( cSkyHorizonColor,
cSkyApexColor,

                                              saturate(  vBumpNormalWS.y ) ),
                                  vBumpNormalWS.yyy * 0.5 + 0.5 );


    float3 cSunLight = cSunColor *
                    ( cDiffuse * saturate( dot( vBumpNormalWS,
vSunDirection ) ) +
                      cSpec * pow( saturate( dot( vReflectWS,
vSunDirection ) ), 5 ) );


    float3 cLight = cSkyLight * 0.4 + cSunLight * 0.6;
    return cLight;


}   // End of ComputeHemisphericLighting(..)



//----------------------------------------float SampleNoise( float3
vPositionOS, float3 vNormalOS, float fViewDistance )
{
    // Pick the best planar projection for generating noise map UVs based
    // on object position
```

```
float3 vTmpNormal = abs( vNormalOS );
float2 vNoiseUV;
if ( ( vTmpNormal.x > vTmpNormal.y ) && ( vTmpNormal.x > vTmpNormal.z ) )
{
   // Plane's normal points mostly along x-axis
   vNoiseUV = vPositionOS.zy;
}
else if ( ( vTmpNormal.y > vTmpNormal.x ) && ( vTmpNormal.y >
vTmpNormal.z ) )
{
   // Plane's normal points mostly along y-axis
   vNoiseUV = vPositionOS.xz;
}
else
{
   // Plane's normal points mostly along z-axis
   vNoiseUV = vPositionOS.xy;
}


float fNoiseFrequency = 150;
float4 vNoise   = tex2D( sNoiseMap, vNoiseUV * fNoiseFrequency / 8.0 );
      vNoise.x = dot( vNoise, float4( 0.25, 0.25, 0.25, 0.25 ) );

float4 vNoise2   = tex2D( sNoiseMap, vNoiseUV * fNoiseFrequency / 128.0 );
      vNoise2.x = dot( vNoise2, float4( 0.25, 0.25, 0.25, 0.25 ));

float4 vNoise3   = tex2D( sNoiseMap, vNoiseUV * fNoiseFrequency );
      vNoise3.x = dot( vNoise3, float4( 0.25, 0.25, 0.25, 0.25 ) );

return lerp( vNoise.x, (vNoise.x + vNoise2.x * vNoise3.x )/( 2.0 ), 1.0 -
             saturate( 1.0 / fViewDistance ) );


} // End of SampleNoise(..)
```

```
//-----------------------------------float3x3
MakeFromToRotationMatrixFast ( float3 vFrom, float3 vTo )
{
    float3x3 mResult;

    float3 vV = cross( vFrom, vTo );
    float  fE = dot( vFrom, vTo );
    float  fH = 1.0 / (1.0 + fE);

    mResult[0][0] = fE + fH   * vV.x * vV.x;
    mResult[1][0] = fH * vV.x * vV.y + vV.z;
    mResult[2][0] = fH * vV.x * vV.z - vV.y;

    mResult[0][1] = fH * vV.x * vV.y - vV.z;
    mResult[1][1] = fE + fH   * vV.y * vV.y;
    mResult[2][1] = fH * vV.y * vV.z + vV.x;

    mResult[0][2] = fH * vV.x * vV.z + vV.y;
    mResult[1][2] = fH * vV.y * vV.z - vV.x;
    mResult[2][2] = fE + fH   * vV.z * vV.z;

    return mResult;

} // End of MakeFromToRotationMatrixFast(..)




//-----------------------------------// Computes lighting by
computing a normal directly from a displacement map using
// central differences approach, and then procedurally determines snow
placement
// based on terrain slope.
//-----------------------------------float4
PSLightingFromDisplacement( PsInput i ) : COLOR0
{
```

```
// Compute view vector
float3 vViewWS       = g_vCameraPosition - i.vPositionWS;
float3 fViewDistance = length( vViewWS );
       vViewWS       = normalize( vViewWS );


// Calculate displaced normal and tangent frame
float3 vPositionDummy;
float3 vNormalWS;
float3 vTangentWS;
float3 vBinormalWS;
DisplaceVertexAndCalculateNormal( i.vPositionWS, i.vTexCoord, QUAD_NORMAL,
                                  QUAD_TANGENT, QUAD_BINORMAL,
                                  vPositionDummy, vNormalWS,
vTangentWS, vBinormalWS);



float3x3  mTangent = { vTangentWS, vBinormalWS, vNormalWS };


// Sample rock normal map
float3 cRockNormal   = tex2D( sRockNormalMap, i.vTexCoord *
c_fRockDetailRepeatRate );
float3 vRockNormalTS = cRockNormal * 2.0 - 1.0f;


float3 cRockNormal2      = tex2D( sRockNormalMap,
            i.vTexCoord * c_fRockDetailRepeatRate *
c_fRockDetailRepeatMultiplier );
       cRockNormal2.xy *= 2.0;
       cRockNormal2      = normalize( cRockNormal2 ) ;
float3 vRockNormal2TS    = cRockNormal2 * 2.0 - 1.0f;


vRockNormalTS  = normalize( vRockNormalTS + vRockNormal2TS );


// Convert rock normal to world-space and calculate new tangent frame
float3   vRockNormalWS   = normalize( mul( vRockNormalTS, mTangent ) );
```

```
    float3x3 mRockNormalRotation = MakeFromToRotationMatrixFast(vNormalWS,
vRockNormalWS);
    float   vRockTangentWS    = mul( mRockNormalRotation, vTangentWS );
    float3  vRockBinormalWS   = mul( mRockNormalRotation, vBinormalWS );
    float3x3 mRockTangent     = { vRockTangentWS, vRockBinormalWS,
vRockNormalWS };


    // Snow accumulation a la ruby4
    float fSnowAccum =
      saturate( smoothstep( c_fSnowRockMin, c_fSnowRockMin + c_fSnowRockFade,
              saturate( vRockNormalWS.y ) ) +
              smoothstep( c_fSnowMin, c_fSnowMin + c_fSnowFade,
              saturate( vNormalWS.y ) ) );


    // Dither the snow
    float fNoise = SampleNoise( i.vPositionWS, QUAD_NORMAL, fViewDistance );


    float fLerp  = saturate( 1.0 / fViewDistance );
        fLerp  = fLerp * fLerp;
    float fDelta = saturate( 1.0 / fLerp) * 0.275;


    fSnowAccum = lerp( fSnowAccum,
       1.0 – smoothstep( fSnowAccum - fDelta, fSnowAccum + fDelta, fNoise ),
fLerp );


    // Sample snow detail normal map
    float3 cSnowDetail   = tex2D( sSnowNormalMap, i.vTexCoord *
c_fSnowDetailRepeatRate );
    float3 vSnowDetailTS = cSnowDetail * 2.0 - 1.0;
    float3 vSnowNormalWS = mul( vSnowDetailTS, mTangent );


    // Sample base texture:
    //   We're using two taps of the basemap at different repeat rates and
```

```
    // averaging them to create interesting color variations.
    float4 cBase   = tex2D( sBaseMap, i.vTexCoord * c_fRockDetailRepeatRate );
            cBase += tex2D( sBaseMap,
        i.vTexCoord * c_fRockDetailRepeatRate *
c_fRockColorDetailRepeatMultiplier );
            cBase  = cBase * 0.25;


    // Snow color (detail-mapped, white)
    float3 cSnowDiffuse = 2;
    float3 cSnowSpec    = 1;
    float3 cSnowColor   = ComputeHemisphericLighting( cSnowDiffuse, cSnowSpec,
vViewWS, vSnowNormalWS );


    // Rock color (unbumped, using basemap)
    float3 cRockDiffuse = cBase.xyz * 1.3;
    float3 cRockSpec    = 0.4;
    float3 cRockColor   = ComputeHemisphericLighting( cRockDiffuse,
cRockSpec, vViewWS, vRockNormalWS );


    // Final color (lerp between rock and snow)
    float3 cFinal  = lerp( cRockColor, cSnowColor, fSnowAccum );
    float4 cOutput = saturate( float4( cFinal, 1 ) );


    return cOutput;


}   // End of PSLightingFromDisplacement(..)
```


PERFORMANCE ANALYSIS

We measured performance for our application on a quad-core AMD Phenom X4 processor–based system with 2GB of RAM and an ATI Radeon graphics card. Table 1.3.2 provides a detailed overview of the results. We notice that adaptive tessellation renders at frame rates close to the original low-resolution rates (less than 1% difference). In the case of rendering the original low-resolution input mesh as well as with rendering using continuous tessellation, we render the mesh as indexed primitives, whereas with adaptive tessellation, we use non-indexed primitives. As mentioned earlier in this article, given the results of using adaptive tessellation, we notice the lack of any serious performance penalties due to rendering with non-indexed primitives in the adaptive tessellation case. Instead, the performance is easily comparable to the cost of rendering the original low-resolution mesh, even though the resulting rendered terrain surface is of significantly higher quality when rendered with adaptive tessellation. Even by simply turning on adaptive tessellation in faraway views, we double the polygon count for the rendered mesh.

TABLE 1.3.2   Performance data for comparing rendering terrain patch with different rendering modes

Rendering Mode	Polygon Count	Faraway View		Close-up View	
		Rendering Time			
		ATI Radeon HD	ATI Radeon HD 2900 XD	ATI Radeon HD 4870	ATI Radeon HD 2900 XT
Original low-resolution input mesh (N_L)	4K triangles	852 fps	359 fps	850 fps	275 fps
Tessellated mesh, continuous tessellation (N_T)[1]	1.6M triangles	232 fps	143 fps	213 fps	101 fps
Tessellated mesh, adaptive tessellation (N^A)	Dynamic, $N_T \leq N_A \leq N_L$	845 fps	356 fps	574 fps	207 fps

[1] The relationship between the polygonal count of the input mesh and the continuously tessellated mesh can be expressed as $N_T = 411 \times N_L$ on Direct3D 10 generation hardware.

Note that rendering terrain with adaptive tessellation results in much higher-quality visual results while maintaining rendering times close to the original, low-resolution mesh rendering.

ON THE DVD

Note that we provide a sample application implementing this system on the DVD-ROM shipping with the book.

ACKNOWLEDGMENTS

We thank Joshua Barczak and Christopher Oat from the AMD Game Computing Applications Group for their fruitful discussions during development of this technique, review of the chapter, and additional code and modifications for some of the shader functions included in this chapter. The procedural snow shader had been developed by Christopher Oat for the AMD Ruby: Whiteout Demo (http://ati.amd.com/developer/demos/rhd2000.html). Additionally, all of the art was created by Abe Wiley from AMD Game Computing Applications Group.

REFERENCES

[AMD09] AMD Radeon SDK and Documents. 2009. http://developer.amd.com/gpu/radeon/pages/RadeonSDKSamplesDocuments.aspx

[AnderssonTatarchuk07] Andersson, J. and Tatarchuk, N. Frostbite Rendering Architecture and Real-time Procedural Shading & Texturing Techniques. Game Developer Conference Presentation. March 5–9, 2007, San Francisco. Slides

[AsirvathamHoppe05] Asirvatham, A. and Hoppe, H. 2005. Terrain rendering using GPU-based geometry clipmaps. *GPU Gems 2*, M. Pharr and R. Fernando, eds., Addison-Wesley, March 2005. http://research.microsoft.com/~hoppe/proj/gpugcm/

[Blow00] Blow, J. 2000. Terrain Rendering Research for Games. SIGGRAPH 2000, Course 39: Games Research: The Science of Interactive Entertainment. SIGGRAPH 2000, New Orleans, August 2000.

[DWS*97] Duchaineau, M., Wolinsky, M., Sigeti, D. E., Miller, M. C., Aldrich, C., and Mineev-Weinstein, M. B. 1997. ROAMing Terrain: Real-time Optimally Adapting Meshes. In *Proceedings of IEEE Visualization*, pp. 81–88.

[LKR*96] Lindstrom, P., Koller, D., Ribarsky, W., Hodges, L. F., Faust, N., and Turner, G. A. 1996. Real-time, continuous level of detail rendering of height fields. *Proceedings of ACM SIGGRAPH 96*, August 1996, pp. 109–118.

[Persson06] Persson, E. 2006. Render to Vertex Buffer Programming. ATI Technologies Technical Report, March 2006. http://developer.amd.com/media/gpu_assets/R2VB_programming.pdf

[TatarchukBarczak09] Tatarchuk, N., and Barczak, J. 2009. Dynamic Terrain Rendering on GPU Using Real-Time Tessellation. In *ShaderX⁷: Advanced Rendering*. Engel, W., Ed. Charles River Media, Cambridge, Mass.

[WorldMachine08] World Machine 2: The Next Generation in Terrain Modeling. http://www.world-machine.com/

1.4 Adaptive Re-Meshing for Displacement Mapping

Rafael P. Torchelsen, Carlos A. Dietrich, Luís Fernando, M. S. Silva, Rui Bastos, and João L. D. Comba

INTRODUCTION

The displacement-mapping technique is defined by two simple elements: a coarse representation of a mesh (a *base mesh*) and a map that encodes information to displace the geometric coordinates of mesh vertices (a *displacement map*). Several factors might be taken into consideration when establishing a correspondence between mesh vertices and a displacement map. For instance, if the displacement function has a great change of values in a certain area, this will only be properly applied if there are enough mesh vertices to sample that area. Re-meshing or subdividing the mesh to increase sampling can solve this problem, which can be done in a uniform or adaptive fashion. A uniform subdivision might be a suitable solution, depending on how the base mesh is created [Szirmay-Kalos08, Lee00], but often tends to create unnecessary vertices on regions where they are not needed. Alternatively, adaptive subdivision is more involved, but gives control over where subdivision should be performed [Dyken04, Doggett00, Amor05]. The work of Szimay-Kalos et al. [Szirmay-Kalos08] presents a survey of displacement-mapping techniques.

Displacement-mapping techniques are very useful for modeling objects with different levels of detail (LODs). Due to their simplicity and optimized use of computational resources, displacement-mapping techniques have been applied in several games (see the presentation of Andersson et al. [Andersson07]), in particular, for rendering terrains, where the benefits of these techniques are well exploited. An LOD representation for meshes is important for games, as there are many demands on performance from all parts of the game engine, such as artificial intelligence computations, physics, gameplay, and so on. Displacement mapping offers such an efficient way and serves as a basis for LOD algorithms. These combine a refinement step preserving details of the mesh with a simplification step that reduces memory usage and avoids unnecessary transfers between the CPU and the GPU.

The subdivision approaches usually do not guarantee that *all* information stored in a displacement map is well sampled by the base mesh. For instance, the approaches might not enforce a valid one-to-one mapping between a vertex of the base mesh and a rectangular region of the displacement map (which usually corresponds to a texel in the displacement map). This happens because subdivision is typically guided by the current camera position, and only considers the distance of the surface to the camera, thus ignoring the frequency of the signal encoded in the displacement map.

In this article, we overcome this sampling problem using a new subdivision algorithm that defines a near one-to-one relationship between the number of texels of the displacement map and the vertices of the base mesh. Our procedure is also adaptive, and therefore aims to obtain an optimal representation of the information contained in a displacement map, while avoiding unnecessary subdivision of uniform-subdivision approaches.

The main characteristics of our proposal are summarized as follows:

- **Adaptability:** The subdivision algorithm is guided by the displacement map information in such way to establish a near one-to-one mapping between mesh vertices and texels.

- **GPU-friendly:** The algorithm proposed here is fully parallel. We leverage this fact by performing both the subdivision and the displacement application in the geometry shader of the GPU.

- **LOD rendering guided by displacement map information:** Details are preserved based on the frequency of the signal stored in the displacement map.

- **Simplicity:** Although the method is based on recent parameterization techniques (which can be complicated), it is simple to implement.

DISPLACEMENT MAP

Displacement maps can be manually constructed or extracted automatically by measuring the distance between a base mesh and the original mesh. The purpose of the technique is to reduce the memory usage of an original mesh by replacing the original mesh with a base mesh and a displacement map. The latter has a smaller memory footprint than the original mesh and allows the reconstruction of the original mesh at runtime.

Tewari et al. [Tewari04] describe a possible approach to extract displacement information, where the extraction is guided by the amount of detail in the original mesh. In regions with higher-frequency details, they increase the size of the area allocated to encode the displacement map. Similarly, they reduce the area in lower-frequency detail regions. Figure 1.4.1 illustrates how the same information encoded in a uniform subdivision can be represented in a more compact displacement map using the approach described above.

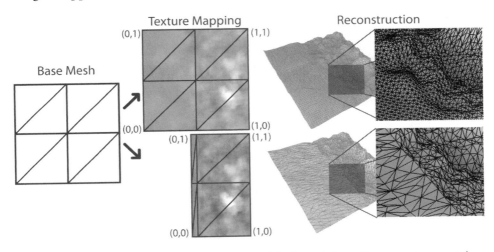

FIGURE 1.4.1   Two reconstructions of the original mesh from the same base mesh. Mapping between mesh vertices and the displacement is displayed in the Texture Mapping column. The one on top uses a uniform distribution of displacements, while the one on the bottom uses an adaptive distribution. The Reconstruction column shows the resulting meshes, with detail images highlighting the differences between these approaches.[1]

An important point to observe is that the reconstruction step is always performed at the highest resolution needed, even if an adaptive distribution of samples in the displacement map was used. Therefore, computation is wasted in regions where a lower-resolution reconstruction would be sufficient (which corresponds to the smaller texels in the texture domain column of Figure 1.4.1). In this work, we show that we can avoid such wasted computation using an adaptive reconstruction algorithm.

ADAPTIVE RE-MESHING FOR DISPLACEMENT MAPPING

The reconstruction step is responsible for constructing a mesh based on the information encoded in the base mesh and the displacement map. We generate a mesh with more detail by subdividing the triangles of the base mesh. The detail encoded in each triangle of the base mesh is estimated by looking to the area of the displacement map reserved for them. Triangles mapped to larger areas of the displacement map encode more information than the triangles mapped to smaller areas, and thus should be subdivided accordingly (Figure 1.4.2).

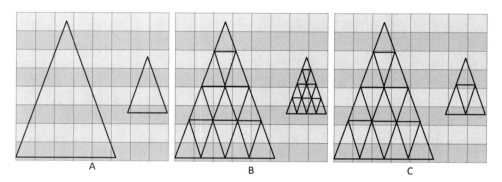

FIGURE 1.4.2   Relationship between the triangle area in texture space and the levels of subdivision. (A) Two triangles of the base mesh are mapped to the texture space represented by the underlying grid. (B) A uniform subdivision for all triangles of the base mesh. Our approach, illustrated in (C), subdivides each triangle according to the number of texels mapped to it.

Central to this proposal is the computation of triangle area, which can be expensive and result in different subdivision levels in adjacent triangles. We overcome this problem by looking at the length of triangle edges in *texture space*. This guarantees consistency between subdivisions, needs only local information, is easily parallelizable, and avoids T-junctions (inconsistent subdivisions between adjacent triangles).

We illustrate this solution with the example in Figure 1.4.3. Suppose we have a horizontal edge crossing from one side to the other of the displacement map. Since the number of texels crossed by this line is equal to the displacement map width, a simple equation to calculate the number of vertices that should be inserted in the edge is to divide the edge length by this width, as shown in Equation 1.4.1. This can be extended to edges with other orientations, and will result in adding more vertices to better sample long edges.

$$\text{Edge Subdivisions} = \frac{1}{\text{Displacement Map Width}} * \text{Edge Length in Texture Space}$$

EQUATION 1.4.1   Each edge of the base mesh is subdivided according to the number of texels it crosses.[2]

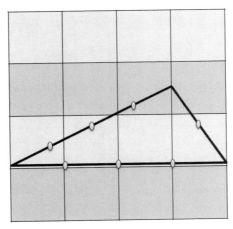

FIGURE 1.4.3   Subdivision of a triangle edge based on its length.[3]

Once we know how many vertices to insert on each edge, we need a tessellation procedure to generate the connections *inside* the triangle. This procedure must be simple, fast, and connect the new vertices consistently. We use pre-defined subdivision patterns (Figure 1.4.4), store them directly in GPU memory, and choose which one to apply according to the number of vertices inserted on each edge. For example, if only two edges require insertion of vertices, we choose the middle pattern. The subdivision pattern is applied recursively until the length of the remaining edges reaches a threshold.

The use of subdivision patterns requires recursive passes when tessellating some triangles. This recursive approach explores the parallelism of current GPUs by distributing the computation through different geometry shader pipelines, thus avoiding the overload of a single pipeline with a given subdivision level. In fact, triangles with different subdivision levels are the whole point of adaptive re-meshing. Figure 1.4.5 illustrates recursive subdivision applied to adapting the base mesh for displacement mapping.

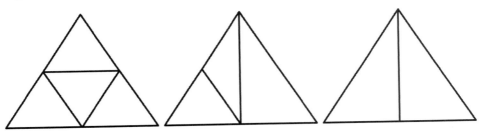

FIGURE 1.4.4   Example of precomputed tessellation patterns for generating subdivisions based on edge lengths. Note that these are only a sample out of seven possible patterns.

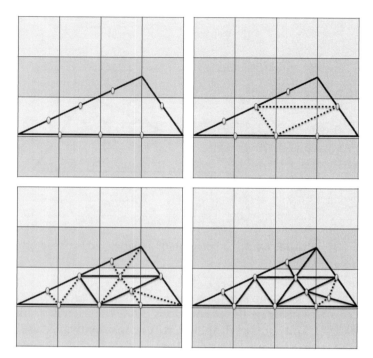

FIGURE 1.4.5 Recursive subdivision of a triangle. The process repeats until the edge length becomes smaller than a pre-defined threshold. Using the side of a texel as the threshold, for example, we have a near one-to-one mapping between texels and new vertices.

LOD

One of the main motivations for using displacement mapping is that the base mesh represents a coarser version of the original mesh. This allows the use of the base mesh even without a displacement map. The use of the base mesh alone is useful, for instance, when the model is far away from the camera and the details inserted by the displacement map would not be perceived. However, if we use the base mesh when the camera is far away, then we need an LOD approach that smoothly adds detail to the base mesh when the model gets closer to the camera.

We modulate the amount of detail by changing the level of subdivision. By decreasing the number of subdivisions in the base mesh, we decrease the number of displacements applied to the model, which results in a less detailed representation of the original mesh. The maximum allowed edge length in texture space (the side of a texel, for instance) is used to modulate the level of subdivision. Decreasing the maximum allowed length represents coarser subdivisions, while longer edge lengths represent higher levels of subdivision.

The distance between the model and the camera is used to modulate the maximum edge length. This provides an LOD technique that increases details near the camera and decreases details as the model moves away from the camera. It is important to observe that while the model is moving away from the camera, regions of the model mapped to small portions of the displacement map converge to the base mesh faster than other regions of the model that map to large areas of the displacement map.

The resulting LOD technique can smoothly insert and remove details while avoiding drastic changes in the model. Furthermore, not only can we smoothly insert details by increasing the subdivision level, but also we can smoothly displace the vertices using geomorph. Figure 1.4.6 illustrates the same dataset from Figure 1.4.1 now using our LOD scheme.

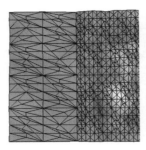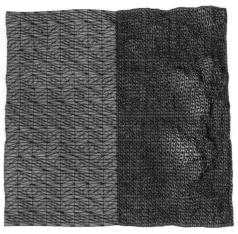

FIGURE 1.4.6   Reconstruction of the original mesh using our LOD scheme. From left to right, the mesh moves closer to the camera (which is perpendicular to the ground). Note that we have a finer tessellation in areas with high-frequency detail.

Instead of computing the LOD according to the distance between a camera and a reference point in the base mesh, we also locally adjust the LOD. For this purpose, we use the middle point of each edge, which defines the subdivision resolution in terms of the proximity to the surface, which is suitable for rendering large surfaces such as a terrain. Figure 1.4.7 illustrates the local modulation of the LOD using the same terrain as Figure 1.4.6. Note that closer to the camera we have more resolution, but the high-frequency regions (mountains) always have a high enough resolution to represent the encoded information, even when the camera is far away, as depicted by the left image.

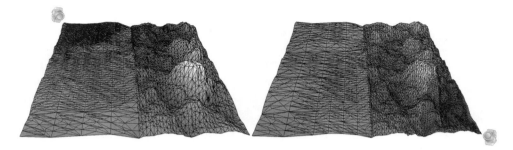

FIGURE 1.4.7 Distribution of resolution according to the distance of the edges to the camera (depicted with an icon in the figure). Distance to the camera is not the only factor that affects base-mesh resolution. High-frequency regions remain with enough resolution, even when they are away from the camera (left).

RESULTS

We measured performance results in a computer with an AMD Athlon 64 Processor 3700+, 2GB RAM and an NVIDIA GeForce 8600 GTS. The first mesh of Figure 1.4.7 has 34,422 vertices and 11,474 triangles, and is rendered in 112 frames per second (FPS). The second mesh has 50,451 vertices and 16,817 triangles running at 108 FPS. Those times include the re-meshing and the displacement of the eight-base-triangle mesh at each frame. The source code for our solution is included in the DVD-ROM accompanying the book.

ON THE DVD

IMPLEMENTATION

We implemented our solution using C++ and GLSL. It is composed of two main steps: a re-meshing (or subdivision) step and a displacement step that generates and renders the mesh. In the first step, we compute, for each triangle of the base mesh, its subdivision pattern according to the number of edges with length beyond a threshold. We implement this step using the geometry shader, which is illustrated in the following code:[4]

```
void main(void) {


int    divisionType=0;
vec3   edgeMiddlePoint
float length=0.0, localmaxlength, distanceFromCamera;
```

```
//first edge
length = distance(gl_TexCoordIn[0][0], gl_TexCoordIn[1][0]);
edgeMiddlePoint    = (gl_PositionIn[0] + gl_PositionIn[1])/2.0;
distanceFromCamera = distance(cameraPosition, edgeMiddlePoint);
distanceFromCamera = maxSubDivisionDistance / distanceFromCamera;
distanceFromCamera = 1.0 - max(distanceFromCamera, 1.0);
localmaxlength     = distanceFromCamera * maxlength;
if (length >= localmaxlength)
  divisionType+=1;


//second edge
length = distance(gl_TexCoordIn[1][0], gl_TexCoordIn[2][0]);
edgeMiddlePoint    = (gl_PositionIn[1] + gl_PositionIn[2])/2.0;
distanceFromCamera = distance(cameraPosition, edgeMiddlePoint);
distanceFromCamera = maxSubDivisionDistance / distanceFromCamera;
distanceFromCamera = 1.0 - max(distanceFromCamera, 1.0);
localmaxlength     = distanceFromCamera * maxlength;
if (length >= localmaxlength)
  divisionType+=2;


//third edge
length = distance(gl_TexCoordIn[2][0], gl_TexCoordIn[0][0]);
edgeMiddlePoint    = (gl_PositionIn[2] + gl_PositionIn[0])/2.0;
distanceFromCamera = distance(cameraPosition, edgeMiddlePoint);
distanceFromCamera = maxSubDivisionDistance / distanceFromCamera;
distanceFromCamera = 1.0 - max(distanceFromCamera, 1.0);
localmaxlength     = distanceFromCamera * maxlength;
if (length >= localmaxlength)
  divisionType+=4;


//according to the edges lengths we choose the
//subdivision pattern and emit the primitives
SubdivideInputTriangle(divisionType);
}
```

The variable `divisionType` encodes the edges that should be subdivided by storing the sum of edges' IDs. IDs 1, 2, and 4 are associated in clockwise order with edges in such a way that the sum of any combination of IDs gives a unique value. Those values range from 0 to 7. Each value is associated with one of the eight possible subdivision patterns: no subdivision, all edges subdivided (Figure 1.4.5, leftmost image), and the three rotations of the middle and rightmost patterns of Figure 1.4.5. After the base mesh is subdivided, we displace all vertices, resulting in the reconstruction of the original mesh.

DEMO

The demo on the DVD-ROM illustrates the technique and the LOD scheme, and includes other terrains and arbitrary surfaces. Our implementation focuses on educational purposes and as a result can be further improved with several optimizations.

CONCLUSION

We have presented a novel multi-resolution displacement-mapping technique that has many desirable features, especially for games: multi-resolution, GPU-friendly, LOD-enabled rendering, simple to implement, and capable of interactive results.

ENDNOTES

[1] For illustration purposes, the dataset of Figure 1.4.1 was manually created. However, this extraction is usually performed automatically based on the difference between the base and the original meshes, with the help of third-party software such as NVIDIAMelody [NVMelody] or AMD GPU MeshMapper [AMDGPU MeshMapper08].

[2] A squared texel was assumed here.

[3] Each edge should have a length not greater than the side of a texel, since we create one vertex for each texel the edge crosses.

[4] This code was not optimized since the main purpose is to illustrate how the process works.

ACKNOWLEDGMENTS

We would like to thank UFRGS (Universidade Federal do Rio Grande do Sul), CNPq processo 140241/2007-8, and NVIDIA for their support.

REFERENCES

[Szirmay-Kalos08] L. Szirmay-Kalos, and T. Umenhoffer. Displacement Mapping on the GPU: State of the Art Survey, *Computer Graphics Forum*, 2008.

[Dyken04] C. Dyken, M. Reimers, and J. Seland. Real-Time GPU Silhouette Refinement Using Adaptively Blended Bézier Patches, *Computer Graphics Forum*, 2004.

[Lee00] A. Lee, H. Moreton, and H. Hoppe. Displaced Subdivision Surfaces, *SIGGRAPH*, 2000.

[Doggett00] M. Doggett and J. Hirche Adaptive View Dependent Tessellation of Displacement Maps, *HWWS '00: Proceedings of the ACM SIGGRAPH/EUROGRAPHICS Workshop on Graphics Hardware*, 2000.

[Amor05] M. Amor, M. Boo, W. Strasser, J. Hirche, and M. Doggett. A Meshing Scheme for Efficient Hardware Implementation of Butterfly Subdivision Using Displacement Mapping, *IEEE Computer Graphics and Applications*, 2005.

[Tewari04] G. Tewari, J. Snyder, P. V. Sander, S. J. Gortler, and H. Hoppe. Signal-specialized parameterization for piecewise linear reconstruction, *SGP '04: Proceedings of the 2004 Eurographics/ACM SIGGRAPH symposium on Geometry processing*, 2004,

[NVMelody] NVIDIA Melody, http://developer.nvidia.com/object/melody_home.html

[AMDGPUMeshMapper] AMD GPU MeshMapper, http://ati.amd.com/developer/gpumeshmapper.html

[Andersson07] J. Andersson and N. Tatarchuk. Rendering Architecture and Real-time Procedural Shading & Texturing Techniques, *GDC 2007*.

1.5 Fast Tessellation of Quadrilateral Patches for Dynamic Levels of Detail

CARLOS A. DIETRICH, LUCIANA P. NEDEL, AND JOÃO L. D. COMBA

INTRODUCTION

In recent years we have observed an increasing demand for high-quality graphics in games, movies, and virtual reality applications. This frequently means huge meshes, giant textures, and sophisticated shading. Together, these requirements may be beyond computational resources for real-time rendering for most consumer GPUs. This problem can be overcome with the help of adaptive mesh resolution, texture streaming, and many other techniques that allow visualization of models in different *levels of detail* (LODs). When the model is far from the viewer or occupies a small region of the viewport, for example, we can replace the original model by a simpler version (with simpler meshes and textures) and have the same rendering result.

LOD techniques in adaptive mesh visualization include ROAM (real-time optimally adapting meshes) [Duchaineau97], progressive meshes [Hoppe96], geometry images [Gu02], and many other very different approaches. The key idea is to produce faces *only where they are needed* for a given scene and camera position, instead of storing a complete high-resolution tessellated mesh in memory and using the simplification and culling algorithms in order to keep a stable frame rate [Müller00]. One of the most interesting of these approaches involves two steps: (1) the generation of a *base coarse mesh*, which resembles the original mesh in shape but with far fewer triangles, and (2) the adoption of an algorithm to refine the base mesh *when* and *where* it is needed. The latter step is known as *tessellation on-the-fly* of the base mesh *patches* (elements of the base mesh, usually triangles or quads) [Niski07]. Each patch is processed as an independent mesh, with its own resolution and textures (Figure 1.5.1b). This technique allows the local adaptation of the mesh, which can be more appropriate than global solutions in many applications [Carr06].

The problem in dealing with independent patches is that we need to ensure consistent tessellations across boundaries, that is, that we don't generate *cracks* or *T-junctions* between the patches (Figure 1.5.1c). Many authors have proposed widely different (and some unusual) solutions to this problem, varying from locally adapting different patch resolutions [Moreton01] to drawing lines between the patches and hiding cracks during the visualization [Balázs04].

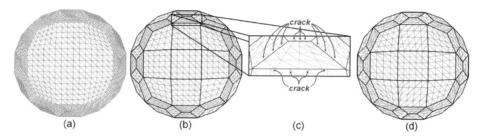

(a)   (b)   (c)   (d)

FIGURE 1.5.1   (a) A simple mesh. (b) Its *base mesh* (superimposed on the original mesh) composed of quadrilateral patches. (c) *Cracks* generated when we subdivide each patch independently. (d) Patch tessellation guided by the number of samples along each edge, guaranteeing seamless tessellations.

In this article we propose a new solution for generating watertight surfaces composed of quadrilateral patches (Figure 1.5.1d). Our method is simple, fast, and can be directly applied to existing applications. Although our discussion is focused on quadrilateral patches, the technique described here can be readily adapted to triangular patches (see the accompanying material).

THE METHOD

It's all about coherence. If you have a patch in a region of the model that contains too much information, you are supposed to subdivide it sooner or later. But that "too much information" characteristic is only visible to the patch itself, since many optimizations are based on the independence between the patches. Therefore, by subdividing the patch, you can create a *crack* between the patch and its adjacent neighbors when they do not know anything about their own neighborhood (see Figure 1.5.1c).

The solution? The decision on how many subdivisions a patch should have must take into consideration the edges shared between adjacent patches [Moreton01]. Let A be a patch that shares an edge ab with another patch B (see Figure 1.5.2). If A decides that ab should be subdivided into eight segments, the patch B will be forced to make the same decision, because the decision on how ab should be subdivided only takes into consideration the information about ab itself.

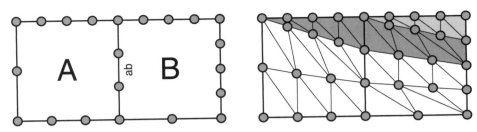

FIGURE 1.5.2   A consistent triangulation (*crack-free*) can be generated between neighbor patches if they first decide how many vertices should be disposed on each edge. Since edges are shared between patches, the decision about how many vertices will be disposed on each edge will be the same.

The problem? Given that we allow a patch to be subdivided into any number of samples, how do we maintain the consistency *inside* each patch (i.e., how do we tessellate the patch to connect the vertices generated on its edges)? The common solution for this problem involves the use of pre-defined tessellation patterns [Boubekeur08]. These patterns are usually very simple, and refined tessellations demand recursive passes through the algorithm. However, we are interested in an efficient method to solve this problem *in one pass*, no matter how many subdivisions are needed in the patch edges.

Our method is based on a simple assumption: Tessellating a quad patch with a different number of subdivisions on each of its edges is as simple as tessellating a quad patch with the same number of subdivisions on all its edges. And why should it be different? When we tessellate a quad patch with n vertices on each of its edges, we build $(n - 1)$ triangle strips of $2(n - 1)$ triangles, as illustrated in Figure 1.5.3. This procedure is very common in displacement mapping or geometry image algorithms, where uniform tessellations of quad patches are created to reconstruct the inherent model surface.

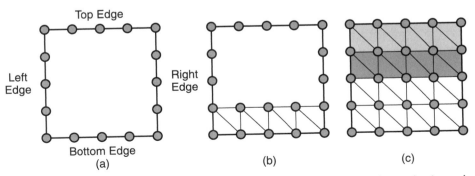

FIGURE 1.5.3   Tessellation of a quad patch with the same number of samples in each edge. (a) The quad patch with five vertices along each edge. (b) The first triangle strip generated at the bottom of the quad. (c) The final set of strips that tessellate the patch.

The uniform tessellation is usually implemented with two nested `for` loops, as illustrated in Listing 1.5.1. The first loop iterates through the triangle strips while the second loop generates the vertices of each strip, two at a time.

Listing 1.5.1 Implementation of a uniform tessellation of a $j \times i$ domain

```
nH — number of vertices in horizontal direction
nV — number of vertices in vertical direction
for i from 0 to (nV − 2) do
    // begin of the triangle strip.
    for j from 0 to (nH − 1) do
        // place a vertex in position (j, i).
        // place a vertex in position (j, i + 1).
    end for
    // end of the triangle strip.
end for
```

The first loop iterates through (nV − 1) triangle strips while the second loop generates 2nH vertices for each strip, resulting in 2(nH − 1) triangles per strip. Each vertex is generated in *parametric* coordinates (which are only valid inside the patch) and then converted to 3D space, using a convex interpolation.

Figure 1.5.4 illustrates all we need to know to create each strip: where it begins (two vertices on the left edge), where it ends (two vertices on the right edge), and the number of vertices in the bottom and top edges of the strip. In the uniform tessellation (as seen in Figure 1.5.3), these variables can be easily calculated, due to the regularity of the subdivision. However, when we take into consideration a varying number of vertices on each edge, these variables should be calculated explicitly. Figure 1.5.5 illustrates an example of such a procedure.

This additional complication does not change the nature of the procedure. We still have two nested `for` loops, the first calculating the parameters for each strip (starting and ending positions and the number of internal vertices) and the second calculating where the vertices will be generated along the strip. Lets take the example illustrated in Figure 1.5.5a again, with only the vertices of the left and right edges (see Figure 1.5.5a). We show that we need to answer just three questions to build the tessellation: (1) how many strips will be needed, (2) where each strip will be located, and (3) how each strip will be tessellated.

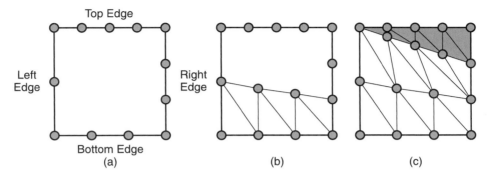

FIGURE 1.5.4 Tessellation of a quad patch with different numbers of vertices on each edge. (a) Quad patch and the vertices distributed along their edges. (b) First triangle strip generated at the bottom of the quad. (c) Final set of strips that tessellate the patch.

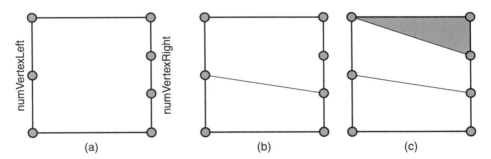

FIGURE 1.5.5   Distribution of triangle strips inside each patch. We need as many triangle strips as the number of gaps between vertices, that is, we need to fill all gaps that exist between vertices.

HOW MANY STRIPS WILL BE NEEDED?

At first, we have to know how many strips will be necessary to tessellate the patch. By taking numVertexLeft and numVertexRight (see Figure 1.5.5a) as the numbers of vertices in the left and right edges of the patch, respectively, the answer to this question is given by numStrips = max(numVertexLeft, numVertexRight) - 1. The reasoning involved here is simple. We need as many triangle strips as gaps between vertices; that is, we need to *fill all gaps* that exist between vertices of the side that has more vertices (see Figure 1.5.5c).

WHERE WILL EACH STRIP BE LOCATED?

The second thing we need to know is where to start and where to end each triangle strip. Since each strip has *two* vertices on each side, we will focus our discussion on the first vertex on the left edge (baseVertexLeft) and the first vertex on the right edge (baseVertexRight), as illustrated in Figure 1.5.6. We already know we have numStrips steps to go through all vertices, and that one side has exactly numStrips "first points." So, all we have to do is to uniformly distribute numStrips steps on the other side vertices. The answer to this question is associated with some quantities that are defined in the third question, and will be discussed right after it.

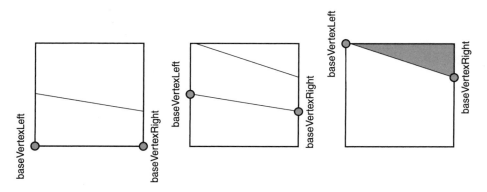

FIGURE 1.5.6 Base points of triangle strips, which determine where the strips begin on the left edge (baseVertexLeft) and where the strips end on the right edge (baseVertexRight).

HOW DO WE TESSELLATE EACH STRIP?

The third thing we need to know is how many points we are supposed to place on the bottom and on the top of each triangle strip. We call these quantities stripNumVertexBottom and stripNumVertexTop, respectively. These quantities are restricted between numVertexBottom and numVertexTop (the number of vertices on the *bottom* and *top* edges of the patch, respectively). The strip tessellation depends on the strip placement, which is discussed in the next section.

A 3D INTERPOLATION TO PLACE TRIANGLE STRIPS

All the quantities involved here (baseVertexLeft, baseVertexRight, numVertexBottom, and numVertexTop) are transitions between two other quantities: baseVertexLeft varies from 0 to numVertexLeft — 1, baseVertexRight varies from 0 to numVertexRight — 1, and stripNumVertexBottom varies between numVertexBottom and numVertexTop. This characteristic allows implementing our first for loop as a simple *Bresenham interpolation* between two points in a 3D parameter space, namely from (0, 0, numVertexBottom) to (numVertexLeft, numVertexRight, numVertexTop). Why? Each point in this 3D line spans one triangle strip, since it contains the values of baseVertexLeft, baseVertexRight, and stripNumVertex Bottom. While this may not seem an intuitive process at first, we illustrate it further in Figure 1.5.7.

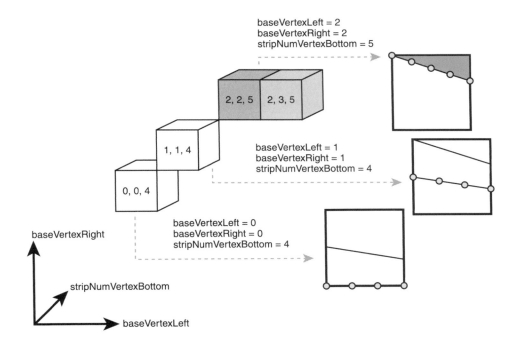

FIGURE 1.5.7   All parameters required to build the tessellation are calculated by a simple *Bresenham interpolation* between two points in a 3D parameter space.

In the example illustrated in Figure 1.5.4, the line starts from the position of the first triangle strip (0 on baseVertexLeft, 0 on baseVertexRight, and 4 on stripNumVertexBottom) and stops at the end of the last triangle strip (2 on baseVertexLeft, 3 on baseVertexRight, and 5 on stripNumVertexBottom). Each point in this 3D line (illustrated by cubes) stores the values of the parameters required to generate one triangle strip.

Figure 1.5.7 shows how the tessellation procedure can be implemented using a Bresenham interpolation. This is a very simple concept. All triangle strips are generated sequentially, and their parameters (starting and ending positions and the number of internal vertices) increase (or decrease) sequentially too, in a linear fashion. The Bresenham interpolation between lower and upper parameter bounds is just a simple way to calculate the intermediate values of these parameters.

A 2D Interpolation to Tessellate Strips

Once we know where our triangle strips are placed, we just need a second for loop to generate internal vertices of each triangle strip, two at a time. We can have a different number of vertices in the bottom (stripNumVertexBottom) and top (stripNumVertexTop) of each strip, which requires a *second* Bresenham interpolation procedure. This procedure implements a 2D interpolation, starting from (0, 0) and going to (stripNumVertexBottom, stripNumVertexTop). Each point of this line stores the parameters required to generate one vertex along the bottom edge of the strip and one vertex along the top edge of the strip, as illustrated in Figure 1.5.8.

The conceptual view of our algorithm, which was described up to this point, is simple and robust. At every pass through the first for loop, one triangle strip is generated. Each triangle strip requires a point on the 3D line to define its position and a sweep through a 2D line for the generation of its internal vertices. The (real) source code is a little bit more involved, due to temporary variables of the 3D

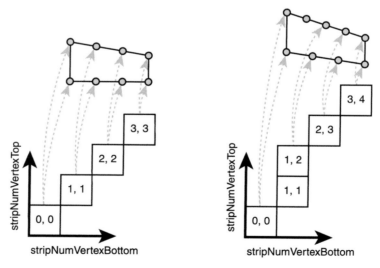

FIGURE 1.5.8 Generation of internal vertices in each strip. A second Bresenham interpolation determines where the vertices will be generated, just like in the first one.

Bresenham interpolation procedure and some optimization hacks. We have included the sample source code illustrating this method on the DVD-ROM, and we strongly suggest reading it in full to understand the underlying algorithm in depth.

RESULTS

We include here some results of the tessellation procedure. Figures 1.5.9 and 1.5.10 illustrate the result of a view-dependent subdivision approach, where each edge is subdivided according to its distance from the viewer. Both meshes are composed of a massive number of patches, which stresses the efficiency of the tessellation procedure.

 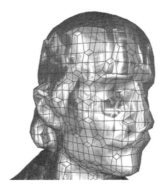 

FIGURE 1.5.9   The *Laçador* dataset (base mesh constructed from a 3D scanning of a Brazilian statue), composed of 16,812 quads (base mesh). The mesh illustrated in the left screenshot is composed of 251,350 triangles and is generated in 48 ms (5.2 million triangles per second) on an Intel Core 2 Duo 2.13 GHz (with 4 GB of RAM).

 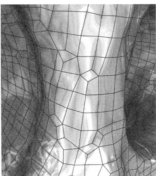 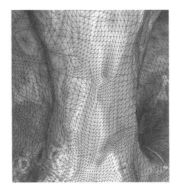

FIGURE 1.5.10   The *engine* dataset, composed of 70,878 quads (base mesh). The mesh illustrated in the left screenshot is composed of 666,030 triangles and is generated in 142 ms (4.6 million triangles per second) on an Intel Core 2 Duo 2.13 GHz (with 4 GB of RAM).

DISCUSSION

This article presented a new procedure to tessellate quad patches in real-time. The procedure is simple, fast, and be can adapted to other patch shapes (triangles, for example). One of the most remarkable characteristics of the procedure is that it is entirely implemented with integer variables (a Bresenham inheritance), which makes it very efficient in CPU-based implementations. We reach performance levels of 5 million triangles per second, starting from a base mesh composed of 16K patches.

We implemented the same algorithm using GLSL. We found that performance ranges greatly from one graphics card model to the next, with some tests on an NVIDIA GeForce 6800 GT showing the same performance as an Intel Core 2 Duo 2.13 GHz (with 4 GB of RAM). We found that performance is increased using a higher-end GPU, such as an NVIDIA GeForce 8800 GTX (7.8 million triangles per second) and an NVIDIA GeForce 9600 GT (10.5 million triangles per second). Future, much improved GPU architectures should show even better performance increases.

ON THE DVD

In a simple analysis, we consider that (a) the geometry shader performance on the specific graphics card and (b) the huge amount of data transferred from CPU to GPU at each frame may be bottlenecks for performance. With our application, we amplify many vertices for a given quad patch with the geometry shaders, and it appears that at the moment, we are highly limited by memory bandwidth for that operation. Each geometry shader is responsible for tessellating one patch at a time (see the accompanying code on the DVD-ROM), and each patch can generate dozens of vertices. The amount of amplified geometry also varies from patch to patch, and therefore, we do not have coherent stream output. The quad mesh (and the subdivision information) is also transferred to the GPU at each frame, which poses a serious limitation in overall system performance. The implementation can be significantly improved, however, if we transfer the quad mesh to a vertex buffer (since it doesn't change on time) and calculate the subdivision level in the vertex shader.

However, with future or alternative GPU architectures, this may be significantly faster. Additionally, another performance consideration for us is the use of integer operations in shaders. Current GPU architectures are designed for floating-point performance (ranging from 16 to 32 bits), and at this time, integer operations can be performed only on one unit of a given single-instruction multiple data (SIMD), rather than utilizing the full vectorization. This incurs additional performance penalty for our implementation.

Another possible improvement is implementing a multi-pass approach, where we would store the triangle strips' parameters in the first pass and tessellate each strip in a second pass. This approach is aligned with the new GPU hardware philosophy and can lead to better results.

REFERENCES

[Balázs04] Á. Balázs, M. Guthe, and R. Klein, "Fat borders: gap filling for efficient view-dependent LOD NURBS rendering," *Computers & Graphics*, Volume 28, Number 1, pages 79–85, 2004.

[Bresenham65] J. Bresenham, "Algorithm for computer control of digital plotter," *IBM System Journal*, Volume 4, Number 1, pages 25–30, 1965.

[Boubekeur08] T. Boubekeur and C. Schlick, "A Flexible kernel for adaptive mesh refinement on GPU," *Computer Graphics Forum*, Volume 27, Number 1, pages 102–114, 2008.

[Carr06] N. A. Carr, J. Hoberock, K. Crane, and J. C. Hart, "Rectangular multi-chart geometry images," In Proceedings of the SGP '06: Fourth Eurographics Symposium on Geometry Processing, pages 181–190, 2006.

[Duchaineau97] M. Duchaineau, M. Wolinsky, D. E. Sigeti, M. C. Miller, C. Aldrich, and M. B. Mineev-Weinstein, "ROAMing terrain: real-time optimally adapting meshes," In Proceedings of the VIS '97: 8th Conference on Visualization, pages 81–88, 1997.

[Gu02] X. Gu, S. Gortler, and H. Hoppe, "Geometry images," In Proceedings of the SIGGRAPH '02: 29th Annual Conference on Computer Graphics and Interactive Techniques, pp. 355–361, 2002.

[Hoppe96] H. Hoppe, "Progressive meshes," In Proceedings of the SIGGRAPH '96: 23rd Annual Conference on Computer Graphics and Interactive Techniques, pages 99–108, 1996.

[Moreton01] H. Moreton, "Watertight tessellation using forward differencing," In Proceedings of the HWWS '01: ACM SIGGRAPH/EUROGRAPHICS Workshop on Graphics Hardware, pages 25–32, 2001.

[Müller00] K. Müller and S. Havemann, "Subdivision Surface Tesselation on the Fly using a Versatile Mesh Data Structure," *Computer Graphics Forum*, Volume 19, Number 3, pages 151–159, 2000.

[Niski07] K. Niski, B. Purnomo, and J. Cohen. "Multi-grained level of detail using a hierarchical seamless texture atlas," in Proceedings of the ACM SIGGRAPH Symposium on Interactive 3D Graphics and Games (SI3D '07), pages 153–160, 2007.

Part II
Rendering Techniques

WESSAM BAHNASSI

In this round of ShaderX, the "Rendering Techniques" section plays on three main themes that reflect some of the trends in real-time computer graphics these days:

- Improvements on the well-known deferred shading method, showing that this approach is becoming more and more popular among rendering engineers
- Customized and advanced shading models, struggling for the eternal quest for better surface shading quality at interactive rates
- Cool tricks of the trade for achieving high performance and quality in a variety of areas

We start with Doug Smith's article, "Quick Noise for GPUs," which builds upon the latest work on real-time implementation of procedural Perlin noise, and achieves attractive performance for ~1MB of video memory only. This opens new venues for using Perlin noise to add texture detail where suitable, or even generate textures from scratch at runtime without completely hogging the GPU.

After that, Gilberto Rosado's "Efficient Soft Particles" shows a neat and simple trick to regain fill-rate performance when rendering soft particles. The technique centralizes around down-sampling and avoiding recalculations where possible.

Stephen Coy's "Simplified High-Quality Anti-Aliased Lines" is a flexible drop-in technique that can be used to draw 3D anti-aliased lines on the screen with arbitrary width and ending shapes, while still interacting properly with the rest of the 3D world. The brilliance of this technique stems from its simple concept, flexibility, low performance and memory cost, and user convenience.

Next, we move into the article "Fast Skin Shading," presented by John Hable, George Borshukov, and Jim Hejl. In this invaluable research, the authors take the latest achievements in state-of-the-art real-time skin rendering, and they push it from demo-only performance to fit in a real-world game's time slot with very little quality compromise, using a number of careful analyses and smart tricks.

131

Christian Schüler discusses a new shading model in his article, "An Efficient and Physically Plausible Real-Time Shading Model." This new model is capable of expressing a very wide range of materials using a set of intuitive controls exposed for artistic control. The results concentrate around high-quality view-dependant material response (i.e., specular and Fresnel effects).

The next contribution, "Graphics Techniques in *Crackdown*," is a rendering postmortem by Hugh Malan, showing the experiences of the rendering team at Realtime Worlds during the *Crackdown* project. You will learn how the game renders many of its elements such as sky, clutter, outlines, and vehicle reflections. Many of these techniques were developed under various time and budget limitations (which is the case for many of us), so we hope this article will provide a useful experience, saving you from having to learn it the hard way.

The final part of the Rendering Techniques section has been strictly dedicated to work on deferred shading. The first of the three articles is David Pangerl's "Deferred Rendering Transparency," which attacks the transparency and translucency rendering limitations found in basic deferred shading. It uses interlacing to store translucent pixels in the same buffer as normal opaque data, thus unifying the whole lighting pipeline on both opaque and translucent objects.

The second contribution to deferred shading is Nicolas Thebieroz's "Deferred Shading with Multisampling Anti-Aliasing in DirectX® 10," which utilizes features in D3D10 and D3D10.1 (i.e., multi-sampled MRTs) to achieve anti-aliasing. This builds on an important optimization that saves us from having to pay the cost of shading for each sample, which makes this technique applicable to real-time applications.

The third and final article in this section is Damian Trebilco's "Light-Indexed Deferred Rendering," which describes a marriage extension between forward and deferred rendering to gain the advantages of both approaches. The article offers a comprehensive coverage over all the implementation details and possible options and how this technique would affect other parts of the pipeline.

We hope our selection of topics for this edition of ShaderX will be an inspiration to you in your future work. Many of the concepts you will face here are novel and can be used as a solid ground upon which to build more advanced techniques. Remember, it might be totally possible to use a trick outside of the context in which it has been framed in here. Personally, such experience is what I would consider innovation, and it is often how new complex techniques are developed!

Welcome!

Wessam Bahanassi

2.1

Quick Noise for GPUs

Doug E. Smith School of Animation, Arts & Design,
Sheridan College, Oakville, ON, Canada

Introduction

Ken Perlin's Noise function [Perlin85] is an invaluable primitive for producing controlled randomness in procedural shaders. For real-time purposes, developers have had to choose between the artifacts of a fast, bilinear texture lookup or a slower, high-quality implementation [Green05]. In this article, we present faster alternatives that are only limited in precision by the underlying hardware.

Background

Perlin Noise is an example of gradient noise. Space is divided into cubical cells with the boundaries defined at integer coordinates. The corners of the cells are set to a value of zero, and their coordinates are hashed to assign a pseudo-random gradient vector. Due to those shared gradients, the value of noise varies smoothly within and across the cells.

The regular zero crossings give noise a vaguely sinusoidal character. The downside is that it can show up as visible grid artifacts. In practice, these artifacts can usually be obscured.

In [Perlin02] the original noise function was improved. The original 256 random gradients were replaced with just 12 gradients. These were arranged as vectors from the center of a cube to each edge's mid-point. The other improvement was to change the cubic blending for a fifth-order function to eliminate artifacts when bump-mapping. Lastly, Perlin established a standard hash table to ensure that different implementations would produce the same results.

The steps involved in generating noise are summarized below:

1. Find which cell contains our sample point.
2. Calculate a smooth weighting factor based on the position within the cell.
3. Assign a pseudo-random gradient to each corner of the cell.
4. For each corner, calculate the dot product of the gradient and the relative sample position.
5. Linearly interpolate the products using the weighting factor.

By design, texturing hardware is efficient at fetching vectors (colors) and linearly interpolating them. If we could postpone calculating the dot products, an implementation could take full advantage of the fast bilinear filtering present in GPUs.

MATH TO THE RESCUE

For simplicity, we will look at the 2D case only in Figure 2.1.1.

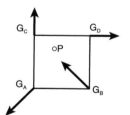

FIGURE 2.1.1   The geometry of a cell. On the left are the corners'
gradient vectors (**G**) at half scale and the sample position (**P**).
On the right are the relative position vectors for each corner (**P**). Notice that they
can all be expressed in terms of the fractional position vector (**F**).

$$N = \text{lerp}\left(w_y, \text{lerp}\left(w_x, \text{dot}(\mathbf{G_A}, \mathbf{P_A}), \text{dot}(\mathbf{G_B}, \mathbf{P_B})\right), \text{lerp}\left(w_x, \text{dot}(\mathbf{G_C}, \mathbf{P_C}), \text{dot}(\mathbf{G_D}, \mathbf{P_D})\right)\right)$$

EQUATION 2.1.1

$$N = (1 - w_y)\left((1 - w_x)\left(G_{Ax}F_x + G_{Ay}F_y \right) + w_x\left(G_{Bx}(F_x - 1) + G_{By}F_y \right) \right)$$
$$+ w_y\left((1 - w_x)\left(G_{Cx}F_x + G_{Cy}(F_y - 1) \right) + w_x\left(G_{Dx}(F_x - 1) + G_{Dx}(F_y - 1) \right) \right)$$

EQUATION 2.1.2

Expanding and factoring out the fractional position results in Equation 2.1.3.

$$N = F_x\Big(\big(1-w_y\big)\big((1-w_x)G_{Ax} + w_xG_{Bx}\big) + w_y\big((1-w_x)G_{Cx} + w_xG_{Dx}\big)\Big)$$
$$+ F_y\Big(\big(1-w_y\big)\big((1-w_x)G_{Ay} + w_xG_{By}\big) + w_y\big((1-w_x)G_{Cy} + w_xG_{Dy}\big)\Big)$$
$$- \Big(\big(1-w_y\big)\big((1-w_x)0 + w_xG_{Bx}\big) + w_y\big((1-w_x)G_{Cy} + w_x(G_{Dx}+ G_{Dy})\big)\Big)$$

EQUATION 2.1.3

All the elements are arranged in terms of a single bilinear interpolation. However, another channel is now required for the extra terms. Define new vectors like so:

$$\mathbf{F'} = (F_x, F_y, -1)$$
$$\mathbf{G_A'} = (G_{Ax}, G_{Ay}, 0)$$
$$\mathbf{G_B'} = (G_{Bx}, G_{By}, G_{Bx})$$
$$\mathbf{G_C'} = (G_{Cx}, G_{Cy}, G_{Cy})$$
$$\mathbf{G_D'} = \big(G_{Dx}, G_{Dy}, (G_{Dx}+ G_{Dy})\big)$$

Giving our final result:

$$N = \mathrm{dot}\Big(\ \mathbf{F'}, \mathrm{lerp}\big(w_y, \mathrm{lerp}(w_x, \mathbf{G_A'}, \mathbf{G_B'}), \mathrm{lerp}(w_x, \mathbf{G_C'}, \mathbf{G_D'})\big)\Big)$$

EQUATION 2.1.4

By using bilinear texture interpolation at the weighted point, the resulting gradient (with extra terms) dotted with the fractional position evaluates to the exact same noise value. The 3D case is similar, except it uses trilinear interpolation. Also, the gradients have four components, and the extra channel must account for Z.

APPLYING IT IN THE REAL WORLD

Unfortunately, the extra terms complicate our implementation. We can put them in the alpha channel of a texture, but the corner diagonally across from the cell origin contains the sum of all the gradient channels. Fortunately, the 12 gradient vectors can never sum outside the range (–2, 2). By halving the range of the alpha channel, we can match the range of the other channels and only need to rescale it in the shader.

The other complication is that the alpha channel contents vary, depending on which cell we are within. This prevents the edges of adjacent cells from overlapping. The simplest solution is to double the dimensions of our texture so that each cell is independent of its neighbors as shown in Figure 2.1.2.

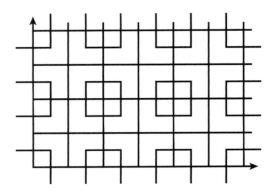

FIGURE 2.1.2   Relation between pixels (light gray) and cells (black).

Here is the `QuickNoiseSmall` HLSL function using a volume of 32×32×32 cells with the result in Figure 2.1.3.

```
sampler3D smpNoiseSmall;
float CELLS = 32;


float QuickNoiseSmall(float3 texCoord)
{
    // Calculate coords
    float3 intCoord = floor(texCoord);
    float3 fracCoord = frac(texCoord);
    float3 smoothCoord = smoothstep(float3(0,0,0), float3(1,1,1), fracCoord);
    float3 sampleCoord = (intCoord + 0.5*smoothCoord)/CELLS + 0.75/CELLS;
    // sample texture
    float4 gradientVec = tex3D(smpNoiseSmall, sampleCoord);

    return dot(gradientVec, float4(fracCoord,-2.0));
}
```

The resulting function compiles to just 9 arithmetic instructions and 1 texture access, occupying a total of 13 instruction slots. In comparison, Green's optimized function requires 42 arithmetic instructions and 9 texture accesses and occupies 58 instruction slots.

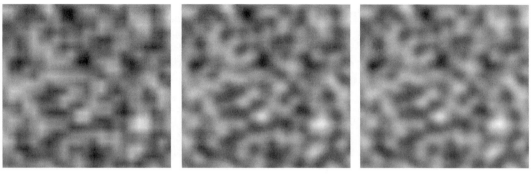

FIGURE 2.1.3   Slices of noise on the XY plane. Precomputed value Noise (left), Quick Noise (center), and Green's implementation (right). At this scale, Quick Noise and Green are virtually indistinguishable. The linear artifacts of value Noise are particularly ugly, with only 2×2×2 samples per cell.

AND NOW THE BAD NEWS

Older GPUs have limited precision when filtering texels, and this is noticeable when Quick Noise is sampled at low frequencies. Banding is visible and tends to accentuate the inherent grid artifacts found in Perlin Noise. The newest GPUs are capable of higher-precision filtering, which should eliminate the banding.

FIGURE 2.1.4   Artifacts in a close-up of Quick Noise (left) and the scaled difference (×16) from the reference (right). Cell boundaries and banding may be noticeable at low frequencies.

Another serious limitation is the small size of the volume that can be represented. The full volume that Perlin supports is 256×256×256. This has proven to be large enough to avoid repeating patterns in most situations. Although the smaller 32×32×32 volume is identical to the subset of the noise volume it represents, it is far too small, and the repetition is very obvious at higher frequencies.

IMPLEMENTATION, THE SEQUEL

At first glance, such a small number of gradients seem inadequate to guarantee randomness. A quick check shows that those 12 gradients give us 12^8—or approximately 430 million unique cells. Since there are only some 16.8 million cells in the entire noise volume, there are clearly more than enough permutations.

However, on a single plane, we end up with 12^4, or only 20,736, combinations. The randomness suffers, but it is a great opportunity. We can easily make a 2D texture atlas of all those combinations. The full 3D volume can be implemented by sampling both the front and back planes of the current cell and linearly interpolating between those samples as shown in Figure 2.1.5.

Given that perm is a table of random values and (X, Y, Z) is the origin of the cell, Perlin's hash takes the form:

$$perm[perm[perm[X] + Y + Z]$$

EQUATION 2.1.1

This complete hash can be calculated through texture lookups. The first texture is accessed at the X and Y coordinates and returns the starting offsets within the permutation table. One lookup will suffice since all four corners of the current cell are packed in the four channels of the texture. The Z value is then added to all four channels. One pair at a time, we use those to index into a second texture. The value returned is either the U or V coordinate of the appropriate cell in the texture atlas.

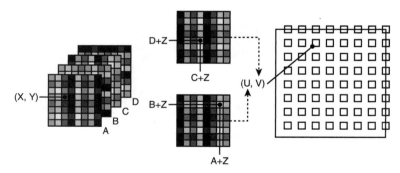

FIGURE 2.1.5 Using dependent texture lookups to find the right cell in the atlas.

Since the Z offset is the last to affect the permutation, the corners at $Z + 1$ will always be the adjacent values in the table. This is exploited to return the coordinates for the $Z + 1$ cell at the same time as the Z cell coordinates.

```
sampler2D smpPermXY;

sampler2D smpPermZ;

sampler2D smpCellAtlas;


float QuickNoiseFull( float3 texCoord )
{
    // Prep coords
    float3 intCoord = floor(texCoord);
    float3 fracCoord = frac(texCoord);
    float3 smoothCoord = smoothstep(float3(0,0,0), float3(1,1,1),
fracCoord);


    // Look-up coords in textures
    float4 packedOffsetXY = tex2D(smpPermXY, (intCoord.xy/256+0.5/256));
    float4 plusZ1 = packedOffsetXY + intCoord.z/256;
    float2 plusZ2 = plusZ1.wz;    // using ps2_0 wzyx swizzle
    float4 coord1 = tex2D(smpPermZ, plusZ1.xy);
    float4 coord2 = tex2D(smpPermZ, plusZ2);
    coord1.zw = coord2.xy;


    // Calculate final sample coordinates
    float2 sampleCoord0 = coord1.xz + (smoothCoord.xy)/512.0;
    float2 sampleCoord1 = coord1.yw + (smoothCoord.xy)/512.0;


    // Sample from atlas and lerp to get gradient
    float4 gradientVec0 = tex2D(smpCellAtlas, sampleCoord0);
    float4 gradientVec1 = tex2D(smpCellAtlas, sampleCoord1);
    gradientVec1.w += 0.5*gradientVec1.z;
    float4 grad = lerp(gradientVec0, gradientVec1, smoothCoord.z);


    return dot(grad, float4(fracCoord,-2.0));
}
```

ON THE DVD

The resulting function compiles to 18 arithmetic instructions and 5 texture accesses occupying approximately 24 instruction slots. Refer to the RenderMonkey and shader files on the DVD-ROM for further details on the shader implementation and texture creation.

RESULTS

The Quick Noise functions occupy far fewer instruction slots than Green. This allows the implementation of procedural shaders on old or limited hardware or more complex shaders on new hardware.

Noise is an ideal primitive for imitating the results of natural processes that would be too tedious to paint by hand. It may also be used to augment traditional texturing by adding detail to otherwise identical assets or in extreme close-ups. The need for very-high-resolution textures is reduced, and more assets can fit in the limited graphics memory.

Noise is also volumetric and does not require unwrapped texture coordinates. It is bandwidth-limited and may be procedurally filtered to avoid aliasing artifacts.

Table 2.1.1   Average values from DirectX preview window in AMD RenderMonkey 1.71. Measured on an IBM Thinkpad T41p with 128MB ATI Mobility FireGL T2 (Radeon 9600 class)

Noise Function	Arithmetic Instructions	Texture Instructions	Instruction Slots	Texture Memory	Volume Size	Frames/ Second
Precomputed	1	1	5	256 KB	323	340
Quick Noise Small	9	1	13	1 MB	323	250
Quick Noise Full	18	5	24	1.75 MB	2563	140
Optimized Green	42	9	58	257 KB	2563	80

FUTURE WORK

The precision issues with Quick Noise at low frequencies might be resolved with a more careful choice of texture formats and better filtering. To date, an elegant way of finding noise derivatives has proven elusive. Shader model 4 implementations have not been explored.

REFERENCES

[Green05] Green, Simon. 2005. "Implementing Improved Perlin Noise." In *GPU Gems 2*, edited by Matt Phar, pp. 409–416. Addison-Wesley.

[Perlin02] Perlin, Ken. 2002. "Improving Noise." In *Computer Graphics (Proceedings of SIGGRAPH 2002)*, pp. 681–682.

[Perlin85] Perlin, Ken. 1985. "An Image Synthesizer." In *Computer Graphics (Proceedings of ACM SIGGRAPH 85)*, pp. 287-–296.

2.2 Efficient Soft Particles

Gilberto Rosado

INTRODUCTION

Particle systems are the standard technique for simulating volumetric phenomena in computer graphics. Particle systems are typically used to render effects such as smoke, dust, fire, and explosions. These particle systems are generally rendered by layering many textured screen-aligned quads using alpha blending. One of the drawbacks of using screen-aligned quads for particles is that there can be a noticeable seam where a quad intersects other geometry in the scene.

The soft particles technique hides these seams. It works by sampling the depth buffer when rendering the particles and fading the particles as they get closer to other geometry. This gives a seamless "soft" look to the particles. However, it can add a significant expense to the particle rendering by requiring the sampling of the depth buffer and a transformation of the depth values in the depth buffer to the camera view space. This transformation is required in order to have a linear distribution of depth values while fading out the particles.

This article introduces a way to make the soft particle technique extremely efficient by doing some preprocessing to the depth buffer. By down-sampling the depth buffer and pretransforming it to view space, the added cost of rendering soft particles is minimized.

Hard Particles vs. Soft Particles

The objectionable seams produced by standard particle systems happen when individual particles intersect other geometry in the world. Figure 2.2.1 and Figure 2.2.2 show the difference between standard particles and soft particles. Notice the seams present in Figure 2.2.1, particularly the way the smoke intersects with the terrain. These seams are even more noticeable when the particles are animated. Figure 2.2.2 uses the soft particle technique, so there are no seams as the smoke intersects the terrain.

FIGURE 2.2.1   A scene rendered with hard particles. Notice the seams that the smoke creates when intersecting with the terrain.

DirectX 10 provides a way to sample the depth buffer as a texture, and [Gilham07] discusses ways to access a depth buffer texture using other APIs. If soft particles cannot be implemented due to depth buffer textures not being available on a particular set of hardware or graphics API, then ways to minimize those seams would be to use smaller particles or to have special code that tries to avoid intersecting the particles with the world.

FIGURE 2.2.2 A scene rendered using soft particles.

IMPLEMENTING SOFT PARTICLES THE STANDARD WAY

The simplest implementation of soft particles is to use a pixel shader that decreases the alpha component of the output color value as the particle gets closer to intersecting the geometry of the currently rendered scene. This can be achieved by comparing the current view space Z position of the particle at that pixel to that currently in the depth buffer. The current values in the depth buffer are projected back to view space using the inverse of the scene's projection matrix.

OPTIMIZING SOFT PARTICLES

In order to minimize the performance impact of adding soft particles to an existing engine, we need to do as much work outside of the pixel shader as possible. Therefore, we must minimize the number of additional instructions and make sure the texture hit is as small as possible. Thankfully, the depth buffer is sampled in a very sequential fashion, so it should make good use of the texture cache. However, even better use of the GPU's texture cache can be achieved by using a down-sampled version of the depth buffer.

A good way to down-sample the depth buffer is to render a screen-aligned quad with a viewport that is half the size along both the X and Y axes using a pixel shader that picks the min or max of the four adjacent texels.

With the down-sampling of the depth buffer, another optimization comes from transforming the depth values to view space Z values during the down-sampling of the depth buffer. This will avoid the transformation in the particle pixel shader.

Now the added instructions to our particle shader have been greatly reduced, and the depth buffer texture has been reduced to a quarter of the original size.

ON THE DVD

The demo on the accompanying DVD-ROM contains a sample implementation of the optimized effect.

RESULTS

Below are the results of our optimization on a GeForce 8800 GT graphics card when rendering 35,000 particles at 1440×900 resolution.

Hard Particles: 4.25 ms

Soft Particles: 5.5 ms

Optimized Soft Particles: 4.35 ms

Down-Sampling Depth Buffer: 0.3 ms

The results show that there is virtually no added cost to rendering soft particles on this graphics card using our optimized technique besides the fixed cost of down-sampling the depth buffer.

Here are the results for a similar scene running at 1440×900 resolution on a much weaker GPU, the GeForce 8400.

Hard Particles: 30 ms

Soft Particles: 60 ms

Optimized Soft Particles: 42 ms

Down-Sampling Depth Buffer: 1.8 ms

There is a significant cost to creating soft particles on the GeForce 8400 GPU, but in this particular scene we saved about 18 ms by using the down-sampled, view space depth buffer.

CONCLUSION

In this article, we discussed a method to optimize soft particle rendering that is so efficient as to become nearly free. Since many other graphical effects can be optimized by using a down-sampled or view space depth buffer, adding soft-particles using the technique described in this paper should be practical for many existing game engines.

REFERENCES

[Gilham07] Gilham, David. "Real-Time Depth-of-Field Implemented with a Post-Processing only Technique," *Shader X⁵*, Wolfgang Engel, Ed., Charles River Media, 2007, pp. 163–175.

2.3 Simplified High-Quality Anti-Aliased Lines

Stephen Coy (scoy@microsoft.com)

Microsoft Research

Abstract

In this article, we present a method for rendering high-quality anti-aliased lines. The method is easily implemented on modern GPUs with programmable shaders. Unlike previous methods that required significant fragment processing, our new method only requires a single texture lookup and a multiply in the pixel shader. The resulting lines can be of any width, and the method allows for an arbitrary filter kernel to be applied to the edges. Properly rounded line ends also result from this method. The method is trivially extended to render points.

For this method the filter kernel is precomputed and stored as a small (typically 16×16) texture. The lines are rendered as a strip of six triangles. A vertex shader calculates the locations of the vertices based on the line endpoints and the line width. The filter texture is sampled to provide the coverage amount for each pixel.

Introduction

Our primary motivation for the creation of this tool was to re-create the classic Atari game *Battlezone*. Released in 1980, *Battlezone* was one of the earliest 3D arcade games (if not the first). *Battlezone* used a vector display for its graphics, resulting in beautifully smooth wireframe images. In order to reproduce this level of quality on a conventional raster display, we needed to find a way to generate anti-aliased lines that approach the quality of a vector display. Previous work [McNamara et al. 00] approached the problem by rendering a box around the line.

For each pixel in this box the distance from the pixel center to the line is calculated, and the result is used to index into a 1D texture that represents the convolved filter weights. This requires considerable computation for each individual pixel. Their technique also required extra work to provide high-quality endpoints on the line segments.

METHOD

The key insight into the new method is that the GPU hardware already does most of what is needed. Given a properly aligned texture, no per-pixel computation needs to be done beyond the built-in texture coordinate iteration and texture sampling.

The benefits of our approach are:

- High-quality lines
- Exact line widths
- 2D vector display lines that integrate properly with a 3D, solid shaded world
- Low shader cost (about 34 instructions in the vertex shader and a single texture sample in the fragment shader)

TEXTURE CREATION

Unlike McNamara et al.'s 1D texture, we use a 2D texture that represents a quarter circle of our desired end point. Figure 2.3.1 shows the texture used for the sample code and a close-up of it in use.

 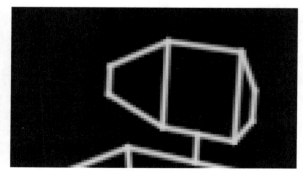

FIGURE 2.3.1   The sample code's texture.

During rendering, the texture is flipped and stretched as needed to fit the shape of the line. By using a 2D texture rather than a 1D ramp, we ensure that the end points can be properly rendered without any extra cost. For the sample implementation, we use a SmoothStep [Upstill 90] function to create the falloff for the edge of the line. Any function can be used. Since this is done as a preprocessing step, the curve can be as complicated as required. We chose the SmoothStep function because the results look good enough and it is quite simple to calculate. In our testing we found that even a linear falloff preformed well visually. Because of the uncertainties involved in understanding how individual monitor gamma curves would affect the result, it was deemed fruitless to try to be any more exact with the solution. Taking the next step and animating the lines then brings into play the rise and decay curves of the pixels on the display device, making the quality of the solution dependent upon the individual device and the speed of the animation. In other words, even though this solution allows for arbitrarily complex falloff curves, you are probably better off just using whatever looks good.

In order to create accurate lines, you must understand the relationship between the filter texture, the desired line width, and the width of the rendered quad. Looking at the filter as a 1D slice, this relationship can be easily shown. For example, Figure 2.3.2 shows how a filter texture would be created for a two-pixel-wide line.

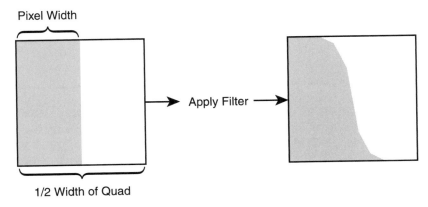

FIGURE 2.3.2 Generation of the filter texture for a two-pixel-wide line.

In this example, the applied filter had a width equal to the pixel width. By increasing this width, the lines can be made to appear softer. This example also shows the pre-filtered pixel width to be exactly half of the texture size. This is not required and is not always desirable. The example shown in Figure 2.3.3 would work fine for half-pixel-wide lines.

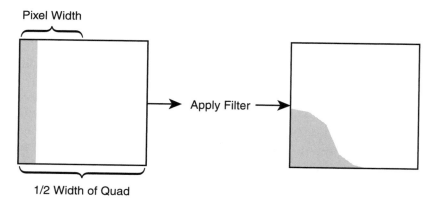

FIGURE 2.3.3   Generation of the filter texture for a half-pixel-wide line.

One caveat that might not be immediately obvious is that mipmaps should not be used in the shader code when sampling the texture. With bilinear filtering, only the filtered texture represents a piece-wise linear approximation of the ideal samples. If mipmapping is employed, then the results will be erroneous.

The ability to employ arbitrary curves also opens the possibility of using the texture to create multiple stroked lines at no extra cost.

VERTEX SETUP

Because the majority of the computation is done per vertex rather than per pixel, we have some freedom about how we choose to split the work between C++ code and the vertex shader. For the reference implementation, we chose to focus on a clear demonstration of the technique rather than absolute performance. The vertex structure contains the positions of both line end points, the line color (RGBA), a set of four weights, and, finally, the radius of the desired line and its inverse. The only thing that differentiates the six vertices from each other is the four weights in each vertex. The first two values, p0 and p1, are either 0.0 or 1.0 and determine to which end of the line the vertices are related (see Figure 2.3.4). The third and fourth weights control where the vertices will end up (relative to the line's end point).

The vertex shader code takes the input points through the transformation from world space to homogeneous space and then into screen space. During this process, it also has to keep track of the Z and W values so that the resulting depth values are correct. The relationship between the Z and W values is especially important.

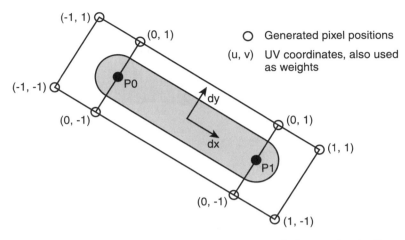

FIGURE 2.3.4   The layout of the vertices as they are expanded to render the line segment.

The Z value must be maintained for correct depth comparison, while the W value must be calculated to force the correct texture interpolation. Even though the line is in 3D space, we want to interpolate the texture as if it was in 2D space. The details of this process are shown in the shader code in Appendix A at the end of this article and screenshots are shown in Figures 2.3.5 and 2.3.6.

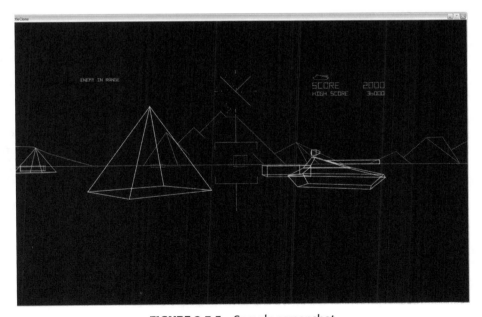

FIGURE 2.3.5   Sample screenshot.

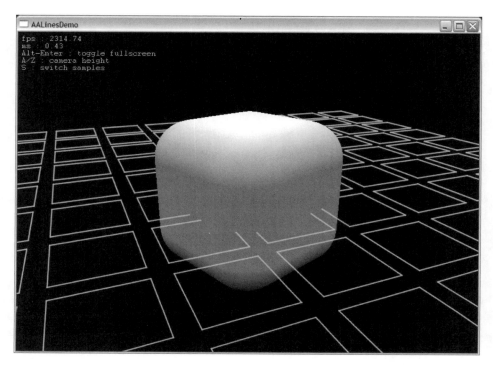

FIGURE 2.3.6   Another screenshot showing the lines interacting with solid shaded objects.

VARIATIONS ON THE THEME

The implementation accompanying this article can act as a basis for several variations:

- The destination contribution to the alpha blending can be changed from `InvSrcAlpha` to `One`. This creates an additive blending effect that more strongly shows where the lines overlap. This is most effective when line colors are not already in full intensity. This also has the advantage of eliminating any differences caused by draw order when lines of different colors overlap.

- If the scene does not require intermixing 3D solid shaded objects with the rendered lines, then the vertex shader can be simplified even further since the need for tracking depth is eliminated.

- The sample implementation uses zero-length lines to represent points. This could easily be special-cased to make them more efficient.

- By using a solid texture (or eliminating the texture altogether), you can create jaggy lines of an exact fixed width.

- The sample implementation assumes that each collection of lines uses a single color. This color could be moved into the vertex structure to allow multiple colors to be used in a single draw call.

CONCLUSION

In this article, we have presented a simple and efficient method for rendering high-quality, anti-aliased lines. The technique has two key advantages over previously published methods. First, by taking advantage of the GPU's texturing capability, we are able to avoid almost all per-fragment processing. Second, the technique allows for correct integration with 3D solid shaded scenes.

APPENDIX A: THE SHADER CODE

```
//
// AALines.fx
//


//
// Global variables
//
float4x4  g_matWorld;             // World matrix for object
float4x4  g_matWorldViewProjection; // World * View * Projection matrix


float4    g_Color;
texture   g_FilterTexture;


sampler FilterTextureSampler =
sampler_state
{
  Texture = <g_FilterTexture>;
  MipFilter = None;                      // Important!
  MinFilter = Linear;
```

```
   MagFilter = Linear;
  AddressU = Mirror;
  AddressV = Mirror;
};



//
// Vertex shader output structure.
//
struct VS_OUTPUT
{
  float4 position   : POSITION;
  float4 textureUV   : TEXCOORD0;  // vertex texture coords
};


//
// Vertex shader for AA lines
//
VS_OUTPUT
VS( float3 pos0   : POSITION0,
  float3 pos1   : POSITION1,
  float4 weights : TEXCOORD0,
  float  radius  : TEXCOORD1,
  float  aspect  : TEXCOORD2 )
{
  VS_OUTPUT  Output;

  // Transform the input points.
  float4 p0 = mul( float4( pos0, 1.0f ), g_matWorldViewProjection );
  float4 p1 = mul( float4( pos1, 1.0f ), g_matWorldViewProjection );

  // Warp transformed points by aspect ratio.
  float4 w0 = p0;
  float4 w1 = p1;
```

```
w0.y /= aspect;
w1.y /= aspect;

// Calc vectors between points in screen space.
float2 delta2 = w1.xy / w1.z - w0.xy / w0.z;
float3 delta_p;

delta_p.xy = delta2;
delta_p.z = w1.z - w0.z;

//
// Calc UV basis vectors.
//
// Calc U
float  len = length( delta2 );
float3 U = delta_p / len;

// Create V orthogonal to U.
float3 V;
V.x = U.y;
V.y = -U.x;
V.z = 0;

// Calculate output position based on this
// vertex's weights.
Output.position = p0 * weights.x + p1 * weights.y;

// Calc offset part of position.
float3 offset = U * weights.z + V * weights.w;

// Apply line thickness.
offset.xy *= radius;

// Unwarp by inverse of aspect ratio.
```

```
    offset.y *= aspect;


    // Undo perspective divide since the hardware will do it.
    Output.position.xy += offset * Output.position.z;


    // Set up UVs. We have to use projected sampling rather
    // than regular sampling because we don't want to get
    // perspective correction.
    Output.textureUV.x = weights.z;
    Output.textureUV.y = weights.w;
    Output.textureUV.z = 0.0f;
    Output.textureUV.w = 1.0f;


    return Output;
}   // end of VS()


//
// Pixel shader
//
float 4
PS( VS_OUTPUT In )
{
    float4 result;


    result = g_Color * tex2Dproj( FilterTextureSampler, In.textureUV );


    return result;
}   // end of PS()



//
// AAlines technique.
//
technique AALines
```

```
{
  pass P0
  {
    VertexShader = compile vs_2_0 VS();
    PixelShader = compile ps_2_0 PS();

    AlphaRef = 1;
    AlphaTestEnable = false;
    AlphaFunc = GreaterEqual;

    // Set up blend renderstates
    AlphaBlendEnable = true;
    SrcBlend = SrcAlpha;
    DestBlend = InvSrcAlpha;  // Change to "One" and use a color that's
not fully saturated
    BlendOp = Add;        // to show overlapping areas more strongly.

    CullMode = None;

    Lighting = false;

    ZEnable = true;
    ZFunc = LessEqual;
    ZWriteEnable = false;
  }
}
```

REFERENCES

[McNamara et al. 00] Robert McNamara, Joel McCormack, and Norman P. Jouppi. "Prefiltered Antialiased Lines Using Half-Plane Distance Functions." In *Proceedings of the ACM SIGGRAPH/ EUROGRAPHICS Workshop on Graphics Hardware* (Interlaken, Switzerland, August 21–22, 2000). S. N. Spencer, Ed. HWWS '00.

[Upstill 90] Steve Upstill (1990). *The RenderMan Companion: A Programmer's Guide to Realistic Computer Graphics. Reading*, Mass: Addison-Wesley. ISBN 0-201-50868-0. OCLC 19741379

2.4 Fast Skin Shading

John Hable, George Borshukov, and Jim Hejl

Introduction

Rendering realistic skin is a difficult problem in computer graphics, and especially in real-time. Most real-time applications that re-create heads use normal maps and diffuse maps to create an object with the shape and color of a head. However, these applications often use the same generic lighting model for skin that they use for cardboard, concrete, and plastic. Consequently, most heads rendered in-game do not "feel" like skin because the lighting model does not accurately model how light affects skin.

Skin looks very different from a pure diffuse surface such as cardboard. One of the fundamental differences between skin and other lighting models is that light bounces around inside of skin. Skin has several layers with differing levels of translucency, whereas a "pure" diffuse model is based on the assumption that when light hits an object, the light scatters equally in all directions. This model is fast to compute, but in order to make CG skin look like real skin, it is necessary to take into account the way light bleeds throughout an object.

This article discusses an implementation of quickly simulating how light transfers underneath skin. This article contains few new advancements, but rather, it synthesizes other people's great work and applies optimizations. Specifically, this article's goal is to make realistic skin shading practical in typical games on the current generation of consoles, such as the PlayStation 3 and Xbox 360. For the theory of making realistic subsurface scattering, rather than adding new information, we will try to synthesize existing art into this standalone article. Then, we will discuss several new variations on these techniques that allow fast subsurface scattering to be used in several in-development games at Electronic Arts.

BACKGROUND AND EXISTING ART

The complete theory of light transfer underneath skin is quite complicated and beyond the scope of this article. For a great discussion, see d'Eon and Luebke's chapter in *GPU Gems 3* [d'EonGPUGems07]. In brief, subsurface scattering happens in three steps. First, the light hits the skin. Second, light bounces around underneath the skin. Third, light exits the skin and is viewed by the camera. We simulate the first step by rendering diffuse light to a light map. The bouncing of the light is simulated by blurring the light map. Finally, light exiting is simulated by multiplying the blurred light by the diffuse map of the face.

While there are numerous techniques for skin shading, this article will talk about texture space diffusion. The idea is quite simple: Render the lights into UV space, blur those lights to simulate subsurface scattering, and render. The first use of this technique was by Borshukov and Lewis in the *Matrix* sequels [Borshukov03, Borshukov05]. They rendered the light to a map in texture-space, blurred that map, and used the blurred light in lighting calculations. To increase realism, they used different blur kernels for the red, green, and blue color channels, since light red, green, and blue light scatter differently in real skin. For the blur kernel, they used the formula $1/(1 + Radius)^p$, where p was chosen based on extensive photographic reference. They used 2.75 for red, 3.25 for green, and 3.50 for blue (Figure 2.4.1).

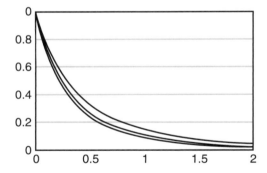

FIGURE 2.4.1 The formula $1/(1 + r)^p$ when p is 3.50, 3.25, and 2.75. The bottom curve is for $p = 3.50$.

This idea was applied to real-time by Gosselin [Gosselin04], using a Poisson sampling, and Green [Green04], using a Gaussian blur. This work laid the foundation for the Adrianne and Doug Jones demos by NVIDIA [NVIDIA 06, NVIDIA 07] that set the current high bar for skin shading in real-time. The main technical leap in these demos was decomposing the dipole function into the addition of separable Gaussian blurs. These demos also showed several other features including finding a good set of shading parameters for real skin, compensating for UV stretching, popularizing a good specular model skin [Kelemen01], and making this information accessible.

In our opinion, the Doug Jones demo sets the clear standard for high-quality skin shading in real-time. The only problem is that "real-time" for a tech demo is quite different from being fast enough to use in a game in real-use cases. The Doug Jones demo fully taxes the processor of a high-end graphics card. In contrast, most games must run on less powerful consoles. Also, the commercial games must render an entire world, which only leaves a small fraction of time for skin shading. The premise of this article is that the Doug Jones demo is the high standard for skin shading, and the goal of this article is to show various ways to scale the Doug Jones demo down so that it is fast enough for a console but still retains as much quality as possible.

SPECULAR AND DIFFUSE

The most common lighting model in computer games is diffuse shading with a specular highlight. When light hits an object, it does one of two things. In the first case, light hits an object, gets absorbed, and then light of a different color is emitted. In the other case, light does not get absorbed and "skips" off the edge. The first case is called *diffuse shading*, and the second case is generally called *specular*. We will handle these cases in order.

DIFFUSE

The diffuse case is much more fundamentally difficult because rendering diffuse lighting at a single point on skin requires knowing the incoming light intensities at nearby points. The first problem is simulating this light transfer if we had infinite computational time, and the second problem is performing that calculation quickly.

Fortunately, the problem of finding a diffusion dipole is nearly a solved problem. Donner and Jensen [Donner05] performed extensive analysis. In their work, they found different curves that show the intensity of red, green, and blue at output points a given distance away from the source of incoming light. For the Doug Jones demo, d'Eon and Leubke found sums of Gaussian blurs that closely match those curves.

Decomposing a dipole into a sum of blurs has several benefits. The first is that it allows that demo to run in real-time, since performing five 7×7 Gaussian blurs is more than an order of magnitude faster than performing one 50×50 blur. The second benefit is that it allows an intuitive way to tweak the numbers. While the artistic effect of changing these numbers is not exactly obvious, it provides a good starting point for changing the look for different skin types. Table 2.4.1 shows the numbers that Eugene d'Eon and David Leubke list as a good starting point for light, Caucasian skin.

One thing to notice is that the red channel is far blurrier than the blue and green. This happens because in the real world, red light scatters farther in skin than the green and blue wavelengths.

Table 2.4.1   The weights used by Eugene d'Eon and David Luebke [d'EonGPUGems07]

Variance (mm^2)	Red	Green	Blue
0.0064	0.233	0.455	0.649
0.0484	0.100	0.336	0.344
0.187	0.118	0.198	0
0.567	0.113	0.007	0.007
1.99	0.358	0.004	0
7.41	0.078	0	0

The Doug Jones demo takes the incoming light and renders it to a light map. That demo blurs the light map several times, and then combines them together. This raises the issue of how the diffuse map alters the light. Does the diffuse map affect the light going in or the light going out? We will discuss that issue more later. The short answer is that we advocate applying the diffuse map to the outgoing light in most cases, but it depends on your specific circumstances.

One final improvement in the Doug Jones demo is using a texture to compensate for the stretching in the UV map. In a typical UV map, certain areas of the face will be greatly distorted—in particular, the nose and the ears. A stretch texture helps avoid this artifact. Also, the first weight set is not actually used in the blur. To preserve sharpness, that weight is used in the final lighting calculation. So you can think of that first blur as the non-scattered lighting that immediately enters the skin and exits without traversing. That is the core algorithm for subsurface scattering as described in *GPU Gems 3*. Now, we will explain our optimizations to improve performance.

OUR CONTRIBUTIONS

The first big problem with the technique as described is the blurs. If you use five blurs, since Gaussian blurs are separable, each blur is actually two passes, one for the horizontal and one for the vertical. At 7 taps per pass, each blur requires 14 taps, so the total cost is 14×5 = 70 taps. Then later on, we have the cost of reading those textures. This procedure very accurately calculates a 50×50 blur in a way that is much faster than a naïve implementation that would take 2,500 taps. However, with a carefully chosen sampling pattern, we can get significantly better performance with minimal additional error.

Our contribution to improve d'Eon and Leubke's technique is to simulate that same blur in fewer taps, and we have achieved acceptable results using 12 or fewer samples. We generate our blur kernel based on the same dipole. After trying many approaches, we found that the best way to simulate this blur is to use two "rings." We divide each ring into 6 sections for a total of 12 sections. Then, in each section, we do a jittered sample. Then, we sample the full kernel with our 12 weights. Keep in mind that there are actually 13 weights because there is an implied weight in the center.

Note that you can use a different sampling pattern. The first weight is for the light that comes in and directly comes out. The next six weights simulate the "mid-level" blurring. The final six weights are mainly for the wide red blurring. Since the red bleeds much farther than the green and blue, the outer ring is primarily for the red channel.

```
float3 blurJitteredWeights[13] =
{
    { 0.220441, 0.437000, 0.635000 },
    { 0.076356, 0.064487, 0.039097 },
    { 0.116515, 0.103222, 0.064912 },
    { 0.064844, 0.086388, 0.062272 },
    { 0.131798, 0.151695, 0.103676 },
    { 0.025690, 0.042728, 0.033003 },
    { 0.048593, 0.064740, 0.046131 },
    { 0.048092, 0.003042, 0.000400 },
    { 0.048845, 0.005406, 0.001222 },
    { 0.051322, 0.006034, 0.001420 },
    { 0.061428, 0.009152, 0.002511 },
    { 0.030936, 0.002868, 0.000652 },
    { 0.073580, 0.023239, 0.009703 },
};
float2 blurJitteredSamples[13] =
{
    { 0.000000,   0.000000 },
```

```
    { 1.633992,    0.036795 },
    { 0.177801,    1.717593 },
    { -0.194906,   0.091094 },
    { -0.239737,  -0.220217 },
    { -0.003530,  -0.118219 },
    { 1.320107,   -0.181542 },
    { 5.970690,    0.253378 },
    { -1.089250,   4.958349 },
    { -4.015465,   4.156699 },
    { -4.063099,  -4.110150 },
    { -0.638605,  -6.297663 },
    { 2.542348,   -3.245901 },
};
```

Since using a sum of Gaussian blurs is a good way to describe subsurface scattering, we describe the blur in this way. Then, in an offline process, we combine the sum of the blurs into a single blur, and then sample. This approach provides us with an intuitive way to tweak the blur for different skin types.

Plugging in these numbers, we actually have a different blur for each R, G, and B channel. Additionally, all of these samples can be done in exactly one pass instead of 10 passes, which greatly assists with memory. Note that these numbers are scaled by a constant. One other interesting feature is that since these are all done in the same pass, we don't actually need to do a separate blur pass. In the final pixel shader, we can perform the 12 texture reads if we so desire.

The second optimization is that while writing the light map texture, we can poke a hole in the depth buffer and use High-Z to only perform the blur on front-facing polygons. During the initial render to light map pass, we can set the depth to $dot(N,V) \times 0.5 + 0.5$, where N is the world normal vector and V is the normalized world-space vector from the camera to the point. Using this formula, a point facing directly at the camera would have an output depth of 1, and a point facing directly away would have an output depth of 0 (see Figure 2.4.2).

Here is the shader code for the blur pass.

```
float3 totalColor = 0;
float2 stretch = tex2D(StretchTextureBlurred, uv.xy).rg;
float shadow = tex2D(LightMap, uv.xy).a;
for (int i = 1; i <= 12; i++)
    totalColor += SubsurfaceJitterSampler(uv.xy, stretch, i);
```

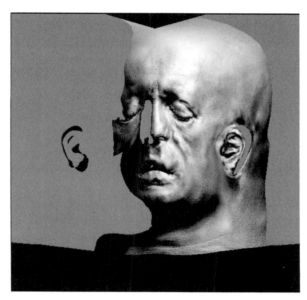

FIGURE 2.4.2   We can render the depth and poke a hole in the depth buffer during our light map render pass. Then, while rendering the blur, we can turn on High-Z, which will allow the blur to only be rendered on the visible pixels. This approach prevents wasted computation on either the black areas (which were never rendered to) or the gray areas (which fail the depth test).

During the blur pass, while rendering the quad, we can render with depth. If we desired, we could render to a depth of 0.5, which would only perform the depth on front-facing normals. In practice, we want to push this buffer back a little bit because while any single triangle is either visible or not visible, due to interpolation, some visible points may have a normal that points away from the viewer. Alternatively, if we are using DirectX10 hardware, we can use a geometry shader to determine if the face is front-facing or not in the final image and use that to poke a hole in the depth buffer that way.

One issue the *GPU Gems* chapter discusses is the idea that the diffuse map should affect the light coming in and the light coming out. For the Adrianne demo, the diffuse map primarily affected light coming in and less light coming out. In the Doug Jones demo, it was split evenly between the two.

We have found that for real video games, our diffuse textures for faces are DXT1-compressed. Additionally, we render the light map to an fp16 RGBA buffer. So while a 1024×1024 DXT1 diffuse texture will take 500k, a 1024×1024 fp16 RGBA buffer requires 8 MB. As a result, the light map blur texture is much smaller than the source textures used, and our light map buffer is generally 512×512 or smaller.

When the light map texture gets this small, applying the diffuse map at all to this incoming light causes the diffuse texture to lose too much sharpness.

Additionally, our textures are based on photos, as opposed to painted by hand. When that happens, a certain amount of blurriness is built into the capture process. That is why we advocate using the diffuse texture only on outgoing light.

Due to this resolution issue, we apply the sharpest of the blurs during the final stage. During the final render, we sample the light map and multiply it by the diffuse map, but we also recalculate the diffuse shading and multiply by the diffuse map again for the sharpest blur.

One final trick you can do is to put the shadow in the alpha channel of the light map. One disadvantage of doing the lighting this way is that we have to calculate the lighting twice per pixel. In reality, this is not much of a problem because usually calculating the diffuse component is cheaper than the specular component. However, this can get very expensive for shadows. In most games, one shadow is used for characters, and in this case, we can put the shadow term in the unused alpha channel. Then during the final pass, we just read the shadow. Note that this will blur the shadow slightly, but we have found that this adds a nice effect because it softens the shadow's jagged edges (see Figure 2.4.3).

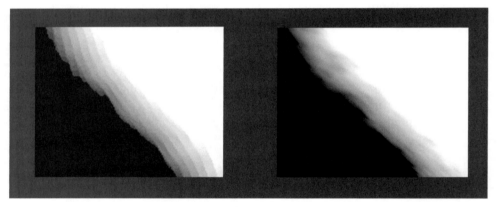

FIGURE 2.4.3 On the left is the shadow computed in the final pass, and on the right we have used the light-mapped shadow. This helps hide shadow artifacts.

Using these techniques, it is practical to render a high-quality head in real-time in a real game, but we have also found that we can have multiple heads rendered simultaneously with subsurface scattering. In most cases we have a fixed amount of memory dedicated to subsurface scattering. How we allocate this buffer varies heavily based on the application.

In the case of a two-person fighting game, an obvious choice would be one map for each person. For more general-purpose cases such as first-person shooters, it is impractical to have subsurface scattering on tens or hundreds of heads. However, with a first-person camera, it is very rare to have an extreme close-up of more than one character at a time. Games can take advantage of this by having more memory allocated to close characters' heads than far characters' heads. In many cases, games can get better results by dedicating a large portion of memory to the closest character and dividing the rest among remaining characters.

SPECULAR

As mentioned before, there are two classifications of light that shades an object. First, there is light that gets absorbed by the surface and then retransmitted, which we call diffuse. Second, there is light that skips right off the surface, which we call specular.

The specular case is much easier. To get real-world reference of specular highlights, you can perform tricks with polarized lenses to separate the diffuse and specular components. Then, modeling the specular term is as easy (or hard) as finding a mathematical model that looks similar to the images. One interesting note is that skin is actually very shiny. In fact, it almost looks like metal.

Most games use a Phong model to approximate the specular highlight of skin. However, when you look at the specular highlights of real skin, it becomes clear that the Phong model will not suffice, and that it is not possible to get an accurate specular falloff using a single Phong lobe. We use the same model that the Doug Jones head uses. We directly use the model that d'Eon and Leubke advocate [d'EonGPUGems07], which is Kelemen-Szirmay-Kalos [Kelemen01]. See Figure 2.4.4 for a comparison. A full discussion of this lighting model is beyond the scope of this article, so we recommend reading d'Eon and Leubke's excellent discussion.

Sill, we will reiterate a few points. There are three important qualities that a better specular model gives you.

1. The model is split into several lobes, and in our case, we use four. By having several lobes, we can get both the soft specular look as well as the tight specular look.
2. There is a built-in Fresnel term.
3. The specular highlight is brighter at grazing angles.

Granted, that model is pretty expensive for consoles, and if it is too expensive, you will have to find a good way to scale it down. In d'Eon and Leubke's chapter where they discuss the Doug Jones demo, they advocate pre-integrating the specular into a texture. If that solution does not appeal to you or is not feasible, here are some other ideas. For the first aspect, one cheap way is to use several Phong lobes.

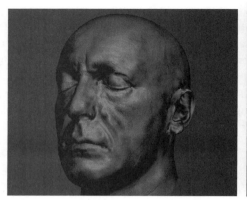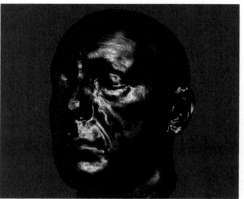

FIGURE 2.4.4 The left image shows the Roberto head with Kelemen-Szirmay-Kalos specular, and the right image shows the same head with the Phong model.

For the Fresnel, you can add that as well to the Phong term. The specular highlight being brighter at grazing angles could be done with other approximations. Ideally, you should try to use Kelemen-Szirmay-Kalos, but even if it is too expensive, implement it anyway as reference.

VARIATION ACROSS THE FACE

One other aspect of rendering is that the lighting model at all points on the face is not equal. Different parts of the face are shinier than others, and have different subsurface scattering effects. There are several ways to implement this variation.

The first and most standard way to add variation is by including a specular map. Additionally, we can also add a term for how tight the specular highlight is. For example, the nose usually has a tighter specular highlight than the cheek. MERL has done some research with measuring the specular highlight and solved this data for several lighting models [Weyrich06]. Using this data will not dramatically affect the results, but it does change the feel of the face, and we highly recommend using it.

The MERL team also measured the subsurface scattering properties of different skin types. It is a good set of data to use for creating a map of how "subsurfacy" different areas of the face are. Once again, adding this map does not dramatically change the look, but it does make a difference. In our data, we have only provided one kernel. We could imagine using the MERL data to create different blur kernels for different types of skin. For example, an older dark-skinned male would have a different kernel than a young white female. So far, we have only used a global scalar to change skin types while using the same kernel for all of them but with a global scalar.

Here is the final shader.

```
float diffuse = saturate(dot(lightVec, normal));
float finalShadow = tex2D(LightmapCombinedBlur, uv.xy).w;


float3 realModelColor = pow(tex2D(HeadDiffuse, uv.xy), 2.2);
float4 outColor = float4(0, 0, 0, 1);
float3 linearLightColor = pow(lightColor, 2.2) * lightBrightness;


float3 diffusePoint = Kd * linearLightColor * diffuse * finalShadow;


float lightmapAmount = tex2D(StretchTexture, uv.xy).b;
float3 diffuseBlurred = Kd * tex2D(LightmapCombinedBlur, float2(uv.x,
uv.y)).rgb;
diffuseColor = blurJitteredWeights[0] * diffusePoint +
               lerp((float3(1,1,1) – blurJitteredWeights[0]) *
               diffusePoint, diffuseBlurred, lightmapAmount);


specular = KelemenSzirmayKalosSpec(normalize(viewVec), normal, lightVec,
                                  eccentricity, rolloff, weight);
outColor.rgb = Ao * Ka * realModelColor +
               (diffuseColor * realModelColor +
               Ks * linearLightColor * specular * finalShadow);
```

DATA PREPARATION

The decisions made in creating the source data greatly affect the final skin render-ing quality. A head with poor normal and diffuse maps will not suddenly look good when subsurface scattering is applied. The process of creating a good head is quite involved, but in general, we highly recommend using scanned data and reference as much as possible to achieve photorealistic results. Scanning gives the best results, and the head used in this demo was a scan from XYZRGB. It also needs to be stressed that gamma correction is absolutely essential. It is not a coincidence that the games that are generally discussed as having the best graphics (*Half-Life 2, Halo 3, Gears of War*, and *Crysis*) all do proper gamma correction of their diffuse maps. See Gritz and d'Eon's chapter [Gritz07] for more details.

The visual impact of subsurface scattering depends heavily on the type of character being used. The more "subsurfacy" the skin of the target character, the more that will be gained from doing subsurface scattering. In fact, we have found that people with more subsurface scattering are harder to re-create digitally than people with less subsurface scattering. In particular, younger people are harder than older people, light skin is harder than dark skin, a more realistic look is harder than a more artistic or processed look, women are harder than men, and attractive people are harder then unattractive people.

Normal maps are important too. As we discussed earlier, the specular highlight on a real face is very bumpy. Also, the subsurface scattering softens the look. Since most artists try to paint normals based on what they see, they have a tendency to soften the normals to match the subsurface look of skin, but real skin is much bumpier. When using this technique, characters look best with bumpier normals that match what their skin actually looks like.

CONCLUSION

The color plate in the middle of this book shows some comparison screenshots of our implementation of the "true" method with multiple blur kernels and our approximation of it. In general, they look very close, while our version runs 10 times faster. On the Xbox 360, we can perform the blur step on a 512×512 buffer in 0.45 ms.

There are a few ways in which our technique does not look as good as the Doug Jones demo. The first one is that a certain "fleshiness" gets lost. By using so few kernel points, this technique does not accurately simulate the really wide blur of the red channel. It is hard to explain, and you do not see it in the images, but when you view the demos side by side, you can see that something subtle is missing. Also, we have some problems with stretching. With using multiple blurs, in the cases where areas of low stretch meet areas of high stretch, we get more noticeable blurring artifacts, such as around the ears.

We definitely feel that our technique creates skin that actually looks like skin, and the different blur kernels for the red, green, and blue channels are the key ingredient. Since the red bleeds farther than the green and blue, imagine a single small bump with a white light on one side. On the side of the bump that points toward the light, the intensity coming in is equal in red, green, and blue, but the red scatters farther, which gives that side of the bump a cyanish look. Meanwhile, since the red light travels farther, it will appear more on the opposite side of the bump, but the green and blue light will not travel as far, so that side looks reddish. That is one of the most important, yet hard-to-define, properties of skin shading. Having the normals toward the light be more cyan and the normals away more red is, in our opinion, the key to the distinctive look of skin.

Our belief is that most games will get better results by using fewer lights with an accurate lighting model than by using more lights with a simpler model and higher-res textures. In other words, doing one light plus ambient with an accurate lighting model will work better than many lights with the standard diffuse plus specular-Phong lighting model.

ACKNOWLEDGMENTS

We would like to thank XYZRGB for providing the high-quality scans of the Roberto face that is used in these images.

REFERENCES

[Borshukov03] George Borshukov and J. P. Lewis. "Realistic Human Face Rendering for *The Matrix Reloaded*," in *ACM SIGGRAPH 2003 Sketches and Applications*, 2003.

[Borshukov05] George Borshukov and J. P. Lewis. "Fast Subsurface Scattering," in *ACM SIGGRAPH 2005 Course on Digital Face Cloning*, 2005.

[d'EonGPUGems07] Eugene d'Eon and David Luebke, "Advanced Techniques for Realistic Real-Time Skin Rendering," in *GPU Gems 3*, edited by Hubert Nguyen, pp. 293–348, 2007.

[Donner05] Craig Donner and Henrik Wann Jensen, "Light Diffusion in Multi-Layered Translucent Materials," in *ACM Transactions on Graphics* (Proceedings of SIGGRAPH 2005), 24(3).

[Gosselin04] David Gosselin, "Real-Time Skin Rendering," presented at Game Developers Conference 2004, available online at http://ati.de/developer/gdc/gosselin_skin.pdf.

[Green04] Simon Green, "Real-Time Approximations to Subsurface Scattering," in *GPU Gems*, edited by Randima Fernando, pp. 263–278. Addison-Wesley.

[Gritz07] Larry Gritz and Eugene d'Eon, "The Importance of Being Linear," in *GPU Gems 3*, edited by Hubert Nguyen, pp. 529–542, 2007.

[Kelemen01] Csaba Kelemen and Lásló Szirmay-Kalos, "A Microfacet Based Coupled Specular-Matte BRDF Model with Importance Sampling," presented at Eurographics, 2001.

[NVIDIA 06] NVIDIA Corporation, "Adrainne," available online at http://www.nzone.com/object/nzone_adrianne_home.html, 2006.

[NVIDIA 07] NVIDIA Corporation, "Human Head," available online at http://www.nzone.com/object/nzone_humanhead_home.html, 2007.

[Weyrich06] Tim Weyrich, W. Matusik, H. Pfister, B. Bickel, C. Donner, C. Tu, J. McAndless, J. Lee, A. Ngan, H. W. Jensen, and M. Gross, "Analysis of Human Faces Using a Measurement-Based Skin Reflectance Model," in *ACM Transactions on Graphics* (Proceedings of SIGGRAPH 2006), 25(3), pp. 1013–1024.

2.5

An Efficient and Physically Plausible Real-Time Shading Model

CHRISTIAN SCHÜLER

INTRODUCTION

This article is a contribution to the ongoing race for visual fidelity. We will learn a mathematical model for surface shading that captures a wide range of materials while still being computationally efficient and practical with regard to content creation. The model can reproduce both metals and dielectrics, such as paper, wood, leather, varnish, paint, chrome, gold, and more. It does so with only a few parameters: two colors and a scalar measure of surface roughness. An alpha channel as either surface mask or surface transparency completes the parameterization via two common RGBA textures.

The intended target audience of this article includes authors of shader programs and technical artists. Knowledge of bidirectional reflection distribution function (BRDF) theory is helpful but not required. We will be discussing a *local illumination model* that is about one point on a surface and the light received and emitted from this point in various *directions*. This article assumes that any global questions are already solved; these include questions of occlusion, visibility, and generally what amount of light can be seen from which direction.

The outline is as follows: First, we will review two influential shading models (Blinn-Phong and Cook-Torrance), as they serve as the basis for our development. We will also briefly review some physics of light-surface interaction. This will lead the way to the formulation of the new model. Finally, we will discuss the practical issues of content creation and display gamma.

175

REVIEW: BLINN-PHONG AND COOK-TORRANCE

One of the earliest and most ubiquitous shading models is due to Bui-Tuong Phong together with its modification by Jim Blinn [Phong75, Blinn77]. It is an empirical model (i.e., "made-up") for a point on a surface lit by a number of discrete point light sources. The spectral intensity of this point, as seen by a viewer, is decomposed into four components. These are, in order of increasing computational cost, the *ambient*, *diffuse*, and *specular* components (ignoring the emissive component; see also Figure 2.5.1). They are characterized as follows:

- The ambient component models a uniform field as a crude approximation for the combined effect of all indirect light. Ambient illumination is assumed to have equal intensity from all directions.

- The diffuse component assumes a Lambertian response to direct illumination from a discrete light source. This response is simply proportional to the dot product between surface normal and light direction.

- The specular component models the effect of mirror images (highlights) of discrete light sources via a simple formula. The fuzziness of these mirror images can be adjusted by an additional parameter that controls the appearance of surface roughness. At this point, the models differ in their approach: While the Phong model generates perfect reflections of fuzzed light sources, the Blinn model generates fuzzy reflections of perfect point lights. Both models are idealizations, but in reality, the Blinn model is closer to the observation more often.

Being designed for computer graphics 30 years ago, the advantage of the Blinn-Phong model is simply speed. The numerous disadvantages are both artistic (a trademark plastic look, limited expressiveness, and the uniform ambient term is lacking) and technical (it is not energy conserving and has somewhat arbitrary parameters).

On the other hand is the Cook-Torrance model, developed rigorously from the theory of micro-facets [Cook81]. This model puts the specular component on a physical basis, while the diffuse and ambient components are the same. The full Cook-Torrance model is expensive to compute, but it makes the important contribution of separating the specular component into three factors: a *distribution* factor accounting for surface roughness, a *geometry* factor accounting for self-shadowing and occlusion, and the *Fresnel* term (see Figure 2.5.2). This separation allows searching for approximations to each of these factors independently, which we will do later.

FIGURE 2.5.1   Components of the Blinn-Phong model for a single-point light. Top left: ambient component; top right: diffuse component; bottom left: specular component; bottom right: sum of all components.

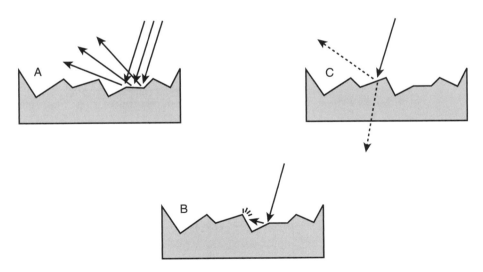

FIGURE 2.5.2   The three factors of the micro-facet model. A: distribution of micro-facets; B: geometric self-occlusion; C: Fresnel reflectance.

SOME PHYSICS OF LIGHT-SURFACE INTERACTION

The situation we are trying to model is that of light (an electromagnetic wave) traveling in a medium (air) and hitting another medium (the solid material). The light wave changes traveling speeds at the boundary, which causes part of it to be reflected back (the specular component according to our model). The remaining part passes the boundary into the second medium. However, the story does not end here because the light that passes can still return after some internal scattering (the diffuse component according to our model). Figure 2.5.3 illustrates these two principles of action.

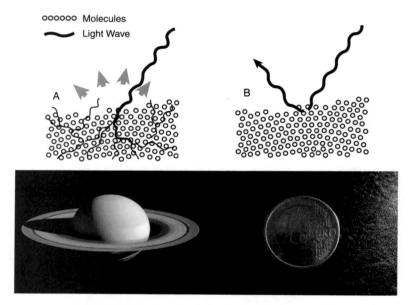

FIGURE 2.5.3 Idealized physical reflection models.
A: purely diffuse (subsurface) reflection; B: purely specular (Fresnel) reflection.

We can draw several conclusions from these observations.

■ Specular reflection happens on the surface. This is why the specular component is colorless most of the time: The reflected light never has the opportunity to enter the substrate and take on its color.

■ The amount of specular reflection on the surface is connected to the *refractive index* of the underlying material. This is why some metals, such as gold and copper, do have a colored specular reflection: Their refractive indices vary with wavelength.

■ Diffuse reflection, in the sense of our model, is a subsurface effect. This is why metals have no diffuse component. An electromagnetic wave cannot penetrate an electrical conductor; it is short-circuited right at the surface. Therefore, the diffuse component of a metal is simply black (that is for atomic metal of course; if a metal is painted, enameled, or rusty, it is a not a metal in the sense of surface shading).

TOWARD AN IMPROVED SHADING MODEL

While experimenting with shading models a few years back, it soon became apparent that a fundamental deviation from the Blinn-Phong model was needed.

As explained in the previous section, materials look most metallic if they have no diffuse component, but artists usually implemented a metallic look with a grayish diffuse texture and some specular added on top of it. When artists were told to leave the diffuse texture black, suddenly the ambient illumination was gone, since virtually all shading models link the ambient illumination to the diffuse texture. A new shading model would at least need to account for the specular component even under pure ambient illumination. In reality, we need individual terms for ambient diffuse and ambient specular reflection for anything more interesting than a uniform ambient field.

Another significant improvement comes from implementing the *Fresnel effect*. Surfaces become more reflective in the limit of a grazing angle. This is again a natural phenomenon connected to wave traveling speed. See Figure 2.5.4 for a real-world observation of the Fresnel effect.

FIGURE 2.5.4   Fresnel effect in the real world. A wooden desk lit by a halogen lamp from different view angles. The specular highlight becomes more intense from left to right.

The last important aspect is *energy conservation*. A glossy surface concentrates the energy of reflected light in a small range of directions. A rough surface spreads the energy of reflected light over a large range of directions. The glossiness of a surface therefore determines both the width and scale factors for the specular reflection image. Failing to account for energy normalization results in the material parameters not being well separated.

Mathematical Formulation

Conventions

The following direction vectors are used in the lighting calculations: The surface normal $\vec{N}$, the direction pointing toward the viewer $\vec{V}$, the direction toward the light source $\vec{L}$, the reflection of the view direction $\vec{R}$, and finally the vector $\vec{H}$ as a bisector between view and light directions. All vectors are assumed to be of unit length. See also Figure 2.5.5.

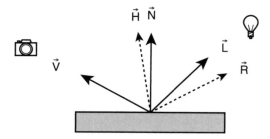

FIGURE 2.5.5 Direction vectors used in lighting calculations.

On a high level, the shading model calculates radiance from a point on a surface with normal $\vec{N}$, observed by a viewer into direction $\vec{V}$ and being lit by irradiance E. We choose I (for intensity) as the symbol for radiance, to prevent confusion with the light direction. Total radiance is the sum of the diffuse and specular parts.

$$I = I_{diffuse} + I_{specular}$$

The ambient term no longer appears as a first-class component. Instead, we offer two general illumination models that can be mixed freely (see Figure 2.5.6).

■ Illumination by a discrete set of light sources: This model has n lights, with the ith light into direction $\vec{L}^i$ and irradiance E^i_{light}.

▪ Illumination by a continuous two-hemisphere (sky and ground): This model has differently colored lower and upper hemispheres with irradiances E_{lower} and E_{upper} and with the up direction assumed as $\vec{Z}$.

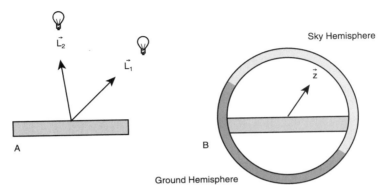

FIGURE 2.5.6   Illumination models. A: discrete light sources; B: continuous two-hemisphere model.

DIFFUSE COMPONENT

The diffuse component is straightforward, assuming a Lambertian reflectance. The material constant $k_{diffuse}$ accounts for the average subsurface absorption (diffuse color). The formulae for different illumination models are then given as

$$I_{diffusediscrete} = k_{diffuse} \sum_{lights} \vec{N} \cdot \vec{L}^{i} \, E^{i}_{light},$$

$$I_{diffusehemisphere} = k_{diffuse} \, \text{lerp} \left\{ E_{lower}, E_{upper}, \frac{1 + \vec{N} \cdot \vec{z}}{2} \right\}.$$

Here, the function $\text{lerp}(a,b,t) = a + t(b-a)$ is the linear interpolation between a and b for $0 \le t \le 1$, an intrinsic function of the HLSL language. The shading model assumes that any global effects, for example, visibility and distance attenuation, are already factored into the available E. Visibility for the hemispheres can be precomputed as ambient occlusion. The two-hemisphere model is the solution of a simple integral (see the appendix at the end of this article).

SPECULAR COMPONENT

The specular component is more involved; the results are displayed first:

$$I_{speculardiscrete} = k_{specular} \sum_{lights} \frac{1+e}{8(\vec{L}^i \cdot \vec{H}^i)^3} (\vec{N} \cdot \vec{H}^i)^e \, \vec{N} \cdot \vec{L}^i \, E^i_{light},$$

$$I_{specularhemisphere} = F(g\vec{N} \cdot \vec{V}) lerp \left\{ E_{lower}, E_{upper}, clamp \left[\frac{\vec{R} \cdot \vec{z}}{1-g}, -1, 1 \right] \right\},$$

$$e = 2^{12g},$$

$$F(t) = lerp\{k_{specular}, min(60k_{specular}, 1), (1-t)^4\}.$$

Here, the function clamp$(x,a,b) = min(max(x,a),b)$ also denotes an intrinsic HLSL function, which limits a value x between lower and upper bounds. The discrete model is motivated from Cook-Torrance, but is dramatically simplified with many factors lumped together (see the appendix at the end of this article for a complete derivation).

The result only differs by an additional factor $\frac{(1+e)\vec{N} \cdot \vec{L}}{8(\vec{L} \cdot \vec{H})^3}$ from the original Blinn-Phong model. It includes the specular exponent e, which is derived from a surface glossiness parameter g in the range 0–1 (rough to smooth).

The two-hemisphere model was developed empirically. The idea was to "look up" the hemisphere via the reflection vector $\vec{R}$ instead of the surface normal $\vec{N}$, and to scale the transition zone between the two hemispheres with the surface roughness. It includes $F(\ldots)$, which is a simplified Fresnel term, scaled such that the highest values are only reached for smooth surfaces.

DISPLAY GAMMA

The response of a common display device is not linear with respect to the contents of the framebuffer, but rather follows a power law. The inverse exponent of this function is called *gamma*. This non-linearity will affect our shading calculations in two major ways, namely:

- Unfaithful representation of intensity (premature darkening)
- Unfaithful representation of color sums

Premature darkening is observed for intensities that are already low. For instance, a 2% reflection of the sky on a dark water surface would be perfectly visible, but after the display has raised this to some power, it is gone. Distance attenuation is also affected, since the attenuation law is raised to the power of the gamma value, making lights fade unnaturally fast if left uncorrected.

The second effect is observed, because the display of a sum (e.g., a gray pixel) is no longer proportional to the sum of displays (e.g., a checkered pattern of black and white pixels). This affects all color mixtures, from anti-aliasing, texture filtering, and light sums to accumulation of shading terms. Adding the specular contribution on top of a diffuse one easily results in clipping and washout if left uncorrected.

The benefit in having a power law is the numerical compression of dynamic range. The sRGB standard has settled on a gamma value of 2.2, which is followed by virtually any current display technology. The 2.2 display gamma expands the dynamic range of an image with 8-bit precision to the equivalent of 17.6 bits (or a contrast of about 1:200k).

A practical shading model must account for display gamma on two fronts: texture input and shading output. Textures typically have at most 8 bits of precision and are authored via their display on a screen, so they have display gamma inherent. Texture colors must be raised to the power of 2.2 before they enter the shading calculation as intensities. There exists a feature on most graphics hardware to perform this as part of the texture sampler with approximate precision; it is activated either as a sampler state (DirectX 9) or as a surface format (DirectX 10 and OpenGL). The conversion can also be performed explicitly in shader code, which results in higher fidelity, especially for lower values, but makes the shader code make assumptions about the texture format.

To account for display gamma on the output side, there are multiple scenarios.

- **Low dynamic range framebuffer with display gamma (traditional case).** In this case the shader must raise the output color to a power of 0.45 (inverse display gamma) before it is written into the framebuffer. This makes sure the intensity that was calculated is actually displayed. There also exists a hardware feature for this; it is activated as a render state (DirectX 9 and OpenGL) or via the surface format of the render target (DirectX 10). In DirectX 10 and OpenGL, this state also affects framebuffer blending, which means a power of 2.2 is applied before the blending operation and a power of 0.45 afterward. If the hardware features are not used, it may be practical to assume a gamma of 2.0, so a simple squaring and square root can do the conversions.

- **Low dynamic range framebuffer, no display gamma.** The display gamma is already accounted for by a lookup table ("gamma ramp"), so the shader can output calculation results verbatim. This is not recommended since an LDR framebuffer does not have enough precision.

- **High dynamic range framebuffer.** An HDR framebuffer is usually not displayed directly but converted into an LDR framebuffer for display via tone mapping. The tone map operator needs to account for the display gamma. The shader can output calculation results verbatim into the HDR framebuffer.

AUTHORING MODEL PARAMETERS

The shading model discussed so far has three parameters that determine material appearance. These are $k_{diffuse}$, the diffuse reflectance; $k_{specular}$, the specular reflectance for normal incidence (face-on); and g, a measure of surface roughness. Together with a surface mask (the [insert α-channel) these are four parameters, two colors and two scalars, which fit nicely in two RGBA textures. In this way, all parameters of the shading model are spatially varying, which allows us to batch a large collection of different appearances onto a single texture atlas.

The "specular color" on a texture, after gamma conversion, becomes $k_{specular}$, which is connected to the refractive index and as such describes a physical property. The shading model then varies this reflectance based on view angle and surface roughness. An artist should therefore use the g parameter to create variety, but not vary the $k_{specular}$ for a given material. For instance, the varying specular effect on the parts of a concrete floor is due to variance in glossiness; the $k_{specular}$ of the rock minerals is the same for the entire surface.

Table 2.5.1 lists as examples the theoretical values for some materials, derived numerically from spectral data [LuxPop]. As a rule of thumb, all metals have near unit reflectance ($k_{specular}$ is close to white), and all dielectrics have reflectances in the single-digit percent range.

APPLICATIONS AND EXTENSIONS

Applications of the discussed shading model are shown in scenes from the game *Velvet Assassin*, courtesy of Replay Studios GmbH. The main contribution is the unification of different materials into the same parameter set, allowing for large texture atlases. Color plate number 1 shows an interior scene with many materials (including cloth, wood, glass, and brass), with a magnification of a syringe on a plate in the inlet. Color plate number 2 shows how glass vs. stone can be achieved on the same texture, with glass shards in the inlet. Color plate number 3 shows how wet vs. dry can be achieved on the same texture, with an opposite view in the inlet.

Possible extensions to the shading model are (a) the inclusion of an environment map for both diffuse and specular components with varying glossiness and (b) the correct handling of transparency with respect to Fresnel law. These topics weren't discussed in this article for reasons of scope, but the scenes shown in the color plates have both of these effects.

TABLE 2.5.1 Reflectivity and corresponding specular color by gamma conversion of selected materials

	Reflectance normal	Specular gray level or color
Water	0.02	44
Glass	0.03	56
Polystyrene	0.05	66
Calcite	0.06	72
Alumina	0.08	80
Diamond	0.17–0.18	114;115;117
Silicon	0.34–0.49	157;163;187
Copper	0.49–0.92	245;214;184
Gold	0.39–0.96	251;233;166
Silver	0.94–0.99	252;250;239

Note: The value for polystyrene can be used as typical for plastics and organic materials. The values for calcite and alumina can be used as typical for rock minerals (sapphires and rubies are also made from alumina). The metal examples are for pure and clean metals.

APPENDIX

DIFFUSE REFLECTION OF THE TWO-HEMISPHERE

A point on the surface is illuminated by complementary parts of a lower and an upper hemisphere. The result is a linear interpolation between irradiances E_{lower} and E_{upper} by some interpolation parameter t. With an angle α defined as the angle between surface normal $\vec{N}$ and up-direction $\vec{Z}$, we can formulate t as the fraction of how much the upper hemisphere contributes to total irradiance, weighted by a Lambertian factor:

$$I_{diffusehemishere} = k_{diffuse} lerp(E_{lower}, E_{upper}, t),$$

$$E_{upper}(\alpha) = \int_{\varphi=0}^{\pi} \int_{\theta=\alpha}^{\pi} \sin^2\varphi \sin\theta d\varphi d\theta = \frac{\pi + \pi\cos\alpha}{2}$$

$$t = \frac{E_{upper}(\alpha)}{E_{upper}(0)} = \frac{1 + \cos\alpha}{2}$$

NORMALIZING THE BLINN-PHONG SPECULAR HIGHLIGHT

The specular highlight of the Blinn-Phong model reflects less energy with increasing specular exponent e, because the shape of the highlight gets smaller without it getting brighter. A normalization factor must scale the term $(\vec{N} \cdot \vec{H})^e$ such that it integrates to one over all directions. An integral over all possible $\vec{H}$ evaluates to

$$I(e) = \int_{\vec{H}} (\vec{N} \cdot \vec{H})^e d\omega^* = \int_{\varphi=0}^{2\pi} \int_{\theta=0}^{\pi/2} \cos\theta \sin^e\theta \, d\varphi d\theta = \frac{2\pi}{1+e}.$$

(*the differential solid angle)

An additional factor of ½ is introduced when changing variables from $\vec{H}$ to $\vec{V}$ because of the different angular distance covered. The complete normalization factor is therefore

$$\frac{1}{2} \frac{I(0)}{I(e)} = \frac{1+e}{2}$$

SIMPLIFYING THE COOK-TORRANCE MODEL

The micro-facet model has a distribution factor D, a Fresnel factor F, and the geometric self-occlusion factor G in the form

$$I_{speculardiscrete,DFG} = \sum_{lights} \frac{D^i F^i G^i}{4\vec{N} \cdot \vec{V}} E^i_{light}$$

If D is the Beckmann distribution and F is the full Fresnel equations, this is the original Cook-Torrance model. This model is available as a technique "CookTorranceFull" in the accompanying HLSL effect file on the DVD-ROM. In the first step, D is replaced by the normalized Blinn-Phong distribution (see above), and F becomes a simplified Fresnel term. This model is available as "CookTorranceSimplified" in the effect file with the factors

$$D = \frac{1+e}{2}(\vec{N} \cdot \vec{H})^e,$$

$$F = \text{lerp}\left\{k_{specular}, \min(60k_{specular}, 1), (1 - \vec{L} \cdot \vec{H})^4\right\},$$

$$G = \min\left\{\frac{2\vec{N} \cdot \vec{H}\min(\vec{N} \cdot \vec{V}, \vec{N} \cdot \vec{L})}{\vec{L} \cdot \vec{H}}, 1\right\}.$$

The next optimization draws from work in [Kelemen01]. It is observed that the geometry factor divided by ($\vec{N} \cdot \vec{V}$) could safely be replaced by a much simpler term, making G redundant. This implementation is available as "KelemenSzirmayKalos" in the effect file on the DVD-ROM. The simplified formula is:

$$I_{speculardiscrete,DF} = \sum_{lights} \frac{D^i F^i}{4(\vec{L}^i \cdot \vec{H}^i)^2} \, \vec{N} \cdot \vec{L}^i \, E^i_{light}$$

The final aggressive optimization exploits the fact that both the Fresnel factor and the remains of G are functions of $\vec{L} \cdot \vec{H}$. A simpler formula can be found that roughly exhibits a comparable combined effect, giving up Fresnel color shift. This version is linear in $k_{specular}$ again, allowing it to be factored out. An implementation is available as a technique named "Optimized" in the effect file. The formula is as previously shown:

$$I_{speculardiscrete} = k_{specular} \sum_{lights} \frac{1 + e}{8(\vec{L}^i \cdot \vec{H}^i)^3} (\vec{N} \cdot \vec{H}^i)^e \, \vec{N} \cdot \vec{L}^i \, E^i_{light}$$

REFERENCES

[Blinn77] James F. Blinn, "Models of light reflection for computer synthesized pictures," *Proc. 4th Annual Conference on Computer Graphics and Interactive Techniques*, pp. 192–198, 1977.

[Cook81] Robert L. Cook and Kenneth E. Torrance, "A reflectance model for computer graphics," *Computer Graphics*, vol. 15(3), pp. 307–316, August 1981.

[Kelemen01] Csaba Kelemen and László Szirmay-Kalos, "A microfacet based coupled specular-matte BRDF model with importance sampling," *Eurographics* 2001 / N.N. short presenation.

[LuxPop] Thin film and bulk index of refraction and photonics calculations; available online at http://www.luxpop.com

[Phong75] Bui-Tuong Phong, "Illumination for Computer Generated Pictures," *Communications of the ACM*, vol. 18(6), pp. 311–317, June 1975.

2.6 Graphics Techniques in *Crackdown*

HUGH MALAN, REALTIME WORLDS

INTRODUCTION

Crackdown was a four-year-long open-world action-adventure game project, initially developed for the original Xbox. The project was shifted to the Xbox 360 halfway through.

Since the rendering time budget was allotted, finding the render time to allow new features had to be done by optimizing the existing code for time or memory. Clutter, vehicle reflections, water reflections, car drop-shadows, the parallax window shader, and many lighting tweaks were added in this way.

As a result of the hard render time and memory restrictions, we often had to look for solutions in places that probably would not be considered with a larger budget. Our solutions for clutter and vehicle reflections are examples of bottom-dollar technology that worked unexpectedly well.

The techniques covered in this article are the sky, clutter, outlines, deferred lighting, and vehicle reflections.

SKY

Figures 2.6.1 and 2.6.2 are in-game captures of *Crackdown's* sky, demonstrating the features of the shader.

FIGURE 2.6.1 Daytime sky.

FIGURE 2.6.2 Sky at dusk.

The shader provides self-shadowing and rim lighting, and the clouds animate slowly over time.

The sky uses the atmospheric scattering approximation described by [Neil05] for sky color; our only addition is the animated cloud layer.

The cloud animation and lighting is effectively a 2D effect. It is controlled by three texture layers; each holds a tilable pattern of cloud density. The maps hold the density and the two partial derivatives of that density, packed into the RGB components.[1] The maps are sampled and the densities summed to find the final cloud density (and its partial derivatives) for the current pixel. The three texture layers are not all comparable: One contains large-scale details (coarse map); the other two contain small-scale details (detail maps). For *Crackdown*, the two detail maps used the same texture as a space-saving measure. It was sampled twice, once at position *XY* and the second time for location *YX*, to effectively rotate and flip the map to try to hide the fact it had been used twice.

The maps are scrolled slowly in different directions and with different speeds to produce the effect of clouds forming and evaporating. To make the movement of the cloud border more complex, the resulting density was scaled and offset, so 0.2 was remapped to 0 (1 was left unchanged). This is equivalent to allowing slightly negative values in the density maps. The change produces large areas with density 0. Without it, the underlying cross-scroll effect is obvious. This change adds a single instruction (mad_sat) and is intended to make the effect a little more difficult to see.

The cloud lighting is a function of cloud density and derivative. The lighting function is very simple, but bears a faint resemblance to a simple physical model of light scattering in a cloud. It is described in [Rost06].

The most important features of cloud lighting that we can simulate easily in the pixel shader are that:

- Wispy clouds are completely brightly lit.
- Dense clouds are brightly lit on the side from which the light is coming; they are dark on the other side.

In the shader, the final color and opacity are computed as follows.

- Opacity is simply proportional to cloud density.
- Color is more complex. It begins with the calculation of the large-scale cloud brightness, implementing the two cloud lighting bullet points above:

$$saturate\ (base\_brightness + dot(coarse\_surface\_normal, light\_direction) \times cloud\_density$$

The base cloud color is quite bright by default (*base_brightness* is roughly 0.8).

If *cloud_density* is low, then the result will be bright. Only if the surface normal of the coarse cloud map points away from the light and the cloud is dense will the result be dark. This emulates self-shadowing and rim lighting.

The cloud lighting in *Crackdown* is based on this equation, but has been extended with artist-controllable colors. The lit cloud color, shadowed cloud color, detail color change, and other such colors can all be set separately, and are animated as part of the day-night cycle. Also, the partial derivatives of the sum of all three layers (with a disproportionate contribution from the detail layers) is used to pick out the small cloud features.

IMPLEMENTATION NOTES

Since the effect is 2D, it would be easy to render it by applying it to a plane at a constant height, but this looks completely wrong. Since the world is a sphere, a layer of clouds will also be a sphere. This may sound academic, but there is a dramatic difference in appearance near the horizon, and a cloud plane looks noticeably wrong.

Since a spherical surface patch is used instead of a plane, then the tangent-space light direction will not be constant. The light direction has to be transformed into tangent space in the same way that a light vector might be transformed into tangent space for normal-mapped lighting.

The UV offset of the cloud layers was also based on the camera position, so the clouds scroll past overhead. This was set up so it was noticeable but not attention-grabbing at top speeds.

The sky shading (Sean O'Neil's method) gave excellent realistic results, but not the dramatic "graphic novel" look. Setting up the sky parameters so sunrise and sunset were fiery required a dense atmosphere, which made midday dull and reddish. The solution was to animate the atmosphere parameters during the day-night cycle, providing both the dramatic sunrise and the deep blue skies at midday. This was complicated by the fact that some of the parameters changed by several orders of magnitude between sunrise and midday, and so the interpolation between keyframes for those parameters had to be done in log space. Even the sun direction had to be keyframed to avoid unsightly results during the morning and afternoon. In the final version, sunrise and sunset last disproportionately long for maximum drama, and the transition to the midday blue sky happens relatively quickly.

Lastly, the color tone of distant buildings needed to match up with the sky at the horizon. The full calculation for the sky shader was too expensive to be used even just for the distant buildings, so a much simpler color blend was used for them based on distance and height. The sky shader was extended with this simple color blend so very distant buildings were tinted with the same color as the sky near them.

CLUTTER

Clutter was added near the end of *Crackdown's* development, and is responsible for adding a great deal of detail to the scene. Geometric detail provides city features down to roughly a few feet, and the detail maps provide features a few inches in size. Conceptually, the goal of clutter was to provide interesting features at scales in between. As can be seen from the screenshots in Figures 6.2.3 and 6.2.4, the city looks simple and much less interesting without clutter.

FIGURE 2.6.3   Clutter off.

FIGURE 2.6.4   Clutter on.

Since the aim was to provide a large variety of objects, and the budgets for block size were set, the per-instance size of each piece of clutter had to be as small as possible, and the render cost had to be minimized.

Each clutter instance had to contain position, orientation, and clutter type; to minimize render cost we couldn't afford a separate draw call for each kind of clutter, so some kind of instanced geometry method was required. [Dudash04] describes the standard method for implementing instanced geometry.

The instanced geometry was implemented in a slightly unusual way: Each type of clutter was a single quad, and the vertex position data for each of the different types of clutter was stored in the shader constants. The positions of the vertices were packed into the shader constants with three bytes to a float, so each four-component vector held the geometry for a single clutter type. The UVs were not user-editable. The texture for each clutter type was 64×64 and packed into a 1024×2048 map (see Figure 2.6.5), so the vertex program computes UVs for the corners of the region of the texture map belonging to this kind of clutter.

The placement, orientation, and type of each clutter instance were stored in a vertex buffer; each instance required 8 bytes (the format is described below).

At render time, the only vertex buffer read is the one containing the list of clutter instance data. Indexed quads are drawn, with one quad per clutter instance. The index buffer is a dummy; it contains 0,1,2,3,…, and needs to be four times larger than the maximum number of possible clutter pieces in a block (a dummy index buffer was the simplest solution on the XBox360, where `SetStreamSourceFreq()` is not available).

For index k, the vertex program reads entry $k/4$ from the vertex buffer to find the position, orientation, and type of the current piece of clutter. The value of k module 4 specifies which corner of the quad is being processed.

The 8 bytes for each instance are interpreted as follows.

The first DWORD specifies the position of this clutter instance. It is a 3D vector in 11-11-10 format, with each coordinate being a fraction within the bounding box of the relevant block, which is usually about 150–200 meters across.

This was not quite accurate enough. The 11-bit components were used for the horizontal coordinates, but a 1-bit change meant a movement of about 7–10 cm. The artists placing the clutter had been having suspicions that some of the clutter was getting lost; it turned out that half of it was hiding behind walls and under floors because the position had been rounded the wrong way. The precision problems were fixed by carefully rounding the coordinates of position the appropriate way to bring it into view and adding some depth bias to avoid z-fighting problems.

FIGURE 2.6.5   Clutter texture map used in *Crackdown*.

The second DWORD is a 4D vector in 8-8-8-8 format, and provides orientation and clutter type. The orientation was defined by the first three 8-bit values (call them *a*, *b*, and *c*) with the fourth value *d* controlling clutter type.

The three basis vectors were set up as follows. The values a and b are scaled to the range $[-1, +1]$ and used to form the vector $(a, 1, b)$. It is normalized, and the result is the vector q (in *Crackdown's* coordinate system, Y is up).

The rotation around that vector is controlled by c. It is scaled to the range $(0, 2\pi)$, and the vector $(\cos c, 0, \sin c)$ is computed. This vector is guaranteed not to be parallel to q, so the cross-product with q can be taken and normalized without risks of degeneracy. The result is vector p. The third vector r is the cross-product of p, and q. p, q, and r form an orthonormal basis, which is used to transform the raw vertex positions of the clutter type to the correct orientation (q is local up, p is forward, and r is right expressed in world space).

This setup allowed a maximum rotation of 45 degrees from horizontal, which was enough to accurately align clutter to the streets and most slopes in *Crackdown*. Posters, graffiti, and stains on walls were accomplished by modeling that sort of clutter vertically; the 45-degree restriction on rotation meant that a poster cannot be rotated to lie on the ground.

For clutter type c, the four-component vector in shader constant c contains the encoded vertex position. Depending on the value of k module 4 the X, Y, Z, or W component of that vector is read. The resulting float is unpacked to give the clutter vertex position with $\text{frac}(v, v \times 256.0, v \times 65536.0)$. The divisor of 256 ($2^8$) was chosen because it yields 24 bits of precision (3×8), which is only slightly more than the 23-bit mantissa, so at most one bit of precision is expected to be lost from one of the components (it would be possible to squeeze a few more bits of precision out by extracting data from the exponent too, but this was already more precision than we required).

The unpacked vector is then transformed into the space defined by the three basis vectors p, q, and r and offset to the correct position in world space.

This technology might sound quite basic and inflexible, but since the vertices of each kind of clutter can be placed without restriction, in principle it is possible to model anything by breaking it down into quads. The tools were set up to allow collections of quads to form larger structures that would be placed together as a group, and to automatically break down quads using larger textures to 32×32 pieces. The artists then built a huge variety of simple items such as crushed cups, coffee cup lids, food wrappers, leftover kebabs, faint stains, vomit, bloodstains, graffiti, bullet holes, and so on (see Figure 2.6.6).

The individual pieces were collected into "clumps." For instance, a crushed cup or bottle on a stain, or food wrappers with assorted stains and leftover food, or two crossed quads forming a small weed (see Figure 2.6.7).

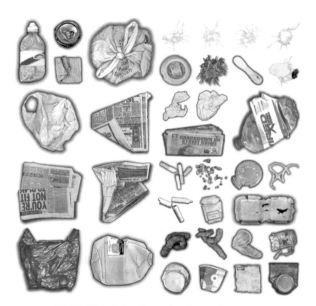

FIGURE 2.6.6   Sample clutter images.

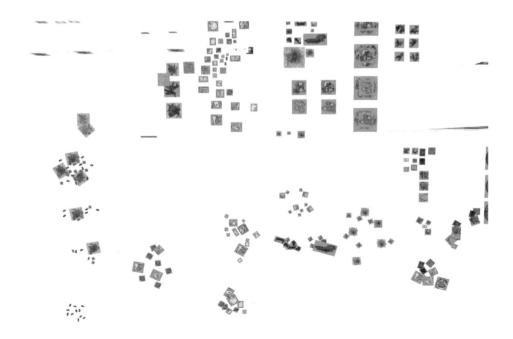

FIGURE 2.6.7   Clutter clumps: groupings of clutter pieces.

The artists then placed the clumps throughout the city. MaxScript procedures were built to spray clutter of a certain category into the world (such as party remains, firefights, greenery, stains, posters). This allowed the artists to quickly place large amounts of clutter in a category appropriate to the environment. So near a bin there might be a lot of waste paper, plastic bags, and other such items crushed into the pavement. Near Guerra's nightclub there are flyers dropped on the ground. In some of the back alleys are shell casings, bloodstains, graffiti, and bullet holes.

This feature is similar in some ways to texture bombing, in that it allows decals to be scattered across the surface. However, since real geometry is used, the decals can stand out from the surface (to provide weeds, bushes, and boxes). It is relatively easy to set up tools to allow the artists to place and edit the clutter, and there are no hard limits on the number of overlapping items that can be placed at a particular point. The downsides stem from the use of a second render pass; no lighting calculations can be shared, so some arithmetic and logic unit (ALU) has to be repeated. Also, it becomes difficult to match clutter items precisely to texture features.

The use of geometry opens up a lot of interesting possibilities that we did not have time to explore for *Crackdown*. The memory and render time it used were minimal. Most blocks used only a few hundred clutter items. If the budget was lifted to allow 10 or 100 times more items, the clutter density might have been high enough for it to embellish the surface texture, rather than just provide decals. One simple idea is to add non-periodic features to surfaces, such as a scattering of discolored or protruding bricks in a wall, or using a parallax shader to provide the appearance of missing or damaged bricks in the wall without paying the price for the parallax shader for the entire surface. Edge fins may be able to provide the appearance of jagged, non-periodic edges on man-made constructions such as concrete structures or brick walls.

Clutter ended up being a very successful feature. It added a great deal of graphical detail to the game for a low render and memory cost, and relatively little artist time. Of all the features described here, clutter probably improved the perceived quality of *Crackdown's* graphics the most.

OUTLINES

Outlines were implemented as a post-process effect, using the per-pixel normal and depth buffer (see [Decaudin96] for a description of the use of per-pixel normals and the depth buffer to detect edges and creases to create the outlines). Figure 2.6.8 shows the outline effect.

Figures 2.6.9 to 2.6.11 show the source per-pixel normal texture and the effect on the final image.

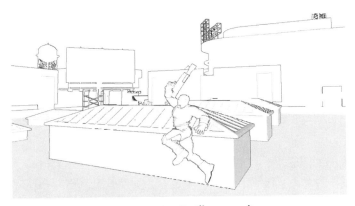

FIGURE 2.6.8   Outline opacity.

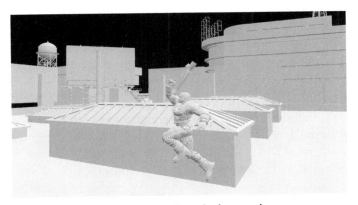

FIGURE 2.6.9   Per-pixel normals.

FIGURE 2.6.10   Image without outlines.

FIGURE 2.6.11   Final composite.

To achieve the desired "graphic novel" look, we wanted very thick anti-aliased outlines, but since render performance was a major concern for project management, if the render time was anything more than a handful of milliseconds, we were in danger of it being cut.

Thicker or smoother outlines result in a larger sample area and more texture reads, but render time is roughly proportional to the number of texture reads. We went through myriads of different variations; in the end we used the resolved result from the 2×MSAA (multisampling anti-aliasing) normal buffer and the depth buffer, reading five samples in a cross-pattern.

The normal texture is read using bilinear filtering. The samples are offset by half a texel, so four texels are sampled and averaged with a single read. This means a 20-pixel neighborhood in the normal texture is used to calculate the outlines.

The depth texture cannot be sampled with the same finesse since the format is floating point. The same five-point sample pattern is used, though this means that some texels are skipped and there is the danger of artifacts due to undersampling.

The per-pixel normals and depths are averaged, and the darkness of the outline depends on the difference between the averaged result and the values at the current pixel.

For a planar surface the per-pixel normal will be constant, so the average normal will match the current pixel. The depth will similarly match, so planar surfaces will not be darkened. Pixels near the edge of an object will have some samples with a depth value substantially different from others, so the averaged depth will be quite different from the current pixel depth and an outline will form. (The per-pixel normal may be constant. Imagine looking down at the edge of a table onto the floor. All nearby pixels have normals pointing "u.")

Pixels near an internal crease on an object may have quite similar depth values, but abruptly different normals, so an outline will appear there too. The contribution of these two different effects had to be carefully balanced to provide consistent outlines.

Since the source per-pixel normal texture used is anti-aliased, it helps provide the (somewhat) anti-aliased edge to the outlines.

Since the outlines only appear for objects included in the depth-normal pass, objects that suddenly appear in or disappear from the depth-normal pass will have their outlines appear or disappear. This is most noticeable for the way the player character and props fade away when they get too close to the camera. The outline change is masked by dropping the opacity from 100% to 60% in one frame (so the object becomes quite transparent at the same time as the outlines disappear) and fading down to 0% smoothly after that.

The outlines fade away in the distance, and the fade depth was set up so the outlines would completely disappear before the first environment levels of detail (LODs) transition happens.

One other problem was due to tiling. A full 1280×720 2×MSAA image cannot fit into EDRAM on the Xenon. It has to be rendered in two sections. The first tile fills in the top half of the normal and depth buffers, and the second tile completes them. Since the outlines sample three pixels in each direction around a pixel, there were problems when rendering the bottom three rows of the first tile because the outline shader would be sampling off the bottom of that tile into uninitialized or stale areas of the normal and depth buffer. The solution we used was to overlap the two tiles by four pixels: the second tile redraws the bottom four rows of the first tile.

Outlines were difficult and time-consuming to develop, and required a great deal of tweaking of many other graphics components to avoid or reduce the quality problems. The final version required little render time and provided the thick anti-aliased outlines around everything, which was the goal.

DEFERRED RENDERING

Deferred lighting has the greatest advantage over standard lighting when there are numerous localized lights, and the frequently changing set of relevant objects that each interacts with ([Hargreaves04] has an introduction covering how deferred lighting can be implemented on the GPU).

The goal of looking out from the top of a building at night and seeing myriads of streetlights (and to a lesser extent, car headlights) was a strong argument for the use of deferred lighting. The fact that the per-pixel normal buffer and depth buffer would also be used by the outlines and no other screen-sized buffers would be required made the proposition a lot more palatable. The standard problem with deferred lighting and other deferred effects is that they do not benefit from MSAA. In *Crackdown's* case, the lighting would only affect a fraction of the pixels onscreen, so only a corresponding fraction of the edges would suffer, and the outlines would help cover up artifacts on those edges too.

Since there were so many differences between standard deferred lighting and the approach we used, we gave the name "afterlights" to the deferred lights in *Crackdown* to avoid confusion. Figures 2.6.12 and 2.6.13 demonstrate the effects provided by the afterlights.

The deferred lighting used in *Crackdown* is relatively simple. As mentioned previously, the only per-pixel quantities stored are the normal and depth resolved out after the depth-normal prepass. Although surface color is not stored, its effect is simulated in the following way.

FIGURE 2.6.12   Deferred effects disabled.

The afterlights are applied after the main color pass, and while rendering opaque surfaces in the main color pass the alpha channel is set to a value proportional to the brightness of the surface color. When the afterlights are blended into the frame buffer, they are modulated by the destination alpha, so their effect varies depending on surface color. Lights are usually modulated by surface color by multiplying each component of the light by surface color.

Here, the dest-alpha modulation means a single scalar is used for all three channels, but it was vital. Without it, surfaces tend to look very flat when lit by afterlights.

FIGURE 2.6.13 Deferred effects enabled: headlights, streetlights, and undercar shadows.

Afterlights were used for streetlights, car headlights, searchlights on the lighthouse and Agency tower, and in effects such as muzzle flashes and explosions. To provide as many lights onscreen as possible, all the lights of a single species are drawn in a single call using instanced geometry. A cube is rendered for each light; back-face culling is enabled, so each pixel within the volume is drawn once rather than twice. Z-testing is enabled too, so pixels of the light cube that are behind geometry will be culled early by the hardware, and will not have the costly pixel shader executed for them at all.

The vertex program does the standard transformation into homogeneous clip space, and sets up the screen texture coordinate (i.e., texture coordinates corresponding to the vertex position onscreen, used to read from the screen-sized depth and normal textures). The pixel shader requires this texture coordinate to match the position of the pixel currently being shaded.

The obvious choice is to pass the homogeneous position down to the pixel shader and use a projective texture map mode, but unfortunately this failed in some cases.

The solution we used in *Crackdown* was for the vertex program to rescale the homogeneous position of the vertex so the Z and W components are constant for all vertices making up the bounding geometry of a particular afterlight. The values chosen are found by taking the cube center point, moving toward the camera by the light radius, and projecting the resulting position. This provides geometry guaranteed to be outside the light radius, but as far back as possible so as many pixels as possible are culled by the depth buffer.

This approach fails in some cases. For instance, if the camera is within the light sphere, the resulting point is behind the camera, and so the resulting geometry would not be rendered as it was behind the camera too. In this case, the vertex program generates a screen-covering quad.

The pixel shader samples the depth buffer and per-pixel normal textures, and computes the normal and position for the pixel currently being shaded. Spherical lights simply compute the dot product between the vector from the light to the pixel and the surface normal, and attenuate the effect based on distance.

Headlights and searchlights were more complex. As well as the direct lighting effect, an in-scatter effect was simulated. This was simulated by defining an ellipse in screen-space, with the major axis along the headlight direction. If the current pixel was within the light volume, the in-scatter effect was reduced based on depth. In practice, this did not work very well. For instance, at the top of the Agency tower the searchlights produce phantom glows when they point away from you. Headlights of cars going the other way produce similar phantoms just after they pass you. A better solution would probably have been to simulate in-scatter using a group of crossed quads.

The most successful use is probably for the streetlights. At night, all 3,000 (or so) streetlights are rendered. From a sufficiently high vantage point, hundreds of lights can be seen. In principle, the lights could be individually moved, recolored, and turned off at no extra cost. No extra CPU work such as per-light culling was required to achieve this. Even the first time the streetlights were hooked into the afterlights, the render time was acceptable. The streetlight effect also included a glare card, not provided by afterlights (see Figure 2.6.14).

FIGURE 2.6.14   An early afterlight test.

To avoid frame rate dips when many car headlights cover the entire screen (such as in a multi-car pileup at night), the afterlights are rendered to a half-size off-screen buffer. This made it quite unlikely that there would be afterlight fill-rate problems, but it meant that the quality of the lighting suffered. The worst artifact is the strobing effect seen in the pools of light under highway streetlights when driving at high speed. The pool is only a few pixels high so it suffers from undersampling. Some undersampling artifacts can be seen on the streetlight post in Figure 2.6.13.

A few other deferred effects were implemented in *Crackdown* such as soft shadows under cars and the cracks on the ground that appear after a hard landing. We hoped to add soft underfoot shadows and some localized darkening on walls close to the characters and perhaps props to simulate ambient occlusion effects, but these features did not make the cut.

Vehicle Reflections

The question, "Can we have vehicle reflections?" came up many times throughout the development of *Crackdown*. It kept coming up despite the fact that the answer was always a unanimous "no." Code to render a dynamic cube map had been added, but the render time required was unaffordably high, so the feature was cut and considered dead.

In the final months of the project, we came up with a very cheap and simple hack that gave the impression of dynamic reflections on vehicles. I do not know the full story of how it was approved (the little I have heard is unprintable), but it was allowed in. Here is how it works.

The sharp transition between light to dark in a reflection is the quality that implies that a surface is shiny. In comparison, smudged, dirty, or matte finishes have blurred transitions. The dynamic part of *Crackdown's* car reflections is a very sharp transition between light and dark, in a pattern that roughly matches the car's surroundings.

Conceptually, the pixel shader ray-marches through a height field of the city to determine whether a pixel on the car is reflecting light or dark.

For both practical and political reasons, we simply could not afford to increase GPU time at all, so we used the absolutely cheapest possible implementation we could find. The "raymarch" is just a single sample of the height field with a carefully chosen position. To fit our memory budget, the city-wide height field is a single static 768×768 16-bpp map with no mipmaps, which meant each texel is roughly 10 feet across. (DVD transfer rate was a very limited resource, so streaming anything was also not an option. All data had to remain in memory.) The resulting color is chosen from two constant colors. There is no attempt to vary the color from building to building, no change in color with height, no distance fogging, and no anti-aliasing of the reflection edge.

The height field is packed in a way that accurately reproduces the abrupt height changes of buildings in a city. The texture map holds three channels of information; two (A and B) specify height fields, and the third (C—"choice value") selects which of the two height fields to use at that point. The choice is made depending on whether the sampled value is over or under 0.5; the values of each texel are set up so the interpolated value crosses the 0.5 threshold as close as possible to the building edge. The A and B values are set up to be the height of the ground and top of the building.

In the pixel shader, the texture is sampled with bilinear filtering. If the C value is >=0.5, then the height to use is based on the A channel; otherwise, the B channel is used.

The pixel shader for the car computes the reflected eye-surface vector (which is also used to sample the reflection cube map), and steps a specific distance from the reflection point in that direction to find the point p. The height field is sampled at that location; if the height of the height field is lower than the height of p, then the reflection color is bright; otherwise, the reflection color is dark.

This means that the samples are taken in a roughly hemispherical shape around the car. The step distance was 0.005 units in UV space, which is 3.84 texels—roughly 40 feet. The distance was chosen so that the sample would not step through an entire row of buildings. However, features smaller than this distance will be undersampled. A thin wall would show up as a thin stripe in the reflection, which is completely incorrect.

We can get away with this in *Crackdown* because the environment is filled with thick rows of buildings, and there were very few places where the overstep problem was noticeable. Thin barriers on the sides of bridges and the decorative columns by the tunnel entrance in Los Muertos are examples of the few problem areas. They were fixed by retouching them out of the raw height field image.

However, building corners are everywhere, and if you know what you are looking for, it is fairly straightforward to position the car and camera in such a way that a sharp corner appears in the reflection.

In practice, if you do not know what you are looking for, or the camera and car are not in just the right arrangement, it is not that noticeable. Also, the car is a complex shape, so even the reflection of simple forms will have kinks and curves, so when a building corner (or other such artifact) does appear, it is easy to overlook.

Thin features overhead such as walkways, pipes, and bridges are not a problem at all; they appear as a thin stripe in the reflection, which looks plausible.

The other implication of the fixed step distance is that distant features will never appear in the reflection. As you drive toward a building, it will only appear when you reach the critical radius, and will grow from small to large in the reflection as the car gets closer.

There are several effects that this method does reproduce. When driving down a street, the reflection silhouette of the buildings will have a shape that matches their heights and gaps at cross-streets. The highway has a small gap between the two lanes. This gap shows up as a light stripe in the reflection as you drive under it. Figures 2.6.15 and 2.6.16 show the car reflections in action.

FIGURE 2.6.15   Car reflections. Note the reflection of the overhead bridge in the car roof.

FIGURE 2.6.16   Car reflections. The overhead bridge is reflected in the back window.

As shown in Figure 2.6.17, height is handled too. If the car is on a bridge, the reflection will be clear. Underneath, the dark shape of the same bridge is visible. Unlike a single shared cube map, each car reflects the environment local to it. For instance, cars that enter a tunnel ahead of you will have the dark reflection pass over them at the appropriate time.

FIGURE 2.6.17   Car reflections. The two cars have quite different reflections.

IMPLEMENTATION NOTES

For *Crackdown*, we used a 768×768 5-6-5 16-bpp texture with the choice value C stored in the red, 5-bit channel; the two height fields were stored in green and blue and so had a 6- and 5-bit channel each. We also experimented with using a smaller texture with a higher bit depth, and a larger texture with lower bit depth (DXT5), but the 16-bpp uncompressed texture was by far the best use of our memory budget. It required a little over 1 MB: 1,179,648 bytes.

The Xenon texture sampling mode could be tweaked to make it automatically scale the C channel to the range $[-1, +1]$, which allowed the comparison to be made against zero, thereby saving an instruction.

Errors in the location of the building edge stand out much more than inaccuracies in the height of the top and bottom of the building. This would suggest putting the choice value C into the highest-precision channel available, as it controls the transition between height fields. In practice, 5 bits were sufficient. A full explanation for this choice is given in the texture map setup section below.

It is possible to get away with quite a bit of error in the height fields. The height range we settled on has a maximum representable height of roughly 85 m, so the height is stored in steps of 2.6 m or 1.3 m in the 5-bit and 6-bit channels, respectively. The height field that mainly provides the ground level is put into the 6-bit G channel to benefit from the extra precision, since the cars will mostly be on the ground level. Nevertheless, there are some reflection artifacts due to lack of height precision that can be seen while driving on some steep hills in the Volk district.

Before we added this feature to *Crackdown*, the car paint shader calculated the reflection vector and sampled a static cube map. Adding code to step along the reflection ray by the fixed distance, sample the height field, and tint the cube map sample by the light or dark reflection was in theory just a handful of instructions, but it ended up not changing the final shader instruction count, due mainly to good fortune with the shader compiler. Since the shader was already very ALU-heavy, the cost of the additional texture read could be absorbed.

TEXTURE MAP SETUP

The source, high-resolution map we used was a 6144×6144 image rendered in 3dsMax using an orthographic camera. This resolution is eight times the 768×768 final map's size. It was rendered by loading all the second-highest LOD data into a single scene, which was near the limit of what 3dsMax could handle.

This 6144×6144 texture was touched up by hand to fix the various problem areas that arose, such as the Los Muertos pillars mentioned above. There were a few isolated black or white pixels that were rendering errors; a preprocess step cleaned them up. The preprocessor would also "grow" all features outward by two pixels in each direction to round them off and reduce the risk of undersampling (specifically, for each pixel a 4×4 neighborhood was searched and the maximum height found). Raw and processed images are shown below in Figures 2.6.18 and 2.6.19, respectively.

The texture map setup is built on the observation that if, when bilinearly filtering a texture, the four corner values are a linear function of position, then the interpolated value will also be a linear function of position.

This is useful for setting up the channel that controls the height field choice. If the value is a linear function of position, then the boundary where the value crosses the threshold value will be a straight line. This is ideal for most building edges.

So in principle, the choice value near a straight building edge can be defined to be a linear function of distance from the edge, taking the value 0.5 on the edge.

Specifically,

$$0.5 + s \times d \times k$$

where d is the distance from the edge (measured in texels), and s is +1 or −1 depending on which height field is the correct one to use on that side of the line. k is a scale applied to bring the values to within the [0, 1] range. The only texels that matter are those that border the edge; all others can be safely clamped to 0 or 1. This function crosses 0.5 at the edge. It is a linear function of position near straight edges, and provides an acceptable behavior for more complex edges.

The next question is how to define the regions where each height field is valid, and here things become murkier. The choice function partitions the world into subsets: areas where the A height field is valid and complementary areas where the B height field is valid. If the city was made out of very simple buildings (such as cuboids), then it would be possible to define the A height field to be used for all the building tops and B everywhere else. Of course, the city in *Crackdown* is much more complex than this, so a more sophisticated partitioning was desirable.

The approach we took for *Crackdown* worked as follows. The source, high-resolution height field was blurred. Points where the original value was greater than the blurred value were specified to use the B channel, and all others used the A channel. Figure 2.6.18 shows three sample cross-sections; the red and blue sections beneath the cross-section correspond to whether the A and B height field is valid at that point. Case (a) shows a simple building on a flat plane. The B height field is used for the top of the building and the A height field for the ground. Case (b) is slightly more complex, and the height field assignment changes in the middle of a flat roof. This is legal and moral; the height fields can be set up in a manner that provides the roof profile exactly, but this behavior is not ideal. The height field switch in the middle of the middle-height roof is not required. However, case (c) requires the height field switch, and establishing whether the height field regions can be divided into concentric rings (thereby allowing the simple partitioning) is far from trivial.

The packed, low-resolution map requires two height-field values and a choice value for each texel. The choice value C is set by first sampling the corresponding point in the high-res map to find whether the A or B map is used. This sets the s value in the above equation; d is found by searching the neighborhood in the high-res maps for the closest transition between A and B height fields.

In practice, it was acceptable to set up the choice value by simply searching in the four directions along the axes. Doing a full search of the neighborhood did not improve quality that much. For an eight times supersampled source image, the range of results is {−7.5, −6.5, ..., +7.5}, which fits into 5 bits with no loss of precision. It is for this reason that the choice values had no need of the 6-bit channel.

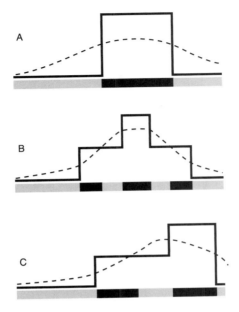

FIGURE 2.6.18   Blurred heights for partitioning.

One option for calculating the *A* and *B* value is to use an expensive method such as hill-climbing, but we found that a simple and cheap weighted average was sufficient. The height was sampled from a 16×16 neighborhood in the high-res height field, with a per-sample weight of 1/squared distance. When setting up the *A* channel, only entries using the *A* height field in the high-res map are considered and vice versa. The 16×16 size of the neighborhood region is chosen because it is exactly the area in the world that would be affected by a change to that low-res texel. In the event that no pixels in the neighborhood (for instance) are *A* when we are setting up the *A* channel, we can be certain that the value used for the low-res *A* texel will have no effect.

Figures 2.6.19 to 2.6.27 show the various images. Figure 2.6.19 is a 512×512 subset of the source 6144×6144 height field rendered out of 3dsMax. Figure 2.6.20 is the cleaned-up version. In Figure 2.6.19, there are some spurious black and white pixels, for example, a white pixel on the edge of the building in the top right at 2 o'clock, and a black region on the right of the building at 9 o'clock. Figure 2.6.20 shows that these artifacts have been cleaned up by the preprocess step. The Los Muertos pillars mentioned above are the two dots in the upper left-hand corner of the maps. They were painted out of the production maps but are shown here for reference.

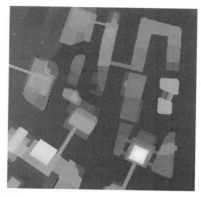

FIGURE 2.6.19 Section of the original height field, rendered in 3dsMax. Note the odd black or white pixel. 512×512.

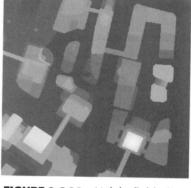

FIGURE 2.6.20 Height field after automatic cleanup. Spurious black or white areas fixed. 512×512.

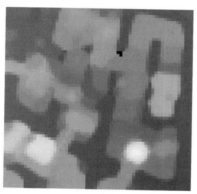

FIGURE 2.6.21 Packed height field *A*. 64×64.

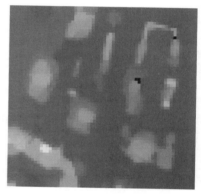

FIGURE 2.6.22 Packed height field *B*. 64×64.

FIGURE 2.6.23 Choice value *C*. 64×64.

Figure 2.6.24 is the height field reconstructed from the packed 64×64 map. Each 8×8 square at 8 bpp is packed into a single 16-bpp texel, so the compression is 32:1. It does look low-quality in comparison to the original, but the only use for this height field is for car reflections, and in practice the approximation is acceptable.

Figure 2.6.25 shows the absolute per-pixel reconstruction error. The sprinkling of bright pixels along an edge shows the errors in the edge's location, which is less than a texel or two in most cases. Complex areas have much lower quality.

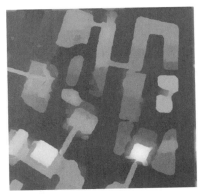

FIGURE 2.6.24   Height field reconstructed from packed 64×64 image. 512×512.

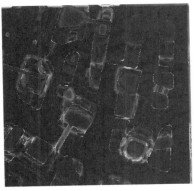

FIGURE 2.6.25   Absolute error between original and reconstruction. 512×512.

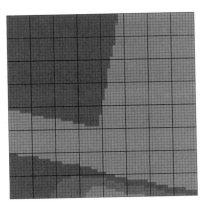

FIGURE 2.6.26   64×64 section of original height field. Black lines indicate the relative size of each texel in the packed height field.

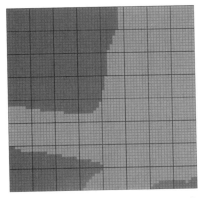

FIGURE 2.6.27   64×64 section of reconstructed height field. Black lines indicate the relative size of each texel in the packed height field.

The overhead bridge mentioned in the description for Figures 2.6.15 and 2.6.16 is included in these height field images. In the 512×512 maps it can be seen on the far left, slightly above the center and running left-right off the left-hand side of the image. The cars are driving toward 6 o'clock.

The fake reflections were a huge asset to the vehicles. Without them, the cars looked dull and very poor. The technique described here has many limitations and quality problems, so the reflections can only stand up to a small amount of inspection before inaccuracies can be seen. But given how cheap they are to render and how little memory they require, when compared to the benefits they provided, they provided exceptional value for us.

This method for packing a height field in a way that preserves straight edges and abrupt transitions may be useful for other data, such as precalculated shadow maps.

CONCLUSION

This article described a number of rendering techniques that were used in the game *Crackdown*. These are sky, clutter, outlines, deferred lighting, and car reflections.

For the reasons described in the introduction, these features are relatively cheap, and can be implemented cheaply and independently. The aim of this article is to present enough information about these methods' benefits and costs for them to be easily judged, and for the weaknesses and quality problems to be detailed well enough for there to be no surprises if they are employed.

ENDNOTES

[1] Packing z, dz/dx, and dz/dy into the components of a vector means adding a second packed function sample, and scaling by a constant can be vectorized. They are the addition of two vectors and the scaling of a vector by a constant, respectively.

ACKNOWLEDGMENTS

Providing the dense crowd, shadows, and high-quality vista, and implementing all the other graphics features on discontinued middleware was a struggle. A lot of people made major contributions to *Crackdown's* graphics, and it would be unfair to them for an article on *Crackdown's* graphics to only have my name associated with it. Everyone involved in the graphics provided bug fixes and optimizations too numerous to be mentioned here; here is only the most significant and visible result from each person's work.

A programmer from Xen single-handedly wrote and supported the particle system runtime and editor, the shadow system, the water tech, and the window shader solution, and provided some vital optimizations to the renderer. He managed to add precompiled command buffer support, without which we would have had to cut the LOD1 block count, and *Crackdown's* vista would have been much lower quality.

George Harris worked on graphics (among many other things) from the first prototype all the way to the end. He built or helped build a great deal of the graphics tech, and fixed bugs in all of it. He built and supported most of the prop and car rendering system, including the damage and part separation, and vehicle morphing. He also worked long hours on a long list of unglamorous and unpleasant but necessary tasks, such as the regular breakage of the specular highlight.

Neil Duffield, Dave Lees, and Peter Walsh provided the crowd technology and distant vehicles. Dave Lees also retrofitted the alpha-blended render pass, and added occlusion culling for props and cars. Peter Walsh integrated SpeedTree, and dramatically improved its render time and memory use.

Kutta Srinivasan implemented *Crackdown's* anti-aliasing. Crackdown's depth-normal prepass was not natively supported by the standard tiled rendering technology, and we were searching in vain for alternative AA methods until Kutta found a solution.

REFERENCES

[Decaudin96], Decaudin, P. "Cartoon Looking Rendering of 3D Scenes," Research Report INRIA #2919, June 1996.

[Dudash04] Dudash, B. "Mesh instancing," nVidia Technical Report, May 2004. Can be found online at http://developer.download.nvidia.com/SDK/9.5/Samples/DEMOS/Direct3D9/src/HLSL_Instancing/docs/HLSL_Instancing.pdf

[Hargreaves04] Hargreaves, S., "Deferred shading," Game Developers Conference, March 2004. Can be found online at http://myati.com/developer/gdc/D3DTutorial_DeferredShading.pdf.

[Neil05] O'Neil, S. "Accurate Atmospheric Scattering," *GPU Gems 2,* Chapter 16.

[Rost06] Rost, R. "OpenGL(R) Shading Language (2nd edition)," Chapter 20.6.

2.7 Deferred Rendering Transparency

DAVID PANGERL, DAVID@ACTALOGIC.COM

FIGURE 2.7.1 Images with transparent objects rendered using deferred rendering transparency.

INTRODUCTION

Transparency is an integral part of any rendering engine. When you render glass, water, smoke, fire, or decals, it requires some level of transparency. Unfortunately, it is one of the most problematic areas for a deferred renderer [HARRIS07].

This article describes an efficient algorithm for rendering transparent objects with deferred rendering.

Deferred rendering transparency provides *lighting consistency* between opaque and transparent objects with texture and/or vertex alpha. The core idea of the method is to interlace transparent objects with opaque ones in the geometry phase, then perform lighting, and then de-interlace and blend them in the composition phase.

The method itself requires only transparency alpha to be saved in the G-buffer, and no other additional data and no pipeline changes. The general performance hit of the method is about 2.2%, making it attractive for production use.

TRANSPARENCY

Transparency (or translucency or alpha compositing) is the process of combining a partially transparent color with its background.

Rendering transparency (also known as alpha blending) requires two colors, c_s (source color) and c_d (destination color), and a transparency level a (usually a part of source color) to be composited with the next alpha blend formula:

$$c_0 = c_s a + c_d(1-a)$$

or:

$$c_0 = c_d + (c_s - c_d)a$$

DEFERRED RENDERING

Deferred rendering (also known as deferred shading) is a combination of the conventional forward rendering technique with the advantages of image space techniques [DEERING88].

Deferred rendering is usually performed in four phases.

1. **Geometry phase:** This is actually the only phase that uses object mesh data; objects, color, position, normal, and additional lighting factors are rendered into render targets.

2. **Lighting phase:** Lights are applied in screen-space.

3. **Composition phase:** The color buffer from the geometry phase and lighting from the lighting phase are combined.

4. **Post-processing phase:** Various effects are applied to create the final image, for example, motion blur, volumetric fog, DOF, HDR.

Transparency with deferred rendering is usually solved by splitting the rendering pipeline in two parts [HARRIS07].

1. **Render opaque objects:** Render all opaque objects with deferred rendering; perform all three deferred rendering phases to get final composite image.

2. **Render transparent objects:** Render all transparent objects sorted back to front with traditional rendering to get the final image with all transparent objects and alpha channel, and then blend it over the deferred rendering final composite image.

The biggest problem in this method is lighting inconsistency (since deferred rendering can handle lights more efficiently than traditional forward rendering). Another problem is the additional administration and code required to handle the split pipelines and traditional rendering required for transparent objects.

One solution to the problem could be *alpha-to-coverage* [MEYERS07]. Unfortunately, it requires a high level of supersampling to blend dithered samples into the final image, which is not usually supported with deferred rendering.

My contribution is a new approach for supporting transparency in deferred rendering: an algorithm that solves the lighting consistency problem of the transparent objects when using the deferred rendering method.

The advantages of this approach are:

■ **Lighting consistency:** Opaque and transparent objects use the same lighting pipeline, resulting in the same lighting quality. Opaque objects can gradually fade out without any lighting glitches.

■ **Simple and robust:** The method requires no pipeline changes and no additional object sorting (which is usually required for transparency rendering) or any other object separation between opaque and transparent objects. It can handle both vertex- and texture-level transparency with no additional coding.

■ **Speed:** The method adds only 7 to 10 pixel shader instructions and two texture fetches and requires no additional render targets switching.

OVERVIEW

Deferred rendering transparency requires two pixel shader code fragments to be inserted into the existing deferred rendering implementation: one in the geometry phase, which interlaces transparent objects, and one in the composition phase, which de-interlaces and blends transparent objects with background.

In the G-buffer creation phase, all transparent pixels are rendered interlaced (Figure 2.7.2); only every odd horizontal line is rendered (implementation can be easily adjusted for vertical lines or zigzags), and pixel alpha values are stored in color alpha channels. This is done with a very simple pixel shader fragment that uses pixel shader 3 VPOS register (it can also be done with a vertex shader-prepared variable on pixel shader 2 hardware) and an alpha test that filters out odd lines where alpha is set to zero.

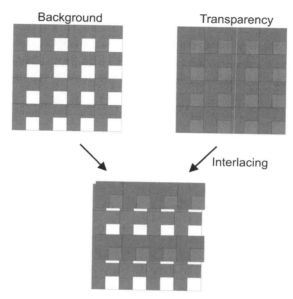

FIGURE 2.7.2   The color buffer after the G-buffer creation phase. Transparency is shown in smaller rectangles in the lower left corner of each pixel.

In the composition phase, the minimal alpha value is taken from the current pixel and the pixel above (or below). If the minimal alpha is less than 1, then both pixels are blended together and de-interlaced with the transparency formula (Figure 2.7.3).

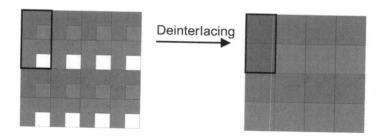

FIGURE 2.7.3   Compositing and de-interlacing the image. Within each two rows, the minimum alpha value across the two vertically adjacent pixels is taken, and the two pixels are blended.

RENDERING

This section explains the technique in detail. Note that the implementation described here is written for pixel shader 3, but it can be easily adopted for pixel shader 2. Also, while we use horizontal lines to perform the transparency blend, vertical or zigzag patterns can be also implemented.

GEOMETRY PHASE

In the G-buffer creation phase, we render all objects: opaque and transparent, and in any order (no need to alpha sort or draw transparent objects separately). However, sorting from front to back is usually better since current hardware can do rejects very fast.

When rendering during this phase, we activate alpha testing with a zero reference value and the test function set to `Greater`.

```
AlphaTestEnable  = true;

AlphaFunc        = Greater;

AlphaRef         = 0;
```

The pixel shader sets the alpha value of transparent pixels in odd lines to zero, so they get skipped by the alpha test, while pixels in even lines are left unchanged. This trick produces interlaced transparent objects that will be combined into the final image in the composition phase. The code below is responsible for calculating the correct alpha value for interlacing:

```
float alpha = tColor.a;

if (alpha < 0.99)
    alpha *= frac(inSPos.y * 0.5) < 0.1;
```

The output alpha value must be stored in an alpha channel (e.g., along with the RGB color).

After this phase, we execute the lighting pass normally without any changes. Then we move to the next phase.

COMPOSITION PHASE

In this phase, color and lighting render targets are composed into a final composite image.

The pixel shader de-interlaces and blends transparent objects with the background. Note that all pixels must be processed; otherwise, transparent objects will not get de-interlaced (so image masking techniques like stencil testing must be handled with care).

The pixel shader basically samples at two positions: color and light at the current pixel and one pixel above. The minimal alpha value between both colors is calculated and is used to blend the two pixel values.

Although this basic de-interlacing approach is fast, it introduces some artifacts that are shown in Figure 2.7.4.

FIGURE 2.7.4   Artifacts showing at the edges of the alpha-blended part of the geometry due to the simplistic de-interlacing approach used to compose the final image.

One quick fix for this problem is to sample one more pixel below, take the minimal alpha value between the three pixels we have, and use the result as the blend value.

Here is the new pixel shader code for the composition phase to handle de-interlacing:

```
float2 uv1 = inTex0 — float2(0, TDeviceSize.y);
float2 uv2 = inTex0 + float2(0, TDeviceSize.y);

float4 colorA = tex2D(Color0PointSampler, inTex0); // Current pixel
float4 colorB = tex2D(Color0SamplerPoint, uv1); // Pixel above
float4 colorC = tex2D(Color0SamplerPoint, uv2); // Pixel below
float4 lightA = tex2D(Color1PointSampler, inTex0); // Current pixel
float4 lightB = tex2D(Color1SamplerPoint, uv1); // Pixel above

colorB.a = min(colorB.a, colorC.a);

float a = colorA.a;
if (colorB.a < colorA.a)
```

```
    a = 1 - colorB.a;

float4 color = lerp(colorB, colorA, a);
float4 light = lerp(lightB, lightA, a);

// now use color and light in the usual lighting calculations
```

where TDeviceSize.y is

$$\frac{1}{\text{deviceheight}}$$

RESULTS DISCUSSION

PERFORMANCE

All tests were performed on a PC with Intel 2.4GHz, 2GB RAM, NVIDIA GeForce 8800 GTS. The transparency implementation has added the following number of instructions over the base deferred rendering technique:

Geometry phase:

7 arithmetic instructions

0 texture instructions

Composition phase:

10 arithmetic instructions

3 texture instructions (point sampled)

The test draws a regular full-screen quad in normal deferred rendering mode and then with transparency. The results are shown in Table 2.7.1

TABLE 2.7.1 Results of the test

	800x600 FS	800x600 Win	1280x1024 Win	1600x1200 FS	1600x1200 Win
Normal	554 fps	527 fps	196 fps	142 fps	138 fps
DRT	542 fps	515 fps	192 fps	139 fps	135 fps
Speed Hit	2.2%	2.3%	2.0%	2.1%	2.2%

DOWNSIDES

The deferred rendering transparency technique proposed in this article has a few downsides:

- **Vertical blur:** A slightly visible two-pixel vertical blur is produced on transparent objects due to interlacing information loss. This anomaly can be solved with vertical oversampling to preserve all information for transparent objects. However, the performance cost of doing that is significant.

- **Jaggy edges:** The simple de-interlacing process described here can produce slightly visible jaggy edges on transparent objects.

- **Only one transparency layer:** This is basically a limitation of the algorithm. Only the closest transparent object is visible.

SUMMARY AND FUTURE WORK

This article presented a deferred rendering transparency algorithm. The main contribution of this new algorithm is lighting consistency between opaque and transparent objects, which results in implementation simplicity and high-speed performance.

The algorithm still has several areas open for future work:

- **Better de-interlacing:** A better de-interlacing process in the composition phase can reduce the effect of jagged edges, and possibly reduce the number of texture reads.

- **Blending modes:** By having an additional pixel attribute, other useful blending modes can be implemented (e.g., multiply, add, overlay).

- **Vertical blur:** Additional research needs to be done to find a fast and simple solution to this problem (e.g., storing two 8-bit color values in a 16-bit render target).

REFERENCES

[MEYERS07] Alpha-to-coverage in depth, Kevin Meyers, ShaderX⁵, 2007.

[HARRIS07] Deferred shading, Shawn Hargreaves, Mark Harris, GDC, 2004.

[DEERING88] The triangle processor and normal vector shader: a VLSI system for high performance graphics, Michael Deering, SIGGRAPH, 1988.

2.8 Deferred Shading with Multisampling Anti-Aliasing in DirectX 10

NICOLAS THIBIEROZ, ADVANCED MICRO DEVICES, INC.

INTRODUCTION

Deferred shading is a rendering technique now commonly used in games. *Ghost Recon: Advanced Warfighter I* and *II, S.T.A.L.K.E.R. Clear Skies, Splinter Cell 4, Tabula Rasa,* and numerous other titles released and in development have all been seduced by the inherent advantages of deferred shading. Other games have chosen a hybrid approach borrowing elements from deferred shading [Carsten07] [Sweeney07]. Unfortunately, one major drawback of these techniques is their inability to take advantage of the graphic hardware's full-screen multisampling anti-aliasing (MSAA) capabilities with legacy APIs such as DirectX 9 and OpenGL 2.1. As a result, games using these APIs have had to take drastic measures to overcome this limitation. In most cases a full-screen anti-aliasing option is simply not supported, leading to the obvious and dreaded "jaggies" inherent to aliasing issues. In other cases a custom full-screen anti-aliasing filter is proposed [Shishkovtsov05], whereby polygon edges are detected and selectively blurred. Unfortunately, the latter option can be quite a costly process, and is a poor-quality replacement for real MSAA due to using adjacent pixels from the fixed-resolution surface to perform the blurring.

The DirectX 10 graphics API from Microsoft finally includes the tools required to allow MSAA to be used robustly with deferred shading algorithms. In particular, the features introduced in DirectX 10.1 make it a fairly straightforward process, while DirectX 10.0 still requires some extra work to achieve identical results. This article provides details on optimized algorithms enabling MSAA to be used with deferred shading using those APIs.

225

Readers already familiar with the basic concepts of deferred shading may want to skip the section "Deferred Shading Principles" and start directly at "MSAA Requirements for Deferred Shading." On the other hand, readers wanting to read an in-depth description of the technique on legacy APIs are encouraged to consult previous literature on the subject, e.g., [Thibieroz04] [Calver03] [Pritchard04] [Hargreaves04].

DEFERRED SHADING PRINCIPLES

Deferred shading is the concept of writing out geometric and material properties for every visible pixel in a scene into a collection of textures that are then subsequently fetched during later passes to apply shading operations on a per-pixel basis. The term *deferred shading* originates from the fact that shading operations are only performed once hidden surface removal has been determined and properties for all opaque pixels in the scene have been stored. This is different from a *forward renderer* whereby pixels are typically shaded as objects are being rendered with one or several geometry passes.

Deferred shading can be decomposed into two main phases (other common rendering phases such as post-processing are mostly agnostic to the rendering technique used and will therefore not be covered in detail here): the G-Buffer building pass and the shading passes. The G-Buffer building pass has the responsibility of storing the properties of every screen pixel, while the shading passes apply lighting or other shading effects by fetching the G-Buffer data. Each shading pass typically processes an area of pixels corresponding to the contributions of the current light. This allows efficient optimizations whereby the 2D projection of a light volume is rendered in order to limit the processing cost to only the pixels affected by the light. For example, a sphere volume would be rendered for point lights, while spot lights would typically use some kind of conic shape. In contrast, an ambient light affecting all pixels in the scene would require a full-screen quad (or triangle). This approach enables lights to be treated like any other objects in the 3D engine. Also, the decoupling of the G-Buffer creation phase from the lighting phase has beneficial results with regard to reducing pixel processing cost, reducing states changes, improving batch performance, and in general allowing a more elegant structure and management of the 3D engine. Because of those advantages, deferred shading is often considered ideal for scenes composed of a large number of lights. Figure 2.8.1 illustrates the deferred shading phases.

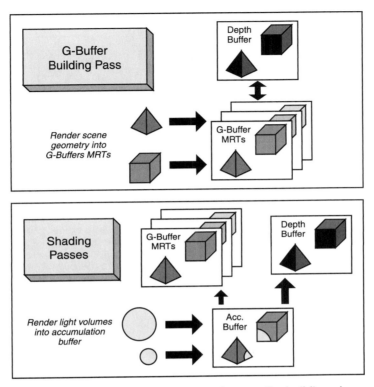

FIGURE 2.8.1   Deferred shading phases. The G-Buffer building phase writes geometric and material properties of the scene into a set of three arbitrary render targets making up the G-Buffer. The shading passes then render 2D projections of light volumes to shade pixels in range of the light. The pixel properties of each lit pixel are fetched from the G-Buffer textures at a 1:1 mapping ratio, and the light equation is subsequently calculated and output into the accumulation buffer.

MSAA REQUIREMENTS FOR DEFERRED SHADING

MSAA BASICS

MSAA allows a scene to be rendered at a higher resolution without having to pay the cost of shading more pixels. MSAA performs pixel shading on a *per-pixel* basis, while depth-stencil testing occurs on a *per-sample* basis. Samples successfully passing the depth-stencil test therefore have the pixel shader output stored into their respective entries in the multisampled render target. Once all rendering has been performed, the color samples for each pixel are averaged together (this process is called the *MSAA resolve* operation) to produce the final, anti-aliased pixel color. Figure 2.8.2 illustrates this concept.

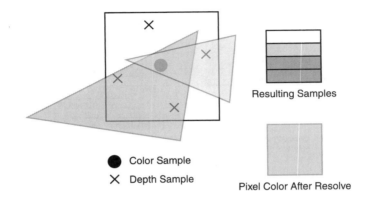

FIGURE 2.8.2   Multisampling anti-aliasing. The pixel represented by a square has two triangles (blue and yellow) crossing some of its sample points. The black dot represents the pixel sample location (pixel center); this is where the pixel shader is executed. The cross symbol corresponds to the location of the multisamples where the depth tests are performed. Samples passing the depth test receive the output of the pixel shader. At resolve time sample colors are averaged together to produce the final, anti-aliased result.

MULTISAMPLING MULTIPLE RENDER TARGETS

The G-Buffer writing phase of deferred shading algorithms relies on multiple render targets (MRTs) to store all the geometric and material properties for the scene. Typical properties such as depth, diffuse color, normal vector, gloss factor, and so on require a certain amount of destination storage that usually cannot be accommodated with a single render target. Therefore, binding multiple render targets during the G-Buffer writing phase is necessary, and in order to support MSAA with deferred shading, all those render targets must be rendered with MSAA. Unfortunately, real-time graphics APIs prior to DirectX 10 did not allow MSAA to work in conjunction with MRTs. One work-around to this problem is to build each G-Buffer's render target individually by binding it as the sole destination in its own geometry pass. However, the multiple passes (one per render target) required for this work-around have quite a high performance cost and defeat the single geometry pass advantage made possible by deferred shading in the first place. One other work-around would be to pack all required G-Buffer properties into a single "fat" render target format (e.g., 128-bits-per pixel formats). Once again, legacy API or hardware limitations with regard to supported formats and the availability of suitable packing and unpacking instructions impose too many limitations for this solution to be really useful.

DirectX 10 now allows MSAA to be used with up to eight multiple render targets. Although not strictly required by DirectX 10.0, existing DirectX 10 graphic hardware supports MSAA on a wide variety of useful render target formats such as 16-bit per channel floating-point surfaces, allowing greater flexibility for the G-Buffer configuration desired. Note that DirectX 10.1 pushes the minimum requirements further by imposing that four-sample MSAA be supported on 64-bit surfaces for compliant implementations.

PER-SAMPLE PIXEL SHADER EXECUTION

Although one may think that the ability to apply MSAA onto multiple render targets is enough to benefit from gorgeous anti-aliased visuals out of a deferred shading engine, the reality is quite different.

With a forward renderer each object is shaded and rendered directly into a multisampled surface that represents the colors of the completed scene. Once all objects have been rendered, a resolve operation is required to convert the multisampled render target into a final, anti-aliased image that can be queued up to the back buffer for the next `Present()` call.

In the case of deferred shading, the G-Buffer's multisampled render targets are simply intermediate storage buffers leading to the construction of the final image. They must therefore be preserved in multisampled form so that the color of each sample can be constructed using its unique per-sample properties stored in the G-Buffer. Once all shading contributions to the scene have been rendered onto the multisampled accumulation buffer, *then* the resolve operation can take place on this buffer to produce the final, anti-aliased image. In other words, the G-Buffer's multisampled render targets should not be resolved into anti-aliased versions of themselves before being used in the shading passes, as doing so will introduce visual artifacts on edge pixels.

Resolving G-Buffer properties like normal vectors or depth makes little sense, and will lead to incorrect results being produced. For example, if half the samples of a given pixel have different depth values stored in the G-Buffer, then the averaged depth produced by the resolve operation no longer has any relevance to the scene, and is very likely to cause incorrect lighting due to a completely new depth value being introduced. A similar case occurs when any samples in a given pixel have different normals: Even if a custom resolve operation is performed (e.g., to preserve normalized vectors through spherical interpolation), the issue remains that the vector produced by the resolve operation is a completely new quantity that did not arise from the G-Buffer writing phase, and therefore does not correspond to the geometric properties of the scene. Figure 2.8.3 provides an illustration of the difference arising when G-Buffer quantities are resolved prior to being fetched for the shading passes.

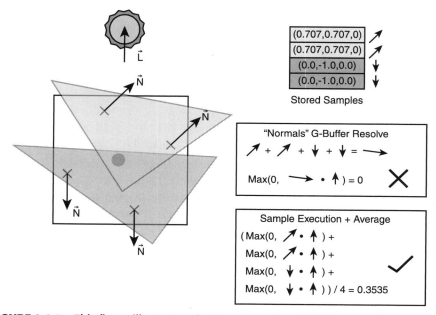

FIGURE 2.8.3   This figure illustrates what happens when G-Buffer normal vectors are resolved prior to being used in the light equation, instead of averaging the results of the light equation at each sample. Two triangles are rendered over a pixel, with each triangle covering two sample points. Resolving (averaging) the normals of all samples yields a vector that is now facing away from the light, even after renormalization. As a result, the light equation (a simple saturated dot product between the normal and the light vector) returns 0. In contrast, the correct method of applying the light equation on each sample and then averaging the results produces a positive value. Resolving quantities such as normal vectors or depth will result in incorrect colors on polygon edges, preventing any form of effective anti-aliasing.

To guarantee correct MSAA in a deferred shading context, the shading passes must therefore ensure that all calculations are performed on a per-sample basis and that the resulting per-sample output color is accumulated into a multisampled buffer. Because this "accumulation" buffer contains sample *colors* it will be subject to the final resolve operation once all shading and subsequent passes are done. To implement this functionality, the GPU must be able to execute a pixel shader at sample frequency: Input attributes are evaluated at a sample location (as opposed to a pixel location), the pixel shader code runs once for every sample, and each sample output is written out to a multisampled render target. DirectX 10.1 supports this feature directly and provides the fastest and most straightforward implementation. GPUs only supporting DirectX 10.0 can still implement this feature, but with less flexibility and performance, details of which are covered in the next section "Implementation."

IMPLEMENTATION

The following describes the basic steps of the algorithm allowing MSAA to be used with deferred shading and how they compare with the usual steps of rendering in single sample mode (i.e., without multisampling).

CREATION OF MULTISAMPLED RESOURCES

The following resources need to be created as multisampled.

- The G-Buffer render targets
- The accumulation buffer receiving the contribution of shading passes and further rendering
- The depth-stencil buffer

The creation of multisampled render targets is done through the `CreateTexture2D()` API, by setting the `SampleDesc` field of the `D3D10_TEXTURE2D_DESC` structure to the desired multisampling configuration.

G-BUFFER WRITING PHASE

There is very little difference between writing to single-sampled G-Buffer render targets and writing to multisampled ones. The only change required is to simply enable multisampling rasterization by creating and setting an appropriate rasterizer state. This can be done by enabling the `MultisampleEnable` field of the `D3D10_RASTERIZER_DESC` structure used during the creation of the state object. With the rasterizer state object set, all rendering is written out to the G-Buffer render targets in multisampled mode.

EDGE DETECTION PHASE

In order to produce accurate results for MSAA, it is essential that the pixel shaders used during the shading passes are executed at per-sample frequency. Executing a pixel shader for every sample has a significant impact on performance, though, especially if a high number of shading passes are rendered or a high number of multisamples are used. Instead of running the pixel shader code once per pixel, the code is now run as many times as there are samples (e.g., with 4x MSAA the pixel shader would execute four times: one for each sample). In order to avoid paying such a high performance cost, a sensible optimization is to detect pixels whose samples have different values and only perform per-sample pixel shader execution on those "edge" pixels. Remaining pixels whose samples share the same value would only be operated on at pixel frequency. By definition, MSAA produces differing samples on triangle edges; however, other rendering operations such as alpha-to-coverage or transparency anti-aliasing also output results on a per-sample granularity. In any case, the number of edge pixels is typically only a fraction of the total number of pixels in the scene, so the performance savings of only executing per-sample pixel shader code on those are fully justified.

The detection of edge pixels relies on the rendering of a full-screen quad (or triangle) with a pixel shader used to determine whether samples fetched from the G-Buffer are identical or not. Different methods can be used for pixel edge detection. For a perfect result, one would have to fetch and compare all samples of all G-Buffer textures. However, this approach can cause a performance concern due to the numerous texture fetches it requires.

The output of the edge detection pass is written out to the stencil buffer. After being cleared to 0, the stencil buffer sets the top stencil bit of every sample if a pixel edge is detected. For this to work, the pixel shader must discard non-edge pixels, and "let through" the ones detected as edges. Note that no color buffer is bound to this render pass, as the only output required is stored in the stencil buffer. Listing 2.8.1 shows the code used to detect pixel edges.

Listing 2.8.1 Pixel shader code used for pixel edge detection

```
// Pixel shader to detect pixel edges
// Used with the following depth-stencil state values:
// DepthEnable =      TRUE
// DepthFunc =        Always
// DepthWriteMask = ZERO
// StencilEnable =    TRUE
// Front/BackFaceStencilFail =      Keep
// Front/BackfaceStencilDepthFail = Keep
// Front/BackfaceStencilPass =      Replace;
// Front/BackfaceStencilFunc =      Always;
// The stencil reference value is set to 0x80
float4 PSMarkStencilWithEdgePixels( PS_INPUT input ) : SV_TARGET
{
    // Fetch and compare samples from GBuffer to determine if pixel
    // is an edge pixel or not
```

```
bool bIsEdge = DetectEdgePixel(input);

// Discard pixel if non-edge (only mark stencil for edge pixels)
if (!bIsEdge) discard;

// Return color (will have no effect since no color buffer bound)
return float4(1,1,1,1);
}
```

DetectEdgePixel() has the responsibility of determining whether the current pixel is an edge pixel. If the function returns FALSE (non-edge), then all samples are equal, and the pixel will be discarded, leaving the default value of 0 in all stencil samples for this pixel. If the function returns TRUE, then the pixel continues its way in the graphics pipeline, causing a 0x80 value to be written out to the stencil samples.

Centroid-Based Edge Detection

An optimized way to detect edges is to leverage the GPU's fixed function resolve feature. Because this process is usually hard-coded in the hardware, it produces a resolved output faster than the equivalent "custom" approach requiring individual samples to be fetched through the use of dedicated instructions. The edge detection method used relies on the centroid functionality that was introduced in DirectX 9. Centroid sampling is used to adjust the sample position of an interpolated pixel shader input so that it is contained within the area defined by the multisamples covered by the triangle. Centroid sampling is generally useful in cases where sampling could generate incorrect results on edge pixels when the triangle does not cover the pixel center. DirectX 10 allows pixel shader inputs to be evaluated at a centroid location by appending the keyword _CENTROID to the semantics declaration. Figure 2.8.4 illustrates the concept of declaring an iterated pixel shader input as centroid and how it compares with the default mode.

Centroid sampling can be used to determine whether a sample belongs to an edge pixel or not. A vertex shader writes a variable unique to every pixel (e.g., position data) into two outputs, while the associated pixel shader declares two inputs: one without and one with centroid sampling enabled. During the G-Buffer building phase the pixel shader then compares the centroid-enabled input with the one without it: Differing values mean that samples were only partially covered by the triangle, indicating an edge pixel. A "centroid value" of 1.0 is then written out to a selected area of the G-Buffer (previously cleared to 0.0) to indicate that the covered samples belong to an edge pixel. Once the G-Buffer writing phase is complete, a fixed-function resolve is performed to average the G-Buffer render target containing the centroid value. If this value is not exactly 0, then the current pixel is an edge pixel.

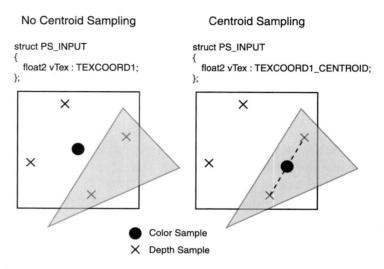

FIGURE 2.8.4 On the left the iterated pixel shader input vTex is interpolated normally: This pixel shader input will always be evaluated at the center of the pixel regardless of whether it is covered by the triangle. On the right the same input is declared with the _CENTROID keyword, forcing a centroid evaluation of the input. Since the two rightmost depth samples are covered by the triangle, the centroid sample location is contained within this area (typically midway between the two points).

This MSAA edge detection technique is quite fast, especially compared to a custom method of comparing every G-Buffer normal and depth samples. It only requires a few bits of storage in a G-Buffer render target. The number of bits reserved for this purpose must be large enough to accommodate the result of the fixed-function resolve operation without triggering a loss of precision that could lead to false negatives. The number of storage bits required is therefore as large as the bit encoding needed to represent the number of multisamples used, plus one bit to avoid any rounding-to-zero behavior. Thus, 4 bits of storage in the G-Buffer is enough to store edge detection data for up to 8x multisampling anti-aliasing.

For example, if only one sample out of eight was to receive the centroid value of 1.0 due to being the only one covered by a triangle, then the resolved (averaged) value of all samples belonging to this pixel would be $1 + 0 + 0 + 0 + 0 + 0 + 0 + 0 = 1 / 8 = 0.125$. This result quantizes to a value between 0001b and 0010b in 4-bit binary representation, enough to guarantee a non-zero result. Since only a few bits are required to store the centroid value for each sample, the remaining bits available in the selected G-Buffer render target channel can be used to pack other properties, for example, a bit field indicating various attributes of the pixel material. In this case the resolve process still safeguards the result of the centroid value resolve, and all that's needed is to adjust the edge test accordingly. For example, a pixel detected as an edge would add 240/255 to an 8-bit destination channel so that only the four top bits are used. After resolve, the test simply has to determine whether the averaged centroid value is above 15 to indicate an edge.

Unfortunately, this method cannot be used to detect non-polygonal edges, so it will not work with techniques like alpha-to-coverage or multisampled alpha testing. If such features are required, then an alternative edge detection algorithm relying on pure detection of differing samples should be used on such primitives.

SHADING PASSES

The shading passes are the "meat" of the algorithm, as this is where most of the changes to enable MSAA are required. The purpose of the shading passes is to add light contributions to the accumulation buffer. Light volumes are typically rendered as 2D projections in screen space so that only pixels affected by the light are processed, enabling significant performance savings. One way to do this is by using a two-sided stencil to mark the pixels inside a volume in a first "pre-pass" and then applying the light equation onto only those marked pixels. This technique has the advantage of generating a perfect "mask" of all pixels affected by the light. Another method commonly used is to detect whether the camera is inside or outside a convex light volume. If outside, the front faces of the volume are rendered; if inside, then the back faces of the volume are rendered with an inverted depth test. The latter approach has the advantage of not requiring an additional pass or any stencil testing, but it may be less effective when the camera is outside the volume due to the possibility of false positives being generated.

Regardless of the method used to render light volumes, the use of MSAA with deferred shading relies on the ability to apply lighting equations on a per-sample basis. In order to avoid redundant and costly processing, this operation is only performed on samples belonging to pixel edges, as detected in the previous phase. Such samples are therefore processed individually by the pixel shader, with their output written out to their respective samples in the accumulation buffer. Because the remaining non-edge pixels share the same sample values, they are then rendered at pixel frequency, which means the result of the pixel shader calculation is output to all samples passing the depth-stencil test.

Per-Sample Pixel Shader Execution: The DX10.1 Method

Shader model 4.1 as available in DX10.1 exposes a feature allowing the execution of a pixel shader at sample frequency, enabling single-pass processing of all samples belonging to edge pixels. To request a pixel shader to run at sample frequency, the `sample` keyword must be declared on at least one of the interpolated pixel shader inputs, or the `SV_SAMPLEINDEX` semantic must be used. Below is an example pixel shader input structure that will trigger a per-sample pixel shader execution.

```
struct PS_INPUT_EDGE_SAMPLE
{
    float4 Pos    : SV_POSITION;
    uint uSample  : SV_SAMPLEINDEX;
};
```

The `uSample` input declared with the `SV_SAMPLEINDEX` semantic is a *system value* that returns a zero-based index of the sample being executed by the pixel shader. This index is used by the pixel shader code to fetch data from the G-Buffers corresponding to the sample being processed. The pixel shader code therefore executes once for every sample using the inputs provided at each iteration. Access to an individual texture sample is achieved by using the `Load()` shader instruction, which takes the pixel screen coordinates and the sample number to retrieve as input parameters. Listing 2.8.2 shows the pixel shader used during the shading passes to process edge samples.

To ensure that only samples belonging to edge pixels are processed, the stencil test has to be set up accordingly before running the aforementioned pixel shader. This can be done by simply setting the stencil test properties so that the test passes if the stencil buffer value equals the value written to the stencil buffer during the edge detection pass (0×80 was used in Listing 2.8.2). The depth test to use depends on whether the camera is inside or outside the light volume.

Listing 2.8.2 The pixel shader applies the light equation on a per-sample basis for all edge samples. The sample index is used to fetch sample properties from the multisampled G-Buffer textures. The pixel shader output is written to the sample corresponding to the current sample being processed

```
// Multisampled G-Buffer textures declaration
Texture2DMS <float4, NUM_SAMPLES> txMRT0;
Texture2DMS <float4, NUM_SAMPLES> txMRT1;
Texture2DMS <float4, NUM_SAMPLES> txMRT2;
```

```
// Pixel shader for shading pass of edge samples in DX10.1
// This shader is run at sample frequency


// Used with the following depth-stencil state values so that only
// samples belonging to edge pixels are rendered, as detected in
// the previous stencil pass.
// StencilEnable =    TRUE
// StencilReadMask = 0x80
// Front/BackFaceStencilFail =      Keep
// Front/BackfaceStencilDepthFail = Keep
// Front/BackfaceStencilPass =      Keep;
// Front/BackfaceStencilFunc =      Equal;
// The stencil reference value is set to 0x80
float4 PSLightPass_EdgeSampleOnly( PS_INPUT_EDGE_SAMPLE input ) : SV_TARGET
{
    // Convert screen coordinates to integer
    int3 nScreenCoordinates = int3(input.Pos.xy, 0);


    // Sample G-Buffer textures for current sample
    float4 MRT0 = txMRT0.Load( nScreenCoordinates, input.uSample);
    float4 MRT1 = txMRT1.Load( nScreenCoordinates, input.uSample);
    float4 MRT2 = txMRT2.Load( nScreenCoordinates, input.uSample);


    // Apply light equation to this sample
    float4 vColor = LightEquation(MRT0, MRT1, MRT2);


    // Return calculated sample color
    return vColor;
}
```

Per-Sample Pixel Shader Execution: The DX10.0 Method

DirectX 10.0 does not support the concept of running a pixel shader at sample frequency. However, it is still possible to achieve an identical result by adopting a multi-pass approach. The idea is to render the light volumes as many times as the number of samples, only enabling output to a single sample each pass. Although the pixel shader is then run per-pixel, the `OMSetBlendState()` API is set up to ensure that only one sample is written out. The pixel shader to execute at each pass fetches the G-Buffer samples corresponding to the sample currently being processed. Listing 2.8.3 shows the pixel shader code to achieve this result.

This method produces results identical to the DX10.1 method detailed in the previous section, at the cost of extra render passes and slightly reduced texture cache effectiveness due to repeated access of the same G-Buffer areas multiple times.

Listing 2.8.3 Pixel shader code run as part of a multi-pass rendering operation to emulate per-sample execution in DX10.0

```
// Multisampled G-Buffer textures declaration
Texture2DMS <float4, NUM_SAMPLES> txMRT0;

Texture2DMS <float4, NUM_SAMPLES> txMRT1;

Texture2DMS <float4, NUM_SAMPLES> txMRT2;


// Pixel shader for shading pass of edge samples in DX10.0
// This shader is run at pixel frequency and is executed once for
// each sample as part of a multipass operation.
// A single sample will be output each pass through the use of:
// pDev10->OMSetBlendState(&BS, &BlendFactor, 1<<nCurrentSample);


// Used with the following depth-stencil state values so that only
// samples belonging to edge pixels are rendered, as detected in
// the previous stencil pass.
// StencilEnable =    TRUE
// StencilReadMask = 0x80
// Front/BackFaceStencilFail =      Keep
// Front/BackfaceStencilDepthFail = Keep
// Front/BackfaceStencilPass =      Keep;
// Front/BackfaceStencilFunc =      Equal;
// The stencil reference value is set to 0x80
float4 PSLightPass_SingleSampleOnly( float4 Pos : SV_POSITION,
                                     uniform uint nSample )
                                  : SV_TARGET
```

```
{
    // Convert screen coordinates to integer
    int3 nScreenCoordinates = int3(Pos.xy, 0);


    // Sample G-Buffer textures for input sample
    float4 MRT0 = txMRT0.Load( nScreenCoordinates, nSample);
    float4 MRT1 = txMRT1.Load( nScreenCoordinates, nSample);
    float4 MRT2 = txMRT2.Load( nScreenCoordinates, nSample);


    // Apply light equation to this sample
    float4 vColor = LightEquation(MRT0, MRT1, MRT2);


    // Return calculated color
    return vColor;
}
```

Each light volume from the shading passes is rendered as many times as there are samples in the chosen multisampling configuration. The global sample mask is set up so that only the sample corresponding to the current pass is output into the multisampled accumulation buffer. The light equation is only applied to the selected sample by fetching the appropriate G-Buffer samples. Note that the Load() API requires the sample index to be a literal value, so several versions of this shader should be compiled (one for every sample index).

Non-Edge Pixels

Regardless of the method used (DX10.1 or DX10.0), once all samples belonging to edge pixels have been rendered into the accumulation buffer, it is the turn of non-edge pixels to add their contribution. By definition, non-edge pixels share the same data across all samples, so the pixel shader need only fetch G-Buffer data for the first sample. The pixel shader code is therefore fairly straightforward and is a simple modification to Listing 2.8.3 whereby the sample to fetch is hard-coded to be sample 0. To ensure that only non-edge pixels are processed, the stencil test is set up differently so that the stencil test passes if bit 8 is *not* equal to the reference value (still set to 0×80).

POST-PROCESSING

Once all light volumes have been rendered, the multisampled accumulation buffer contains color samples representing the scene; it is therefore suited to any further operations required by the graphic engine and can be resolved as normal prior to being used in some post-processing operations or before the final copy to the back buffer.

ASSESSMENT OF ALTERNATIVE IMPLEMENTATION

ON-THE-FLY RESOLVES

It can be tempting to think that per-sample execution frequency is not strictly required for correct multisampling of deferred shading engines and that instead, an "on-the-fly" resolve approach could be taken to add per-pixel color contributions during the shading passes. The on-the-fly resolve approach consists in fetching all the samples belonging to a pixel, calculating their respective color contributions, and then averaging (resolving) the results so that a single pixel color is accumulated into a render target. This technique presents the advantage that only per-sample access to multisampled resources is required for it to work (which is supported on all DirectX 10.0 implementations), but it can also be subject to significant inefficiencies and even errors.

First, the render target used for accumulation of the shading passes' output will still need to be multisampled despite writing whole pixel color values. This is because the depth buffer itself is multisampled, and it is not possible to mix a multisampled depth buffer with a non-multisampled color render target. The depth buffer is quite essential to improve the performance of shading passes through Z culling optimizations, so not binding it is not an option.

The second issue requires a good knowledge of DirectX 10 multisampling rules to be understood. It is important to point out that a notable difference between having multisampling enabled or not is the value of the incoming depth used as input to the depth-stencil test. With multisampling disabled, the same interpolated depth value (evaluated at the pixel center) is input to the depth test of each sample. With multisampling enabled, the interpolated depth is evaluated at each sample, providing a unique input depth to the depth test of each sample. In *both* cases depth tests, stencil tests, and backend operations such as blending operate on a *per-sample* basis. When rendering a light volume with depth or stencil optimizations, there will be cases where some samples of a pixel pass the depth-stencil tests while others do not (this will happen along the edges of objects inside the volume and regardless of whether MSAA is enabled or not). Unfortunately, the pixel shader used with the on-the-fly resolve method averages all samples regardless of whether they actually pass the depth-stencil test, and output the resolved value into the samples that passed the depth test. The multisampled accumulation buffer may therefore contain different values per sample when it was supposed to contain a unique value representing the average of all samples. This requires a resolve operation at the backend to take into account the value of all samples; unfortunately, this process creates lower color intensities on edge pixels (by averaging some samples containing values that are already the result of an averaging operation), resulting in a considerable reduction in anti-aliasing effectiveness as illustrated on the right-hand side of Figure 2.8.5.

FIGURE 2.8.5 Comparison of rendering method used during the shading passes. On the left the pixel shader outputs an individual per-sample color for every sample belonging to edge pixels, resulting in efficient anti-aliasing. On the right the shading is performed per-pixel by averaging lighting contributions of all samples (on-the-fly resolve). Notice the reduced effectiveness of anti-aliasing for the latter method due to darker colors being produced.

It is possible to overcome this problem by ensuring that pixel edge samples are always fully covered by a light volume; in this case the result of the on-the-fly resolve will be written out to all samples, and the final resolve need only take a single sample to produce the final output. Unfortunately, ensuring that pixel edge samples are always covered means that early depth or stencil culling optimizations may not be used (as they will produce per-sample outputs), so a light volume would have to be rendered integrally (e.g., using an alternative technique such as scissoring). Naturally, this will increase the fill-rate and pixel processing cost and should therefore not be considered a good solution.

The last issue with this method is the inability to perform further drawing operations requiring per-sample access after the shading passes. This limitation can be drastically restrictive, for example, when high-dynamic-range-correct rendering needs to be applied to the scene [Persson08].

CONCLUSION

This article has shown how to implement a correct deferred shading implementation in combination with multisampling anti-aliasing. Because of the significant memory cost associated with the creation of multisampled resources, it pays off to be economical on the G-Buffer configuration chosen. Reducing the number of render targets and their bit depth will not only provide savings in video memory but will also result in higher performance. The use of a proper edge detection filter is also essential to the implementation since executing shading passes on too many samples rapidly results in unacceptable performance issues.

REFERENCES

[Thibieroz04] Nicolas Thibieroz, "Deferred Shading with Multiple Render Targets," *ShaderX²: Shader Programming Tips & Tricks with DirectX 9*, Wolfgang Engel, ed., Wordware Publishing, 2004, pp. 251–269.

[Calver03] Dean Calver, "Photo-Realistic Deferred Lighting," white paper, available at http://www.beyond3d.com/content/articles/19

[Shishkovtsov05] Oles Shishkovtsov, "Deferred Shading in S.T.A.L.K.E.R.," *GPU Gems 2*, Matt Pharr, ed., Addison Wesley, 2005, pp. 143–166.

[Pritchard04] Rich Geldreich, Matt Pritchard, & John Brooks, "Deferred Lighting and Shading," GDC 2004 presentation, available at: http://www.gdconf.com/conference/archives/2004/pritchard_matt.ppt

[Hargreaves04] Shawn Hargreaves, "Deferred Shading," presentation, GDC 2004, available at http://ati.amd.com/developer/gdc/D3DTutorial_DeferredShading.pdf

[Carsten07] Carsten Wenzel, "Real-time Atmospheric Effects in Games Revisited," GDC 2007 presentation, available at http://developer.amd.com/assets/D3DTutorial_Crytek.pdf

[Sweeney07], EVGA Gaming, "Q&A with Tim Sweeney," available at http://www.evga.com/gaming/gaming_news/gn_100.asp

[Persson08] Emil Persson, "Post-Tonemapping Resolve for High-Quality HDR Anti-aliasing in D3D10," *ShaderX⁶: Advanced Rendering Techniques*, Wolfgang Engel, ed., Course Technology CENGAGE Learning, 2008, pp. 161–164.

2.9 Light-Indexed Deferred Rendering

DAMIAN TREBILCO

INTRODUCTION

Current rasterization-based renderers utilize one of two main techniques for lighting: forward rendering and deferred rendering [Calver07] [Shish05] [Koonce07]. However, both of these techniques have disadvantages.

Forward rendering does not scale well with complex lighting scenes, and standard deferred rendering suffers from high memory usage. Standard deferred rendering also has trouble with transparency, multi-sample anti-aliasing (MSAA), and per-material lighting schemes.

This article presents a middle ground technique that keeps the key advantages of both forward and deferred rendering: minimal memory usage while being able to handle complex lighting scenes on a per-material basis.

RENDERING CONCEPT

Typical deferred rendering stores the material properties at each fragment and renders lights by accessing the fragment's data. This implementation aims to do the reverse: Store the light properties at each fragment and access these properties when rendering the main scene using forward-pass rendering.

The most direct way of achieving this is to store light direction, color, and attenuation at each fragment. However, this approach limits the number of lights that can influence each fragment, as storing these properties consumes a large amount of buffer storage space.

Some recent work by Wolfgang Engel with "Light Pre-Pass Rendering" [Engel08] provides one solution to this problem. This is achieved by storing surface normals in a pre-pass, calculating diffuse and specular terms for each light, and adding the results to a light buffer. These lighting terms are then used in a forward material rendering pass to do the lighting. However, this technique requires that all materials be lit with the same lighting scheme and requires a normal output pre-pass.

LIGHT-INDEXED DEFERRED RENDERING

This new approach simply assigns each light a unique index and then stores this index at each fragment the light hits, rather than storing all the light or material properties per fragment. These indices can then be used in a fragment shader to look up into a lighting properties table for data to light the fragment.

This technique can be broken down into three basic render passes.

1. Render depth only pre-pass.
2. Disable depth writes (keep depth testing only) and render light volumes into a light index texture. Standard deferred lighting and shadow volume techniques can be used to find what fragments are hit by each light volume.
3. Render geometry using standard forward rendering. Lighting is done using the light index texture to access lighting properties in each shader.

The problem with steps 2 and 3 occurs when lights overlap. If light volumes could not overlap, then step 2 could simply write the light index to the texture, which can be directly accessed in step 3.

In order to support multiple light indices per fragment, it would be ideal to store the first light index in the texture's red channel, the second light index in the blue index, and so on. To do this, a light index packing scheme will be needed.

Presented here are three light index packing schemes that use differing amounts of CPU and GPU processing time. The *CPU sorting* method is purely CPU based, while the *bit shifting* method is a purely GPU-based technique. The *multi-pass max blend equation* method uses a moderate amount of GPU processing time with the option to use the CPU to offload some work.

LIGHT INDEX PACKING: CPU SORTING

An easy CPU-based solution for light index packing involves sorting the scene lights based on light volume overlap. Assuming 8-bit light indices and an RGBA8 light index texture, four overlapping light indices can be rendered using the following steps:

- On the CPU, create four arrays to hold light volume data. Then for each scene light, find the light data array it can be added to without intersecting any of the existing lights in the array (e.g., attempt to add to array one, then attempt to add to array two, etc.). If a light cannot be added, it will have to be discarded or stored to be processed in a second pass.

- Clear the light index color buffer to zero.

- Enable writing to the *red* channel only and render light volumes from light data array 1.

- Enable writing to the *green* channel only and render light volumes from light data array 2.

- Enable writing to the *blue* channel only and render light volumes from light data array 3.

- Enable writing to the *alpha* channel only and render light volumes from light data array 4.

The advantage of this method is:

- No unpacking in the fragment shader is needed.

The disadvantage to packing light indices this way is:

- Requires sorting the scene lights on the CPU.

Using this packing method, lights can be prioritized by sorting the important lights first. The light overlap count and number of total scene lights can be varied by changing the number of render targets and the bit-depth of the render targets.

If a scene is mostly made up of static lights, these lights can be presorted into light volume arrays or have an intersection tree generated for fast runtime access.

LIGHT INDEX PACKING: MULTI-PASS MAX BLEND EQUATION

A GPU-based solution to storing multiple indices based on the fragment pass was suggested by Timothy Farrar [Farrar07], and has been modified to better support light-indexed rendering.

Assuming 8-bit light indices and an RGBA8 light index texture, four overlapping light indices can be rendered using the following steps:

- Clear color and stencil buffers to zero.

- Set blend equation mode to MAX.

- Mask out writes to blue and alpha channels.

- Set the stencil to increment on stencil pass and set the stencil compare value to only pass on values <2 (only allow a maximum of two writes per fragment).
- Render the light volumes and output (index, 1.0–index) in the red and green channels.
- Mask out writes to *red* and *green* channels and enable *blue* and *alpha* channels.
- Set the stencil to decrement on stencil failure and set the stencil compare value to only pass on values equal to 0.
- Render the light volumes and output (index, 1.0–index) in the blue and alpha channels.

Unpacking for each light index is done as follows (a zero index is assumed to be no light):

- Index1 = red channel
- Index2 = 1.0–blue channel (ignore if equal to red channel)
- Index3 = green
- Index4 = 1.0–alpha channel (ignore if equal to green channel)

The advantage of this method is:

- Simple unpack

The disadvantages to packing light indices this way are:

- Only supports a maximum of four overlapping lights.
- Requires two passes of the light volumes for four light indices.
- Uses the stencil buffer, which may be needed by shadow volumes or the light volume passes. If only two light indices are needed, then the stencil buffer does not need to be used.
- If only one or three lights hit a fragment, light indices 1, 2 or 3, 4 will be the same index.

Using this packing method, lights can be prioritized by using the high and low indices for primary important lights and the mid-range indices for secondary lights.

This method can also be combined with the CPU sorting technique above to sort the scene lights into two light data arrays. Each array is allowed intersecting lights as long as no more than two lights share the same intersecting space. Each array can then be rendered (red-green pass and then blue-alpha pass) without the need of the stencil buffer.

LIGHT INDEX PACKING: BIT SHIFTING

Another GPU-based solution to light index packing involves bit shifting and packing.

Again, assuming 8-bit light indices and an RGBA8 light index texture, four overlapping light indices can be rendered using the following steps:

- Clear the color buffer to zero.

- Set the blend mode to `ONE`, `CONSTANT_COLOR` where the constant color is set to 0.25. This shifts existing color bits down two places (`>> 2 = * 0.25`) and adds the two new bits to the top of the number.

- Render the light volumes and break the 8-bit index value into four 2-bit values and output each 2-bit value into RGBA channels as high bits, for example, red channel = (`index & 0x3`) `<< 6`. This index splitting can be done offline and simply supplied as an output color to the light volume pass.

Unpacking for each light index requires a video card that can do bit logic in shaders (shader model 4) or with some floating-point emulation. The following GLSL code uses floating-point math to unpack each light index into a 0...1 range—suitable for looking up into a light index texture of 256 values:

```
#define NUM_LIGHTS 256.0

// Look up the bit planes texture
vec4 packedLight = texture2DProj(BitPlaneTexture, projectSpace);


// Unpack each lighting channel
vec4 unpackConst = vec4(4.0, 16.0, 64.0 , 256.0) / NUM_LIGHTS;


// Expand the packed light values to the 0.. 255 range
vec4 floorValues = ceil(packedLight * 254.5);


float lightIndex[4];
for(int i=0; i< 4; i++)
{
   packedLight = floorValues * 0.25; // Shift two bits down
   floorValues = floor(packedLight); // Remove shifted bits
   lightIndex[i] = dot((packedLight - floorValues), unpackConst);
}
```

Bit packing also allows a lot of different light overlap counts and scene light count combinations. Some of the possible combinations are listed in Table 2.9.1.

TABLE 2.9.1 Bit-packing combinations

Lights Per Fragment	Scene Light Count	Details
2	15	1×8-bit channel Light index written directly out (4 bits)
4	15	2×8-bit channels Light index split into 2×2-bit values
8	15	1×RGBA8 surface Light index split into 4×1-bit values
16	15	2×RGBA8 surfaces (2 render targets) Light index split into 4×1-bit values Output to one render target at a time and use the stencil buffer like in multi-pass max blend equation when eight overlaps have been reached (requires two passes of light volume geometry)
1	255	1×8-bit channel Light index written directly out (8 bits)
2	255	2×8-bit channels Light index split into 2×4-bit values
4	255	1×RGBA8 surface Light index split into 4×2-bit values
8	255	2×RGBA8 surfaces (two render targets) Light index split into 8×1-bit values
16	255	4×RGBA8 surfaces (four render targets) Light index split into 8×1-bit values Output to two render targets at a time and use the stencil buffer like in multi-pass max blend equation when eight overlaps have been reached (requires two passes of light volume geometry)
1	65,535*	2×8-bit channels Light index split into 2×8-bit values
2	65,535	1×RGBA8 surface Light index split into 4×4-bit values

| 4 | 65,535 | 2×RGBA8 surfaces (two render targets) Light index split into 8×2-bit values |
| 8 | 65,535 | 4×RGBA8 surfaces (four render targets) Light index split into 16×1-bit values |

** Note that when 65,535 lights are used, it is advisable to split the light index into two indexes and look up into a 256×256 light data table.

The advantages of this bit packing method are:

■ It scales based on the number of scene lights and the overlap requirements.
■ Typically, it renders in a single pass without using additional buffers (e.g., stencil).

The disadvantages of packing light indices this way are:

■ Complex unpacking.
■ Requires hardware to be bit-precise in blending and floating-point math.

Using this bit packing method, lights can be prioritized by rendering the lowest-priority lights first. If more lights than the pack limit are reached, older lights will be discarded when blending.

LIGHT INDEX GEOMETRY LIGHTING

Once a light index packing technique is chosen, the next step is to update each standard forward-rendered shader to use the light indices.

If using multiple light indices, it is recommended that all lighting calculations be done in world or view space. This is because lighting data can be supplied in world or view space, and surface data is typically in tangent or model space. It is typically more efficient to transform the surface data once into the lighting space than to transform each light's data into the surface's space. However, using world space for lighting can cause precision issues for large worlds.

The next step is to decide how to supply a light data lookup table to the fragment shader and what data should be contained within it.

The obvious choice for supplying light data is one or more point-sampled textures. Textures have the advantage of being widely supported, but care has to be used to ensure that when updating dynamic data in the textures, the GPU pipeline is not stalled. Multiple textures can be used in alternate frames to help ensure that an update is not attempted on a texture currently being used by the GPU. If a scene is made up of static lights in world space, no per-frame updates are required, and single textures can be used. Another choice to supply lighting data is to use constant buffers (as available in Direct3D 10), but this article will focus on the texture approach.

The type of data needed depends on the lighting types you want to support. We will focus on point lights, as you can emulate a parallel light with a distant point light and spotlights can be partially emulated by rendering a cone volume. Point lights require position, attenuation, and light color data. All this data could be supplied in one 2D texture—using the x axis as the light index and the y axis as the light property. However, it is more practical to split the light properties into different textures based on the update frequency and format requirements. Experiment with different formats and splits to determine what is fastest for the target hardware.

For the test application provided on the accompanying DVD-ROM (see Figure 2.9.1), we decided that colors would be updated infrequently and only needed low precision. Therefore, colors are supplied in a 1D RGBA8 texture. Position and attenuation lighting data need more precision and are supplied in a 1D 32-bit per component RGBA floating-point texture. The RGB values represent the light position in view space, with the alpha component containing (1/light radius) for attenuation. Using 8-bit light indices (255 lights), the total size of these light data textures is a tiny 5 KB.

Note that light index zero represents the "none" or "NULL" light, and the light buffers for this index should be filled with values that cannot affect the final rendering (e.g., black light color).

Once each light property has been looked up using a light index, standard lighting equations can be used. On modern hardware it may be beneficial to "early out" of processing when a light index of zero is reached.

COMBINING WITH OTHER RENDERING TECHNIQUES

Many lighting techniques work well in isolation, but fail when combined with other techniques used in an application. This section will discuss ways of combining light-indexed deferred rendering (LIDR) with other common rendering methods.

MULTI-SAMPLE ANTI-ALIASING

Typically, the biggest disadvantage with deferred rendering has been supporting Multi-sample anti-aliasing (MSAA). Fortunately, there are several solutions for LIDR.

FIGURE 2.9.1 Screenshot from the provided test application on the DVD-ROM. The scene consists of ~40,000 triangles with 255 lights. Running on an NVIDIA Geforce 6800 GT at 1024×768 resolution, the application compares light-indexed deferred rendering (LIDR) with multi-pass forward rendering. Frame rates measured: 82 frames per second (FPS) with 1 overlap LIDR, 62 FPS with 2 overlap LIDR, 37 FPS with 4 overlap LIDR, and 12 FPS with multi-pass forward rendering.

MSAA TECHNIQUE 1: MSAA TEXTURE SURFACE

Render all targets (depth or stencil, light index texture, main scene) to MSAA surfaces. Then, when doing the forward render pass, sample the light index texture using the screen *X,Y* and current sample index. Sampling an MSAA texture is possible with Direct3D 10 and current console hardware.

While traditional deferred rendering can also use this technique for MSAA, it suffers from two major disadvantages:

- Already large "fat buffers" are made 2/4/8 times the size.
- Lighting calculations have to be done for all samples (2/4/8 times the fragment work), or samples have to be interpolated that only give approximate lighting. LIDR only needs to perform lighting on fragments actually generated on edges.

MSAA TECHNIQUE 2: LIGHT VOLUME FRONT FACES

Typically, when rendering light volumes in deferred rendering, only surfaces that intersect the light volume are marked and lit. This is generally accomplished by a "shadow–volume-like" technique of rendering back faces—incrementing stencil where depth is greater than zero—and then rendering front faces and only accepting when depth is less than zero and stencil is not zero. By only rendering front faces where depth is less than, all future lookups by fragments in the forward rendering pass will get all possible lights that could hit the fragment.

This front face method has the advantage of using a standard non-MSAA texture, but has a major problem with light intersections. Previously, only lights that hit a surface were counted in the packing of light indices. By only rendering front faces, all light volumes that intersect the ray from the eye to the surface will be counted in the packing count. This wastes fragment shader cycles in processing lights that may not hit the surface and can easily saturate the number of lights a surface supports.

Using this technique, it is also possible to leave out the depth pre-pass (in very vertex-limited scenes) at the cost of saturating the surface light index count faster.

TRANSPARENCY

Transparency has also been a major problem with deferred rendering. However, by using the light volume front faces technique as discussed in the multi-sample anti-aliasing section, semi-transparent objects can be rendered after opaque objects using the same light index texture. This is because all light volumes that intersect the ray from the eye to an opaque surface are included in the light index texture. Therefore, in the rendering of semi-transparent objects, the forward render pass will have access to all lights that could possibly hit each fragment.

SHADOWS

There are several ways of combining LIDR with shadows, depending on what shadowing technique is used.

No Combined Shadows

The easiest way to integrate LIDR into an application with shadows is to only use it with non-shadowing lights. This is possible, as LIDR uses the standard forward rendering when applying lights.

For example, an application may render shadows only from one primary directional light and have lots of non-shadowing point or PFX lights. Each shader that handles the directional light shadowing simply needs to be updated to access the

LIDR lights. Another option is to do the LIDR lights as a separate pass after the shadow pass.

SHADOW VOLUMES

Shadow volumes work easily with LIDR lights. Once the shadow volume has marked the stencil buffer to indicate where the shadowed areas are, the light volumes can be rendered to ignore these areas. However, this will not work if you are using the light volume front faces technique for MSAA and transparency support.

SHADOW MAPS

Shadow maps can be supported in a few ways depending on the requirements.

- **Pre-pass:** By accessing the buffer depth value when rendering the light volume pass, a shadow map texture can be compared to determine if a fragment is in shadow. If hard shadows are acceptable, the shader can simply call "discard" when a fragment is in shadow. If soft shadows are desired, a "shadow intensity" value can be output in a separate render target. These shadow intensity values need to be bit-packed and unpacked in a way similar to the light index values and accessed in the forward pass to attenuate the lighting.

- **Final pass:** By packing the shadow maps into a 3D texture or a 2D texture array (Direct3D 10), the light index can be used to access a shadow map and do the shadow calculation in the forward rendering pass. This requires additional light table data for the shadow map matrices and may be difficult to support for shadowed point lights (possibly use six consecutive shadow map indices). If using this technique, it is recommended that only a limited light index range has shadows, for example, light indices 0 to 3 have shadows.

CONSTRAINING LIGHTS TO SURFACES

One of deferred rendering's greatest strengths is that all surfaces are lit equally. Unfortunately, this can also be a problem. Artists sometimes like to light scenes with lights that only affect some surfaces. This can be solved with traditional deferred rendering by rendering out another index to indicate light surface interaction, but this requires yet more buffer space and more logic in the scene lighting passes.

With LIDR, however, all that is needed is to supply different light lookup tables for the forward render pass. Lights that should not hit a surface can be nulled out by using a black color or adjusting the attenuation.

If no LIDR lighting is to hit a surface, the surface shader can simply have the LIDR calculations taken out. A common case of this might be a scene with static lights baked into a light map for static geometry. These static lights can then be rendered at runtime with LIDR for access by dynamic surfaces. Static geometry surfaces can ignore all LIDR lights and simply use the light map for lighting.

MULTI-LIGHT TYPE SUPPORT

Most scenes are made up of a combination of different light types, from simple directional lights to spot lights with projected textures. Unfortunately, multiple light types per scene are not easily handled with LIDR. Some possible solutions are:

- Only use LIDR for a single light type. For example, if a scene is made up of one directional light and multiple point lights, the point lights can use LIDR while the directional light is rendered using standard forward rendering. The directional light could also be "faked" as a distant point light.

- Store a flag with the light data indicating the light type. This can involve complicated shader logic and may not be practical for many different lighting types.

- Use different light index buffers for each light type. This may waste index buffer space if light types are not evenly distributed. This technique also involves complicated shader logic or multiple passes of the scene geometry for each light type.

LIGHTING TECHNIQUE COMPARISON

As with all rendering techniques, LIDR has both advantages and disadvantages. To highlight these, a comparison of LIDR with other common rendering techniques is given.

When comparing LIDR with standard deferred and light-pre-pass rendering, LIDR uses smaller buffer sizes, lighting techniques can vary per material, and transparency can be supported. MSAA is supported by all techniques but uses less memory with LIDR. In addition, LIDR can be layered on an existing forward renderer (assuming a depth pre-pass) and only needs lighting reflection vectors to be calculated once.

In comparing LIDR with multi-pass or multi-light forward rendering, LIDR scales well based on the number of lights, geometry does not have to broken up for individual lighting, and object-light interactions do not have to be calculated on the CPU.

Depending on the scene, significant overdraw can also be saved when using LIDR (e.g., small lights on a terrain). LIDR can also support lights that are "mesh" shaped.

However, there are significant disadvantages to using LIDR. The main one is the limit of how many lights can hit a fragment at once (current implementation has a maximum of 16). Scenes with few objects and lights would be faster with other techniques, as each material shader has a fixed lighting overhead. Shadows and "exotic" light types (e.g., projected textures) are also more difficult to support with LIDR.

FUTURE WORK

FAKE RADIOSITY

Using LIDR it may be possible to "fake" one-bounce radiosity. This may be accomplished by:

- Rendering the scene from light projection and storing depth and color values.

- Rendering hundreds of small point light spheres into the scene using LIDR. Inside the vertex shader, look up the depth texture from the previous light projection pass to position each light in the scene. Look up the color buffer from the same light projection pass to get the light color.

Using this technique it may be possible to emulate the first bounce in a radiosity lighting pass or implement splatting indirect illumination [Dach06].

BUFFER SHARING

Most implementations of LIDR need a separate buffer to store the light indices. However, on some hardware it may be possible to reuse the final color buffer as the light index texture. This is because accesses to the index texture are only ever for the current fragment position.

CONCLUSION

The technique presented in this article, light-indexed deferred rendering (LIDR), has been shown to be an efficient middle ground between standard forward rendering and deferred rendering techniques. LIDR handles many lights with linear scaling and with only one or two passes of the scene vertex data. LIDR also has only minimal memory requirements with one screen-sized texture for index data and small lookup tables for lighting data. With some minor changes, LIDR can also be made to handle the difficult deferred rendering cases of MSAA and transparency.

Existing applications that use forward rendering can also easily be modified to layer LIDR on top of existing lighting solutions.

Future developments on this technique will be made available on the projects Web site at http://code.google.com/p/lightindexed-deferredrender/.

REFERENCES

[Calver07] Calver, Dean, "Photo-realistic Deferred Lighting," available online at http://www.beyond3d.com/content/articles/19/1, March 11, 2007.

[Shish05] Shishkovtsov, Oles, "Deferred Shading in STALKER," *GPU Gems 2*, Addison-Wesley Professional, 2005, pg. 143.

[Koonce07] Koonce, Rusty, "Deferred Shading in Tabula Rasa," *GPU Gems 3*, Addison-Wesley Professional, 2007, pg. 429.

[Engel08] Engel, Wolfgang, "Designing a Renderer for Multiple Lights - The Light Pre-Pass Renderer" in this volume.

[Farrar07] Farrar, Timothy, "Output data packing," OpenGL forum post available online at http://www.opengl.org/discussion_boards/ubbthreads.php?ubb=showflat&Number=230242#Post230242, October 31, 2007.

[Dach06] Dachsbacher, Carsten and Stamminger, Marc, "Splatting indirect illumination," *Proceedings of the 2006 Symposium on Interactive 3D Graphics and Games*, March 14–17, 2006, Redwood City, California.

Part

III

Image Space

CHRISTOPHER OAT

In this section we will cover a number of real-time, image space algorithms. Image space algorithms have many nice properties. In particular, their run-time cost is generally a function of screen resolution, which makes them scale nicely as graphics processors become more powerful. These techniques are also frequently easy to add to game engines as they require little to no engine modification; just some shader code and the ability to draw full screen quads. However, while screen-space techniques are often easy to implement and efficient to execute, these techniques can have a massive impact on the visual quality and style of a game. The articles in this section are devoted to post-processing using importance sampling, efficient motion blur, and flow-based image abstraction.

Image filtering shaders are often bottlenecked by their heavy use of texture fetch instructions. Our first article, "Efficient Post-Processing with Importance Sampling," by Balázs Tóth, László Szirmay-Kalos, and Tamás Umenhoffer, seeks to maximize the image quality of image space algorithms while minimizing the number of texture fetches they require. The authors supply several practical examples of this technique using popular image filtering applications such as tone mapping, depth of field, and ambient occlusion.

Motion blur is an important visual element that provides vital perceptual cues about an object's motion relative to the viewer. Motion blur is a critical component in offline CG movie making but its runtime costs remain a challenge to programmers looking to add this effect to their interactive applications. In "Efficient Real-Time Motion Blur for Multiple Rigid Objects," Ben Padget discusses an algorithm for image space motion blur that is highly efficient, both in terms of computation as well as memory consumption, while still providing nice visual results.

The final article in this section is "Real-Time Image Abstraction by Directed Filtering," by Jan Eric Kyprianidis and Jürgen Döllner. The authors present a real-time framework for converting ordinary images and videos into stylized illustrations.

This technique can be implemented entirely on the GPU making it suitable for use in real-time applications, such as games, which seek to provide a unique look to their virtual environments.

The popularity of real-time image space algorithms continues to grow. While choosing articles for this section it was challenging to neatly sort techniques into "image space" and "non-image space" categories. Increasingly, rendering algorithms that we may not typically think of as "image space" are adopting image space components. In addition to this section, I also encourage readers to investigate Section 6, "Global Illumination," which covers several global illumination, ambient occlusion, and subsurface scattering techniques that take advantage of screen-space computations.

3.1 Efficient Post-Processing with Importance Sampling

BALÁZS TÓTH, LÁSZLÓ SZIRMAY-KALOS, AND TAMÁS UMENHOFFER

INTRODUCTION

Texture filtering is critical to many rendering and post-processing methods. If we do it naively, the fragment shader needs to access texture memory many times to fetch values in the neighborhood of the processed texel. This article presents an efficient filtering algorithm that minimizes the number of texture fetches. The algorithm is based on *importance sampling* and exploits the bilinear filtering hardware. We also present applications in one, two, and three dimensions, such as *tone mapping with glow*, *depth of field*, and *real-time local ambient occlusion*.

PROBLEM STATEMENT

Many rendering and post-processing algorithms are equivalent to the evaluation of spatial integrals. The general form of a 2D image filter is

$$L'(X,Y) = \int_{-\infty}^{\infty} \int_{-\infty}^{\infty} L(X-x, Y-y) w(X,Y,x,y) dx dy$$

where $L'(X,Y)$ is the filtered value at pixel X,Y, $L(X,Y)$ is the original image, and $w(X,Y,x,y)$ is the filter kernel for this pixel. If the same filter kernel is used for all pixels, that is, when kernel w is independent of pixel coordinates X,Y, then the filter is *spatial-invariant*. For example, the spatial invariant 2D *Gaussian filter* of variance σ^2 has the following kernel:

$$w(x,y) = \frac{1}{2\pi\sigma^2} e^{-\frac{x^2+y^2}{2\sigma^2}}$$

259

The square root of the variance is called the *standard deviation* and is denoted by σ.

The integrals of the filter are usually approximated by finite sums:

$$L'(X,Y) \approx \sum_{i=-N/2}^{N/2} \sum_{j=-N/2}^{N/2} L(X-i,Y-j)w(i,j)$$

This discrete integral approximation requires the evaluation of N^2 kernel values, multiplications, and additions, which is rather costly when repeated for every pixel of the screen.

The computation cost can be reduced for spatial-invariant *separable* filters. In the case of separable filters the two-variate filter kernel can be expressed in a product form:

$$w(x,y) = w_x(x) \cdot w_y(y)$$

For spatial-invariant separable filters, the double integral can be computed in two passes. The first pass results in the following 2D function:

$$L_h(X,Y) \approx \sum_{i=-N/2}^{N/2} L(X-i,Y)w_x(i)$$

Then the resulting image is filtered again with a similar 1D filter, but in the vertical direction:

$$L'(X,Y) \approx \sum_{i=-N/2}^{N/2} L_h(X,Y-i)w_y(i)$$

With this trick the filtering cost of a pixel can be reduced from N^2 to $2N$ kernel evaluations and multiplications, which may still be too high in interactive applications.

THE APPROACH OF IMPORTANCE SAMPLING

In order to reduce the number of samples, instead of sampling the integration domain regularly, importance sampling takes more samples where the filter kernel is large. Let us consider the 1D convolution,

$$L'(X) = \int_{-\infty}^{\infty} L(X-x)w(x)dx$$

and find the integral $\tau(x)$ of the kernel and its inverse $x(\tau)$ so that the following conditions hold:

$$\frac{d\tau}{dx} = w(x),$$

that is,

$$\tau(x) = \int_{-\infty}^{x} w(t)dt$$

If kernel $w(t)$ is a probability density, that is, it is non-negative and integrates to 1, then $\tau(x)$ is non-decreasing, $\tau(-\infty) = 0$, and $\tau(\infty) = 1$. In fact, $\tau(x)$ is the *cumulative distribution function* of the probability density.

If filter kernel w is known, then $x(\tau)$ can be computed and inverted offline for a sufficient number of uniformly distributed sample points. Substituting the $x(\tau)$ function into the filtering integral we obtain

$$L'(X) = \int_{-\infty}^{\infty} L(X - x)w(x)dx = \int_{-\infty}^{\infty} L(X - x)\frac{d\tau}{dx}\,dx = \int_{\tau(-\infty)}^{\tau(\infty)} L(X - x(\tau))d\tau = \int_{0}^{1} L(X - x(\tau))d\tau$$

Approximating the transformed integral taking uniformly distributed samples in τ corresponds to a quadrature of the original integral taking M nonuniform samples in x. In one dimension we compute $x(\tau)$ for $\tau = 1/(2M), 3/(2M), \ldots, (2M-1)/(2M)$

$$L'(X) = \int_{0}^{1} L(X - x(\tau))d\tau \approx \frac{1}{M}\sum_{i=1}^{M} L\left(X - x\left(\frac{2i-1}{2M}\right)\right)$$

This way we take samples densely where the filter kernel is large and fetch samples less often farther away, but do not apply weighting (Figure 3.1.1).

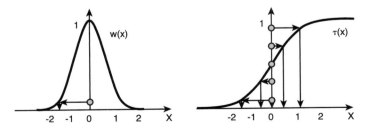

FIGURE 3.1.1   The kernel of the Gaussian filter of unit variance (left) and its cumulative distribution function $\tau(x) = \Phi(x)$. Sampling according to the inverse of this function is equivalent to taking uniform samples on the vertical abscissa and mapping it to the horizontal one.

The nonuniform sample positions are not necessarily on the grid, but may be in between the texel centers. Such samples can be obtained assuming the original function to be piece-wise linear and exploiting the texture filtering hardware to provide us with these interpolated values at no additional cost [Sigg05].

Note that nonuniform sampling allows us to use a smaller number of samples than uniform sampling ($M < N$) while providing the same accuracy. Nonuniform sampling does not access every texel in the neighborhood since far from the center of the filter kernel the weighting would eliminate the contribution anyway, so taking dense samples far from the center would be a waste of time.

The implementation of this approach is quite straightforward. Function $x(\tau)$ is computed by integrating the filter kernel and inverting the integral. For the Gaussian filter, $\tau(x)$ is the cumulative probability distribution function of the normal distribution, that is, the famous Φ-function, $\tau(x) = \Phi(x/\sigma)$ [Wikipedia]. Values of its inverse can be hardwired into the shader. For example, if $M = 5$, we need the following precomputed values:

$$x(1/10) = -1.282\sigma, \; x(3/10) = -0.524\sigma, \; x(5/10) = 0, \; x(7/10) = 0.524\sigma, \; x(9/10) = 1.282\sigma.$$

The fragment shader implementing this idea along one dimension is shown below. The shader gets the texture coordinates of the current fragment in Tex, and filters the input image stored in texture InputImage. The horizontal resolution of the image is HRES. The standard deviation σ of the Gaussian filter is passed in global variable sigma.

```
float4 FilterImportancePS(in float2 Tex : TEXCOORD0) : COLOR {
    float2 du1 = float2(0.524/HRES * sigma, 0);
    float2 du2 = float2(1.282/HRES * sigma, 0);
    float3 filtered = tex2D(InputImage, Tex - du2) +
                      tex2D(InputImage, Tex - du1) +
                      tex2D(InputImage, Tex) +
                      tex2D(InputImage, Tex + du1) +
                      tex2D(InputImage, Tex + du2);
    return float4(filtered/5, 1);
}
```

In one dimension, importance sampling takes an optimally uniform series $1/(2M), 3/(2M), \ldots, (2M-1)/(2M)$ in the unit interval, and transforms its elements with the inverse of the cumulative distribution (τ^{-1}) to obtain the nonuniform set of offsets for sampling. In two or higher dimensions the same concept is applied, but unfortunately we do not have the optimally uniform distribution of points in a unit square or in higher dimensional unit cubes. Regular grids, which repeat the same 1D series independently along the coordinate axes, get very nonuniform in higher dimensions (we have large gaps between the rows and columns). Better options are the *low-discrepancy series*, such as the *Halton* or *Hammersley* series, or we can also produce our own uniform sample set with an iterative relaxation algorithm. An initial set of points are put into an (arbitrary dimensional) cube, and we assume that points repel each other. By moving the points in the direction of the resulting force and repeating this step iteratively, a uniform distribution, the Poisson disc distribution, can be obtained.

In the following sections we present three applications for the discussed importance-based filtering scheme. Tone mapping and glow (also called bloom) require spatial-invariant Gaussian filtering, which can be executed as a pass of one-variate horizontal and then vertical filtering. Then depth of field is attacked, where the filter size is not spatial-invariant. Thus, the two dimensions cannot be simply separated, but we apply the 2D version of the discussed importance sampling scheme. Finally, a 3D example is taken, the low-variance computation of screen-space ambient occlusion.

Tone Mapping with Glow

Off-the-shelf monitors can only produce light intensity in a limited, *low dynamic range* (LDR). Therefore, the values written into the frame buffer are unsigned bytes in the range of [0x00, 0xff], representing values in [0,1], where 1 corresponds to the maximum intensity of the monitor. However, realistic rendering often results in *high dynamic range* (HDR) luminance values that are not restricted to the range of the monitors. The mapping of HDR image values to displayable LDR values is called *tone mapping* [Reinhard06]. The conversion is based on the luminance to which the human eye is adapted. Assuming that our view spans over the image, the adaptation luminance will be the average luminance of the whole image.

The main steps of tone mapping are as follows. The luminance value of every pixel is obtained with the standard CIE XYZ transform:

$$Y = 0.2126R + 0.7152G + 0.0722B$$

and these values are averaged to get adaptation luminance Y'. Since the human visual system is sensitive to relative differences rather than to absolute ones, the geometric average is computed instead of the arithmetic mean. The geometric average can be calculated by obtaining the logarithm of the pixel luminances, generating the arithmetic mean of these logarithms, and finally applying exponentiation. Having adaptation luminance Y', pixel luminance values Y are first mapped to relative luminance Y_r:

$$Y_r = \frac{\alpha Y}{Y'}$$

where α is a user-defined constant of the mapping, which is called the *key*. The relative luminance values are then mapped to displayable pixel intensities using the following function:

$$D = \frac{Y_r(1 + Y_r/Y_w^2)}{1 + Y_r}$$

where Y_w is another user-defined value representing the relative luminance that is expected to be mapped onto the maximum monitor intensity. Colors of relative luminance higher than Y_w will burn out.

Having the display luminance, the original $[R,G,B]$ data is scaled with it to provide color information $[r,g,b]$:

$$[r,g,b] = [R,G,B]\frac{D}{Y}$$

The user-defined key value controls where the average luminance is mapped in the $[0,1]$ region.

Glow or *bloom* occurs when a very bright object causes the neighboring pixels to be brighter than they would be normally. It is caused by scattering in the lens and other parts of the eye, giving a glow around the light and dimming contrast elsewhere. To produce glow, first we distinguish pixels where glowing parts are seen from the rest by selecting pixels where the luminance is significantly higher than the average. The HDR color of glowing parts is distributed to the pixels nearby, using a Gaussian blur, which results in a *glow map*. The glow map is added to the HDR image before tone mapping.

IMPLEMENTATION OF GLOW

Note that in this process we use Gaussian filtering during the computation of the glow map. The variance is constant; thus, this is a spatial-invariant separable filter, which can be realized by two 1D filtering steps, which can exploit the proposed importance sampling scheme, which fetches samples nonuniformly, but with a distribution specified by the cumulative distribution of the Gaussian.

Figure 3.1.2 shows a game scene rendered with this algorithm.

FIGURE 3.1.2   The Moria scene with tone mapping and glow.

DEPTH OF FIELD

Computer graphics algorithms usually apply the pinhole camera model, while real cameras have lenses of finite dimensions, which let through rays coming from different directions. As a result, parts of the scene are sharp only if they are located at a specific focal distance.

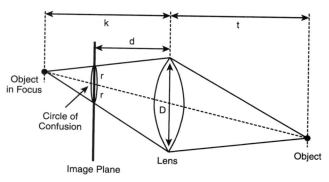

FIGURE 3.1.3 The computation of the circle of confusion.

According to geometric optics (see Figure 3.1.3), if the *focal length* of a lens is f and an object point is at distance t from the lens, then the corresponding image point will be in sharp focus on an image plane at distance k behind the lens, where f, t, and k satisfy the following equation:

$$\frac{1}{f} = \frac{1}{k} + \frac{1}{t}$$

If the image plane is not at a proper distance k from the lens of diameter D, but at distance d, then the object point is mapped not onto a point but onto a circle of radius r:

$$r = \frac{|k - d|}{k}\frac{D}{2}$$

This circle is called the *circle of confusion* corresponding to the given object point. It expresses that the color of the object point affects the color of not only a single pixel but all pixels falling into the circle.

A given camera setting can be specified by the *focal distance P*, which is the distance of those objects from the lens that appear in sharp focus on the image plane (note that the focal distance must not be confused with the focal length).

The focal distance and the distance of the image plane also satisfy the basic relation of the geometric optics:

$$\frac{1}{f} = \frac{1}{d} + \frac{1}{P}$$

Putting the three equations together, we obtain the following formula for the radius of the circle of confusion:

$$r = \left| \frac{1}{t} - \frac{1}{P} \right| \frac{Dd}{2}$$

According to this formula, the radius is proportional to the difference of the reciprocals of the object distance and of the focal distance. Since the projective transform and the homogeneous division translate camera space depth z to screen space depth Z, as $Z = a + b/z$, where a and b depend on the front and back clipping space distances (yet another camera parameter), the radius of the circle of confusion is just proportional to the difference of the object's depth coordinate and the focal distance, interpreting them in screen-space:

$$r = |Z - P'|S$$

where Z is the screen-space depth of the point, P' is the distance of the focal plane transformed to screen-space, and $S = Ddb/2$ is the camera's scaling parameter composed from the size of the lens, the distance of the image plane, and the front and back clipping plane distances.

This theory of depth of field describes the phenomenon from the point of view of object points projected onto the view plane. The power reflected by a point is distributed in a circle, usually nonuniformly, producing higher power density in the center. The affected region grows with the area of the circle, but the contribution to a particular point decreases proportionally. However, in rendering we take an opposite approach and should consider the phenomenon from the point of view of the pixels of the image. If we can assume that the depth is similar in the neighborhood to the depth of the current fragment, the colors of the neighborhood pixels should be blended with the current color, using a filter that decreases with the distance to a negligible value when the distance is greater than the radius of the circle of confusion. A good candidate for such filters is the Gaussian filter setting its standard deviation σ to the radius of the circle of confusion.

DEPTH-OF-FIELD IMPLEMENTATION

Depth-of-field simulation consists of two phases. In the first pass, the scene is rendered into textures of color and depth values. In the second pass, the final image is computed from the prepared textures with blurring. Blurring is performed using a variable-sized Gaussian filter since the variance (i.e., the circle of confusion) changes from pixel to pixel, making the filtering process not spatially invariant. Note that this prohibits us from replacing the 2D filtering with two 1D filtering phases. So we have to implement the method as a real 2D filtering scheme, which makes importance sampling even more indispensable. The depth-of-field shader should use 2D offset positions stored in a precomputed array, which is generated by the previously discussed importance sampling method. We have two options. On the one hand, we can exploit the separability of the 2D Gaussian filter and repeat the method proposed for 1D filtering to independently find the x and y coordinates of the sample locations. The other possibility is to replace Cartesian coordinates by polar coordinates r, ϕ in the filtering integral:

$$\int_{-\infty}^{\infty}\int_{-\infty}^{\infty} L(X-x,Y-y) \frac{1}{2\pi\sigma^2} e^{-\frac{x^2+y^2}{2\sigma^2}} dxdy = \int_{\phi=0}^{2\pi}\int_{r=0}^{\infty} L(X-r\cos\phi,Y-r\sin\phi) \frac{1}{2\pi\sigma^2} e^{-\frac{r^2}{2\sigma^2}} rdrd\phi$$

This filter can be separated to a filter for angles ϕ, where the filter kernel is constant $1/2\pi$ in the filtering domain $[0,2\pi]$, and to filter for radius r, where the filtering kernel is

$$w(r) = \frac{1}{\sigma^2} e^{-\frac{r^2}{2\sigma^2}} r$$

Since the filtering kernel of polar angle ϕ is constant, such samples are taken uniformly in the angular domain $[0,2\pi]$. Considering distance r, the cumulative distribution

$$\tau(r) = \int_0^r \frac{1}{\sigma^2} e^{-\frac{t^2}{2\sigma^2}} tdt = 1 - e^{-\frac{r^2}{2\sigma^2}}$$

can be analytically inverted:

$$r = \sigma\sqrt{-2\log(1-\tau)}$$

Despite the analytical expression, it is still worth precomputing the sample location offsets and passing them to the shader as a global variable (`filterTaps[i]` in the program below). This array is constructed by taking NUM_DOF_TAPS number of uniformly distributed (τ, υ) samples in the unit square, transforming them as $(\sqrt{-2\log(1-\tau)}, 2\pi\upsilon)$ to (r, ϕ) polar coordinate pairs, and finally obtaining the offset positions in Cartesian coordinates. The offset positions will be multiplied by the radius of the circle of confusion (σ) in the shader since this parameter varies from fragment to fragment.

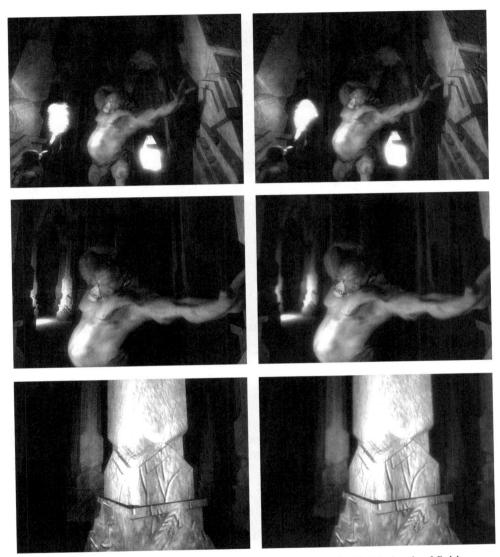

FIGURE 3.1.4 The Moria scene without (left) and with (right) depth of field.

The fragment shader gets the location of the current fragment and its depth value in screen coordinates, computes the circle of confusion radius `sizeCoC`, and scales the sample offset with this value. The original color image is fetched at the offset positions, and the colors are added up without any additional weighting.

```
float4 DepthBlurPS(in float2 Tex :TEXCOORD0): COLOR {
    float4 colorSum = tex2D(InputImage, Tex);      // Center sample
    float  depth = tex2D(depthMapSampler, Tex).a; // Current depth
    float sizeCoC = abs(depth - FOCAL_DISTANCE) * DOF_SCALE;
    for (int i = 0; i < NUM_DOF_TAPS; i++) {// Filter
        float2 tapCoord = Tex + filterTaps[i].xy * sizeCoC;
        colorSum += tex2D(InputImage, tapCoord);
    }
    return colorSum / (NUM_DOF_TAPS + 1); // Normalize
}
```

Note that this implementation assumes that the depth values are similar in the neighborhood as the depth of the current pixel. If this assumption fails, artifacts may show up, which can be reduced by skipping those candidate fragments where the depth difference is too large.

REAL-TIME OBSCURANCE AND AMBIENT OCCLUSION

The *obscurance* [Iones03] model approximates the indirect lighting at point $\check{X}$ of the scene by

$$L^i(\check{x}) \approx a(\check{x})W(\check{x})L^a$$

where a is the albedo, L^a is the ambient light intensity, and W is the obscurance value of the point, which expresses how open this point is for ambient illumination. A point is *open* in a direction if no occluder can be found close by. The obscurance value is defined by

$$W(\check{x}) = \frac{1}{\pi} \int \mu(d(\check{\omega})) \cos\theta d\omega$$

where d is the distance of the occluding surface in direction $\check{\omega}$ enclosing angle θ with the surface normal, and μ is a fuzzy measure of openness. If d is small, then the point is closed, and thus the fuzzy measure is small. If the distance is large, the point gets more open. We consider just a neighborhood of radius R, and assume the point to be totally open if the occluder is farther.

Ambient occlusion is a special case of this model that uses a clear, non-fuzzy distinction of open and closed directions [Hayden02]. If the occluder is closer than R, then the point is closed; otherwise it is open, which can be modeled by a step-like fuzzy membership function. However, better results can be obtained with smoother membership functions, as proposed by Mendez et al. [Mendez05]. For example, $\mu(d) = \sqrt{d/R}$ works well in practice.

The evaluation of the directional integral of the obscurance formula requires rays to be traced in many directions, which is rather costly. The expensive ray tracing operation can be replaced by a simple containment test if neighborhood R is small enough to allow the assumption that the ray intersects the surface at most once in the R-interval. This imposes restrictions on the surface curvature.

In order to find an efficient method for the evaluation of obscurance, we express it as a 3D integral. First, the fuzzy measure is expressed as

$$\mu(d) = \int_0^d \frac{d\mu(r)}{dr} \, dr = \int_0^R \frac{d\mu(r)}{dr} \, \epsilon(d-r)dr$$

where $\epsilon(r)$ is the step function, which is 1 if r is not negative and zero otherwise. Substituting this integral into the obscurance formula we get

$$W(\tilde{x}) = \int_\Omega \int_0^R \frac{d\mu(r)}{dr} \frac{\cos\theta}{\pi} \epsilon(d-r)drd\omega$$

Let us consider a ray of equation $\tilde{x} + \tilde{\omega}r$ where the shaded point is the origin, $\tilde{\omega}$ is the direction, and distance r is the ray parameter. If we assume that the ray intersects the surface at most once in the R-neighborhood, then ϵ $(d\text{-}r)$ is equivalent to the condition that the ray has not intersected the surface yet. If it has not intersected the surface, and other objects are far, then this condition is equivalent to the visibility of the sample point $\tilde{x} + \tilde{\omega}r$, which can be checked using the content of the z-buffer [Mittring07] (Figure 3.1.5). Note that this integral is a filtering scheme where we filter the 0, 1 values of visibility indicator ϵ with the following kernel:

$$W(r, \tilde{\omega}) = \frac{d\mu(r)}{dr} \frac{\cos\theta}{\pi}$$

This filter is the product of a density $d\mu(r)/dr$ of distances and density $\cos\theta/\pi$ of ray directions.

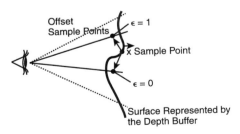

Offset Sample Points
$\epsilon = 1$
x Sample Point
$\epsilon = 0$
Surface Represented by the Depth Buffer

FIGURE 3.1.5 The idea of replacing ray tracing with visibility tests using the content of the depth buffer as a sampled representation of the surface.

IMPLEMENTATION OF REAL-TIME OBSCURANCE

To construct the nonuniform locations representing the filter kernel, we start with point set [τ, υ,ξ], which is uniformly distributed in a 3D unit cube, and transform the uniform distribution to mimic the filtering kernel. As the first step of the transformation, two coordinates [τ, υ] are transformed to a direction that has cosine distribution. Let us consider a unit radius sphere centered at the considered point. The sphere intersects the tangent plane *xy* in a circle. If we take points in a unit radius circle uniformly, and then map the points up onto the sphere, we get samples with a cosine distribution. In order to generate uniformly distributed points in a unit radius circle, we take values τ, υ and transform them linearly from [0,1] to [−1,1]. The two scalars are considered as *x,y* coordinates of a 2D point, and it is checked whether the point is inside the unit radius circle. If not, this pair is rejected, and another pair is taken until we get a point that is really in the circle, and finally project it up to the unit sphere.

After we find a cosine distributed direction, distance *r* is sampled with density $d\mu(r)/dr$. If we take the third coordinate ξ of the uniform 3D point set, $r = \mu^{-1}(\xi)$ will have exactly the required density. Sample points generated this way are stored in a global array OFFSET. These points correspond to translations in the tangent space.

During runtime, the post-processing filter computes obscurance from the depth buffer (depthMap) storing camera space *z* values. The shader gets the current point's texture coordinates (Tex) and its projection onto the first clipping plane (Dir). From the projection and the stored depth, the point is reconstructed in camera space. The shader program transforms the offsets of OFFSET to camera space (cOff) and translates the camera space point with them, obtaining sampleCPos in camera space and then by projection transformation sampleSPos in screen-space. The visibility of the translated point is checked by projecting it onto the screen and comparing its depth to the depth obtained in the direction of the translated point. If the sample point passes the depth test, then the value 1 is added to the filtered variable; otherwise, the variable is not changed. Note that to transform the offsets from tangent space to camera space we need the camera space normal vector of the current point. We can store these normals in the first three channels of the texture depthMap storing depth values.

```
float4 SSAOPS(in float2 Tex : TEXCOORD0, // pixel coords in [0,1]
          in float4 Dir : TEXCOORD1, // on front clipping plane
             ) : COLOR {
    float depth = tex2D(depthMap, Tex).a;  // camera space depth
    Dir.xyz /= Dir.w;
```

```
float3 Pos = Dir.xyz * depth / Dir.z; // camera space location
float3 T, B, N;                        // Determine tangent space
N = tex2D(depthMap, Tex).rgb;          // camera space normal
T = cross(N, float3(0, 1, 0));
B = cross(N, T);
float3x3 TangentToView = float3x3(T, B, N);


float occ = 0;
for(int k = 0; k < NUM_SAMPLES; k++) {
    // Transform offsets from tangent space to camera space
    float3 cOff = mul(OFFSET[k].xyz, TangentToView) * R;
    float3 sampleCPos = cPos + cOff; // pos in camera space


    // Compute screen coordinates
    float4 sampleCPos = mul(float4(sampleCPos, 1), projMatrix);
    float2 sampleSPos = sampleCPos.xy / sampleCPos.w;
    sampleSPos.y *= -1;
    sampleSPos = (sampleSPos + 1.0) * 0.5;


    // Read depth buffer
    float sampleDepth = tex2D(depthMap, sampleSPos).a;


    // Compare sample depth with depth buffer value
    if(sampleDepth >= sampleCPos.z)          occ++;
    else if(sampleCPos.z - sampleDepth > R) occ++;
}
occ = occ / NUM_SAMPLES; // Normalize
return occ * tex2D(InputImage, Tex); // Compose with shaded image
}
```

If the offsets are generated from different uniform values in neighboring pixels, then noise would show up. The same samples would make the error correlated and replace noise with "stripes." Unfortunately, both stripes and pixel noise are quite disturbing. In order to reduce the error without taking an excessive number of samples, we can apply *interleaved sampling*, that is, different uniform series in the pixels of a 4×4 pixel pattern, and repeat the same sample structure periodically. The errors in the pixels of a 4×4 pattern are uncorrelated, and can be successfully reduced by an averaging of the same size. With this trick, 16 samples are enough to generate smooth results (see Figure 3.1.6).

FIGURE 3.1.6 The Rocky Scene and the Space Station Scene rendered with classical ambient reflection model $a(\breve{x})L^a$ (top row), obscurance only (middle row), and using the obscurance reflection model $a(\breve{x})W(\breve{x})L^a$. The obscurance values are generated from 16 samples per pixel in real-time, and are smoothed by interleaved sampling.

COMPARISONS TO UNIFORM SAMPLING

In order to demonstrate the power of importance sampling, we also implemented the depth-of-field algorithm and the obscurance computation using uniform sampling.

Depth of field with uniform samples   Depth of field with importance sampling

FIGURE 3.1.7 Comparison of uniform sampling and importance sampling in the depth-of-field algorithm.

The reference depth-of-field algorithm takes uniform pixel samples from a regular grid. Figure 3.1.7 compares its results to the image obtained with importance sampling. In both cases we took only nine samples per pixel, and the frame rates were also similar. Note that the regular sampling pattern becomes visible in the reference algorithm, creating stripe-like artifacts, which are successfully eliminated by importance sampling.

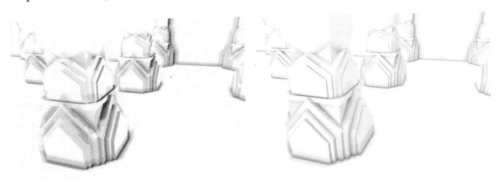

Obscurance with uniform samples   Obscurance with importance sampling

FIGURE 3.1.8 Comparison of uniform sampling and importance sampling in the obscurance method using the square root membership function.

Figure 3.1.8 shows the advantages of importance sampling in obscurance computation using the square root membership function proposed by Mendez. The reference image on the left is obtained by uniform directions and distances. In order to show the differences, we turned interleaved sampling off and took 32 samples per pixel.

CONCLUSION

This article presents a method to improve the efficiency of filtering algorithms and three applications to demonstrate the power of the method. The first application is a separable Gaussian filtering used for tone mapping and glow. The second application is a spatial-variant 2D-filter-producing depth-of-field effect. The final application filters in 3D and provides real-time ambient occlusion. A real-time demo is implemented using DirectX 9.

ACKNOWLEDGMENTS

This work was completed in the framework of the GameTools project (www.game-tools.org/) and supported by OTKA ref. No. T042735 of the Hungarian Academy of Sciences.

REFERENCES

[Sigg05] C. Sigg and M. Hadwiger. Fast Third-Order Texture Filtering. In *GPU Gems 2: Programming Techniques for High-Performance Graphics and General-Purpose Computation*, Matt Pharr (ed.), Addison-Wesley, 2005. pp. 313–329.

[Wikipedia] Normal distribution. http://en.wikipedia.org/wiki/Normal_distribution

[Reinhard06] E. Reinhard, G. Ward, S. Pattanaik, and P. Debevec. *High Dynamic Range Imaging*. Morgan Kaufmann, 2006.

[Iones03] A. Iones, A. Krupkin, M. Sbert, and S. Zhukov. Fast realistic lighting for video games. *IEEE Computer Graphics and Applications*, Vol. 23, No 3, 2003. pp. 54–64.

[Hayden02] L. Hayden. *Production-Ready Global Illumination*. SIGGRAPH Course notes 16. 2002.

[Mendez05] A. Mendez, M. Sbert, J. Cata, N. Sunyer, and S. Funtane. Real-time Obscurances with Color Bleeding. In *ShaderX⁴: Advanced Rendering Techniques*, Wolfgang Engel (ed.) Charles River Media. 2005. pp. 121–134.

[Mittring07] Martin Mittring. Finding Next Gen - CryEngine 2. In *Advanced Real-Time Rendering in 3D Graphics and Games Course*, Siggraph 2007. pp. 97–121.

3.2 Efficient Real-Time Motion Blur for Multiple Rigid Objects

BEN PADGET, ROCKSTAR GAMES, SAN DIEGO

INTRODUCTION

Motion blur is an important visual effect in many types of games. It adds a perceptual cue that indicates an object's motion relative to other scene elements and increases realism. Many different techniques for simulating motion blur have been developed over the years. One approach, described in [Green03], performs motion blur on a per-object basis. This produces good-quality results, but the cost can be prohibitive if the number of moving objects in the scene is high. A better solution is to decouple the cost of the blur from the number of objects in the scene. This can be achieved by computing the motion blur as a post-process effect. In this type of implementation, a velocity buffer is used to store screen-space velocity at each pixel [Shimizu03]. Each pixel in the scene image is then blurred along its corresponding screen-space velocity vector. By performing motion blur as a post-process, the cost is dependent only on screen resolution and thus is decoupled from scene complexity. Generating a velocity buffer requires extra memory and either the use of multiple render targets or two draw passes of the scene geometry. By restricting the motion blur to operating at an object level, we can do away with the velocity buffer and compute per-pixel velocity vectors in the same shader that does our blurring.

The technique described here removes the need for a velocity buffer, thus eliminating the cost of both generating and storing a velocity buffer. In practice this roughly doubles the speed of the effect and reduces memory cost to zero. However, since we store a single velocity vector for each object in the scene, this technique is not suited for articulated characters or other situations where different parts of an object can have different velocities. Since this technique is a post-process effect, transparent objects are not handled well. Each pixel in the frame buffer can only have one object ID, so semitransparent objects will either blur with the background or blur the background with themselves.

OVERVIEW

Consider a scene with no moving objects in it. In this situation motion blur will result only from camera movement. One way to blur this scene would be to compute the previous frame buffer position for each pixel in the scene and use that to generate a screen-space velocity vector that is then used for blurring. To compute the previous frame position, the previous frame's composite matrix is downloaded into a pixel shader constant. We then compute the world space position from the screen coordinates and the depth of each pixel. This world position is then transformed by the previous frame's composite matrix to obtain the previous frame's screen position. This technique was first described in [Rosado07].

This technique can easily be extended to handle a number of moving objects. The first step is to assign each object an integer ID. When the object is drawn, this ID is written to the stencil buffer. When we have finished rendering scene geometry, we download the previous frame matrix of each object into a pixel shader constant. We then run our motion blur shader on the entire frame. The pixel shader reads the object indices from the stencil buffer and uses those to index into the array of previous frame matrices we downloaded. This is used to generate a screen-space velocity for each pixel, and we then blur the scene with this vector. The number of objects that can be handled in this manner is restricted only by the number of available pixel shader constants.

CPU-SIDE WORK

The CPU is responsible for managing the object IDs and computing the previous frame composite matrices. Each object stores its previous frame composite matrix, which it caches after rendering itself. These are then registered with a class responsible for managing the blur object IDs, which stores the previous frame composite matrix and returns an object ID. The object then writes this object ID to the stencil buffer when it renders. After all scene objects have been rendered, the array of previous frame matrices is uploaded to pixel shader constant memory on the GPU.

GPU-SIDE WORK

The motion blur is rendered at the end of the frame as a post-process effect. The first task of the pixel shader is to reconstruct the world space position of the current pixel. To compute this we use the normalized screen-space coordinates along with the current depth. Once we have the current world position of the pixel, we read the object ID of the current pixel from the stencil buffer and use this to index into the array of previous frame matrices. Then we transform the world position by the previous frame matrix to get the previous frame screen position of the pixel. We then subtract this from the previous frame position to get the velocity vector of the pixel and blur along this vector.

```
float depth = tex2D(DepthMapSampler, texCoord);

float stencil = tex2D(StencilSampler, texCoord);


float4x4 prevMtx = PrevFrameMotionBlurMtxs[stencil];


float3 screenPos = float3(IN.texCoord.xy * FrameBufferSize.xy,
                          1.0f - depth);


float4 woldPos4 = mul(float4(screenPos, 1.0f),
                      WorldViewProjInverse);

worldPos.xyz /= worldPos4.w;


float4 oldScreenPos = mul(float4(worldPos4.xyz, 1.0f), prevMtx);

oldScreenPos.xy /= oldScreenPos.w;


float2 blurDir = screenPos.xy - oldScreenPos.xy;

blurDir /= FrameBufferSize.xy;
```

BLURRING AND HALO FIXING

Once we have determined the pixel velocity, we use it to blur the scene. We do this by averaging the colors of the pixels along the velocity vector. There are several different approaches to performing the blur. It is possible to dynamically alter the number of blur samples at each pixel according to the length of the velocity vector. This leads to a lower cost in areas where there is little blur happening. The savings can be significant in applications where the camera is stationary or slow moving.

One potential problem with post-process motion blur is that objects with different velocities will blend with one another. Depending on the application, this may be undesirable. If your camera is slow moving or stationary in the scene, blending moving objects with the background will generally look realistic. However, when the camera is tracking a moving object, this blending between objects can lead to artifacts. The movement of the camera will cause the background geometry to blur (see Figure 3.2.1). When the background geometry is blurred, it will sample pixels belonging to the tracked object. This will result in a blurry halo around the tracked object. Since the object that the camera is tracking is stationary within the frame one would expect a crisp edge around it.

FIGURE 3.2.1 A moving background with a static object (left) leads to object and background pixels blending together. A moving object against a static background (right) looks correct when this happens.

The halos are fairly easy to fix since we already have objects tagged. When the pixel shader is collecting blur samples, we simply discard samples that come from a different object than the current one we are processing.

```
float3 sampleAverage = 0.0f;

for (int i = 0; i < numSamples; i++)
{
        float2 currentVel = pixelVelocity * (i+1);
        float2 texCoord = IN.texCoord0.xy + currentVelocityStep;

        float3 sample0 = tex2D(QuarterSizeMap,
                        IN.texCoord0.xy+currentVel);
        float stencilVal0 = tex2D(StencilSampler,
                        IN.texCoord0.xy + currentVel);
        float stencilDist0 = stencilVal0-basePixelStencil;
        stencilDist0 = stencilDist0 < 1.0f ? 0 : stencilDist0;
```

```
    float3 sample1 = tex2D(QuarterSizeMap,
                    IN.texCoord0.xy-currentVel);
    float stencilVal1 = tex2D(StencilSampler,
                      IN.texCoord0.xy-currentVel);
    float stencilDist1 = stencilVal1-basePixelStencil;
    stencilDist1 = stencilDist1 < 1.0f ? 0 : stencilDist1;


    sampleAverage += float4(sample0*stencilDist0,
                    stencilDist0);
    sampleAverage += float4(sample1*stencilDist1,
                    stencilDist1);
}
float3 finalColor = sampleAverage.xyz / sampleAverage.w;
```

A side effect of the halo-fixing step is that it creates a hard edge between objects with different velocities (see Figure 3.2.2). This artifact is exacerbated if the blur is performed on a lower-resolution target to increase performance. This causes the hard halo-fixed edges to exhibit pixel artifacts equal in size to the low-resolution target. In practice, however, these are not visually disturbing since they only occur on objects that are moving quickly across the screen.

FIGURE 3.2.2   Halo fixing leads to crisp edges around objects in the scene. This looks correct for a static object against a moving background (left) but less correct for a moving object against a static background (right).

INTEGRATION WITH A POST-PROCESSING PIPELINE

This method of blurring is well suited for integration into an existing post-process pipeline. In our implementation we reuse a half-resolution frame buffer texture that has been previously generated. Depth of field could also be combined into the same pixel shader as the motion blur.

COPING WITH HARDWARE LIMITATIONS

The motion blur technique described above requires a GPU that is capable of indexing into constant registers in the pixel shader. If your platform is not capable of this, you can store the object matrices in a 1D floating-point texture.

Platforms that do not grant general stencil buffer read access to pixel shaders can instead put object IDs into the alpha channel of the frame buffer. If you use this method, it may become necessary to draw alpha-blended objects twice, once normally and then again to fill the frame buffer alpha channel with the correct value. Alternatively, an additional render target can be used to avoid extra passes over alpha-blended objects.

CONCLUSION

Replacing a velocity map implementation of motion blur with the method presented here has many advantages, but there are some tradeoffs. This method is best suited for rigid objects, such as cars, because it records a single velocity vector for each object. The technique is very fast, however. Adding velocity vector calculation to the same shader as the blurring makes sense from a performance standpoint, since the velocity vector calculation consists mainly of arithmetic instructions, and the blurring operation relies on numerous texture reads. In practice, we achieved performance of just under two milliseconds for the entire blur operation on an Xbox 360 running in 720p resolution.

ACKNOWLEDGMENTS

I would like to thank Wolfgang Engel, Thomas Johnston, Raymond Kerr, and Steve Reed for discussing this motion blur technique with me and for providing their valuable insights.

REFERENCES

[Shimizu03] Clement Shimizu, Amit Shesh, Baoquan Chen, "Hardware Accelerated Motion Blur Generation," University of Minnesota Computer Science Department Technical Report 2003, available online at www.dtc.umn.edu/~ashesh/our_papers/motion-blur.pdf

[Green03] Simon Green, "Stupid OpenGL Shader Tricks," Games Developers Conference 2003, available online at http://developer.nvidia.com/docs/IO/8230/GDC2003_OpenGLShaderTricks.pdf

[Rosado07] Gilberto Rosado, "Motion Blur as a Post-Processing Effect," *GPU Gems 3*, Hubert Nguyen, ed., Addison Wesley Professional, 2007

3.3 Real-Time Image Abstraction by Directed Filtering

JAN ERIC KYPRIANIDIS AND JÜRGEN DÖLLNER

FIGURE 3.3.1 An image abstracted using our framework.
Left: Original image (Copyright Anthony Santella). Right: Abstracted result.

INTRODUCTION

In this chapter we present a framework of automatic image processing techniques that create high-quality, simplified, stylistic illustrations from color images, videos, and 3D renderings. Our method extends the approach of [Winnemöller06] to use iterated bilateral filtering for abstraction and Difference-of-Gaussians (DoG) for edge detection. We present enhancements to these techniques to improve the quality of the output by adapting them to the local orientation of the input.

To smooth low-contrast regions while preserving edges, we present a fast separable implementation of the bilateral filter. Our approach works by aligning the bilateral filter with the local structure of the image. The first pass filters in the direction of the gradient, and the second pass filters in the direction of the tangent. To extract salient edges, we present a fast two-pass algorithm. A 1D DoG filter is applied in the direction of the gradient, followed by a second pass that applies smoothing along flow curves that are derived from the local structure of the image. Both techniques require a smooth vector field that represents local orientation. We show how such a vector field can be computed from the eigenvectors of the smoothed structure tensor. Besides gradient calculation, only linear separable smoothing with a box or Gaussian filter is necessary.

A schematic overview of our framework is shown in Figure 3.3.2. Input is typically an image, a frame of a video, or the output of a 3D rendering. We start with the construction of the flow field by calculating the structure tensor. The structure tensor is then smoothed, and the eigenvector corresponding to the local tangent direction is stored in a texture map. Then the input is iteratively abstracted by using the orientation-aligned bilateral filter. We perform a total of n_a iterations. We apply color quantization to the result. After $n_e < n_a$ iterations, we extract edges from the intermediate result using the separable flow-based DoG filter. In our examples we use n_α and $n_a = 4$. Finally, the extracted edges are superimposed on the output of the color quantization.

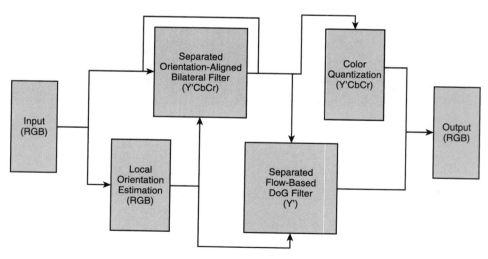

FIGURE 3.3.2   Overview of our abstraction framework.

COLOR SPACE CONVERSION

Our framework uses different color spaces. The flow field construction is performed in RGB color space. This has the advantage that the computation is not affected by noise that may be introduced through color space conversion.

Applying the bilateral filter in RGB color space may result in unwanted color bleeding artifacts [Tomasi98]. Therefore, a color space that separates luminance and chrominance should be used. In our previous work [Kyprianidis08] as well as in [Winnemöller06], the CIE-Lab color space is used. For simplicity, we use the Y'CbCr color space here, which is a popular standard in the television industry. Conversion from RGB to Y'CbCr can be performed using the following matrix whose coefficients are based on the ITUR BT.601 specification:

$$
\begin{pmatrix} Y' \\ C_b \\ C_r \end{pmatrix} = \begin{pmatrix} 0.299 & 0.587 & 0.114 \\ -0.169 & 0.331 & 0.500 \\ 0.500 & -0.419 & 0.081 \end{pmatrix} \cdot \begin{pmatrix} r \\ g \\ b \end{pmatrix}
$$

The inverse transform from RGB to Y'CbCr is given by

$$
\begin{pmatrix} r \\ g \\ b \end{pmatrix} = \begin{pmatrix} 1 & 0 & 1.402 \\ 1 & -0.344 & 0.714 \\ 1 & 1.772 & 0 \end{pmatrix} \cdot \begin{pmatrix} Y' \\ C_b \\ C_r \end{pmatrix}
$$

Color space conversion is only necessary before bilateral filtering and during the final composition step, where the detected edges are superimposed on the output of the color quantization.

FLOW FIELD CONSTRUCTION

The basic idea behind flow field construction is to find a local direction in which the rate of change is minimized. Our approach is based on the eigenvalues of the structure tensor [van Vliet95]. To make full use of RGB color information during computation, we combine it with Di Zenzo's multi-image gradient method [Cumani89]. Let $f(x,y)$ denote the RGB color value of the input image at pixel (x,y). We begin by calculating an approximation to the directional derivatives in the x- and y-directions using the Sobel filter:

$$
\begin{aligned}
f_x(x_0,y_0) = &-f(x_0 - 1, y_0 - 1) - 2f(x_0 - 1, y_0) - f(x_0 - 1, y_0 + 1) \\
&+ f(x_0 + 1, y_0 - 1) + 2f(x_0 + 1, y_0) + f(x_0 + 1, y_0 + 1)
\end{aligned}
$$

$$f_y(x_0,y_0) = -f(x_0 - 1, y_0 - 1) - 2f(x_0, y_0 - 1) - f(x_0 + 1, y_0 - 1)$$
$$+ f(x_0 - 1, y_0 + 1) + 2f(x_0, y_0 + 1) + f(x_0 + 1, y_0 + 1)$$

The structure tensor at (x_0, y_0) is then given by

$$(g_{ij})(x_0,y_0) = \begin{pmatrix} E & F \\ F & G \end{pmatrix} = \begin{pmatrix} \langle f_x(x_0,y_0), f_x(x_0,y_0) \rangle & \langle f_x(x_0,y_0), f_y(x_0,y_0) \rangle \\ \langle f_x(x_0,y_0), f_y(x_0,y_0) \rangle & \langle f_y(x_0,y_0), f_y(x_0,y_0) \rangle \end{pmatrix}$$

The induced quadratic form measures the squared rate of change of f in a certain direction. We are interested in the extremal values and the corresponding directions. From linear algebra we know that the extremal values are given by the square roots of the eigenvalues:

$$\lambda_{1,2} = \frac{E + G \pm \sqrt{(E - G)^2 + 4F^2}}{2}$$

The corresponding eigenvectors are

$$v_1 = \begin{pmatrix} F \\ \lambda_1 - E \end{pmatrix} \qquad v_2 = \begin{pmatrix} \lambda_1 - G \\ F \end{pmatrix}$$

Since the structure tensor is a symmetric positive semidefinite matrix, the eigenvalues are non-negative real numbers and are orthogonal to each other. The eigenvector points in the direction of maximum change. The eigenvector points in the direction of the minimum rate of change.

By calculating the eigenvectors v_2 for every point of an image, we get a vector field that is aligned to local edge orientation, as shown in Figure 3.3.3a. Unfortunately, this vector field has discontinuities, and, accordingly, tracing its flow curves does not give good results. In order to smooth the vector field, we apply smoothing to the structure tensor. The smoothing of the structure tensor is a linear operation, but the effect on the eigenvector field is highly non-linear. Vectors of higher magnitude and vectors that point in similar directions get more weight. Also, vectors pointing in the opposite direction do not cancel out. The effect on the vector field is similar to the non-linear edge tangent flow filter (ETF) from [Kang07]. The advantage of our approach is that it only requires linear separable smoothing. That means the filter can be implemented as two passes, reducing the computational complexity from $O(r^2)$ to $O(r)$ per pixel. Furthermore, our approach creates good results without requiring multiple iterations. The result of applying a 5×5 Gaussian filter is shown in Figure 3.3.3b. Even better results can be achieved using a 7×7 or 9×9 Gaussian filter.

 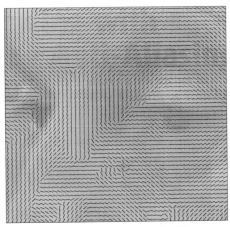

(a) Without Smoothing   (b) Smoothed with 5x5 Gaussian Filter

FIGURE 3.3.3 Tangent field induced by the structure tensor.
(a) Before smoothing. (b) After smoothing.

Our implementation uses three rendering passes to construct the flow field. In the first pass we calculate the gradients and the structure tensor. The structure is stored as a triple (E,F,G) in a temporary texture (Listing 3.3.1). The second pass takes this temporary texture as input and applies a 1D Gaussian filter with kernel [14641] in the horizontal direction (Listing 3.3.2). The third pass applies the Gaussian filter in the vertical direction and then calculates the eigenvector v_2 (Listing 3.3.3). Our algorithms require a normalized direction. We therefore store the normalized eigenvector in the first and second component and the length of the eigenvector in the third component of the texture map. We refer to this texture as the tangent flow map (tfm).

Listing 3.3.1 Fragment shader for calculating the structure tensor

```
uniform sampler2D img;

void main (void) {
    ivec2 uv = ivec2(gl_FragCoord.xy);
    vec4 c = texelFetch2D(img, uv, 0);

    vec4 u = (
            -1.0 * texelFetch2D(img, uv + ivec2(-1, -1), 0) +
```

```
                   -2.0 * texelFetch2D(img, uv + ivec2(-1,  0), 0) +
                   -1.0 * texelFetch2D(img, uv + ivec2(-1,  1), 0) +
                   +1.0 * texelFetch2D(img, uv + ivec2( 1, -1), 0) +
                   +2.0 * texelFetch2D(img, uv + ivec2( 1,  0), 0) +
                   +1.0 * texelFetch2D(img, uv + ivec2( 1,  1), 0)
                   ) / 4.0;

        vec4 v = (
                   -1.0 * texelFetch2D(img, uv + ivec2(-1, -1), 0) +
                   -2.0 * texelFetch2D(img, uv + ivec2( 0, -1), 0) +
                   -1.0 * texelFetch2D(img, uv + ivec2( 1, -1), 0) +
                   +1.0 * texelFetch2D(img, uv + ivec2(-1,  1), 0) +
                   +2.0 * texelFetch2D(img, uv + ivec2( 0,  1), 0) +
                   +1.0 * texelFetch2D(img, uv + ivec2( 1,  1), 0)
                   ) / 4.0;

        gl_FragColor = vec4(vec3(dot(u.xyz, u.xyz),
                                 dot(v.xyz, v.xyz),
                                 dot(u.xyz, v.xyz)), 1.0);
    }
```

Listing 3.3.2 Fragment shader for smoothing the structure in the horizontal direction

```
    uniform sampler2D img;

    void main (void) {
        ivec2 uv = ivec2(gl_FragCoord.xy);
        gl_FragColor = vec4(vec3(
            1.0/16.0 * texelFetch2D(img, uv + ivec2(0, -2), 0).xyz +
            4.0/16.0 * texelFetch2D(img, uv + ivec2(0, -1), 0).xyz +
            6.0/16.0 * texelFetch2D(img, uv + ivec2(0,  0), 0).xyz +
            4.0/16.0 * texelFetch2D(img, uv + ivec2(0,  1), 0).xyz +
            1.0/16.0 * texelFetch2D(img, uv + ivec2(0,  2), 0).xyz
        ), 1.0);
    }
```

Listing 3.3.3 Fragment shader for smoothing the structure in the vertical direction and calculation of the flow field

```
uniform sampler2D img;

void main (void) {
    ivec2 uv = ivec2(gl_FragCoord.xy);

    vec3 g = vec3(
        1.0/16.0 * texelFetch2D(img, uv + ivec2(-2, 0), 0).xyz +
        4.0/16.0 * texelFetch2D(img, uv + ivec2(-1, 0), 0).xyz +
        6.0/16.0 * texelFetch2D(img, uv + ivec2( 0, 0), 0).xyz +
        4.0/16.0 * texelFetch2D(img, uv + ivec2( 1, 0), 0).xyz +
        1.0/16.0 * texelFetch2D(img, uv + ivec2( 2, 0), 0).xyz
    );

    float lambda1 = 0.5 * (g.y + g.x +
            sqrt(g.y*g.y - 2.0*g.x*g.y + g.x*g.x + 4.0*g.z*g.z));
    vec2 d = vec2(g.x - lambda1, g.z);

    gl_FragColor = (length(d) > 0.0)?
        vec4(normalize(d), sqrt(lambda1), 1.0) :
        vec4(0.0, 1.0, 0.0, 1.0);
}
```

ORIENTATION-ALIGNED BILATERAL FILTER

The bilateral filter is a non-linear filter that smoothes images while preserving edges [Paris07]. It is based on two weighting functions. The first one gives more weight to pixels that are close to the filter center, and the second one gives more weight to pixels whose colors are similar to the color at the filter's center. This has the effect that regions of similar color are smoothed, while regions with detail are preserved.

For an image f, the bilateral filter is defined by

$$\frac{\displaystyle\sum_{x\in\Omega(x_0)} f(x)G_{\sigma_d}(\|x - x_0\|)G_{\sigma_r}(\|f(x) - f(x_0)\|)}{\displaystyle\sum_{x\in\Omega(x_0)} G_{\sigma_d}(\|x - x_0\|)G_{\sigma_r}(\|f(x) - f(x_0)\|)}$$

where x_0 denotes the center of the filter neighborhood $\Omega(x_0)$. For the closeness function G_{σ_d} and the similarity function G_{σ_r}, we use 1D Gaussian functions with standard deviation σ:

$$G_\sigma(t) = \frac{1}{\sqrt{2\pi\sigma}}\exp\left(\frac{t^2}{2\sigma^2}\right)$$

To achieve a non-linear diffusion effect, the bilateral filter must be applied recursively. We are therefore interested in a fast computation of the bilateral filter. Computing the bilateral filter is expensive because it is not separable. A simple implementation requires evaluation of the full kernel. Several acceleration schemes have been presented in the research literature. A very simple approach is to perform a brute-force separation [Pham05]. Unfortunately, this results in horizontal and vertical artifacts, especially when applied recursively.

By aligning the xy-separable bilateral filter [Pham05] with the local orientation, these horizontal and vertical artifacts can be avoided. The first pass filters in the gradient's direction, and the second pass filters in the tangent's direction (Figure 3.3.4). A comparison of our approach with other methods is shown in Figure 3.3.5.

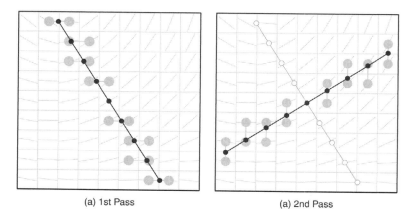

(a) 1st Pass   (a) 2nd Pass

FIGURE 3.3.4   Orientation-aligned bilateral filter. Gray points indicate sampling positions that are linearly interpolated. (a) First pass filters in the direction of the gradient. (b) Second pass filters in the direction of the tangent.

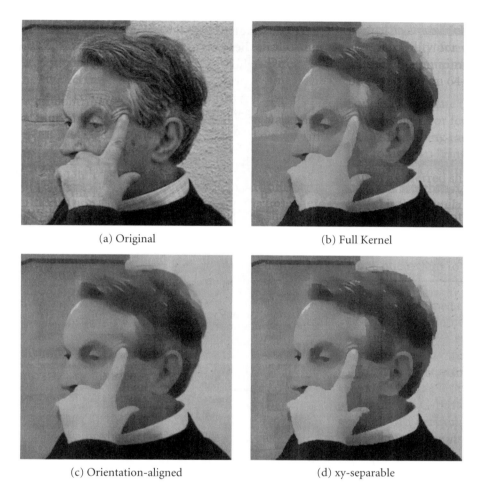

(a) Original   (b) Full Kernel

(c) Orientation-aligned   (d) xy-separable

FIGURE 3.3.5   Comparison of different bilateral filter implementations ($\sigma_d = 3.0$, $\sigma_r = 4.25\%$).

This approach requires sampling along the two directions. Simply sampling with unit-step length would result in nonuniformly distributed samples when the nearest texture filtering is used. In the case of bilinear texture filtering, the four neighboring pixels would be averaged. This is undesirable for the bilateral filter, since it would result in smoothing of pixels lying on different sides of an edge. A possible solution would be to implement a custom "bilateral" bilinear texture filtering in the shader. Since this would both make the shader more complex and require more texture lookups, we use a different approach that allows us to use the built-in bilinear texture filtering unit of the GPU.

We perform sampling in gradient and tangent directions using a constant step vector that has unit size along either the *x* or *y* axis. When used with bilinear texture filtering, this results in two neighboring pixels being linearly interpolated. This is shown in Figure 3.3.4, where the gray points indicate the sampling positions. A positive side effect of this approach is that we get anti-aliasing on the edge boundaries. The step length can easily be calculated using the intercept theorem, as illustrated in Figure 3.3.6. Our fragment shader implementation is shown in Listing 3.3.4.

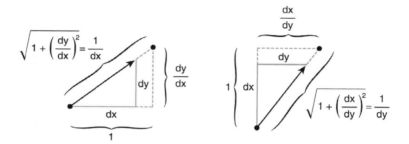

FIGURE 3.3.6 Calculation of the step length for the orientation-aligned bilateral filter using the intercept theorem.

Listing 3.3.4 Fragment shader for the orientation-aligned bilateral filter

```
uniform sampler2D img;
uniform sampler2D tfm;
uniform int pass;
uniform float sigma_d;
uniform float sigma_r;

void main (void) {
    float twoSigmaD2 = 2.0 * sigma_d * sigma_d;
    float twoSigmaR2 = 2.0 * sigma_r * sigma_r;
    vec2 uv = gl_TexCoord[0].xy;

    vec2 t = texture2D(tfm, uv).xy;
    vec2 dir = (pass == 0)? vec2(t.y, -t.x) : t;
    vec2 dabs = abs(dir);
    float ds = 1.0 / ((dabs.x > dabs.y)? dabs.x : dabs.y);
```

```
dir /= textureSize2D(img, 0);

vec3 center = texture2D(img, uv).rgb;
vec3 sum = center;
float norm = 1.0;

float halfWidth = 2.0 * sigma_d;
for (float d = ds; d <= halfWidth; d += ds) {
    vec3 c0 = texture2D(img, uv + d * dir).rgb;
    vec3 c1 = texture2D(img, uv - d * dir).rgb;
    float e0 = length(c0 - center);
    float e1 = length(c1 - center);

    float kerneld = exp( - d *d / twoSigmaD2 );
    float kernele0 = exp( - e0 *e0 / twoSigmaR2 );
    float kernele1 = exp( - e1 *e1 / twoSigmaR2 );
    norm += kerneld * kernele0;
    norm += kerneld * kernele1;

    sum += kerneld * kernele0 * c0;
    sum += kerneld * kernele1 * c1;
}
sum /= norm;
gl_FragColor = vec4(sum, 1.0);
}
```

Separable Flow-Based Difference-of-Gaussians

Edges are extracted from the luminance channel after n_e iterations of the bilateral filter. In our examples we typically use a single iteration. This preprocessing is required to avoid the detection of edges that are due to noise.

The Marr and Hildreth edge detector [Marr80] works by computing the Laplacian-of-Gaussian and detecting the zero crossings in the result. The Laplacian-of-Gaussian can be approximated as the difference of two Gaussians.

This variant is called Difference-of-Gaussians (DoG):

$$\sum_{x \in \Omega(x_0)} G_{\sigma_e}(\|x - x_0\|) - \tau \cdot G_{\sigma_{e'}}(\|x - x_0\|)$$

The parameter $\sigma_{e'}$ is set to $1.6 \cdot \sigma_e$ to approximate the Laplacian-of-Gaussian; τ controls the sensitivity of the edge detection. For smaller values, τ detects less noise, but important edges may be missed. We use $\tau = 0.99$ in our examples.

DoG edges look frayed and don't reproduce straight line or curve segments very well (Figure 3.3.7a). By construction, the gradient points in the direction of maximum rate of change. Thus, if a point lies on an edge, it is most likely found in the direction of the gradient, and applying a 1D DoG filter in this direction gives the maximum filter response. Because of this insight, the DoG filter is replaced by a flow-guided anisotropic filter in [Kang07]. Compared to DoG edges, these Flow-based Difference-of-Gaussians (FDoG) edges create more coherent lines.

(a) Isotropic DoG   (b) Separable flow-based DoG

FIGURE 3.3.7 Comparison of isotropic DoG vs. separable flow-based DoG.

Comparable high-quality results can be achieved by a separable implementation with corresponding reduced computational complexity (Figure 3.3.7b). During the first pass a 1D DoG filter in the gradient's direction is applied. This is followed by a second pass that applies smoothing along the streamlines of the flow field and performs thresholding (Figure 3.3.8).

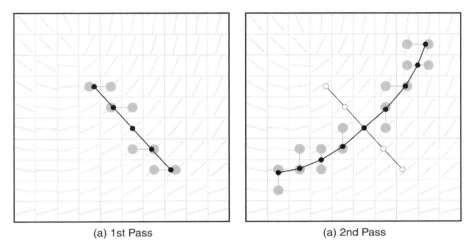

(a) 1st Pass   (a) 2nd Pass

FIGURE 3.3.8   Separable flow-based DoG. Gray points indicate sampling positions that are linearly interpolated. (a) First pass filters in the direction of the gradient. (b) Second pass filters along the flow curves induced by the tangent field.

To evaluate the 1D DoG filter in the direction of the gradient, we use the same approach as described in the previous section. The corresponding fragment shader implementation is shown in Listing 3.3.5.

Listing 3.3.5 Fragment shader for the first pass of the separable flow-based DoG filter

```glsl
uniform sampler2D img;

uniform sampler2D tfm;

uniform float sigma_e;

uniform float sigma_r;

uniform float tau;


void main() {
    float twoSigmaESquared = 2.0 * sigma_e * sigma_e;

    float twoSigmaRSquared = 2.0 * sigma_r * sigma_r;

    vec2 uv = gl_TexCoord[0].xy;
```

```
vec2 t = texture2D(tfm, uv).xy;
vec2 n = vec2(t.y, -t.x);
vec2 nabs = abs(n);
float ds = 1.0 / ((nabs.x > nabs.y)? nabs.x : nabs.y);
n /= vec2(textureSize2D(img, 0));


vec2 sum = texture2D( img, uv ).xx;
vec2 norm = vec2(1.0, 1.0);


float halfWidth = 2.0 * sigma_r;
for( float d = ds; d <= halfWidth; d += ds ) {
    vec2 kernel = vec2( exp( -d * d / twoSigmaESquared ),
                        exp( -d * d / twoSigmaRSquared ));
    norm += 2.0 * kernel;


    vec2 L0 = texture2D( img, uv - d*n ).xx;
    vec2 L1 = texture2D( img, uv + d*n ).xx;


    sum += kernel * ( L0 + L1 );
}
sum /= norm;


float diff = 100.0 * (sum.x - tau * sum.y);
gl_FragColor = vec4(vec3(diff), 1.0);
}
```

To average the calculated filter response, we apply a 1D Gaussian filter along the streamlines induced by the flow field. To calculate the sampling positions we adapt the approach for sampling along a line, but in this case the situation is more complex. At every sampling position, a new step direction and a new step length must be calculated. The step direction is calculated using the eigenvector v_2. Since v_2 does not define a particular direction, the direction with the smaller change in orientation is chosen. By construction, only linear interpolation between two neighboring pixels is necessary. The eigenvector v_2 is sampled using nearest-neighbor filtering. Figure 3.3.9 illustrates the calculation of the step length for the case dx < dy.

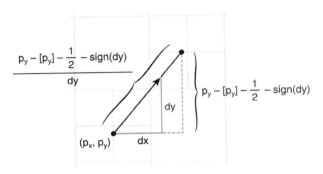

FIGURE 3.3.9 Figure calculation of the step length for the separable flow-based DoG filter illustrated for the case $dx < dy$.

As a final step, thresholding is applied. We use the smooth step function approach described in [Winnemöller06]. Instead of the tanh function, we use the smoothstep function:

$$T(h) = \begin{cases} 1 & h > 0 \\ 2\text{smoothstep}\,(2,2,\varphi_e \cdot h) & h \leq 0 \end{cases}$$

The parameter φ_e controls the sharpness of the edge output. To smooth aliasing artifacts caused by thresholding, we optionally process the thresholded output using a 3×3 Gaussian filter. Our fragment shader implementations are shown in Listings 3.3.6 and 3.3.7.

Listing 3.3.6 Function for flow curve step calculation

```
struct lic_t {
    vec2 p;        // current position
    vec2 t;        // previous tangent
    float w;       // total length
    float dw;      // length of current step
};

void step(inout lic_t s) {
    vec2 t = texture2D(tfm, s.p).xy;
    if (dot(t, s.t) < 0.0) t = -t;
```

```
        s.t = t;

        s.dw = (abs(t.x) > abs(t.y))?
            abs((fract(s.p.x) - 0.5 - sign(t.x)) / t.x) :
            abs((fract(s.p.y) - 0.5 - sign(t.y)) / t.y);

        s.p += t * s.dw / textureSize2D(tfm, 0);
        s.w += s.dw;
    }
```

Listing 3.3.7 Fragment shader for the second pass of the separable flow-based DoG filter

```
uniform sampler2D img;
uniform sampler2D tfm;
uniform float sigma_m;
uniform float phi;

void main (void) {
    float twoSigmaMSquared = 2.0 * sigma_m * sigma_m;
    float halfWidth = 2.0 * sigma_m;
    vec2 uv = gl_TexCoord[0].xy;

    float H = texture2D( img, uv ).x;
    float w = 1.0;

    lic_t a, b;
    a.p = b.p = uv;
    a.t = texture2D( tfm, uv ).xy / textureSize2D(tfm, 0);
    b.t = -a.t;
    a.w = b.w = 0.0;
```

```
while (a.w < halfWidth) {

    step(a);

    float k = a.dw * exp(-a.w * a.w / twoSigmaMSquared);

    H += k * texture2D(img, a.p).x;

    w += k;

}

while (b.w < halfWidth) {

    step(b);

    float k = b.dw * exp(-b.w * b.w / twoSigmaMSquared);

    H += k * texture2D(img, b.p).x;

    w += k;

}

H /= w;


float edge = ( H > 0.0 )?

            1.0 : 2.0 * smoothstep(-2.0, 2.0, phi * H );

gl_FragColor = vec4(vec3(edge), 1.0);

}
```

COLOR QUANTIZATION

For color quantization, we use a simplified version of the approach described in
[Winnemöller06]. Suppose that c is the input color in Y'CbCr color space, and
nbins is the number of quantization levels. To avoid a sharp transition between
different quantization levels, we use the smoothstep function as shown in the following code:

```
float qn = floor(c.x * float(nbins) + 0.5) / float(nbins);

float qs = smoothstep(-2.0, 2.0, phi_q*(c.x - qn) * 100.0)-0.5;

float qc = qn + qs / float(nbins);
```

The parameter phi_q controls the smoothness of the transition. In our examples
we use phi_q = 3.4, which results in a cartoon-like effect.

CONCLUSIONS

We presented a framework of image processing techniques that can be used for real-time image abstraction. A smooth vector field whose flow curves follow salient image features can be constructed from the eigenvalues of the smoothed structure tensor in a highly efficient way. Aligning the filter to the local structure can increase the quality of the xy-separable bilateral filter. Flow-based DoG filtering can be implemented as a separable algorithm. It outperforms the classical DoG filter in quality and is efficient to compute. Source code for a sample application is provided on the DVD-ROM accompanying this book.

ON THE DVD

ACKNOWLEDGMENTS

The authors would like to thank Pascal Barla, Tassilo Glander, Stefan Maaß, Haik Lorenz, and Christian Richardt and for their comments, Matthias Trapp for helpful discussions about GPU programming, and the section editor, Christopher Oat, for his support. This work was supported by the German Research Foundation (DFG), grant DO 697/5-1.

REFERENCES

[Cumani89] Cumani, A., "Edge Detection in Multispectral Images," Technical report, Istituto Elettrotecnico Nazionale "Galileo Ferraris" (1989).

[Kang07] Kang, H., Lee, S., and Chui, C. K., "Coherent line drawing," *Proc. ACM NPAR* (2007): pp. 43–50.

[Kyprianidis08] Kyprianidis, J. E., and Döllner, J., "Image abstraction by structure adaptive filtering," *Proc. EG UK Theory and Practice of Computer Graphics* (2008): pp. 51–58

[Marr80] Marr, D., Hildreth R. C., "Theory of edge detection," *Proc. Royal Society London* 207 (1980): pp. 187–217.

[Paris07] Paris S., Kornprobst P., Tumblin J., and Durand F., "A gentle introduction to bilateral filtering and its applications," ACM SIGGRAPH courses (2007).

[Pham05] Pham, T. Q., and van Vliet, L., "Separable bilateral filtering for fast video preprocessing," IEEE International Conference on Multimedia and Expo (2005).

[Tomasi98] Tomasi, C., and Manduchi, R., "Bilateral filtering for gray and color images," *Proc. International Conference on Computer Vision* (1998): pp. 839–846.

[van Vliet95] van Vliet L., Verbeek P., "Estimators for orientation and anisotropy in digitized images," *Proc. ASCI, Conference of the Advanced School for Computing and Imaging*, Heijen (1995): vol. 95, pp. 16–18.

[Winnemöller06] Winnemöller, H., Olsen, S. C., and Gooch, B., "Real-time video abstraction," *ACM Transactions on Graphics* (2006): Vol. 25, no. 3, 1221–1226.

Part IV | Shadows

SAM MARTIN

You should at least consider it curious that the highly specific subject of "shadows" continues to play such a major part in current graphics research. Although the problem is as old as the computer graphics industry itself, anyone who has attempted to use a modern shadowing solution will tell you that the problem of real-time shadowing is not yet adequately solved. The evils of aliasing, the complications of soft shadowing, greedy memory consumption, and heavy rendering costs— they still conspire to disappoint artists the world over.

But is the situation really all that gloomy? Well, no. Shadows are indeed proving to be a tough subject but regular advances in the field have arrived at a comforting rate, and in this section of the book you will find both consolidation and innovation.

Amongst a sea of alternatives, cascaded shadow maps [Engel06] [Zhang07] is one technique that has found a warm reception amongst developers for its practicality and effectiveness. A successful implementation is not without its challenges and it is this topic that Fan Zhang, Alexander Zapriagaev, and Allan Bentham address head-on in the article, "Practical Cascaded Shadow Maps."

The effects of fluids and gases on light transport are frequently neglected, but Chris Wyman and Shaun Ramsey describe an approach to modelling their influence in, "A Hybrid Method for Interactive Shadows in Participating Media."

High-dynamic range environment maps can provide a particularly effective and natural means of lighting a scene. The lighting can be computed dynamically with spherical harmonics as in [Ramamoorthi01], but this ignores the effect of visibility. If the geometry can be assumed to be static, then the visibility information can be precomputed [Sloan02], but efficient handling of dynamic geometry is still an active field of research. Mark Colbert and Jaroslav Křivánek present a novel algorithm for environment lighting with dynamic visibility in "Real-Time Dynamic Shadows for Image-Based Lighting."

The notable main alternative to the splitting approach used in cascaded shadow maps are warped projections, such as [Stamminger02]. Ray Tran presents a new technique for harnessing the benefits of both camps through a novel hybrid in "Facetted Shadow Mapping for Large Dynamic Game Environments."

REFERENCES

[Engel06] Wolfgang Engel, "Cascaded Shadow Maps", ShaderX⁵, 2006

[Zhang07] Fan Zhang, Hanqiu Sun, Leilei Xu and Le Kit Lun, "Parallel-split shadow maps for large-scale virtual environments", ACM VRCIA'06

[Stamminger02] Stamminger, Marc and George Drettakis, "Perspective Shadow Maps", ACM SIGGRAPH 2002

[Ramamoorthi01] Ravi Ramamoorthi, Pat Hanrahan, "An Efficient Representation for Irradiance Environment Maps" ACM SIGGRAPH 2001

[Sloan02] Peter-Pike Sloan, Jan Kautz, and John Snyder, "Precomputed Radiance Transfer for Real-Time Rendering in Dynamic, Low-Frequency Lighting Environments", ACM SIGGRAPH 2002

4.1 Practical Cascaded Shadow Maps

FAN ZHANG, ALEXANDER ZAPRJAGAEV, ALLAN BENTHAM

INTRODUCTION

Like any other visual effect in real-time applications, practical shadow algorithms should allow developers to trade cost and quality. Although it is a popular real-time shadowing technique, *shadow mapping* [Williams78] cannot achieve this goal in complicated scenes, because it does not adequately trade performance cost for quality. Numerous extensions to this algorithm have been developed toward achieving this goal. *Cascaded shadow maps* (CSMs) [Engel06][Forsyth05] are an example of such an extension and have recently been attracting more attention with graphics hardware becoming more powerful. This technique can handle the *dueling frusta* case in shadow mapping, in which the light and view directions are nearly opposite. Furthermore, unlike warping algorithms [Stamminger02][Wimmer04][Martin04], CSMs do not require careful tuning and special tricks to handle extreme cases. We note that a similar idea was independently developed by Zhang et al. in the concurrent work on *parallel-split shadow maps* (PSSMs) [Zhang07][Zhang06]. This paper does not differentiate between the papers, as the basic idea is the same.

Although the prototyping of CSMs is quite simple, integrating CSMs into real games requires us to carefully consider several issues, some of which were not mentioned in the original CSM algorithm. This article discusses practical implementation issues of CSMs, which we have experienced in the Unigine project (see Figure 4.1.1), outlined as follows.

FIGURE 4.1.1 Cascaded shadow maps in Unigine.

- **Flickering of shadow quality:** This problem is also referred to as *swimming*, which exists in all view-dependent shadow-mapping techniques. To improve available shadow map texture resolution, a popular method is to focus the shadow map on visible objects. Such view-dependent processing can result in different rasterizations in consecutive frames. The flickering of shadow quality is thus perceived. To see this artifact, please refer to the video on the accompanying DVD-ROM. This article presents two methods to handle this issue.

- **Storage strategy:** In CSMs, shadow map textures can be stored in a variety of ways. For example, the most intuitive way is to store each shadow map in a separate texture. However, this storage strategy places considerable demand on the available interpolators. As a result, it is not an ideal choice for complex shading systems that already require a large number of simultaneous textures. Therefore, we should choose the storage strategy that best suits the requirements of the project. This article presents a detailed discussion of different strategies.

- **Non-optimized split selection:** The *practical split scheme* proposed by Zhang et al. [Zhang07] provides a practical solution for choosing the corresponding shadow map for a given pixel being rasterized. However, in some extreme cases such as when the light and view directions are nearly parallel, this scheme is not optimal. This article presents the solution we used in the Unigine project.

- **Correct computation of texture coordinates:** In typical CSM implementations, the vertex shader feeds all possible texture coordinates to the pixel shader for texture lookup. An alternative is to output the world-space position from the vertex shader. The pixel shader computes the texture coordinates from this world-space position after the split index is determined. The major advantage of this alternative is only using a single interpolator. However, as we will explain in this article, this method is mathematically incorrect because it results in an incorrect interpolation during rasterization.

- **Filter across splits:** A filtering operation is usually needed in shadow mapping to produce anti-aliased shadows. A recent development in this field is *prefiltering* (i.e., filtering happens before depth comparison) the shadow map texture by exploiting the built-in filtering capabilities available on graphics hardware. This is made possible by the insightful ideas presented in literature on Variance Shadow Maps (VSMs) [Donnelly06][Lauritzen07b][Lauritzen08], Convolution Shadow Maps (CSMs) [Annen07], and Exponential Shadow Maps (ESMs) [Salvi07] [Annen08]. Though these filtering methods and CSMs are orthogonal, combining them requires careful consideration of discontinuity at split positions. This article explains how this problem occurs and presents two solutions.

The remainder of this article details each of the above issues and provides a summary.

FLICKERING OF SHADOW QUALITY

The flicking issue results from different rasterizations of the shadow maps as frames lapse, and is visually represented by the swimming of the shadow quality. Figure 4.1.2 illustrates the flickering problem in a scene containing a static light and a moving observer. Notice the degradation of quality between the two consecutive frames. Such a large change between two consecutive frames causes this degradation to be very noticeable to the user. Ideally, if such degradation is unavoidable, it should happen gradually.

FIGURE 4.1.2   Flickering issue. The shadow quality significantly changes between two consecutive frames, in which the light is static and the observer is moving.

Here we have an important note: Resolving the flickering issues for any given shadow map resolution will still not help reduce the spatial aliasing. In other words, the flickering issue aggravates the spatial aliasing in sequential frames. If a low-resolution shadow map produces jaggy shadows in a static frame, even if you handle the flickering issue when the light and/or viewer is moving, the jaggy shadow boundaries will not be sharp because spatial aliasing requires more dense sampling rates. The solutions to the flickering issue presented in this section just make your shadow quality view-independent.

To better understand how different rasterizations could aggravate the flickering issue, we demonstrate a few representative scenarios in Figure 4.1.3. This figure shows you how a point of interest (denoted by the red dot) is rasterized into texture pixels (denoted by green dots).

- **Scale:** In the top case in the figure, when the texel size (usually measured in the world space) of the shadow map changes in the next frame, the texel corresponding to the point of interest is now different. The shadow-testing result thus might be different from that in the previous frame. We refer to this case as the *scale problem*.

- **Offset:** The middle case illustrates different rasterizations of the point of interest, which is caused by a sub-texel offset due to the limited precision of the floating numbers. Note that this case happens almost every time your camera is changed. The reason is that transforming a point from the object space to the texture space (by vector-matrix multiplication) always results in a loss of precision. We refer to this case as the *offset problem*.

- **Scale + offset:** In practice, scale and offset problems usually happen together, as shown in the bottom case. To increase the available shadow map resolution, a popular and useful preprocessing technique is to focus the shadow map on the bounding shape (illustrated by the axis-aligned bounding box) of visible objects (simply represented by the view frustum). As we can see, due to the instability of the bounding box, when the viewer is moving, the shadow map can be significantly changed such that both the scale and offset problems simultaneously occur.

We present two methods to remove the flickering effect between different rasterizations. Each of them has its disadvantages and advantages. Depending on if shadows are required to be filtered or not, you can choose one of these methods as the solution to this problem in your project. Our solutions to the flickering issue are intended to make your shadow rasterization view-independent. The spatial aliasing caused by insufficient shadow map resolution needs to be handled separately.

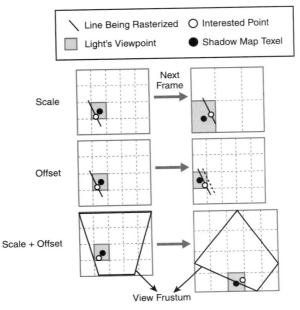

FIGURE 4.1.3   Three example scenarios of the flickering problem.
Top row: Varying of the texel size (i.e., scale problem).
Middle row: Sub-texel offset (i.e., offset problem).
Bottom row: Focusing the shadow map on the bounding box
of the view frustum results in both scale and offset problems.

EXACT SOLUTION

As explained earlier, an exact solution to the flickering needs to solve both scale and offset problems. In such exact solutions [Valient07] (see Figure 4.1.4), each shadow map is focused on the split's bounding sphere rather than the split's bounding box. The symmetric characteristic of the sphere removes the scale problem, because the shadow map size (in the world space) is now stabilized. Furthermore, to avoid the offset problem, the light's position is accordingly adjusted in the world space such that the sphere center is contained by the center of the shadow map. As a reference, we show the pseudo code for this solution in Listing 4.1.1.

The advantage of this solution is that flickering is correctly removed, as shown in Figure 4.1.5. On the other hand, although the flickering problem is well handled, a considerable portion of shadow map resolution is wasted. More importantly, most modern games use filtering techniques to help anti-aliasing; an approximate solution to the flickering issue is usually enough because a slight flickering will be hidden by filtering anyway. Finally, warping algorithms cannot use this solution due to the nonuniform texel distribution.

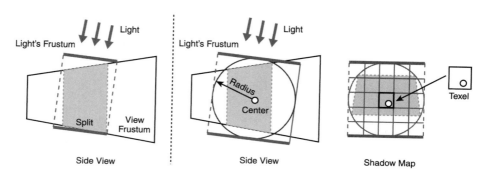

FIGURE 4.1.4 Left: Typical CSM implementations focus each shadow map on the axis-aligned bounding box in the light's post-perspective space. Right: Exact solutions focus each shadow map on the bounding sphere of the corresponding split (left), and fix the position of the sphere center (measured by the texel size) in world space.

Listing 4.1.1 Exact solution to the flickering issue

```
//Step 1: calculate the light basis

vector3 direction = normalize(WORLD.getColumn3(2)); //z axis of the light
coordinates system

vector3 side = normalize(WORLD getColumn3(1)); //x axis of the light
coordinates system

vector3 up = normalize(WORLD. getColumn3(0));  //y axis of the light
coordinates system

// Update all splits

for(int i = 0; i < numSplits; i++){ //'numSplits' is the number of spWlits

    // Step 2: calculate the bounding sphere' bs' of each split 'split[i]'

    Sphere bs = CalculateBoundingSphere(split[i]);

    // get the sphere center's position in world space

    vector3 center = INVWORLDVIEW * bs.getCenter();

    //get the sphere radius

    float radius = bs.getRadius();

    // adjust the sphere's center to make sure it is transformed into the
center of the shadow map

    float x = ceilf(dot(center,up) * sizeSM / radiu) * radius / sizeSM; //
'sizeSM' is texture size

    float y = ceilf(dot(center,side) * sizeSM / radius) * radius / sizeSM;
```

```
center = up * x + side * y + direction * dot(center,direction);


    // Step 3: update the split-specific view matrix 'matrixView[i]' and
projection matrix 'matrixProjection[i]'
    matrixProjections[i] = MatrixOrthoProjection(-radius,  radius,
radius, -radius, near, far);
    vector3 origin = center – direction * far; // get the light's position
    matrixView[i] = MatrixLookAt(origin, center, up);

}
```

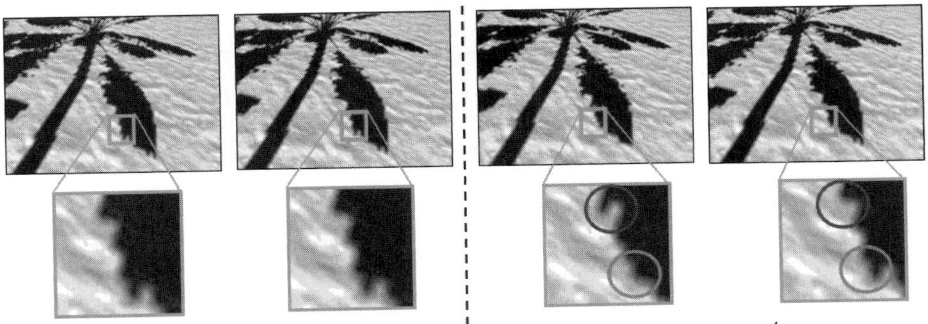

frame N   frame N+1   frame N   frame N+1

FIGURE 4.1.5   Comparison of shadow quality. Left: The shadows stay the same in two successive frames using the exact solution. Right: Flickering issue occurring in the original CSM implementation. The differences are marked by colored circles.

APPROXIMATED SOLUTION

As we have pointed out above, the main disadvantage of the exact solution is that a large amount of shadow map resolution is wasted. The reason is simple: The sphere is not the best approximation of the view frustum from the light's viewpoint. In many situations, it is not acceptable to sacrifice texture resolution *purely* to prevent flickering. An approximate solution that allows more efficient use of the texture resolution may be more desirable.

Let's revisit the flickering issue from a mathematical view. During the rasterization of the shadow map, every fragment's position is *quantized* in terms of the *measure unit*—the texel size. If the position is quantized differently across two frames, the offset problem happens. Therefore, removal of the offset problem requires stabilizing the quantization of positions relative to the frustum. Likewise, in order to avoid the scale problem, the same requirement is needed for the *scale value*—the change of texel size. In exact solutions, the texel size (in world space) stays the same due to the symmetry of the sphere; that is, the scale value is always 1.

To quantize the scale value, we assume the scale value varies smoothly in successive frames. This assumption is valid in many cases. With this assumption, we can quantize the scale value into a *pre-defined* range of discrete levels (see Figure 4.1.6). In our experiments, we empirically found 64 to be a good candidate for this. Quantization of offset values in exact and approximated solutions is the same. Pseudo code for the approximated solution is shown in Listing 4.1.2.

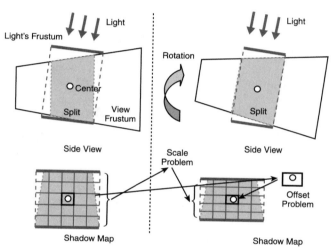

FIGURE 4.1.6 Approximated solution. The left and right columns show two frames before and after, respectively, of a slight rotation of the view frustum.

This solution results in much better utilization of shadow map resolution and much better shadow quality when combined with filtering techniques. On the other hand, the disadvantage is that, without filtering there is a possibility that some minor flickering may still occur.

Listing 4.1.2 Approximated solution to the flickering issue

```
// calculate the scale values

// Notes: in the light's post-perspective space, both width and height of
the view port are 2. The dimension of the shadow map for a specific split
is the bounding coordinates of the split's corner points in this space.
'maxX' and 'minX' stand for the maximum and minimum x values respectively.
'maxY' and 'minY' stand for the maximum and minimum y values respectively.
```

```
float scaleX = 2.0f / (maxX - minX); // scale value for x dimension
float scaleY = 2.0f / (maxY - minY); // scale value for y dimension
//the scale values will be quantized into 64 discrete levels
float scaleQuantizer = 64.0f;
// quantize scale
scaleX = 1.0f / ceilf(1.0f / scaleX * scaleQuantizer) * scaleQuantizer;
scaleY = 1.0f / ceilf(1.0f / scaleY * scaleQuantizer) * scaleQuantizer;


// calculate offset values
float offsetX = -0.5f * (maxX + minX) * scaleX; // offset value for x
dimension
float offsetY = -0.5f * (maxY + minY) * scaleY; // offset value for y
dimension
// quantize offset
float halfTextureSize = 0.5f * sizeSM;
offsetX = ceilf(offsetX * halfTextureSize) / halfTextureSize;
offsetY = ceilf(offsetY * halfTextureSize) / halfTextureSize;
```

STORAGE STRATEGY

The original CSM algorithm does *not* impose any restriction on how to store shadow maps. These textures can be stored in separate textures [Zhang07][Engel06], packed into a single texture atlas [Valient07][Lloyd06], encapsulated into a cube map [Zhang07], or directly stored in a texture array on modern GPUs [Zhang07]. Packing CSMs into an atlas texture (see Figure 4.1.7) reserves more texture samplers for other purposes. Considering this, our project uses this strategy.

Variant storage strategies of CSMs are discussed below.

- **Texture arrays:** According to our experiments, storing CSMs in a texture array [Zhang07] works well on NVIDIA Geforce 8xxx graphics cards. However, sampling texture arrays is only supported by Direct3D 10.1 or above.

- **Cube maps:** In this method, additional shader instructions are needed for the lookup of texture coordinates and simulating the border color addressing mode [Zhang07]. Furthermore, if the number of splits is small (a typical setting is four), there's a waste of video memory because this method always allocates six shadow maps.

- **Multiple textures:** The simplest way is to store each shadow map in a separate texture [Zhang06]. This method, however, makes it difficult to implement filtering techniques (e.g., percentage closer filtering [PCF]) on DX9-level hardware because it requires the support of texture arrays. More importantly, considering that DX9-level hardware supports up to 16 textures, this method is not very suitable for complicated shading systems that use a large number of textures simultaneously.

- **Texture atlas:** In this method, all shadow maps are packed into a single large texture. Although the maximum texture size allowed by hardware imposes a restriction on the atlas resolution, this method brings a few practical advantages.
  - Working equally on DX9 and DX10 hardware.
  - Very efficient usage of video memory, especially when four splits are used.
  - Reserving more texture samplers for other purposes.
  - Filtering CSMs can be done in a single rendering pass.

With the above observations, the atlas strategy has become more and more popular in modern games. The default setting in Unigine uses four splits, which is enough in most cases. Although we are limited by maximum texture dimension (e.g., 2048×2048 on PS 2.0 hardware), in our experiments the shadow quality is far better *and* more robust than that of warping techniques with the same texture resolution. We show the pseudo code for computing texture coordinates in the atlas strategy in Listing 4.1.3.

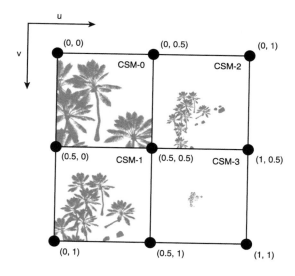

FIGURE 4.1.7 An example of the texture atlas containing four shadow maps. Texture coordinates for corner points of each shadow map are given also.

NON-OPTIMIZED SPLIT SELECTION

The original CSM algorithm uses the eye's view-space depth to select the shadow map for every pixel being rasterized. This method works well in the most general cases. However, once the light becomes almost parallel with the view direction, the shadow map selected for the current point might *not* be optimal. For example, consider a point p in the second split as shown in Figure 4.1.8. It is covered by all three shadow maps. On the other hand, in order to get the highest shadow quality at this position, we should choose the first (rather than the second) shadow map.

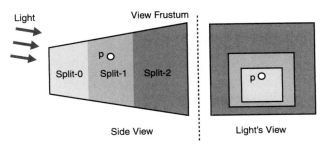

FIGURE 4.1.8   The best split index selection for p is 0 rather than 1 in the original CSMs.

An optimized split-selection schema in this case is illustrated in Figure 4.1.9. When the angle between the light direction and view direction is very small, the standard split selection wastes a lot of texture resolution. To further improve shadow quality in such cases, we always select the shadow map with higher resolution. The pixel shader in Listing 4.1.3 illustrates how to achieve this goal using the atlas strategy.

Listing 4.1.3 Pixel shader for the optimized split selection in the atlas strategy

```
//Note: 4 shadow maps are stored into an atlas as shown in Figure 4.1.4. '
matrixWorld2Texture[4]' stores texture matrices, 'PS_Input.world_position'
stores the world position in the input of pixel shader.


float shadow = 0.0;
// get the potential texture coordinates in the first shadow map
float4 texcoord = mul(matrixWorld2Texture[0], PS_Input.world_position);
```

```
// projective coordinates
texcoord.xyz = texcoord.xyz / texcoord.w;
// see Figure 4.1.4, if the range of x and y locates in [0, 0.5], then
this point is contained by the 1st SM
if(max(abs(texcoord.x - 0.25),abs(texcoord.y - 0.25)) >= 0.25) {
        // if this point is not contained by the 1st SM, then do the same
test for the 2nd SM
        // see Figure 4.1.4,  0<=x<=0.5 and 0.5<=y<=1 for the 2nd SM.
        texcoord = mul(matrixWorld2Texture[1], PS_Input.world_position);
        texcoord.xyz = texcoord.xyz / texcoord.w;
        if(max(abs(texcoord.x - 0.25),abs(texcoord.y - 0.75)) >= 0.25) {
                //test for the 3rd SM in which  0.5<=x<=1 and 0<=y<=0.5
                texcoord = mul(matrixWorld2Texture[2],
PS_Input.world_position);
                texcoord.xyz = texcoord.xyz / texcoord.w;
                if(max(abs(texcoord.x - 0.75),abs(texcoord.y - 0.25>= 0.25) {
                        //test for the last SM in which  0.5<=x<=1
and 0.5<=y<=1
                        texcoord = mul(matrixWorld2Texture[3],
PS_Input.world_position);
                        texcoord.xyz = texcoord.xyz / texcoord.w;
                        if(max(abs(texcoord.x - 0.75),abs(texcoord.y - 0.75))
>= 0.25) {
                                shadow = 1.0;
                        }
                }
        }
}
if(shadow != 1.0) {
        //get shadow value, where 'samaplerAtlas' is the sampler the atlas.
        shadow = tex2D(samaplerAtlas, texcoord);
}
```

As you can see from Figure 4.1.9, shadow rendering is improved in our optimized method. Notice that we've used the exact solution to handle the filtering issue in this figure. That's why the splits in the optimized method have circular boundaries.

FIGURE 4.1.9 Top row: shadow quality in the optimized method and original method. The shadow details are zoomed in the colored rectangles. Bottom row: colorized visualization of splits in two methods.

CORRECT COMPUTATION OF TEXTURE COORDINATES

Typical CSM implementations (e.g., [Zhang07]) output all possible texture coordinates from the vertex shader to the pixel shader. Subsequently, in the pixel shader, once we've determined which split the current pixel is in, the associated texture coordinates are used for texture lookup. Refer to the pseudo code for "Method 1" in Listing 4.1.4. The main disadvantage of this method is that several interpolators are used. For example, three interpolators are required for CSM(3) in Listing 4.1.4, where CSM(3) stands for splitting the view frustum into three splits. This situation becomes more serious when the number of interpolators is limited, which is very common for complex shaders.

In order to reduce the number of interpolators required in CSMs, another popular (but incorrect) alternative is to output only the world-space position from the vertex shader to the pixel shader, and then accordingly compute the texture coordinates in the pixel shader after the split index is determined. As you can see, the code in Listing 4.1.3 also uses this method. However, this method is *mathematically* incorrect (but NOT visually noticeable in most practical cases). This method is illustrated as Method 2 in Listing 4.1.4. In the next section, we will show that Method 2 actually results in an incorrect interpolation during rasterization. One note for the pseudo code is that you can use a simple dot product to determine the split index in practice.

Listing 4.1.4 Comparison of two methods for computing texture coordinates

```
Note: we assume 3 shadow maps are used in the following pseudo code.

/************************Method 1********************************/
//DATA STRUCTURE
struct VS_OUTPUT
{
  float4 position : POSITION; // screen-space posit
  float4 tex0 : TEXCOORD0; // texture position for CSM0
  float4 tex1 : TEXCOORD1; // texture position for CSM1
  float4 tex2 : TEXCOORD2; // texture position for CSM2
}


//VERTEX SHADER
float4 posWorldSpace = mul(VSInput.position, WORLD); // world-space position
VSOutput.position = mul(posWorldSpace, matrixViewProj); // screen-space
position

VSOutput.tex0 = mul(posWorldSpace, matrixTexture[0]); // texture position
for CSM0

VSOutput.tex1 = mul(posWorldSpace, matrixTexture[1]); // texture position
for CSM1

VSOutput.tex2 = mul(posWorldSpace, matrixTexture[2]); // texture position
for CSM2


//PIXEL SHADER
float shadow; //final illumination result
int split = …; //we ignore the code for computing the split index 'split'
here
```

```
if (split < 1)  //if the current pixel is in the first split
    shadow = tex2DProj(samplerCSM0, PSInput.tex0); //depth comparison
else if… //the rest code is ignored


/************************Method 2********************************/
//DATA STRUCTURE
struct VS_OUTPUT
{
  float4 position : POSITION; // screen-space posit
  float4 tex0 : TEXCOORD0; // world-space position
}


//VERTEX SHADER
VSOutput.position = mul(VSInput.position, WORLDVIEWPROJ); // screen-space
position
VSOutput.tex0 = mul(VSInput.position, WORLD); // world-space position


//PIXEL SHADER
float shadow; //final illumination result
float4 texCoords; //texture coordinates
int split = …; //we ignore the code for computing the split index 'split'
here
if (split < 1)  //if the current pixel is in the first split
{
    texCoords = mul(PSInput.tex0, matrixWorld2Texture[split]); //compute
texture coordinates
    shadow = tex2DProj(samplerCSM0, texCoords); //depth comparison
}
else if… //the rest code is ignored
```

Any attributes passed to the pixel shader are *perspective-interpolated* from the vertex shader output. Listing 4.1.5 shows that the texture coordinates used in the pixel shader are different between the two methods. It means that the interpolated texture coordinates in the second method are wrong in theory. The resultant visual artifacts are usually not noticeable when the scene is well tessellated. However, the problem can become noticeable for scenes that contain large triangles.

Listing 4.1.5 Comparison of the perspective-interpolation in two methods

```
/*********************Method 1 (correct perspective interpolation)
*********************/
//VERTEX SHADER
//denote 'position' and 'tex0' as two vectors, shown as follows
VSOutput.position ↔ (x, y, z, w)
VSOutput.tex ↔ (s, t, u, v)


//PIXEL SHADER
//texture coordinates are perspective-interpolated from the output of the
vertex shader,
PSInput.tex0 ↔ ( lerp(s/w) / lerp(1/w), //x component
                 lerp (t/w) / lerp(1/w), //y component
                 lerp (u/w) /lerp(1/w), //z component
                 lerp (v/w) /lerp(1/w) ) //w component


/*********************Method 2 (wrong perspective interpolation)
*********************/
//VERTEX SHADER
//denote 'position' and 'tex0' as two vectors, shown as follows
VSOutput.position ↔ (x, y, z, w)
VSOutput.tex0 ↔ (x_world, y_world, z_world, w_world)


//PIXEL SHADER
//world-space positions are perspective-interpolated from the output of
the vertex shader,
PSInput.tex0 ↔ ( lerp(x_world /w) / lerp(1/w), //x component
                 lerp (y_world /w) / lerp(1/w), //y component
                 lerp (z_world /w) /lerp(1/w), //z component
                 lerp (w_world /w) /lerp(1/w) ) //w component
// texture coordinates are then
texCoords = mul(PSInput.tex0, matrixWorld2Texture) ≠ (s, t, u, v)!
```

As we explained in Listing 4.1.5, the correct computation of texture coordinates in the second rendering pass requires us to get the correct world-space position for each fragment. We have a short note here: There are various ways to correctly construct the world-space position as part of a *deferred shading* pass, which are beyond the scope of this article. This will require one extra vector-matrix multiplication, that is, the vector of the screen-space coordinates and the inverse matrix from screen-space to world space. Various methods exist for calculating the world position from screen-space coordinates. In particular, readers can refer to deferred shading methods for more details. Finally, you could simply pass the inverse matrix from your application to the GPU.

According to our experience in practice, in the case that the interpolators are quite important and limited, we suggest that developers use the alternative Method 2 *but* with a clear understanding of the potential problem behind it. A similar example in computer graphics is *Gouraud shading*. Although the bilinear interpolation used in Gouraud shading is not theoretically correct, the shading result is usually fine for diffuse objects.

FILTERING ACROSS SPLITS

The splitting planes in CSM introduce discontinuities that can interfere with texture filtering. We need to pay special attention to filtering at split boundaries to avoid visual artifacts. This problem is very similar to filtering cube maps [Isidoro05]. Current hardware regards each face in a cube map as a separate 2D texture and does not filter across cube map faces. This can cause noticeable discontinuities to appear at face borders. Therefore, we need a practical solution for this issue in CSMs.

A significant advantage of pre-filtering techniques over PCF is that shadow maps can be filtered like standard textures by using the GPU hardware's built-in filtering functionality.

As illustrated in Figure 4.1.10, graphics hardware computes the screen-space texture derivatives (for a transformed quad) to determine the texture filtering width and *levels-of-detail* (LODs) selection in the *mipmap* chain [Akenine02]. This procedure works well for filtering a single texture, but it does not work across splits in CSMs.

To understand why CSM splits do not work with hardware filtering, it will help to understand how the derivative instruction is implemented in graphics hardware. As illustrated in Figure 4.1.11, when computing the derivative of a variable u, the value of u is computed at both the current fragment and the neighbor fragment.

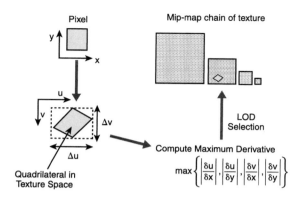

FIGURE 4.1.10 Mipmap LOD selection in hardware.

The difference between the two values is returned as the derivative result. Notice that, due to the nature of the SIMD (i.e., single-instruction-multiple-data) architecture in GPUs, the derivative computation is very efficient.

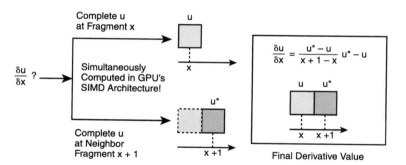

FIGURE 4.1.11 How a modern GPU computes derivatives.

The reliance of the derivative instruction on neighboring pixels causes it to produce invalid results across CSM splits (see Figure 4.1.12). Fragments on the same quad can belong to two different shadow maps along split boundaries, so the texture coordinates transformed by different texture matrices result in meaningless derivatives. As a result, noticeable "seam" artifacts appear at split boundaries.

Notice that this problem does not appear in techniques that filter *after* the depth comparison, such as *percentage closer filtering* (PCF) [Reeves87]. Filtering after the depth comparison avoids the hardware's built-in filtering and therefore avoids the derivative computation and split boundary artifacts.

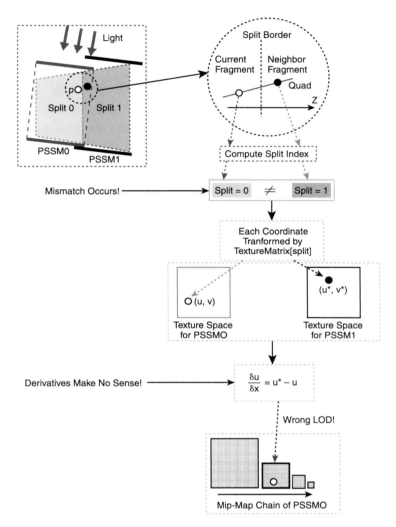

FIGURE 4.1.12 Wrong LOD selection can happen when fragments in the same quad belong to different splits.

From our previous analysis, artifacts at split boundaries occur when an incorrect LOD is used in texture filtering. This problem was first analyzed and solved in *parallel-split variance shadow maps* (PSVSMs) [Lauritzen07a]. In theory, an analytic solution is needed to select the correct LOD in the mipmap chain. In practice, the approximate method proposed in PSVSMs solves this problem well without sacrificing performance. You can choose either one according to your implementation. In the following, we outline both methods.

Method Used in PSVSMs

The idea is based on the observation that the problem results from different split indices being used for fragments in the same quad. In other words, the filtering discontinuity can be avoided by keeping split indices consistent over the quad.

Figure 4.1.13 illustrates how we can use the hardware's derivative instructions to implement this idea. For simplicity, let's consider the fragment in 1D space first. When the mismatch of split indices at neighboring fragments occurs, there's a difference of 1 between the two indices, denoted by *split* and *split**. To detect if the mismatch occurs, we just need to check if ***ddx(split)*** is non-zero because ***ddx(split)*** = *split** − *split* (see Figure 4.1.11). Our goal is to keep the split index the same for both fragments, for example, *split* (notice that you can also choose *split**). However, since ***ddx(split)*** always returns 1, the problem is how to deduce the value of *split*. We use another smart trick employed with PSVSMs. Let's treat 2^{split} as a variable, ***ddx***$(2^{split}) = 2^{split*} − 2^{split} = 2^{split}$. A simple *log* will give you the original split value. Even simpler, you can replace the *log* operation with a predefined lookup table to improve performance.

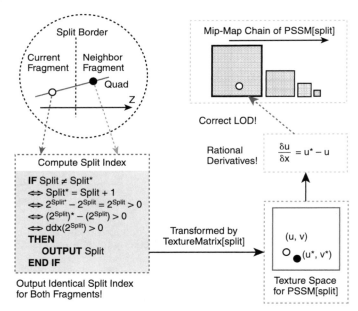

FIGURE 4.1.13 Solving mismatch of split indices in PSVSMs.

Generalizing the analysis to 2D screen-space, we need to compute all derivatives to deduce a consistent split index, as shown in Listing 4.1.6.

Listing 4.1.6 Keep the consistent split index fragments on the same quad

```
// CONSTANTS
const int SPLIT_NUM = 3; //number of splits


// PIXEL SHADER
int powerSplitIndex = pow(2, splitIndex);   // 2^splitIndex
int dx = abs(ddx(powerSplitIndex));   // d(2^splitIndex)/ dx
int dy = abs(ddy(powerSplitIndex));   // d(2^splitIndex)/ dy
int dxy = abs(ddx(dy));   // d²(2^splitIndex)/dxdy
int split = max(dxy, max(dx, dy));   // get the maximum derivative value
if(powerSplitIndex>0) // if mismatch happens
    splitIndex = log(powerSplitIndex); // update split index
```

ANALYTIC METHOD

In this method, the derivative is no longer computed in the split-specific texture space because it will cause the wrong LOD selection, as previously explained. The idea of this method is based on the observation that there's obviously no problem for hardware to compute derivatives when using a single shadow map texture. For a given shadow map in CSMs, as long as we can find the relationship between the derivatives in standard shadow mapping (for the whole view frustum) and the derivatives in the texture space of the given shadow map (for a split), the correct split-specific derivatives should be derivable from the former. This idea is illustrated by Figure 4.1.14. On the other hand, it's very easy to tell there's only a scale difference between the derivatives in the two texture spaces. In Figure 4.1.14, you can easily tell there's a difference of translation and scale between the texture coordinates

$$d = \frac{D+S}{D}$$ (for the whole view frustum) and u (for the split only).

$$M = \begin{bmatrix} d & 0 & 0 & F_x \\ 0 & d & 0 & F_y \\ 0 & 0 & d & F_z \\ 0 & 0 & 0 & S \end{bmatrix}$$

Therefore, the difference between the derivatives and

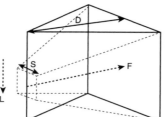 (remember this is what we want) is a scale ratio. The corresponding pseudo code is illustrated in Listing 4.1.7.

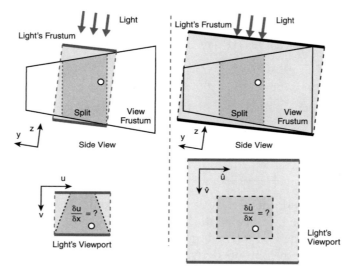

FIGURE 4.1.14   Analytic method to compute derivatives.

Listing 4.1.7 Analytic method for computing derivatives

```
// CONSTANTS

// Refer to [Zhang07], transforming from the texture space for the whole
view frustum to the texture space for a specific split only requires a
SCALE transformation and a TRANSLATION transformation.

float2 scale; //scale values in x and y dimensions

float2 translate; //translation values in x and y dimensions


// PIXEL SHADER

// Step 1: Take derivatives in standard shadow mapping
```

```
// NOTE: 'PosLight' stands for the position in light's clip space for the
whole view frustum!
float2 LightTexCoord = PSInput.PosLight.xy / PSInput.PosLight.w; //
project texture coordinates
float2 dtdx = ddx(LightTexCoord); //take derivative
float2 dtdy = ddy(LightTexCoord); //take derivative


// Step 2: Apply split-specific scale/translate to texture coordinates and
derivatives
scale = scale * float2(0.5, -0.5);
translate = translate * float2(0.5, -0.5) + 0.5;
LightTexCoord = scale * LightTexCoord + translate; //NDC to texture space
dtdx *= Scale;
dtdy *= Scale;
```

Finally, as an optional improvement when you combine CSMs and filtering techniques, you can use a self-adjusting filtering kernel size when using filtering. Ideally, generating a consistent blurring effect over all splits needs a *varying* kernel size due to the foreshortening effect. Although a small and constant filtering width (e.g., 2×2) can still blur shadows well, a self-adjusted filtering size is necessary in some cases such as when applying warping algorithms into each shadow map. It's actually very easy to provide such a varying kernel. We just need to scale the original constant filtering width by the ratio of the size of the current split and to the size of whole view frustum from the light's point of view, as shown in Listing 4.1.8.

Listing 4.1.8 Self-adjusted filtering kernel size

```
// Scale values for x and y respectively
float scaleX, scaleY;


// Compute the required scale for the current split in light's post-
perspective space
// 'maxX' and 'minX' stand for the maximum and minimum x values respectively.
// 'maxY' and 'minY' stand for the maximum and minimum y values respectively.
scaleX = 2.0f / (maxX - minX);
scaleY = 2.0f / (maxY - minY);
```

```
// Assume the original constant filtering size is 2x2
float2 vFilteringKenerlSize(2.0f, 2.0f);
// Update the filtering size
vFilteringKenerlSize.x *= scaleX;
vFilteringKenerlSize.y *= scaleY;
```

CONCLUSION

This chapter has discussed a few practical issues in *cascaded shadow maps* (CSMs). For each of these issues, we have analyzed the cause and subsequently presented the solutions. We hope the methods presented in this article can help developers improve their CSM implementations and motivate further research on this topic.

ACKNOWLEDGMENTS

Thanks to Sam Martin for his valuable review comments. Thanks to David Lam, Andrew Lauritzen, Adrian Egli, Oskari Nyman, and Marco Salvi for their early reviews. Special thanks to David Lam for his patient and careful proofreading, and to Andrew Lauritzen for insightful suggestions and sample code and for inspiring the second method for the filtering issue.

REFERENCES

[Akenine02] Thomas Akenine-Moller and Eric Haines. *Real-Time Rendering* (2nd Edition). A. K. Peters Limited, 2002.

[Annen07] Thomas Annen, Tom Mertens, Philippe Bekaert, Hans-Peter Seidel, and Jan Kautz. "Convolution Shadow Maps." In *Proceedings of the Eurographics Symposium on Rendering 2007*, pp. 51–60.

[Annen08] Thomas Annen, Tom Mertens, Hans-Peter Seidel, Eddy Flerackers, and Jan Kautz. "Convolution Shadow Maps." In *Proceedings of Graphics Interface 2008*, pp. 155–161.

[Donnelly06] William Donnelly and Andrew Lauritzen. 2006. "Variance Shadow Maps." In *Proceedings of the Symposium on Interactive 3D Graphics and Games 2006*, pp. 161–165.

[Engel06] Wolfgang Engel. "Cascaded Shadow Maps." *ShaderX⁵*, edited by Wolfgang Engel. Charles River Media, 2006, pp. 197–206.

[Forsyth05] Tom Forsyth. "Shadowbuffer Frustum Partitioning," *ShaderX⁴*, edited by Wolfgang Engel. Charles River Media, 2005, pp. 289–297.

[Isidoro05] John R. Isidoro. " Filtering Cubemaps - Angular Extent Filtering and Edge Seam Fixup Methods," Siggraph'05 Sketch Presentation, 2005. (also available at http://ati.amd.com/developer/SIGGRAPH05/Isidoro-CubeMapFiltering.pdf).

[Lauritzen07a] Andrew Lauritzen. "Parallel-Split Variance Shadow Maps," In Proceedings of Graphics Interface 2007 (poster).

[Lauritzen07b] Andrew Lauritzen. "Summed-Area Variance Shadow Maps." *GPU Gems3*, edited by Hubert Nguyen. Addison Wesley. 2007, pp. 157–182.

[Lauritzen08] Andrew Lauritzen and Michael McCool. "Layered Variance Shadow Maps," In *Proceedings of Graphics Interface 2008*, pp. 139–146.

[Lloyd06] Brandon Lloyd, David Tuft, Sung-Eui Yoon, and Dinesh Manocha. 2006. "Warping and Partitioning for Low Error Shadow Maps." In *Proceedings of the Eurographics Symposium on Rendering 2006*, pp. 215–226.

[Martin04] Tobias Martin and Tiow-Seng Tan. "Anti-Aliasing and Continuity with Trapezoidal Shadow Maps." In *Proceedings of the Eurographics Symposium on Rendering 2004*, 2004, pp. 153–160.

[Reeves87] William Reeves, David Salesin, and Robert Cook. "Rendering Antialiased Shadows with Depth Maps." In *Computer Graphics* (Proceedings of SIGGRAPH 1987), 1987, 21(3), pp. 283–291.

[Salvi07] Marco Salvi. "Rendering Filtered Shadows with Exponential Shadow Maps." *ShaderX⁶*, edited by Wolfgang Engel. Charles River Media, 2007, pp. 257–274.

[Stamminger02] Marc Stamminger and George Drettakis. "Perspective Shadow Maps." In *Proceedings of SIGGRAPH 2002*, 2002, pp. 557–562.

[Valient07] Michal Valient. "Stable Rendering of Cascaded Shadow Maps," *ShaderX⁶*, edited by Wolfgang Engel. Charles River Media, 2007, pp. 231–238.

[Williams78] Lance Williams. "Casting Curved Shadows on Curved Surfaces." In *Computer Graphics* (Proceedings of SIGGRAPH 1978) 12(3), 1978, pp. 270–274.

[Wimmer04] Michael Wimmer, Daniel Scherzer, and Werner Purgathofer. "Light Space Perspective Shadow Maps." In *Proceedings of the Eurographics Symposium on Rendering 2004*, pp. 143–152.

[Zhang06] Fan Zhang, Hanqiu Sun, Leilei Xu, and Lee Kit Lun. "Parallel-Split Shadow Maps for Largescale Virtual Environments," *In Proceedings of the 2006 ACM International Conference on Virtual Reality Continuum and Its Applications* (VRCIA'2006), 2006, pp. 311–318.

[Zhang07] Fan Zhang, Hanqiu Sun, and Oskari Nyman. "Parallel-Split Shadow Maps on Programmable GPUs." *GPU Gems3*, edited by Hubert Nguyen. Addison Wesley. 2007, pp. 203–237.

4.2 A Hybrid Method for Interactive Shadows in Homogeneous Media

CHRIS WYMAN AND SHAUN RAMSEY

INTRODUCTION

For many applications both realism and interactivity are vital, yet attempts to improve one often come at the cost of the other. To make interactive realism tractable, a variety of simplifications are commonplace. For instance, materials are often assumed to be ideally diffuse, light emission only occurs from idealized point lights, and this light only interacts on the surface of scene geometry. Clearly, these simplifications rule out many common environments, and recent research and development has focused on identifying other, less severe approximations that would allow interactive rendering in more complex scenes.

In the case of *participating media*, where light interacts not only with surfaces but also with particles inside a volume, rendering APIs such as OpenGL and DirectX have long included ad hoc approximations that fade geometry as a function of distance. This approach is amenable to hardware acceleration, allowing the rendering of reasonably plausible fog at virtually no cost. Unfortunately, this method lacks many behaviors of participating media, as computations still occur only at surfaces. In particular, the glow around light sources and the ubiquitous light shafts, or "god rays," that appear on cloudy days are not possible.

Recent research has developed additional techniques that solve some of these problems. Work in cloud rendering has long considered a variety of scattering effects, though these approaches typically consider only this special case of participating media. Another avenue of research has developed participating media models largely independent of illumination or visibility concerns. Two examples of this are the Hoffman and Preetham [Hoffman03] and Sun et al. [Sun05] models, which provide much more realistic scattering than the DirectX and OpenGL vertex fog approximations yet come at only a small additional cost. While models such as these capture scattering effects such as glows near light sources, they generally assume that lights are always visible throughout the volume and thus cannot generate light shafts.

This article proposes a method to augment these models to allow light shafts, or alternatively their inverse, shadow shafts. Our approach uses a hybrid GPU ray-marching technique augmented by shadow volumes to accelerate ray marching and eliminate aliasing inherent in sampling light along a ray. The idea is to combine two techniques used to render realistic shadow shafts: ray marching [Imagire07] and shadow volumes [Biri06, James03]. Our results, shown in Figure 4.2.1, give real-time believable volumetric shafts from complex objects.

In the rest of this article, we first give a brief overview of participating media and existing single-scattering models used in interactive rendering. We then introduce our hybrid in a simplified environment using point light sources, followed by an extension to allow the use of textured spotlights. Implementation details and a discussion of the results round out the chapter.

FIGURE 4.2.1 Interactive volumetric light shafts and shadows rendered at up to 80 frames per second using our hybrid approach. The fairy forest uses a white point light. The other two scenes use textured lights where the inset shows the texture used.

PARTICIPATING MEDIA REVIEW

To understand the rationale for our hybrid, we first review single-scattering approximations for participating media, such as Sun et al. [Sun05], and then discuss how these models interact with ray marching and shadow volume techniques.

When light interacts with volumetric media, multiple particles of different sizes, orientations, and material properties may absorb, scatter, or reflect the light before it reaches our eyes. In many environments these particles can be safely ignored, effectively assuming the media has no effect on transient light. While this is a reasonable assumption in some settings, the increasing desire to render scenes with complex atmospheric effects and to include depth cues gained by accounting for scattering suggests more complex models are necessary. To relax this approximation without excessive additional computation, people often restrict light to scatter no more than once along its path. With this approach, the paths of light look similar to the dark path shown in Figure 4.2.2. From the eye to point S, at every distance x there is some probability that light scatters toward the eye from the direction of the light. As we assume light only scatters once, this reflected light reaches the eye without further scattering.

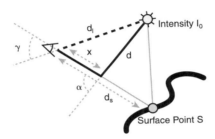

FIGURE 4.2.2   Important paths of light in single-scattering participating media. d_s and d_l are the distances from the eye to the surface and the light, x is the distance to a point on the viewing ray, γ is the angle between the viewing ray and the light direction, and $d(x)$ is the distance from the light to this point.

Using math similar to that proposed by Nishita et al. [Nishita87], the radiance L can be represented in a single-scattering model by:

$$L = L_s e^{-(K_a + K_s)d_s} + \int_0^{d_s} K_s \rho(\alpha) \frac{1_0(x)}{d(x)^2} e^{-(K_a + K_s)(d(x) + x)} dx,$$

where L_s is the radiance of the surface at point s, K_a, and K_s are the media's absorption and scattering coefficients, $\rho(\alpha)$ is its scattering phase function, and $I_0(x)$ is the radiance of the light visible at point x. The first term represents the color of the surface attenuated by particles in the air, similar to the color computed via hardware fog models. The second term represents color scattered toward the light by particles in the air.

This integral can be numerically sampled by approximating the integral as a sum. Unfortunately, this requires relatively fine sampling to eliminate aliasing along visibility boundaries. As a ray weaves in and out of volumetric light shafts, sufficient samples must be used to identify every transition. Just as lines in a 2D image become aliased, with some slopes appearing worse than others, shadow volumes in this discretely sampled 3D volume appear aliased when samples on adjacent rays switch from being illuminated to shadowed. Adaptively increasing sampling near shadow boundaries could reduce aliasing reasonably cheaply. Unfortunately, the locations of light shafts in complex and dynamic scenes are unknown a priori, so expensive, uniformly high sampling rates may be necessary to locate all such boundaries.

A different approach uses shadow volumes to identify when eye rays enter and leave shadowed regions. This subdivides the integral into distinct, fully illuminated intervals. For the situation shown in Figure 4.2.3, for instance, the integral above could be divided as:

$$\int_0^{d_s} f(x)dx = \int_0^{d_1} f(x)dx + \int_{d_2}^{d_3} f(x)dx + \int_{d_4}^{d_5} f(x)dx,$$

where

$$f(x) = K_s I_0(x)\rho(\alpha)e^{-(K_a + K_s)(d(x) + x)}/d(x)^2.$$

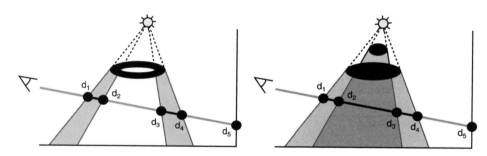

FIGURE 4.2.3 When using shadow volumes, scattering computations can be limited to only illuminated segments of a ray, such as $d_2 d_3$ and $d_4 d_5$. However, front- and back-facing shadow volumes must be paired correctly, to avoid incorrectly shading the left and right cases similarly.

For some illumination models, including [Sun05], each of these integrals can be precomputed and stored to texture, reducing runtime computations to a few texture lookups. This significantly increases rendering performance.

While this method avoids aliasing along shadow boundaries and missing shadow shafts, the shadow volumes must first be sorted to correctly pair front and back faces along each illuminated region and in order to ignore extraneous, completely shadowed polygons, such as those in Figure 4.2.3. While depth-peeling techniques can sort shadow polygons, shadow volumes for complex geometry can have arbitrarily high depth complexity, leading to arbitrarily large numbers of depth-peeling passes.

Hybrid Approach

Our method combines ray marching and shadow volumes in order to eliminate the sorting costs of the shadow volume approach and to reduce aliasing and sampling requirements needed for naïve ray marching. For clarity, we first discuss how our method works for simple point lights, and then discuss how this technique extends to handle textured "spotlights" (or projective textures), such as those shown in Figure 4.2.1.

Our basic assumption is that many volumetric shadows will be relatively simple, covering only a limited region of screen-space and a limited volume of the environment. For very complex environments, such as a hazy jungle scene or illumination through a chain-link fence, this assumption clearly breaks. However, in these scenarios, we would argue that only the nearest shafts of light are comprehensible to human viewers, and more distant ones could be ignored or approximated more cheaply, for instance, by representing the illumination as a texture and projecting it onto the scene.

Given our assumption, we observe that dense samples along a ray are only needed to identify sharp illumination boundaries under point lights. Once illumination boundaries have been identified, Sun et al.'s precomputed lighting model can be used to analytically determine scattering over each lit interval. We propose that shadow volumes can be used to limit ray marching to pixels on the screen that encounter volumetric shadows, and ray marching can be used to identify shadow boundaries, avoiding the cost of sorting the shadow polygons.

This technique can be viewed as a six-step process.

1. Render a shadow map from the light, used in step 5 to sample visibility while ray marching.

2. Render shadow volumes, as seen from the eye, storing distance to frontmost and backmost polygons.

3. Render scene geometry, as seen from the eye, attenuated by $e^{-(K_a + K_s)d_s}$.

4. Use an analytic fog model, such as Sun et al.'s, directly for eye pixels encountering no shadow quads.

5. Ray march from the back shadow quad to the front shadow quad, using the shadow map to identify illuminated regions. Use the analytic fog model to account for scattering inside each fully illuminated interval.

6. Combine attenuated scene (step 3) and scattering (steps 4 and 5) contributions.

While described as a six-step process, it can be implemented in four passes, combining steps 4, 5, and 6 into a single pass over a screen-sized quad. Please note that step 2 can be performed in a single pass by rendering depth (z) and inverted depth ($1 - z$) for front- and back-facing polygons, respectively, and either using GL_MIN blending to accumulate front and back depths to different color channels or using geometry shaders to output them to different buffers.

Our hybrid method has three advantages over ray marching: It completely avoids aliasing at two shadow boundaries (the ones closest and furthest from the eye), it avoids ray marching for all pixels that do not encounter volumetric shadows, and it avoids sampling the regions of the ray in front of the foremost shadow polygon and behind the backmost polygon. It also avoids the sorting of shadow polygons that is necessary when using a pure shadow volume approach.

Results using this algorithm are shown in Figure 4.2.4 on objects and scenes of various complexities, ranging from a few thousand polygons (sphere) up to more than 700,000 polygons (the "Yeah Right" model).

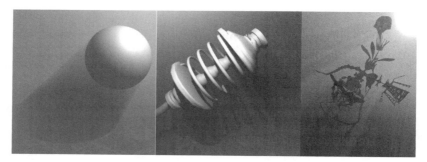

FIGURE 4.2.4 Our hybrid approach shown using models of varying complexity under a single, white point light.

ADDING TEXTURED LIGHT SOURCES

While our approach provides impressive results, simple point light sources are insufficient for many scenes, and more complex lighting may be necessary. For example, a spotlight may restrict illumination to a shaft of light, and a stained glass window creates shafts of light with varying colors and intensities.

Our initial hybrid categorizes rays into two categories: those that need ray marching and those that do not. Along each ray, our hybrid further identifies intervals whose illumination can be trivially computed without ray marching. Unfortunately, with illumination that varies throughout the volume, such as that from a stained glass window, lit intervals must be sampled to capture lighting variations.

While a clear separation between ray intervals that do and do not need sampling no longer exists, there is still a difference between these intervals. Fully illuminated ray segments only need sampling to capture lighting variations, whereas regions between shadow volumes must be sampled for both lighting *and* visibility variations (i.e., shadows). We observe that this is an important distinction. Visibility variations tend to cause relatively sharp boundaries that lead to god rays and shadow shafts, whereas illumination variations tend to give rise to much subtler variations. We suggest this is due to the diffusing nature of light undergoing multiple scattering events and the fact that only a tiny portion of the light is scattered in any region, making less abrupt lighting changes difficult to see.

We can use this observation, along with our hybrid, to sample ray intervals with different frequencies. Regions where visibility varies must be sampled relatively densely. Regions with only illumination changes can be sampled more coarsely, using step size and ray direction to select an appropriate level in a mipmapped illumination texture. To clarify, this mipmapping process effectively applies a low-pass filter on the illumination and allows us to sample arbitrarily coarsely depending on desired frame rate and quality. Similar coarsened sampling for visibility introduces artifacts, so we must continue to densely sample regions where visibility changes.

We change our original six-step process into an eight-step process to incorporate the additional sampling needed and the addition of a light frustum (along the boundary of the projective texture):

1. Render a shadow map from the light.
2. Render shadow volumes, storing distance to foremost and backmost polygons.
3. Render the light frustum from the eye, storing distance to its front and back.
4. Render scene geometry from the eye, attenuated by $e^{-(K_a + K_s)d_s}$.
5. Outside the light frustum, set the scattering to zero.
6. Inside the light frustum, march from back to front for pixels entirely outside the shadow volumes. At each sample point, sample just the illumination $I_0(\mathbf{x})$, using an appropriate mipmap level based on step size and orientation.
7. For pixels encountering shadow volumes, ray march through three distinct intervals inside the light frustum: behind the shadow polygons, between the shadow polygons, and in front of the shadows. Sample the illumination $I_0(\mathbf{x})$ for each illuminated segment.
8. Combine the attenuated scene (step 4) and scattering (steps 6 and 7) contributions.

This approach still allows ray marching to be completely eliminated outside the light's frustum. Inside the illuminated frustum, the three segments described in step 7 can be sampled with different granularity. Results using a variety of geometry and lighting are shown in Figure 4.2.5.

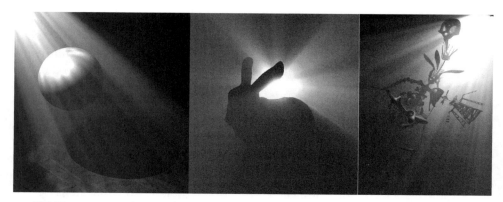

FIGURE 4.2.5 Using our hybrid approach under multi-colored textured spotlights allows sampling at different granularity along different segments of each viewing ray, allowing images like these to be rendered at up to 80 frames per second.

IMPLEMENTATION DETAILS

While the overall algorithm is straightforward, we encountered various additional optimizations and implementation issues that needed addressing. We found computing scattering at full-screen resolution excessive; computing scattering at 256^2 was sufficient for high-quality $1,024^2$ renderings. This coarser resolution is acceptable because participating media has a diffusing effect and generally contributes only a small portion of the scene's illumination. Sharp lighting variations simply become blurred in these environments. Typically, a 3^2 Gaussian filter eliminates most artifacts when upsampling this lower-resolution scattering image, but light leakage occurs when blurring across depth discontinuities, so an edge-preserving filter is needed. We used a 3^2 bilateral filter [Tomasi98] to eliminate light leakage, though the accompanying demo on this book's DVD-ROM uses a simplified edge-preserving filter based on a 3^2 tent filter that provides similar quality. The idea behind both filters is that a weight of a texel in the coarse image is zeroed if scattering was computed at a drastically different depth from a pixel in the final image, which can be implemented as per the following GLSL pseudo code.

```
vec4 FilterNeighborFogContributions( float depthOfPixel )
{
```

```
vec4 colorSum = vec4(0), weightSum = vec4(0);

for ( texels T_ij in 3x3 texel neighborhood of current pixel )
{
    float texelDepth = DistanceToObjectOccludedByFog( T_ij );

    if ( abs( texelDepth - depthOfPixel ) < distanceThreshold )
    {
        float weight = NonEdgePreservingFilterWeight( T_ij );

        colorSum += weight * LowResolutionFogColor( T_ij );

        weightSum += weight;
    }
    // else texel T_ij is ignored and not used by filter
}
return colorSum / weightSum;
}
```

Sun et al.'s model precomputes the integrals described above, requiring two texture lookups to evaluate each interval. However, their model was designed to analytically compute one integral per pixel, so costs for texture coordinate computation played only a small role in overall performance. In their model, the scattering integral is approximated as

$$\int_0^{d_s} f(x)dx \approx I_0(x)A_0 \left[F(A_1,A_2) - F\left(A_1, \frac{\gamma}{2}\right) \right],$$

where A_0, A_1, and A_2 are functions of d_l, d_s, K_s, and γ given by

$$A_0(d_l,\gamma,K_s) = \frac{K_s e^{-K_s d_l \cos\gamma}}{2\pi d_l \sin\gamma}, \quad A_1(d_l,\gamma,K_s) = K_s d_l \sin\gamma,$$

$$A_2(d_l,\gamma,d_s) = \frac{\pi}{4} + \frac{1}{2} \arctan\left(\frac{d_s - d_l \cos\gamma}{d_l \sin\gamma}\right)$$

and $F(u,v) = \int_0^v e^{-u\tan\xi}d\xi$ is precomputed and stored in a texture. While A_0 and A_1 are independent of distance along the viewing ray, A_2 with its expensive arctangent must be recomputed every step along the ray. We found reparameterizing F as a function of $\cos\gamma$ and x, both values already cheaply computed inside the shader, and dynamically recomputing the reparameterization F' as necessary saved a significant amount of time. In this case, we used

$$\int_0^{d_s} f(x)dx \approx \sum I_0(x_{start})[F'(\cos\gamma,x_{end}) - F'(\cos\gamma,x_{start})]$$

where $F'(\cos\gamma,x) = A_0(d_1,\gamma,K_s)F(A_1(d_1,\gamma,K_s),A_2(d_1,\gamma,x))$ and must be recomputed whenever the distance to the light d_l or the scattering coefficient K_s change. This reparameterization can be performed via the following GLSL pseudo code shader, which generates a 2D table storing $F'(\cos\gamma,x)$ in a texture, where the x-coordinate represents $\cos\gamma$ in the range $[-1..1]$ and the y-coordinate represents the distance x, in the range $[0..far]$.

```
uniform sampler2D fTex;   // Tabulated precomputed F integral
uniform vec2 fTexRange;   // Maximal u,v values sampled in fTex
uniform vec2 imageSize;   // Output buffer size, in pixels.
void main( void )
{
    float X = (gl_FragCoord.y / imageSize) * distToFarPlane;
    float cosGamma = 2 *( gl_FragCoord.x / imageSize) - 1;
    float sinGamma = sqrt( 1 - cosGamma * cosGamma );
    float gamma_2  = 0.5 * atan( sinGamma, cosGamma );
    float distToLight = DistanceFromCurrentEyePointToLight();
    float A_0 = k_s * exp( -k_s * cosGamma * distToLight ) /
                    ( 6.28319 * distToLight * sinGamma );
    float A_1 = k_s * distToLight * sinGamma;
    float A_2 = 0.78540 +
                0.5 * atan ( ( X - distToLight * cosGamma ) /
                            ( distToLight * sinGamma ) );
    vec2 fCoord = vec2( A_1, A_2 ) / fTexRange;
    gl_FragColor = A_0 * texture2D( fTex, fCoord );
}
```

One key to reducing the number of samples used during ray marching is to intelligently pick the sample locations. Imagire et al. [Imagire07] chose to sample along planes perpendicular to the viewing direction, using a slicing technique.

Unfortunately, this adds correlation between sampling locations that causes aliasing along shadow boundaries. For our simple point light hybrid, we found that uniformly subdividing the region between front and back shadow volumes, as shown in Figure 4.2.6, worked satisfactorily. While this still correlates samples, the correlation planes lie roughly parallel to shadow volumes, reducing aliasing significantly. Unfortunately, under textured spotlights the resulting crease in the sampling planes causes an abrupt and noticeable change in the scattered illumination. To avoid this, we sample the interval Δ along each eye ray, where this interval depends on the angle between eye and light viewing directions:

$$\Delta = \frac{d_{front}\sin\varphi}{\sin(\beta - \frac{\varphi}{2})}$$

where d_{front} is the distance to the light of the point along the front-facing shadow volume (i.e., the closest black points in Figure 4.2.6), φ is the light field-of-view, and β is the angle between viewing and light orientations. Unfortunately, the denominator blows up as β approaches

$$\frac{\varphi}{2},$$

so we approximate this as $\Delta' \approx 6 * d_{front}\sin\varphi$ to avoid this error. This leads to sampling planes similar to those in the right of Figure 4.2.6. Sampling this whole interval Δ' is unnecessary, since some samples may be occluded by geometry. Having samples correlated along planes parallel to neither the light nor the eye avoids many aliasing issues and avoids introducing artifacts where sampling planes intersect.

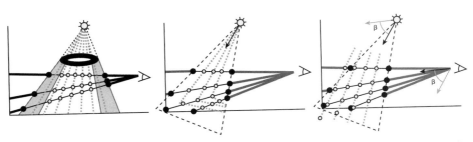

FIGURE 4.2.6   When marching between shadow polygons under a point light, sampling the front-to-back distance uniformly (left) significantly reduces aliasing, especially compared to naïve ray marching the whole ray. However, this leads to a sudden change in sampling planes (center) clearly visible under textured illumination, so a slightly wasteful sampling (right) that aligns sample planes partway between the eye and light views yields much higher quality, even though some samples are discarded.

Another technique that reduces aliasing uses a variance shadow map (VSM) [Donnelly06], rather than a standard shadow map, when sampling visibility during ray marching. This allows shadow map queries to return non-binary values and helps smooth shadow boundaries. While this reduces the number of ray steps required, variance shadow maps cost slightly more to generate, and we found this cost roughly equal to the performance gained by using fewer samples. However, in applications with already computed VSMs, they provide an additional method for reducing sampling costs.

RESULTS

ON THE DVD

We implemented our technique using OpenGL and GLSL, with provided timings from an NVIDIA GeForce 8800 GTX on a 2.66 GHz multi-core Xeon processor. Our prototype implementation is provided on the accompanying DVD-ROM. Timings from Table 4.2.1 are all computed when rendering $1,024^2$ final images, and for reference are compared with costs for naïve, brute force ray tracing and a rendering without volumetric shadows.

The ray samples required for high quality vary dramatically, depending on the complexity of the scene and the light source. For consistency, the timings provided in Table 4.2.1 all use the same sampling rates, determined based on a sampling rate that provided alias-free results for most of our scenes. For brute force marching, our point light hybrid, and our textured light hybrid, respectively, we used 150, 50, and 150 ray samples per pixel. For simple scenes, such as the sphere, our hybrid required many fewer samples for good quality. In more complex scenes, for example, using the "YeahRight" model, the sampling rate needed to be doubled (300 samples per pixel) to eliminate aliasing at shadow boundaries.

We found that limiting ray stepping to inside the shadow volume typically gave a 3–8 times speedup over brute force ray marching, and computing scattering at lower resolution increases performance by another 25–100%. When using our textured light hybrid, the performance improvement is somewhat less pronounced, especially in scenes where the light frustum covers most of the view.

CONCLUSIONS

This article presented a hybrid for rendering volumetric shadows that combines ray marching and shadow volumes. The basic idea works only for point light sources, but can be extended to intelligently sample illumination and visibility under more complex textured spotlights. Under both lighting conditions, our technique runs in real time for simple scenes, remains interactive for more complex geometry, and outperforms brute-force ray marching while giving comparable results.

ON THE DVD

Further examples, videos, an executable demo, code, and discussion are available either on the accompanying DVD-ROM, the technical paper [Wyman08], or on the project Web page at www.cs.uiowa.edu/~cwyman/publications/.

TABLE 4.2.1 A comparison of our hybrid's costs to those for a brute force, ray marching approach and a rendering without volumetric shadows

Scene (# triangles)	No volume shadows	Brute force ray marching	Hybrid with point light		Hybrid with textured light	
			10242 fog	2562 fog	10242 fog	2562 fog
Sphere (20k)	120.5 fps 8.3 ms	12.9 fps 77.5 ms	85.0 fps 11.8 ms	99.6 fps 10.0 ms	45.5 fps 21.9 ms	83.5 fps 12.0 ms
Sphere (32k)	160.7 fps 6.2 ms	14.6 fps 68.5 ms	76.8 fps 13.0 ms	112.5 fps 8.9 ms	18.0 fps 55.6 ms	72.5 fps 13.8 ms
Bunny (70k)	135.0 fps 7.4 ms	11.9 fps 84.0 ms	47.5 fps 21.1 ms	87.5 fps 11.4 ms	32.3 fps 31.0 ms	81.3 fps 12.3 ms
Fairy (155k)	121.9 fps 8.2 ms	12.3 fps 81.3 ms	38.5 fps 25.9 ms	72.1 fps 13.9 ms	35.9 fps 27.9 ms	78.3 fps 12.8 ms
Buddha (250k)	96.1 fps 10.4 ms	12.2 fps 82.0 ms	50.2 fps 19.9 ms	61.4 fps 16.3 ms	28.3 fps 35.3 ms	61.7 fps 16.2 ms
YeahRight (755k)	57.3 fps 17.5 ms	11.1 fps 90.1 ms	26.3 fps 38.0 ms	33.8 fps 29.6 ms	16.1 fps 62.1 ms	40.9 fps 24.4 ms

Note: Timings are provided in both frames per second (fps) and milliseconds per frame (ms). Note that for both hybrid techniques, we show times for scattering computed either at full screen (10242) or 1/16 screen size (2562).

REFERENCES

[Biri06] Biri, V., Arques, D., and Michelin, S. "Real time rendering of atmospheric scattering and volumetric shadows." *Journal of WSCG*, Vol 14, pages 65–72, 2006.

[Donnelly06] Donnelly, W. and Lauritzen, A. "Variance shadow maps." In *Proceedings of ACM Symposium on Interactive 3D Graphics and Games*, pages 161–165, 2006.

[Hoffman03] Hoffman, N. and Preetham, A. "Real-time light-atmosphere interactions for outdoor scenes." In *Graphics Programming Methods*, pages 337–352. Charles River Media, 2003.

[Imagire07] Imagire, T., Johan, H., Tamura, N., and Nishita, T. "Anti-aliased and real-time rendering of scenes with light scattering effects." *The Visual Computer*, 23(9), pages 935–944, 2007.

[James03] James, R. "True volumetric shadows." In *Graphics Programming Methods*, pages 353–366. Charles River Media, 2003.

[Nishita87] Nishita, T., Miyawaki, Y., and Nakamae, E. "A shading model for atmospheric scattering considering luminous distribution of light sources." In *Proceedings of ACM SIGGRAPH*, pages 303–310, 1987.

[Sun05] Sun, B., Ramamoorthi, R., Narasimhan, S., and Nayar, S. "A practical analytic single scattering model for real time rendering." *ACM Transactions on Graphics*, 24(3), pages 1040–1049, 2005.

[Tomasi98] Tomasi, C. and Manduchi, R. "Bilateral filtering for gray and color images." In *Proceedings of IEEE International Conference on Computer Vision*, pages 839–846, 1998.

[Wyman08] Wyman, C. and Ramsey, S. "Interactive Volumetric Shadows in Participating Media with Single Scattering." In *Proceedings of the IEEE Symposium on Interactive Ray Tracing*, 2008.

4.3 Real-Time Dynamic Shadows for Image-Based Lighting

MARK COLBERT, JAROSLAV KŘIVÁNEK

INTRODUCTION

We describe the implementation of a simple real-time GPU-based algorithm to compute a spherical harmonic-based visibility function for environment lighting. Visibility can be computed at the vertices or texels of an object and be used for fully dynamic shadow computation on diffuse as well as glossy surfaces in scenes illuminated by an environment map where geometry, illumination, and materials are allowed to change in real-time, at about 70 FPS (see Figure 4.3.1). The algorithm first appeared in our paper [Křivánek08]; this article describes it in more detail with a special focus on practical implementation issues. In addition, we provide full source code of a demo application on the DVD-ROM. The demo is written in C++ with DirectX and HLSL for the GPU shaders. The code snippets in the article use the same languages.

ON THE DVD

FIGURE 4.3.1 Using our technique, shadows for dynamic scenes can be computed in real-time without any precomputation for both diffuse surfaces (left) as well as complex, spatially varying, glossy surface reflection (right). For these two images, the boxes render at 70 FPS, and the rusty robot renders at 75.8 FPS for a 1k × 1k on an NVIDIA 8800 GTX.

RELATED WORK

Rendering of objects illuminated by high-dynamic-range (HDR) environment maps provides images of remarkable visual quality [Debevec02]. Existing real-time rendering algorithms based on precomputed radiance transfer [Kautz05] suffer from long precomputation times precluding their use in dynamic scenes. Other real-time algorithms support dynamic scenes at the expense of visibility. However, the absence of shadows can compromise image quality since shadows play an important role in understanding a scene. Annen et al. [Annen08] recently proposed an alternative technique for real-time soft shadows due to environment maps that is more accurate than ours. However, it is slower and consumes significantly more memory.

ALGORITHM OVERVIEW

For realistic shadows under complex environment lighting, we first determine the directions in the environment that cast the strongest shadows. Using importance sampling, we find high-intensity areas in an environment map ("Environment Map Importance Sampling" section). To find the occluding geometry, we then render orthographic shadow maps for the sampled directions. However, evaluating all these shadow maps for every pixel of every frame can be computationally burdensome. As an efficient alternative, we convert the occlusion defined per shadow map into a filtered *visibility map* defined per object ("Visibility Map Generation").

Once the visibility map is computed, we can use it to render images with shadows. For diffuse reflections, we use a simple dot product operation per pixel ("Rendering Shadows on Diffuse Surfaces"). For glossy reflections, we adapt the *filtered importance sampling* algorithm [Colbert07, Křivánek08], where we add shadows by attenuating the contribution of each filtered sample using the visibility map ("Rendering Shadows on Glossy Surfaces").

ENVIRONMENT MAP IMPORTANCE SAMPLING

Importance sampling is used to generate directions from which we will create the shadow maps. Our goal is to find more samples in directions where the environment map intensity is large, that is, produce the sample directions proportionally to the environment map luminance. The rationale is that the brightest parts of the environment cast the most pronounced shadows, so we want to compute the shadow maps for these directions.

We use a latitude-longitude mapping to associate a direction on the sphere with 2D texture coordinates, since the sampling procedure works in the rectangular texture domain. A pixel of the environment map with texture coordinates of (u, v) corresponds to the direction whose spherical coordinates are

$\varphi = 2\pi u$

$\theta = \pi(1 - v)$ **EQUATION 4.3.1**

The Cartesian coordinates of the direction can be computed as:

$x = \sin\theta \, \cos\varphi$

$y = \sin\theta \, \sin\varphi$

$z = \cos\theta$ **EQUATION 4.3.2**

Before importance sampling starts, the RGB color of each pixel of the environment map is converted to luminance using the formula, $Y = 0.2126 \, R + 0.7152 \, G + 0.0722 \, B$. The luminance is multiplied by the factor $\sin \Theta$, where Θ is the elevation angle corresponding to each pixel, in order to compensate for the stretching near the poles due to the latitude-longitude mapping. This step gives us a luminance map of our lighting environment that we can use for sampling.

Formally, the luminance map is an unnormalized *probability mass function* (PMF). In general, a PMF is just a set of probabilities that a number of events will take place. In our case an event means choosing a particular pixel of the 2D environment map in the sampling procedure. In order to call our luminance map a PMF, we should first normalize it by scaling every pixel's value such that all pixels sum to one. However, we can skip this costly explicit normalization step. Instead, we perform an implicit normalization by rescaling the random numbers used for sampling by the sum of all environment map pixels.

Our sampling problem is defined in 2D, but we can easily simplify it to sampling two 1D functions: First, we pick a row of the environment map and, second, we pick a pixel within the selected row. To select the row, we use the *marginal* PMF, which is simply the sum of luminances for each row of the environment map. This way, rows with brighter pixels are more likely to be sampled than rows with dim pixels. After selecting a row, we pick a pixel according to the 1D PMF given by the pixel luminances in the selected row. This concept is illustrated in Figure 4.3.2.

Now all we need to perform sampling is a procedure to randomly pick an element according to a 1D PMF. Imagine that you stack the probabilities in the PMF next to each other as shown in Figure 4.3.3. If we choose a random number, where there exists an equal likelihood that any value between 0 and 1 will be produced, then more numbers will map to the higher-probability item, the third probability in our example, and thus we will sample that direction more often. The stacking of the PMF is formally known as the discrete cumulative distribution function (CDF).

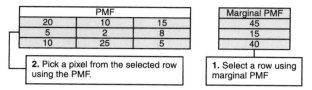

FIGURE 4.3.2 Sampling from a 2D probability mass function (PMF). First, a row is selected using the 1D marginal PMF (given by the sum of the probabilities in each row). Second, a pixel in the selected row is picked using the 1D PMF for the selected row.

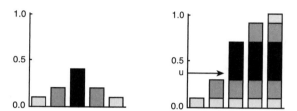

FIGURE 4.3.3 The discrete cumulative distribution function (CDF). By stacking the PMF of each column (left), we obtain a CDF (right). Using a random number u between zero and one, we can find the column whose CDF range contains u. Continuing this process, we get a distribution of column samples proportional to the PMF. In this case, since the third column is larger than the others, we will have more samples from that column.

Sampling from the PMF thus reduces to generating a random number u uniformly distributed between zero and the sum of all probabilities, and finding the first entry in the CDF larger than u. Binary search can be used for this purpose.

It would be undesirable if two or more samples were generated very close to each other, which could easily happen with purely random sampling. To prevent this sample clumping, we generate quasi-random numbers using the folded Hammersley sequence [Pharr04], which provides good sample distributions.

Let us now summarize the sampling procedure.

1. Generate the conditional CDF for each row of the environment map by accumulating the pixel luminances.

2. Generate the marginal CDF by accumulating the values of the last pixel of each row's conditional CDF.

3. Generate tuples $(\xi_{0,i}, \xi_{1,i})$ using the folded Hammersley sequence. Here, the number of tuples is equal to the number of samples we want to generate.

4. For each sample direction i:

    a. Pick a row by finding the first entry of the marginal CDF larger than $\xi_{0,i} * \Sigma$, where the normalizing factor Σ is the sum of all pixels in the PMF map.

b. Use the second value in the tuple, $\xi_{1,i}$, to pick a column in the row.

c. Compute the sample direction using Equations 4.3.1 and 4.3.2.

The end result of the above procedure is a set of sample directions generated proportionally to the environment map luminance. Figure 4.3.4 shows the resulting distribution of samples for two environment maps.

FIGURE 4.3.4 Sample distribution for two environment maps (St. Peters Cathedral and Pisa).

VISIBILITY MAP GENERATION

In order to capture visibility along our sample directions, we render shadow maps. We set an orthographic camera on a bounding sphere of the scene in the sample direction and render the scene into a depth buffer.

We only have a few shadow maps at our disposal, due to the limited computation resources. As we will see in the sections "Rendering Shadows on Diffuse Surfaces" and "Rendering Shadows on Glossy Surfaces," we need to evaluate the visibility at any point for any direction to render images with shadows. Therefore, we interpolate the visibility information in the shadow maps to any direction. To this end, we exploit the good directional interpolation properties of spherical harmonics (SH) and convert the shadow maps to an SH-based *visibility map*.

The visibility map is simply a texture of SH coefficients mapped to scene meshes. For that reason, the meshes must be equipped with a smooth, nonoverlapping parameterization (i.e., texture coordinates). Each mesh in the scene has its own visibility map. Each texel of the visibility map stores 16 spherical harmonic coefficients that approximate the visibility function for each direction around the texel position (directions pointing inside the object have zero visibility). The *visibility function* at point **p** is a spherical function (i.e., it takes a direction as an argument) defined as follows:

$$V_p(\omega) = \begin{cases} 0 & \text{a ray from } \mathbf{p} \text{ in direction } \omega \text{ hits scene geometry} \\ 1 & \text{otherwise} \end{cases}$$

Figure 4.3.5 illustrates the visibility function for a simple scene.

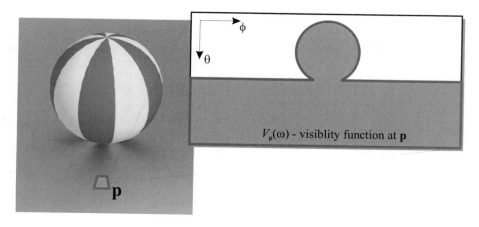

FIGURE 4.3.5 Visibility function $V_p(\omega)$ is a spherical function that returns 1 for all occluded directions and 0 otherwise.

In the rest of this section, we describe the construction of the visibility map. First, we give a brief introduction to spherical harmonics. After that we describe the fitting procedure used to find the SH coefficients in the visibility map from the shadow maps. Finally, we describe the filtering procedure used to alleviate occasional aliasing artifacts caused by the use of low-resolution shadow maps. The use of the visibility map for shadow rendering is described in the subsequent sections.

SPHERICAL HARMONICS

Spherical harmonics are basis functions that can be used to approximate any spherical function (including the visibility function) as follows:

$$V(\omega) = \sum_{i=0}^{n^2-1} w_i Y_i(\omega)$$

EQUATION 4.3.3

Here, ω denotes a direction, $V(\omega)$ is our visibility function, and $Y_i(\omega)$ are the spherical harmonic functions. Common nomenclature indexes the SH bases using two indices, l and m. We prefer to stick with the single index i since it makes the formulas easier to read. The coefficients, or weights, w_i tell us how "similar" each of the spherical harmonics functions is to the function being approximated ($V(\omega)$ in our case). Storing these coefficients enables us to reconstruct the visibility for any direction. The number of functions we sum determines the accuracy of the approximation; the larger the order n, the more precise the approximation. However, increasing n quadratically increases our coefficients. In our implementation, we use order 4 (16 coefficients) to represent the visibility function at a point. In order to evaluate Equation 4.3.3, we need a code to evaluate the SH functions themselves, which can be found in the demo source on the DVD-ROM or in [Green03]. This reference also provides a thorough introduction on the use of spherical harmonics for rendering.

ON THE DVD

One may ask why we bother using spherical harmonics to represent the visibility function. Why not use the shadow maps directly for rendering? In our implementation we use 16 or 32 shadow maps that give us a sparse, nonuniform, directional sampling of the visibility function. Using spherical harmonics to represent the visibility provides an efficient and smooth means of interpolating between these nonuniform directions.

FITTING THE SPHERICAL HARMONICS COEFFICIENTS

Equation 4.3.3 tells us how to evaluate the visibility function from the stored coefficients. That will be useful for using the visibility map to render shadows as described in "Rendering Shadows on Glossy Surfaces." This section focuses on how we compute these coefficients for each texel of the visibility map from the shadow maps. We will start with the theory and move on to the implementation.

Theory

Consider the visibility function for one texel of the visibility map (which maps to a point **p** on an object surface with normal **n**). We have m visibility samples that can be evaluated using the shadow map test, and we want to compute 16 coefficients w_i that give the best approximation (in the least squares sense) of the visibility in the sample directions:

$$w = \operatorname*{argmin}_{w} \sum_{j=1}^{m} \left(V(\omega_j) \lfloor \mathbf{n} \cdot \omega_j \rfloor - \sum_{i=0}^{15} w_i Y_i(\omega_j) \right)^2.$$

EQUATION 4.3.4

We denote the 16-component coefficient vector as **w**. Notice that we actually fit the visibility function multiplied by the cosine of the angle between the surface normal at **p** and the visibility sample direction ω_j, (i.e., the dot product $\mathbf{n} \cdot \omega_j$), clamped to zero for negative values. This has two advantages: First, it makes shading on diffuse surfaces trivial, as we will see in "Rendering Shadows on Diffuse Surfaces," and, second, it produces more accurate fitting results than fitting the visibility function alone.

We want to find the coefficient vector **w** that minimizes the function in Equation 4.3.4, so we take its derivative with respect to **w**, set it equal to zero and solve for **w**. In matrix form, the solution can be written as

$$\mathbf{w} = \mathbf{Y}^+\mathbf{b} \quad \textbf{EQUATION 4.3.5}$$

One column of matrix **Y** corresponds to one spherical harmonic function evaluated for the m sample directions, and the column vector **b** is composed of the values of the function we are trying to fit:

$$\mathbf{Y} = \begin{bmatrix} Y_0(\omega_1) & Y_1(\omega_1) & \cdots & Y_{15}(\omega_1) \\ Y_0(\omega_2) & Y_1(\omega_2) & \cdots & Y_{15}(\omega_2) \\ \vdots & \vdots & \ddots & \vdots \\ Y_0(\omega_m) & Y_1(\omega_m) & \cdots & Y_{15}(\omega_m) \end{bmatrix} \quad \mathbf{b} = \begin{bmatrix} V(\omega_1)\lfloor \mathbf{n} \cdot \omega_1 \rfloor \\ V(\omega_2)\lfloor \mathbf{n} \cdot \omega_2 \rfloor \\ \vdots \\ V(\omega_m)\lfloor \mathbf{n} \cdot \omega_m \rfloor \end{bmatrix}$$

EQUATION 4.3.6

The Moore-Penrose pseudo-inverse, denoted by the + superscript, finds a matrix that is "as close to as possible" to the inverse of matrix **Y**, even though **Y** may be (and it usually is) singular. To find the pseudo-inverse, we first perform the *singular value decomposition* (SVD) of **Y**, which expresses **Y** as a product of two *orthogonal* matrices[1] **U** and **V**^{T} and a diagonal matrix Σ composed of (non-negative) *singular values* σ_i.

$$\mathbf{Y} = \mathbf{U}\Sigma\mathbf{V}^T$$

We use the `svdcmp()` routine from the numerical recipes book [Press92] to compute the SVD in our implementation. Using the SVD, the pseudo-inverse $\mathbf{Y}^+$ can be computed as

$$\mathbf{Y}^+ = \mathbf{V}\Sigma^+\mathbf{U}^T$$

where the diagonal matrix Σ^+ is composed of the inverted non-zero singular values:

$$\sigma_i^+ = \begin{cases} \dfrac{\sigma_i}{\sigma_i^2 + \alpha^2} & \sigma_i > \epsilon \\ 0 & \text{otherwise} \end{cases}$$

EQUATION 4.3.7

Here, instead of taking the true inverse of the singular values (i.e., $1/\sigma_i$), we use Tikhonov regularization by introducing the α^2 term in the denominator to avoid over-fitting the data. The actual values for α and ϵ are left as user parameters since they are sensitive to the scene, much the way the bias and offset are for regular shadow maps.

Let us now summarize the computation of the $\mathbf{Y}^+$ matrix.

1. Compute the **Y** matrix using Equation 4.3.6.
2. Use the `svdcmp()` routine to find the **U**, Σ, and **V** matrices.
3. Compute the Σ^+ matrix using Equation 4.3.7.
4. Compute $\mathbf{Y}^+$ as $\mathbf{V}\,\Sigma^+\,\mathbf{U}^T$.

We refer to [Colbert08, Bishop06] for the derivation of this result. The keyword to look for is *normal equations* for a least-squares problem.

GPU Implementation

With the coefficient vector expressed as the matrix-vector multiplication in Equation 4.3.5, we can independently "accumulate" the contributions from the individual visibility samples (i.e., the shadow maps). We exploit this property in our GPU implementation.

Whenever the environment map changes, we compute the $\mathbf{Y}^+$ matrix on the CPU and upload it to the GPU constant registers. Recall that there is a separate visibility map for each mesh in the scene. In order to generate the visibility map for a mesh, we bind its visibility map textures as four `float4` render targets and accumulate the coefficients by rendering multiple passes. We render the mesh to the visibility map using the mesh's UV coordinates as screen-space positions. In practice we process eight shadow maps in one pass, but for simplicity, we will show code snippets for two shadow maps processed at the same time.

The main purpose of the *vertex shader* is to transform the mesh vertices to the texture coordinate space:

```
OUT.hpos  = float4(IN.uv*float2(2,-2)+float2(-1,1),0,1);
```

As an optimization, the vertex shader computes the cosine factors later used to multiply the visibility function for fitting:

```
float3 n = normalize(mul(IN.normal, g_mWorld));
OUT.cos0.x = max(0,dot(n,g_dir[0]));
OUT.cos0.y = max(0,dot(n,g_dir[1]));
...
```

The vertex shader also transforms the vertex position `IN.pos` to the coordinate frame of individual shadow maps:

```
OUT.smplHPos0 = mul(IN.pos,g_mSmplWorldViewProj[0]);
OUT.smplHPos1 = mul(IN.pos,g_mSmplWorldViewProj[1]);
...
```

The *pixel shader* first computes the vector **b** composed of the values:

```
float4 b[2]; // length 8 = number of visibility samples (i.e. shdw maps)

// shadow map tests yield V(omega_i)
b[0].x = tex2Dproj(ShadowMapSampler[0], IN.smplHPos0).r;
b[0].y = tex2Dproj(ShadowMapSampler[1], IN.smplHPos1).r;
...


// multiply by the cosine terms
b[0] *= IN.cos0;
b[1] *= IN.cos1;
```

The last step of the pixel shader performs the matrix-vector multiplication $\mathbf{w} = \mathbf{Y}^+\mathbf{b}$:

```
OUT.w0 = OUT.w1 = OUT.w2 = OUT.w3 = 0;


int k=0;
```

```
for (int i=0; i<2; i++)
{
  for (int j=0; j<4; j++,k+=4)
  {
    OUT.w0 += Yplus[k+0]*b[i][j];
    OUT.w1 += Yplus[k+1]*b[i][j];
    OUT.w2 += Yplus[k+2]*b[i][j];
    OUT.w3 += Yplus[k+3]*b[i][j];
  }
}
```

ON THE DVD

An example of the resulting coefficients is visualized in the accompanying demo on the DVD-ROM as well as Figure 4.3.6.

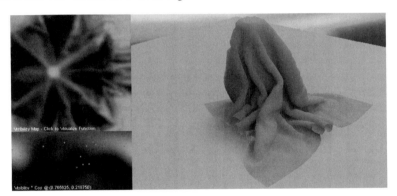

FIGURE 4.3.6   The first three SH coefficients visualized in RGB (upper left) for the draping cloth (right). The resulting visibility function for a single point in the map is displayed in the lower left, where the sample directions are highlighted.

VISIBILITY MAP FILTERING

The directional discretization due to the visibility sampling is smoothed out by the use of spherical harmonics. Nonetheless, spatial discretization caused by the use of low-resolution shadow maps may lead to artifacts as shown in Figure 4.3.7a. We perform low-pass filtering (i.e., blurring) of the spherical harmonics coefficients in the visibility map texture to suppress these artifacts (see Figure 4.3.7b). We convolve the visibility map with a 2D Gaussian filter discretized in a 9×9 window. Since the 2D Gaussian is separable[2], we can perform the 2D convolution as a sequence of two 1D convolutions, one in the horizontal and the second in the vertical direction. The two 1D convolutions are more efficient than one 2D convolution.

Before the actual filtering starts, we compute the normal map for the mesh and bind it to `NMapSampler`. The normal map is simply a texture containing the normal vector for the mapped texel position. We use the normal map to weight the contribution of surrounding pixels in order to avoid filtering over edges. While this normal weighting breaks the separability of the Gaussian filter, we find that computing the weighted filter in two 1D passes still provides a good approximation.

The filtering itself starts by computing the 1D filter window `filtWeights`, which is then uploaded to the GPU constant registers:

```
for (int i=-4; i<=4; i++)
{
    filtWeights[i+4] = expf(- float(i*i) / (2.f*5.f));
}
```

The horizontal convolution proceeds by rendering a screen-space quad with dimensions of the visibility map. The *vertex shader* computes nine texture coordinates offset by –4, –3, …, 4 pixels, respectively. These are sent to the pixel shader, where they are used to look up visibility map values inside the filter window.

In the *pixel shader*, we first compute the actual weights for each pixel in the filter window. The weight is given as a product of the Gaussian computed on the CPU and a normal attenuation term that avoids filtering over edges. The shader fragment for first two pixels is shown below:

```
// lookup the normal map at the filter center
float3 bn = tex2D(NMapSampler,uv2.xy).xyz;


// compute weights for pixels in the filter window
float4 weights[3];
float norm_atten = max(0,dot(tex2D(NMapSampler,uv0.xy).xyz,bn))
weights[0][0] = norm_atten * filtWeights[0];


norm_atten = max(0,dot(tex2D(NMapSampler,uv0.zw).xyz,bn));
weights[0][1] = norm_atten * filtWeights[1];
...
```

The next step uses the computed weights to perform the filtering:

```
float4 coeff[4];
for (int i=0; i<4; i++)
```

```
{
  coeff[i]  = tex2D(SHVisMapSampler[i],uv0.xy)*weights[0][0];

  coeff[i] += tex2D(SHVisMapSampler[i],uv0.zw)*weights[0][1];

  ...

}
```

As a last step, we normalize the filtered value:

```
float total = dot(weights[0],float4(1,1,1,1)) +
              dot(weights[1],float4(1,1,1,1)) + weights[2][0];


OUT.coeff0 = coeff[0]/total;    OUT.coeff1 = coeff[1]/total;

OUT.coeff2 = coeff[2]/total;    OUT.coeff3 = coeff[3]/total;
```

Filtering in the vertical direction is applied on the result of the horizontal filtering step. The only difference in the shader code is the computation of the texture coordinate offset in the vertex shader.

(a)   (b)

FIGURE 4.3.7   Jittering artifacts due to the limited resolution of the shadow maps (a) are suppressed with the normal-dependent spatial filtering (b).

RENDERING SHADOWS ON DIFFUSE SURFACES

To render diffuse surfaces with shadows, we exploit techniques from spherical harmonic-based precomputed radiance transfer (PRT) [Kautz05]. We convert the environment map to a vector of SH coefficients so the environment lighting follows the same representation as the SH visibility function. To perform the conversion, we use the code available from [Ramamoorthi01], which we extend to handle fourth-order spherical harmonics. When rendering, we upload the environment map SH coefficients to the GPU as shader constants. Diffuse shading is then computed in a pixel shader as a dot product of the environment map coefficients and the visibility coefficients:

```
float3 SHDiffuseShading(const float4 shVisCoeff[4])
{
  float3 res;
  float4 t;

  t[0] = dot(shVisCoeff[0], g_rEnvCoeff[0]);
  t[1] = dot(shVisCoeff[1], g_rEnvCoeff[1]);
  t[2] = dot(shVisCoeff[2], g_rEnvCoeff[2]);
  t[3] = dot(shVisCoeff[3], g_rEnvCoeff[3]);
  res.r = dot(t,float4(1,1,1,1));

  t[0] = dot(shVisCoeff[0], g_gEnvCoeff[0]);
  t[1] = dot(shVisCoeff[1], g_gEnvCoeff[1]);
  t[2] = dot(shVisCoeff[2], g_gEnvCoeff[2]);
  t[3] = dot(shVisCoeff[3], g_gEnvCoeff[3]);
  res.g = dot(t,float4(1,1,1,1));

  t[0] = dot(shVisCoeff[0], g_bEnvCoeff[0]);
  t[1] = dot(shVisCoeff[1], g_bEnvCoeff[1]);
  t[2] = dot(shVisCoeff[2], g_bEnvCoeff[2]);
  t[3] = dot(shVisCoeff[3], g_bEnvCoeff[3]);
  res.b = dot(t,float4(1,1,1,1));

  return res;
}
```

RENDERING SHADOWS ON GLOSSY SURFACES

For rendering glossy reflections under environment lighting, we use the *filtered importance sampling* (FIS) algorithm described in detail in [Colbert07, Křivánek08].

FIGURES 1 Dynamic weather effects.
This figure shows the dynamic weather system in *Project Gotham Racing 4*
for Xbox 360. Different parameters create different types of precipitation;
rain in the top picture smoothly blends into snow on the bottom.

FIGURE 2 More dynamic weather effects in *Project Gotham Racing 4* for Xbox 360.

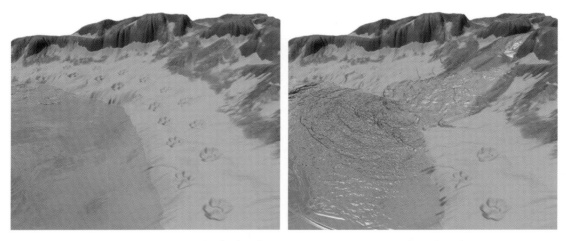

FIGURE 3 Interactive hydraulic erosion. Here, a river erodes a beach. Both the erosion simulation and the rendering run on the GPU in real time.

FIGURE 4   A scene composed from four layers of material (displayed as different colors).

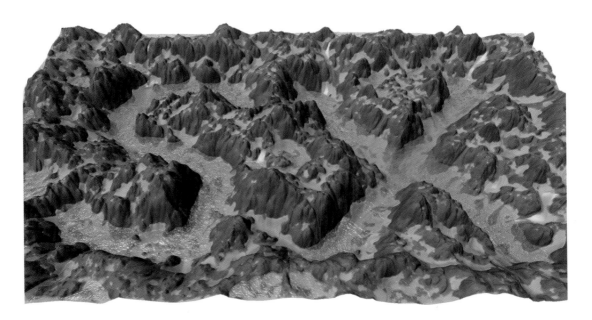

FIGURE 5   Rain eroding a 2,048×1,024 terrain.

FIGURE 6 Terrain rendering. Real-time rendering of terrain with displacement-map–based lighting and procedurally generated snow placement.

FIGURE 7 An interior scene with many materials (including cloth, wood, glass, and brass), with a magnification of a syringe on a plate in the inset.

FIGURE 8 Orientation-aligned bilateral filter: $n_a = 4$, $\sigma_d = 3.0$, $\sigma_r = 4.25\%$.
Separable flow-based DoG: $n_e = 1$, $\sigma_e = 1.0$, $\sigma_m = 3.0$.
Color quantization: $q = 8$, $\varphi = 3.4$. Original images courtesy of philip.greenspun.com.

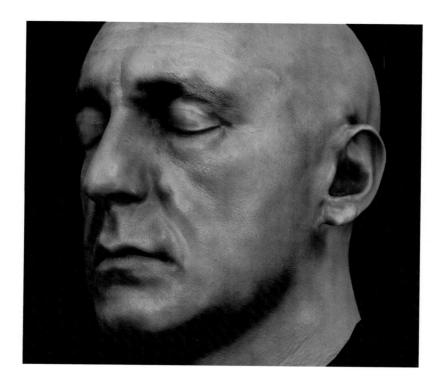

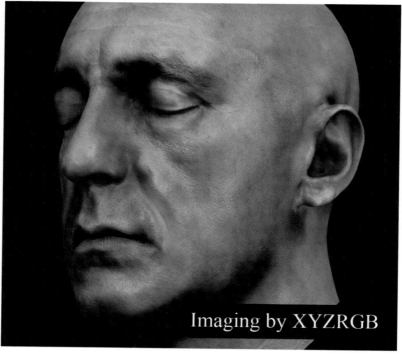

Imaging by XYZRGB

FIGURES 9 These images show a comparison between an implementation of texture-space diffusion as described by d'Eon and Leubke (top) and an optimized implementation (bottom).

FIGURE 10 This shows how glass and stone can be achieved on the same texture, with glass shards in the inset.

FIGURE 11 Interactive volumetric light shafts and shadows rendered at up to 80 frames per second using a hybrid approach. The fairy forest uses a white point light, the other two scenes use textured lights, and the inset shows the texture used.

FIGURE 12   This shows how wet and dry can be achieved on the same texture, with an opposite view in the inset.

The shading calculation in FIS involves generating sample directions proportionally to the bidirectional reflection distribution function, performing a filtered lookup in a mipmap of the environment for each sample direction, and summing the sample contributions together.

To generate shadows, we additionally attenuate the contribution of each sample by the visibility for the sample direction reconstructed from the SH coefficients using Equation 4.3.3. Note that for convenience in diffuse shading, we actually represent the visibility multiplied by the cosine term. However, multiplication by the cosine term is not desirable for shading of glossy surfaces. Therefore, we explicitly divide the contribution of each sample by the cosine term to compensate the multiplication included with the visibility function.

RESULTS

IMAGE QUALITY

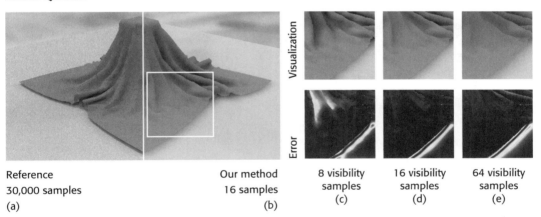

Reference
30,000 samples
(a)

Our method
16 samples
(b)

Visualization

Error

8 visibility
samples
(c)

16 visibility
samples
(d)

64 visibility
samples
(e)

FIGURE 4.3.8   A visual comparison of a ray-traced solution for the shadow (a) versus our approximation (b). As seen in (c–e) our method provides a good approximation when compared to a reference solution. As the number of samples increases, the fit improves (c, d) but the filtering may over-blur the shadow, causing additional error (e).

As seen in Figure 4.3.1 and Figure 4.3.8, our method captures the appearance of the shadows cast from an environment light source in both a qualitative and quantitative manner. As our approach is based on shadow mapping, the quality of the result requires scene-specific parameter tweaking to combat the spatial and depth aliasing in the shadow maps. For instance, an appropriate offset and bias must be selected to account for quantization errors in the shadow depth map.

Moreover, the size of the filter kernel as well as the amount of regularization used for the least squares fit relates to resolution of the shadow maps and the distribution of the important samples. However, since the algorithm operates in real-time, these parameters can either be set until appearing visually correct or fitted to match a reference solution for a single frame.

RUNTIME PERFORMANCE

Illustrating the algorithm's runtimes, Figure 4.3.9 depicts the near linear performance when adjusting the number of filtered importance samples, the number of shadow-mapped importance samples, and the number of polygons in the scene on an NVIDIA 8800 GTX. In each case, these performance curves demonstrate the simple tradeoff between visual quality and the cost of computation. Moreover, since our performance behaves linearly and GPUs continue to perform parallel operations at faster rates, our methods can be adapted to improve visual performance on future hardware by simply adding more samples.

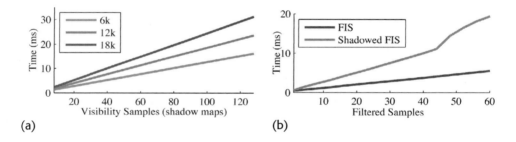

FIGURE 4.3.9 (a) The execution time for generating the SH coefficients for visibility and rendering a diffuse surface with differing polygon count. (b) Time for rendering a glossy sphere at a resolution of 512 × 512 with (red) and without (blue) visibility. The non-linearity at 45 samples results from an optimization shift on the GPU due to the increased number of instructions.

More examples, animations, and the latest version of the demo are available at http://www.mcl.ucf.edu/shaderx7. The demo is written in C++ using DirectX and requires a GPU supporting Shader Model 3.0.

CONCLUSION

This article presents a simple technique to generate shadows in scenes illuminated by an environment map. The shadows are approximate but visually plausible. While our technique is not per-pixel accurate, we provide solutions good enough for complex pre-visualizations in film or visually pleasing shadows in a gaming environment.

ENDNOTES

[1] A matrix is *orthogonal* if the scalar product of any of its columns, i and j, is nonzero if and only if $i = j$. The inverse of an orthogonal matrix is equal to its transpose.

[2] A 2D function $f(x,y)$ is *separable* if it can be written as a product of two 1D functions, that is, $f(x,y) = h(x) \cdot g(y)$.

ACKNOWLEDGMENTS

This work has been supported by the Ministry of Education, Youth and Sports of the Czech Republic under the research program LC-06008 (Center for Computer Graphics) and by the Media Convergence Lab at the University of Central Florida. Special thanks to Alex Zelenin for the robot model.

REFERENCES

[Annen08] T. Annen, Z. Dong, T. Mertens, P. Bekaert, H.-P. Seidel, and J. Kautz, "Real-time, All-frequency Shadows in Dynamic Scenes," *ACM Trans. Graph.* (Proc. of SIGGRAPH 2008), 27(3), 2008.

[Bishop06] C. H. Bishop, *Pattern Recognition and Machine Learning*, Springer-Verlag New York, 2006.

[Colbert08] M. Colbert, "Appearance-Driven Material Design," PhD Thesis, University of Central Florida, 2008.

[Colbert07] M. Colbert and J. Křivánek, "GPU-Based Importance Sampling," *GPU Gems 3*, Addison-Wesley Professional, 2007, pp. 459–475.

[Debevec02] P. Debevec, "Image-Based Lighting," In *IEEE Comp. Graph. App.* 22(2), pp. 26–34.

[Green03] R. Green, "Spherical Harmonic Lighting: The Gritty Details," In Game Developers' Conference, 2003.

[Křivánek08] J. Křivánek and M. Colbert, "Real-time Shading with Filtered Importance Sampling," *Computer Graphics Forum* (Proc. of Eurographics Symposium on Rendering), 27(4), 2008.

[Kautz05] J. Kautz, J. Lehtinen, and P.-P. Sloan, "Precomputed Radiance Transfer: Theory and Practice," In SIGGRAPH '05 Courses, 2005.

[Pharr04] M. Pharr and G. Humphreys, *Physically Based Rendering: from Theory to Implementation*, Morgan Kaufmann, 2004.

[Press92] W. H. Press, B. P. Flannery, S. A. Teukolsky, and W. T. Vetterling, *Numerical Recipes in C: The Art of Scientific Computing*, Cambridge University Press; 2nd edition, 1992.

[Ramamoorthi01] R. Ramamoorthi, "An Efficient Representation for Irradiance Environment Maps," http://www1.cs.columbia.edu/~ravir/papers/envmap/, 2001.

4.4 Facetted Shadow Mapping for Large Dynamic Game Environments

RAY TRAN

INTRODUCTION

Shadows play an important role in providing a convincing representation of the game world to the game player, and with the current generation of game consoles and the GPUs they employ, rendering soft dynamic shadows even in large dynamic game environments has become possible.

This article presents a novel shadowing algorithm that was used in the game *Grand Theft Auto IV* (*GTA4*). In the following section we discuss the challenges posed when developing a shadow system in large dynamic game environments and describe how our approach addressed these challenges. We then review existing shadowing techniques that have influenced the development of our new approach and show how our approach overcomes some issues with these techniques. A detailed description of our approach, including source code examples, is then provided, showing how to construct facetted shadow maps and how to use them when applying shadows to a scene.

THE CHALLENGES

In this section we describe some of the challenges faced when developing a shadow system for a game environment and explain the motivation behind some of the choices made in developing the facetted shadow approach. It should be noted that facetted shadow maps are suitable for light sources that can be simulated as global directional lights in a game environment, such as the sun or the moon. When choosing a shadow approach for a game, you need to consider the requirements of your scene, and for *GTA4* these were:

- **Dynamic time of day:** The relative sun position would continuously change as time passed in the game world, starting in the east at dawn and swinging around to the west at dusk. Precalculating shadows for a continuously changing sun was therefore not possible without producing a large amount of data.

- **Consistent shadowing:** To produce a convincing environment, our aim was to have all objects cast and receive shadows using a consistent approach. It was important for all shadows to match the originating light source.

- **High-detail soft shadows:** Our aim was to produce highly detailed shadows without harsh edges.

- **Low memory usage:** Fitting the dense game world into memory is a real challenge. A shadow system that has low memory usage was required.

- **Low streaming bandwidth:** It is often impossible for large games such as *GTA4* to fit entirely in the fixed memory available on a game console, so you have to stream data in and out from a secondary storage device. A shadow system that has a small impact on streaming bandwidth was desirable.

The development of the facetted approach allowed us to meet these requirements in *GTA4*: "The real-time shadows are working across every object and surface in the game with everything self-shadowing and casting onto everything else" (Aaron Garbut, Art Director, Rockstar North) [Bramwell08].

EXISTING SHADOW MAP APPROACHES

There have been many adaptations of the original shadow map approach presented in [Williams78]. We will focus on approaches that can be implemented on current console hardware and have influenced the development of the facetted approach—broadly divided into two categories: warped shadow maps and split shadow maps.

- **Warped shadow maps:** These include perspective shadow maps [Stamminger02] and several variants of perspective shadow maps including light space perspective shadow maps [Wimmer04] and trapezoid shadow maps [Martin04]. These warping techniques use a special projection matrix to warp the shadow map so that the important parts, close to the viewpoint of the scene, appear larger in the shadow map and therefore reduce aliasing artifacts. Perspective shadow maps suffer from *dueling frusta* problems, which occur when a certain range of light directions and view directions prevent a good projection matrix from being formulated. This problem has largely prevented their wide use in games that have varying light directions and unconstrained camera directions.

- **Split shadow maps:** These include cascaded shadow maps [Engel06] and a similar technique called parallel-split shadow maps [Zhang07]. These splitting techniques divide up the view frustum into several parts, rendering each part as a separate map or tile. By varying the size of each tile or the area that each tile covers, it is possible to render more detail into tiles closer to the view point and reduce aliasing in those tiles. Split shadow maps are widely used in games, as they do not suffer from dueling frusta problems and there are efficient methods to correctly choose which of the tiles should be used when applying shadows. Split shadow maps suffer from an artifact that can be seen on the border between tiles where there is a differing texel density.

The facetted shadow map approach uses both warping and splitting to reduce aliasing. The key advantage over other split shadow maps is that it is possible to apply a filter across the splits, but it does not suffer from dueling frusta issues.

FACETTED SHADOW MAP APPROACH

In a facetted shadow map the scene is split into several equal-sized parts or facets (Figure 4.4.1). All facets sit on the same map, and the arrangement of each facet within the map allows filtering from one facet to an adjacent facet, avoiding the visible artifact found in other split shadow maps. Each facet has an individual projection matrix formulated to warp the objects in that facet, which is used when creating the facet and when using the facet to apply shadows.

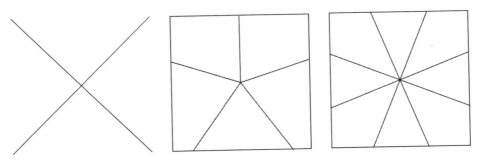

FIGURE 4.4.1   These pictures show possible facet arrangements of four, five, and eight facets.

FIGURE 4.4.2 (Top left) A standard shadow map. (Top right) A facetted shadow map with four facets. (Bottom left) An eight-facet facetted shadow map. (Bottom right) An isolated facet from an eight-facet arrangement. The dark area would normally be clipped because other facets making up the shadow map would occupy this area.

Notice in Figure 4.4.2 that the trees in the center of the facetted shadow maps are bigger than they would appear in the standard shadow map and thus have more shadow information close to the center of the map, reducing aliasing where the viewpoint would be located. Also note that when trees fall into more than one facet, the edges of the facets line up even though the warp direction is different for each facet. This allows filtering across facet boundaries.

CREATING AND USING FACETTED SHADOW MAPS

The formulation of the perspective projection matrix for each of the facets depends on the size of the region in the scene in which you want to cast shadows and the desired detail at the center of the map. Three values are required to create a facet projection matrix equation: **F**, D, and S, where:

- **F** is the facet direction—a vector in the direction of the perspective warp.

- D is the distance to the edge of the shadow map—a scalar value in world space.

- S is the detail level of at the center of the shadow map—a scalar value in world space.

The units of D and S should match the units in the game world and should remain constant across all facets. **F** should be normalized and have a magnitude of 1.0 and can be described as the direction of the line that bisects each facet, perpendicular to the light direction. Figure 4.4.3 illustrates how **F**, D, and S relate to a single facet; **L** is the light direction:

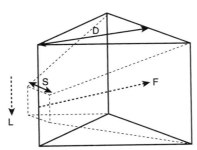

FIGURE 4.4.3   The magnitude of S is the width of the near clip plane on the dotted frustum, most of which will be clipped by the facet shown as the triangular wedge.

A derived value of d is calculated from D and S:

$$d = \frac{D + S}{D}$$

d is then used in the facet projection matrix, **M**:

$$\mathbf{M} = \begin{bmatrix} d & 0 & 0 & F_x \\ 0 & d & 0 & F_y \\ 0 & 0 & d & F_z \\ 0 & 0 & 0 & S \end{bmatrix}$$

The values chosen for *S* and *D* will affect the severity of the warping and therefore the detail that is stored in the shadow map closer or further from the center point. The greater the detail required at the center (controlled by *S*) and the larger the desired total area covered by the shadow map (controlled by *D*), the more severe the warping will be. This means it is possible to balance where the pixels of a fixed-size shadow map are used in a scene.

From an implementation standpoint, the facet projection matrix should be combined with the world matrix and light view matrix and applied together in a vertex shader, and polygons produced for each facet should be clipped along the edges of that facet. Clipping can be achieved by using the stencil buffer to cut out the shape of the facet on the map, or by dropping pixels rendered outside the facet (using instructions such as clip() or texkill) or by simply enabling hardware clipping planes.

Here is an example vertex shader for rendering to a facet:

```
//note that all three matrices can be combined to a single matrix
void VS_RenderShadowFacet(in float4 pos : POSITION, in int facetIndex, out
float4 posOut: POSITION)
{
        //transform into world space
        float4 worldPos=mul(pos, worldMatrix);

        //transform into shadow view space
        float4 lightPos=mul(worldPos, lightViewMatrix);

        //output projected position
        posOut=mul(lightPos, facetProjectionMatrix[facetIndex]);
}
```

To use a facetted shadow map to determine whether a test point is in shadow, you need to determine which of the facets the test point falls in, and then transform the test point by the same matrix formulated to create the facet. A comparison can be made between the depth of the transformed point and the depth read from the shadow map. After the facet has been selected, the approach is essentially the same as using individual perspective shadow maps as described in [Stamminger02].

To determine which of the facet projection matrices to use, you can perform a dot product between **F**, the direction vector for each facet in the map, and choose the facet with the highest dot product. You can alternatively calculate the angle of the test point and rescale it to the index of the matrix directly. Here is an example pixel shader function demonstrating the use of an angle to index the facet matrix:

```
//this function returns 0.0 if in position is in shadow and 1.0 if not in
shadow
float PS_GetShadowFactor(float4 pos)
{
    //transform into world space
    float4 worldPos=mul(pos, worldMatrix);


    //transform world position into light view space
    float4 lightPos=mul(worldPos, lightViewMatrix);


    //calculate the angle per facet in radians - this value can be
precalculated and reciprocated to avoid using a divide instruction
    float facetAngle=(2.0*PI)/NUM_FACETS;


    //calculate facet index by calculating the angle, then dividing by
the facet angle
    float angle=atan2(lightPos.x,lightPos.y)+PI;
    int facetIndex=(angle/facetAngle);


    //once the facet index is found the facetted map can be treated as a
standard perspective shadow map
    float4 facetPos=mul(lightPos, facetProjectionMatrix[facetIndex]);
    float2 facetUV=((facetPos.xy/facetPos.w)*0.5)+0.5;


    float facetDepth=facetPos.z/facetPos.w;
    float shadowMapDepth=tex2D(FacettedShadowMapSampler, facetUV);


    if (shadowMapDepth<facetDepth)
        return 0.0;
    else
        return 1.0;
}
```

The example code above takes a single "tap." It does not apply an averaging filter to the shadow result. Using multiple taps can help hide aliasing and give a softer shadow. Facetted shadow maps can be used with all shadow filtering methods, because apart from having to determine the correct facet matrix to use, once a facetted shadow map is constructed it is possible treat it as you would an unwarped orthographic shadow map. The filtering technique used to produce softer shadows in *GTA4* was a four-tap rotated disk-filtering technique.

RESULTS

The end results can be qualitatively assessed by playing *GTA4* or looking at the color pictures found on the front cover of this book. In terms of performance, in a typical scene, the rendering of the facetted shadow map would take between 10 and 15% of the total frame time. Table 4.4.1 shows results taken from *GTA4*. Each scene corresponds to a color picture found on the front cover of this book from top to bottom:

TABLE 4.4.1 Results from *GTA4*

Firefly Island	2,364,288 vertices	11,928,880 pixels	4.31 ms
Star Junction	1,315,401 vertices	10,434,240 pixels	3.78 ms
Applejack St	1,429,142 vertices	11,447,552 pixels	3.64 ms

The relationship between vertex count, pixel count, and time taken to render a facetted shadow map is not linear and is dependant on the composition of each individual scene.

Memory usage was kept very low. The facetted shadow map used in *GTA4* used a total of only 6.4 MB for a 1,280×1,280 shadow map. Clearly, a larger map would increase the quality of the shadows and reduce aliasing, but this was not an option for *GTA4* due to memory constraints.

CONCLUSION

This article described a shadow mapping method suitable for large-scale dynamic game environments under the constraints of current game console hardware. The technique has some advantages over some existing shadow map approaches and was used to good effect in *GTA4*.

Future developments for the facetted approach may include using geometry shaders to render to many or all facets at once, by generating extra vertices on the facet boundaries as required. Further investigation into methods to offset the center of the facet map, and adjust facet projection matrices accordingly, could result in reduced aliasing in some combinations of light direction and viewing direction.

ACKNOWLEDGMENTS

We would like to give thanks to all those involved in the creation of *GTA4*, and special thanks to Adam Fowler for his support and guidance throughout the development process, Aaron Garbut for constantly pushing for graphical excellence, and Wolfgang Engel for making this article possible.

REFERENCES

[Williams78] L. Williams, "Casting Curved Shadows on Curved Surfaces," ACM SIGGRAPH 1978.

[Stamminger02] Marc Stamminger and George Drettakis, "Perspective Shadow Maps," ACM SIGGRAPH 2002.

[Wimmer04] Michael Wimmer, Daniel Scherzer, and Werner Purgathofer, "Light Space Perspective Shadow Maps," Eurographics 2004.

[Martin04] Tobias Martin and Tiow-Seng Tan, "Anti-Alias and Continuity with Trapezoidal Shadow Maps," Eurographics 2004.

[Engel06] Wolfgang Engel, "Cascaded Shadow Maps," *Shader X 5*, 2006

[Zhang07] Fan Zhang, Hanqiu Sun, Leilei Xu, and Le Kit Lun, "Parallel-Split Shadow Maps for Large-Scale Virtual Environments," ACM VRCIA'06.

[Bramwell08] Tom Bramwell, "CGSociety Feature: GTA IV – Under the Hood," available online at http://features.cgsociety.org/story_custom.php?story_id=4499, 2008.

Part V

Environmental Effects

MATTHIAS WLOKA, VISUAL CONCEPTS, TAKE TWO INC.

The "Environmental Effects" section presents articles about how to render aspects of a game's environment convincingly and efficiently. This year we have three contributions that advance the state of the art.

First, Charlie Birtwistle and Stephen McAuley of Bizarre Creations describe how their recent game *Project Gotham Racing 4* implements "Dynamic Weather Effects." They render rain or any other type of precipitation using a particle system that employs only a fraction of the number of particles typically used for these purposes. They exploit the observation that a particle system whose particles wrap around to a small, axis-aligned cube tiles seamlessly over the world. Even better, rendering such a cube's worth of particles in front of the camera creates the illusion of an infinite expanse of rain, despite the small number of particles that require simulation and rendering. In addition, particles persist in the world even if the camera is dynamic. They also address how to make it not rain indoors. Their demo

ON THE DVD

on the book's DVD-ROM comes with full source code.

Second, Ondřej Šťava, Bedřich Beneš, and Jaroslav Křivánek present "Interactive Hydraulic Erosion on the GPU." Their technique emulates how water, both flowing and still, shapes terrain via erosion and deposition processes. Their implementation uses the GPU to both simulate these processes and render the results. The accom-

ON THE DVD

panying demo on the book's DVD-ROM shows that the result is real-time, even for large, high-resolution terrains. The technique is thus highly valuable as an extension for interactive terrain modeling tools.

Third and last, James Sun from the Keystone Game Studio in Taiwan introduces a novel sky geometry in "Advanced Geometry for Complex Sky Representation." The article observes that for each projection type, such as a planar, cylindrical, or spherical projection, there exists an ideal sky geometry that represents that projection with minimal distortions, i.e., sky planes, cylinders, or hemispheres. To avoid rendering multiple sky geometries when requiring multiple projection types, James shows how to construct a single sky geometry that integrates all three projection types while minimizing projection inaccuracies.

All good stuff: Enjoy!

5.1 Dynamic Weather Effects

CHARLIE BIRTWISTLE AND STEPHEN MCAULEY, BIZARRE CREATIONS LTD.

INTRODUCTION

Well-implemented weather effects such as rain, fog, and lightning greatly add to the realism of an outdoor scene. Rain and other types of precipitation are the most challenging to render convincingly in real-time. This article presents an innovative method of rendering rain, snow, sleet, and hail that smoothly blends between any type and density of precipitation and is highly art directable.

Prior approaches to rendering precipitation fall into one of two classes: particles or image space.

Using one particle to model each drop of precipitation is still the most common solution. These particle systems, however, have a high computational cost directly proportional to the number of particles in use. While particle rendering consumes GPU cycles, particle simulation either runs on the CPU, or consumes additional GPU cycles [Tariq07].

Image space techniques use layers of scrolling textures to model precipitation [Wang05] [Tatarchuk07]. These techniques only consume GPU cycles for simulation and rendering. They are, however, inherently 2D and thus suffer from artifacts when moving the camera, especially at high speeds, making them unsuitable for many games.

Neither of the above methods suits our needs for *Project Gotham Racing 4* (see Figure 5.1.1 and the color plates): Particle systems are too costly for the desired number of particles, and an image space approach creates too many visual artifacts.

FIGURE 5.1.1   Screenshot of our dynamic weather system in *Project Gotham Racing 4* for the Xbox 360, developed by Bizarre Creations and published by Microsoft.

PARTICLE SIMULATION AND RENDERING

Our solution simulates and renders only a small subset of all particles in the world. In particular, we choose a world space axis-aligned cube near the origin that is 30 m on a side and randomly populate it with a fixed number, that is, 10,000 particles. We only simulate these 10,000 particles. Particles that fall or blow out of this cube immediately wrap around to reenter the cube from the opposite side. Thus, this cube always contains the same number of particles throughout the simulation.

Because the particles in the cube always wrap in all directions, it is possible to tile the cube in any direction without visible boundaries, akin to the wrap texture addressing mode. In fact, arbitrarily placing any world space axis-aligned cube of the same dimensions into the world encloses the identical set of particles as contained in the original cube near the origin (see also Figure 5.1.2).

Our particle simulation simply offsets each particle by gravity and wind. The CPU computes both offsets every frame and passes the result as simple offset vectors to the vertex shader. The vertex shader thus computes a particle's current position every time it renders; that is, we only ever store the initial particle positions in a static vertex buffer. The fmod function ensures that each particle wraps back into the original cube:

```
float3 offsets  = gravityOffset + windOffset;
float3 position = fmod(initialPosition + offsets, BoxSize);
```

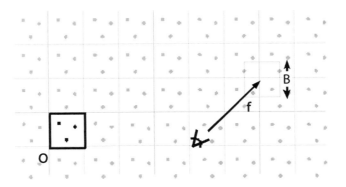

FIGURE 5.1.2   A world space axis-aligned box at the origin contains a
fixed number of particles and tiles over the entire world. Any world space
axis-aligned box of the same dimensions contains the identical set of particles.
We place one such box in front of the camera.

When the CPU computes the current `gravityOffset`, it simply adds a delta value to the previous `gravityOffset` result. The delta value is user-controlled; larger offsets simulate heavier particles. This delta value may be time-varying to emulate changing weights of particles. Computing the `windOffset` is analogous. In particular, we use a Perlin noise function for the wind direction that gives the appearance of ever-changing wind currents. To avoid eventual overflows in these offset vectors, the CPU also needs to apply the `fmod` function. The `gravityOffset` and `windOffset` vectors are the same for all particles.

To efficiently render this world of particles, we choose a cube directly in front of the camera and render the particles within it (see Figure 5.1.2). In other words, all particles are additionally offset by the camera position and a forward offset that is the view direction scaled by the distance of the cube to the camera:

```
float3 offsets   = gravityOffset + windOffset;
      offsets  -= cameraPosition + forwardOffset + BoxSize/2;
float3 position  = fmod(initialPosition + offsets, BoxSize);
      position += cameraPosition + forwardOffset - BoxSize/2;
```

We choose the original cube's dimensions, that is, 30 m on a side (see above), and the cube's distance to the camera so that particles between the camera and the cube are clipped by the near plane or otherwise invisible, and particles beyond the far sides of the cube are too far to be visible, or are convincingly represented as distance fog.

To increase visual complexity we render the set of particles inside the cube multiple times. Each set of particles runs a different instance of our simulation and uses an additional random, but constant, 3D offset vector:

```
float3 offsets  = gravityOffset[i] + windOffset[i] + randomOffset[i];
        offsets += cameraPosition + forwardOffset + BoxSize/2;
float3 position = fmod(initialPosition + offsets, BoxSize);
        position += cameraPosition + forwardOffset - BoxSize/2;
```

We find that 1 to 20 simulation instances and thus particle set renderings provide sufficient variation to look believable. More than 20 instances make the precipitation look too dense, and have too much performance overhead. The actual number of instances varies with the type of precipitation and is artist-controlled.

The above pseudo code is incorrect due to a small, but important, implementation detail: The fmod function produces results in the range [-BoxSize, BoxSize], that is, negative values wrap to [-BoxSize, 0], and positive values wrap to [0, BoxSize]. Yet we expect all values to wrap to the range [0, BoxSize].

To account for this behavior we apply fmod to the sum of the offset vectors, which is thus guaranteed to be in the range [-BoxSize, BoxSize]. We generate all initial particle positions in the range [BoxSize, 2BoxSize]. The sum of the initial particle position and its offsets are thus always positive and in the range [0, 3BoxSize]. Applying fmod to this sum thus creates a result in the desired range [0, BoxSize]:

```
float3 offsets  = gravityOffset[i] + windOffset[i] + randomOffset[i];
        offsets += cameraPosition + forwardOffset + BoxSize/2;
        offsets  = fmod( offsets, BoxSize );
float3 position = fmod(initialPosition + offsets, BoxSize);
        position += cameraPosition + forwardOffset − BoxSize/2;
```

RENDERING MOTION-BLURRED PARTICLES

Precipitation particles draw as an indexed triangle list or, if the GPU supports it, as a quad list from the static vertex buffer of initial positions. Each position in the static vertex buffer generates a quad via instancing with a stream of four pairs of UV coordinates. The quad's construction ensures it is always camera facing.

While real rain consists of fast-moving droplets of water, viewing these through a camera with finite exposure times results in motion-blurred streaks. To emulate motion blur we require two positions for every particle: its current position and its previous position. The current position is the result of our particle simulation (see "Particle Simulation and Rendering" above). Because all particles in a simulation instance move identically, they all share the same velocity (see "Particle Simulation and Rendering" above). A particle's previous position is thus equal to the current position minus a global, per simulation instance velocity. To directly control the length of the streaks, we scale this velocity by a user-controlled constant.

The screen-space positions of the top and bottom vertices of each particle are thus the previous and current positions transformed by the previous and current view projection matrices, respectively (see also Listing 5.1.1).

Listing 5.1.1 Computing the screen-space positions of the bottom and top vertices of each motion-blurred particle

```
float4 worldPosPrev = worldPos + g_vVelocity * g_fHeightScale;

      worldPosPrev.w = 1.0f;

float4 bottom = mul(worldPos,      g_mViewProj);

float4 top    = mul(worldPosPrev, g_mViewProjPrev);
```

Next we calculate how to offset a particle's vertices to the left and right so that the particle faces the camera and is rectangular. The difference between the top and bottom vertices in screen-space is a 2D vector $\mathbf{v} = \text{top} - \text{bottom}$. We compute a vector $\mathbf{w}$ as

$$\mathbf{v} = \begin{bmatrix} x \\ y \end{bmatrix} \qquad \mathbf{w} = \begin{bmatrix} -y \\ x \end{bmatrix}$$

EQUATION 5.1.1

that is perpendicular to $\mathbf{v}$. Offsetting the top and bottom positions of a particle by $\mathbf{w}$ and $-\mathbf{w}$ results in a camera-facing and rectangular billboard (see also Figure 5.1.3).

Listing 5.1.2 provides the code to construct per-particle, camera-facing quads. It uses a vertex's UV coordinates to decide how to offset each vertex.

Listing 5.1.2 Vertex shader code to construct camera-facing quads

```
float4 ConstructBillboard(float4 position, float2 uv)

{

    float4 worldPos = position;
```

```
        float4 worldPosPrev = position + g_vVelocity * g_fHeightScale;
        worldPosPrev.w = 1.0f;


        float4 bottom  = mul(worldPos,      g_mViewProj);
        float4 topPrev = mul(worldPosPrev, g_mViewProjPrev);
        float2 dir     = (topPrev.xy/topPrev.w) - (bottom.xy/bottom.w);
        float2 dirPerp = normalize(float2(-dir.y, dir.x));


        float4 projPos;
        projPos     = lerp(topPrev, bottom, uv.y);
        projPos.xy += (0.5f - uv.x) * dirPerp * g_fWidthScale;
        return projPos;
}
```

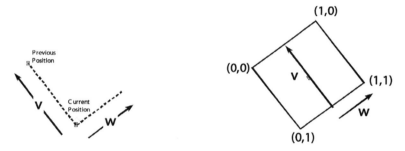

FIGURE 5.1.3 The screen-space vectors **v** and **w** are perpendicular and span a camera-facing rectangle for every particle.

The above implementation of motion blur, however, suffers from two visual problems. First, the faster the camera moves, the brighter the rain becomes. The cause of this effect is that all particles retain the same brightness regardless of their screen size or how much they stretch. We thus fade each particle proportional to its screen-space velocity, as shown in Listing 5.1.3.

Listing 5.1.3 Fading out fast-moving particles

```
...

float4 bottom  = mul(worldPos,      g_mViewProj);
float4 top     = mul(worldPosPrev, g_mViewProj);
```

```
float4 topPrev = mul(worldPosPrev, g_mViewProjPrev);


float2 dir     = (top.xy/top.w) - (bottom.xy/bottom.w);
float2 dirPrev = (topPrev.xy/topPrev.w) - (bottom.xy/bottom.w);


float len      = length(dir);
float lenPrev  = length(dirPrev);
float lenColorScale = saturate(len/lenPrev);
...
```

The second visual problem appears when moving through rain at high speeds (see Figure 5.1.4), even when scaling the rain's brightness as described above. To avoid this hyperspace effect we altogether fade out precipitation when it is moving at extremely high velocities.

FIGURE 5.1.4   An example of the hyperspace effect.

To further improve the look of particles, adding extra information to the vertex buffer provides particles with size and color variation. In addition, a texture atlas of various precipitation sprites increases the appearance of randomness.

At present, precipitation is unlit. We suggest picking the nearest two lights to the camera and using them to light the rain using Tariq's method of using a texture atlas of rain drops illuminated from different angles [Tariq07].

Occlusion

To produce believable precipitation we also account for occlusion. Rain is absent in indoor regions, such as tunnels and buildings, and generally in areas under cover, such as bridges.

Our first attempt at solving this problem uses a height map of the world to compare it with the *y* coordinate of the world position of each precipitation particle pixel. If the pixel is beneath the height map, then it is under cover, and we set its alpha value to zero, making it invisible. This technique, however, becomes problematic for real-world scenes because they require height map textures of impractically high resolution.

Our current solution instead uses multiple occlusion boxes. An occlusion box is a cuboid that contains a height map (see Figure 5.1.5). It represents a rectangular covered region: Any pixel whose world-space position is below the occlusion box, or is inside the occlusion box but below the height map, sets its alpha value to zero.

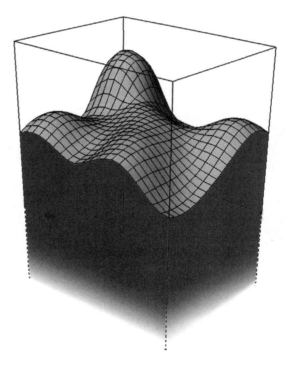

FIGURE 5.1.5 An occlusion box contains a height map that occludes everything beneath it.

To sample a height map in a pixel shader we must transform world space into texture space. We use the matrix that transforms the occlusion box into the unit cube ranging from $(0, 0, 0)$ to $(1, 1, 1)$. The resulting x- and z-coordinates then serve as UV coordinates, while the y-coordinate is compared with the height map sample (see Listing 5.1.4).

Listing 5.1.4 Testing whether an occlusion box covers a precipitation particle pixel

```
// Returns 0.0f if occluded, 1.0f otherwise
float TestOcclusionBox(float3 worldPosition, float4x4 boxMatrix,
                       sampler2D boxTexture)
{
    float3 uv = mul(float4(worldPosition, 1.0f), boxMatrix).xyz;
    float height = tex2D(boxTexture, uv.xz).x;
    float3 uvclamp = saturate(uv);

    if (uvclamp.x == uv.x && uvclamp.z == uv.z && uv.y < height)
        return 0.0f;

    return 1.0f;
}
```

Although artists place any number of occlusion boxes in a scene, for performance reasons a shader only tests a few of them at a time. To determine which occlusion boxes to test in the pixel shader, we first frustum cull all occlusion boxes before drawing the rain. We then sort the remaining occlusion boxes by increasing distance from the camera, and finally select the nearest two for testing in the pixel shader.

If the GPU supports vertex texturing and the implementation is pixel-shader bound, then a possible optimization is to let the vertex shader calculate occlusion. Occluded particles send all their post-transform vertices to $(0, 0, 0, 0)$, and the hardware's degenerate triangle test then rejects the particle's quad.

DYNAMIC, ARTIST-CONTROLLED WEATHER

We expose six main parameters of our technique to artists. They use these parameters to model different precipitation types, such as light rainfall or heavy snow fall. In the game, we interpolate these settings to smoothly blend between various types of precipitation. For instance, a scene can move from dry weather to light rainfall to heavy snowfall (see Figure 1.5.6 and the color plates). These main parameters are described below.

- Density is the number of layers of precipitation to render. Fractional values alpha-blend layers in. For instance, 9.5 layers means we draw 10 layers, but the last layer draws with only 50% opacity.

- The speed of falling precipitation: High-density particles, for example, rain drops, have high speed, while low-density particles, for example, snow, have low speed.

- The current wind strength, and how much it affects the precipitation.

- The length of the blur of the particles: Rain uses higher values than snow.

- The width of the particles: Snow generally consists of square billboards, while rain renders as narrow rectangles.

- Each precipitation type has an associated texture atlas depicting its particles. We currently do not blend between textures, and thus any scene transitioning from rain to snow (or vice versa) must use the same texture for both particles. It is, however, relatively easy to find textures that work well for a range of precipitation types.

FIGURE 5.1.6 Different parameters create different types of precipitation.
Rain in the first picture smoothly blends into snow in the second.

ADDITIONAL EFFECTS

Unfortunately, the above technique to render rain in itself is insufficient to convincingly depict realistic weather. Secondary effects such as impact splashes, rippling puddles, and drops running down windows help integrate rain into a world [Tatarchuk06] [Tatarchuk06a].

Other important effects include lightning: An implementation may either use lightning maps [Tatarchuk06a] or a volumetric lightning model [Wenzel07]. For sheet lightning, we find that momentarily increasing the sun's intensity to an extremely high value yields acceptable results and is free to use, since dim sun light already contributes to the rain's illumination. This trick also generates free lightning shadows if the sun is already a shadow caster.

Fog is also relevant for creating believable weather. Volumetric fog [Wenzel07] is far more realistic than simple hardware fog, although it is computationally much more expensive. Fog volumes may also simulate patches of fog [Grün05][Wenzel07].

Wind that is affecting precipitation also needs to affect other susceptible objects, such as trees or telephone wires. Vegetation animation [Sousa07] is extendable to fill that role.

Finally, although this book is about graphics programming, sound is crucial. From the pitter-patter of rain to loud thunder, good audio enhances the realism of a scene and even covers up any lack of realism in the graphics.

CONCLUSION

This article describes a new method of rendering precipitation. This method is computationally less expensive than traditional particle-based methods and has none of the visual artifacts of image-space post-processing effects. Moreover, the method smoothly blends between any type and density of precipitation, allowing for a dynamic weather system.

The article also discusses various extensions to the technique to improve visual quality. One important extension is how to solve occlusion, for example, allowing for environments with both outdoor and indoor areas. The article introduces the concept of occlusion boxes that employ user-positioned height maps within a scene.

We use a vertex-based approach that is fixed cost and runs entirely on the GPU using Direct3D 9 and Shader Model 2.0. As such, it reacts properly to wind and copes with unrestricted camera movement of any speed without visual artifacts.

Currently, the problems of this technique consist of the performance of its vertex shader and the few hundred kilobytes of memory used for the vertex buffer storing the initial particle positions. Compressing the vertex data as much as possible is thus an improvement. Since all particle positions are within a limited box, representing positions as 16-bit integers provides sufficient resolution. Using 8-bit integers for texture coordinates also suffices.

If Direct3D 10 is available, using a geometry shader to create billboards reduces vertex shader computations fourfold, since the position of each particle quad computes only once, instead of once per vertex.

ON THE DVD
The accompanying DVD-ROM contains a demo of our technique. The demo uses Direct3D 9 and HLSL and includes the source code.

ACKNOWLEDGMENTS

The authors thank everyone at Bizarre Creations for their help and support in developing this technique, and in particular Andy King for his assistance in creating assets for this article.

REFERENCES

[Grün05] Grün, Holger and Spoerl, Marco, "Ray-Traced Fog Volumes," in *ShaderX⁴*, edited by Wolfgang Engel, Charles River Media, 2005: pp. 143–155.

[Sousa07] Sousa, Tiago, "Vegetation Procedural Animation and Shading in Crysis," *GPU Gems 3*, edited by Hubert Nguyen, Addison Wesley 2007, pp: 373–385.

[Tariq07] Tariq, Sarah, "Rain," available online at http://developer.download.nvidia.com/SDK/10/direct3d/Source/rain/doc/RainSDKWhitePaper.pdf.

[Tatarchuk06] Tatarchuk, Natalya, "ToyShop Revealed," Game Developers Conference 2006, available online at http://ati.amd.com/developer/gdc/2006/GDC06-ATI_Session-Tatarchuk-ToyShop.pdf.

[Tatarchuk06a] Tatarchuk, Natalya, "Artist-Directable Real-Time Rain Rendering in City Environments," Course 26: Advanced Real-Time Rendering in 3D Graphics and Games, SIGGRAPH 2006, available online at http://ati.amd.com/developer/siggraph06/Tatarchuk-Rain.pdf.

[Tatarchuk07] Tatarchuk, Natalya, "Rendering Multiple Layers of Rain with a Postprocessing Composite Effect," *ShaderX⁵*, edited by Wolfgang Engel, Charles River Media, 2007: pp. 303–313.

[Wang05] Wang, Niniane and Wade, Bretton, "Let It Snow, Let It Snow, Let It Snow (and Rain)," *Game Programming Gems 5*, edited by Kim Pallister, Charles River Media, 2005: pp. 507–513.

[Wenzel07] Wenzel, Carsten, "Real-time Atmospheric Effects in Games Revisited," Game Developers Conference 2007, available online at http://ati.amd.com/developer/gdc/2007/D3DTutorial_Crytek.pdf.

5.2 Interactive Hydraulic Erosion on the GPU

Ondřej Šťava, Bedřich Beneš, Purdue University and

Jaroslav Křivánek, Czech Technical University in Prague

Introduction

The way in which water interacts with terrain is an important natural phenomenon that has been extensively studied in computer graphics for more than 15 years. Recent work focuses on real-time water simulation, splashing fluids, waves, and bubbles [Bridson2008, Hong2008]. We describe an algorithm that simulates how water moves over a terrain and how water erodes the terrain in the process. The erosion model includes the effects of both running and still water. Our method is thus able to compute erosion caused by rain, rivers, lakes, creeks, or oceans (see Figure 5.2.1 and the color plates). We also show how to effectively couple the hydraulic erosion simulation with visualization. Our algorithm executes all the simulation and visualization computations on the GPU in real-time.

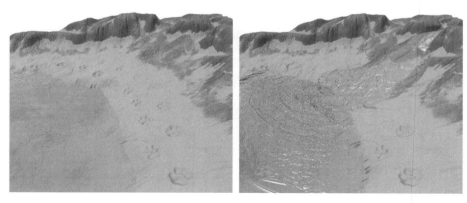

FIGURE 5.2.1   A river erodes a beach. Both the erosion simulation and the rendering run on the GPU in real-time.

An earlier article [Št'ava2008] describes the theoretical aspects of our hydraulic erosion model. This article focuses on the technical implementation details.

We use a set of layers that are input as 2D images to describe a terrain [Beneš2001]. Each layer represents a different material that allows simulating erosion of a wide range of terrains such as sand on hard rock. It also makes material erosion and deposition computations efficient. Water level is set as one of these layers or is defined by discrete water inputs. Similarly, discrete water sinks define the water outlets. The erosion and deposition process always occurs on the topmost layer.

The simulation works in discrete time steps of constant duration: The duration is 50 ms. Each time step consists of several operations (see Figure 5.2.2).

1. Compute water movement.
2. Simulate erosion:
   a. Force-based erosion: erosion and deposition due to moving water
   b. Still water erosion: erosion due to dissolved materials acting like a viscid fluid and thus smoothing terrain
   c. Terrain slippage: erosion due to gravity

In the following sections we discuss these operations in detail and describe their GPU implementation using OpenGL and Cg.

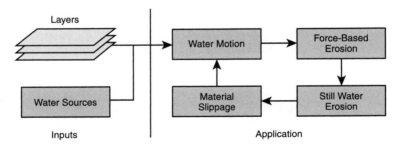

FIGURE 5.2.2 A collection of 2D images define material layers that represent the terrain. Water sources and sinks define the production and consumption of water. Our algorithm operates in discrete time steps, each of which cycles through several operations shown at the right.

DATA STRUCTURES

As mentioned above, we model terrain as a collection of layers. We assume that each material layer is homogenous. Each layer is a 2D texture and represents a regular, nonoverlapping height field. Consequently, we cannot reproduce full 3D terrain features such as caves or overhangs. Similarly, water level is also a 2D height field stored in a texture.

We use multiple textures to store and thus discretize various simulation quantities, such as layer thickness $d_k(x,y)$, water height $w(x,y)$, regolith thickness $r(x,y)$, level of sediment $s(x,y)$, and water and regolith output flow $f_{i,j}(x,y)$. Because our simulation is sensitive to small differences of these quantities, we use 32-bit floating-point textures. Depending on the dimensionality of each quantity, texture formats vary from one-component, for example, for water height or regolith thickness, to four-component, for example, for output flows.

Without loss of generality, we limit the maximum number of input layers that define the terrain materials' thickness to four, because four layers typically suffice for modeling most common terrains [Št'ava2008] (see also Figure 5.2.3 and the color plates). This limitation then allows us to pack all input layers into a single texture. Users are also free to specify less than four input layers. To compute overall terrain height at a given location—without using costly for loops to iterate over all components in use—we precompute a layer mask (see Listing 5.2.1).

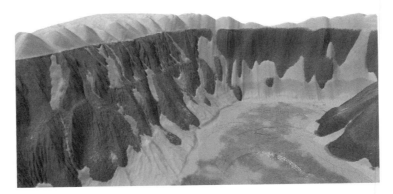

FIGURE 5.2.3   A scene composed from four layers of material (displayed as different colors).

Listing 5.2.1 Computing the total height at a terrain position via a layer mask

```
// compute total height for one texel
float4 getLayerMask(float layers) {
    float4 maskVec = float4(layers,layers-1,layers-2,layers-3);
    return min(float4(1.0), max(float4(0.0), maskVec));
}
```

```
// get total height of a terrain at a given position
float getTotalHeight(float layers, float4 layerData) {
    float4 maskVec = getLayerMask(layers);
    return dot(layerData, maskVec);
}
```

WATER MOVEMENT

The basis of our water simulation is a shallow-water simulation using the virtual-pipe model [Mei2007]: Neighboring cells exchange water through a virtual pipe connecting each cell to its four neighbors (see Figure 5.2.4). A large difference in pressure between connected cells accelerates the flow.

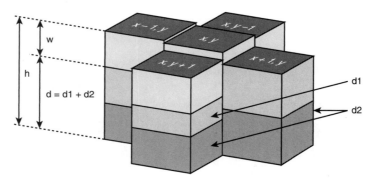

FIGURE 5.2.4   A multilayered 2D texture that is stored on the GPU represents the scene consisting of the terrain and water.

A two-step procedure computes water movement. First, a water-level texture stores the current amount of water in each cell. From this texture we compute output flows of all four virtual pipes for all cells and store the results in an output flow texture (see Listing 5.2.2). This output flow texture thus has four components: one component each for the left, right, top, and bottom pipes of a cell. Second, we use the output flow texture from the first step to compute the new amount of water in all cells: We add all inflows to the current amount of water and subtract all outflows. The inflows are the sum of the outflows of pipes from neighboring cells connecting to the current cell and available from the output flow texture. The water-level texture provides the current amount of water, and finally, the output flow texture also lists all outflows of a cell (see also Listing 5.2.3).

Listing 5.2.2 Pseudo code for computing outflows

Inputs:

```
float   layers;                         // number of layers in the simulation
float   waterC;                         // height of the water
float4  terrainC;                       // height of the terrain
float   waterNeigh[4];                  // height of water at neighbors
float4  terrainNeigh[4];                // height at neighboring cells
const float          gravity  = 10;     // acceleration due to the gravity
const float          cellSize = 1;      // distance between neighboring cells
const float  damping = 0.999;           // affects the water "viscosity"
const float          css      = 1;      // cross-sectional area of a pipe
const float          timeStep = 0.      // size of a time step
```

Pseudo code:

```
// the total height of the central cell
float totalHC = waterC + getTotalHeight(layers, terrainC);
// the total height of the neighboring cells
float4 totalH = waterNeigh + getTotalHeightNeig(layers,terrainNeigh);
// the difference between the center cell and the neighbors
float4 heightDif = float4(totalHC) — totalH;
// acceleration between the center cell and the neighbors
float4 accel = gravity*heightDif/cellSize;
// the new outflow values for the given cell
float4 outflow = damping*oldOutflow + timeStep*css*accel;
// make sure that the outflows are always positive
outflow = max(float4(0.0), outflow);
// the total sum of outflow from the cell has to be smaller than the
// total amount of water in it, otherwise the outflows are scaled down
float maxWater = cellSize * cellSize * waterC;
float waterOut = Sum(outflow) * timeStep;
if (waterOut == 0.0)
outflow = float4(0.0);
```

```
else {

float waterScaleFactor = maxWater / waterOut;

     if (waterScaleFactor < 1.0)

outflow = outflow * waterScaleFactor;

}

return outflow;
```

Listing 5.2.3 Pseudo code for computing the new water amount per cell

Inputs:

```
float4 flowC;                      // outflow from the center cell

float4 flowL, flowR, flowT,        // outflows from the left, right, top

     flowB;                        // and bottom cell neighbors

float      waterC;                 // old water amount of the cell

const float  cellSize = 1;         // distance between neighboring cells

const float  timeStep = 0.05;      // size of a time step
```

Pseudo code:

```
// compute the total output flow in the processed cell

float inflows  = flowR.x + flowL.y + flowB.z + flowT.w;

float outflows = flowC.x + flowC.y + flowC.z + flowC.w;

return waterC + (timeStep * (inflows - outflows))/(cellSize*cellSize);
```

EROSION

Three different erosion algorithms act on our terrain: force-based erosion [Mei2007], still water erosion [Beneš2007], and direct material transportation through terrain slippage [Musgrave1989].

FORCE-BASED EROSION

The force-based hydraulic erosion algorithm calculates the forces of water running over terrain; it is well suited for simulating fast rivers or rain. We expand Mei et al.'s method [Mei2007] to include a second-order accuracy advection method [Selle2007].

It requires us to compute water velocity and the sediment transport capacity of each cell. These quantities then let us redistribute terrain sediments.

Our computation of water movement (see "Water Movement" above) provides us with three textures: the current amount of water in each cell, the previous amount of water in each cell, and the output flow for each cell. Water velocity per cell derives directly from those quantities (see Listing 5.2.4).

Listing 5.2.4 Pseudo code for computing per-cell water velocity

Inputs:

```
float4 flowC;                    // outflow from the central cell
float4 flowL, flowR, flowT,      // outflows from the left, right, top
       flowB;                    // and bottom cells
float      waterC, waterCOl      // current/previous water amount/cell
const float  cellSize = 1;       // distance between neighboring cells
```

Pseudo code:

```
float2 velocityData;
velocityData.x = (flowL.y + flowC.y - flowR.x - flowC.x) / 2.0;
velocityData.y = (flowT.w + flowC.w - flowB.z - flowC.z) / 2.0;
float velocityFactor = cellSize * (waterC + waterCOld) / 2.0;
if (velocityFactor > 0.0)  velocityData /= velocityFactor;
return velocityData;
```

We define the sediment transport capacity $S_k^m(x,y)$ of the flow as:

$$S_k^m(x,y) = \|\mathbf{v}(x,y)\| C_k \sin\alpha(x,y) \quad \textbf{EQUATION 5.2.1}$$

where k is the layer, C_k is a per-layer sediment capacity constant (between $10^{[mw]4}$ for rock and 10^{-1} for sand), $v(x, y)$ is water velocity (see above), and $\alpha(x,y)$ is the tilt angle of the terrain. A separate rendering pass computes up-to-date terrain normals and associated tilt angles:

```
tiltAngle = acos(dot(normal, float3(0,0,1))
```

We then compare the actual level of sediment $S^a(x,y)$ with $S_k^m(x,y)$ (see Equation 5.2.1). If the actual level is larger, some sediment deposits onto the terrain's top layer; otherwise, some sediment dissolves into the water.

Note that even terrains with multiple layers always deposit sediments only into the topmost layer. Any layer, however, can participate in the dissolution step, since there may not be enough material in any one layer k to fully saturate the water. Layers process in top-to-bottom order (see Listing 5.2.5).

Because this step updates the level of sediment, as well as the individual terrain layers, we render into multiple textures simultaneously using the multiple-render targets (MRT) feature of OpenGL. A frame-buffer object in OpenGL, however, supports only MRT textures of the same internal format. In our case, the sediment-level texture has only one component, whereas a multiple-component texture represents the terrain layers. We therefore render the sediment level into a temporary texture with the same format as the terrain texture even though it wastes memory. Because reading from a multiple-component 32-bit floating-point texture is slower than reading a one-component 32-bit floating-point texture, and because we read the sediment level texture multiple times during a frame, we copy the temporary multiple-component sediment texture to a single-component sediment texture as an optimization.

Listing 5.2.5 Pseudo code for multiple layer deposition and dissolution of sediment during force-based erosion

---

Inputs:

```
float  layers;                  // number of layers in the simulation

float2 velocity;                // velocity of the flow

float4 terrain;                 // actual height of individual layers

float  sediment;                // sediment in the water

float       tiltAngle;          // tilt angle of the terrain

float  dissolvingConst[4];      // dissolving constant for each layer

float  depositionConst;         // deposition constant (top-most
layer)

float  capacityConst[4];        // sediment cap. const. for each layer
```

Pseudo code:

```
if (sediment > MaxSediment(layers-1)) {
// if the amount of sediment is larger than the maximum amount
// of sediment then a portion of it is deposited to the terrain
     float sedimentDif =
     depositionConst * (sediment − MaxSediment(layers-1));
```

```
terrainOut[layers-1] += sedimentDif;

sedimentOut -= sedimentDif;

} else {

        // else perform the dissolution

        float layersHeight = 0.0;

        for (int k = layers-1; k >= 0; k-) {

float maxSediment = MaxSediment(k) - layersHeight;

                if (maxSediment < sediment)

                        break;

float actLayerHeight = GetLayerHeight(k);

layersHeight += actLayerHeight;

float sedimentDif = dissolvingConst[k] *

        (sediment - maxSediment);

                // limit the dissolution to the actual layer thickness,

                // but not for the bottommost layer

                if (k > 0)

                        sedimentDif = min(actLayerHeight, sedimentDif);

                terrainOut[k] -= sedimentDif;

                sedimentOut  += sedimentDif;

        }

}
```

In Listing 5.2.5, constant parameters define the material properties. We use values ranging from 0.15 to 0.9 for both dissolving and deposition constants and from 10^{-4} to 10^{-1} for the sediment capacity constants.

After calculating the sediment level in each cell, we advect the sediment via the water velocity field using the MacCormack advection scheme [Selle2007]. The following three equations describe how to do that:

$$\hat{S}^{n+1} = A(S^n) \quad \text{EQUATION 5.2.2}$$

$$\hat{S}^n = A^R(\hat{S}^{n+1}) \quad \text{EQUATION 5.2.3}$$

$$S^{n+1} = \hat{S}^{n+1} + \frac{1}{2}(S^n - \hat{S}^n) \quad \text{EQUATION 5.2.4}$$

where A is a standard semi-Lagrangian advection scheme (as described in Listing 5.2.6), and A^R is a reversed semi-Lagrangian scheme where all velocities have negative values. To ensure the unconditional stability of this method, the third equation applies a limiter to the final value of the result. The limiter is the range obtained from the nodes used in the bilinear interpolation of the first semi-Lagrangian pass (see Equation 5.2.2). Crane et al. [Crane2008] describe the algorithm in detail.

Listing 5.2.6 Pseudo code for the semi-Lagrangian advection

Inputs:

```
const float   cellSize = 1;           // distance between neighboring cells
const float   timeStep = 0.05;        // size of a time step
float2 pos;                           // position of the cell center
float2 velocity;                      // velocity at the cell center
sampler sourceField;                  // a field to be advected
```

Pseudo code:

```
float2 targetPos = pos - (timeStep * velocity) / cellSize;
// perform a bilinear interpolation on the source field (sediment)
return bilerp1f(targetPos, sourceField);
```

STILL WATER EROSION

In the dissolution-based erosion algorithm [Beneš2007], slow-moving water penetrates the bottom and creates a layer of slowly moving regolith (see Figure 5.2.5). As long as water feeds into this layer, it remains liquid, and a simulation similar to high-viscous fluid simulations computes its movement. When the water evaporates and the layer's level decreases, deposition occurs: The soft layer hardens and changes back to soil.

The material constant (between 10^{-4} and 10^{-2}) and Equation 5.2.5 below determine the maximum penetration depth for each layer k:

$$r_k^m(x,y) = \min(c_k, w(x,y)) \quad \text{EQUATION 5.2.5}$$

where $w(x,y)$ represents the actual water depth at a given cell. The process of deposition and dissolution is essentially the same as for the force-based erosion (see "Force-Based Erosion" above). The only difference is that our implementation assumes that the dissolution and the deposition constants are equal to one; therefore, material transfers between the regolith and the terrain are instantaneous.

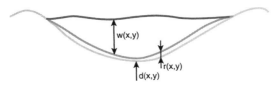

FIGURE 5.2.5   Terrain with a layer of regolith *r(x,y)* at the bottom of the pool.

Our implementation of still water erosion thus derives directly from our implementations of water movement (see "Water Movement" above) and force-based erosion (see "Force-Based Erosion" above). Still water erosion computes in three passes.

First, deposition and dissolution uses the same code as in Listing 5.2.5, except that the deposition and dissolution constants are set to one, and r_k^m (see Equation 5.2.5 above) replaces the maximum amount of sediment for each layer. Second, the code in Listing 5.2.2 computes the regolith output flows. To treat the regolith as a viscid fluid we significantly lower the damping constant: We use a value of 0.15 in our simulations. Third, and finally, the code in Listing 5.2.3 updates the regolith levels using the regolith output flows computed in the previous pass.

TERRAIN SLIPPAGE

Sand and soil can also slip down, yet internal tension prevents continuous falling [Musgrave1989]. A material property called the talus angle characterizes this behavior, for example, the talus angle of dry sand is 30.

To simulate slippage we compare the gradient at every location to a material's talus angle. If the gradient exceeds the talus angle, we shift some amount of terrain material to the location below. A virtual pipes method moves material between cells. We use the code from Listing 5.2.2 to compute slippage outflows, except that we set damping to zero and compute height differences differently. The modified code to compute height differences for the purpose of slippage simulation is shown in Listing 5.2.7.

Listing 5.2.7   We also use the virtual pipe model to compute terrain movement due to slippage. Slippage depends on a per-material talus angle that influences how we compute height differences between neighboring cells

Inputs:

```
float   layered;        // id of processed layer
float4  layerC;         // height of a layer
```

```
float4   layerNeigh[4];                    // height at neighboring cells
const float cellSize   = 1;                // distance between neighboring cells
const float talusAngle = 30;               // the talus angle
```

Pseudo code:

```
// compute the maximum allowed height difference between neighbors
float maxHeightDif = cellSize * tan(talusAngle);
// compute the total height on a layer at the central cell
float totalHC = getTotalHeight(layerId+1, layerC);
// compute the total height on a layer at the neighboring cells
float4 totalH = getTotalHeight4f(layerId+1, layerNeigh);
// compute the difference between the center cell and the neighbors
float4 heightDif = float4(totalHC) – totalH - maxHeightDif;
```

In multilayer terrains, a slipping lower layer affects all layers above it. Therefore, we calculate slippage for terrain layers sequentially in a bottom-to-top order. Because a single texture stores all our terrain layers in its multiple components, we need to be careful to only update one layer at a time without corrupting the other layers. To update each layer we use the code from Listing 5.2.3; that is, the code runs once for each layer. To only update the current layer we disable frame buffer writes to all color channels except the one representing the current layer.

BOUNDARIES

Our algorithm uses neighboring cells for various computations. Because the simulation domain is finite, we require boundary conditions. One solution is to use a periodic boundary representing a torus topology. Our solution is to extend the domain by one cell in each direction. We call these new cells ghost cells (see also Figure 5.2.6). Ghost cells do not execute any of our algorithms; they only serve to store values. A ghost cell always contains the same value as its neighboring boundary cell. This scheme ensures that, for example, the outflow from the border cells to the ghost cells is always zero (see Listing 5.2.2), and therefore water never leaves the domain. We implement this solution by setting the texture wrap mode to clamp for all textures in use.

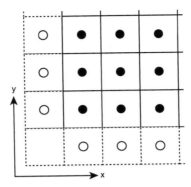

FIGURE 5.2.6   Solid circles mark regular cells; empty circles denote ghost cells.

RENDERING

We render our evolving terrain in two passes. The first pass renders the terrain, and the second pass renders the water. In each pass a vertex shader displaces a predefined vertex grid by the terrain and water heights, respectively. Both fragment shaders compute per-pixel normals every frame [Lengyel2002]. The per-pixel normal is the cross-product of the tangent vectors in the x and y directions:

$$N(x,y) = \begin{bmatrix} d(x-1,y) - d(x+1,y) \\ d(x,y-1) - d(x,y+1) \\ 2l \end{bmatrix}$$

EQUATION 5.2.6

where $d(x, y)$ is the height of the terrain or water at position (x, y), and l is the distance between two neighboring cells.

To compute the color of terrain with multiple material layers, the pixel shader combines the various layer materials together in top-to-bottom order. A thickness threshold for each material determines the level of material opacity. If the layer thickness is less than the threshold, only a proportional fraction of that material's color contributes to the final color (see Listing 5.2.8).

Water renders as a semitransparent and specular surface. The difference between terrain and water heights determines the water's transparency. The surface of the water reflects an environment map to emulate a specular term. Fresnel's formula [Wloka2002] modulates this specular term. To limit z-fighting between water and terrain, we discard all water fragments whose distance from the terrain surface is below a threshold value of 0.1 m, although ideally this threshold is calculated from the terrain size and camera settings.

Listing 5.2.8 Computing the frame buffer color of multilayer terrains

Inputs:

```
float       layers;                 // number of layers
float4 terrain;                     // height of individual layers
float  thresholdThickness[4];       // threshold thickness of the
layers
float3 layerColor[4];               // color of individual layers
```

Pseudo code:

```
float remainingThickness = 1.0;
float3 finalColor = float3(0.0);
// process all layers above the bottommost layer
for (int i=layers-1; i>=1; i—) {
      float layerHeight = getLayerHeight(i, terrain);
      float thickness = min(thresholdThickness[i], layerHeight);
   float thicknessFactor = thickness/thresholdThickness[i];
      finalColor += layerColor[i]*thicknessFactor;
      remainingThickness -= thicknessFactor;
}
// process the final layer
finalColor += layerColor[0] * remainingThickness;
```

RESULTS AND CONCLUSION

ON THE DVD

An application implementing our technique with the full source code is available on the book's accompanying DVD-ROM. It requires Direct3D 10 and is capable of rendering a four-layer terrain with a grid resolution of 2048×1024 at 20 fps on an NVIDIA GeForce 8800 GTX GPU. Figure 5.2.7 (see also the color plates) demonstrates the results of continuous rain eroding such a large terrain. This real-time performance, even for large and detailed terrains, makes our method a highly functional tool for interactive terrain modeling. Users may interactively add water sinks and sources, control rain intensity, change material properties, or create lakes and rivers; a realistic terrain shape always emerges due to the realistic simulation of hydraulic erosion. In addition to terrain modeling, we foresee hydraulic erosion as a next step of improving realistic physics within computer games.

FIGURE 5.2.7   Rain eroding a 2048×1024 terrain.

ACKNOWLEDGMENT

This work is supported by the Ministry of Education, Youth and Sports of the Czech Republic under the research program LC-06008 (Center for Computer Graphics).

REFERENCES

[Beneš2001] Beneš, B., and Forsbach, R., "Layered Data Representation for Visual Simulation of Terrain Erosion." In SCCG '01: Proceedings of the 17th Spring Conference on Computer Graphics, IEEE Computer Society, Washington, DC, USA, 80 (2001).

[Beneš2007] Beneš B., "Real-Time Erosion Using Shallow Water Simulation." In VRIPHYS '07: Proc. of Workshop in Virtual Reality Interactions and Physical Simulation (2007).

[Bridson2008] Bridson, R. *Fluid Simulation for Computer Graphics*, A K Peters, 2008.

[Crane2008] Crane, K., Llamas I., and Tariq S., "Real-Time Simulation and Rendering of 3D Fluids," *GPU Gems 3*, Addison-Wesley (2008).

[Hong2008] Hong, J.-M., Lee, H.-Y., Yoon, J.-C., Kim, C.-H. "Bubbles Alive." In Proc. of SIGGRAPH'08, 2008

[Mei2007] Mei, X., Decaudin, P., and Hu, B.-G., "Fast Hydraulic Erosion Simulation and Visualization on GPU." In Proc. of Pacific Graphics (2007), pp. 47–56.

[Lengyel2002] Lengyel E., *Mathematics for 3D Game Programming & Computer Graphics*. Charles River Media, Massachusetts, USA (2002).

[Musgrave1989] Musgrave, F. K., Kolb, C. E., and Mace, R. S., "The Synthesis and Rendering of Eroded Fractal Terrains," in Proc. of SIGGRAPH'89, 1989, 41–50.

[Selle2007] Selle A., Fedkiw, R., Kim B., Liu, Y., and Rossignac J., "An Unconditionally Stable MacCormack Method." *J. Sci. Comput.* (2007).

[Št'ava2008] Št'ava, O., Beneš, B., Brisbin, M., and Křivánek, J., "Interactive Terrain Modeling Using Hydraulic Erosion," In Eurographics/SIGGRAPH Symposium on Computer Animation 2008.

[Wloka2002] Wloka M., "Fresnel Reflection," NVIDIA Technical Report, 2002.

5.3 Advanced Geometry for Complex Sky Representation

JAMES SUN, KEYSTONE GAME STUDIO, TAIWAN

INTRODUCTION

Sky is essential in completing a graphical representation of a world. While articles on sky rendering usually focus on shading algorithms, we examine the geometric aspects instead. Sky geometries typically consist of cubes, spheres, cylinders, or planes. These shapes, however, have limitations that make them sub-optimal for rendering sky. This article introduces a simple, single geometrical representation for sky, which overcomes the limitations of current sky geometries.

Current sky representations use simple primitive types such as hemispheres, cylinders, cubes, and planes [Bell98] [Sempe01] [Valve08]. Each of these primitive types is the geometrical equivalent of a projection type. These projections provide a local coordinate system (i.e., uv-coordinates) to shaders to compute specific phenomena and map textures onto the geometry.

A sky hemisphere, for example, corresponds to a spherical projection. Spherical projections are useful for effects such as atmospheric scattering. A sky cylinder represents a cylindrical projection and excels at depicting distant clouds, distance fog, or distant objects. A sky plane is a planar projection that is good for rendering low-flying clouds.

Each primitive type accurately represents its corresponding projection, but distorts any other projection types. When you require multiple projections, the current solution is to use multiple primitives. Using multiple primitives to render sky, however, is inefficient: Sky pixels draw multiple times [Flannery07], use inter-penetrating alpha sorting [Scheuermann04], and cause multiple render state changes [Torgo07].

We propose a single sky geometry that accurately represents multiple projection types. This geometry lets us draw sky efficiently with a single draw call. In particular, all sky pixels draw exactly once, that is, there is no overdraw; there is no need for alpha blending; and there are no render state changes.

GEOMETRY GENERATION

Our sky geometry fits a cylindrical projection to an infinite planar mapping through a hemispherical projection. In addition, every vertex in this geometry stores uv-coordinates for all desired projection types. The vertex distribution of this sky geometry allows us to accurately represent planar, cylindrical, and spherical mappings.

The following paragraphs describe how to construct this geometry. While it is possible to build this geometry manually in any 3D software package, using a script to generate it automatically is less tedious and more accurate.

We first create two 2D splines, named sA and sB. Spline sA is parallel to the y-axis and represents a cylindrical projection. Spline sB is parallel to the x-axis and represents a planar projection. Now offset sB upward to a height representing the height of planar clouds. Then, offset sA to the right by a quarter of the height of sB (see also Figure 5.3.1). We then insert n equidistant control points on sA between $y = 0$ and where y intersects sB (see also Figure 5.3.2). We recommend using at least $n = 16$ control points. Using $n = 32$ control points generates distortion-free results. These control points are named pA0 through pAn. Larger values of n increase the accuracy of representing the various mappings, but also increase the number of triangles of the sky geometry, thus impacting memory and rendering resources.

We continue by adding a ray i for each control point pAi in sA. Each ray connects the origin with one control point in sA and ends when it intersects sB. The intersection point of ray i with sB is pBi (see also Figure 5.3.3). These radial rays represent a spherical projection. Recall that sA represents a cylindrical projection and that sB represents a planar projection. If each point pAi were in the same location as pBi, then a spline connecting these points accurately represents all three of these projections. Fortunately, cylindrical projections are constant along their projection direction, so we can change the x-coordinates of all points pAi arbitrarily without fundamentally altering the original cylindrical projection. Similarly, planar projections are constant along the plane normal, so we can change the y-coordinates of all points pBi arbitrarily. We thus construct new points pCi by shifting pAi sideways until they line up under pBi, that is, pCi = (pBi.x, pAi.y) (see also Figure 5.3.3).

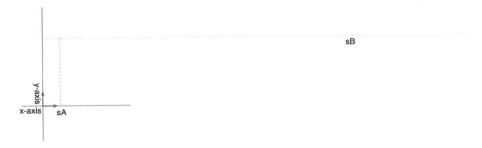

FIGURE 5.3.1   The sky geometry derives from two 2D splines: sA and sB. We construct these two splines by making sA vertical and offset to the right and making sB horizontal and offset to the top.

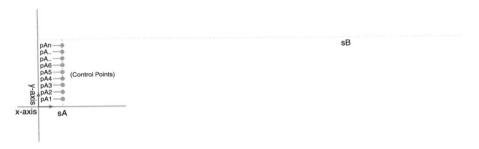

FIGURE 5.3.2   Spline sA contains n equidistant control points.

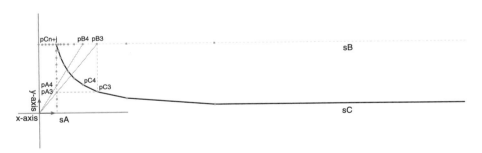

FIGURE 5.3.3   Rays emanating from the origin and traveling through sA's control points pAi intersect sB at points pBi. Points pCi derive from pBi's x-coordinate and pAi's y-coordinate.

We then insert an additional m control points pC$n + j$ by subdividing sB between $x = 0$ and where x intersects sA. Again, about $m = 16$ equidistant control points suffice, and $m = 32$ control points yields nearly distortion-free results. Interpolating all points pCi defines a spline sC.

Revolving spline sC by at least $l = 16$ steps around the y-axis creates a 3D shape similar to that of a hyperboloid or a capped volcano. Using $l = 32$ steps provides excellent-looking results and is the geometry we use for rendering skies (see Figure 5.3.4). Because points pCi are the intersection of a spherical, a cylindrical, and a planar projection, our sky geometry simultaneously approximates all radial, planar, and cylindrical projections.

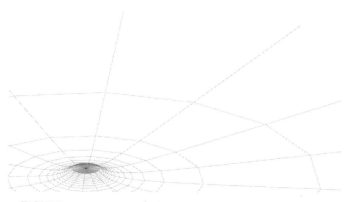

FIGURE 5.3.4 Interpolating points pCi yields a spline sC.
Revolving sC around the y-axis results in our sky geometry that
simultaneously represents a spherical, a cylindrical, and a planar mapping.

All that is left to do is to store uv-coordinates for each desired mapping: For each vertex project the vertex position according to the mapping and store the result in a UV channel. Note that projections need to be centered and based at the center of the geometry.

CONCLUSION

This article demonstrates an easy technique to render sky efficiently. We create a single geometry that stores three distinct mapping types. Thus, all sky elements and effects render exactly once using the same geometry and a single shader, and as a result, GPU efficiency increases.

Because planar, cylindrical, and hemispherical mappings influence the construction of our sky geometry, the vertex distribution of this geometry minimizes distortions due to linear uv-interpolation between vertices. Accordingly, a relatively coarse tessellation suffices to render without visible distortions in any of the mappings. We find that a spline sC (see "Geometry Generation" above) with a total of 64 control points and rotated around the y-axis in 32 steps generates relatively distortion-free results, yet only contains 64×32 = 2,048 quads, that is, 4,096 triangles. For typical view angles only about 1,500 triangles of those 4,096 triangles are usually visible.

The storage requirements of our sky geometry are the number of vertices times per-vertex size. Vertices store position data and up to three UV sets.

In future work, it may be possible to construct this sky geometry on the fly, thus significantly reducing storage requirements. If such construction code is able to only generate the currently visible subset, it also substantially reduces the GPU's vertex processing load.

Another possible improvement is to replace the straight spline sB (see "Geometry Generation" above) with a slightly curved, convex spline. The geometry construction works the same way as long as sB is monotonically non-increasing.

Finally, our method assumes that the eye is at the center of the world and only sees the top half of the sky. This assumption, however, is easily enforceable by always centering the sky on the eye and keeping the player relatively low on the ground.

REFERENCES

[Bell98] Gavin Bell, "Creating Backgrounds for 3D Games," available online at www.gamasutra.com/features/19981023/bell_01.htm, October 23, 1998.

[Flannery07] Simon Flannery, "Overdraw," available online at www.pixeltangent.com/index.php?start=11, 2007.

[Scheuermann04] Thorsten Scheuermann, "Practical Real-Time Hair Rendering and Shading," available online at http://ati.amd.com/developer/techreports.html, 2004.

[Sempe01] Luis R. Sempe, "Sky Domes," available online at www.spheregames.com/index.php?p=templates/pages/tutorials, October, 2001.

[Torgo07] Torgo3000, "Performance Art," available online at http://blogs.technet.com/torgo3000/archive/2007/06/01/performance-art.aspx, 2007.

[Valve08] The Valve Developer Community, "3D Skybox," available online at http://developer.valvesoftware.com/wiki/3D_Skybox, 2008.

Part

VI

Global Illumination Effects

CARSTEN DACHSBACHER

ASSISTANT PROFESSOR AT VISUS/UNIVERSITY OF STUTTGART

Since *ShaderX⁵* the global illumination section is an integral part of this book. This is not surprising given the demand for high quality rendering in games and interactive applications, and the increase in computation power and flexibility of GPUs. In this section, we have a collection of interesting articles covering techniques ranging from real-time effects used in shipped games and demos, to illumination computations which might be part of future engines.

The illumination effect that probably gained the most attention recently is ambient occlusion and this becomes obvious if one counts the number of articles that deal with this technique in this section. Vladimir Kajalin describes the screen-space ambient occlusion approach used in *Crysis*, which made these techniques popular. In general, working in image space has many advantages, such as good scaling with scene complexity and no need for special tessellation or parameterization. To this end, Louis Bavoil and Miguel Sainz present extensions and intelligent sampling strategies to increase the quality of ambient occlusion rendering. Angelo Pesce presents an interesting alternative to the brute force sampling methods adapting the idea of variance shadow maps. There are two more articles dealing with ambient occlusion: Jeremy Shopf, Joshua Barczak, Thorsten Scheuermann, and Christopher Oat decided to go a completely different way and represent objects with simple proxy geometry to compute the occlusion analytically. Dave Bookout computes ambient occlusion per vertex using a finite element approach and shifting the work load from fragment processing into geometry shaders.

Emmanuel Briney, Victor Ceitelis, and David Crémoux describe a system for rendering realistic lighting, effectively combining ambient occlusion effects and screen-space indirect lighting.

Hyunwoo Ki deals with the rendering of another effect that is very important for realistic lighting: translucency. His article describes an efficient way to compute sub-surface scattering based on extended shadow maps.

László Szécsi describes his system for rendering global illumination solutions based on the instant radiosity method. To render indirect illumination he combines several established techniques, among others ray tracing on the GPU to compute photon paths, and achieves interactive to real-time frame rates.

6.1 Screen-Space Ambient Occlusion

VLADIMIR KAJALIN

INTRODUCTION

Ambient occlusion (AO) is a well-known computer graphics method for approximating global illumination. It is an important instrument to improve the perception of scene topology for the human eye [Luft06]. AO provides a good ratio between quality and speed, but it was never feasible to run it completely in real-time for complex and completely dynamic 3D environments in time-critical applications such as computer games, where it needs to be computed per frame within a few milliseconds.

This article will describe the algorithm and implementation of the approach that was successfully used in the PC game *Crysis*, released in 2007 (see Figure 6.1.1).

FIGURE 6.1.1 Visualization of screen-space AO component of a typical game scene in *Crysis*.

THE PROBLEMS

Most of the existing AO methods suffer from the following problems.

- **Heavy preprocessing.** Most techniques precompute AO information in a pre-process on a per-object or per-level basis. This means level designers or artists often have to wait several minutes or hours before they can see their work in a final game environment.

- **Dependency on scene complexity.** In most cases, complex and detailed scenes require much more processing time, higher memory consumption, and additional programming efforts.

- **Inconsistency between static and dynamic geometry processing.** A common way of handling AO is precomputing high-quality AO for static geometry to store it in textures and to use fast but low-quality real-time solutions for dynamic geometry. This leads to visual inconsistency between the static and dynamic components of a scene. Some of these problems can be tackled by more complex code, but complexity here is quickly exceeding the benefits.

- **Complications in implementation.** Developing a good AO compiler featuring an efficient ray-tracer, a good texture packer, and other components that can handle huge game levels full of various types of objects costs a lot of time and programming efforts. At runtime the precomputed data needs to be streamed from media and processed by the engine. Here, it competes with other systems on valuable resources such as memory, CPU, and IO bandwidth.

Our approach allows a simple and efficient approximation of AO effects entirely in real-time, free from all the problems listed above. The algorithm is executed solely on the GPU and implemented as a simple pixel shader, analyzing the scene depth buffer and extracting the occlusion factor for every pixel on the screen.

PREVIOUS WORK

The idea of extracting ambient occlusion from the scene depth buffer is not new, but it has not received enough attention in the past. The solution described in [Shanmugam07] handles near and high-frequency local ambient occlusion using a screen-space approach. More distant parts of the scene are handled using a low-detailed approximation of the scene geometry, where each object is represented as a sphere. In comparison to [Shanmugam07], our approach handles an entire scene using a single homogenous solution and is independent of scene complexity.

OVERVIEW OF THE APPROACH

Let's see how a screen-space solution can work in the simplest case. For every pixel P of the screen, we would like to compute the occlusion factor due to the surrounding geometry. Similar to most offline AO compilers, we trace many 3D rays from point P into the surrounding space and check how many of these rays hit geometry as shown in Figure 6.1.2. In order to do that on a GPU, we need a texture containing information about the scene geometry. Since we want this to be fully dynamic without any preprocess, the scene depth target seems a good candidate for the task, as the depth buffer provides a discrete sampling of the (visible) surfaces. In our renderer we had this information already available because we exported the z values to a texture in an early z pass. What problems might we encounter with such a simple brute force approach, and how we can solve them?

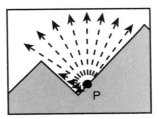

FIGURE 6.1.2   Typical way of computing the AO value for some point P. Black rays are hitting the geometry surface. Red rays don't hit anything.

■ **Geometry outside of the camera frustum does not cast occlusion.** Information about occluders outside the camera view is missing, which leads to visual artifacts such as no darkening at the edges of the screen. This is true, but only to a certain degree. In most cases, depth values of a scene behind the edges of the screen are very similar to the values right at the border of the screen. This property of scene depth allows us to solve at least half of the cases that initially looked problematic. Another factor that helps us is the fact that human vision may not recognize small high-frequency details at long distance and at the same time may not recognize big low-frequency occlusion at very close proximity. Basically, the size of the most important details is fixed in screen-space. This leads to the conclusion that the size of an area taken into account for occlusion may be relatively small and fixed in screen-space. In practice, values of about 10% of the screen size work well. Such a solution provides a general method of computing AO for any pixel on the screen. It may handle nicely, for example, AO of a human face right in front of the camera, and at the same time huge objects such as mountains or buildings in the background (see Figure 6.1.1).

- **Geometry occluded by other geometry does not cast occlusion.** A single depth buffer cannot provide a full description of the scene topology, and information about some hidden parts of the scene may be missing. This statement is true, but in reality this problem causes few problems. Several complex solutions may be developed in order to overcome this issue, but we think artifacts that are unnoticeable to the average user are acceptable, especially because we aim for an efficient real-time solution. In the implementation described, only the foremost pixels, or basically only visible pixels, are taken into account for occlusion.

- **It will require a lot of ray tracing for every pixel on the screen.** In the case of a brute force solution for good visual quality, hundreds of rays have to be traced for every pixel on the screen, which is not affordable on current hardware. Below we describe several approximations and optimizations to allow good visual quality using a minimal number of texture reads.

- **No unified solution for alpha-blended surfaces.** As the technique depends on existing depth values, it's problematic to support alpha-blended surfaces. At this stage there's simply no good solution for the current hardware generation. In *Crysis*, the usage of alpha blending was limited to only particles and a few other special cases when screen-space (SS) AO was not required and not used.

AMOUNT OF GEOMETRY

Tracing many "real" rays through the depth buffer for every screen pixel (marching along the rays requires multiple texture fetches per ray) is not efficient enough on current hardware generation, so we have to find a simple approximation of this operation. Instead of computing the amount of occlusion produced by geometry hits through ray-tracing, we approximate it by the amount of solid geometry (ratio between solid and empty space) around a point of interest.

In order to do this we sample the 3D space around point P (using a predefined kernel of offset points distributed in the surrounding sphere) and for every sample point we check whether we are inside the geometry or not (see Figure 6.1.3). This can be implemented by a simple comparison between the screen-space depth of the 3D sample point and the value stored in the depth buffer at the same screen position. If the depth value of a sample point is greater than the depth buffer value, the sample point is considered to be inside the geometry.

In the case of a flat wall in front of the camera, half of the samples will appear inside the wall and half outside (Figure 6.1.4, left) so the visibility ratio is approximately 0.5. In the corner of the room (Figure 6.1.4, center) the amount of geometry is about 0.75, and the corner appears darker.

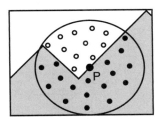

FIGURE 6.1.3   Computing the amount of solid geometry around a point P. The ratio between solid and empty space approximates the amount of occlusion.

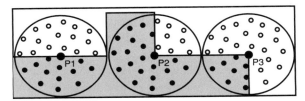

FIGURE 6.1.4   Several scenarios of AO computation. P1 is located on the flat plane, P2 in the corner, and P3 on the edge.

An interesting situation occurs, for example, on the edges of the box (Figure 6.1.4, right). The amount of geometry is about 0.25, and pixels on the edge appear brighter than on the rest of the object. At first sight such behavior may be considered a visual artifact (since in real-life the surface normal is taken into account and edges do not appearing brighter), but we found that by not fixing this "artifact" we can make more geometry features recognizable to the viewer and improve the overall 3D perception of the scene geometry (Figure 6.1.5).

FIGURE 6.1.5   Example showing the benefits from edges highlighting.

DISTANCE ATTENUATION

Special computations of the distance attenuation for individual sample points are not necessary in our implementation because we solve it using a nonuniform way of distributing offset points in the sampling kernel. The density of sample points near the center of the kernel is higher than near the surface of the sphere. This way, the amount of occlusion from far geometry is weighted less than from near geometry. Additionally, since the kernel sphere is projected to a 2D screen, the density of samples near point P in screen-space is higher than on the projected sphere's boundaries. Such a distribution of sample points makes occlusion from near geometry stronger and more precise. This way, after summing up all accessibility values from all sample points, we get an overall accessibility for a point P, taking into account distance attenuation.

DEPTH RANGE CHECK

In some cases our method will fail, causing false occlusion from near objects to far objects in the background. This occurs when information about correct occluders is missing in the scene depth buffer. In order to compensate, an additional depth range check is used. Occlusion from sample points having a too big depth difference compared to the center point P is faded out or ignored completely and replaced with a fixed default value.

RANDOMLY ROTATED KERNEL AND HIGH-FREQUENCY NOISE

Since we are talking about usage of AO in time-critical applications such as computer games, we have to limit the number of texture fetches to a small number. We used 16 fetches per pixel. Such a small amount of samples would result in an image like Figure 6.1.6, which quality-wise is clearly not good enough to be acceptable.

FIGURE 6.1.6 SSAO computed without random rotation of the sampling kernel.

A common solution to improve quality with a small sample count is to use a randomly rotated kernel of sample vectors [Isidoro06]. This way we get a virtually much higher sample count, and the overall quality will improve. Unfortunately, we also introduce a lot of noise in the final picture. A common method to reduce the noise is to blur the image. Since we don't want to loose details, we can not use a big blur radius. We pick a 4×4-pixel blurring area size, which means we will be able to completely remove very-high-frequency components of the noise only in the image. In order to produce only high-frequency noise during the depth buffer sampling stage, we repeat orientations of our kernel every 4×4 screen pixels. This means that in the case of a flat wall in front of the camera, we will get a screen filled by the same tiled 4×4 pixels pattern, and then using a 4×4 post-blur step (with equal weighs for each of the 4×4 pixels), we will be able to completely remove noise (see Figure 6.1.7).

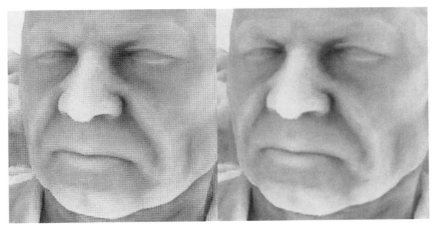

FIGURE 6.1.7   On the left, the post-blur step is disabled.
On the right, post-blur is enabled.

Since each pixel in our 4×4 pattern gets a unique orientation of the kernel, we effectively simulate 256 unique vectors for every 4×4-pixel block, allowing good visual quality.

EDGE-PRESERVING BLUR

A simple blur may introduce some leaks between dark and bright areas of the AO image. For example, incorrect brightness may be noticeable on the silhouette edges of a dark object on a bright background. In order to avoid leaking, we use a more advanced version of the blur, taking into account depth discontinuities and blending only pixels with a similar depth. Other techniques used interleaved sampling strategies before, and they also blended the samples in the final pass [Wald02] [Segovia06].

IMPLEMENTATION

The SSAO technique requires a scene depth buffer that is available to the pixel shader. This requirement doesn't seem to be a problem since at the time we developed the technique, most graphics engines already did a z pre-pass, and some already stored the scene depth in a texture for later use. A z pre-pass allows reduction of the overdraw during consequent passes, and a scene depth texture can be used in many advanced effects such as soft particles, depth of field, atmospheric effects, deferred lighting, and shadow mapping [Wenzel07] [Mittring07].

We can run the SSAO technique after the scene depth texture becomes available. We draw a full-screen quad into the AO render target using the SSAO shader. After that, by rendering another full-screen quad, we blur the AO values with the blur method described above. The output render target will contain AO values that may be used during light passes. Usually, the AO value modulates ambient lighting, but for some stylized looks it can be even applied to diffuse and specular components.

SSAO PIXEL SHADER

Here we present an example of the pixel shader function computing SSAO. It is not the fastest implementation since the main purpose of this example is to help the reader understand the algorithm. This code will compile into more than 200 instructions. An optimized and vectorized but much less readable version of this code was used in *Crysis*, where it was compiled into about 86 instructions.

```
float ComputeSSAO(
    // 4x4 texture containing 16 random vectors
    sampler2D sRotSampler4x4,
    // scene depth target containing normalized
    // from 0 to 1 linear depth
    sampler2D sSceneDepthSampler,
    // texture coordinates of current pixel
    float2 screenTC,
    // dimensions of the screen
    float2 screenSize,
    // far clipping plane distance in meters
    float farClipDist)
{
```

```
// get rotation vector, rotation is tiled every 4 screen pixels
float2 rotationTC = screenTC * screenSize / 4;
float3 vRotation = 2*tex2D(sRotSampler4x4, rotationTC).rgb-1;

// create rotation matrix from rotation vector
float3x3 rotMat;
float h = 1 / (1 + vRotation.z);
rotMat._m00= h*vRotation.y*vRotation.y+vRotation.z;
rotMat._m01=-h*vRotation.y*vRotation.x;
rotMat._m02=-vRotation.x;
rotMat._m10=-h*vRotation.y*vRotation.x;
rotMat._m11= h*vRotation.x*vRotation.x+vRotation.z;
rotMat._m12=-vRotation.y; rotMat._m20= vRotation.x;
rotMat._m21= vRotation.y; rotMat._m22= vRotation.z;

// get depth of current pixel and convert into meters
float fSceneDepthP = tex2D( sSceneDepthSampler, screenTC ).r *
                  farClipDist;

// parameters affecting offset points number and distribution
const int nSamplesNum = 16; // may be 8, 16 or 24
float offsetScale = 0.01;
const float offsetScaleStep = 1 + 2.4/nSamplesNum;

float Accessibility = 0;

// sample area and accumulate accessibility
for(int i=0; i<(nSamplesNum/8); i++)
for(int x=-1; x<=1; x+=2)
for(int y=-1; y<=1; y+=2)
for(int z=-1; z<=1; z+=2) {
  // generate offset vector (this code line is executed only
  // at shader compile stage)
```

```
    // here we use cube corners and give it different lengths
    float3 vOffset = normalize(float3( x, y, z )) *
                        ( offsetScale *= offsetScaleStep );


    // rotate offset vector by rotation matrix
    float3 vRotatedOffset = mul( vOffset, rotMat );


    // get center pixel 3d coordinates in screen space
    float3 vSamplePos = float3( screenTC, fSceneDepthP );


    // shift coordinates by offset vector (range convert
    // and width depth value)
    vSamplePos += float3( vRotatedOffset.xy,
                        vRotatedOffset.z * fSceneDepthP * 2);


    // read scene depth at sampling point and convert into meters
    float fSceneDepthS = tex2D( sSceneDepthSampler,
                        vSamplePos.xy ) * farClipDist;


    // check if depths of both pixels are close enough and
    // sampling point should affect our center pixel
    float fRangeIsInvalid = saturate( ( ( fSceneDepthP -
                        fSceneDepthS ) / fSceneDepthS ) );


    // accumulate accessibility, use default value of 0.5
    // if right computations are not possible
    Accessibility += lerp( fSceneDepthS > vSamplePos.z, 0.5,
                    fRangeIsInvalid );
}

// get average value
Accessibility = Accessibility / nSamplesNum;
```

```
    // amplify and saturate if necessary
    return saturate( Accessibility*Accessibility + Accessibility );
}
```

FUTURE IMPROVEMENTS

SSAO is a new technique and has a lot of untapped potential for quality and speed improvements, and we cover only few of them here.

For every pixel on the screen our shader does many reads from a relatively large-sized texture at completely different positions, causing heavy texture cache trashing. Even code vectorization and reducing the shader instruction count two to three times wasn't increasing speed because of the texture lookup performance. One way to get better performance is to use a downscaled version of depth texture. In *Crysis* this optimization allowed us to roughly double the speed of the SSAO shader. Another possible example of code optimization is to replace the rotation of offset vectors using matrix operations with faster mirroring of the vector by plane. The mirror trick has been used in *Crysis* and is described in [Mittring07].

An interesting possibility would be to take scene normals into account. One of the obvious benefits from it can be to use a normal in order to concentrate more samples in front of the face and avoid wasting half of the samples for self-occlusion.

The SSAO technique is an approximation of the ambient occlusion, which itself is an approximation of the indirect lighting. The SSAO technique can be extended to approximate indirect lighting even better by taking into account colors of the scene. Such a screen-space indirect lighting solution (SSIL would be a good name) result is a more plausible approximation of indirect lighting taking into account brightness and colors of surfaces. An image-space indirect lighting technique has been described by [Dachsbacher05].

RESULTS AND CONCLUSION

This article described the implementation of a technique for computing AO using only the scene depth buffer. Several optimizations and approximations were developed in order to speed up the process while maintaining high visual quality. Performance-wise, the implementation presented here requires 3 milliseconds per frame on an NVIDIA GeForce 8800 GTX at 1280×720 screen resolution, including the aforementioned post-blur step. Such a good performance makes it finally possible to use real-time AO in time-critical applications such as computer games.

During the development of *Crysis*, after researching multiple AO solutions, we found that SSAO is a very effective solution for us. Major benefits we found are improved game production, support for dynamic content, simple implementation, and adjustable quality. As a disadvantage we can mention the requirement for a good graphic card like the GeForce 8800, which was relatively expensive at the time of the *Crysis* release. Nowadays such hardware is a usual component in a gamer PC, and soon nothing will prevent SSAO from running on most computers or game consoles; we expect that in the near future all graphics engines will support SSAO (or SSIL) as a common feature.

Acknowledgments

Special thanks to the Crytek team for helping me develop this technique.

References

[Dachsbacher05] Carsten Dachsbacher, Marc Stamminger, "Reflective Shadow Maps," Proceedings of the 2005 Symposium on Interactive 3D Graphics and Games

[Isidoro06] John R. Isidoro, "Shadow Mapping: GPU-based Tips and Techniques," GDC 2006

[Luft06] Thomas Luft, Carsten Colditz, Oliver Deussen, "Image Enhancement by Unsharp Masking the Depth Buffer," International Conference on Computer Graphics and Interactive Techniques (SIGGRAPH), 2006

[Mittring07] Martin Mittring, "Finding Next Gen - CryEngine 2," Advanced Real-Time Rendering in 3D Graphics and Games Course, SIGGRAPH 2007

[Segovia06] Benjamin Segovia, Jean-Claude Iehl , Richard Mitanchey, Bernard Péroche, "Non-Interleaved Deferred Shading of Interleaved Sample Patterns," Proceedings of SIGGRAPH/Eurographics Workshop on Graphics Hardware 2006

[Shanmugam07] Perumaal Shanmugam, Okan Arikan, "Hardware Accelerated Ambient Occlusion Techniques on GPUs," Proceedings of the 2007 Symposium on Interactive 3D Graphics and Games

[Wald02] Ingo Wald, Thomas Kollig, Carsten Benthin, Alexander Keller, Philipp Slusallek, "Interactive Global Illumination Using Fast Ray Tracing," Proceedings of the 13th EUROGRAPHICS Workshop on Rendering, 2002

[Wenzel07] Carsten Wenzel, "Real-Time Atmospheric Effects in Games Revisited," Conference Session GDC 2007

6.2 Image-Space Horizon-Based Ambient Occlusion

Louis Bavoil and Miguel Sainz

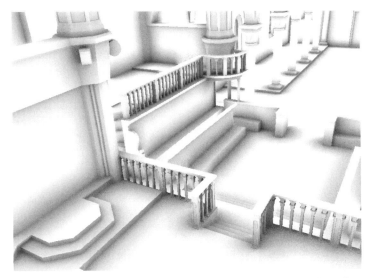

FIGURE 6.2.1 Image rendered with our horizon-based algorithm.

INTRODUCTION

AMBIENT OCCLUSION

Ambient occlusion is a lighting model that approximates the amount of light reaching a point on a diffuse surface based on its directly visible occluders. It gives perceptual clues of depth, curvature, and spatial proximity. The term *ambient occlusion* was introduced by [Landis02] and more precisely defined in [Christensen03].

425

[Langer99] used the same model for approximating the lighting on a cloudy day, and [Zhukov98] presented a similar lighting model called obscurances.

One way of rendering ambient occlusion is to trace rays from a surface point P in the hemisphere oriented around the normal **n** at P, and count how many of these rays intersect any surrounding object within a given radius of influence R, normalizing the result by the number of rays. The radius of influence R is important to control the set of potential occluders.

A first form of ambient occlusion uses a cosine-weighted distribution, tracing more rays toward the normal. This form is described by the following integral defined over the normal-oriented unit hemisphere Ω at point P:

$$A_1 = 1 - \frac{1}{\pi} \int_\Omega V(\vec{\omega})(\vec{\omega} . \vec{n}) d\omega$$

EQUATION 6.2.1

where $V(\vec{\omega})$ is the visibility function returning 1 if a ray starting from P in direction $\vec{\omega}$ intersects an occluder around P within a given radius of influence R, and 0 otherwise (Figure 6.2.2), and $d\omega$ is an elementary solid angle on the hemisphere Ω.

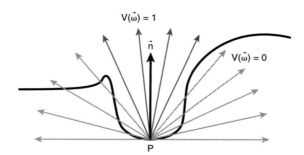

FIGURE 6.2.2 Rays distributed in the normal-oriented hemisphere.

The $(\vec{\omega} . \vec{n})$ cosine term in the ambient occlusion of the type described in Equation 6.2.1 is the response to the diffuse reflection of the ambient light on the surface. Responses to other light sources should be added to A_1 to produce the final color.

A second form of ambient occlusion used by [Pharr04] and [Hegeman06] does not include the cosine term in its definition:

$$A_2 = 1 - \frac{1}{2\pi} \int_\Omega V(\vec{\omega}) d\omega$$

EQUATION 6.2.2

In this case, the ambient occlusion term A_2 can be considered as the shadow contribution from an environment light. Like for regular shadowing, it should be multiplied with the direct lighting term, as described by [Hegeman06].

We follow the latter approach and solve the following ambient occlusion integral:

$$A = 1 - \frac{1}{2\pi} \int_{\Omega} V(\vec{\omega}) W(\vec{\omega}) d\omega$$

EQUATION 6.2.3

where $W(\vec{\omega})$ is an attenuation function based on the distance between P and the occluder in direction $V(\vec{\omega})$. The purpose of the attenuation function is to soften sharp occlusion boundaries due to occluders at a distance R strongly influencing the ambient occlusion once they begin to be sampled. See Figure 6.2.3.

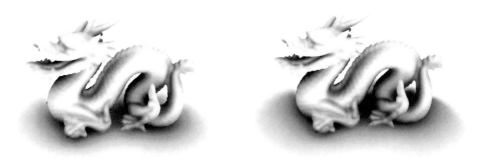

FIGURE 6.2.3   Ambient occlusion rendered with our algorithm, with and without an attenuation function.

In real-time graphics, for static scenes, ambient occlusion terms can be precomputed at vertices or in light maps. The problem with most techniques is that they require scene-dependent precomputations, which makes them impractical for complex scenes with arbitrary dynamic geometry.

Screen-Space Ambient Occlusion

The term *screen-space ambient occlusion* (SSAO) was introduced by [Mittring07]. [Shanmugam07] and [Fox08] described different SSAO algorithms. The general idea is to use the depth buffer of the scene being rendered as a discrete approximation of the scene geometry. Although this approach uses a single layer of depth and no information is available outside the view frustum, it produces plausible results as seen in Figure 6.2.1.

Per-pixel ambient occlusion is computed in a postprocessing pass that samples a depth image rendered from the camera (eye's point of view). This approach requires no scene-dependent precomputations.

The image-based algorithm from [Shanmugam07] fits a microsphere around every pixel in the depth buffer and accumulates the ambient occlusion contribution from each microsphere occluder. The algorithm assumes that any microsphere is visible from P and does not take mutual occlusion between spheres into account. For large radii of influence, this accumulation approach produces unrealistic over-occlusion that cannot be simply fixed using a uniform scale factor.

The crease shading algorithm from [Fox08] uses the same approach as [Shanmugam07] but without the microspheres. As it accumulates occlusion, the algorithm ignores the solid angles. This can be seen as an approximation of [Shanmugam07], where all the microspheres have the same solid angle.

The algorithm presented by [Mittring07] and [Moller08] distributes points in 3D space in a sphere around P and compares the depth of each 3D sample with the corresponding depth in the depth buffer, similar to shadow mapping. This algorithm assumes that points that are above the height field are visible from the surface point P, which is not always true (see Figure 6.2.4).

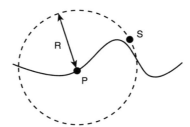

FIGURE 6.2.4   Sample S is above the height field but is not visible from P.

SAMPLING THE HEMISPHERE

Equation 6.2.3 can be integrated using a Monte Carlo approach, sampling directions on the normal-oriented hemisphere and evaluating the visibility function V and the attenuation function W for each sampled direction. In offline renderers, this is typically done by analytically intersecting 3D rays with the scene geometry, using a precomputed acceleration structure to avoid testing each ray with every primitive.

INPUT BUFFERS FOR IMAGE SPACE AMBIENT OCCLUSION

DEPTH IMAGE

We store eye-space z coordinates in the depth image, and we reconstruct 3D eye-space positions from the 2D pixel coordinates and the associated depth value, assuming that the depths are being generated at the pixel centers. Now that we have this depth image available, the problem is how to integrate Equation 6.2.3 for every pixel on the screen.

NORMALS

As shown in Figure 6.2.2, the hemisphere is defined based on the normal direction, such that all the sampled directions have $(\vec{\omega}.\vec{n}) > 0$. The reason for this is that the integration domain for Equation 6.2.3 is the positive hemisphere defined by the surface normal and the point being evaluated.

In the following, we assume that we have a depth image rendered from the eye's point of view, along with the associated per-pixel normals.

IMAGE SPACE AMBIENT OCCLUSION WITH RAY MARCHING

In this section, we describe a brute force algorithm for rendering ambient occlusion based on tracing rays in image space using a per-pixel depth and normal buffers. This algorithm will provide the reader a basis to understand the mechanics of the integration of the ambient occlusion in screen-space. Further in the chapter we will present our approach that follows similar underlying principles.

INTERSECTING A RAY WITH A HEIGHT FIELD

A simple and robust way to render ambient occlusion in image space is to consider the depth image as a height field, and intersect 3D rays with it, by stepping on the height field along a 2D ray segment and testing at each step if the ray crosses the height field surface. This same approach is also referred to as grid tracing [Musgrave88], image-based ray tracing [Lischinski98], discrete ray tracing [Yagel92], linear search [Policarpo05] [Tatarchuk06], rasterization-based intersection [Baboud06], scan-line conversion [Xie07], and 2D iterative search [Davis07]. In this article, we refer to it as ray marching, following the naming from [Perlin89].

For intersecting a ray with a height field, assuming that the ray is traced in a direction going through the normal-oriented hemisphere, we approximate the intersection point by taking the first sample for which the current position along the ray is below the height field (see Figure 6.2.5).

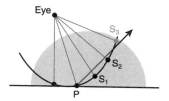

FIGURE 6.2.5   Intersecting a ray with a depth image by stepping along the ray and comparing the depths of the samples with the associated depths along the ray.

We define the end point E to be at distance R from P along the current direction. Ray-marching algorithms then step from P to E with a uniform step size. The ray marching can be done by projecting P and E first and then stepping in image space (uv = uv + step), or by stepping in 3D space (P = P + step) and projecting every sample point into image space to sample the depth image.

AVOIDING OUTLIERS

The height field that we are working on has depth discontinuities between objects (for instance, see Figure 6.2.6).

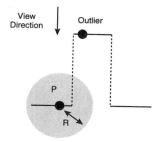

FIGURE 6.2.6   A surface point P and an outlier outside of the radius of influence R from P.

To avoid any artifacts from intersecting portions of the height field belonging to outliers (see Figure 6.2.6), we simply ignore samples that are outside the radius of influence R by computing the distance r between P and the sample position for every sample along the ray segment.

MONTE CARLO INTEGRATION

If we define for each pixel a tangent-binormal-normal (TBN) basis, the normal-oriented hemisphere can be sampled using a spherical coordinate system with the zenith axis aligned with the normal at the current point P. To integrate the ambient occlusion from Equation 6.2.3 using this approach, we would need N_d directions

(θ angles), N_r rays per direction (ϕ angles), and N_s steps per ray. When a ray intersects the depth image at point S, an ambient occlusion contribution $W(\|P - S\|)/(N_r N_s)$ would be added to the current ambient occlusion for surface point P. The per-pixel complexity of the algorithm is $O(N_d N_r N_s)$. For a given direction θ around the normal, the ray-marching algorithm traces one ray per ϕ angle, and in practice, to get good results at least three rays per direction are required.

OUR ALGORITHM

HORIZON CULLING

We assume that the height field from the depth image is continuous, which tends to be true in practice when ignoring outliers outside of the radius of influence from P. To simplify this explanation, we can assume that the attenuation function is $W(\bar{\omega}) = 1$. In this case, there exists a horizon angle below which all the rays are guaranteed to intersect the height field. This is a property of height fields used for occlusion culling [Rogers85] and horizon mapping [Max86] [Sloan00].

Given a horizon point H inside the radius of influence R, the ambient occlusion contribution subtended by the horizon angle (P,T,H) and the distance $\|P\text{-}H\|$ can be integrated analytically (see Figure 6.2.7). The problem is then how to find an accurate horizon angle in a given direction.

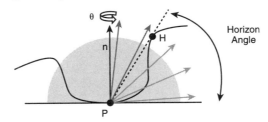

FIGURE 6.2.7   Horizon angle defined in tangent space for a particular direction θ. The rays with angles lower than the horizon angle intersect the depth image, and the others do not.

REFORMULATING THE AMBIENT OCCLUSION INTEGRAL

WORKING IN IMAGE SPACE

Instead of distributing directions in eye space based on the TBN basis at the surface point P (as described in "Ray Marching" above), our new algorithm distributes directions in image space around the current pixel. This works because a property of the perspective projection is that lines in eye space project to lines in image space.

Our algorithm samples depths in image space by stepping along 2D directions, and it integrates the ambient occlusion by using 3D eye-space positions.

SNAPPING TEXTURE COORDINATES

For each 3D sample S, to avoid any discrepancy between the fetched S.z and the exact depth associated with the offset S.xy, before sampling the depth buffer, we snap the (u,v) coordinates to pixel centers when reconstructing S.xy from (u,v). Because of this snapping requirement, we cannot use optimizations based on maximum mipmaps such as [Dachsbacher07] where the 2D locations of the depth samples in the mip levels would be unknown.

EYE-SPACE BASIS

Our algorithm distributes rays in the hemisphere by using the eye-space XYZ basis, not the tangent-space TBN basis. We effectively rotate the TBN basis to face the camera. We are assuming a left-handed projection, so the camera is looking toward the Z > 0, parallel to the Z axis.

We parameterize the integral using spherical coordinates, with the zenith axis aligned with the Z axis in eye-space, and the azimuth angle θ around Z and the elevation angle ϕ. In the coordinate system, the ambient occlusion integral from Equation 6.2.3 can be expressed by Equation 6.2.4 (see Figure 6.2.8a):

$$A = 1 - \frac{1}{2\pi} \int_{\theta=-\pi}^{\pi} \int_{\phi=t(\theta)}^{t(\theta)+\pi/2} V(\vec{\omega})W(\vec{\omega})d\omega$$

EQUATION 6.2.4

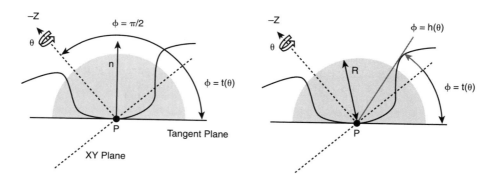

FIGURE 6.2.8   (a) Parameterization of the normal-oriented hemisphere.
(b) The horizon angle h(θ).

Similarly to horizon mapping [Max86] [Sloan00], we split the unit sphere by a horizon line defined by the signed horizon angle $h(\theta)$ relative to the XY plane going through P and perpendicular to Z. In addition, we split the hemisphere by a tangent line defined by the signed angle $t(\theta)$ between the tangent plane and the XY plane (see Figure 6.2.8b).

Assuming that the neighborhood of **P** defined within the radius of influence R is a continuous height field, rays that would normally be traced below the horizon are known to intersect an occluder, that is, $V(\vec{\omega}) = 1$ for all ϕ between $t(\theta)$ and $h(\theta)$. Then Equation 6.2.3 can be rewritten as

$$A = 1 - \frac{1}{2\pi} \int_{\theta=-\pi}^{\pi} \int_{\phi=t(\theta)}^{h(\theta)} W(\vec{\omega}) \cos(\phi) d\phi d\theta \qquad \text{EQUATION 6.2.5}$$

We assume that a uniform distribution of directions in image space approximately corresponds to a uniform distribution of θ angles in eye space.

INCREMENTAL HORIZON ANGLE

We step in the depth image in direction θ with a uniform step size and reconstruct the eye-space positions S_i from the sampled depths. The signed elevation angles $\phi(S_i)$ are given by

$$\tan\phi(S_i) = \frac{(P - S_i).z}{\|(P - S_i).xy\|} \qquad \text{EQUATION 6.2.6}$$

In this sampling process, we ignore samples that are outside the radius of influence R, that is, $\|S_i - P\| > R$. We also keep track of the maximum elevation angle (incremental horizon angle h) as shown in Figure 6.2.9. If the elevation angle $\phi(S_i)$ of the current sample is not greater than $\phi(S_{i-1})$, then we ignore sample S_i and go to the next sample. Otherwise, we compute the ambient occlusion contributed by the sample.

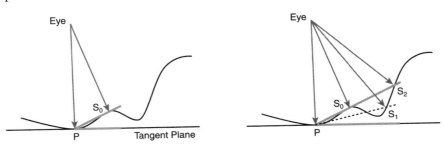

FIGURE 6.2.9 Horizon angles for a given direction after one sample (left) and after three samples (right).

ATTENUATION FUNCTION

Up to this point, we have been assuming that $W(\vec{\omega}) = 1$. The attenuation function is important to avoid any discontinuities in the ambient occlusion and can be defined as a function of the distance to the horizon point ([Dimitrov08] [Bavoil08]). This would approximate $W(\vec{\omega}_i)$ by the lowest attenuation for all samples along the direction $\vec{\omega}$, and therefore this results in over-attenuating the ambient occlusion. We found that it made a significant difference to evaluate the attenuation function $W(\vec{\omega}_i)$ for every sample.

In offline rendering, the attenuation function $W(r)$ (referred to as "falloff" in [Gritz06]) is typically set to a linear decay $W(r) = (1 - r)$, where r is the distance to the occluder, normalized by the radius of influence R. To attenuate the samples near the middle of R less, we use the following quadratic attenuation function: $W(r) = (1 - r^2)$, which attenuates less than the linear attenuation function.

INTEGRATING THE AMBIENT OCCLUSION

By sampling along a line on the image and skipping the samples that do not increase the horizon angle as shown on Figure 6.2.9, we get a partitioning of the elevation angles $\phi \in [t(\theta), h(\theta)]$ with $t(\theta) = \phi_0 \leq \phi_1 \leq \phi_2 \leq \ldots \leq \phi_{N_s} = h(\theta)$, which we use to integrate Equation 6.2.5. We use a piecewise constant approximation of $W(\vec{\omega})$, where $\vec{\omega}_i$ is the 3D direction associated with $\phi = \phi_i$:

$$\int_{\phi=t(\theta)}^{h(\theta)} W(\vec{\omega})\cos\phi\,d\phi = \sum_{i=1}^{N_s} \int_{\phi=\phi_{i-1}}^{\phi_i} W(\vec{\omega}_i)\cos\phi\,d\phi$$

EQUATION 6.2.7

which yields the following incremental computation of the ambient occlusion:

$$A = 1 - \frac{1}{2\pi} \int_{\theta=-\pi}^{\pi} \sum_{i=1}^{N_s} W(\vec{\omega}_i)(\sin\phi_i - \sin\phi_{i-1})\,d\theta$$

EQUATION 6.2.8

To integrate Equation 6.2.8, for every 2D direction θ, we step on the depth image, and for every sample S_i, we compute $\tan(\phi(S_i))$ and $\sin(\phi(S_i))$. This works correctly when the samples S_i all have the same exact θ angle relative to the Z axis. However, because we need to snap the sample coordinates to the pixel centers, the θ_i angles of the snapped sample coordinates are slightly different from the θ_i angles of the true non-snapped coordinates. Taking the difference of $\sin(\phi(S_i))$ and $\sin(\phi(S_{i-1}))$, where S_i and S_{i-1} have perturbed θ angles, may generate objectionable false-occlusion artifacts.

To solve this issue, we compute a $\sin(t_i)$ value per sample S_i, and we rewrite the integral in terms of differences between $\sin(\phi_i)$ and $\sin(t_i)$. This can be seen as grounding the height $\sin(\phi_i)$ of each sample by the height $\sin(t_i)$ of its associated tangent. Equation 6.2.9 describes the grounded form of our horizon-based integral:

$$A = 1 - \frac{1}{2\pi} \int_{\theta=-\pi}^{\pi} \sum_{i=1}^{N_s} W(\vec{\omega}_i)[(\sin\phi_i - \sin t_i) - (\sin\phi_{i-1} - \sin t_{i-1})]d\theta$$

EQUATION 6.2.9

The advantage of using per-sample tangents with Equation 6.2.9 is that the integral does not produce any false-occlusion artifacts when the θ angles are perturbed by per-sample snapping.

IMPLEMENTATION CONSIDERATIONS

Provided we have a linear depth buffer and a normal buffer, we can proceed to compute the per-pixel ambient occlusion by rendering a full-screen quad into an ambient occlusion buffer (8 bits, 1 channel). In the following subsections we present details on implementation tradeoffs in order to perform an efficient screen-space ambient occlusion integration.

PER-PIXEL NORMALS

Normals are typically defined at vertices of a mesh and smoothed using linear interpolation during rasterization. Because per-vertex smoothed normals are by definition not orthogonal to their associated triangles, the resulting interpolated per-pixel normals will not be either, and this may generate artifacts especially visible for large triangles (low tessellated scenes). Therefore, we prefer to compute per-pixel normals in the pixel shader by taking derivates of eye-space coordinates instead of interpolated per-vertex normals.

In our implementation we have seen that 8 bits per component provides enough precision for the normal buffer, so we use a R8G8B8A8_SNORM normal texture.

COMBINING WITH THE COLOR BUFFER

There are multiple ways the ambient occlusion can be applied to a scene. For applications that use a depth pre-pass before shading, the ambient occlusion can be rendered right after the depth pre-pass and applied in a flexible manner during shading. Otherwise, the ambient occlusion should be multiplied over the current scene's color buffer right after shading the opaque objects.

We apply the ambient occlusion pass on the opaque geometry only, before any semitransparent objects are rendered over it.

Our ambient occlusion term does not include cosine terms, so it makes the most sense to consider it as an ambient shadow and apply it by multiplying the ambient terms. In our results, we simply multiply the ambient occlusion over the full shaded colors, including direct lighting terms.

DIRECTIONS AND JITTERING

For each angle θ, we sample the depth image along a line segment in image space. The eye-space radius of influence R is projected onto the image plane, and its projected size is subdivided into N_s steps of uniform lengths.

We pick N_d 2D directions θ in image space around the current pixel, which correspond to directions around the Z axis in eye space (see Figure 6.2.10). To avoid banding artifacts, we rotate the 2D directions by a random per-pixel angle, and we jitter the samples along each direction. These randomized values are precomputed and stored in a tiled texture containing $(\cos(\alpha),\sin(\alpha),\beta)$, where $\alpha \in [0,2\pi/Nd]$ and $\beta \in [0,1)$. The sample locations for a given direction θ are

$$uv(S_i) = uv(P) + (\beta + i)(\Delta u, \Delta v)R(\alpha) \quad \text{EQUATION 6.2.10}$$

where $R(\alpha)$ is a 2×2 rotation matrix, and $(\Delta u, \Delta v)$ is the step size in direction θ.

Note that this sampling distribution is biased toward P. This is not a problem, though, since our integration does not assume a uniform distribution. In fact, having more samples near the center is important for improving the quality of contact occlusion, because the nearer the samples are to the center, the less attenuated they are likely to be.

To account for the pixel-snapping requirements of the algorithm, we would be required to snap each of these $uv(S_i)$ texture coordinates. However, it is more efficient to snap the texture coordinate of the initial sample S_0 and then snap the step size to guarantee that we always sample at pixel centers (see Figure 6.2.10). However, using such snapped directions generates banding for high numbers of steps or for small radii of influence, due to the limited number of possible directions.

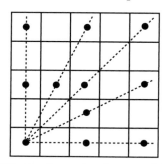

FIGURE 6.2.10   Example of snapped directions.

VARIABLE STEP SIZE

The step size is the distance in uv texture space between two consecutive samples along a given direction of integration. To compute it, we start by projecting the size of the radius of influence R from eye space to clip space, using similar triangles (Figure 6.2.11).

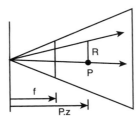

FIGURE 6.2.11   Projecting the radius of influence R into uv space.

The projected size of the radius R on the focal plane is $R_{uv} = fR/P.z$, where f is the focal length vector defined as (cotan(fovy/2) height/width, cotan(fovy/2)). We then compute the uv-space step size $(\Delta u, \Delta v) = (R_{uv} / 2) / (N_s + 1)$, and early exit if this step size is smaller than one texel in the X or the Y directions to guarantee, at most, one sample per texel.

EYE-SPACE TANGENT VECTORS

For a given direction θ, we start the ambient occlusion integration by computing a tangent vector T in eye space. Given a step size in texture space Δuv associated with direction θ and given the plane equation for the tangent plane at P defined using the eye-space normal at P, the tangent vector T can be computed by intersecting a view ray with the tangent plane, as shown on Figure 6.2.12.

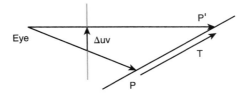

FIGURE 6.2.12   Tangent vector associated with a step size Δuv.

We use a simpler method to compute the tangent T using a screen-aligned basis (dPdu, dPdv) for the tangent plane, where

$\Delta P = \Delta u\ dPdu + \Delta v\ dPdv$ **EQUATION 6.2.11**

This means that when (u,v) moves to (u,v) + (Δu, Δv), P moves to P + ΔP, which defines a tangent vector $T(\theta) = T(\Delta u, \Delta v) = \Delta P$.

For an orthogonal projection, (u,v) is linearly related to the eye-space coordinates (x,y). However, for perspective projections, the relationship between texture-space (u,v) and eye-space (x,y) is not linear except when the plane has a constant depth. We found that the error introduced by the non-linearity does not generate any visible artifacts compared to ray casting. For efficiency, we use Equation 6.2.11 even though it is not perspective correct.

ANGLE BIAS

When the level of tessellation of the geometry used in the scene is low, the ambient occlusion contribution tends to magnify the creases due to large polygons that produce unpleasant artifacts (see Figure 6.2.13). If increasing the polygon count in the scene is not possible, this effect can be eliminated by adding an angle bias to the horizon calculation (see Figure 6.2.14). Moreover, using an angle bias removes artifacts generated by clamping to edge when sampling depth.

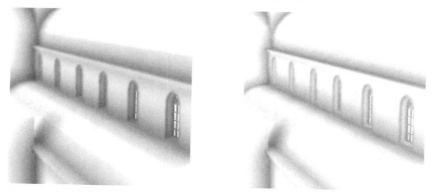

FIGURE 6.2.13   (a) Low-tessellated mesh. (b) Adding an angle bias fixes the creases.

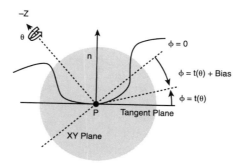

FIGURE 6.2.14   The angle bias ignores directions with tangent angles below the bias.

CROSS-BILATERAL FILTER

Depending on the number of sampling directions and the use of jittered sampling, the result of the ambient occlusion pass presents a certain degree of noise. This can be reduced by blurring the ambient occlusion image. To preserve sharp geometric edges between foreground and background objects, we use a cross-bilateral filter based on the depth delta from the kernel center [Eisemann04].

The size of the filter kernel is a parameter. The values we found to work quite well for normal settings are between 9×9 and 21×21 pixels. As the number of directions and the number of steps increase, the blur kernel can be reduced considerably. Although bilateral filters are mathematically non-separable, similarly to [Segovia06], we have obtained good performance results by separating the filter in X and Y with very minimal visual artifacts.

MULTISAMPLE ANTIALIASING

For integrating the ambient occlusion with multisample antialiasing (MSAA), we take as input multisample depth and normal textures generated using multiple render targets (rendering colors, depths, and normals in the same pass). First, we resolve the depth and normal textures with a full-screen pass that copies one of the samples per pixel into non-multisample depth and normal textures. Second, we perform the ambient occlusion full-screen pass, which takes as input the previously generated textures and writes into a non-multisample ambient occlusion texture. Finally, we apply our two blur passes over the ambient occlusion, taking as input the multisample depth texture and the non-multisample ambient occlusion texture.

Since the blur is performed on the non-multisample ambient occlusion texture, it tends to magnify bleeding artifacts at the edges (see Figure 6.2.15). To overcome this problem we add an edge detection pass [Cantlay07] followed by a supersampling blur pass only for the edges that compute the blur for each depth sample per pixel, and averages the results.

FIGURE 6.2.15   (a) Original image. (b) Edge bleeding with a naïve blur.
(c) Running a supersampling blur at the edges reduces the leaking and the aliasing.

WORKING AT LOWER RESOLUTION

Since ambient occlusion is a soft global illumination effect, it is not required to support higher-frequency textures and silhouettes, and hence the calculations can be performed at a coarser level. As a performance optimization with little impact in visual quality, we propose to run the ambient occlusion pass in a half resolution buffer and up-sample the result during the edge-preserving Gaussian blur. As we will see in the experiments section, this solution is a good balance point.

SUMMARY OF THE PARAMETERS

Overall, our implementation has the following parameters that control quality and performance.

- The radius of influence R, in eye space
- The number of directions N_d distributed in image space around every pixel
- The number of steps per direction N_s (see Figure 6.2.16)
- The angle bias (see Figure 6.2.13)
- A scale factor multiplying the ambient occlusion
- The blur kernel size in pixels
- The depth variance for the cross-bilateral filter

RESULTS

In this section, we present some results of our screen-space ambient occlusion algorithm. All the experiments have been run on an Intel Core2Duo CPU, with 2 GB of RAM, using the indicated GPUs. The data sets used for these experiments are the Stanford Dragon, the Sibenik Cathedral, and the Cornell box.

To test the performance of the algorithm, we use the Sibenik dataset with three different GeForce GPUs: 8600 GTS, 8800GT, and 8800 GTX Ultra. Table 6.2.1 contains frames per second at 1600×1200 resolution for the cases of:

- No AO/no blur: Represents the speed-of-light reference.
- No AO: Only applies the blur.
- 4,4: Uses four directions and four samples per direction.
- 8,8: Uses eight directions and eight samples per direction.
- 16,16: Uses 16 directions and 16 samples per direction.

TABLE 6.2.1 The blur size in all the results was 9×9. The half resolution AO results did not have MSAA enabled

| | Frames Per Second—1600x1200 | | | | |
	No AO/No Blur	No AO	4/4	8/8	16/16
Half Resolution AO					
8600 GTS	88	43	26	15	6
8800 GT	234	127	81	48	20
8800 Ultra	301	155	100	59	24
1x MSAA					
8600 GTS	86	42	10	4.2	1.5
8800 GT	234	128	26	10	4
8800 Ultra	299	155	41	17	5.8
4x MSAA					
8600 GTS	38	26	8.8	4.2	1.5
8800 GT	88	67	22	9.8	3.9
8800 Ultra	138	97	36	16	5.7

In Figure 6.2.16, we show the visual quality that can be achieved with different numbers of samples. For the cases where only four directions and four steps per direction are used, we can easily obtain very visible and smooth creases. As we increase the number of total samples, more subtle details come to life, bringing more details in the scene. The main problem at low sample rate is the need for extra blur strength to compensate for the noise generated during jittering.

As for final results, we show in Figure 6.2.17 the ability of the ambient occlusion contribution to provide proper depth cues and realism to a rendered scene. We show the separate diffuse pass and the ambient occlusion pass for the dragon model and the result of combining them together into a final image.

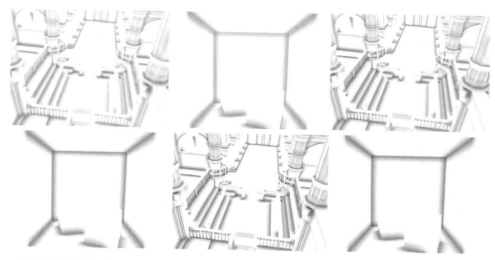

FIGURE 6.2.16 From top to bottom, three views of two datasets showing the quality variation of the ambient occlusion when using 4/4, 8/8, and 16/16 directions and steps. The blur kernel size has been adjusted accordingly to compensate for the lack of samples.

FIGURE 6.2.17 From top to bottom, diffuse shading on the dragon model, ambient occlusion calculated using our approach, and the final composited image.

ACKNOWLEDGMENTS

We thank Rouslan Dimitrov for the fruitful discussions in the early stages of our ambient occlusion research. We also thank Jason Mitchell, Naty Hoffman, and Nelson Max for the helpful discussions during the I3D '08 conference.

REFERENCES

[Baboud06] Baboud, L. and Decoret, X. "Rendering geometry with relief textures." In GI '06: Proceedings of Graphics Interface 2006, Canadian Information Processing Society, Toronto, Ont., Canada, Canada, 195–201, 2006.

[Bavoil08] Bavoil, L., Sainz, M., Dimitrov, R. "Image-space horizon-based ambient occlusion." ACM SIGGRAPH 2008 talks, 2008.

[Cantlay07] Cantlay, I. "High-Speed, Off-Screen Particles." GPU Gems 3, 2007.

[Christensen03] Christensen, P. H. "Global illumination and all that." In ACM SIGGRAPH Course 9 (RenderMan, Theory and Practice), 2003.

[Dachsbacher07] Dachsbacher, C. and Tatarchuk, N. "Prism parallax occlusion mapping with accurate silhouette generation." Symposium on Interactive 3D Graphics and Games, Poster, 2007.

[Davis07] Davis, S. T. and Wyman, C. "Interactive refractions with total internal reflection." In GI '07: Proceedings of Graphics Interface 2007.

[Dimitrov08] Dimitrov, R., Bavoil, L., and Sainz, M. "Horizon split ambient occlusion." Symposium on Interactive 3D Graphics and Games, Poster, 2008.

[Eisemann04] Eisemann, E. and Durand, F. "Flash photography enhancement via intrinsic relighting." ACM Transactions on Graphics (Proceedings of SIGGRAPH Conference), Volume 23, 2004.

[Gritz06] Gritz, L. Gelato 2.1 technical reference. Tech. rep., NVIDIA, 2006.

[Landis02] Landis, H., "Production Ready Global Illumination." ACM SIGGRAPH Course 16: Renderman in Production, 2002.

[Langer99] Langer, M., and Bulthoff, H., "Perception of Shape From Shading on a Cloudy Day." Technical Report, 1999.

[Lischinski98] Lischinski, D. and Rapoport, A. "Image-based rendering for non-diffuse synthetic scenes." Proc. Ninth Eurographics Workshop on Rendering, in Rendering Techniques '98, pp. 301–314, 1998.

[Max86] Max, N. L. "Horizon mapping: shadows for bump-mapped surfaces." In Proceedings of Computer Graphics Tokyo '86 on Advanced Computer Graphics, 1986.

[Mittring07] Mittring, M., "Finding next gen: CryEngine 2." In ACM SIGGRAPH 2007 courses, 2007, 97–121.

[Moller08] Akenine-Möller, T., Haines, E., and Hoffman, N. *Real-Time Rendering* (third edition). 2008.

[Musgrave88] Musgrave, F. K. "Grid tracing: fast ray tracing for height fields." Technical Report YALEU/DCS/RR-639, Yale University, Dept. of Computer Science Research, 1988.

[Perlin89] Perlin, K. and Hoffert, E. "Hypertexture." *Computer Graphics* (Proceedings of ACM SIGGRAPH Conference), Vol. 23, No. 3, 1989.

[Pharr04] Pharr, M. and Green, S., "Ambient Occlusion." GPU Gems, 2004.

[Hegeman06] Hegeman, K., and Premoze, S., Ashikhmin, M., Drettakis, G., "Approximate ambient occlusion for trees." Symposium on Interactive 3D Graphics and Games, 2006.

[Policarpo05] Policarpo, F., Oliveira, M. M., and Comba, J. "Real-time relief mapping on arbitrary polygonal surfaces." Symposium on Interactive 3D Graphics and Games, 2005, 155–162.

[Segovia06] Segovia B., Iehl J. C., Mitanchey, R., and Péroche, B. "Non-interleaved deferred shading of interleaved sample patterns." Proceedings of SIGGRAPH/Eurographics Workshop on Graphics Hardware 2006.

[Shanmugam07] Shanmugam, P., and Arikan, O. "Hardware accelerated ambient occlusion techniques on GPUs." Symposium on Interactive 3D Graphics and Games, 2007, 73–80.

[Fox08] Fox, M. and Compton, S. "Ambient Occlusive Crease Shading." Game Developer Magazine, March 2008.

[Rogers85] Rogers, D. "Procedural elements for computer graphics", 1985.

[Sloan00] Sloan, P.-P. J. and Cohen, M. F. "Interactive horizon mapping." In Proceedings of the Eurographics Workshop on Rendering Techniques 2000.

[Tatarchuk06] Tatarchuk, N. "Practical parallax occlusion mapping with approximate soft shadows for detailed surface rendering." In ACM SIGGRAPH 2006 Courses, 2006, 81–112.

[Xie07] Xie, F., Tabellion, E., Pearce, A. "Soft Shadows by Ray Tracing Multilayer Transparent Shadow Maps." Eurographics Symposium on Rendering, 2007.

[Yagel92] Yagel, R., Cohen, D., and Kaufman, A. "Discrete ray tracing." IEEE Computer Graphics & Applications, 1992.

[Zhukov98] Zhukov, S., Inoes, A., and Kronin, G. "An ambient light illumination model." In Rendering Techniques '98, G. Drettakis and N. Max, Eds., Eurographics, 1998, 45–56.

6.3 Deferred Occlusion from Analytic Surfaces

Jeremy Shopf, Joshua Barczak, Thorsten Scheuermann, and Christopher Oat

FIGURE 6.3.1 Ambient occlusion from a large mass of ping-pong balls calculated using our method.

INTRODUCTION

Ambient occlusion (AO) is an often-used approximation to global illumination. It provides a sense of surface shape and spatial context. AO is the attenuation of ambient light over incoming directions due to occlusion. It is calculated by integrating the visibility function at a point. Calculating occlusion due to near and distant surfaces in a scene can be an expensive process.

We alleviate this problem by calculating AO from analytic surfaces such as spheres, planes, and cuboids in a deferred manner and splatting it onto the scene.

By restricting occlusion to objects for which we have an analytic description, we can formulate a closed-form approximation of AO at a point. Evaluating a closed-form equation to calculate AO for an object was inspired by the Ambient Occlusion Fields work [Kontkanen05].

We start by rendering scene depth and surface normals to off-screen render targets. Then, to approximate occlusion for a given pixel, we sample the rendered normal and depth buffers and evaluate our analytic occlusion equation for a single occluder. By calculating AO in screen space, we ensure that we are performing visibility calculations only on visible surfaces. By rendering bounding proxy geometry for each occluder, we restrict this computation to pixels where the occlusion will be visible. The resulting occlusion for each object is accumulated into an AO buffer that is then used to attenuate surface shading.

We present a discussion of our implementation, some applications, and a few optimizations.

METHOD

Our deferred AO pipeline consists of three simple steps. Our first pass is to render scene depth and surface normals to an off-screen render target.

During the second pass, the scene is rendered to the back buffer using desired lighting techniques.

In the third pass, we render the proxy geometry for each object that will occlude the scene. In the case of our 5,000 ping-pong ball scene, we render a cube for each ball. It is important that the width of the cube encompass the 3D extent of the occlusion due to a spherical ping-pong ball. For efficiency's sake, we restrict the domain of the sphere's occlusion to distances where the occlusion is visually significant, as performed in [Dachsbacher06]. We use a bounding cube rather than a bounding sphere because a cube can be represented using fewer triangles, and therefore it is much more efficient to draw. We have chosen 3D proxy geometry over a view-aligned 2D quad so that we do not have to dynamically adjust the bounds of the proxy based on distance from the camera. 3D proxy geometry also allows us to use depth culling to eliminate unnecessary computation from non-visible surfaces.

A pixel shader that evaluates the analytic occlusion of the sphere is executed for each front-facing fragment generated by the proxy geometry. The occlusion values are accumulated into a single-channel AO buffer using multiplicative blending [Kontkanen05], which we then composite onto the rendered scene in the back buffer using alpha blending to darken occluded pixels.

Analytic Occlusion from a Sphere

The formula for occlusion from a sphere, taking into account the cosine falloff of incoming lighting, is as follows (refer to Figure 6.3.2):

$$AO(r,d) = \cos\alpha \left(\frac{r}{d}\right)^2$$

where r is the radius of the occluding sphere and d is the distance from the occluding sphere to the shaded point. We refer the reader to the derivation of this formula in [Quilez07].

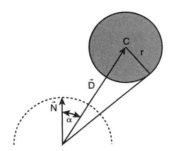

FIGURE 6.3.2   Quantities used to calculate sphere AO.

To handle spheres that are partially or totally below the horizon, we add an extra term to the occlusion value $AO(r,d)$. We simply linearly interpolate between the occlusion value and zero based on the distance of the center of the sphere from the horizon relative to the diameter of the sphere. It is also possible to get an approximation of this falloff by precomputing it using Monte Carlo integration techniques into a texture that is indexed by distance and angle relative to the horizon (assuming a constant sphere radius).

Below is an HLSL function for computing AO due to a sphere.

```
float SphereOcclusion( float3 vPositionWS, float3 vNormalWS,
                       float4 vSphereCenterAndRadius )
{
    // Compute vector from point we are shading to center of sphere
    float3 vSphereDirWS =
        vSphereCenterPosAndRadius.xyz - vPositionWS;
    float fRadius = vSphereCenterPosAndRadius.w;
```

```
// Compute the height of the sphere above the horizon
float fHeightAboveHorizon = dot( vNormalWS, vSphereDirWS );


// Find the cosine of the sphere's angular height above horizon
float fCosAlpha = dot( normalize(vNormalWS),
                       normalize(vSphereDirWS) );


// Reduce occulsion as sphere falls below horizon
float fHorizonScale =
    saturate((fHeightAboveHorizon + fRadius)/(2.0*fRadius));


// Distance from point we are shading to sphere center
float fDist = length( vSphereDirWS );


float fFactor = fRadius/fDist;
float fOcclusion = fCosAlpha*(fFactor*fFactor)*fHorizonScale


return fOcclusion;
}
```

ANALYTIC OCCLUSION FROM A TRIANGLE OR QUAD

Calculating AO from triangles and quads is more difficult, as there is no simple way to handle the horizon case. Special care must be taken in these AO shaders to alleviate this problem of over-darkening when the occluders pass below the horizon of the point we are shading.

To calculate the AO from a triangle or quadrilateral, the following three steps are performed.

1. **Setup:** Provide vertices of polygon (V_i) to the pixel shader through constant store or VBs.
2. **Clip:** Move all vertices below the horizon of the shaded point **P** to the horizon so that occlusion is not improperly calculated using regions below the horizon.
3. **Calculate:** Calculate occlusion using contour integral discussed in [Baum89].

Clip

When computing AO, we must ensure that all vertices and edges that will be used to compute AO are in the hemisphere of the point we are shading. Failing to do this will lead to artifacts and over-darkening. In order to get correct AO we must clip out the portion of the polygon that is below the horizon.

First, we calculate the signed distance of each vertex from the plane defined by **P** and **N**. Depending on which vertices are above or below the horizon, we perform different actions. If all vertices have a positive distance, they are above the plane, and there is no need to clip. If all vertices have negative distance, the entire polygon is below the plane, and we can ignore any occlusion from the polygon. For other cases, the vertices must be moved to the horizon plane. The new vertex positions can be calculated using ray-plane intersection tests. If one vertex is below, an extra vertex must be added, as illustrated in Figure 6.3.3. Our AO calculation works for general non-self-intersecting polygons.

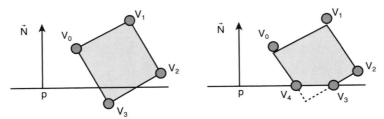

FIGURE 6.3.3 Clipping performed when one vertex is below the horizon.

Calculate

The formula for computing the visibility of a convex polygon at a point is quite simple. The following equation was used in [Baum89] to analytically compute form factors in radiosity calculations. For a differential receiver like the point p, the form factor is equal to the occlusion of the hemisphere. The equations for computing the AO from a polygon and the required quantities are shown in Figure 6.3.4. Quads and triangles can be used to represent simple objects such as cuboids (Figure 6.3.5).

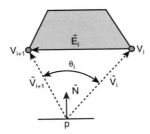

FIGURE 6.3.4 Quantities used to compute AO from a general polygon.

$$AO = \frac{1}{2\pi} \sum_i N \cdot \Gamma_i \qquad\qquad \Gamma_i = \frac{\vec{E}_i \times \vec{V}_i}{|\vec{E}_i \times \vec{V}_i|} \cdot \theta_i$$

where $\mathbf{N}$ is the surface normal of the occluded point P, $\vec{E}_i$ is the edge between $\mathbf{V}_i$ and $\mathbf{V}_{i+1}$ in the occluding surface, $\vec{V}_i$ is the vector computed as $\mathbf{V}_i$ - $\mathbf{P}$, and θ_i is the angle (in radians) between $\vec{V}_i$ and $\vec{V}_{i+1}$.

The HLSL function for computing the AO value for a quad is shown below.

```
float QuadOcclusion( float3 vVertsIn[4], float3 vPosWS, float3 vNormalWS )
{
    float3 vV_i[4] = { normalize(vVertsIn[0] - vPosWS),
                       normalize(vVertsIn[1] - vPosWS),
                       normalize(vVertsIn[2] - vPosWS),
                       normalize(vVertsIn[3] - vPosWS) };
    // Calculate occlusion
    float4 fD1 = acos( dot(vV_i[0], vV_i[1]) );
    float4 fD2 = acos( dot(vV_i[1], vV_i[2]) );
    float4 fD3 = acos( dot(vV_i[2], vV_i[3]) );
    float4 fD4 = acos( dot(vV_i[3], vV_i[0]) );

    float3 vCross1 = normalize( cross( vV_i[0], vV_i[1] )) * fD1;
    float3 vCross2 = normalize( cross( vV_i[1], vV_i[2] )) * fD2;
    float3 vCross3 = normalize( cross( vV_i[2], vV_i[3] )) * fD3;
    float3 vCross4 = normalize( cross( vV_i[3], vV_i[0] )) * fD4;

    float4 fOcclusion = dot( vNormalWS, vCross1 ) +
                        dot( vNormalWS, vCross2 ) +
                        dot( vNormalWS, vCross3 ) +
                        dot( vNormalWS, vCross4 );

    return fOcclusion/(2*PI);
}
```

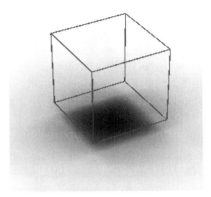

FIGURE 6.3.5   AO from six quads.

ANALYTIC OCCLUSION FROM OTHER SURFACES

We have illustrated the use of spheres, triangles, and quads here, but this method can be used with any shape for which you have an analytic description and some way to handle the horizon case. Bunnell demonstrated the use of discs to calculate ambient occlusion [Bunnell05]. Cylinders are also worth exploring: For example, a collection of cylinders and spheres could be used as proxy geometry for a character model to use for casting AO from the character into the scene.

OPTIMIZATION

OPTIMIZATION #1: COMPUTE MULTIPLE PIXELS AND DE-SWIZZLE

Our method for computing occlusion consists of many scalar math operations. While a good shader compiler will perform some vectorization for vector or very long instruction word (VLIW) hardware targets, this packing is limited by dependencies between instructions. By reformulating our shader to compute occlusion for four pixels at once, the compiler has four independent sets of instructions that can be much more easily vectorized. This can be achieved by rendering occlusion into a ¼ resolution render target and computing occlusion for four points per-pixel and storing the results in the RGBA channels of the target. Thus, each invocation of the pixel shader will compute and store four occlusion values. Running this modified shader through the AMD GPU ShaderAnalyzer [AMD08] shows a 15% improvement in ALU utilization when performing AO computation on four pixels at once. It should be noted that it is not necessary to manually vectorize the high-level shader code. The compiler did a much better job vectorizing the code than we could manage to do by hand (using ATI's shader compiler).

The largest gain in performance (in our scenario of 5,000 spheres) from computing four occlusion values per pixel comes from blending four channels per pixel rather than blending a single scalar for each of four individual pixels. While the output bandwidth from the pixel shader is the same, the overall number of blends is one-fourth. The render backends that perform blending are designed to blend four color channels in parallel. Thus, blending to single-channel targets only utilizes 25% of the total blend capabilities of the GPU.

Unfortunately, computing AO in this packed fashion requires a de-swizzle of the final AO values from a four-channel half-resolution texture to a one-channel full-resolution texture so that they are blended onto the scene correctly. The overhead of this de-swizzle operation is small relative to the improvement in ALU and blend unit utilization.

Overall, computing four pixels in one fragment shader invocation provided a 30% improvement in rendering performance in our example scene.

OPTIMIZATION #2: DEPTH EXTENTS EARLY-OUT

Depending on the nature of the scene, a significant performance improvement could be gained by culling ambient occlusion computations on fragments that could not possibly be occluded because the points are outside of the depth-bounds of the proxy. This is done by performing a depth extents test at the beginning of the AO shader and killing the pixel before the AO calculation is done. If there are coherent regions of pixels that are outside the valid depth extents, a significant savings in performance can be achieved because the entire thread group (fragments that are executed in lock-step) can be discarded before executing the remainder of the AO shader. If your objects exist in a scene where there is no significant distance between the objects and the background, then the overhead of testing the depth will be greater than any performance gains from culling unnecessary computations.

OPTIMIZATION #3: COMPUTE AT LOWER RESOLUTION AND UP-SAMPLE

Because ambient occlusion is typically low frequency, computing it per pixel is often unnecessary. There are existing methods that allow computation to be performed at a lower resolution and then up-sampled to final screen resolution.

The first, bilateral up-sampling, takes uniform samples and uses weighted bilinear interpolation to up-sample the AO values. This weighting ensures that values are not interpolated across discontinuities in the AO buffer.

The second, push-pull up-sampling [Guennebaud07], takes adaptive samples and uses a form of hierarchical down-sampling and up-sampling to fill in gaps. The initial samples are computed adaptively based on the orientation of the receiving surface relative to the view and discontinuities in the depth buffer.

A third, simpler method involves computing shading at a lower resolution and up-sampling using bilinear filtering where possible [Dachsbacher05]. A single-channel discontinuity buffer (same resolution as the low-res buffer previously discussed) is calculated based on angles between adjacent normals and distances in world space between adjacent depth values. This buffer contains binary values indicating whether or not each pixel is at a discontinuity. If one or none of the low-resolution samples are in the discontinuity buffer, bilinear filtering is used (normalizing the weights if using three samples) to up-sample. If two or more of the low-resolution samples are in the discontinuity buffer, the low-resolution calculations are performed at full resolution.

CONCLUSION

AO from analytic surfaces is preferable over depth-based screen-space AO (such as [Mittring07] and [Shanmugam07]) because it does not rely on noisy stochastic sampling techniques. Depth-buffer-based methods do not account for occlusion from back-facing polygons and must resort to multiple passes to handle these cases, while our analytic technique inherently handles this. Unlike other screen-space AO techniques that tend to be texture fetch heavy, our method consists mainly of ALU. The ALU throughput of contemporary graphics processors is growing much faster than fetch power. Therefore ALU-heavy methods are favorable in increasingly bandwidth-limited systems.

It is also important to note that you can selectively calculate AO by only splatting the objects for which you want to occlude visibility in the scene. This is desirable in game scenarios where some objects are required to have more importance or visual impact. In the ping-pong demo, the ping-pong balls were the most important element of the scene, so only the AO due to the balls has been rendered (Figure 6.3.6).

FIGURE 6.3.6   Diffuse shading without and with ambient occlusion. Note the greater sense of depth and spatial context due to contact shadows.

REFERENCES

[AMD08] AMD GPU ShaderAnalyzer, Available online at: http://developer.amd.com/gpu, 2008.

[Baum89] Daniel R. Baum, Holly E. Rushmeier, and James M. Winget, "Improving Radiosity Solutions Through the Use of Analytically Determined Form-factors," Proceedings of the 16th Annual Conference on Computer Graphics and Interactive Techniques, ACM, 1989, pp. 325–334.

[Bunnell05] Micheal Bunnell, "Dynamic Ambient Occlusion and Indirect Lighting," In *GPU Gems 2*, Ed. Matt Pharr, Addison-Wesley, 2005, pp. 223–233.

[Dachsbacher06] Carsten Dachsbacher and Marc Stamminger, "Splatting Indirect Illumination," Proceedings of the 2006 Symposium on Interactive 3D Graphics and Games, ACM, 2006, pp. 93–100.

[Dachsbacher05] Carsten Dachsbacher and Marc Stamminger, "Reflective Shadow Maps," Proceedings of the 2005 Symposium on Interactive 3D Graphics and Games, ACM, 2005, pp. 203–231.

[Guennebaud07] Gael Guennebaud, Loic Barthe, and Mathias Paulin, "High-Quality Adaptive Soft Shadow Mapping," *Computer Graphics Forum*, Volume 26, Issue 3, pp. 525–533.

[Kontkanen05] Janne Kontkanen and Samuli Laine, "Ambient Occlusion Fields," Proceedings of the 2005 Symposium on Interactive 3D Graphics and Games, ACM, 2005, pp. 41–48.

[Mittring07] Martin Mittring, "Finding Next Gen: CryEngine 2," SIGGRAPH '07 Course Notes, ACM, 2007, pp. 97121.

[Quilez07] Iñigo Quilez, "Sphere Ambient Occlusion," Available online at http://rgba.scenesp.org/iq/computer/articles/sphereao/sphereao.htm, 2007.

[Shanmugam07] Perumaal Shanmugam and Okan Arikan, "Hardware Accelerated Ambient Occlusion Techniques on GPUs," Proceedings of the 2007 Symposium on Interactive 3D Graphics and Games, ACM, 2007, pp. 73–80.

6.4 Fast Fake Global Illumination

EMMANUEL BRINEY, VICTOR CEITELIS, AND DAVID CRÉMOUX, MKO GAMES

INTRODUCTION

A long time ago, the challenge of graphical effects development was to synchronize the rendering with the vertical blank. Today, main game technology is focused on realistic rendering, but the most important aspect of games is the feeling of reality: It has to be as close to reality as possible but not essentially physically correct. Graphic effects also have to be fast to render and must take advantage of multi-threaded architectures on current-generation consoles, such as the Xbox 360 or PlayStation 3. Global illumination is an important field of realistic rendering. We present four techniques that concern the two main parts of global illumination: visibility (ambient occlusion) and irradiance (radiosity). These techniques are fast, easy to integrate, and scalable.

AMBIENT OCCLUSION PROBES

Self–ambient occlusion on skinned objects is really hard to implement in real-time because it requires dynamic neighborhood data [Bun05][Hob07]. However, we don't need to be very accurate to get a convincing effect, so we propose to approximate occluders.

How Does It Work?

We must keep the equations for computing occlusion as simple as possible to get the most out of the GPU's horsepower. An aligned disk-like shape seems to be very efficient, and we approximate the occlusion from a single disk with

$$Occ_i = \frac{A_i}{dot(\vec{v},\vec{v})} \times saturate(dot(\vec{n},\vec{v}))$$

where A_i is the occluder area, $\vec{n}$ is the receiver normal, and $\vec{v}$ is the vector from the receiver to the occluder center. From a mathematical point of view, probes are just simple Lambertian negative lights with linear attenuation at short range (<1 m).

We have tried two formulations to combine all contributions—an additive one:

$$AO = saturate\left(1 - \sum_i Occ_i\right)$$

and a multiplicative one:

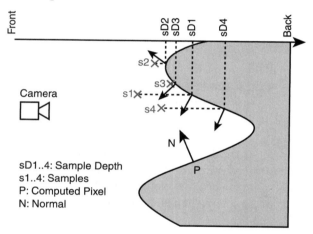

sD1..4: Sample Depth
s1..4: Samples
P: Computed Pixel
N: Normal

The multiplicative formula is easier to tweak and gives better results at a slightly increased cost of about 5%.

We need the position (three floats) and the visible area of the virtual occluder (scalar value) to calculate its contribution: only a `float4` is necessary for each ambient occlusion (AO) probe. We use the normal in the pixel shader to perform the occlusion computation. As a consequence, our method supports per-pixel normal modifications such as normal mapping, relief mapping, and their extensions.

We attach the ambient occlusion probes to bones in order to make them follow the animations. The probes need to be placed inside the geometry of the standard mesh. An AO probe can be seen as a dark light. Because we don't want this to influence the external faces of the mesh, it's necessary to place the probes inside the geometry. In this way the Lambertian dot product result will be negative, and the mesh containing the dark light is not darkened by it.

How Do You Use It?

Incorporating AO probes into existing data is trivial: We implement a naming convention on dummies (or lights) and bind them to shader constants (see Figure 6.4.1).

FIGURE 6.4.1   (a) Software AO rendering. (b) Our rendering using 18 AO probes. (c) Wireframe view of the mesh with AO probes.

Advantages, Restrictions, and Future

It is easy to integrate this technique into an existing engine. It is scalable, and only a few probes are required to achieve a good ambient occlusion feeling.

It works well for single characters, but adding AO probes to an entire scene is harder because in this case, we need to manage AO probes in the exact same way that lights are usually managed, with a selector, dealing with popping artifacts, and optimizing them with an LOD system.

This is the pixel shader code for multiplicative AO probes:

```
uniform float4 AOProbe[NBPROBES];

float AOFromProbes(float3 WPos, float3 WNorm)
{
    float AO = 1;
    for (unsigned int ProbeID = 0 ; ProbeID < NBPROBES ; ProbeID++)
    {
        float A = AOProbe[ProbeID].w;
        float3 v = AOProbe[ProbeID].xyz - WPos;
        float Occ = A*saturate(dot(WNorm,v))/dot(v,v);
        AO *= saturate(1 - Occ);
    }
    return AO;
}
```

SCREEN-SPACE AMBIENT OCCLUSION

This technique uses the depth buffer as a sampling of the scene geometry and for estimating visibility information used in ambient occlusion computations. We use it in the rendering process to visually emphasize the volume of the scene's objects. It doesn't accurately simulate ambient occlusion, but emphasizes the volumetric effect of the objects.

Moreover, the complexity of this technique, as with other screen-space techniques, depends on the resolution. This makes it a good technique to add an impression of depth to a scene or objects at low integration cost.

Several techniques have been developed since the Crytek article on screen-space ambient occlusion (SSAO) [Mit07]. The technique, presented in 2007, has evolved to more accurate ones, but most of them require a lot of samples per pixel. Our goal is to provide an efficient and parameterized sampling that allows us to keep the required samples per pixel down to a reasonable number and is customizable enough to avoid all artifacts generated by SSAO and to get better results.

HOW DOES IT WORK?

First, we perform the sampling in world space for each pixel to gather the AO information. AO is supposed to follow the Lambertian emissive law, so the results are more accurate if we sample the pixels along the normal.

We can control the sampling with two parameters (see Figure 6.4.2): The first one controls the influence of the normal of the computed pixel (`Directivity`) (see Figure 6.4.3), and the second controls the spread of the sampling around the computed pixel (`KernelSize`) (see Figure 6.4.4). We could see a behavior due to the screen-space with this sampling: The SSAO sampling spread tends to get bigger when it is far from the camera because there is no depth information taken into account in our sampling. Thus, we introduce an attenuation parameter that is used to adjust the two main parameters with regard to the distance of the computed pixel from the camera. Thus, the SSAO sampling remains a local operation.

Next we need to validate and compute the contribution of each sample (see Figure 6.4.5). We first compare the depth of the sample and the depth of the computed pixel. The sample is taken into account only if the computed pixel is behind the sample: Only those samples contribute to the occlusion for the computed pixel.

Next we adjust the sample contribution depending on its depth difference from the computed pixel: The farther a sample is from the computed pixel, the less it contributes to its occlusion. This `Bias` parameter gets rid of the common SSAO artifact of black borders around objects (see Figure 6.4.6).

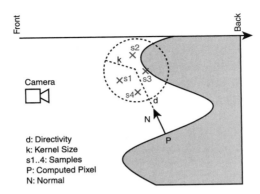

FIGURE 6.4.2   Sampling for one pixel.

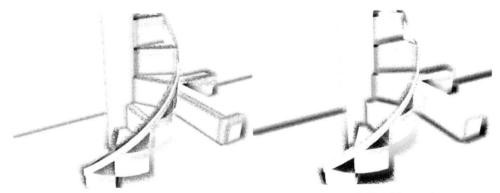

FIGURE 6.4.3   Influence of directivity on a sampling: (left) without the Directivity parameter; (right) with the Directivity parameter.

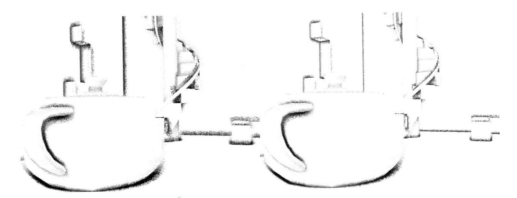

FIGURE 6.4.4   Influence of attenuation on sampling: (left) without the Attenuation parameter; (right) with the Attenuation parameter.

The last factor varies the ambient occlusion contribution of a sample: How do the sample and the computed pixel see each other? This factor is expressed by the geometric term of the rendering equation. In our approximation, a simple dot between the sample normal and the computed pixel normal can simulate this. This factor also has a side effect; it removes another common effect of basic SSAO: the uncontrolled shading of almost planar surfaces (see Figure 6.4.7).

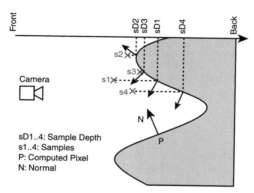

FIGURE 6.4.5 Validate samples with their depths and normals.

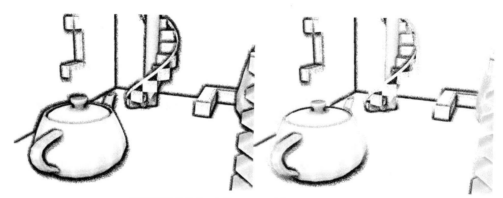

FIGURE 6.4.6 Influence of bias on sampling:
(left) without the Bias parameter; (right) with the Bias parameter.

With this sort of sampling, we only need four samples to get acceptable and good-looking results (see Figure 6.4.8). We sum and average all contributing samples to get the ambient occlusion for the computed pixel. The result is then stored in one channel of a texture.

FIGURE 6.4.7   Influence of the `Geometric` factor on sampling: (left) without the `Geometric` factor; (right) with the `Geometric` factor.

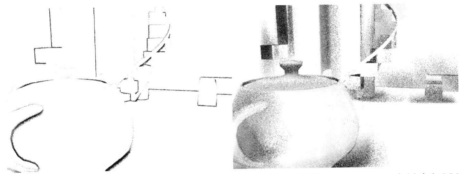

FIGURE 6.4.8   Playing with parameters: from very sharp (left) to very spread (right) SSAO.

How Do You Use It?

As input data, we need a buffer that contains world-normal and depth information for each pixel of the scene.

The effect requires three general render passes: The first pass computes the AO contribution approximation of the scene. Then we need to filter and blur to avoid noise artifacts. The final pass then simply merges the AO contribution with the scene.

Advantages, Restrictions, and Future

As we are working in screen-space, we only have information that lies within the screen, so the SSAO can produce a strong appearance of occlusion at screen borders sometimes, especially when the camera moves. The computed AO is still a local effect, so we don't have large and smooth AO from big objects that, for example, influence a whole set of objects.

The whole set of parameters allows us to tweak this technique very sharply and to adapt it to a lot of different configurations of scenes: close-ups, wide angle, and so on. Also, the code for the pixel shader doesn't go above approximately 100 instructions in DirectX 9.0, which makes it fast on modern hardware.

SCREEN-SPACE RADIOSITY

With our SSAO technique, we compute geometric, positional, and visibility information from a screen-space configuration. By using a rendering of the scene, we can extract color information for a given pixel surrounding. In other words, we should be able to compute a fake local radiance transfer: a screen-space radiosity (SSRad).

HOW DOES IT WORK?

We use the same method to sample color information as we do in SSAO and with the same set of parameters.

As in SSAO, we only need four samples to get acceptable results. We simply add and average all samples for a given pixel. It gives us three color parameters for each pixel, and we save them in a three-channel target. In the final process, we merge the contribution with the scene to colorize the areas in question.

HOW DO YOU USE IT?

The constraints and the process are the same as with SSAO. In addition, we need a rendering of the scene to gather color information.

ADVANTAGES, RESTRICTIONS, AND FUTURE

This technique only allows us to compute a local radiosity effect, which is more similar to local color bleeding. For a better result we could add an emitting factor that could control how much light is emitted from each object to other objects in the scene. We could also add object information for each pixel during rendering to avoid color gathering from the same object of the computed pixel.

FAKE RADIOSITY

Radiosity greatly improves the realism of rendered scenes, and there are many different algorithms, but most of them are not suitable for high-frame-rate real-time applications such as video games. In order to give the feeling of radiosity, we chose to simplify the algorithm. Our fake radiosity technique is focused on the model of the first light bounce between objects, and considers only diffuse lighting.

THE MAIN IDEA

We present an extension of the irradiance volume technique [Gre98][Oat07]. We need to capture the irradiance in the 3D space (Figure 6.4.9); we choose to use a spherical harmonics (SH) grid. An SH grid is a set of SH coefficients placed in world space. Such a grid will be stored in several volumes of texels, that is, 3D textures.

FIGURE 6.4.9 Capturing the irradiance environment of a scene.

When fetching these volume textures representing the irradiance, the samplers get the right SH coefficients. As the same time, we profit from the filtering hardware's capabilities to do interpolation between SH coefficients: The bilinear filtering of 3D textures does the computation of SH coefficients gradients for us.

This technique is similar to the well-known light-mapping technique, but instead of capturing lights in 2D, we do it in 3D, and instead of using RGBA texels, we use SH coefficients.

LIGHT PRINT

As we need the light print of every object in the world, we do a preprocess phase, which generates lighting representation for all separate objects: At each position in the 3D grid, we generate an environment cube map. We chose to compress the cube maps with the help of SH [Ram01] because we can't afford to use such an amount of cube maps, due to memory and bandwidth constraints. We obtain SH coefficients, and we store them in volume textures (see Figure 6.4.10). This preprocessing step could be very time-consuming; the cube map projection in SH basis time is dependant on the cube maps' resolution. In practice, a low-resolution, 8×8 per cube face gives good results.

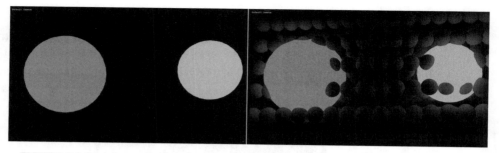

FIGURE 6.4.10 An example of capturing the light print of simple spheres, converting each cube map to SH coefficients, and saving them in 3D textures.

SPHERICAL HARMONICS COEFFICIENT BLENDING

Once we have our 3D textures, we mix them in order to have a dynamic behavior. We use a mini 3D rasterizer on the CPU. It uses a thread, or a parallel processor like the PS3's SPU. Currently, we just add the SH coefficients. It's like using additive blending. We can use a multiplicative or subtractive blending mode for other results, which could be used to simulate multiplicative AO. If we don't need dynamic lighting, we only use the static background 3D volume SH texture as the light source in the final pixel shader.

IMPLEMENTATION

In our current implementation, we use a 64×64×64 SH grid, but this technique is scalable, and we can increase the resolution to obtain more details, but at a high frame rate cost.

The final pixel shader is very simple. We pick our SH coefficients from the position of the fragment being rasterized. We use seven slots of textures. With SH of order 3, we need nine `float3` coefficients per band: 27 (9 ×x 3) floats, stored in seven `float4`s. The following HLSL code illustrates how to fetch the SH coefficients from the SH volume textures.

```
float3 ComputeDiffuse3DSH(float4 WorldNormal,float3 kPos)
{
    float3 npos  =
(float3(kPos.x/fScaleX,kPos.y/fScaleY,kPos.z/fScaleZ)+0.5);

    float4 cAr = tex3D(S0,npos).rgba;
    float4 cAg = tex3D(S1,npos).rgba;
```

```
    float4 cAb = tex3D(S2,npos).rgba;

    float4 cBr = tex3D(S3,npos).rgba;

    float4 cBg = tex3D(S4,npos).rgba;

    float4 cBb = tex3D(S5,npos).rgba;

    float4 cCc = tex3D(S6,npos).rgba;


    return ComputeDiffuseSH(WorldNormal,cAr,cAg,cAb,cBr,cBg,cBb,cCc);

}
```

ON THE DVD
Use an offline tool (the executable is included on the DVD-ROM) to capture the object lighting environment. It takes an input mesh as argument, and outputs a 3D volume texture, representing the light print of the object. During the render loop, we lock our seven volume textures, and the mini rasterizer writes the SH volume textures of each dynamic object in the previously locked seven volume textures. Due to the preprocessing step, this implementation can't handle skinned objects.

IMPROVEMENTS AND ALTERNATIVE

There are other methods to store lighting information. For example, we can use ambient cubes instead of SH. Ambient cubes [Mit06] are environment cube maps with a 1×1 resolution, which allow the compression of an entire environment map in just six RGB colors. To generate them, we have to blur our cube maps, and store them in six RGBA 3D volume textures instead of seven RGBA16F 3D textures with SH.

An optimization technique should be developed to maximize the SH volume space, using an indirection texture to address texels, but this is a well-known and common problem in light-mapping techniques, which is not addressed in this article. The interested reader is referred to [Che08]. To improve performance and reduce bandwidth, we can use quantized SH coefficients, for example, using one byte per SH coefficients instead of four [Ko08].

As in our technique all objects generate light, we can simulate point lighting by using a simple colored sphere. This can be combined with precomputed radiance transfer (PRT) rendering because we have a spatial grid of environment probes.

If the application is already CPU bound, we could use the GPU for the 3D rasterizer process. In this case we divide our volumes in 2D textures and render each object in a 2D grid, with the right transformation applied.

We focused on a DX9 implementation, targeting the Xbox 360 and the PS3, but DirectX 10.1 allows us to use cube map arrays, which accelerate the process [Hud08].

CONCLUSION

In this article, we presented four complementary techniques, which render at high frame rates, give good-looking results, and are easy to use.

ACKNOWLEDGMENTS

Special thanks to Stéphane Fradet of MKO Games for asset production on the demo.

REFERENCES

[Bun05] Michael Bunnell. "Dynamic Ambient Occlusion and Indirect Lighting." *GPU Gems 2*, 2005.

[Hob07] Jared Hoberock and Yuntao Jia. "High-Quality Ambient Occlusion." *GPU Gems 3*, 2007.

[Mit07] Mittring Martin. Finding Next Gen – Cry Engine 2, Advanced Real-Time Rendering in 3D Graphics and Games Course, SIGGRAPH 2007.

[Oat07] Chris Oat. "Irradiance Volumes for Real-Time Rendering." *ShaderX5*, 2007.

[Ko08] Jerome Ko, Manchor Ko, and Matthias Zwicker. "Practical Methods for a PRT-Based Shader Using Spherical Harmonics." *ShaderX6*, 2008.

[Che08] Hao Chen. "Lighting And Material Of Halo3." GDC 2008.

[Hud08] Richard Huddy, DirectX 10.1 "DirectX 10 and then some…." Game Developer Conference 2008.

[Gre98] Gene Greger, Peter Shirley, Philip M. Hubbard, and Donald P. Greenberg. "The Irradiance Volume." *IEEE Computer Graphics & Applications*, 18(2):32–43, 1998.

[Ram01] Ravi Ramamoorthi and Pat Hanrahan. "An Efficient Representation for Irradiance Environment Maps." SIGGRAPH 2001, pages 497–500.

[Mit06] Jason Mitchell, Gary McTaggart, and Chris Green. "Course Shading in the Valve Source Engine." SIGGRAPH 2006.

6.5 Real-Time Subsurface Scattering Using Shadow Maps

HYUNWOO KI

INTRODUCTION

Physically based lighting provides a high level of realism in 3D games and VR systems. Light is not only reflected at the nonmetallic surfaces, but also scatters below the surface and leaves at a different position. This phenomenon, known as *subsurface scattering*, makes the appearance of an object translucent, soft, and smooth. The light distribution within highly scattering media tends to become isotropic. As a result, the media exhibits geometric blurring, while within optically thin or highly curved media, the light often scatters "once" and exits the media. Such *single scattering* represents geometric details and leads to a characteristic appearance according to the light and viewing directions and the anisotropy of the media. Unfortunately, since simulation of subsurface scattering is computationally costly, many solutions exist in an offline context only or require lengthy precomputation [Hanrahan1993; Jensen2001; Sloan2003; Hao2004; Wang2005].

This article discusses drawbacks of previous real-time techniques, and introduces a simple technique to approximate single scattering that overcomes many of these drawbacks. We use shadow maps [Williams1978] as a key ingredient, and our technique is motivated by [Hery2003; Dachsbacher2003; Green2004; Ki2008]. By using the shadow maps, we can avoid costly ray tracing and exploit the power of modern graphics hardware. Furthermore, an adaptive deterministic sampling strategy dramatically reduces the number of samples. Finally, jittering in the shadow map projection eliminates aliasing and simulates soft shadows at shadow boundaries. Figure 6.5.1 shows the value of this technique compared to ray tracing and diffuse shading. This technique, called *subsurface-scatter mapping*, fully runs on graphics hardware at hundreds of frames per second without any precomputation.

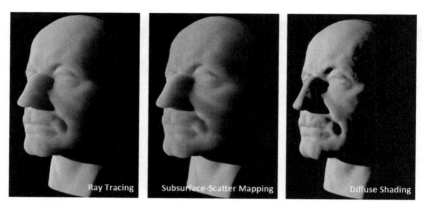

FIGURE 6.5.1 Subsurface-scatter mapping enables rendering of translucent objects to run in real-time. This technique provides comparable quality to ray tracing.

RELATED WORK

[Jensen2001] proposed an efficient *bidirectional scattering surface reflectance distribution function* (BSSRDF) model to render translucent materials in an offline context, which is composed of single scattering by [Hanrahan1993] and multiple scattering by a dipole diffusion approximation. Many attempts have been made to render translucent materials in real-time. [Lensch2002; Sloan2003; Hao2004] precomputed vertex-to-vertex light transfer, but their techniques ignored physically based single scattering of light. [Wang2005] proposed the first interactive method, based on a wavelet precomputed radiance transfer, including both single and multiple scattering. However, it cannot support local lights and requires considerable storage and precomputation. Moreover, none of the above methods can handle animated objects and shadows caused by other objects, which are important features for real-time applications such as games, since their highly expensive precomputation is executed on a static, single object. [Mertens2003] employed a radiosity-like approach to real-time multiple scattering. However, its quality and speed highly depend on the complexity of geometry and topology of an object, and it also ignored single scattering.

Shadow mapping [Williams1978] is a very popular method for generation of hard shadows. [Hery2003] approximated subsurface scattering using a traditional depth shadow map for the RenderMan in an offline context. [Green2004] also used a depth shadow map, but it is not physically based. [Dachsbacher2003; d'Eon2007; Ki2008] used *rich* shadow maps to evaluate multiple scattering, but single scattering is also ignored. Our technique is also strongly based on shadow mapping. For brevity, this article assumes that the reader has a basic knowledge of shadow mapping.

THEORY

The outgoing radiance L_o at the surface point x_o in the direction $\vec{\omega}_o$ is computed as

$$L_o(x_o,\vec{\omega}_o) = \int_A \int_{2\pi} S(x_i,\vec{\omega}_i;x_o,\vec{\omega}_o)L_i(x_i,\vec{\omega}_i)(\vec{n} \cdot \vec{\omega}_i)d\omega_i dA_{x_i},$$

EQUATION 6.5.1

where L_i is the incident radiance and S is the BSSRDF. For homogeneous and semi-infinite media, we can estimate the BSSRDF as the sum of single scattering by ray tracing and multiple scattering by light diffusion [Jensen2001].

We can compute the single-scattering term by integrating the incident radiance along the refracted outgoing path:

$$L_o^{(1)}(x_o,\vec{\omega}_o)$$
$$= \sigma_s(x_o)\int_{2\pi}\int_0^\infty F \cdot p(\vec{\omega}'_i,\vec{\omega}'_o)\exp(-s'_o\sigma_t(x_o))\exp(-s'_i\sigma_t(x_i))L_i(x_i,\vec{\omega}_i)(\vec{n} \cdot \vec{\omega}_i)dsd\vec{\omega}_i,$$

EQUATION 6.5.2

where the Fresnel transmittance as the boundary condition is $F = F_t(\eta,\vec{\omega}_o)F_t(\eta,\vec{\omega}_1)$, and η is the relative index of refraction. Here, the phase function of Henyey-Greenstein is $p(\cos j) = 1 - g^2/4\pi(1 + g^2 - g \cos j)^{3/2}$, absorption and scattering coefficients are σ_a and σ_s, and the extinction coefficient is $\sigma_t = \sigma_a + \sigma_s$. In this article, we focus on the approximation of the single scattering term using shadow maps.

As shown in Figure 6.5.2, if the surface is locally flat and the extinction coefficients of the incident and outgoing surface points are the same, then we can rearrange Equation 6.5.2 as

$$L_o^{(1)}(x_o,\vec{\omega}_o)$$
$$= \sigma_s F_t(\eta,\vec{\omega}_o)\int_{2\pi}p(\vec{\omega}'_i,\vec{\omega}'_o)\int_0^\infty \exp(-(s'_o + s'_i)\sigma_t)F_t(\eta,\vec{\omega}_i)L_i(x_i,\vec{\omega}_i)(\vec{n} \cdot \vec{\omega}_i)dsd\vec{\omega}_i.$$

EQUATION 6.5.3

For simplicity, if we assume that primary lights are point or directional sources, and we only handle direct illumination from these lights, the transmitted irradiance through x_i in direction $\vec{\omega}_i$ is simply computed as

$$E_t(x_i,\vec{\omega}_i,\eta) = att \cdot F_t(\eta,\vec{\omega}_i)I_i(x_i,\vec{\omega}_i)(\vec{n} \cdot \vec{\omega}_i),$$ EQUATION 6.5.4

where F_t is the incident Fresnel transmittance and I_i is the intensity of the light. The attenuation term *att* varies according to the type of the light, for example, $att = 1/d^2$, where d is the distance between the light and surface point for a spot light.

Now, substituting Equation 6.5.3 into Equation 6.5.4 and using the standard Monte Carlo estimation by generating N light and M path samples according to their probability density functions (PDFs), f, we get

$$L_o^{(1)}(x_o, \vec{\omega}_o)$$

$$\approx \sigma_s F_t(\eta, \vec{\omega}_o) \frac{1}{N} \frac{1}{M} \sum_{j=1}^{N} p(\vec{\omega}'_i, \vec{\omega}'_o) \sum_{k=1}^{M} \frac{\exp(-(s'_{i,j} + s'_{o,k})\sigma_t)}{f(s'_{o,k})} \frac{E_t(x_{j,k}, \vec{\omega}_{j,k}, \eta)}{f(\vec{\omega}_{j,k})}.$$

EQUATION 6.5.5

In order to construct a PDF for a light $f(\vec{\omega}_{j,k})$, we could use uniform sampling, power proportional sampling, and other strategies. For brevity, this article does not describe such light sampling strategies, and thus we trivially use uniform sampling (i.e., the same PDF for every light). Efficiently constructing a PDF for a path $f(s'_{o,k})$ and computing s'_i are the main issues of this article.

A dipole method offers a good approximation of multiple scattering for homogeneous, optically thick media [Jensen2001]. A detailed discussion of multiple scattering is outside the scope of this article. The references section lists a number of excellent academic papers that provide detailed explanations of the dipole approximation. [Mertens2003; Dachsbacher2003; Ki2008] proposed real-time techniques based on the dipole approximation using graphics hardware without (lengthy) precomputation. We especially integrated our method with [Ki2008] for the renderings in the color plate.

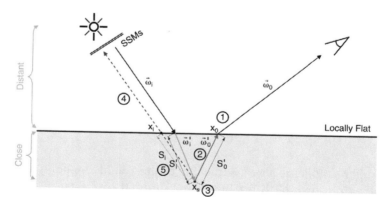

FIGURE 6.5.2 We estimate the refracted incident path, s'_i, and the irradiance in the direction $\vec{\omega}_o$ using an approach similar to shadow mapping. (1) At the outgoing surface point being shaded, (2) we sample the refracted outgoing path, s'_o, and then (3) compute the subsurface intersection, x_s. (4) Next, we transform x_s into the light-space and find the surface intersection, x_i. (5) Finally, we approximate s'_i with s_i using Snell's law.

ALGORITHM

We use a general two-pass algorithm for real-time subsurface scattering: creation of *subsurface-scatter maps* (SSMs) and rendering translucent objects using the SSMs. The first step is similar to the traditional shadow map creation. We render the scene to render-target textures from each light's point of view; however, in addition to depth, we store the transmitted irradiance, position, material ID, and normal in three textures. Then, we estimate the illumination due to subsurface scattering of light using the SSMs. Vertex shaders only perform simple operations such as transformation, whereas pixel shaders perform complex operations such as evaluation of the BSSRDF. We describe the algorithm in depth in the following subsections.

CREATION OF SUBSURFACE-SCATTER MAPS

The first step, the creation of SSMs, is very simple. The SSMs are render-target textures that store the information of the first surfaces from a light source. We render the scene from each light's point of view, similar to creation of a shadow map, but we store transmitted irradiance, position and material ID, and normal and depth in three textures. The transmitted irradiance is computed using Equation 6.5.4. The depth information is used for shadow mapping to compute direct illumination. The other information is required for the evaluation of subsurface scattering. We reuse the SSMs created in the previous frame if lights and objects do not move. Figure 6.5.3 shows an example of the SSMs.

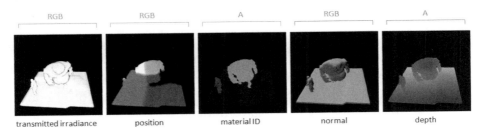

FIGURE 6.5.3   An example of subsurface-scatter maps (SSMs). We store the transmitted irradiance, position and material ID, and normal and depth in three render-target textures.

RENDERING OF TRANSLUCENT OBJECTS USING SSMS

The next step is rendering the translucent objects using SSMs from the camera's point of view. In order to compute the single-scattered illumination from Equation 6.5.5, we should integrate the single-scattered path illustrated in Figure 6.5.2. By applying importance sampling to the integration path, we sample a refracted outgoing path, $s'_o = -\log(\xi)/\sigma_t$, with $f(s'_o) = \exp(-\sigma_t s'_o)$, where ξ is a random number of $[0,1)$.

Standard Monte Carlo sampling requires a large number of samples. Fortunately, we can efficiently reduce the number of samples with deterministic sampling because the integration is of low dimension. As a completely deterministic strategy, we use a set of uniformly distributed numbers of ξ_k without randomness. More precisely, a kth path sample is $s'_{o,k} = -\log(\xi_k)/\sigma_t$ with $\xi_k = k - 0.5/M_j$. Here, k is the positive integer from 1 to M_j, and M_j is the number of path samples for a light j.

After sampling the refracted outgoing path length s'_o, we should compute the incident refracted path length s'_i. It is difficult to accurately compute s'_i for arbitrary objects. However, if we assume that the surface is locally flat and the light is located at a great distance compared with the mean free path of the media, we can approximate s'_i with s_i using Equation 6.5.6, which is derived from Snell's law [Jensen2001].

$$s'_i = s_i \frac{|\vec{\omega}_i \cdot \vec{n}_i|}{\sqrt{1 - (1/\eta)^2(1 - |\vec{\omega}_i \cdot \vec{n}_i|^2)}} .$$ **EQUATION 6.5.6**

In order to compute the observed path length s_i we need to find the surface intersection x_i. Using an approach similar to shadow mapping, we transform the subsurface intersection $x_s = x_o + \vec{\omega}'_o s'_o$ (in world-space coordinates) into the respective projected position as seen by the light by multiplying the light-space perspective matrix. Then, we read an SSM storing the surface's position and material ID. The position read from the SSM corresponds to x_i. Note that we must compare the material ID with the ID of the currently rendered object because subsurface scattering is a local phenomenon within each object. It plays a role in generating shadows occluded by other objects similar to object ID shadow maps [Ambroz2005].

With concave objects we sometimes cannot find the first surface intersection if the intersection is located in a self-shadowed region because the SSMs only contain the information of the closest surface points seen from the light. Figure 6.5.4 illustrates this problem. Since we ignore indirect illumination, we do not want to contribute transmitted irradiance through the undesired surface intersection $\tilde{x}_i$ to the outgoing radiance L_o at the surface point x_o. In other words, we want to consider that x_o in direction $\vec{\omega}_i$ is self-shadowed.

By using a layered depth map we can solve this problem. We first create an additional depth map using depth peeling [Everitt2001] to capture the second surface from the light. Next, we find x_i from x_s and do a depth test with the depth map storing the second surface. If a depth value in the depth map is closer than x_s, we consider that x_i is self-shadowed, and thus we skip the estimation of the illumination at this path sample.

In practice, we could represent the self-shadowing without such layered depth maps. The reason is that the light energy decreases exponentially with distance within the media, and other terms in Equation 6.5.5 also attenuate the light energy.

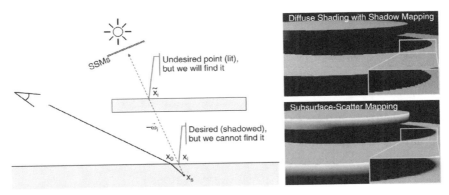

FIGURE 6.5.4   If an object is concave, we cannot find the incident surface point correctly. However, we could represent the self-shadowing of the object without additional visibility tests in many cases because the light traveling the path from the undesired surface point $\hat{x}_i$ to the outgoing surface point x_o will be attenuated exponentially, and as a result the light energy tends to become zero.

For example, the isotropic phase function is $1/4\pi$, and therefore the transmitted irradiance through $\hat{x}_i$ tends to become zero. If a medium is optically very thin or highly anisotropic visual errors appear, however, we have obtained plausible results in many cases, as shown in Figures 6.5.1, 6.5.4, 6.5.5, and 6.5.6.

After computing the incident and outgoing path length, s'_i and s'_o, we read the transmitted irradiance E_t and the normal from the SSMs. To quickly evaluate the Fresnel and phase functions we can use approximations of [Schlick1994]. We included these approximations in the shader code of the demo program. Of course, we could also tabulate these functions and replace the computations by texture lookups. Listing 6.5.1 displays pseudo code to estimate single scattering as described in this subsection.

Listing 6.5.1   Pseudo code of subsurface-scatter mapping

```
wo_prime = ComputeOutgoingRefractedDir( eta, n );
Fto = ApproximateFresnelTransmittance( eta, cosT );


for ( int k = 0; k < Mj; ++k )
{
so_prime = SampleOutgoingPath( k );
weight = ComputeWeight( so_prime, sigma_t );
xs = xo + wo_prime * so_prime;
```

```
xs_l = xs * matLightVP;
xs_l = ( xs_l * 0.5 + 0.5 * xs_l.w ) / xs_l.w;
xi_id = tex2Dlod( PositionIDSSM, xs_l );
if ( TestMaterialID( xi_id.w ) )
{
ni = tex2Dlod( NormalDepthSSM, xs_l ).xyz;
si = distance( xp, xi_id.xyz );
si_prime = ApproximateSiPrime( si, cosI, eta );
Et = tex2Dlod( IrradianceSSM, xs_l ).xyz;
p = ApproximateHGPhaseFunction( cosJ, g );
SS += ComputeSingleScattering(Et, p, weight, si_prime, so_prime);
}
}
SS *= sigma_s * Fto * ( 1 / Mj );
```

RENDERING OPTIMIZATIONS

Jittering

Although our deterministic sampling can dramatically reduce the number of samples, it causes banding artifacts at shadow boundaries because the sampled points are suddenly shadowed or illuminated. To reduce the artifact we can use more samples, but this reduces rendering speed. Instead, we use jittering of the SSM coordinates for each path sample to eliminate the artifact, as well as to simulate fake soft shadows. Jittering converts low-frequency aliasing to high-frequency noise to which human vision is less sensitive (Figure 6.5.5). Additionally, it also eliminates a jaggy artifact at shadow boundaries due to the low resolution of SSMs, which is an open problem of all image-space algorithms. As current graphics hardware does not support random number generation, we generate and store random numbers in a 2D texture on the CPU and then use the texture on the GPU. To maintain temporal coherence, we reuse this texture for every frame. Noticeable patterns did not occur in our tests.

Adaptive Sampling

Another optimization to reduce the sampling artifacts of aliasing and noise is to employ an adaptive sampling strategy that first detects shadow boundaries and

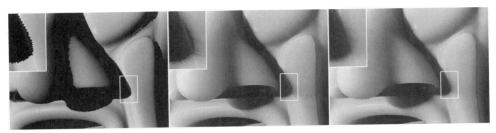

FIGURE 6.5.5   Jittering eliminates aliasing at shadow boundaries. (Left) Diffuse shading with shadow mapping; (center) subsurface-scatter mapping without jittering; (right) subsurface-scatter mapping with jittering.

then draws more samples in these regions. If a pixel being shaded contains many "dim" light rays whose contributions are very small (e.g., luminance less than 0.05), but the pixel is not completely black, then we assume that this pixel is located at shadow boundaries, and thus we use path samples twice. In our implementation we use such adaptive sampling if a pixel contains 20 ~ 85% dim light rays. Figure 6.5.6 shows the effect of using the adaptive sampling.

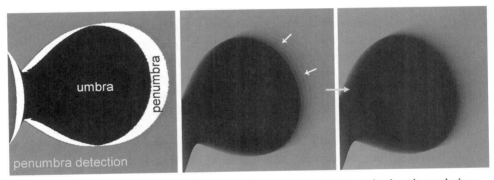

FIGURE 6.5.6   Adaptive sampling efficiently reduces artifacts at shadow boundaries.

Levels of Detail (LODs)

As stated before, although using many samples produces nice images without artifacts, it is too expensive for real-time applications. As last optimization strategy, we use a simple LOD technique. We first compute the LOD level considering the partial derivative of the current pixel with respect to the screen-space using the pixel shader code presented Listing 6.5.2. Then we adjust the total number of samples according to the LOD level.

Listing 6.5.2 Pixel shader code to select the LOD level

```
float SelectLodLevel( float2 screenCoord, float2 resolution)
{
float2 texCoord = screenCoord * 0.5f + 0.5f;
float2 dx = ddx( texCoord * resolution.x );
float2 dy = ddy( texCoord * resolution.y );
float d = max( dot( dx, dx ), dot( dy, dy ) );
return log2( sqrt( d ) );
}
```

RESULTS

We implemented subsurface-scatter mapping on an NVIDIA GeForce GTX 280 graphics card using Direct3D 9 and HLSL with pixel shader model 3. Figure 6.5.1 shows a side-by-side comparison between ray tracing, subsurface-scatter mapping (10 path samples with adaptive sampling, and 2048×2048 SSMs), and diffuse shading. We used the marble coefficients [Jensen2001] as the optical property. Single scattering represents translucency and blurred shadows that cannot be captured by diffuse shading. Our technique provides a visually comparable quality to ray tracing, but it runs very fast at approximately 118 fps. There are two major reasons for this: First, we can avoid costly ray-object intersection tests, and accelerate computation of functions by exploiting rich shadow maps on graphics hardware. Furthermore, we can render pixels highly parallel. Second, by employing simple deterministic sampling, the variance in the Monte Carlo integration becomes dramatically lower than the reference solution, and thus our technique works very well with a small number of samples.

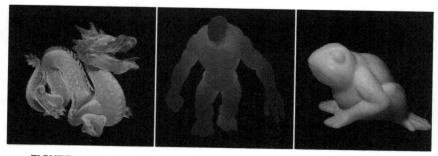

FIGURE 6.5.7 Translucent objects with single and multiple scattering.

TABLE 6.5.1 Rendering performance at 1280×960 frame buffer

No.	Rendering Conditions	FPS
1	Deterministic sampling. Static light and object (L&O)	410.85
2	Deterministic sampling. Dynamic L&O	363.07
3	Deterministic sampling with jittering. Dynamic L&O	228.14
4	Adaptive sampling with jittering. Dynamic L&O	225.95
5	Deterministic sampling with 2× samples. Dynamic L&O	155.62
6	Adaptive sampling with jittering + direct illumination. Dynamic L&O	210.90

CONCLUSION

This article presented a simple technique for real-time rendering of translucent objects due to subsurface scattering. We used rich shadow maps to store irradiance and geometric properties and to approximate ray tracing. Consequently, this technique has problems inherited from shadow mapping such as aliasing. Jittering and adaptive sampling can efficiently reduce artifacts at shadow boundaries and simulate fake soft shadows. We hope that this technique will inspire developers to improve the realism of many real-time applications such as 3D games and VR systems.

ACKNOWLEDGMENTS

ON THE DVD

We would like to thank Carsten Dachsbacher for allowing us to use his Reflective Shadow Maps code in *ShaderX⁴*. The implementation of our subsurface-scatter mapping included on the DVD-ROM is based on Dachsbacher's code. Reference images in Figure 6.5.1 (left and right heads) are provided by Rui Wang with his kind permission.

REFERENCES

[Hanrahan1993] Hanrahan, Pat et al. "Reflection from Layered Surfaces due to Subsurface Scattering." *SIGGRAPH1993*, pp. 165–174.

[Jensen2001] Jensen, Henrik Wann et al. "A Practical Model for Subsurface Light Transport." *SIGGRAPH 2001*, pp. 511–518.

[Sloan2003] Sloan, Peter-Pike et al. "Clustered Principal Components for Precomputed Radiance Transfer." *ACM Transactions on Graphics*, 22, 3 (July 2003), pp. 382–391.

[Hao2004] Hao, Xuejun et al. "Real-time Rendering of Translucent Meshes." *ACM Transactions on Graphics,* 23, 2 (April 2004), pp. 120–142, 2004.

[Wang2005] Wang, Rui et al. "All-Frequency Interactive Relighting of Translucent Objects with Single and Multiple Scattering." *ACM Transactions on Graphics*, 24, 3 (Jul. 2005), pp. 1202–1207.

[Williams1978] Williams, Lance. "Casting Curved Shadows on Curved Surfaces." *SIGGRAPH 1978*, pp. 270–274.

[Hery2003] Hery, Christophe. "Implementing a Skin BSSRDF." *ACM SIGGRAPH 2003 Course 9*, pp. 73–88.

[Dachsbacher2003] Carsten, Dachsbacher et al. "Translucent Shadow Maps." In *Proceedings of the 14th Eurographics Workshop on Rendering* (Leuven, Belgium, June 25 - 27, 2003), pp. 197–201.

[Green2004] Green, Steve. "Real-Time Approximations to Subsurface Scattering." *GPU Gems*, Chapter 16, pp. 263–278, 2004.

[Ki2008] Ki, Hyunwoo et al. "A GPU-Based Light Hierarchy for Real-Time Approximate Illumination." *The Visual Computer,* Volume 24, Numbers 7-9, (July 2008), pp. 649–658.

[Lensch2002] Lensch, Hendrik P.A. et al. "Interactive Rendering of Translucent Objects." In *Proceedings of Pacific Graphics 2002*, pp. 214–224.

[Mertens2003] Mertens, Tom et al. "Interactive Rendering of Translucent Deformable Objects." In *Proceedings of the 14th Eurographics Workshop on Rendering* (Leuven, Belgium, June 25–27, 2003), pp. 130–140.

[d'Eon2007] d'Eon, Eugene et al. "Efficient Rendering of Human Skin." In *Proceedings of the 18th Eurographics Symposium on Rendering 2007*, pp. 147–157, 2007.

[Ambroz2005] Ambroz, David. "Shadow Maps—Problems & Solutions." http://www.shadowstechniques.com/presentations/mff_shadowmaps.pdf, December, 2005.

[Everitt2001] Everitt, Cass. "Interactive Order-Independent Transparency." Technical Report, NVIDIA Corporation. Available online at http://developer.nvidia.com/object/Interactive_Order_Transparency.html, May 2001.

[Schlick1994] Schlick, Christophe. "An Inexpensive BRDF Model for Physically-Based Rendering." *Computer Graphics Forum*, 13, 3 (1994), pp. 233–246.

6.6

Instant Radiosity with GPU Photon Tracing and Approximate Indirect Shadows

LÁSZLÓ SZÉCSI

INTRODUCTION

Today, computer games can hardly make concessions in the realism of lighting algorithms. Specular and diffuse reflections, caustics, soft shadows, and indirect illumination have all been achieved [SKSL08]. However, as more interaction with the virtual world is called for, algorithms assuming static geometry and relying on precomputation are becoming too restrictive. In this article, we tailor the instant radiosity algorithm to render indirect illumination in dynamic scenes, using GPU ray tracing and ideas from screen-space occlusion.

Instant radiosity [Keller97] is also known as indirect photon mapping. It involves a photon tracing phase, where hit points along the light paths are stored as a sampled representation of the scene radiance. In the second, gathering phase, the indirect illumination due to this radiance is rendered by treating the photon hits as virtual point lights (VPLs). There are two time-consuming operations: ray tracing for photon shooting and testing the visibility of the VPLs from the shaded surface point during final gathering. In *ShaderX⁶* [Laine08] described how to distribute the cost of rendering depth shadow maps for the VPLs to multiple frames, reaching real-time performance. They generated VPLs from a single primary point light without ray tracing, rendering single-bounce indirect illumination only.

In this article, we abandon depth shadow maps for a differently sampled representation of the scene geometry, which does not depend on the number of VPLs. We generate photon hits using real GPU ray tracing, thus allowing for area light sources and indirect illumination due to caustics.

479

TECHNIQUES WE BUILD ON

BOUNDING INTERVAL HIERARCHY

For GPU ray tracing, we use the bounding interval hierarchy (BIH) [Wächter06] as an acceleration structure. It is also known as the bounding kd-tree or the skd-tree. It is like kd-trees in that it uses axis-aligned planes to partition primitives into cells, and is like bounding volume hierarchies in that these cells enclose primitives that belong to them (Figure 6.6.1). BIH construction is similar to kd-tree construction. Starting with a single box-shaped root cell enclosing all primitives, primitives of cells are sorted recursively into two groups along one coordinate axis until cells are small enough. The strategy for choosing the axis, grouping primitives, and terminating the recursion is usually based on the surface area heuristics (SAH) [MacDonald90]. SAH predicts the cost of ray tracing for a cell as the surface area of the cell multiplied by the number of primitives within. The data structure is a binary tree, where leaf nodes contain the axis and locations of child cell extrema, and leaf nodes also reference the list of associated primitives. The ray traversal starts from the root cell: The child cells are recursively processed in the order of the ray passing through them. If the BIH tree and the primitives are encoded in texture or buffer resources, the algorithm can be implemented as a GPU shader.

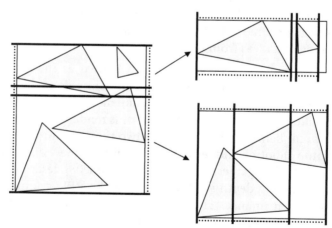

FIGURE 6.6.1   A bounding volume hierarchy tree.

APPROXIMATE RAY TRACING WITH DISTANCE IMPOSTORS

Szirmay et al. [Szirmay05] have proposed distance impostors for rendering ray-tracing effects in real-time. The rays are not intersected with the actual surrounding geometry, but with a sampled representation stored in a cube texture. The texture is created by rendering the environment geometry from a reference point with a shader that outputs the distance from the camera. The intersection point can be found using iterative lookups in this texture. The method works best with a somewhat remote environment; supporting local intersections requires elaborate and demanding multilayer schemes [Umenhoffer07]. We will use this technique to trace shadow rays toward virtual point lights, against the off-screen (outside of the view frustum) part of the geometry.

SCREEN-SPACE AMBIENT OCCLUSION

The screen-space ambient occlusion method [Mittring07] also uses sampled geometry, but focuses on local effects. The depth buffer of the actual on-screen world, or a texture of similar information content, is queried at several sampling locations in the vicinity of the shaded point to find whether the local features of the surface block light coming from a certain direction. Omnidirectional ambient lighting is usually assumed. We will extend this approach to deal with somewhat more distant, but on-screen, occluders, and modulate the contribution of virtual point lights with the acquired shadowing factor.

PYRAMIDAL DISPLACEMENT MAPS

We use depth or height maps as a sampled representation of geometry for tracing shadow rays. Prefiltering these maps allows us to make individual samples more important, evaluating shadows with fewer texture reads. Using a minimum filter to build a mipmap-like hierarchy as described in [Oh06] provides a natural bounding volume representation of the height field. The authors describe how to traverse this structure rigorously to find a ray intersection point. We will not perform this expensive operation for every insignificant shadow ray, but we will use the pyramidal minimum data structure to get quick approximations for point samples on rays.

ALGORITHM OVERVIEW

The workflow of the rendering process is depicted in Figure 6.6.2. After loading geometry meshes, a BIH is constructed for each of them and stored in GPU textures. If the meshes themselves are animated, the BIHs can be updated efficiently when necessary [Wald07], but we are not addressing that in this article. The refitting algorithm could easily be implemented on the GPU to avoid texture upload overhead.

At the beginning of every frame, the positions and orientations of scene entities—as computed by the animation logic—are taken, and an acceleration structure is built over them. Every entity refers to the BIH of its mesh. Photons are traced using this two-level acceleration scheme. First, the light sources are sent to the

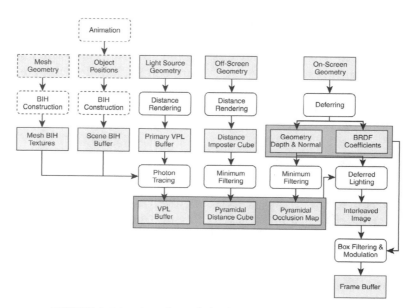

FIGURE 6.6.2 Overview of shader passes and resources.

pipeline, where the geometry shader outputs light samples as VPLs. Then, using these VPLs as starting points, the rays are traced against the BIHs to create photon paths, and thus, new VPLs. Note that we do not need to differentiate between direct and indirect lighting, as both are represented by VPLs now. Direct illumination of non-area light sources that do not require light sampling could be handled by conventional lighting and shadowing techniques.

Before the lighting phase, the distance cube and occlusion maps have to be built. First, the off-screen geometry is rendered onto a cube map to obtain environment distance impostors. Second, the geometry within the view frustum is rendered as in deferred shading: depth, normal, and material information is output to a geometry and a bidirectional reflection distribution function (BRDF) texture. The geometry buffer is not only used for deferred shading, but it is the first level of the occlusion map at the same time.

The deferred lighting pass performs deferred shading, but uses the interleaved technique [Segovia06]. Therefore, in every pixel, we only use a subset of VPLs. Elements of the VPL buffer are evenly distributed between pixels of every 4×4 neighborhood. In the shader, these VPLs are tested for visibility against both the on-screen and off-screen geometry. The visibility information is used to modulate the lighting from the VPLs. The resulting image then must be filtered with a geometry-sensitive 4×4 box kernel to gather the contribution of all VPLs in every pixel. Modulation by the texture color is performed only after this to avoid blurring.

SCENE REPRESENTATION FOR RAY TRACING

The virtual world is built up of entities of given position and orientation, referencing meshes that define their geometry. See Figure 6.6.3 for the data structure layout over GPU resources. For each mesh, a BIH is constructed and stored in textures. Every mesh has a BIH tree texture and a triangle texture that contains triangle data, the ones belonging to the same cell in continuous blocks. These 1D textures are organized into texture arrays so that the appropriate mesh can be selected from the ray-tracing shader. The BIH textures consist of four channels of 16-bit signed integer texels, each corresponding to a node of the tree. We use the compact layout, meaning the children of node n are nodes $2n + 1$ and $2n + 2$. The texture size limits the maximum depth of the tree. Every such texel stores the minimum and the maximum value of the left and right child cells as fixed-point normalized values. Thus, the AABB of the mesh must be mapped to the positive unit cube. Figure 6.6.4 shows an overview of transformations and coordinate spaces that are used. All stored values will be positive, and thus we use the signs of the first three channels to encode the subdivision axis: The channel corresponding to the axis should be positive. The sign of the value in the fourth channel is used to flag a leaf node. A leaf node texel is interpreted differently. It contains two indices into the list of triangles: the start and the end of the section that belongs to the cell.

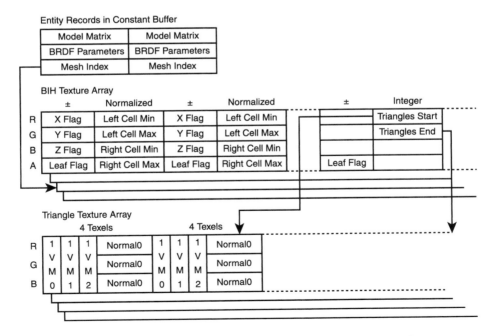

FIGURE 6.6.3   GPU representation of entities, BIHs, and triangles.

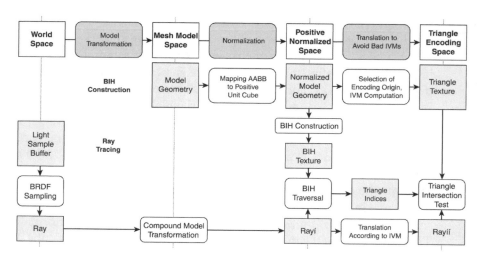

FIGURE 6.6.4 Coordinate spaces and transformations used when building and traversing BIHs.

The triangle texture has three channels of 16-bit floats, and encodes triangles in texel groups of four. Three texels contain a preprocessed representation of the triangle, and the fourth stores the shading normals in 8-bit signed normalized format, mapping each normal to a single float. A mesh can have at most 2,096 triangles, because of the texture size. More complex meshes would need to be simplified or divided into smaller submeshes. Also, we assume these small meshes have uniform material properties, so no texture lookup is required. Note that reading normals and texture coordinates from the original vertex buffer would also be possible.

The data structure for the scene entities must be rebuilt every frame in an animated scene. It is presented to the ray-tracing shader as a shader constant buffer. For every entity, it contains the model transformation, the material properties, and the index of the mesh in the array of BIH textures.

RAY-TRIANGLE INTERSECTION

The intersection computation is always performed in a local coordinate frame called the triangle encoding space. The ray parameters and the results must be transformed as shown in Figure 6.6.4. First, we find an intersection point with the triangle's plane, and then decide whether the point is within the triangle. Let us write the equation of the plane as

$$\mathbf{r} \cdot \mathbf{q}^T = \mathbf{q} \cdot \mathbf{q}^T,$$

where the superscript T denotes a column vector, and **q** is the point on the triangle's plane that is nearest to the origin. If **q** is zero, this is not a proper plane equation. We avoid this special case by choosing from eight coordinate spaces to encode a triangle: those having their origins at the corners of the positive unit cube. We always choose the one where the origin is the most distant from the plane. Which space we have used can always be found out from the sign vector of **q**. The parametric ray equation is

$$\mathbf{r}(t) = \mathbf{o} + \mathbf{d}t,$$

where **o** is the origin of the ray, **d** is the normalized ray direction, and t is the distance along the ray. From the plane and ray equations the ray parameter of the intersection t^* can be expressed as

$$t^* = \frac{\mathbf{q} \cdot \mathbf{q}^T - \mathbf{o} \cdot \mathbf{q}^T}{\mathbf{d} \cdot \mathbf{q}^T}.$$

The hit point **p** can be obtained by substituting t^* back into the ray equation.

We have to decide whether the point is within the triangle, and find the barycentric coordinates of the point. If the triangle vertex positions are vectors $\mathbf{v}_0, \mathbf{v}_1, \mathbf{v}_{2'}$, the barycentric coordinate vector **b** of point **p** is defined to fulfill the following equation:

$$\mathbf{b} \cdot \begin{bmatrix} \mathbf{v}_0 \\ \mathbf{v}_1 \\ \mathbf{v}_{2'} \end{bmatrix} = \mathbf{p}.$$

The barycentric coordinate elements can be seen as weights assigned to the triangle vertices. The linear combination of the vertex positions with these weights must give point **p**. If all three barycentric weights are positive, then the point is within the triangle. The weights can also be used to interpolate normals given at the vertices.

Using the above definition, **b** can be expressed as

$$\mathbf{b} = \mathbf{p} \cdot \begin{bmatrix} \mathbf{v}_0 \\ \mathbf{v}_1 \\ \mathbf{v}_{2'} \end{bmatrix}^{-1},$$

using the inverse of the 3×3 matrix assembled from the vertex coordinates. Let us call the inverse of the vertex position matrix the IVM. Thus, in order to evaluate intersection, we need **q** and the IVM. All three vertices satisfy the plane equation.

This can be written in a single vector equation as

$$
\begin{bmatrix} \mathbf{v}_0 \\ \mathbf{v}_1 \\ \mathbf{v}_{2,} \end{bmatrix} \cdot \mathbf{q}^\mathsf{T} = \begin{bmatrix} \mathbf{q} \cdot \mathbf{q}^\mathsf{T} \\ \mathbf{q} \cdot \mathbf{q}^\mathsf{T} \\ \mathbf{q} \cdot \mathbf{q}^\mathsf{T} \end{bmatrix}.
$$

Multiplying with the IVM and dividing by $\mathbf{q} \cdot \mathbf{q}^\mathsf{T}$, we get

$$
\frac{\mathbf{q}^\mathsf{T}}{\mathbf{q} \cdot \mathbf{q}^\mathsf{T}} = \begin{bmatrix} \mathbf{v}_0 \\ \mathbf{v}_1 \\ \mathbf{v}_{2,} \end{bmatrix}^{-1} \cdot \begin{bmatrix} 1 \\ 1 \\ 1 \end{bmatrix}.
$$

Thus, by summing the columns of the IVM, we get a vector $\mathbf{q}' = \mathbf{q}/\mathbf{q} \cdot \mathbf{q}^\mathsf{T}$ that has the same direction as $\mathbf{q}$ and the reciprocal of its length. Thus, $\mathbf{q}$ can be found as $\mathbf{q}'/\mathbf{q}' \cdot \mathbf{q}'^\mathsf{T}$.

This way $\mathbf{q}$ can easily be computed from the IVM, which is thus all we need to perform intersection computations. With nine floating-point values, it is a minimal representation for a triangle, with a footprint equal to the vertex positions themselves. The HLSL function for intersection is given in Listing 6.6.1.

Listing 6.6.1 HLSL function for intersection

```
void intersectTriangle( float3 o, float3 d, float3 ivm0, float3
ivm1,float3 ivm2,

    inout float tBest, out bool hit, out float3 b ) {


    float3 q = ivm0 + ivm1 + ivm2; q /= dot(q, q);     // compute q from
IVM
    o -= q < 0;                                        // encoding
translation
    hit = false; b = 0;
    float tStar = (dot(q, q) - dot(o, q)) / dot(d, q); // intersection
with plane

    if(tStar > 0 && tStart < tBest) {
        float3 p = o + (d * tStar);                    // ray equation
        b.x = dot(ivm0, p);                            // compute
barycentric
```

```
          b.y = dot(ivm1, p);
          b.z = dot(ivm2, p);
          if(all(b > 0)) {      tBest = tStar;      hit = true; }      // hit
on triangle
      }
  }
```

For simplicity, we store shading normals, encoded to 8 bits per direction, in the same texture as the IVMs. After the closest intersection has been found, the normals of the triangle vertices are expanded into 3D vectors and interpolated using the barycentric coordinates.

BIH TRAVERSAL

With a ray to trace, we first traverse the scene BIH. For every entity, we transform the ray to the normalized model space of the mesh, where its bounding box is the positive unit cube. If there is an intersection with the box, the mesh BIH is traversed for an intersection. We use the classic stack-using kd-tree traversal technique. As the tree depth is limited, we can use a finite array as the stack. The intersections with the four bounding planes and then the extrema of the segments within the child cells can be evaluated in parallel using vector operations as shown in the source code in Listing 6.6.2

Listing 6.6.2 Evaluating using vector operations

```
// transform ray to normalized model space
o = mul( float4(o, 1), entities[meshIndex].modelMatrixInverse ).xyz;
d = mul( float4(d, 0), entities[meshIndex].modelMatrixInverse ).xyz;
// d is not normalized so that ray parameters of entities are comparable
float3 rd = float3(1, 1, 1) / d;                     // inverse ray direction

float3 traversalStack[24];
float2 raySegment = float2(0.0, bestDepth);          // tMin, tMax
uint iNode = 0;                                      // traversed node
uint stackPointer = 1;                               // initialize stack
traversalStack[0] = float3(raySegment, asfloat(iNode));
```

```
while(stackPointer > 0) {
    float3 nextNode = traversalStack[-stackPointer];     // pop
    raySegment = nextNode.xy;
    raySegment.y = min(bestDepth, raySegment.y);
    if(raySegment.x > raySegment.y) continue;            // skip sub-tree
    iNode = asuint(nextNode.z);

    float4 node = BIHTextureArray.Load(uint3(iNode, meshIndex, 0));
    if(node.w > 0) {                                     // if not a leaf
        uint nearChild = (iNode << 1) + 1;               // index of
left child
        uint farChild = nearChild;
        float3 axis = step(node.xyz, 0);                 // splitting axis
        float4 bounds = abs(node);                       // splitting bounds

        //compute intersections with cutting planes
        float4 tBounds = (bounds - dot(o, axis).xxxx) * dot(rd, axis);

        if(dot(rd, axis) > 0.0)        farChild += 1;    // right is far
        else {
            tBounds.xyzw = tBounds.wzyx;                 // right to left
            nearChild += 1;                              // right is near
        }

        //compute ray segments within child cells
        float4 childSegs;
        childSegs.xz = max(raySegment.xx, tBounds.xz);
        childSegs.yw = min(raySegment.yy, tBounds.yw);

        traversalStack[stackPointer++] =                 // push child jobs
float3(childSegs.xy, asfloat(nearChild));
        traversalStack[stackPointer++] =
float3(childSegs.xy, asfloat(farChild));
```

```
        }
    } else {
        // intersect triangles rawNode.x to rawNode.y, updating
bestDepth
    }
}
```

LIGHT SOURCE SAMPLING

Light sources are ordinary mesh-based scene entities, but they emit light. The light source sampling pass is initiated by rendering the meshes of the light sources. The geometry shader emits a number of VPL records proportional to the area of the triangle, uniformly distributed on the surface. The stream output feature of the pipeline is used to write the results into a buffer. Subsequent pipeline stages are not required.

PHOTON SHOOTING

The photon shooting pass is also implemented in a geometry shader with the stream output. The light sample buffer is rendered as a point list, and results are appended to the VPL buffer. The shader performs the random walk algorithm to generate new photon path nodes. We use BRDF sampling, taking random numbers from a pre-filled buffer. Both with diffuse and specular reflections, this comes down to generating a point on the unit hemisphere with a cosine distribution to some power. We generate points on the unit disc and project them up. The random buffer contains pairs made up of a random planar unit vector and a random scalar between 0 and 1. In the shader, the appropriate power of the scalar is taken (one half in the diffuse case), giving the distance of the sample point from the origin. The random planar direction is scaled with this value. Then the third coordinate for a point on the hemisphere is computed.

The random direction is used to trace a ray using the algorithm described above. The hit point is emitted as a VPL into the output stream. The process can be repeated to obtain more samples or multiple reflections. The original light sample is also written to the output to provide direct illumination.

VPL MANAGEMENT

In order to keep photon shooting real-time, and to avoid temporal artifacts, only a few photon paths are generated in every frame. The resulting VPLs are always appended to the end of the buffer. Therefore, another pass has to copy the buffer, eliminating old records from the start. This pass is also responsible for precomputing view-dependent VPL data: the VPL positions in clipping space coordinates. This way we do not need to perform all of the aforementioned matrix multiplications for every pixel in the lighting and shadowing shaders. In the next frame, new elements will be appended to this new VPL buffer, and the view-dependent data recalculated, allowing for a moving camera.

RENDERING THE DISTANCE IMPOSTOR CUBE MAP

The scene geometry is rendered onto the faces of a cube map using the render target array architecture of DX10. The reference camera position is placed a convenient distance within the visible scene. In the pixel shader, all fragments that are within the view frustum of the original camera are discarded, rendering only the off-screen geometry. The distance from the reference position is written to the render target.

RENDERING DEFERRING TEXTURES

The on-screen geometry is rendered to create viewport-sized textures used for deferred shading. The geometry texture contains the clipping-space depth and the surface normal of the points visible in the pixels, and the BRDF texture contains its material parameters. The use is fourfold. First, the expensive lighting pass is only performed for visible pixels, as in deferred shading. Second, the geometry information is needed for the geometry-sensitive box filtering of the interleaved lighting image. Third, the BRDF data is needed to modulate the filtered lighting results. Fourth, the depth information from the geometry texture is a sampled representation of the on-screen geometry, against which we can trace the shadow rays toward VPLs.

BUILDING PYRAMIDAL OCCLUSION MAPS

Filtered occlusion maps are generated by filtering the depth component of the geometry texture by taking the minimum of all samples. It is practical to use the gather functionality of the HLSL texture object, which returns four values in a single vector.

The same applies for the distance impostor cube map. The neighborhood minima are thus accumulated in textures.

LIGHTING

The lighting pixel shader is initiated by rendering a full-viewport quad. This is where all the previously built resources are used. It performs deferred shading on the geometry texture. It loops over some, but not all, elements of the VPL buffer, different ones in neighboring pixels, thus producing an interleaved image. Lighting is performed using the classic point-to-point form factor formula

$$F = \frac{\cos\theta\cos\psi}{d^2} \, ,$$

where d is the distance of the shaded point and the VPL, θ is the light incidence angle, and ψ is the angle between the light vector and the VPL normal. In order to avoid light spikes near VPLs, we use a bit more complex formula than usual. If the squared distance from the plane of VPL, $N^2 = d^2\cos^2\psi$, is smaller than a threshold value N_c^2, the form factor is

$$F = \frac{\cos\theta\sqrt{N_c^2/\delta^2}}{\delta^2} \, ,$$

where

$$\delta^2 = d^2(1 - \cos^2\psi) + N_c^2 \, .$$

This is the same as moving the points that are below the threshold curve of the VPL onto the curve, along the VPL's surface normal, and evaluating the form factor there. As opposed to simple clamping, this also removes dark edges, not only light spikes.

SHADOWS DUE TO OFF-SCREEN GEOMETRY

The shadow ray from the shaded point to the VPL is traced against the distance impostor cube. If there is an occluding piece of geometry, it can be found in the cube map somewhere between the direction toward the VPL and the direction of the point where the shadow ray exits the main camera's view frustum (see Figure 6.6.5). Various search algorithms developed for displacement mapping can be used [Szirmay08], but we exploit our minimum maps for efficiency. The first sample along the ray is taken just outside the view frustum, and the sample is then advanced along the ray up to the minimum distance read at the first sample point. If the distance is less than the distance of the sample point, then we continue the search on the distance map filtered with a smaller kernel, or deem the VPL to be occluded. In practice, we are content with taking only two samples to obtain approximate results.

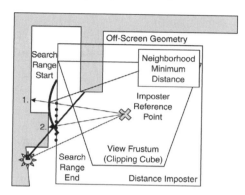

FIGURE 6.6.5 Occluder search in a pyramidal depth impostor cube map.

SHADOWS DUE TO ON-SCREEN GEOMETRY

Tracing a shadow ray over the depth field of the viewport is similar to looking up the distance impostor in that it is a search along a line. The VPL position in homogenous clipping space coordinates is given in the VPL buffer. We have to clip the line segment connecting the shaded point and the VPL to the unit cube. This is because we are only interested in the on-screen ray segment, we want to avoid reading out of the depth texture, and we need to handle VPLs behind the camera (which do not have a valid projection onto the viewport) properly. After homogenous division we obtain a ray within the view frustum over the viewport. We use a simple stepping search along the ray to find a possible intersection point. At locations near the shaded point, high accuracy is desired, so there we use unfiltered depth information. As we move further, we take larger steps, but use more coarsely filtered levels of the pyramidal depth map. If the minimum depth of the neighborhood is less than the depth of the sample, the VPL is deemed to be occluded. We use the smooth-step HLSL function for a soft comparison. This is clearly a crude approximation, but acceptable if we consider VPLs to be area lights: Occlusions nearer to the VPL should be softer. Note that if we look at the near samples only, we are practically reproducing the screen-space occlusion algorithm, only with the VPLs substituting for the random directional samples. The visibility factors of all occlusion tests are multiplied, as a single occlusion is enough to block the light. As we use smooth step functions when comparing distances, we are not merely multiplying ones and zeros.

Adaptive Geometry-Sensitive Box Filtering

In the image resulting after the lighting and shadowing pass, VPL contributions are distributed into 4×4 pixel neighborhoods. This has to be filtered as described in *ShaderX⁶* [Laine08], taking geometry into account, and discarding samples where the surface normal or the position is very different. The information for this is available in the geometry texture. In order to avoid loss of quality near geometric discontinuities without sacrificing performance, we made the box-filtering algorithm more adaptive. First the 16 samples from the 4×4 neighborhood are taken and averaged. If one or more samples have been rejected, another 16 samples are taken from an extended neighborhood to account for the rejected ones. These are also tested for validity. This way we can be sure that every group of VPLs is represented in the final color of every pixel.

Performance

The complete algorithm uses a dozen passes with different shaders, some of which are quite complex. The two most demanding elements that define the overall performance are the photon shooting and lighting passes. The test scene (Figure 6.6.6) had 10,000 triangles in five entities; we used 512 VPLs, with 64 new ones shot in every frame. The viewport resolution was 512×512, and the hardware was a GeForce 8800 GTX. Under these conditions, both photon shooting and lighting with shadows took under 10 msec, achieving an overall frame rate over 50 fps.

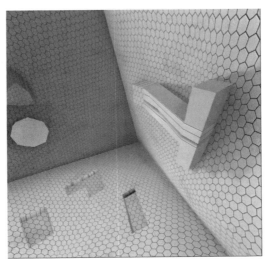

FIGURE 6.6.6   Screenshot of the test scene with indirect shadows.

CONCLUSION

This performance is clearly below but in a similar order of magnitude to those achieved in *ShaderX⁶*. However, we allow for at least four times as many VPLs, which can cover not only indirect illumination but also samples of area light sources. Multiple reflection photon paths are supported, and the dynamics of the scene are not limited. We can conclude that it is feasible to implement a complete global illumination solution like instant radiosity on the GPU, achieving real-time frame rates. With the expected increase in graphics hardware performance, similar techniques can and will be applied in interactive applications, even computer games.

REFERENCES

[Keller97] A. Keller. "Instant radiosity," Proceedings of the 24th Annual Conference on Computer Graphics and Interactive Techniques, 1997. pp. 49–56.

[Laine08] S. Laine, H. Saransaari, J. Kontkanen, J. Lehtinen, T. Aila. "Incremental instant radiosity," *ShaderX⁶ Advanced Rendering Techniques*, Wolfgang Engel (editor), Charles River Media, Hingham, Massachusetts, 2008. pp. 381–391.

[MacDonald90] J. D. MacDonald, K. S. Booth. "Heuristics for ray tracing using space subdivision," *The Visual Computer*, volume 6, number 3, Springer, 1990. pp 153–166.

[Mittring07] M. Mittring. "Finding next gen: CryEngine 2," *International Conference on Computer Graphics and Interactive Techniques*, ACM Press New York, NY, USA, 2007. pp. 97–121.

[Oh06] K. Oh, H. Ki, C. H. Lee. "Pyramidal displacement mapping: a GPU based artifacts-free ray tracing through an image pyramid," *Proceedings of the ACM Symposium on Virtual Reality Software and Technology*, ACM Press New York, NY, USA, 2006. pp. 75–82.

[Segovia06] B. Segovia, J.C. Iehl, R. Mitanchey, B. Peroche. "Non-interleaved deferred shading of interleaved sample patterns," Proceedings of the 21st ACM SIGGRAPH/Eurographics Symposium on Graphics Hardware: Vienna, Austria, volume 3, number 4, 2006. pp. 53–60.

[Szirmay08] L. Szirmay-Kalos, T. Umenhoffer. "Displacement mapping on the GPU – state of the art," *Computer Graphics Forum*, volume 27, number 1, 2008.

[Szirmay05] L. Szirmay-Kalos, B. Aszódi, I. Lazányi, M. Premecz. "Approximate ray-tracing on the GPU with distance impostors," *Computer Graphics Forum*, volume 24, number 3, 2005. pp. 695–704.

[SKSL08] L. Szirmay-Kalos, L. Szécsi, M. Sbert. *GPU-Based Techniques for Global Illumination Effects*, Morgan and Claypool Publishers, 2008.

[Umenhoffer07] T. Umenhoffer, G. Patow, L. Szirmay-Kalos. "Robust multiple specular reflections and refractions," *GPU Gems 3*, Addison-Wesley, 2007.

[Wald07] I. Wald, S. Boulos, P. Shirley. "Ray tracing deformable scenes using dynamic bounding volume hierarchies," *ACM Transactions on Graphics*, volume 26, number 1, 2007. pp.. 1–18.

[Wächter06] C. Wächter, A. Keller. "Instant ray tracing: the bounding interval hierarchy," Rendering Techniques 2006: Eurographics Symposium on Rendering, Nicosia, Cyprus, June 26–28, 2006.

6.7 Variance Methods for Screen-Space Ambient Occlusion

Angelo Pesce

AMBIENT LIGHTING

Traditionally, in real-time computer graphics, surface response to light has been divided into two major components: diffuse lighting and specular lighting.

The diffuse (Lambertian) component models materials that scatter a light ray hitting its surface with the same probability over all possible outgoing directions. The specular component, on the other hand, has a lobe of directions into which most of the light is scattered, it is view-dependent, and it models the material glossiness.

Given some light sources, we can easily derive how much light at each visible point scatters toward our view point by evaluating those two components. As this computation involves only the lights and the shaded point, it is called a local lighting model for shading.

Unfortunately, such a model is not sufficient to re-create realistic-looking images, as it does not convey any information about the relations of the objects in the scene, and objects appear to be floating due to the lack of shadows. In general, computing global effects is very hard on GPUs, as it requires computing visibility between arbitrary points on all surfaces in our scene (even the not directly visible ones!).

What GPUs are good at is computing visibility for a huge number of coherent viewing directions, via the z-buffer algorithm. This has enabled us to compute the direct interaction of scene objects with a narrow class of light emitters: those that emit light in a coherent fashion, for example, directional lights, point lights, and spot lights. Objects interact directly with light sources by blocking some of the light rays from further propagation in the scene, in other words, by casting shadows.

This limited global illumination model is also called direct lighting. While it's a huge improvement over the local model, it still lacks the indirect lighting part: Objects not only block light rays, but scatter them in all directions, some striking our image plane and others reaching other objects, thus acting as light sources. Disregarding this lighting results in overly darkened scenes, and shadows appear as completely black.

To compensate for this an ambient term is used that is the diffuse response of the material to a light that is present everywhere in the environment and that emits light in every direction.

AMBIENT OCCLUSION

We have a further improvement on this model if we consider the shadowing term for the ambient light. This means that, for each surface point, we sum up for each incoming direction how far a ray can travel (accumulating ambient light) before it is blocked by another object. This computation is incredibly expensive to do, as it requires a huge number of visibility queries (it was first introduced as an offline rendering technique by Industrial Light and Magic; see [Landis2002]).

Fortunately, as ambient lighting is the lowest-frequency term of our illumination, its shadows are of a low frequency. Thus, we can use a ray tracer to compute the shadowing amount offline, bake the results into a texture or the geometry's vertices, and interpolate.

This technique is what usually "ambient occlusion" refers to, and it is able to generate astonishing results: We have shadows in the not-directly-lit regions, and we are able to see spatial relationships—not only between surfaces in the scene, but also conveying information about volumes and depth (see [Langer00]). It was a breakthrough as important as casted shadows for realistic rendering.

DYNAMIC AMBIENT OCCLUSION

The major problem of baking techniques is that they don't work at all for dynamic scenes. Thus, various dynamic ambient occlusion techniques have been developed, ranging from object space techniques [Bunnell05], trying to achieve fast visibility computations using approximate occluders (spheres or discs), to screen-space techniques, approximating ambient occlusion by considering only the visible surfaces as occluders, to hybrid methods combining both approaches [Shanmugam07] [Sloan07].

The rest of this article will focus on screen-space techniques, as they are applicable right now, but reading about the other references is recommended as well.

SCREEN-SPACE AMBIENT OCCLUSION

Screen-space ambient occlusion (SSAO) techniques became very popular after their adoption in the game *Crysis* by Crytek [Mittring07]. They use the scene z-buffer to reconstruct the world-space position of the visible samples in a frame. Those samples are used as locations where we want to compute the ambient occlusion and approximations of the occluders.

From each pixel, we can trace visibility rays in screen-space, walking over the z-buffer (a technique very similar to relief mapping [Oliveira00] [Sloan00]) until an intersection is found. However, if we assume that all surfaces close to a given point are always visible from that point, then we can avoid ray marching and simply consider a number of samples in a circular region around our shaded point in the z-buffer and use them as occluders.

This is possible, as ambient occlusion quickly becomes irrelevant as we travel away from our sample point, and we can do our search in a small radius (in world space) around the sample where that local visibility assumption usually holds (see also [Arikan05]).

However, this technique has three drawbacks: over-darkening caused by local visibility assumption (easily recognizable for large search radii, especially in the center of large flat polygons), over-darkening caused by the z-buffer scene visibility approximation (as we can't see what's behind the first layer of visible surfaces, which could be solved by depth peeling), and noise caused by the sampling method (the sampling pattern usually changes across pixels to turn disturbing patterns into noise).

The latter is the problem we want to solve with our technique, or, in other words, we try to get better quality from fewer samples.

UNSHARP MASKING

Another simple technique to achieve the visual effect of defining the edges and volumes in the scene is unsharp masking of the z-buffer, subtracting a blurred version of the z-buffer from the original depth [Luft06] [Fox08].

This is different from SSAO, as SSAO computes for each pixel the mean number of neighboring pixels failing the z-test against the pixel's z-buffer value (if we disregard the inverse square law of attenuation). The z-buffer test is a binary decision, not a linear operation, and as a consequence, comparing the z-value with the mean of neighboring z-values does not compute the same result.

On the other hand, it is convenient, as the mean z-buffer value can be computed very quickly with a separable, two-pass blur filter, and we can account for varying neighbor sizes (necessary due to the projection of the 3D sampling sphere in view space) by mipmapping the blurred buffer.

Variance Maps and SSAO

This problem is very similar to the problem of shadow map filtering, where we take a number of samples around the pixel in the shadow map and test them against the shaded surface depth value (as seen from the light source) [Reeves87].

Recently, a solution to that problem has been found called variance shadow maps (VSMs) [Donnelly06], which are based on the simple and elegant idea of expressing the depth values as a probability distribution. What do we do when counting how many samples around our point are occluding it? We are estimating the probability of our point being occluded by surfaces in a certain area.

Instead of doing that, VSMs reconstruct a probability distribution (PDF) in that area, and then compute the probability of that PDF exceeding the sample point depth.

Chebyshev's inequality is a tool that enables us to do this computation: Given the first two moments of an arbitrary PDF, it computes an upper bound on the probability for that PDF for values being greater than a certain threshold.

The first two moments are the mean and the variance. Computing them is easy: We just take the average of our depth values for the former, and the average of the squared depths for the latter (so we have to save two values per pixel, instead of one). We want to do this "locally," that is, we do a moving average that can be simply computed with a separable box filter.

VSMs map very nicely to this problem, as they seem to not show many of the typical artifacts that this technique has when applied to shadow computations. Further, it is able to capture high-frequency occlusion details with very high quality. It does not perform equally well with low-frequency ambient occlusion components generated by distant surfaces because VSMs require huge amounts of floating-point accuracy in order to express such surfaces, and they violate the local visibility assumption.

This first approach has one remaining problem: We only compute the probability of a surface point being occluded, disregarding the distance attenuation of the other surfaces' occlusion. This can generate wrong occlusion values, especially in regions of high variance. An easy workaround is to directly use the estimated variance to artificially lower the computed occlusion value.

The final algorithm operates in three steps:

1. Render scene depth and squared depth into an off-screen buffer.
2. Blur this buffer, using a two-pass separable box filter, into a second one, giving us the mean and the mean of squared values; from those we can compute the variance.

3. For each pixel we evaluate the occlusion probability using its depth value, the mean and the variance. That—the slightly increased by a fraction of the variance—is our ambient occlusion value.

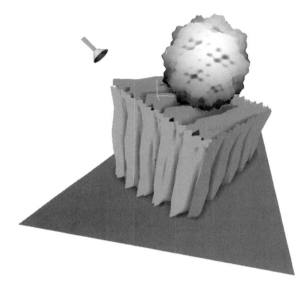

FIGURE 6.7.1   The results.

REFERENCES

[Bunnell05] Michael Bunnel: Dynamic Ambient Occlusion and Indirect Lighting, *GPU Gems 2*

[Shanmugam07] Perumaal Shanmugam, Okan Arikan: Hardware accelerated ambient occlusion techniques on GPUs, *ACM Proceedings of the 2007 Symposium on Interactive 3D Graphics and Games*

[Sloan07] Peter-Pike Sloan, Naga K. Govindaraju, Derek Nowrouzezahrai, John Snyder: Image-Based Proxy Accumulation for Real-Time Soft Global Illumination, *Proceedings of the 15th Pacific Conference on Computer Graphics and Applications*

[Mittring07] Martin Mittring: Finding Next Gen CryEngine2 in Advanced Real-Time Rendering in 3D Graphics and Games Course, Siggraph 2007

[Oliveira00] Manuel M. Oliveira, Gary Bishop, David McAllister: Relief Texture Mapping, *Proceedings of ACM Siggraph 2000*

[Arikan05] Okan Arikan, David Forsyth, James O'Brien: Fast and Detailed Approximate Global Illumination by Irradiance Decomposition, *Proceedings of ACM Siggraph 2005*

[Luft06] Thomas Luft, Carsten Colditz, Olivier Deussen: Image Enhancement by Unsharp Masking the Depth Buffer, *Proceedings of ACM Siggraph 2006*

[Fox08] Megan Fox, Stuart Compton: Ambient Occlusive Crease Shading, *Game Developer Magazine*, March 2008

[Reeves87] William T. Reeves, David Salesin, Robert L. Cook: Rendering Antialiased Shadows with Depth Maps, *Proceedings of ACM Siggraph 1987*

[Donnelly06] William Donnelly, Andrew Lauritzen: Variance Shadow Maps, 2006 Symposium On Interactive 3D Graphics and Games

[Sloan00] Peter-Pike Sloan, Micheal F. Cohen, Interactive Horizon Mapping, Eurographics Rendering Workshop 2000

[Langer00] Michael S. Langer, Heinrich H. Bulthoff: Depth Discrimination from Shading under Diffuse Lighting

[Landis2002] Hayden Landis: Production-Ready Global Illumination, RenderMan in Production, ACM Siggraph 2002, Course 16.

6.8 Per-Pixel Ambient Occlusion Using Geometry Shaders

Dave Bookout, Intel Corporation

Introduction

As GPUs become more powerful and more computational time is used for advanced lighting techniques, global illumination approximations have become feasible for interactive applications. Ambient occlusion, a global illumination technique common in offline rendering, varies the amount of ambient light that reaches a surface based on the amount of nearby shadowing geometry. An effective approximation for ambient occlusion [Bunnell05] performs per-vertex lighting calculations with a simplified mesh. The approximation allows for implementations more suitable to modern GPUs and real-time graphics APIs than the implementations developed previously. This chapter modifies that original algorithm to perform the occlusion calculations per pixel and leverages the geometry shader available in DirectX Shader Model 4.0 to greatly simplify the implementation. The results are shown in Figure 6.8.1.

FIGURE 6.8.1 A model rendered with ambient occlusion and without ambient occlusion.

BACKGROUND

Ambient occlusion is used to vary the ambient lighting term for a surface point by determining how much nearby geometry is shadowing that point or, conversely, how much of the environment is visible from that point. Most real-time implementations require a preprocessing stage that determines the visibility of some selection of points on a model's surface. The visibility test may involve ray tracing over a hemisphere centered at the point or rendering hundreds of shadow maps and, in effect, reversing the ray cast [Pharr04]. Another approach is to ignore the visibility determination and assume that every point can occlude every other point. Starting with this assumption, [Bunnell05] replaced all geometry with disks positioned at each vertex. Per-vertex occlusion values were then calculated and interpolated across the triangle faces for the final rendering. [Hoberock08] extended the algorithm to perform per-pixel calculations.

OUR APPROACH

ALGORITHM

The base algorithm is similar to [Bunnell05]. To calculate the ambient occlusion per pixel, the positions and normals of the geometry visible from the camera are determined. The geometry in the scene is approximated by a collection of disks as shown in Figure 6.8.2. Assuming that the input geometry is a triangle mesh, the disk approximation roughly corresponds to the triangles in the mesh. Each disk blocks the light reaching a point based on its relative orientation and distance from that point. For a first approximation, each disk is treated independently of all the others.

[Bunnell05] For each pixel, the occlusion for each disk is calculated. The results are accumulated and then subtracted from the ambient lighting term for that pixel.

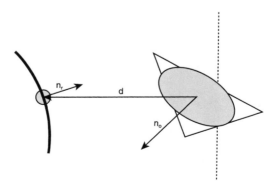

FIGURE 6.8.2   The disk-based approximation for ambient occlusion.

IMPLEMENTATION

The first requirement is to determine the positions and normals of the points in the scene that are visible from the camera's point of view by rendering the scene. The implementation uses two render targets to store the three component view space positions and normals at each pixel. The results will be accessed as textures in the next stage.

The second stage creates the disk-shaped approximations for the geometry. Instead of preprocessing the geometry to build the disk occluders, all of the work is performed in the geometry shader. The geometry shader allows access to the three vertices that make up each triangle. From these points, a single disk is created with an area equal to the triangle's area and a normal equal to the face normal of the triangle. The center of the disc is equal to the midpoint of the triangle, that is, the average of the three vertices.

The output of the geometry shader is a screen-aligned quad that contains this disk information. While the original version of the algorithm placed the disks at the vertices of the mesh, the triangle center approximation is more natural for the geometry shader inputs and avoids any additional mesh preprocessing, or reprocessing in the case of animated geometry, to determine the area for each disk. Also, for per-pixel calculations, placing the disks on the triangle serves as a better approximation for the geometry [Hoberock08].

While previous implementations ([Bunnell05], [Hoberock08]) consider all discs when determining the ambient occlusion for a point, our implementation limits the influence of a disc. Because the influence of a triangle is based on its area, only points within a certain hemisphere of space will be occluded by a disk. The radius of the hemisphere is scaled based on the area of the disc. The screen-aligned quad that the geometry shader outputs is placed to fully cover the hemisphere when the hemisphere is projected onto the screen.

```
[maxvertexcount(5)]
void AmbientOcclusionGS(triangle PS_INPUT_WORLD_NORMAL StreamInput[3],
                inout TriangleStream <PS_AMBIENT_OCCLUSION_INPUT> Stream)
{
    PS_AMBIENT_OCCLUSION_INPUT output = (PS_AMBIENT_OCCLUSION_INPUT)0;
    //set up disk approximation for triangle
    //calculate area, direction, center of the disk
    output.area = TriangleArea(StreamInput[0].viewPos,
                        StreamInput[1].viewPos,
```

```
                                    StreamInput[2].viewPos);
  output.normal = TriangleNormal(StreamInput[0].viewPos,
                                 StreamInput[1].viewPos,
                                 StreamInput[2].viewPos);
  float4 diskCenter  = float4(StreamInput[2].viewPos
                              + StreamInput[1].viewPos
                              + StreamInput[0].viewPos) / 3.0f,
                              1.0f);
  output.vpos = diskCenter.xyz;
  //Move disks behind the camera in front of the camera so disks are not
  //clipped inappropriately.
  diskCenter.z = abs(diskCenter.z);

  //output a screen aligned quad for pixel shader calculations
  float radius = g_influenceScale*output.area;;

  output.hpos = mul(diskCenter + radius*float4(-1.0f, -1.0f, 0.0f, 0.0f),
                    Proj);
  Stream.Append(output);

  output.hpos = mul(diskCenter + radius*float4(-1.0f, 1.0f, 0.0f, 0.0f),
                    Proj);
  Stream.Append(output);

  output.hpos = mul(diskCenter + radius*float4(1.0f, 1.0f, 0.0f, 0.0f),
                    Proj);
  Stream.Append(output);

  output.hpos = mul(diskCenter + radius*float4(1.0f, -1.0f, 0.0f, 0.0f),
                    Proj);
  Stream.Append(output);

  output.hpos = mul(diskCenter + radius*float4(-1.0f, -1.0f, 0.0f, 0.0f),
                    Proj);
```

```
        Stream.Append(output);


        Stream.RestartStrip();
}
```

For each quad, the occlusion term for each pixel that quad covers is calculated. For each pixel, the position and normal of the point visible from the camera as determined in the first pass are used in combination with the disc information passed in with the quad from the geometry shader to determine the occlusion for that pixel from that disc. The result is then subtracted from the current frame buffer value to accumulate the occlusion from all the disks.

```
float ComputeSolidAngle(float3 v,
                        float d2,
                        float3 receiverNormal,
                        float3 emitterNormal,
                        float3 emitterArea)

{
    return (1.0f - rsqrt(emitterArea/d2 + 1))
            * saturate(dot(emitterNormal, v))
            * saturate(4*dot(receiverNormal, v));

}


float4 AmbientOcclusionPS(PS_AMBIENT_OCCLUSION_INPUT input) : SV_TARGET
{
    int3 texCoord = int3(input.hpos.x, input.hpos.y, 0);
    float3 vpos = 2*g_VisiblePositionsTx.Load(texCoord)-1;


    float3 vnorm = 2*g_VisibleNormalsTx.Load(texCoord)-1;
    float3 v = input.vpos - vpos;
    float3 d2 = dot(v, v);
    float f = ComputeSolidAngle(normaize(v), d2, vnorm, input.normal,
input.area);
    return f;

}
```

RESULTS

ARTIFACTS

Because visibility is not calculated and this implementation performs a single pass, the results are generally darker than a more complete solution [Bunnell05]. The additional darkness is caused by double shadowing of a point. For example, given a point and two triangles, the point and one of the triangles may both be occluded by the second triangle (Figure 6.8.3). In this case, both of the triangles will reduce the ambient term of the point independently and cause the point to be too dark. A more accurate solution would consider the two triangles simultaneously. The over-darkening can be alleviated by performing multiple passes so that points that are dark contribute to the occlusion of other points less [Bunnell05]. Our implementation only processes information for visible positions, and does not retain any intermediate calculations, so the intermediate representation necessary for multiple passes is not available.

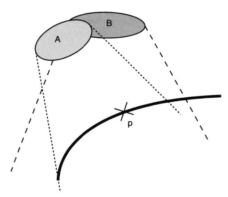

FIGURE 6.8.3 Over-darkening. Because no visibility testing is performed in the algorithm, a single point will be shadowed individually by each disc. When two discs overlap, the point will be too dark.

Additional artifacts occur because of the disk approximation as shown in Figure 6.8.4. Although the calculations are performed per screen pixel, the disk approximations are of triangles of various sizes. Larger triangles have more error and can cause very dark areas or reveal the tessellation artifacts, particularly near the vertices where the disk approximation is less accurate. One could subdivide the triangle in the geometry shader and emit multiple quads for the occlusion calculation. Alternatively, information for multiple discs can be embedded into a single quad.

FIGURE 6.8.4   Artifacts from the disk-based approximation when applied to a low-polygon model.

PERFORMANCE

If every pixel can be occluded by every triangle in the scene, the quads from the geometry shader have to be rendered to the entire screen, which results in enormous fill-rate requirements. To alleviate this, each triangle is given a volume of influence based on its area; larger triangles have larger volumes of influence. The sizes of the quads generated in the geometry shader are scaled to match that volume. Because the occlusion value falls off with the square of the distance, when considering a point, many of the disks can be discarded with little or no visible difference. Also, the volume can be scaled to achieve a desired frame rate while retaining some of the visual detail.

The quads are projected onto the screen with the same perspective projection transform used to render the final scene. In this way, the volume of influence will scale relative to the distance from the camera as shown in Figure 6.8.5. Because triangles behind the camera's near clip plane are discarded, the absolute value of the occluding disk's center is used when projecting to the screen. While this causes disks behind the camera to cover a larger number of pixels than they should, their influence still scales with distance from the camera as shown in Figure 6.8.6.

FIGURE 6.8.5   Visualization of the area of influence of the disks. Darker areas present areas with more occluders.

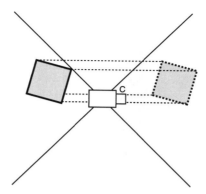

FIGURE 6.8.6 Disks behind the camera would be culled and not contribute to the lighting of the visible points. Disks are moved in front of the camera before projecting.

Because of the high fill-rate requirements for this implementation, scaling down the volume of influence can improve performance significantly. However, if the volume is too small, blocky artifacts will appear at the edges of the quads that are rendered for the occlusion calculations. Also, reducing the quad size does not change the depth of the influence of a disk, so the occlusion term becomes view dependent.

As noted in [Dachsbacher06], for fill-rate-limited algorithms, more complex geometry can be used to limit the fill rate at the expense of more expensive vertex processing. Performance improves until the vertex processing becomes the bottleneck. For ambient occlusion, only points in front of a disc can be occluded by that disc, and, in our approximation, only points within a certain hemisphere around the disc can be occluded. By substituting a pyramid that contains the hemisphere for the original quad, we can decrease the number of pixel writes by ~20% as shown in Figure 6.8.7 and Table 6.8.1.

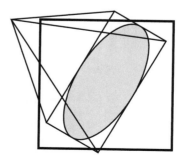

FIGURE 6.8.7 Comparison of using a pyramid versus a quad to approximate the volume that a disk can influence. Much of the time, the pyramid will require less fill rate at the expense of additional geometry processing.

FIGURE 6.8.8   Bunny mesh with 36k vertices.

TABLE 6.8.1 Sample performance of the bunny (actual performance is heavily dependent on the scene composition)

Quad/Pyramid	640x480	1024x768	1280x1024
Max overdraw	3691/2652	3645/2670	3661/2680
Total pixel shader executions	9,939,408/8,240,312	25,448,468/21,095920	45,242,629/37,503,563
FPS	10.0/15.0	4.25/7.5	2.5/4.5

CONCLUSION

This article demonstrates a straightforward approximation of ambient occlusion using the geometry shader to avoid preprocessing the mesh data. Also, the article presented methods for improving performance over the base implementation. Future work will focus on multiple passes for more accurate results and more efficient approximations for the triangle mesh to reduce pixel shader computations and fill-rate requirements.

Acknowledgments

Special thanks to Glen Lewis for providing the army man model.

References

[Bunnell05] Michael Bunnell, "Dynamic Ambient Occlusion and Indirect Lighting," *GPU Gems 2*, Matt Pharr, ed., Addison-Wesley, 2005, pp. 223–233.

[Dachsbacher06] Carsten Dachsbacher and Marc Stamminger, "Splatting Indirect Illumination," *Proceedings of the 2006 Symposium on Interactive 3D Graphics and Games*, ACM Press, 2006, pp. 93–100.

[Hoberock08] Jared Hoberock and Yuntao Jia, "High-Quality Ambient Occlusion," *GPU Gems 3*, Hubert Nguyen, ed., Addison-Wesley, 2008, pp. 257–274.

[Pharr04] Matt Pharr, "Ambient Occlusion," *GPU Gems 1*, Randima Fernando, ed., Addison-Wesley, 2004, pp. 279–292.

Part

VII

Handheld Devices

The "Handheld Devices" section covers the latest development in graphics programming targeting devices that are portable, such as mobile phones, personal organizers, and portable game consoles. The latest generation of GPUs for handheld devices comes with a feature set that is comparable to the latest PC and console GPU feature sets.

In the first article in the section, "Optimizing Your First OpenGL ES Application," Kristof Beets, Mikael Gustavsson, and Erik Olsson use the game *Kodo Evolved* to demonstrate how to optimize performance on POWERVR graphics hardware. The article also covers an overview of the current market that allows developers to evaluate the business potential of mobile phones with GPUs.

User interfaces for games play an important role. Usually, game developers want to use their own user interfaces because this helps provide a seamless game experience and is also easier to port over to other platforms. Ken Catterall describes an implementation of a user interface tailored to handheld devices that looks very nice in his article "Optimized Shaders for Advanced Graphical User Interfaces." This article also shows an example implementation of a "cover flow"–like interface.

The article "Facial Animation for Mobile GPUs," by Andrew Senior, describes a highly optimized routine for facial animation using geometry textures combined with matrix palette skinning.

The last article in this section, "Augmented Reality on Mobile Phones," covers the implementation challenges of augmented reality on handheld devices. Augmented reality can be used as a next-generation user interface on any handheld that has an integrated camera. Sony's eye-based games show some of the potential in this area for games.

Have fun,

Wolf

7.1

Optimizing Your First OpenGL ES Application

KRISTOF BEETS, IMAGINATION TECHNOLOGIES

MIKAEL GUSTAVSSON, JADESTONE

ERIK OLSSON, JADESTONE

INTRODUCTION

With the widespread introduction of OpenGL ES 1.1 hardware accelerated hand-held devices, such as the NOKIA N95, Apple iPhone, Motorola Z10, and Sony Ericsson W960, the addressable market for application and game developers has easily grown to over 100 million devices. This far exceeds the market opportunities offered by either handheld consoles or games consoles. OpenGL ES 2.0 shader-capable devices bring graphics quality and performance for handheld devices to a new level, exceeding today's dedicated handheld consoles' capabilities. These devices are expected to become available toward the end of 2008 and include both ES1.1 and 2.0 API interfaces. This will further fuel the exciting market opportunities offered by accelerated graphics in handheld devices today.

This article looks at the complexities of the mobile market and how developers can effectively address this exciting opportunity in addition to providing the most up-to-date performance guidelines for developing OpenGL ES 1.1 and 2.0 content. These guidelines are based on Imagination Technologies' experience supporting leading OpenGL ES software developers such as Jadestone with their award-winning *Kodo Evolved* game, which is used as a case study throughout this article.

MOBILE DEVELOPMENT

CROSS-PLATFORM DEVELOPMENT

While the mobile market has adopted the Khronos OpenGL ES1.1 and 2.0 APIs as standard for graphics, there is considerably more fragmentation than in other market areas such as the console and PC markets. This fragmentation is linked to a much wider variety of different operating systems (OSes) including several Linux variants, Symbian OS, Windows CE variants, and a whole range of real-time operating systems (QNX, Nucleus, etc.). This is further complicated by a wide variety of graphical user interface (GUI) frameworks including the NOKIA-backed Series 60, Sony Ericsson–backed UIQ, Apple's OS X, and a wide variety of Linux frameworks based around the X Window System. Finally, there is device fragmentation from the many varieties of display size, different numbers of device keys and key mappings, possible touch screen support, and variable amounts of available system memory, not to mention a variety of possible device-specific bugs and features. This situation very quickly results in a wide requirement of different software SKUs to address all the devices on the market.

The only way to deal effectively with such a wide array of platform differences is through the introduction of an abstraction framework that handles the OS- and device-specific functionality, allowing the bulk of the application or game code to be generic.

ON THE DVD

Imagination Technologies faced this fragmentation problem during the creation of its software development kits (PC Emulation version included on the DVD-ROM). These include a basic Shell abstraction framework that efficiently handles OS and platform abstraction and now supports more than 50 different POWERVR 3D hardware-enabled platform configurations. The POWERVR Shell is freely available for developers to use and adapt to their needs.

Many commercial abstraction solutions are also available on the market such as Ideaworks3D Airplay [I3D08], Polarbit Fuse [FUSE08], Acrodea XFORGE [XFORGE08], and so on.

While these solutions simplify the process of supporting a wide range of devices, there is still an effort required of variable complexity with the introduction of a new platform. This makes it impractical to support every single device out there. As a result, most developers are already concentrating their efforts on the most successful and powerful devices on the market to ensure maximum return on investment. Many of these are based on the same underlying POWERVR graphics technology [KISHONTI08], including most of the Nokia N-series devices, Sony Ericsson UIQ devices, and many other well-known platforms from other leading manufacturers.

VARIABLE GRAPHICS FEATURE LEVELS

For the next couple of years, OpenGL ES 1.1, which enables fixed-function graphics capabilities, will remain the dominant solution on the market. This is due to the existing and expected ramp-up in the market as a result of cost-reduced solutions, allowing the feature set to go into mainstream devices. Also, OpenGL ES 2.0 solutions will support the OpenGL ES 1.1 API interface.

OpenGL ES 2.0–capable solutions offer a significantly more advanced feature set by exposing fully programmable graphics functionality in line with the latest PC and console graphics solutions. Initially, this will be restricted to higher-cost devices and thus a smaller market opportunity, but in the long term this will become the dominant API, as it should be easier for developers to port existing titles from the PC and console market to act as an accelerating factor in market adoption.

Again, an abstraction layer can offer the best of both API worlds, and this option should be taken into account when developing new 3D engines for this market, an effort further strengthened by the variability of expected performance levels discussed in the next section.

VARIABLE PERFORMANCE LEVELS

The features and capabilities of handheld converged devices have been rapidly expanding, with mobile phones absorbing an increasing number of features in the past couple of years. These include PDA functions, music playback, video playback, video and still capture, GPS and navigation-functions, gaming, and now full Internet browsing experience. The increasing adoption of more features and capabilities has resulted in a very wide collection of mobile phones with a variable degree of convergence and performance. The wide range of overall capabilities and performance is matched on the graphics side, where Imagination Technologies is anticipating graphics performance to vary by up to 16 times or more between entry-level devices (feature phones) and high-end devices (MID devices, handheld gaming devices). This is based on expected deployment of different POWERVR SGX graphics cores (e.g., SGX520 to SGX540 and beyond) and their variable frequencies (e.g., from sub–100 MHz to over 400 MHz) over the next couple of years.

This is a situation very similar to the PC market, where performance has a similar if not even greater range between entry-level integrated solutions and high-end add-in board solutions. In the PC market this has resulted in configurable complexity levels for applications, ranging from entry-level shaders and low-resolution to advanced shaders at high resolutions with post-processing effects and anti-aliasing. Similar approaches should be considered in the mobile market, where anti-aliasing and filtering offer simple, quality scaling mechanisms (easy to toggle with minimal code effort), but variable shader complexity should also be considered, for example, in combination with level of detail mechanisms [Beets07]. Post-processing is also an option but typically at a high bandwidth cost (see later comments).

BATTERY LIFE IS KEY

Improving battery technology, display technology, silicon process technology, and efficient architectures such as POWERVR's Tile-Based Deferred Rendering (TBDR), all play a major role in delivering long battery life for mobile products, but without careful software design, battery life can quickly become disappointing.

In the 10 years that I have been involved with 3D graphics, there is one key phrase I have had to use numerous times: "Nothing is free in 3D" [Beyond3D04], and on mobile devices this can easily be expanded to "Nothing is free on mobile devices." Everything will use up extra power or contribute to reducing your battery life.

Therefore, compared to other gaming platforms, power consumption must be part of your overall design strategy. For OEMs long battery life is key for their products, and some are already enforcing energy-saving device behavior that can range from limiting the maximum frame rate (e.g., locked to 30 fps) to stopping applications from ever running in the background (e.g., no more dead batteries because a game continued to run in your pocket). Specific tools are also increasingly available to assist the overall power consumption tuning effort as part of software development. A selection of such tools is listed in the "Optimization Utilities Are Key" section of this article.

BANDWIDTH IS LIMITED

While the latest PC graphics cards enjoy 512–bit-wide, high-speed buses to dedicated video memory, handheld devices use unified memory architectures with typically a modest bus width of only 32 or 64 bits to conserve power. This means that minimizing bandwidth usage also becomes a key design goal of handheld software.

When designing algorithms such as AI, physics, or data processing, it is essential to take data flow and cache usage into account, especially avoiding multiple passes across large data sets since this means that the same data is pulled into the chip multiple times, taking up valuable bandwidth. The same factor needs to be taken into account when deciding between various graphics algorithms.

It is not just overall data flow, but also algorithms, that need to be considered. For instance, it is quite common knowledge that blur filters can be implemented using a separable filter approach that first applies a horizontal pass followed by a vertical blur filter pass. While this minimizes the mathematical operations involved, it is a solution that also results in several round trips to and from memory, making it complex to determine the correct approach without actually benchmarking different methods on the platform.

It's difficult to provide overall guidelines, but from a graphics perspective, be aware that render to texture directly translates into extra memory bandwidth usage and that its usage should be minimized using concepts such as render on demand (e.g., lower render update rate driven by content changes). Numerous other elements will influence bandwidth, and various recommendations are offered in the following pages.

OPTIMIZATION UTILITIES ARE KEY

Utilities are key to assisting the overall development and, more specifically, the optimization process. Many of these tools are available from various hardware vendors and even OEMs. Try to use as many of these as possible, but typically what is good for one platform is likely to be good for others, or at least should not be harmful from an overall algorithm point of view. There are, however, some cases where platform-specific optimization should be considered in the form of platform-specific data packages. For example, geometry optimization strategies can differ from platform to platform, and, very likely, texture compression formats will differ from one solution to the other. These cases can easily be handled by using a tool flow that generates optimized data packages for different architectures, and many middleware solutions already support this.

Below is a list of some key development utilities available for free download today:

- POWERVR Insider SDK and utilities:
  http://www.imgtec.com/powervr/insider/powervr-utilities.asp
- NOKIA Series 60 OpenGL SDK:
  http://www.forum.nokia.com/info/sw.nokia.com/id/
  36331d44-414a-4b82-8b20-85f1183e7029/OpenGL_ES_1_1_Plug_in.html
- NOKIA Carbide including performance tools:
  http://www.forum.nokia.com/main/resources/tools_and_sdks/carbide_cpp/
- NOKIA Energy Profiler: http://www.forum.nokia.com/info/sw.nokia.com/id/
  324866e9-0460-4fa4-ac53-01f0c392d40f/Nokia_Energy_Profiler.html
- Sony Ericsson OpenGL ES SDK: http://developer.sonyericsson.com/site/
  global/newsandevents/latestnews/newsjune06/p_opengl_es_sdk_3dhardware
  acc_uiq3phones.jsp

- Apple iPhone SDK including OpenGL ES examples and performance tools: http://developer.apple.com/iphone/
- Intel Development Tools for Mobile Internet Devices: http://www.intel.com/cd/software/products/asmo-na/eng/386925.htm
- AMD OpenGL ES 2.0 Emulator: http://developer.amd.com/GPU/OPENGL/Pages/default.aspx
- acbPocketSoft PowerMeter and TaskMan for power optimization on Windows Mobile: http://www.acbpocketsoft.com/

Many more tools and valuable resources can be found on the Khronos OpenGL ES Resource Pages: http://www.khronos.org/developers/resources/opengles/

Discussion forums offer an opportunity to discuss optimization strategies with colleagues:

- Imagination Technologies Forum: http://www.imgtec.com/forum/default.asp
- Khronos Forum: http://www.khronos.org/message_boards/

GRAPHICS DEVELOPMENT GUIDELINES

This section provides an overview of development guidelines to ensure the best possible graphics experience for your customers with minimal bandwidth usage and maximal battery life. Recommendations are split into a generic section, applicable to both OpenGL ES 1.1 and OpenGL ES 2.0 APIs, and sections dedicated to optimizations for the fixed function API (ES 1.1) and finally the fully shader-based programmable API (ES 2.0).

GENERIC RECOMMENDATIONS

This section provides recommendations applicable to both OpenGL ES 1.1 devices (including POWERVR MBX family–based devices) and OpenGL ES 2.0 devices (including POWERVR SGX family–based devices).

Understand Your Target and Benchmark Your Applications

Unfortunately, no two devices are identical. Even when based on the same graphics IP core or even the same SoC chip solution, there can still be a wide variety of parameters that influence graphics performance such as core clock speed, memory bus speed, exposure of extensions, screen resolutions, operating system, GUI integration, and so on.

There is no easy way around this, and gaining insight into a device's capabilities and performance is essential. Benchmarking, ideally using your own in-house engine with your specific feature set and usage model, should be used to determine the performance level that should be activated for a specific device. In some cases a generic application can be delivered that through an automated or user-controlled benchmark allows tweaking of the graphical quality and complexity levels. This approach is often used in PC applications. As discussed in the previous section, variable quality levels will be essential to effectively target the mobile space unless your development is restricted to a single device. The traditional lowest common denominator approach in the mobile market is no longer acceptable to consumers who expect the best possible experience from their devices.

Jadestone experimented with various quality levels for *Kodo Evolved* and created entry-level and high-end profiles, as illustrated in Figure 7.1.1, with additional quality and performance levels possible in between based on shader scaling and effect selection.

Entry Level Device
OpenGL ES 1.1

Basic Lighting
Single Textured
Simple Translucency

High-End Device
OpenGL ES 2.0

Shadow Maps   Per-Pixel Lighting
Distortion Effects   Day/Night Mode
Fog Effect   Glow Post Process

FIGURE 7.1.1   Quality scaling based on device capabilities.

Do Not Access the Frame Buffer from the CPU

CPU and GPU parallelism is critical for the best possible performance. The latest graphics architectures, including POWERVR SGX, completely decouple CPU and GPU interaction through command buffers in system memory that allow the GPU to operate completely autonomously from the CPU by getting its instructions from system memory without direct CPU interaction. There are, however, a number of API calls that will force a synchronization between the CPU and GPU, the most obvious one being access to the color render target. Access to the frame buffer will force the CPU to stall while the GPU flushes all the commands buffered up in memory; then the GPU is stalled while the CPU operates on the frame buffer. As a result, any mixed CPU-GPU operations (typical in basic Java implementations) that use the CPU and GPU to interact with a single frame buffer should be optimized by mapping all frame buffer operations onto the GPU and thus avoiding stalls and maximizing performance and efficiency.

The latest graphics APIs, including OpenGL ES 1.1 and 2.0, already limit buffer access, for example, making it impossible to access the depth buffer of a scene. However, color buffer access remains available only for one valid usage case: screenshots. All other usage should be avoided.

Batch Your Primitives To Keep the Number of Draw Calls Low

Between the application and the 3D accelerator is a driver layer that translates the industry standard API calls into a format understood by the hardware. This translation requires resources and thus results in extra CPU work for each API call issued. Given that the CPU is a possible limiting performance factor and significant power consumer within the platform, it is essential to try to minimize the number of API calls. The CPU load created by the API is thus minimized, and overall device efficiency is optimized.

This can often be achieved through the concept of batching: grouping operations together as much as possible. Batching can be done on multiple levels, for example, based on render state (e.g., keep all opaque objects together), on texture (e.g., render all objects with the same texture in one go; consider using a texture atlas [one large texture containing multiple subtextures] as used by Jadestone and illustrated in Figure 7.1.2), or on fog colors (aim to use the same color or group all objects with the same color). The overall aim should be to reduce the number of API calls, so instead of 100 draw calls, each drawing a single object, optimally aim to have only a single draw call that draws all 100 objects.

Perform Rough Object Culling on the CPU

Although modern GPUs, such as POWERVR SGX, are very efficient at removing invisible objects, not submitting them for rendering at all is faster still. Your application has more knowledge of the scene contents and positions of objects than the GPU and OpenGL ES driver, and it can use that information to quickly cull objects based on occlusion or view direction. Especially when you're using complex vertex shaders, it is important that you keep the number of vertices submitted reasonably low.

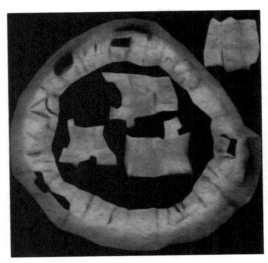
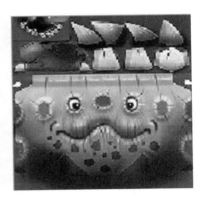

FIGURE 7.1.2   *Kodo Evolved* texture atlas examples for improved batching.

To perform this culling it is important that your application uses efficient spatial data structures. Bounding volumes can help to quickly decide whether an object is completely outside the view frustum. If your application uses a static camera, perform view frustum culling offline.

Jadestone's *Kodo Evolved* uses a fairly static isometric-style view of the scene, enabling extensive usage of offline culling as illustrated in Figure 7.1.3 and Figure 7.1.4.

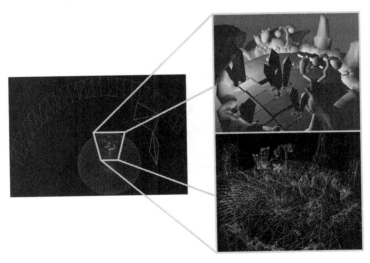

FIGURE 7.1.3   *Kodo Evolved* scene geometry before optimization.
(Left) Complete scene view. (Right) Actual in-game visible area.

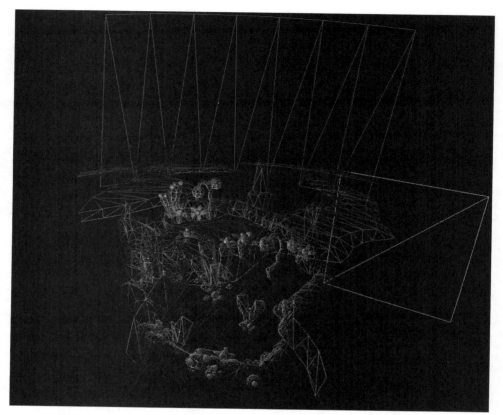

FIGURE 7.1.4 *Kodo Evolved* scene geometry after offline optimization. Note the removal of hidden and off-screen polygons as part of the artwork pipeline.

Don't lose sight of bandwidth, though. The earlier in the process geometry can be culled, the lower the amount of bandwidth used through the overall graphics rendering process. However, don't spend too many cycles or too much bandwidth passing through complex data structures trying to remove individual triangles. Try to find the correct balance between gain and effort for the best results.

Avoid "Discard" or "Alpha Test" Operations

Most, if not all, architectures today deploy advanced "early" hidden surface removal techniques, such as POWERVR's pixel perfect submission-order-independent tile-based deferred rendering approach. However, the usage of some render states or shader operations can make these optimizations ineffective.

The OpenGL ES 2.0 GLSL ES fragment shader operation `discard` can be used to stop fragment processing and prevent any buffer updates for this fragment.

It provides the same functionality as the fixed-function OpenGL ES 1.1 alpha testing but in a programmable fashion.

`discard` for POWERVR SGX and alpha test for MBX are expensive operations because they require the fragment shader to be executed or the fixed function textures to be fetched to determine if a pixel should continue to be processed or not. This effectively makes "early," that is, pre–fragment shader or pre–texture processing, rejection impossible, thus rendering any of these technologies' benefits ineffective.

For this reason you should avoid `discard` and alpha testing whenever possible. Often, the same visual effect can be achieved using the right alpha blend mode and forcing the alpha value to 0 where `discard` would be used. If you really need to use `discard`, make sure that you render objects using this shader after all opaque objects have been submitted to maximize the opportunity for these costly objects to be hidden behind already-submitted opaque geometry.

Use Sensibly Sized Textures, Texture Compression, and Mipmapping

A common misconception is that bigger textures always look better. Using a 1,024×1,024 texture for an object that never covers more than a small part of the screen just wastes storage space. Choose your textures' sizes based on how they will be used. Ideally, you would choose the texture size so about one texel is mapped to every pixel the object covers when it is viewed from the closest distance allowed.

Obviously, memory constraints limit the amount of texture data you can use, and it is rarely possible to use all the texture detail you want. However, when you reduce texture sizes to try to squeeze more textures into memory, try to reduce texture resolution uniformly. It is often better to aim for a scene with uniform—though lower—texture detail across all surfaces than to have highly detailed textures clash with blurry ones.

Non-power-of-two (NPOT) texture support is limited within the OpenGL ES 2.0 core specification. This core specification means that mipmapping is not supported with NPOT textures, and the wrap mode must be set to `CLAMP_TO_EDGE`. The only use of NPOT textures should thus be for screen-sized render targets necessary for post-processing effects. Due to the mipmapping restriction, we do not recommended using NPOT textures for normal texture mapping of meshes.

POWERVR supports a proprietary texture compression format called PVRTC. It boasts very high quality for competitive compression ratios. As with S3TC, this compression format is block-based but benefits from a higher image quality than S3TC, as data from adjacent blocks is also used in the reconstruction of original texture data. PVRTC supports opaque and translucent textures in both 4-bits-per-pixel and 2-bits-per-pixel modes. This reduced memory footprint is advantageous for embedded systems where memory is scarce, and considerably minimizes the memory bandwidth requirements (while improving cache effectiveness).

Figure 7.1.5 shows a 128×128 color texture for the red Kodo character in uncompressed, 4-bpp (bits per pixel) PVRTC and 2-bpp PVRTC formats. The size of the uncompressed image is 64 kB, while the compressed versions are 8 kB and 4 kB, respectively. As can be seen, the image degradation is negligible in the 4-bpp version and probably acceptable in the 2-bpp version.

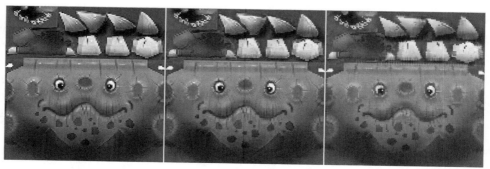

FIGURE 7.1.5 Kodo compression comparison. Uncompressed (left), 4-bbp PVRTC (center), and 2-bbp PVRTC (right).

POWERVR SGX also supports Ericsson Texture Compression (ETC). The ETC format is expected to be supported on a wide range of OpenGL ES 2.0 implementations from multiple vendors, offering good portability. However, it only includes a single 4-bpp RGB format and is thus less flexible than PVRTC.

Mipmaps are smaller, prefiltered variants of a texture image, representing different levels of detail (LODs) of a texture. By using a minification filter mode that uses mipmaps, the hardware can be set up to automatically calculate which level of detail comes closest to mapping one texel of a mipmap to one pixel in the render target, and use the according mipmap for texturing. This automatic selection only works in fragment shaders. In vertex shaders you need to calculate the level of detail parameter yourself and pass it to the `texture2DLod` GLSL ES function.

Using mipmaps has two important advantages. It increases performance by massively improving texture cache efficiency, especially in cases of strong minification. At the same time, using prefiltered textures improves image quality by countering aliasing that would be caused by severe under-filtering of the texture content. This aliasing usually shows itself as a strong shimmering noise on minified textures.

The one drawback of mipmaps is that they require about one-third more texture memory, but this cost can often be considered minor compared to the gains. There are some exceptions where mipmaps should not be used, though. This includes any kind of textures where filtering can't be applied sensibly, such as textures containing indices. Also, textures that are never minified, for example, 2D elements such as fonts or HUDs that are mapped 1:1 to screen pixels, do not need mipmaps.

Mipmaps can be created offline with a utility such as PVRTexTool, which can be found in the POWERVR SDK. Alternatively, you can save the file storage space for mipmaps and generate them at runtime in your application. The OpenGL ES function `glGenerateMipmap` will perform this task for you, but it will not work with PVRTC or ETC textures. These should always be generated offline. This function is also useful when you want to update mipmaps for render target textures.

In combination with certain texture content, especially with high contrast, the lack of filtering *between* mipmap levels can lead to visible seams at mipmap transitions. This is called *mipmap banding*. Trilinear filtering (`GL_LINEAR_MIPMAP_NEAREST`) can effectively eliminate these seams and thus achieve higher image quality. However, this quality comes at a cost, and its usage should be restricted to surfaces where the benefit-cost ratio is highest.

Target a Fixed Frame Rate

The smoothest animations can be achieved by running at a constant frame rate. By having an upper limit for the frame rate, you can save power when scene complexity is low since hardware solutions will automatically power down various SoC components based on workload.

It is important to understand that smoothness of animation is largely determined by the lowest frame rate and that high peaks and average frame rates do not serve to even out stuttering and dips to 10 fps or less. As those maximum frames per second do not contribute much to the perceived smoothness, it makes sense to limit the frame rate to a fixed value that can be achieved at all times and let the hardware idle and save power when the workload is low.

Most LCDs are updated at a rate of around 60 Hz. By setting a swap interval of 2 using `eglSwapInterval`, you can limit the frame rate to a maximum of ~30 fps, which is often considered sufficient for smooth animation for all but the fastest-moving games.

Jadestone's *Kodo Evolved* for OpenGL ES 1.1 runs unlocked at over 60 frames per second on high-end smartphones such as the POWERVR MBX+VGP–enabled Nokia N95, yet the game does not require super high frame rates. To optimize battery life, `eglSwapInterval` was used to reduce the frame rate to a very playable and stable 20 fps, saving considerable amounts of power and thus extending the device battery life and game experience.

Opaque First, Alpha Blend Last, and Discard/Alpha Test Only if You Must

The order in which objects are submitted for rendering can have a huge impact on the number of state changes required and therefore on performance. Additionally, blended objects often need to be rendered back-to-front to get the desired result.

Opaque objects are those that are rendered without framebuffer blending or `discard` in the fragment shader.

Maximum benefit is only possible when `GL_ALPHA_TEST` (see previous), `GL_BLEND`, and `GL_LOGIC_OPS` are enabled only when required, specifically when the object is not opaque. For optimal performance take batching into account: First, render all opaque objects, and at the end of the frame render all translucent objects.

Always submit all opaque objects first, before any transparent ones. Follow these four steps:

1. Separate your objects into three groups: opaque, using `discard`, using blending.
2. Render opaque objects sorted by render state.
3. Render objects using `discard` sorted by render state (but avoid `discard` if possible).
4. Render blended objects sorted back-to-front.

Due to the advanced hidden surface removal mechanism of POWERVR MBX and SGX, you don't need to sort opaque objects by depth for good efficiency. In fact, it would be a waste of CPU cycles to do so. Sort these objects in a way that minimizes render state changes instead. For example, by grouping objects based on the shader program they're using, you can ensure that each shader program used is set exactly once.

Not all state changes are equally costly. Always submit all commands to draw one frame to a render target in one go; don't switch render targets mid-frame. Per frame, sort objects by the shader program used. Inside, those groups try to minimize texture and uniform changes as well as all other state changes.

Interleaved Attributes or Separate Arrays?

There are several ways of storing vertex data in memory. One is to interleave it so all data for one vertex is followed by all data for the next vertex. Another way is to keep each attribute in a sequential array, one array after another or in completely separate locations. It is also possible to mix these two approaches. Interleaved attributes can be considered an array of structs (AoS), while sequential arrays represent a struct of arrays (SoA).

In general, interleaved vertex data provides better performance because all data required to process each vertex can be gathered in one sequential read that greatly improves cache efficiency.

However, if there is a vertex attribute array you want to share between several meshes but don't want to duplicate, putting this attribute into its own sequential array can result in better performance. The same is true if there is one attribute that needs frequent updating while the other attributes remain unchanged.

Avoid Mixing 2D and 3D Within the Same Frame

Mixing 2D and 3D content within the same frame is a common operation. However, it is tricky to get right and can easily result in excessive bandwidth or CPU cycle consumption when implemented naively.

The worst case is when 2D content is rendered using the CPU instead of the GPU. Depending on the platform, this can occur when using OS GDI calls to render text or other 2D content. In this type of situation a synchronization between CPU and GPU is enforced, meaning the CPU will stall while the GPU flushes all outstanding graphics operations; once this is completed, the GPU stalls while the CPU accesses the frame buffer. The loss of parallelism significantly reduces both CPU and GPU performance. On some platforms there might even be intermediate buffer copies, where the 3D scene is copied to another memory location, 2D operations are executed, and then finally the result is copied back into the frame buffer—obviously resulting in disappointing performance and high bandwidth consumption. Where possible, stick to the Khronos APIs to do all your rendering for maximum efficiency, or make sure that you do your own benchmarking to ensure that performance and battery life are not negatively impacted when processing 2D operations using other system calls.

Even when mixing hardware-accelerated 2D and 3D calls through, for example, the Khronos OpenVG and OpenGL ES API interfaces it is essential to minimize the number of switches between these interfaces since the context switch between APIs introduces CPU overhead. Additionally, on some platforms OpenVG and OpenGL ES hardware might not be unified, resulting in synchronization and possible buffer copy operations, as in the case of CPU rendering. Where possible, switches between APIs should be seen as layers, and the number of layer transitions should be minimized. Ideally, all OpenVG and OpenGL ES calls should be grouped and submitted together, resulting in an optimal two-layer approach where typically the OpenGL ES 3D scene is the background layer, with an OpenVG 2D top layer for GUI and overlaid information. High-frequency OpenVG and OpenGL ES interleaving is not recommended and should be avoided.

Avoid Mid-Scene Texture Updates

When you upload textures to the OpenGL ES driver via `glTexImage2D`, the input data is usually in linear scanline format. Internally, though, almost all GPUs use a twiddled layout (i.e., following a plane-filling curve) to greatly improve memory access locality when texturing. Because of this different layout, uploading textures will always require a somewhat expensive reformatting operation, regardless of whether the input pixel format exactly matches the internal pixel format or not.

For this reason it is recommended that you upload all required textures at application or level start-up time in order to avoid any frame rate dips when additional textures are uploaded later on.

You should especially avoid uploading texture data mid-frame to a texture object that has already been used in that frame. On tile-based rendering architectures this enforces the ghosting (keeping a copy) of the original texture data before uploading the new texture data. The tile-based process delays rendering until tiling of the whole frame is completed, meaning that the old texture data has not yet been used to render the actual scene when the application makes a mid-scene texture change.

Allocating and uploading new texture data for usage by the 3D core is a bandwidth-intense operation; this means that changing the contents of an existing texture or creating a new texture during 3D rendering results in a perceptible reduction in performance. Therefore, it is highly recommended that you create and upload all required textures at the start of a game level or when the application loads.

Be Careful with Buffer Copies and Multi-Pass and Excessive Render to Texture

Bandwidth is a limited resource for embedded platforms, making the use of multi-texturing preferable to multi-pass rendering. This reduces the number of required draw calls, the vertex processing work, and the number of state changes. As a result, the overall driver overhead and CPU load is also reduced and obviously also contributes to overall lower bandwidth. Using multi-texturing also avoids the risk of Z-fighting often seen with multi-pass rendering, where the geometry in different passes ends up at slightly different depth positions (e.g., disabling lighting can result in a different driver path and hence potentially different depth values).

Render to texture enables many key differentiating effects in applications, but rendering off-screen targets consumes extra bandwidth and increases processing costs. On mobile platforms off-screen surfaces should be limited in size and color depth. They should be updated "on-demand," for example, when they actually change (no use re-rendering the same data over and over, e.g., the shadow of a static object or character or post-processing of a background that does not change) and ideally at a sensible update rate that could be lower than the overall frame rate (e.g., once every two or even three frames).

In the original emulator version of *Kodo*, Jadestone used render to texture for some effects, namely, to add refraction to some translucent crystals in the scene and to add shadows. Both were later disabled for performance reasons. Using an on-demand approach was not a viable option due to the dynamic nature of the scene; since the shadow-casting light is moving, the shadows change with each frame. Shadows were removed altogether (because of lack of development time to consider alternatives such as stencil-based shadows), and the refractions in the crystals were replaced with simple alpha blending, shown in Figure 7.1.6. As can be seen, the visual difference between using alpha blending and a refraction shader is not enough to warrant the performance drop.

FIGURE 7.1.6   Render to texture comparison. (Left) with shadows and crystal refraction. (Right) Without shadows and alpha blended crystals.

Jadestone originally implemented a dynamic glow effect for the nighttime scenes in *Kodo Evolved*. This involved rendering the whole scene into texture, followed by a high-pass intensity filter operation, followed by a down-sampling blur-filter operation. The result was then blended with the originally rendered scene to create a dynamic glow effect around bright objects. This approach resulted in eight passes through memory, specifically, four writes and four reads, thus using up a significant amount of system bandwidth not typically available on embedded systems. Because the glow effect was largely static, the Imagination Technologies Developer Technology Team proposed the usage of pregenerated glow textures, thus avoiding all render to texture operations and minimizing the cost of alpha-blended areas on screen. The original dynamic and the optimized prerendered dataflow are illustrated in Figure 7.1.7. The final scene geometry with glow objects and proposed glow overlay regions is illustrated in Figure 7.1.8.

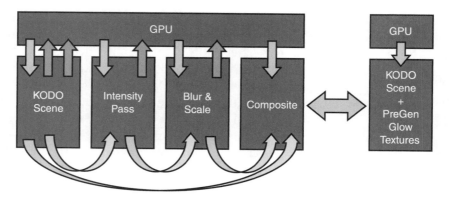

FIGURE 7.1.7 Glow effect data flow: dynamic versus prerendered optimized path.

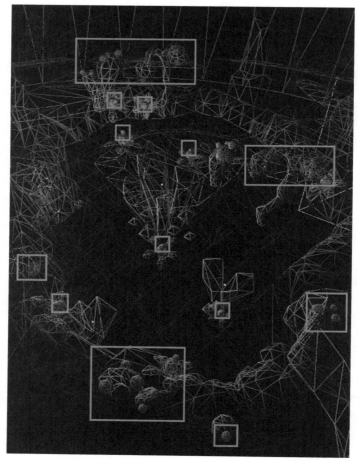

FIGURE 7.1.8 Prerendered glow texture overlay regions.

OpenGL ES 1.1 Recommendations: Fixed-Function API

This section contains recommendations specifically for the fixed-function OpenGL ES 1.1 API interface as supported by both the POWERVR MBX and SGX families of IP cores.

Use Interleaved Strip-Order Geometry Submission

Optimal geometry submission strategies can be different among devices and architectures. For the POWERVR MBX–based devices, the optimal submission mechanism uses interleaved arrays with triangles submitted in strip order. Depending on the device, a multi-draw array extension might be available that significantly facilitates the submission of strip-ordered geometry by allowing multiple strips to be submitted in a single draw call with minimal CPU overhead. On some devices this extension is not exposed, making a single indexed submission in strip order the most optimal submission mechanism; the submission of strips using OpenGL ES 1.1 core functionality requires an API call per strip, resulting in high CPU overhead.

For POWERVR SGX geometry submission guidelines check the OpenGL ES 2.0 recommendations section.

Keep the Number of Lights Down and the Lighting Model Simple

The OpenGL ES 1.1 API fixed-function lighting model is expensive, and implementations must meet conformance, meaning that no short-cuts can be implemented. For optimal performance this means that the number of light sources should be kept low and the complexity of the light model simplified, for example, usage of parallel lights instead of spot lights and careful usage of specular lighting. Performance will be variable, so device-specific benchmarking and variable quality levels should be considered.

OpenGL ES 2.0 Recommendations: Programmable API

This section contains recommendations specifically for the shader-based programmable OpenGL ES 2.0 API interface as supported by the POWERVR SGX family of IP cores.

Perform Calculations per Vertex Instead of per Fragment Where Possible

The number of vertices processed is logically much lower than the total number of fragments, so operations per vertex are considerably cheaper than per fragment.

Note that it is essential to avoid "over-tessellated" geometry within your scene for bandwidth and processing reasons. Scenes where the number of vertices matches, or even exceeds, the number of fragments result in very large numbers of minute triangles that will not actually contribute to the final visible scene; they are so small that no sampling point actually falls within them.

Excessive tessellation can easily be identified by enabling wireframe rendering (using PC-based emulation or development tools; the OpenGL ES API has no immediate support for wireframe). If large parts of your scene look "solid" despite enabling wireframe mode, then the scene is over-tessellated and the geometry complexity is too high for the given display size. Key solutions to this problem are the use of dynamic tessellation for terrains and the use of LOD mechanisms for objects.

Kodo Evolved supports both per-pixel and per-vertex lighting, scaling from a single light source all the way up to eight light sources (scene objects, light-emitting Kodos, etc.) with optional specular components. Lighting is very dynamic within the *Kodo Evolved* environment and plays a key role in the overall day-to-night transition experience, which has an extensive visual impact on the game. Given the high number of light sources, vertex lighting was ultimately preferred over per-pixel lighting. While this had an impact on visual quality, as illustrated in Figure 7.1.9, the per-pixel shader workload was simply not offering enough quality given the extra shader cycle cost. However, the code path remains available for higher-end platforms that will become available over time.

FIGURE 7.1.9   Light comparison: per-pixel (left) versus per-vertex (right).

Use Vertex Buffer Objects and Indexed Geometry

Vertex buffer objects (VBOs) are the preferred way of storing vertex and index data. Since their storage is server (driver) managed, there is no need to copy an array from the client side at every draw call, and the driver is able to perform some transparent optimizations.

Pack all the vertex attributes that are required for a mesh into the same VBO unless there is an attribute you want to share between meshes. You don't have to create one VBO for every mesh. It's a good idea to group meshes that are always rendered together in order to minimize buffer rebinding.

For dynamic vertex data you should have one buffer object for each update frequency. Don't forget to set the right usage flag (STATIC_DRAW, DYNAMIC_DRAW, STREAM_DRAW) when submitting data or allocating storage with glBufferData.

Optimize Your Shaders: Math Look-up Textures

Sometimes it can be a good idea to encode the results of a complex function into a texture and use it as a lookup table instead of performing the necessary calculations in a shader. This is a tradeoff between shader workload, bandwidth and memory usage, and precision.

Before you attempt to use a math lookup texture, always make sure that you're actually shader limited. For small functions, using a lookup table is rarely worth the effort. For example, replacing 3D vector normalization with a normalization cube map lookup may not help performance at all.

If the function parameters, that is, the texture coordinates, vary wildly between adjacent fragments, texture cache efficiency suffers. Using mipmaps will help improve this somewhat, but the loss of high-frequency detail, accompanied by a loss of accuracy, may or may not be desirable, depending on the function represented. As mipmap generation is easy, you can always compare both methods and pick the best one.

One interesting example is to approximate the whole scene's light environment using a single cube map texture lookup. Typically, this gives visually pleasing results with per-pixel quality while avoiding costly per-pixel lighting model evaluations with specular lighting for multiple light sources.

Optimize Your Shaders: Compact Varyings

Varyings represent the outputs from the vertex shader that are interpolated across a triangle and then fed into the fragment shader. Interpolation of varyings is always perspective-correct. Each varying variable requires memory space in the parameter buffer (intermediate storage used by tile-based rendering solutions that are the rule rather than the exception in the embedded market) and processing cycles for interpolation (true for all architectures). Always try to use as few varyings as possible. By choosing a lower precision for varyings, you can reduce the space and memory bandwidth required to store the whole scene in the parameter buffer. mediump may be sufficient for texture coordinates, especially if the textures are relatively small, while colors and normals can usually be stored as lowp vec3/vec4.

POWERVR SGX supports up to eight varying vectors between vertex and fragment shaders.

Optimize Your Shaders: Keep Your Fragment Shaders Short

For complex shaders that run for more than a few cycles per invocation, picking the right algorithm is usually more important than low-level optimizations. Doing research on the latest and greatest shader techniques can be a time-consuming task. To help you with this, the *ShaderX* series of books features plenty of articles that are an excellent source of algorithms and ideas for amazing shader effects. The same is true for the *GPU Gems* series. However, many of these examples target high-end PC hardware and need adaptation, not just porting, to GLSL ES and a reduction in complexity to be useful for mobile and embedded devices.

Keep in mind that these devices are not designed to handle the complex shaders used in the latest PC and console games at full frame rates. Because the number of GLSL ES lines is not always indicative of the number of actual hardware-specific instructions generated by the compiler for that shader, it is hard to give a recommendation based on shader source length. Many shader compilers, including the *PVRUniSCo* offline shader compiler for POWERVR SGX, are able to return instruction statistics for each GLSL line. To find the best balance between shader complexity and performance, you will have to benchmark and analyze your shaders.

Optimize Your Shaders: Maximize the Usage of Non-Dependant Texture Reads

Dependent texture reads are those in which the texture coordinates depend on some calculation in the shader instead of being taken directly from varying variables. Vertex shader texture lookups always count as dependent reads.

Non-dependent reads can easily be prefetched by the hardware and have a low cost. Dependent reads are more complex and consume more cycles. POWERVR SGX variants with an equal number of shader and texture units may therefore become shader limited when performing dependent reads. In this case the processing cost of trilinear filtering can be masked most of the time.

Be careful with dependent reads that are based on a high-frequency function since this will result in widely varying texture fetches. The resulting poor texture cache efficiency will produce high bandwidth usage, and, despite advanced latency (the time it takes for a data request to receive data from system memory), hiding mechanisms such as random accesses might introduce stall cycles during processing, resulting in valuable lost performance. If this type of access is essential for a visual result, ensure that there are enough other operations in flight within the system that can be scheduled while waiting for data to be fetched from memory, such as non-dependant calculations and vertex processing work.

Optimize Your Shaders: Optimize Precision

To achieve high throughput in a variety of tasks, POWERVR SGX was designed with support for multiple precisions. The GLSL ES 1.00 shading language supports three precision modifiers that can be applied to float and integer variables. Because choosing a lower precision can increase performance but also introduce precision artifacts, finding the right balance is very important. The safest method for arriving at the right precision is to start with `highp` for everything (except samplers) and then gradually reduce precision according to the following rules until the first precision problems start to appear.

The following sections provide some baseline recommendations for precision applied to typical graphical operations.

Optimize Your Shaders: `highp` Usage

Float variables with the `highp` precision modifier will be represented as 32-bit floating-point values, adhering largely to the IEEE754 single-precision standard. This precision should be used for all vertex position calculations, including world, view, and projection matrices, as well as any bone matrices used for skinning. It should also be used for most texture coordinate and lighting calculations, as well as any scalar calculations that use complex built-in functions such as `sin`, `cos`, `pow`, `log`, and so on.

With `highp` precision, the embedded pipeline might be acting on scalar values. This is to allow maximum efficiency since a traditional vector-based pipeline would execute unneeded calculations, resulting in extra power consumption. This does mean that calculations must be limited to a minimum width and vectorization should not be used.

Optimize Your Shaders: `mediump` Usage

Variables declared with the `mediump` modifier are represented as 16-bit floating-point values (using a sign bit, 5 exponent bits and 10 mantissa bits), covering the range [65520, −65520]. This precision level typically offers only minor performance improvements over `highp`, with throughput being identical most of the time. It can, however, reduce storage space requirements, and thus it can be very useful for texture coordinate varyings.

With `mediump` precision, the pipelines might act on two-component vectors matching the width of scalar operations.

Optimize Your Shaders: lowp Usage

A variable declared with the `lowp` modifier will use a 10-bit fixed-point format, allowing values in the range [−2, 2] to be represented with a precision of 1/256. The pipelines may process `lowp` variables as three- or four-component vectors. The `lowp` precision is useful mainly for representing colors and any data read from low-precision textures, such as normals, from a normal map. Be careful not to exceed the numerical range of `lowp` floats, especially with intermediate results. Swizzling the components of `lowp` vectors is expensive and should be avoided.

Optimize Your Shaders: Uniform Calculations Are OK

Uniform variables represent values that are constant for all vertices or fragments processed as part of a draw call. Similar to redundant state changes, try to avoid redundant uniform updates in between draw calls. Unlike attributes and varyings, uniform variables can be declared as arrays. Be careful with the number of uniforms you use, though. While a certain number of uniforms can be stored in registers on-chip, large uniform arrays may be stored in system memory, and accessing them comes at a bandwidth and execution time cost.

POWERVR SGX supports up to 512 uniform scalars in the vertex shader and up to 64 uniform scalars in the fragment shader.

The shader compiler for POWERVR SGX is able to extract calculations based on uniforms from the shader and perform these calculations once per draw call using the hardware pipelines. This can be very handy on platforms with weak floating-point support and allows you to offload operations such as matrix-matrix multiplications from the CPU. Make sure the order of operations is chosen so that the uniforms are processed first, though:

```
unform highp mat4 modelview, projection;
attribute vec4 modelPosition;

// Can be extracted
gl_Position = (projection * modelview) * modelPosition;

// Can not be extracted
gl_Position = projection * (modelview * modelPosition);
```

Optimize Your Shaders: Reap the Benefits of Flow Control

POWERVR SGX offers full support for flow control constructs (`if-else`, `for`, and `while` loops) in both vertex and fragment shaders. You can use these without explicitly enabling a language extension in GLSL ES.

When conditional execution depends on the value of a uniform variable, this is called *static flow control,* and the same shader execution path is applied to all vertex or fragment instances in a draw call. *Dynamic flow control* refers to conditional execution based on per-fragment or per-vertex data, for example, textures or vertex attributes.

Static flow control can be used to combine many shaders into one big shader. This is not generally a win, though, and you should benchmark thoroughly when deciding whether to put multiple paths into one shader.

Using dynamic branching in a shader has a certain, non-constant overhead that depends on the exact shader code. Therefore, using dynamic branching is not always a performance win. The branching granularity on SGX is one fragment or one vertex. This means you don't have to worry a lot about making branching coherent for an area of fragments. Apply the following rules when deciding where to apply conditional execution:

- Make use of conditionals to skip unnecessary operations when the condition is met in a significant number of cases.
- If you have to calculate the product of two rather complex functions that sometimes evaluate to 0, use the one that is less complex and more often returns 0 as a condition for executing the other.
- Don't unroll loops manually. The compiler knows when loop unrolling and predication is cheaper than a jump.
- Don't use texture lookups without explicit LOD in a conditionally executed part of a shader.

Optimize Your Shaders: Don't Vectorize Scalar `highp` Calculations

When using `highp` precision, SGX operates on scalars, not vectors. Do not vectorize computations that are naturally scalar. Be careful with the order of operations when you mix scalar and vector computations. Try to keep it scalar as long as possible. For example, when you calculate the product of two scalar values and a vector, multiply the two scalars first.

```
highp vec4 v1, v2;
highp float x, y;


// Bad
v2 = (v1 * x) * y;


// Good
v2 = v1 * (x * y);
```

Optimize Your Shaders: Don't Execute Full Matrix-Vector Multiplications with Sparse Data

If you already know that many elements of a transformation matrix are 0, don't perform a full matrix transform. For example, a typical projection matrix looks like this:

$$
\begin{matrix}
A & 0 & 0 & 0 \\
0 & B & 0 & 0 \\
0 & 0 & C & D \\
0 & 0 & E & 0
\end{matrix}
$$

So if for some reason you had to transform your vertex position to view space, another full matrix transform would be a waste of cycles. In fact, since dividing the matrix by a positive constant will not change the transformation result in homogeneous coordinates, it is sufficient to store just four values.

Similarly, non-projective transformation matrices usually have the fourth row fixed at (0, 0, 0, 1). which means you don't have to store that row at all. Instead you can just store three vec4 rows and replace the matrix-vector multiplication with three dot products as shown below.

```
attribute highp vec3 vertexPos;

uniform highp vec4 modelview[3]; // first three rows of modelview matrix
uniform highp vec4 projection;   // = vec4(A/D, B/D, C/D, E/D)

void main()
{
    // transform from model space to view space
    highp vec3 viewSpacePos;
    viewSpacePos.x = dot(modelview[0], vec4(vertexPos, 1.));
    viewSpacePos.y = dot(modelview[1], vec4(vertexPos, 1.));
    viewSpacePos.z = dot(modelview[2], vec4(vertexPos, 1.));

    // use view space position in calculations
    ...

    // transform from view space to clip space
    gl_Position = viewSpacePos.xyzz * projection;
    gl_Position.z += 1.0;
}
```

Note that if D is negative, you need to negate the projection vector and subtract 1.0 from `gl_Position.z` instead in order to avoid negative W values.

A common mistake in vertex shaders is to perform unnecessary transformations between model space, world space, view space, and clip space. If the model-world transformation is a rigid body transformation (consisting only of rotations, translations, and mirroring), you can perform lighting and similar calculations directly in model space. Transforming uniforms such as light positions and directions to model space is a per-mesh operation, as opposed to transforming the vertex position to world or view space once per vertex. However, if you have to use a certain space, for example, for cubemap reflections, it's often best to use this single space throughout. If you use view space, remember to use the method presented above.

A Developer's Experience: Insight from Jadestone into *KODO Evolved*

Developing the *Kodo Evolved* game prototype provided Jadestone with a number of insights about how well 3D graphics work for mobile games, how shaders can be used in games, and how to work with artists to realize a graphical concept. The increasing performance and capabilities of mobile hardware makes OpenGL ES games more similar to 3D games for PCs or game consoles than previous mobile games. While it is important to be aware of the lower performance of mobile hardware, the key difference between mobile and stationary hardware regarding graphics is probably screen size. Smaller screens with lower resolutions directly affect the design of a game since much less information can be shown simultaneously. This limits the number of objects and amount of detail that it is appropriate to show and which kind of graphical effects are meaningful to use. It also has implications for everything else in the game, such as GUI, game type, and game complexity.

In most aspects, a 3D game for mobile hardware is very similar to a PC or console game. Although the actual game must be smaller and simpler than contemporary stationary games, the accompanying tools can be just as advanced since they are used on a PC. When developing *Kodo Evolved*, we relied heavily on the tools and libraries made available by Imagination Technologies.

The biggest difference regarding this project for Jadestone was definitely that our previous mobile games have all been 2D, but it is clear to us that 3D graphics can be used successfully to make mobile games even better. We think they can be used to incorporate more information on a small screen without making the presentation confusing. For example, the playing field in 3D Kodo was slightly spherical; this looks more interesting, allows more tiles to fit in the view, and would be hard to accomplish in 2D.

We did not use that many shaders in the final version of the game. However, the main advantage of shaders is perhaps not that they enable more advanced effects, but instead, the freedom and precision that they allow. Shaders give the freedom to implement virtually any kind of appearance that can be thought of and the precision to make it work exactly as envisioned. This might involve coming up with a totally new and odd surface effect, but might just as well simply be used to slightly adjust a well-known effect to fit a certain situation. As a result, shaders allow games to look more interesting and stay closer to the artist's vision (Figure 7.1.10).

FIGURE 7.1.10   *Kodo Evolved* concept art.

CONCLUSION

This article provided insight into the complexities of application development for handheld devices including various types of fragmentation (device, performance, features) and possible solutions. The article continued with a variety of recommendations addressing performance, battery life, and image quality topics using Jadestone's *Kodo Evolved* game as a reference.

ACKNOWLEDGMENTS

The author thanks his colleagues at Imagination Technologies who took the time to provide valuable input for this article, in particular, Georg Kolling, Gordon MacLachlan, Mike Hopkins, David Harold, Ken Catterall, Andrew Senior, and finally the whole POWERVR Developer Technology Group for developing the POWERVR SGX Utilities and SDK.

The coauthors would like to thank our colleagues at Jadestone who made our work with *Kodo Evolved* possible, in particular, Tommy Palm, Henrik Pettersson, and Fredrik Englund, as well as Henrik Eriksson at the Royal Institute of Technology in Sweden for the encouragement and help with our master theses. We would also like to thank the people at Imagination Technologies for their dedication and help with porting *Kodo Evolved* to work with their hardware.

REFERENCES

[I3D08] Ideaworks, information available online at:
http://www3.ideaworks3d.com/downloads/Airplay_3.5_GDC_Press_Release.pdf

[FUSE08] Polarbit, information available online at: http://www.polarbit.com/afuse.html

[XFORGE08] Acrodea, information available online at:
http://www.acrodea.com/english/product/x_forge/index.html

[KISHONTI08] Kishonti Informatics LP, GLBenchmark results available online at:
http://www.glbenchmark.com/result.jsp

[Beets07] Kristof Beets, "Every Cycle Counts: Level of Detail Shaders for Handheld Devices." In *ShaderX^6*, Charles River Media, 2008

[Beyond3D04] Beyond3D Forum, available online at:
http://forum.beyond3d.com/showthread.php?t=13511

7.2 Optimized Shaders for Advanced Graphical User Interfaces

KEN CATTERALL, IMAGINATION TECHNOLOGIES

INTRODUCTION

We see today the amazing possibilities of 3D accelerated user interfaces on mobile devices—whether in rotating menus or "flipping" album browsers. It is that extra smoothness and polish that 3D hardware brings that people are coming to expect of their gadgets.

The first generation of OpenGL ES 2.0–enabled devices, with full shader support, is now entering the market, so it is time to look ahead at the kind of advanced UIs this extra freedom will enable us to build. We will also look at the necessary sort of optimizations and power-saving tips that will keep our applications running smoothly and looking cool, without killing battery life.

HANDHELD GUI REQUIREMENTS

The user interface is the one application that everybody must use. It is the first and most important software on the device, and the success of its implementation can make or break the platform. We are seeing a revolution in handheld GUIs, with sophisticated graphics becoming a "must-have" for many customers.

We can already see in the top-of-the-range mobile devices a tendency toward larger screens and flashier menus. Touch screens are gaining in importance, rapidly replacing physical buttons. With the screen now covering 90% of the physical device, the screen effectively becomes the number-one branding opportunity, making high-quality graphics essential in standing out from other devices and applications on the market.

543

Cool, yet Functional

This trend looks set to continue, with developers now looking toward shader-based user interfaces with some truly impressive results (see Figure 7.2.1). At the same time the UI must be usable and useful. Functionality is as important as style, and good performance is of paramount importance for both.

FIGURE 7.2.1   Advanced user interfaces by TAT.

Power consumption is the other important factor to consider. In many cases the GUI will be running, if not all the time, at least far longer and more often than a standard application. It must not be a big draw on the battery, or the system will simply be unusable. Fortunately, there are many ways we can tweak our applications to conserve power, especially in the case of UI, and we will discuss some of these below.

Optimizing for Power Consumption

Limiting Frame Rate and Update On-Demand

The frame rate of your application will, of course, vary with the complexity of your scene, but if your frame rate is too high, you will be needlessly updating and consuming power. At the very least, ensure that v-sync is enabled, but consider also limiting your update rate to about 30 fps, as that is often sufficiently smooth.

Additionally, in the case of a graphical UI, it is also important to consider that your scene might not always be moving. If, for example, it is waiting for user input, the scene may be completely static, in which case it is not necessary to update at all. This may be accomplished, for example, by bypassing the render loop unless a user input is detected.

DIRTY REGIONS

In a typical 3D game you will have a very dynamic, fast-moving environment in which most visible elements will be moving constantly. In the UI, on the other hand, you might have several separate regions largely independent of one another. This depends, of course, on your design, but a good approach could be to render each region into a separate viewport, only updating each as necessary.

BANDWIDTH-REDUCING ALGORITHMS

Be mindful of the data flow in your hardware, especially if you have a composite UI with graphics and video stream overlays, for example. If you are streaming a video into a texture, the naïve approach is to use the video decoder to write the decoded video frame into memory, and then create a texture from this via the graphics driver. First, however, this uses the CPU to copy and optimize the texture data (using texture twiddle, for example, to improve memory access). It is better to use video extensions (such as GL_IMG_texture_stream) that are available on your GPU to access the decoded video directly, saving you from copying the data to and from the CPU every frame (Figure 7.2.2).

For further reading on optimizations and power saving, be sure to refer to documentation provided by mobile hardware suppliers, the performance recommendations in the POWERVR SDK, and Kristof Beets' article on this subject [Beets08].

Data flow for naïve video streaming to texture

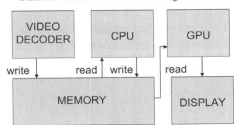

Using video extensions such as GL_IMG_texture_stream

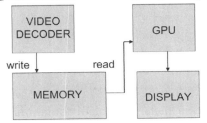

FIGURE 7.2.2   The bandwidth saved by using video stream extensions, thus eliminating the need for a CPU read/write.

OPTIMIZING BLURS

Blurring is a commonly used operation, with a wide variety of applications; it will pop up in all sorts of effects, from image transitions, to post-processing effects (such as depth-of-field, light bloom, or frosted glass, to name a few).

1D BLUR

Here is a simple blur algorithm for a single-directional, horizontal Gaussian blur: Compute a table of Gaussian weights (N values, totaling 1, where N is the size of your Gaussian filter). You will perform N texture reads per pixel, each fractionally offset from the last, and add the resulting colors to create a blurred effect.

Let's start with the straightforward way of coding this:

```
for(int i=0; i<N; i++)
{
    color += texture2D(sampler, texCoord.st + vec2(offsets[i], 0.0))
        * weights[i];
}
```

First, a few notes on optimality for this approach:

- The offsets and the weights should be calculated once, not on a per-frame basis. They will not change unless the blur parameters are dynamically altered, and even then the recalculation should only be done whenever an update is required. If they are not to change at all, consider setting them as constant values in the shader code. If, however, you want to animate the blur, there are some cheaper options you may want to consider (see section below).

- Offset, weights, and texture coordinates should all be in high precision for a nice effect. Since offsets and weights are constant, this should not be too much of a bottleneck. All color values can and should be low precision.

- Remember also to use the GL_LINEAR filtering mode rather than point sampling, as this allows you to sample points in between two texels and get an average, without costing shader cycles to accomplish it. (For example, sampling the center of a 2×2 texture will give you an average of all four pixels). Using the hardware's texture filtering will have much less impact on performance than using the shader for the same end.

The code above is also not optimal in that it contains a dependent texture read—one in which the texture coordinates depend on a calculation in the shader.

It would be better to perform this calculation (adding the offsets) in the vertex shader and then pass the result in as follows:

```
varying highp vec4 texCoordPlusOffsets01;

varying highp vec4 texCoordPlusOffsets23;

varying highp vec4 texCoordPlusOffsets45;


//...etc...


color += texture2D(sampler, texCoordPlusOffsets01.xy)
        * weights[0];
color += texture2D(sampler, texCoordPlusOffsets01.zw)
        * weights[1];
color += texture2D(sampler, texCoordPlusOffsets23.xy)
        * weights[2];
color += texture2D(sampler, texCoordPlusOffsets23.zw)
* weights[3];


//...etc...
```

In this case we are adding the offsets to the texture coordinates in the vertex shader and then passing them through as varyings to the fragment shader. We can pass two sets of texture coordinates per varying, and we can have a total of eight varyings in our shader program, which puts an upper limit on the size of N. Our texture reads now become non-dependent and can be pre-fetched by the graphics hardware [Beets08].

2D BLUR

Since the 2D Gaussian filter is separable, performing a multi-pass blur (for example, a horizontal blur followed by a vertical blur on the resultant image) is equivalent to submitting a 2D filter to the shader and sampling all around the pixel on the first pass. Thus, to create a true blur, the above algorithm can be performed in two passes, one where the offsets apply to the x-coordinate and one where they affect the y-coordinate. This reduces the size of the kernel that needs to be submitted to the shader, but it does require an extra render pass, so it is a good alternative if your hardware supports fast render-to-texture.

In addition, it is good to play with the blur parameters: the size of the kernel (N), the weight function (a Gaussian filter can be replaced with a box filter or other, more exotic types), as well as the offset calculation. In this way you can come up with a variety of interesting effects, often unintentionally. Keep in mind the factors that will affect performance, particularly the value of N.

ANIMATED BLUR

Calculating the Gaussian kernel should be performed on the CPU (it is not a per-pixel or per-vertex operation, so best to keep it out of the shaders). If your blur parameters are unchanging, then, as previously mentioned, the kernel can be pre-computed. However, if your blur is animated, your kernel will need to change every frame. Even then, however, you could (for example) have a table of Gaussian kernels ready before beginning the animation.

Alternatively, here are a few tricks or cheats for your consideration:

1. Forcing the mipmap level. This is a sort of "pixelated" blur, but due to the linear mipmap interpolation, it can look quite effective, as will later be demonstrated in the transition examples (see the mipmap blur section).

2. Create a fully blurred image and interpolate between this and the unblurred image. Obviously, this will not work for a dynamically changing image, such as a render-to-texture.

3. Do some distortion by randomly varying the texture coordinates—not a blur, but this might be just as good depending on the effect you want to achieve.

PROGRESSIVE BLUR

With render-to-texture you can blur an image and then sample the blurred image and re-blur it as many times as you like. If in each iteration the blur is slight, this will result in a very nice and natural blur.

Obviously, each iteration incurs an additional performance hit. However, if we have a still image and use render-to-texture to blur it incrementally each frame, the performance will not suffer, and it will give a nice animated progressive blur effect. Additionally, if the scene being blurred is slowly moving, the effect will create "trails."

OPTIMIZING OTHER POPULAR EFFECTS

LIGHTING EFFECTS

On a GUI, depending on your artistic preference and the overall theme, you may never need to use very advanced lighting at all.

Of course, the availability of programmable shaders makes it possible to apply all kinds of fancy per-pixel lighting. It can be very tempting to have, for instance, multiple specular light sources (with dot-3 bump mapping). Keep in mind, however, that on a (likely) small screen, displaying an even smaller widget, the lighting may be hard to distinguish, and the effect is likely to be minimal.

Tailor the effect to the object to which it is applied. Per-pixel lighting will get expensive if you introduce too many calculations (read: multiple light sources); per-vertex lighting, on the other hand, will not look good unless you have, unsurprisingly, a reasonably large number of vertices. You could have a spinning coin, for example, and this would naturally show off advanced lighting, but if the object doesn't *move*, lighting calculations are next to pointless. Consider using pre-baked lightmaps instead.

Shiny is good, however, and giving your widgets some moving highlights will add the polish that makes a UI attractive. Such highlights need not be the product of expensive calculations, however; with shaders and the proper artistic touch, you can often fake them quite effectively.

How to Fake a Specular Highlight

Often, the effect can be achieved with a very simple sort of cubemap reflection, where the highlight is more or less a white blob that appears somewhere in your cubemap (you may have to orient the cubemap and view angle properly so that the highlight appears on the object) (Figure 7.2.3).

FIGURE 7.2.3   One face of the cubemap. The other five faces are all black.

This kind of cubemap can work quite well for a simple object such as a rectangular widget. Of course, if you want to use a more detailed 3D model, it might be nicer to have a more complete environment map, depending on how well your "simple" highlight shows up. Figure 7.2.4 shows a photo flipper in the style of today's popular music and photo album browsers. We have applied our specular highlight to the flat panels; as they move, the highlight flashes across the object.

FIGURE 7.2.4 A cubemap applied to panel objects.
The specular highlight appears when the panel is tilted at certain angles.

MIRRORING

Another popular effect is to show a semi-transparent "reflection" hovering below your widgets, as if they were mirrored in some invisible surface. This can be inexpensive and very effective if done correctly (by cheating), as it basically boils down to rendering your widgets upside-down with some blending or multi-texturing thrown in. The reason for the blending is that the "reflected" object should look semi-transparent (see 7.2.5). The transparency looks best with a gradient, so that the alpha (opacity) of the reflected image decreases as you move down it.

This gradient effect can often be done without using blending proper. Instead, depending on the background, we can use multi-texturing for the same effect. The simplest method is to have a gradient texture whose color matches the background, and modulate it with the reflected image (this is the approach shown in Figure 7.2.5). Depending on the background, other techniques may be applicable instead; the gradient can be entirely procedural, for example, generated by the shader itself.

FIGURE 7.2.5   (a) Mirrored object in our example UI.
(b) Modulated with gradient texture.

USING BLENDING FOR SOFT EDGES

In our example UI, all the widgets are rectangular panels. Normally we would have to enable anti-aliasing, or else the edges of these rectangles would look jagged. Anti-aliasing can, however, impact bandwidth usage, power consumption, and performance, and on some devices it may not even be enabled.

Instead, we can render a "soft border" around the quads, with a gradient alpha (see Figure 7.2.6). The border is a sort of cutout—a quad with a big hole in the middle. Alpha blending should be enabled for rendering the border only. (Remember to disable GL_BLEND when it is not necessary to have it on. This is very simple to do and can save performance.) Optionally, in your UI you may even be able to do without blending (as with the reflections), if you can get away with just sampling the background texture and mixing it in instead. Note that we cannot do this in our example, as the widgets overlap one another.

VERTEX DEFORMS

Deformations, properly applied, can look very elegant and can serve to add a 3D aspect to a mostly 2D UI. Operations in the vertex shader are also generally cheaper than calculations performed in the fragment shader, although, on the flip side, to get a nice-looking deform one generally needs a 3D mesh of some minimum complexity. (A quad of only four vertices, for example, cannot show a nice deform effect. So to have a "wavy" plane, like a flag or banner, you would need a tessellated quad.)

FIGURE 7.2.6   (a) Hard outlines with aliasing visible.
(b) Blended border objects. (c) Combined result.

BACKGROUND AND POST-PROCESSING

Take a menu screen with some background texture, and draw a panel on top of it. Now, by passing the screen coordinates into the panel's shader you can sample the background texture. (Hint: To get the screen coordinates in OpenGL ES 2.0, it is usually enough to pass through the transformed vertex position; that is, (gl_Position.xy / gl_Position.w); scaled from the range [−1,1] to the range [0,1]. This is assuming your background is full screen. If not, scale appropriately.)

If you just do this your panel will appear invisible, as the textures of panel and background will blend seamlessly. However, in the panel shader you can play with your texture read in an infinite variety of interesting ways.

The background can be anything you like—a striking photograph, or even a 3D scene rendered to texture (but watch the performance in the latter case, and remember that the resolution of the background need be no larger than the screen size you are targeting).

BLURRING

Exactly the same blurring that can be applied to images can be used for post-processing; refer back to the different techniques for implementing blurring. The difference is simply in that we use the screen coordinates and sample the background image. Many post-processing effects use blur filters: to add a glow around bright objects, for example. Remember, however, that blurring is relatively expensive, and effects such as glow can often be replaced by a static texture or updated only as necessary.

SWIRL, AND OTHER POLAR EFFECTS

Polar effects are an example of 2D pixel effects that can be applied quite nicely to a post-processing scenario. The general concept is this: Convert the texture coordinates to polar coordinates, apply some polar function to them, and convert them back before sampling the texture.

The following is a sample of fragment shader code to do a twirl effect, but by varying the central effect function, many other kinds of polar transformations can be performed. The parameters to the function can also be varied to create an animated effect or a transition, as seen in the transition examples later on.

```
// Parameters for swirl effect; these can be animated (use uniforms)
highp float c_radius = 1.5;
highp float c_twirl = 20.0;
highp float param1 = 1.0;


highp vec2 centerPos = vec2(0.5);


// Re-align to be centered around [0.5,0.5] and normalize
highp vec2 texCoordNew = screenCoords.xy;
texCoordNew -= (centerPos-0.5);
```

```
highp vec2 normCoord = 2.0 * texCoordNew — 1.0;
normCoord /= c_radius;


// Convert to polar coordinates.
highp float r = length(normCoord);
highp float phi = atan(normCoord.y, normCoord.x);



// Effect function: Twirl
phi = phi + (1.0 — smoothstep(-param1, param1, r)) * c_twirl;



// Convert back to Cartesian coordinates.
normCoord.x = r * cos(phi);
normCoord.y = r * sin(phi);


// Inverse of earlier realignment
normCoord *= c_radius;
texCoordNew = normCoord / 2.0 + 0.5;
texCoordNew += (centerPos-0.5);


gl_FragColor = texture2D(sBackground, texCoordNew);
```

Note that the conversion to and from polar coordinates uses `length()`, `atan()`, `cos()`, and `sin()` functions, which is not ideal for performance; also note that this effect creates a dependent texture read. There are, however, cheaper post-processing operations that can be visually just as impressive.

LOW-COST EFFECTS (THAT LOOK COOL)

Negation

As post-processing effects go, this one must be among the easiest. Negation is as follows:

```
vec3 texColor = texture2D(sBackground, screenCoords).rgb;
gl_FragColor = vec4(1.0-texColor, 1.0);
```

It's literally that simple. Invert the colors of the background, but pick the right image for the background, and the result will always be eye-catching.

Color Transform

This effect can be applied to any color value but works very well on post-processing. By multiplying the color with a transform matrix, you can change the balance of colors in the scene. The following matrix produces a sepia-toned image.

```
highp mat4 colorMat = mat4(
     0.393, 0.349, 0.272, 0.0,
     0.769, 0.686, 0.534, 0.0,
     0.189, 0.168, 0.131, 0.0,
     0.0,   0.0,   0.0,   1.0
);
lowp vec4 texColorNew = colorMat * texColor;
```

Note that even this can be optimized, as the transformation only actually applies to the RGB values. Thus, a better approach, saving unnecessary calculations, would be:

```
highp mat3 colorMat = mat3(
     0.393, 0.349, 0.272,
     0.769, 0.686, 0.534,
     0.189, 0.168, 0.131
);
lowp vec4 texColorNew = vec4(colorMat * texColor.rgb, texColor.a);
```

TRANSITIONS

You can have many different kinds of transitions in your UI; you will likely require at least a few. By transitions, we mean a change in state of some sort—changing the currently selected item, for example, or moving from one screen to the next. A transition can be as simple as scrolling the widgets across the screen (a simple horizontal translation), or it could be a fadeout or a transition to another shape or image.

Vertex deformations can also be used very effectively for transitions. Instead of having a panel scroll in from off screen, try unfurling it instead.

Photo UI: Example Transitions

Many of the effects described in the previous section can be animated to create a transitional effect, based on some varying time-based parameter extent (i.e., extent = 0.0 marks the start of the transition, and 1.0 marks the end).

Let us look at some of these animated effects in our example UI. Each widget is a simple quad, with a different image applied to the front and the back. We can scroll through the images, or flip them to toggle whether the front or back is showing. The transitions we use are as follows.

Movement Transition: Scrolling and Flipping

Standard rigid-body transformations supply this kind of transition, which we use in our example for scrolling through the cover options, as well as the default "flip" transition that toggles between the front and back face of the cover. This flip simply spins the cover around by way of a rotation in the modelview matrix, using no special shader effects.

It does, however, show off our specular highlight quite nicely (see the earlier section on faking this). This reiterates the point that movement makes all the difference when showing off lighting effects. Similarly, our scrolling motion moves the widgets by rotation and translation and shows off the same effect.

Mipmap Blur (Pixelated Blur) Transition

A very simple yet effective way to blur out a picture is to use a mipmapped texture and simply decrease the level of detail we sample at (by increasing the mip level) as the transition progresses. To transition between two images it is then simply a matter of increasing the mip level to the maximum (1 pixel, solid color), and then switching the images and applying the same process in reverse (see Figure 7.2.7). The work done in the fragment shader is thus no more than a simple texture read, and would look something like:

```
uniform sampler2D      sTexture;
uniform highp float    Lod;            //mip level
varying mediump vec2   TexCoord;


void main()
{
    gl_FragColor = texture2DLod(sTexture, TexCoord, Lod);
}
```

Then the `Lod` parameter would simply vary something like this:

```
if (extent < 0.5)
    Lod = (extent/0.5 * max_lod);
else
    Lod = ((0.5-extent)/0.5 * max_lod);
```

where `max_lod` is the maximum mipmap level for whichever texture we are using, and `extent`, as stated before, varies from 0 to 1. The example here, as mentioned, samples only one texture and switches the textures at the halfway point of the transition; for a possibly smoother transition you could use a linear fade on top of this by sampling both textures at the given mip level and mixing them in the ratio of `extent` to fade from one image to the other.

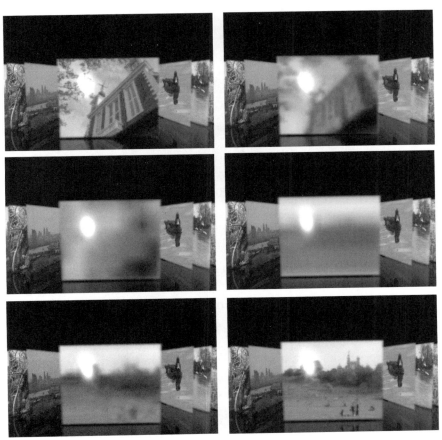

FIGURE 7.2.7   Using mipmap blur to transition images.

Swirl Transition

Here we apply the polar effect mentioned earlier, adapted to work on the cover texture instead of the background image (Figure 7.2.8). The procedure is essentially the same, but the `parameter1` in the effect function is animated using the `extent` uniform, and we are, of course, using normal texture coordinates rather than screen coordinates.

FIGURE 7.2.8 The swirl transition. Warped texture coordinates producing a multi-textured tourbillion.

The actual transition between the images is a simple linear fade, but the swirling animation helps mask this.

Burn Transition

This effect is a flashy-looking transition that is actually a fancy application of some simple dynamic branching.

The core of the effect lies in sampling a noise texture to see if the noise intensity is above a certain threshold (*unburned*) or below it (*burned*). After this it is entirely up to the designer to decide what effect to apply to the regions burned and unburned. By animating the burn threshold, this effect becomes a very nice transition.

We are using in this example the simple texture mapping of each of our two covers for the two regions; in effect, the cover will burn across from one image to the next.

The way in which the burn-line animates is determined entirely by the function that computes the threshold value. In the simplest case we can set `threshold = extent`, so the burns will appear randomly—first wherever the noise texture is darkest and then increasingly as the threshold rises linearly until it reaches the maximum (1.0) and the entire region is thus burned.

Such a threshold function will result in patchy burns, uniformly spread across the noise texture, but by adding a positional factor to the function, we can control where the burns appear first. This can be done using either vertex positions or texture coordinates. Here is a simple function using the y-texture coordinate:

```
highp float yburn = TexCoord.y;
highp float threshold = extent — yburn;
```

This will animate the threshold according to the y-coordinate. At the start of the animation where `extent= 0`, the threshold will be near 0 at the bottom of the texture and near maximum at the top. Thus, we would expect to see more burned regions higher up on the texture. As `extent` increases, the threshold value will scale up across the region, and the burn will sweep across the surface. We can use constant multipliers in the threshold function to vary the speed and scale of the burn.

In the following code, a conditional statement then sets the color according to how the sampled intensity compares with the threshold. At either extreme it samples the two textures we are transitioning between; in the middle, where the intensity is near the threshold, it instead sets the color to either near-black (for just-burned regions), or a fire-colored gradient (for regions currently at the burn line) (Figure 7.2.9). The constants are arbitrary and have been picked to best suit the effect.

```
if (intensity < threshold)
    color = texture2D(sTexture2, TexCoord).rgb;
else if(intensity < 1.5* threshold)
    color = vec3(0.1);
else if(intensity < 1.7* threshold)
    color = vec3(1.0, 15.0 * (intensity-1.5* threshold) ,0.0);
else
    color = texture2D(sTexture, TexCoord).rgb;
```

The nice thing about this effect is that there are no expensive math functions or dependent texture reads—just branching and multi-texturing.

FIGURE 7.2.9   Burn transition, showing burned, unburned, and borderline regions.

CONCLUSION

This article examined some of the exciting possibilities for shader-based mobile UIs. We have seen effects that can be implemented easily and cheaply and discussed how to optimize some that are more expensive. We have also presented an example that has colligated a few of these concepts to create a fun and visually appealing UI that includes reflections and lighting as well as a few examples of interesting transition effects.

ACKNOWLEDGMENTS

The author would like to thank his colleagues at Imagination Technologies, in particular, Andrew Senior for input and original demo code, Kristof Beets for guidance and input, David Harold and Gordon MacLachlan for their corrections and suggestions, and, finally, the Developer Technology group for the POWERVR SDK and Utilities.

REFERENCES

[Beets08] Beets, Kristof; Gustavsson, Mikael; Olsson, Erik; *ShaderX⁷*, "Optimizing your first OpenGL ES Applications"

7.3 Facial Animation for Mobile GPUs

ANDREW SENIOR, IMAGINATION TECHNOLOGIES

INTRODUCTION

With the growing popularity of avatars for mobile communication, this article describes a highly optimized routine for facial animation using geometry textures combined with matrix palette skinning. Geometry textures are used to reduce the overall workload by avoiding per-frame recalculations based on multiple morph targets. This is achieved by encoding these morph targets into textures, thus also removing the limit to the number of morph targets that can be supported compared to more traditional vertex-buffer-based approaches. Using simple blending operations, it is possible to achieve facial animation by only calculating the difference from the previous animation pose, thus reducing the calculation workload significantly compared to recalculating the weighted average of all morph targets for every frame. The geometry texture effectively takes on the role of a cache that can be reused at high speed when the facial expression does not change. Skinning is used for major movements such as head orientation, which cannot be handled effectively using morph targets.

This article will describe the lessons learned during the development of the POWERVR Gremlin demonstration, which runs at interactive frame rates on POWERVR SGX–enabled applications processors. These are expected to ship into the market in 2009.

FACIAL ANIMATION COMPONENTS

The approach to facial animation introduced in this article consists of two components: morphing and skinning. Morphing is used to approximate the fine detail motion in the face, such as expressions, while traditional skinning is used to approximate the major head orientation movements.

561

MORPHING

Morphing is a computer graphics animation technique that generates a smooth transformation from one shape into another shape. In the case of facial animation, morphing is used to transform a face of neutral expression into a variety of different expressions (e.g., happy or sad), often based on morph targets that represent components of expressions (e.g., raised eyebrow, open eye). These can then be combined to generate different overall facial expressions.

The simplest case of morphing requires two meshes. The first mesh is known as the base mesh, and every subsequent mesh is known as a morph target. The base mesh is the default expression and is the mesh that will be deformed on a vertex by vertex basis to form each specific morph target. A morph target is thus effectively a clone of the base mesh, having the same vertex structure and data order but with part of the mesh transformed to represent a different expression.

Because morphing is typically implemented using a simple linear transition between different shapes, it is most effective for limited-distance translation-based animation such as the small subtle changes due to muscle activity within facial expressions. It is much less suited for major changes, such as head orientation, where a linear approximation is not suitable and would lead to incorrect intermediate results.

SKINNING

Skinning is a computer graphics animation technique whereby a model is wrapped around a skeleton. When the skeleton moves, the model will move correspondingly. The model effectively forms a skin over the skeleton joints and is suited for larger orientation changes within animation, such as head orientation, which is based on skeleton movement.

Skinning can easily be added as a post-processing operation on top of the facial morphing effort.

CURRENT APPROACHES AND EFFICIENCY

CPU-BASED MORPHING

OpenGL ES 1.1, the fixed function API from Khronos for embedded graphics devices, does not include support for shaders. This means that morphing using graphics hardware was not possible without extensions and thus typically required the CPU to deform the base model before submission to the hardware for rasterization.

However, given the limited CPU resources, and the impact on battery life of excessive CPU usage, this approach has so far not proven to be viable for handheld and other embedded devices. Additionally, bandwidth usage using a CPU-based approach is high: The whole data set is read into the CPU, morphing is executed, data is written out to memory, and this data base is then read into the GPU for further processing. The mixed CPU-GPU operation forces extra data flow passes through memory, which consume additional power and reduce battery life even further.

VERTEX-SHADER-BASED MORPHING

The introduction of vertex-shader-capable hardware enables the first GPU-accelerated implementations of morphing. This approach typically uses multiple vertex input streams, with each stream representing a different morph target. These input streams are blended together using the vertex shader program. While this approach offloads most of the effort from the CPU, the overall efficiency of this algorithm is very low and bandwidth-intensive. This is because for every frame, all morph targets are streamed into the graphics core, and all the blending is executed even if no change in facial expression is required. On mobile platforms bandwidth and processing resources are scarce, and redundant processing is unacceptable on battery-dependant devices, thus making this traditional, brute force approach unsuitable.

MOBILE APPROACH: MAXIMAL EFFICIENCY IS CRITICAL

The approach described in this article concentrates on maximal efficiency while maintaining a fully flexible and high-quality implementation of facial animation. Specific goals of our approach are:

- Minimal bandwidth usage (e.g., avoid streaming data that is not required)
- Minimal processing usage (e.g., avoid recalculation of the same result over and over each frame, where possible)

The above goals can be satisfied by the introduction of caching and differential calculations. Caching the morph result between frames allows results to be reused quickly and easily without recalculations when the facial expression is static. Additionally, the cached result also allows the use of a "differential" calculation approach. This means we can calculate the "change" compared to the previous cached state rather than scrapping the complete previous result and recombining all morph targets again.

In more detail, this can be achieved by:

- Encoding the morph targets as "geometry" textures, thus allowing the blending of morph targets to be simplified to just blending textures and allowing the result to be cached within an off-screen render target.

- No animation means no calculation since the previous morph position is cached within the render target.

- Differential blending, rather than combining all the texture during every frame, only differences are processed based on the results of the previous morphing operation, which is cached within the render target.

Final display uses the vertex texturing functionality of the hardware to deform the facial geometry based on the animation data contained with the "geometry" render target.

OVERVIEW

This section of the article will go through the processes required to implement morphing including the creation, blending, and finally the usage of the "geometry" textures. An overview of the approach can be seen in Figure 7.3.1.

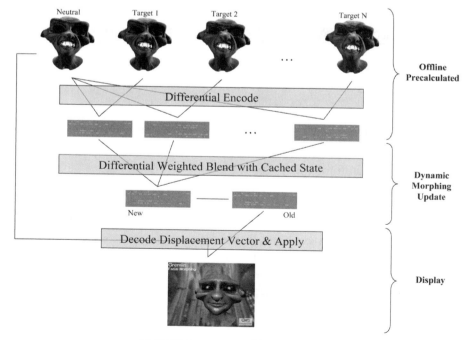

FIGURE 7.3.1 Morphing overview.

ON THE DVD
Full implementation details can be found in the demo source code provided on the DVD-ROM.

GENERATING AND ENCODING GEOMETRY INTO MORPH TARGET TEXTURES

Each pixel within a morph target texture (MTT) represents a single vertex, where the pixel at [0, 0] will correspond to the first vertex, and the pixel at [1, 1] will hold the data for vertex $n*n$, where n is the size of the texture. Storing this data sequentially from left to right within a texture is easiest, but does not offer the best possible efficiency in terms of memory access. Using a space-filling curve approach (similar to twiddled texture data) would be better by avoiding page breaks during memory access.

It is critical to make sure that the geometry buffers for all the morph targets have the exact same data order to ensure that the morphing process blends the correct vertex data together. This can be problematic with geometry optimization tools, and special care is required. Triangle re-ordering optimizations might break the uniform data ordering required for morphing by ordering the data for different morph targets differently.

It is also important to generate and use morph target textures with enough pixels to hold the size of each mesh. Power-of-two textures are recommended, so look for the nearest power-of-two texture dimensions that contain enough storage space for your morph targets. For example, a 256×256 texture offers enough storage space to encode 16,384 vertices. The filtering mode used for geometry textures should always be set to `GL_NEAREST`. This will stop the data from being corrupted by OpenGL's linear interpolation.

Encoding of the full vertex position for a specific morph target within a morph target texture requires high accuracy and would force the use of floating-point or wide-integer texture data formats. Instead, it is more efficient to encode the position relative to an average or neutral base morph target. This base target will later form the geometry that will be "displaced" by the data in the calculated morph target texture. This type of relative encoding enables the use of simple high-performance 8-bit textures since overall displacements between matching facial morph target vertices are expected to be small. Additional accuracy can be gained by the use of per-vertex scaling factors for each axis. This allows each vertex's movement to be encoded with maximal precision and avoids the situation where one large displacement reduces the accuracy of the positioning of all vertices within the morph target. Using per-vertex scaling factors does increase the decoding cost within the shader and also increases the bandwidth usage per vertex, but analysis of real-use cases has shown that this is essential for smooth animation with high enough accuracy. Our approach uses different positive and negative scale factors along each axis, resulting in six scale factors per vertex. This concept is illustrated in Figure 7.3.2.

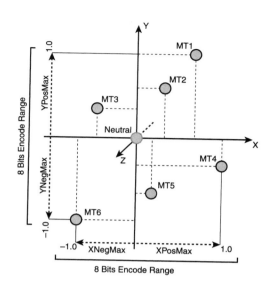

FIGURE 7.3.2 Per-vertex encoding range for six morph targets versus neutral position—simplified to XY plane.

Per-vertex scale factors and vertex encoding can easily be executed through multiple passes through the morphing dataset. This calculation can be done offline since results will be stored as textures. Note that texture compression can be attempted on these textures, but the high-frequency nature of the encoding is likely to give poor results unless data coherency is maximized by encoding neighboring vertices (with similar displacements) in neighboring pixels within the texture. The pseudo code below describes the encoding process:

```
For All Morph Target Meshes
{
    For Each Vertex in Morph Target Mesh
    {
        Compare & Store largest positive displacement along X, Y and Z axis
            relative to neutral mesh in XPosMax, YPosMax, ZPosMax
        Compare & Store largest negative displacement along X, Y and Z axis
            relative to neutral mesh in XNegMax, YNegMax, ZNegMax
    }
}
```

```
For All Morph Target Meshes
{
    For Each Vertex in Morph Target Mesh
    {
        Encode relative position into 8 bits versus the neutral mesh
        with XPosMax, YPosMax, ZPosMax, XNegMax, YNegMax & ZNegMax
        representing a displacement of 1.0 or -1.0
        Store encoded data into Morph Target Texture per Morph Target Mesh
        Store per vertex scale factors inside Neutral Mesh Target Vertex
        Buffer Object dataStore UV mapping data per vertex (linear or
space filling curve)
    }
}
```

Figure 7.3.3 shows an example of an encoded morph target texture for the Gremlin model shown in Figure 7.3.4. Note the high-frequency nature of the data set, which unfortunately renders most texture compression algorithms ineffective. Also, note that a mix of high-contrast values within a gray background is expected, with gray pixels representing neutral nonactive vertices and other pixels representing the final morphed positions of active vertices.

FIGURE 7.3.3   Linear encoded morph target texture.

FIGURE 7.3.4   Morph target matching encoded data in Figure 7.3.3.

UPDATING THE MORPH CACHE TEXTURE

The morph cache texture (MCT) is a special geometry texture that represents the current morph result and thus actually consists of multiple morph target textures blended together. As these morph target textures are already encoded, it is just a matter of adding or subtracting weighted morph target textures from the cache to generate a new morph result. Frame buffer objects should be used to implement this recursive render-to-texture approach (summarized in Figure 7.3.5) efficiently on the GPU.

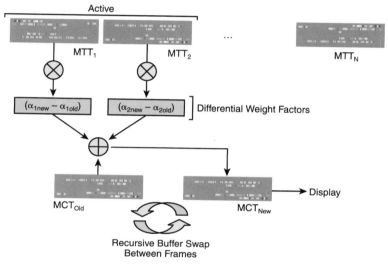

FIGURE 7.3.5 Morph cache texture update based on active morph target textures.

Differential updating of the morph cache texture requires complex management code that ensures that only active morph target textures are differentially blended with the previous result. In other words, if a morph target texture represents the movement of, for example, the left eyebrow, and the left eyebrow position is not changing as part of the animation flow, then this morph target texture should be ignored and cached data maintained.

Note that when using a texture with a size that exceeds the required number of vertices in the mesh, it is possible to speed up computation by only updating the active area of the texture that contains encoded values. Thus, rather than updating the data by drawing a full-screen quad, vertices and UV coordinates can be positioned to only draw, and thus update, a subregion of the morph cache texture. This will save unnecessary pixel processing in the fragment shader (blending of all neutral gray values).

Using the Morph Cache Texture

The morph cache texture represents the current morphed geometry state and needs to be read, decoded, and then used to displace the neutral geometry such that the correct morphed geometry is obtained.

The decode process reads the correct vertex displacement data from the morph cache texture using the texture UV coordinates provided in the vertex stream. This data needs to be decoded by first biasing the result into a −1 to 1 range and can then, using either the minimum or maximum scale factors, be converted into the correct displacement vector. This vector then distorts the neutral mesh into the target expression using a displacement map style approach.

Adding in Skinning

ON THE DVD

Adding skinning support is easy and can simply be done as a post-process operation on top of the morphing implementation described above. Example code can be found on the DVD-ROM as part of the Gremlin Demo. A simpler, easy to understand example is also available as part of the POWERVR SGX OpenGL ES 2.0 SDK.

Figure 7.3.6 illustrates different head orientations obtained through matrix palette skinning in addition to morphing.

FIGURE 7.3.6 Head orientation movement range achieved using skinning.

Conclusion

This article introduced a highly optimized solution for facial animation, and other morphing effects, for mobile embedded platforms. The proposed solution implements texture-based caching allowing efficient data reuse and differential calculations by encoding morph targets into pre-encoded textures, resulting in minimal power and bandwidth consumption and maximized performance.

Acknowledgments

The author thanks his colleagues at Imagination Technologies who took the time to provide valuable input for this article, in particular, Georg Kolling, Gordon MacLachlan, Mike Hopkins, Ken Catterall, Kristof Beets, and finally the whole POWERVR Developer Technology Group for developing the POWERVR SGX Utilities and SDK.

7.4 Augmented Reality on Mobile Phones

DANIEL WAGNER, LUKAS GRUBER, AND DIETER SCHMALSTIEG

GRAZ UNIVERSITY OF TECHNOLOGY

INTRODUCTION

Our motivation comes from research on a novel kind of user interface called augmented reality (AR). The real world as viewed with a camera is augmented with virtual objects, which are spatially registered in the scene. Probably the most widely recognized example is the *Eye of Judgment*, a computer/board game for Sony's PlayStation 3 that puts virtual game characters on playing cards, similar to the image shown in Figure 7.4.1.

 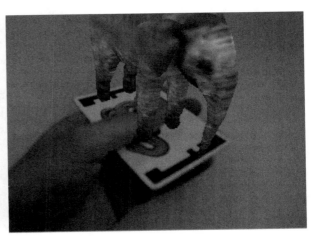

FIGURE 7.4.1 Examples of augmented reality on phones. Left: a virtual character on a square marker. Right: a virtual animal on a tracked playing card. In both cases the live camera feed is drawn as a video background, and the virtual object is rendered on top of it.

Recently, mobile phones with cameras have become attractive as inexpensive AR devices. Mobile phones have a market penetration of 100% in many industrial countries now, and their graphics performance is constantly increasing, primarily driven by the desire for compelling mobile games. Unfortunately, the phone market is highly fragmented in terms of platforms and capabilities, so that delivering a graphics application to a wide user base is a very tedious task.

What is interesting about our work to develop AR experiences on mobile phones is that until recently, AR was considered too demanding to be executed on mobile phones due to the requirement to simultaneously perform video acquisition, image processing, and graphics synthesis in real-time. We have recently shown that compelling AR applications are possible on phones [Sch07]. The solutions we have developed are not limited to AR, but can be applied to any high-performance graphics/video application.

The purpose of this article is to provide some insight in how to approach performance-sensitive issues for mobile phone development, and how to obtain sufficient platform independence to allow dissemination for a reasonably large user base. First, we describe the special needs and techniques of AR applications. The article continues with issues and solutions when developing for Symbian and Windows Mobile, OpenGL ES and Direct3D, software and hardware rendering, and scene-graph as well as video processing issues.

DEVELOPING AUGMENTED REALITY APPLICATIONS

Augmented reality combines real and virtual by accurately combining both in a single view. This works by establishing a single coordinate system that is shared between the real and virtual world. The strategy is to first estimate the position and orientation (pose) of the real camera in the real world. The virtual camera is then set at the very same pose as the real one and hence looks at the same part of the (virtual) scene. Therefore, when drawing virtual content, it shows up at the same place in the rendered image as a real object would in the real world from the point of view of the real camera.

MAINLOOP OF AN AR APPLICATION

Augmented reality applications share many features with typical games. Both aim at running at maximum speed with minimum delay to user input, and both render a mixture of 2D and 3D graphics. In this chapter we outline the typical main loop of an AR application as shown in Figure 7.4.2.

FIGURE 7.4.2   Dataflow in augmented reality on mobile phones.

- **Pre-render actions.** Similar to games, a new frame starts by reacting to user input as well as other data, such as coming in over the network and sending out new requests. Due to the highly graphical focus, the pre-render actions most often modify the scene-graph, before it is rendered later on in the "3D rendering" step.

- **Network sending.** Network communication is slow compared to other data flow inside the application. Hence, it is advised that you split networking up into a sending and receiving part: Data is sent out early in the frame and inter-leaved with computationally expensive actions until the reply is expected.

- **Camera image reading.** Retrieving and processing video images from the camera is an integral part of every AR application, except for those using an optical see-through path, such as with some head-mounted displays (HMD). The received camera image must be converted into a format that suits the needs of the renderer as well as the pose estimator. In many cases this also includes up-scaling the color image to match the screen's resolution.

- **Pose estimation.** This describes the process of calculating the device's position and orientation in 3D space so that virtual content can be put correctly next to real content. There are many different methods of estimating a pose, most of which use special hardware such as magnetic, infrared, or inertial sensors. Since these sensors are not available in mobile phones today, computer vision (ana-lyzing the camera image) is the most obvious way to go.

- **Video background.** Drawing the camera image as a background on the screen simulates a see-through capability as if the phone was a frame rather than a solid object. This method is also called "magic lens."

- **3D rendering.** Now that the video background, representing the real world, is on the screen, the application renders virtual content on top of it. To create a convincing augmentation, the virtual camera has to be set up to use the same parameters as the real one. A general problem with this method is that virtual content always shows up in front of the real content.

- **2D rendering.** Similar to games, most AR applications also show 2D information as well as user interface items on the screen in the form of a heads up display (HUD).

- **Frame flipping.** The creation of visual output finishes with displaying the current back buffer on the screen.

- **Network receiving.** The previous six steps consumed the major part of the overall processing capabilities. Hence, much time has passed since network requests have been sent out, and replies are likely to have arrived by now so that no time is lost waiting.

OFF-AXIS PROJECTION CAMERA

One of the most fundamental differences in rendering between typical 3D applications such as games or graphical editors and AR applications is the way the virtual camera is set up. In order to correctly place virtual next to real objects, the virtual camera has to mimic the real camera's attributes, called the extrinsic and intrinsic parameters.

Extrinsic parameters describe a camera's location and orientation. If a virtual camera is located at the same position as a real camera and points in the same direction, then it observes the same part of the scene as the real camera. Yet this is not fully true, since we have not specified attributes such as zoom yet. Naturally, when zooming out, a camera sees a larger part of a scene than when it is zoomed in. This is where the intrinsic camera parameters come into the game: They describe the camera's focal length (the zoom factor), the principle point (center of projection), the camera's resolution in pixels, and finally the distortion of the camera's lens. Estimating the intrinsic parameters of a camera is a highly complicated issue and beyond of the scope of this article. Fortunately, there exist tools such as the MATLAB camera calibration toolbox that do the job very well and require only minimal insight. All that is required is taking a few pictures of a calibration pattern, and the software gives us all the data we need.

To remain independent of any physical properties, focal length and principle point are typically specified in pixels. Most people assume that the center of projection is in the middle of a camera's image, yet this is not true for most real cameras. In practice, the principle point is easily off by a few percent. Camera resolution, principle point, and focal length are "linear" parameters and can therefore be modeled using a projection matrix. Lens distortion, on the other hand, is a nonlinear effect and is typically treated separately. Most AR applications only correct for radial distortion during the pose estimation (see next section), but ignore it during rendering.

To finally make the virtual camera see exactly the same part as the real one, we need to create a custom projection matrix (called an off-axis projection matrix) that honors the real camera's intrinsic parameters. Figure 7.4.3 shows the differences between a regular "on-axis" and an off-axis camera. In the on-axis case, the viewing direction is perpendicular to the projection plane. In the off-axis case, the viewing direction is perturbed, and the center of projection is not in the middle of the of the camera plane.

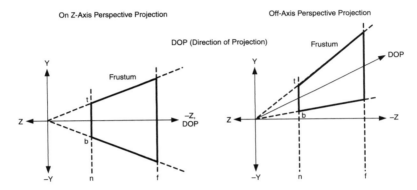

FIGURE 7.4.3   On-axis and off-axis camera models.

To calculate the projection matrix, it is more suitable to imagine the center of projection as fixed at the 0,0,0 coordinate and to shear the camera's viewing frustum. This way, the only thing that changes when going from on- to off-axis are the coordinates of where the frustum's side planes intersect with the near plane, marked with 'n' in Figure 7.4.3. Similarly, the intersections are marked with t (for top) and b (for bottom). The side planes intersect at the l (left) and r (right), but are not visible in Figure 7.4.3, since it shows the camera from the side.

OpenGL ES comes with a `glFrustum()` function that allows us to directly pass these n, f, t, b, l, r values to specify an off-axis projection matrix. The following code snippet shows how to calculate a 4×4 projection matrix directly from the intrinsic parameters. As always in this article, we use row-major order, which means that the resulting matrix has to be transposed in order to be passed to OpenGL ES.

```
// Calculating an off-axis projection matrix from intrinsic parameters
//
float matrix[16];
#define MAT(Y,X)  matrix[Y*4+X]
```

```
float dx = principalPointX-cameraWidth/2, dy=principalPointY-
cameraHeight/2;
float x, y, a, b, c, d;


x =  2.0f * focalLengthX / cameraWidth;
y = -2.0f * focalLengthY / cameraHeight;
a = 2.0f * dx / cameraWidth;
b = -2.0f * (dy+1.0f) / cameraHeight;
c = (farPlane+nearPlane)/(farPlane-nearPlane);
d = - nearPlane *(1.0f+c);


MAT(0,0) = x;      MAT(0,1) = 0.0f;  MAT(0,2) = 0.0f;  MAT(0,3) = 0.0f;
MAT(1,0) = 0.0f;   MAT(1,1) = y;     MAT(1,2) = 0.0f;  MAT(1,3) = 0.0f;
MAT(2,0) = a;      MAT(2,1) = b;     MAT(2,2) = c;     MAT(2,3) = 1.0f;
MAT(3,0) = 0.0f;   MAT(3,1) = 0.0f;  MAT(3,2) = d;     MAT(3,3) = 0.0f;


#undef MAT
```

POSE ESTIMATION

In the previous section we saw how to set up a virtual camera to reflect a real camera's intrinsic parameters. What is still missing is how to calculate the real camera's location and orientation. This process is called pose estimation. In many AR applications pose estimation is done by the use of an attached camera and computer vision algorithms. To make things easier, artificial objects (markers), optimized for easy detection, are deployed in the real scene. Figure 7.4.4 shows two different marker types.

To estimate a camera's pose a set of well-known points must be detected in the camera image. For a planar case, four points are sufficient to uniquely calculate the camera's 3D position and orientation. Hence, many markers have a square shape, which allows using the four corners for pose estimation.

The problem of estimating a camera's pose using a square marker can be split into:

■ Finding squares in the camera image
■ Checking all found squares for being valid markers
■ Estimating the camera's pose relative to one or more valid markers

The remainder of this section gives an overview of the aforementioned three steps. A detailed description goes beyond the scope of this article, but can be found in [Wag07].

Finding squares in the camera image typically starts by performing a thresholding operation that converts a color or grayscale image into pure black and white (see Figure 7.4.4). Next, the software searches for closed contours. Using a pure black and white image, a counter is found by scanning every line from left to right, searching for changes from black to white or white to black. The contour is followed until it ends at either the image border or in the starting position (right-hand image in Figure 7.4.4). Only in the latter case is the contour kept for further processing. Next, a square fitting algorithm rejects all contours that are not quadrilaterals. A quadrilateral is defined by having exactly four corners, so any contour with fewer or more than four corners is discarded. Finally, the quadrilaterals are checked for convexity and minimum size.

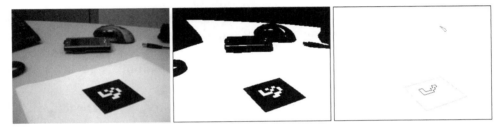

FIGURE 7.4.4   Thresholding and contour detection.

Checking found squares for being valid markers rejects those squares that do not contain a valid marker pattern. To check the pattern, it must be unprojected (unwarped) from the image into its original square shape. It is not sufficient to linearly interpolate the marker square since the pattern has undergone a perspective projection. Hence, we need to find the homography, a 3×3 projection matrix that maps the unprojected 2D marker corners into the image. The homography is defined only up to scale and therefore has eight degrees of freedom. Since any 2D point has two degrees of freedom (corresponding to its x- and y-coordinates) four points are sufficient to solve this linear system, which is typically done using singular value decomposition (SVD) or Cholesky factorization. For details please see [Wag07].

The homography matrix basically defines a local coordinate system that can be used to sample points (see Figure 7.4.5). Although the homography allows us to sample at an arbitrary resolution, it is not possible to reconstruct marker patterns of too small size. Generally, a minimum size of roughly 20×20 pixels in the camera image is sufficient for robust marker detection.

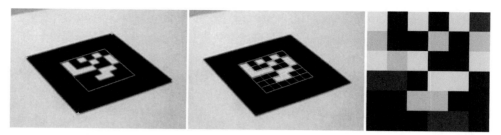

FIGURE 7.4.5 Marker pattern unprojection.

Estimating the camera's pose can be done directly by using the homography calculated in the previous step. Yet this provides only a coarse estimation and requires refinement to prevent jitter (virtual content would not remain stable on the marker). To gain better quality, the corner coordinates are now compensated for lens distortion. Furthermore, while the homography optimizes the algebraic error, we do now optimize the pose for minimal reprojection error. Since projection is a nonlinear operation, a nonlinear optimizer such as Gauss-Newton is required. Although the pose calculated from the homography is not highly accurate, it serves as a good starting point for the Gauss-Newton iteration. Hence, typically only two or three iterations are required.

A 6DOF pose is usually stored as a 3×4 matrix, where the left 3×3 submatrix represents the orientation, and the rightmost column vector presents the position. The representation is optimal for many purposes, since 3D points can be easily transformed by multiplying their homogenous form with the pose matrix. Yet optimizing all 12 values of a 3×4 matrix with six degrees of freedom only is a waste of processing power. Hence, the pose is converted into a more compact six-vector form before the refinement step and then back into its 3×4 matrix form. This six-vector pose (see Figure 7.4.6) is composed of three values for position plus three rotation values of a quaternion (although a quaternion has four values, its length is defined to be one and the fourth value can always be reconstructed). After refinement, the six-vector pose is converted back to a 3×4 matrix that can be extended to a 4×4 matrix for rendering by adding a fourth line of (0 0 0 1).

HANDLING OCCLUSION BETWEEN REAL AND VIRTUAL OBJECTS

Seamless blending between the real and the virtual world is a fundamental target in augmented reality systems. This concerns a set of different topics such as applying real-world lighting onto virtual objects or computing realistic physical interactions. Furthermore, correct occlusion handling between real and virtual objects is an important issue. The visual perception can be disturbed significantly by virtual objects, which occlude real-world objects if the virtual object is actually placed

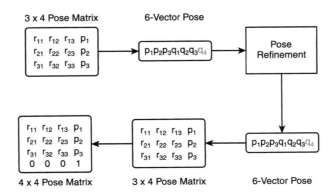

FIGURE 7.4.6 Pose representations during the pose refinement step.

behind the real world object (see Figures 7.4.7 and 7.4.8a). Ignoring occlusion handling can lead to incorrect depth perception, and important parts of the real world information could be lost. The problem is caused by the missing scene-depth information of the real world in the rendering pipeline.

FIGURE 7.4.7 Incorrect occlusion caused by missing scene-depth information.

Several approaches have been developed so far. There are two related methods to handle occlusion between real and virtual objects [Bree96]. The first method (depth-based) tries to gather an entire depth map of the real world. Dynamic scene reconstruction based on multi-vision can create such a depth map, which is then employed in the render pass. The depth values are written directly into the depth buffer to perform a correct depth test with the virtual objects. Although this method reconstructs the depth map of the entire environment, it has some serious drawbacks, especially for mobile devices: Scene reconstruction by stereoscopic vision is based on a two-camera system, which is still uncommon on mobile devices. Moreover, the scene reconstruction is a computationally costly and not very stable task.

The second method (model-based) is more applicable to mobile phones. The idea is to create a so-called "phantom" object, which represents a virtual counterpart of a real-world object. The virtual phantom object is superimposed to its genuine. During rendering only the geometry of the phantom is rendered, and no color output is created. Hence, the z-buffer is filled with the geometric properties of the supposed real-world object, and a correct occlusion can be computed. In Figure 7.4.8a the virtual object V is theoretically occluded by the real-world object A. Figure 7.4.8b shows a phantom for object A. The result is a correct occlusion of the virtual object V.

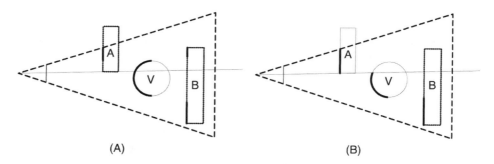

(A) (B)

FIGURE 7.4.8 Visibility without (a) and with (b) a phantom object. Bold lines show visible edges.

The entire workflow for occlusion handling of static real-world objects is presented in the following steps. In Figure 7.4.8a an example of a phantom object is given. Figure 7.4.8b shows the final results.

1. Create a phantom object of the real object model. Only the geometric properties are of interest. Textures and colors do not have to be defined.

2. Add the phantom object to the virtual scene. This additionally implies the possibility of adding physical behavior to the augmented reality application. A collision detection system, for example, could be added to provide physical interaction between real-world objects and virtual objects.

3. Superimpose the phantom object to the real-world object. This task is called the "registration" step. As long as the real-world object does not move, the phantom can be placed relative to the computed pose. In the case of a moving object, the object itself has to be tracked individually.

The render pass can be subdivided into six separate tasks.

1. Clear the z-buffer.
2. Clear the color buffer.
3. Disable RGB color writing.
4. Render phantom objects.
5. Enable RGB color writing.
6. Render virtual objects.

(a)   (b)

FIGURE 7.4.9   The left image shows a superimposed phantom object.
The right image shows the final result of the occlusion handling.

PLATFORM CONSIDERATIONS

The mobile phone market of today is very fragmented in terms of operating systems. Standardized operating systems such as Symbian and Windows Mobile are targeted at the higher end of the market, while the lower end is dominated by proprietary, closed operating systems that can only be extended with Java applications. Java is problematic in that it does not allow performance-critical operations close to the hardware, while the remaining platforms such as iPhone, Blackberry, and Android have proprietary or immature development models. In this article, we are only reporting on our experiences with Windows Mobile and Symbian.

OpenGL ES has been widely accepted as the cross-platform graphics API of choice for mobile phones. It is supported in Windows Mobile, Symbian, iPhone, and other platforms. The first mobile phones with hardware support for the latest OpenGL ES 2.0 standard were expected in 2008–2009. However, Windows Mobile also supports Direct3D Mobile, a direct competitor of OpenGL ES. Direct3D Mobile was introduced with Windows CE 5.0 (the basis for all current Windows Mobile versions), has a feature set similar to Direct3D version 6, and is only available on Windows Mobile phones. In contrast to OpenGL ES, its API is object oriented but targets exactly the same feature set as OpenGL ES 1.1. Although Direct3D is inferior to OpenGL ES in most ways, some phones only come with Direct3D drivers for hardware-accelerated rendering. Hence, supporting both APIs is suggested for a broad coverage of target devices.

Finally, M3G is a scene-graph API for Java that is implemented on top of OpenGL ES. Java code typically runs 4–10 times slower on mobile phones than native code [Pul05]. Hence, most M3G renderers are implemented in native code, preinstalled by the OEM, whereas only the application itself is written in Java. Since M3G is a high-level API, only a little Java code must be executed. Unfortunately, AR requires executing computationally expensive code (e.g., image processing), which is too slow to run in Java on phones. This problem is acerbated, as Java-only phones usually have lower-end hardware, and therefore a Java-based approach was considered not useful for our purposes.

Mobile phone hardware is mostly driven by space and battery power considerations and hence is very different from today's desktop computers [Möl08]. CPUs based on ARM-designs are predominant. Except for some high-end devices, these CPUs do not have floating-point units. Floating-point math must therefore be emulated, which is around 40 times slower than integer math. If present, the GPU is typically part of the mobile phone CPU today, which also means that the GPU and CPU share the same memory.

Basically, any modern mobile phone today has some kind of hardware graphics acceleration, yet most phones today can accelerate only 2D operations for GUI drawing. Even more, the respective hardware units are not directly accessible. Hence, when we write about devices with and without a GPU, we actually mean with and without hardware 3D acceleration.

There are three major obstacles that a platform-independent render engine has to overcome in order to run on a majority of mobile phones as well as on the PC (mostly for development and testing). These are:

- **Operating system.** There is a large and growing number of operating systems currently in use on mobile phones. For simplicity, this article only considers Windows Mobile and Symbian as well as Windows XP.

- **Graphics library.** As mentioned earlier, OpenGL ES is available on every platform, but often only as a software implementation. While this represents a highly portable fallback solution, Direct3D Mobile must also be supported for maximum device coverage.

■ **Hardware vs. software rendering.** Not considering the inherent differences between hardware and software renderer implementations can easily result in a performance drop of 50%.

All three topics listed above require careful consideration when you are aiming for a portable render engine. Additionally, augmented reality applications require fast video retrieval and processing from the built-in camera, as discussed in the next section.

APPLICATION INITIALIZATION

So far, most of the concepts and code snippets presented are actually completely OS independent (ignoring the fact the Direct3D is only available on Windows platforms). The major difference between the platforms lies in the way the application window is created. Additionally, support for user input, file access, sound, and so on have to be considered, but are not discussed here.

Even though an application might run in full screen so that no "window" is visible, most modern operating systems still bind an application to a window, for example, for managing system events. To create a full-screen application, the window is then either enlarged to cover the whole screen (including the omnipresent title and button bars), or the application switches the display into a "real" graphics mode. Some hardware-accelerated implementations even require running in full screen for optimal performance.

WINDOW CREATION ON WINDOWS XP AND WINDOWS MOBILE

Creating a window for rendering on Windows XP and Windows Mobile is very similar and requires a call to a single API function:

```
// Code fragment to create a rendering window on Windows Mobile.
//
window = CreateWindow("MyWindowClass","MyApplication",WS_VISIBLE,
                 CW_USEDEFAULT,CW_USEDEFAULT,
                 GetSystemMetrics(SM_CXSCREEN),
                 GetSystemMetrics(SM_CYSCREEN),
                 NULL,NULL,hInstance,NULL);
```

The code snipped above creates a window that spans the whole screen. The returned handle can be directly used as the window parameter for the `eglCreateWindowSurface` function. On Windows Mobile it is also advised to disable the title and the button bar to make sure that they don't show up in front of the render target:

```
// Code to disable the title and button bar
//
SHFullScreen(GameBase::GetWindow(), SHFS_HIDESIPBUTTON |
SHFS_HIDETASKBAR);
```

WINDOW CREATION ON SYMBIAN

While Windows developers can choose to create simple windows or follow the MFC or ATL application frameworks, Symbian developers have no choice. Even if not put into use, a Symbian application always has to implement the model-view-controller framework. This involves implementing the `CAknApplication` interface, which creates the application's document (derived from `CEikDocument`). The document object then creates the user interface (derived from `CAknAppUi`), which in turn creates the application's view (derived from `CCoeControl`).

A call to the view's `Window()` method finally provides the window pointer that can be passed to the `eglCreateWindowSurface()` function.

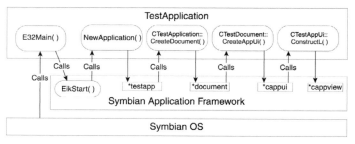

FIGURE 7.4.10 Sequence of initializing a Symbian application.

INITIALIZING OPENGL ES

After the window has been created, the EGL code for setup of the OpenGL ES context is identical for both Windows and Symbian platforms:

```
// Code fragment to create the OpenGL ES rendering context.
//
```

```
const EGLint configAttribs[] =
{
        EGL_RED_SIZE,          5,
        EGL_GREEN_SIZE,        6,
        EGL_BLUE_SIZE,         5,
        EGL_ALPHA_SIZE,        EGL_DONT_CARE,
        EGL_DEPTH_SIZE,        16,
        EGL_STENCIL_SIZE,      EGL_DONT_CARE,
        EGL_SURFACE_TYPE,      EGL_WINDOW_BIT,
        EGL_SAMPLE_BUFFERS,      0,
        EGL_NONE
};


EGLint majorVersion, minorVersion, numConfigs;
EGLDisplay eglDisplay = eglGetDisplay(EGL_DEFAULT_DISPLAY);
eglInitialize(eglDisplay, &majorVersion, &minorVersion);
eglGetConfigs(eglDisplay, NULL, 0, &numConfigs);
eglChooseConfig(eglDisplay, configAttribs, &eglConfig, 1, &numConfigs);
EGLContext eglContext = eglCreateContext(eglDisplay, eglConfig, NULL, NULL);
EGLSurface eglWindowSurface = eglCreateWindowSurface(eglDisplay, eglConfig,
window, NULL);
```

In the code snippet above, which works on Windows as well as Symbian, the window parameter represents either a handle or a pointer to the previously created window. `configAttribs` is an array of type and value pairs. It defines settings such as color depth, stencil size, and so on.

INITIALIZING DIRECT3D MOBILE

Similar to OpenGL ES, Direct3D Mobile requires filling a structure with configuration data. In contrast to OpenGL ES, which uses an array with key-value pairs, Direct3D introduces a specific struct of type D3DMPRESENT_PARAMETERS.

```
D3DMPRESENT_PARAMETERS d3dmpp;
memset( &d3dmpp, 0, sizeof(d3dmpp) );
d3dmpp.Windowed = TRUE;
d3dmpp.SwapEffect = D3DMSWAPEFFECT_DISCARD;
```

```
d3dmpp.BackBufferFormat = D3DMFMT_UNKNOWN;

d3dmpp.EnableAutoDepthStencil = TRUE;

d3dmpp.AutoDepthStencilFormat = D3DMFMT_D16;

pD3DM = Direct3DMobileCreate(D3DM_SDK_VERSION);

pD3DM->CreateDevice(D3DMADAPTER_DEFAULT, D3DMDEVTYPE_DEFAULT, hWnd, 0,
&d3dmpp, & pd3dmDevice);
```

The code above first fills the parameters `struct` with the required settings. Then Direct3D Mobile is initialized, and finally a device object is created that is automatically bound to the previously created window via the `hWnd` parameter.

GRAPHICS API ABSTRACTION

There are two major design choices for how to abstract a graphics API, which both have their clear advantages and weaknesses. Hence, both approaches are common in practice.

A thick-layer approach provides a high-level unified rendering API to the application programmer that most often includes many advanced methods such as rendering of complete levels, sky-boxes, or animated characters. Naturally, such an approach strongly depends on the actual application, for example, the type of game to develop. An advantage of such a high-level approach is that the implementation has full control over the wrapped graphics API and can therefore gain optimal performance. Furthermore, such an approach can effectively hide even large differences of APIs. For example, a high-level renderer could provide exactly the same API, while wrapping a polygon rasterizer (such as Direct3D or OpenGL) or a ray-tracer or a volume renderer. Even though the latter two approaches might not use the concept of polygonal data at all, the high level of abstraction could easily annihilate this fundamental difference.

The alternative to the approach above is a thin-layer wrapper that tries to increase the level of abstraction over the wrapped API as little as possible. The obvious advantage is that only a little code has to be written for a thin layer. At the same time, this approach only works if the various APIs to be wrapped are similar enough to fit under the common thin layer. In practice, most 3D engines put another layer on top of the thin layer, which then adds high-level features.

Although not apparent at first sight, Direct3D Mobile and OpenGL ES 1.x are actually very similar. Although the former implements an object-oriented API, while the latter uses a state machine concept, both APIs target exactly the same kind of feature set, which naturally leads to similar results.

There are three basic design choices for implementing a thin layer approach:

- **Virtual methods.** This is the textbook approach to object-oriented programming. A set of interfaces, specified using pure virtual methods, is defined. Each implementation must implement all methods or the compiler will complain. While this is the most beautiful approach from a pure object-oriented point of view, it severely suffers from low performance if the virtual functions are called at a high frequency. The problem lies in the way virtual methods are implemented. Typically, the compiler creates a function lookup table for each class. When a method is called, the CPU first looks up the method and then calls it. Since the method's address is not known in advance, this flushes the processor pipeline and hence creates a stall. The negative effect depends on the frequency at which these functions are called, as well as the length of the processor pipeline. Although graphics functions are not called that often and mobile phone processors have short pipelines, we do not recommend using this approach.

- **Non-virtual, non-inline methods.** Using this approach, graphics-API-specific functions are wrapped inside an implementation file. Classes are implemented without usage of virtual members, so there is no penalty for virtual function calls anymore. On the other hand, it is not possible to formally specify an interface to be implemented. While virtual methods are resolved at runtime (when the method is called), these methods are resolved at link time. If methods are wrongly declared or not declared at all, the compiler complains. If methods are declared, but implemented, the linker complains. This approach trades object-oriented design principles for faster code: Only when a function is called, can the compiler tell if the function's signature matches the specification.

- **Inline functions.** The usage of inline functions or methods clearly marks the fastest approach. Since the compiler is able to see the actual implementation of the wrapper when a function is called, it can often optimize the wrapper completely away. The downside of this approach is that the whole 3D engine now depends on the graphics API, although hidden from the programmer. Functions are bound at compile time and cannot be switched at runtime by loading a different DLL.

Using the second approach (non-virtual, non-inline methods), the easiest method is to informally define a common API that is implemented by both the OpenGL ES and the Direct3D Mobile wrapper. The wrapper can be outsourced to a separate module for static or dynamic linking (lib or dll). A choice that remains is whether to implement an object-oriented or a C-style API. Since OpenGL ES and Direct3D Mobile each use a different method, the choice seems arbitrary. Yet, considering the problems with writing to static data on certain platforms, such as Symbian, an object-oriented approach provides higher portability.

Most graphics concepts such as lights and materials are mostly the same on both OpenGL ES and Direct3D Mobile. It is therefore advised that you create simple, platform-independent structures for storing their configurations. The following code snippets show example implementations that can be easily interpreted by both wrappers:

```
/// Specifies properties of a light
struct Light {

        enum TYPE {

                TYPE_DIRECTIONAL,

                TYPE_POINT

        };


        TYPE        type;

        Vec3X        position;

        Vec4X        ambient, diffuse, specular;
};


/// Specifies properties of a material
struct Material
{
        Color4X        ambient, diffuse, specular, emission;

        FixedX                shininess;
};
```

Vec3X and Vec4X (as well as Color4X) are 3D and 4D vectors based on 32-bit fixed-point values. FixedX represents a single 32-bit fixed point. While most data types (3D and 4D vectors) are compatible between OpenGL ES and Direct3D, special care has to be taken when it comes to handling of matrices. Both renderers use 4×4 matrices to specify transformations, yet Direct3D (Mobile) expects matrices in row-major order, as most textbooks use it. This way, the internal array stores the matrix entries row by row. OpenGL (ES), on the other hand, expects matrices in a column-major order (see Figure 7.4.11). The render engine developer has to decide which methods to use (most developers prefer row-major) and take care to transpose matrices for the graphics API that does not follow the selected order.

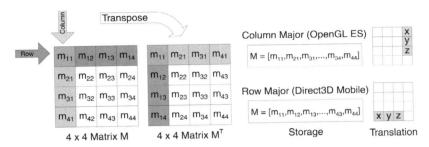

FIGURE 7.4.11   Column major vs. row major matrices.

TEXTURE MANAGEMENT

Other than for lights, materials, and so on, which can be described compactly and efficiently using a common structure, textures require more work. The major difference is that OpenGL ES and Direct3D Mobile do not use the same texture coordinate system: OpenGL ES specifies the origin in the lower-left corner, and Direct3D Mobile in the upper-left corner. Hence, texture coordinates have to be adapted in one direction or the other. Mikey Wetzel gives an excellent overview on the coordinate system differences between OpenGL and Direct3D in *ShaderX*[6] [Wen08]. Instead of adapting texture coordinates, one can also flip the texture image itself. This can easily be done during the loading of textures, but might create problems with textures of other sources such as when using PBuffers.

Textures are always stored in video memory, requiring the developer to keep a handle, either an object ID or pointer that identifies the texture. This suggests the idea of putting this handle into a higher-level object, a texture class that provides additional features, such as loading of textures of bookkeeping texture memory usage.

GEOMETRY MANAGEMENT CONSIDERATIONS

Compared to textures, management of geometry data is much more involved and requires API-specific solutions. This decision is driven by the much more data-intensive nature of geometry as well as the fact that geometry is specified quite differently in OpenGL ES and Direct3D Mobile. There are three main variants of how vertex (and index) data can be specified across the two APIs:

- **Direct3D vertex buffers.** Buffers are created once; updating then requires locking the buffer, writing new data, and finally unlocking. Since all types of vertex data (coordinate, normals, etc.) go into a single buffer, the buffer layout, called "flexible vertex format," has to be specified, and data has to be packed accordingly. For drawing, the vertex (and index buffer) is bound and followed by a call to `DrawPrimitive()` or `DrawIndexedPrimitive()`.

- **OpenGL ES vertex arrays.** Different than both other variants, all geometry data stays in client-side (application allocated) memory when using vertex arrays. Hence, there is no preparation step. All types of vertex data are specified as separate pointers right before rendering the object. Since strides can be specified too, data can be interleaved like for Direct3D, which often results in improved cache coherence. Finally, `glDrawElements()` (for indexed data, also requiring a pointer and index array) or `glDrawArrays()` (for non-indexed) rendering is called.

- **OpenGL ES vertex buffer objects.** Similar to Direct3D, vertex buffers are created once and then bound before usage, such as updating or rendering. The very same render functions (`glDrawElements` and `glDrawArrays`) as for vertex arrays are called, yet the renderer internally uses the bound buffers rather than array pointers.

While Direct3D Mobile always requires using vertex buffers, OpenGL ES comes in two variants: OpenGL ES 1.0 does not know about vertex buffers, which were only added with version 1.1. Instead, data has to be always specified using vertex arrays, which is ineffective for hardware implementations that prefer storing vertex data at the server side (graphics memory). On the other hand, using vertex arrays requires fewer API calls (no buffers need to be created or updated), which can be superior for geometry that is very small or changes on a frame by frame basis. In practice, though, one can expect that hardware OpenGL ES renderers support vertex arrays by implementing them on top of vertex buffers internally, which annihilates the advantage of using vertex arrays in this case, too.

For optimal performance, a renderer must therefore implement support for all three variants. It is obvious that support for Direct3D Mobile vs. OpenGL ES is selected at compile time. Yet also, support for vertex buffers is compile-time dependent, since OpenGL ES 1.0 implementations miss the required API functions and would therefore prevent the application from binding the OpenGL ES DLL at startup. As an alternative, the application could bind the buffer functions manually at startup and thereby dynamically detect vertex buffer support.

In the following we describe how to implement a geometry buffer class that provides a unique API for all three variants. The API of such a geometry buffer can be very simple: As a minimum it must allow specifying vertices, normals, texture coordinates, and colors as well as indices. Furthermore, hints for telling the renderer about the nature of the data (changes often, rarely, never) are useful so that the renderer can decide how to store the data. After all parameters have been set, the object can be rendered using a single call (not taking surface attributes into account). This means that the geometry buffer manages all data storage internally.

GEOMETRY RENDERING WITH DIRECT3D MOBILE

The following code snippet shows in a simplified form (production code would include many checks) how geometry is specified and rendered in Direct3D.

```
// Direct3D Mobile - Creating and filling the vertex buffer
//
unsigned int fvfSize = getFVFSize(geometryFlags);
unsigned int dstStep = fvfSize/4;
unsigned int fvfD3Dflags = getFVFD3DFlags(geometryFlags);
pd3dmDevice ->CreateVertexBuffer(numVertices*fvfSize, 0, fvfD3Dflags,
pool, &pVB));
pVB->Lock(0, 0, (void**)&pVertices, 0);
const float* src = verticesPtr;
float* dst = (float*)pVertices;

for(size_t i=0; i<numVertices; i++)
{
dst[0] = src[0];
dst[1] = src[1];
dst[2] = src[2];
dst += dstStep;
src += 3;
}

if(geometryFlags & FLAGS_NORMALS)
{
  ...
}

pVB->Unlock();

// Direct3D Mobile - Rendering
//
pd3dmDevice->SetStreamSource(0, pVB, fvfSize);
```

```
D3DMPRIMITIVETYPE d3dPrimType =
(D3DMPRIMITIVETYPE)RendererD3D::translatePrimTypeToNative(primType);

size_t numPrims = Render::getPrimCountFromType(primType, numVertices);

PD3DMDevice->DrawPrimitive(d3dPrimType, 0, numPrims);
```

The first two lines calculate the Direct3D flexible vertex format and the vertex size depending on the set of geometry attributes, such as normals, texture coordinates, and so on that will be rendered. Next, a vertex buffer of the correct size is created. The appropriate memory pool (video or system memory) has been determined beforehand. Finally, the vertex data (only 3D coordinates here) is copied into the buffer, which is then unlocked.

For rendering the object, the vertex buffer is specified as a stream source. `DrawPrimitive()` requires passing the primitive type, which has to be translated from a platform-independent value to a Direct3D parameter.

GEOMETRY RENDERING USING OPENGL ES VERTEX ARRAYS

The use of vertex arrays requires that the respective data is stored in client memory. This is different from the Direct3D Mobile and OpenGL ES vertex buffer objects, which store data in server memory. This means that valid vertex arrays must be available each time the object is rendered, which requires deciding who is responsible for maintaining the vertex arrays: The API wrapper can either buffer the data internally (doubling the memory requirements in case the application programmer decides to also keep a copy), or it can simply demand that the application programmer keep the vertex arrays as long as the object is rendered. While the first approach can waste memory, the latter one is dangerous if the programmer does not follow the rules.

Since no OpenGL ES buffers are required in this approach, the following code snippet only shows the rendering part.

```
// OpenGL ES Vertex Arrays — Rendering
//
GLenum mathType = RendererGL::getInternalMathTypeAsGLEnum();

GLenum glPrimType = RendererGL::translatePrimTypeToNative(primType);


glEnableClientState(GL_VERTEX_ARRAY);

glVertexPointer(3, mathType, 0, getVertices());


if(const void* normals = getNormals())
```

```
{
glNormalPointer(mathType, 0, normals);
glEnableClientState(GL_NORMAL_ARRAY);
}
else
glDisableClientState(GL_NORMAL_ARRAY);

If(const void* texCoords = getTextureCoordinate())
{
…
}


glDrawArrays(glPrimType, 0, (GLsizei)numVertices);
```

getInternalMathTypeAsGLEnum() returns either GL_FLOAT or GL_FIXED, depending on whether the engine stores data as floating point or fixed point internally. Like the Direct3D case, a function that translates the platform-independent primitive type to an OpenGL ES parameter is required. Then vertex data (which is expected to always be available) is specified. In case other geometry attributes (normals, etc.) are present, the respective client state is activated. Finally, the 3D object is rendered using a single call.

GEOMETRY RENDERING USING OPENGL ES VERTEX BUFFER OBJECTS

OpenGL ES vertex buffers are very similar to those in Direct3D Mobile, except that each geometry attribute is specified separately, rather than using a single buffer. Each buffer is then bound, and the respective data set is uploaded into server memory.

```
// OpenGL ES Vertex Buffers — Creating and filling the vertex buffer
//
GLenum bufferType = getBufferTypeFromHints();
glGenBuffers(getNumBuffers(), buffers);


glBindBuffer(GL_ARRAY_BUFFER, buffers[VERTEX_BUFFER]);
glBufferData(GL_ARRAY_BUFFER, (GLsizeiptr)(numVertices*sizeof(FixedX)*3),
getVertices(), bufferType);
```

```
if(getNormals())
{
glBindBuffer(GL_ARRAY_BUFFER, buffers[NORMAL_BUFFER]);
glBufferData(GL_ARRAY_BUFFER, (GLsizeiptr)(numVertices*sizeof(FixedX)*3),
getNormals(),bufferType);
}


if(getTextureCoordinates())
{
        …
}


// OpenGL ES Vertex Buffers — Rendering
//
GLenum mathType = RendererGL::getInternalMathTypeAsGLEnum();
GLenum glPrimType = RendererGL::translatePrimTypeToNative(primType);


glEnableClientState(GL_VERTEX_ARRAY);
glBindBuffer(GL_ARRAY_BUFFER, buffers[VERTEX_BUFFER]);


if(Components&Render::PRIM_NORMALS)
{
       glEnableClientState(GL_NORMAL_ARRAY);
       glBindBuffer(GL_ARRAY_BUFFER, buffers[NORMAL_BUFFER]);
}
else
       glDisableClientState(GL_NORMAL_ARRAY);


if(Components&Render::PRIM_TEXCOORDS)
{
       …
}


glDrawArrays(glPrimType, 0, (GLsizei)numVertices);
```

As can be seen, rendering works very similarly to OpenGL ES with vertex arrays, whereas the buffering concept is similar to Direct3D (except for the interleaving).

The API of the envisioned geometry buffer is much simpler than working directly with Direct3D Mobile or OpenGL ES. Specifying data requires only a single call per data type, and rendering is performed with a single function call, too. Of course, this is not because OpenGL ES or Direct3D Mobile would be unreasonably complex. The price for a simplified API is paid with a reduced flexibility, which on the other hand might be perfectly reasonable for a render engine with a clearly defined purpose.

COORDINATE SYSTEMS AND MATRIX STACKS

The final difference between the Direct3D Mobile and OpenGL ES APIs discussed here concerns coordinate systems and how to specify transformations.

OpenGL (ES) uses a right-handed coordinate system, whereas Direct3D (Mobile) uses a left-handed coordinate system. Yet this is not entirely true, since the actual renderer does not care about handedness. In the end the renderer works with 4×4 matrices and does not know about the specific meanings of the matrices in use. On the other hand, OpenGL's "high-level" matrix functions such as `glTranform()`, `glRotate()`, and so on create right-handed matrices. Since there is no counterpart of such operations in Direct3D Mobile, it is advised that you not use these functions anyway and instead write custom routines that stick to one handedness.

The same as for object transformation also applies to projection matrices. Creating custom projections ensures compatibility.

Another difference between OpenGL ES and Direct3D Mobile is that Direct3D Mobile uses three rather than just two matrices to define the object and camera transformation. In addition to the world and projection matrix, Direct3D Mobile knows a view matrix. A renderer that targets both APIs can simply ignore the Direct3D view matrix and use the world matrix to mimic the OpenGL model-view matrix.

Direct3D Mobile does not include any kind of attribute or matrix stacks. Although matrix stacks are available in OpenGL ES, there are several good reasons for not using them and instead creating custom stacks for OpenGL ES, too (assuming that matrix stacks are required by the renderer...):

■ **Portability.** A render engine that runs on top of OpenGL ES and Direct3D Mobile has to implement custom matrix stacks for Direct3D Mobile anyway. Hence, the same mechanism can be used for OpenGL ES, too.

- **Performance.** As pointed out by Atkin [Atk06], most software implementations implement all matrix operations in floating point in order to achieve full precision and numeric range as required for full compliance. Yet many applications do not benefit from the enhanced precision and range, but suffer from the decreased performance due to floating-point usage. With custom matrix operations the developer can decide whether to use floating point or fixed point.

- **Stack size.** The sizes of the matrix stacks are typically very small and easily create problems with large scene-graphs. For example, the typical limit for the projection matrix stack is 2, which is not enough when more than two cameras are present in a scene-graph.

HARDWARE VS. SOFTWARE RENDERING

While both hardware and software implementations of OpenGL ES and Direct3D mobile provide the same feature set, their performance characteristics are different, as the OpenGL ES software implementations tend to be faster. They are typically implemented using runtime code generation to overcome the complexity problem of the pixel pipeline: OpenGL ES allows specifying around a dozen parameters that define the fragments output color. General-purpose code that can cope with all combinations would either be enormously slow or immensely large. Instead, advanced implementations create optimized code for each parameter combination as needed at runtime.

Besides pure software and hardware implementations, mixed approaches are common. Similar to the introduction of hardware 3D support on desktop PCs in the 1990s, some mobile designs today only implement the pixel stage in hardware, while running the vertex stage in the driver and therefore on the CPU.

Hardware rendering obviously has the advantage of providing much more raw processing power than software rendering, which usually removes the need to carefully reduce the vertex count of 3D meshes. Furthermore, texturing is typically as fast as simple Gouraud shading, making texturing a free option to select. Unfortunately, these GPUs, which are primarily targeting games, are often not very fast in uploading textures, which poses a severe problem for efficient rendering of the video background in an AR application.

While pure hardware implementations are usually well balanced, smaller designs often implement only the rasterization stage in hardware. Pure software renderers typically suffer from bottlenecks in the pixel pipeline, whereas mixed designs are more often vertex limited (see Table 7.4.1). The Intel 2700G as well as the NVIDIA Goforce 4500 GPUs are typical examples of mixed designs.

TABLE 7.4.1 Comparing Software, Hardware, and Mixed Implementations

	Pure Software	**Mixed S/W-H/W**	**Pure Hardware**
Vertex stage	Software	Software	Hardware
Pixel stage	Software	Hardware	Hardware
Typical limits	Pixels	Vertices	–
Framebuffer access	Yes	No	No
Fast texturing	No	Yes	Yes

The main bottleneck of pure software renderers is usually the pixel pipeline, especially when making intensive use of texturing. As a unique advantage, these implementations allow direct frame buffer access, which enables copying the video background directly into the frame buffer, thereby bypassing slow texture-mapping routines. Furthermore, since the frame buffer of these designs is always in system memory, this copy operation is extremely fast. Under specific circumstances such as when rendering simple 3D graphics only, a pure software implementation can clearly outperform a built-in graphics chip.

A high-level augmented reality toolkit is therefore required to implement multiple render paths to make optimal use of the strengths of each kind of renderer. It has to provide different routines for 2D graphics operations, such as drawing video background or 2D GUI elements. When running on hardware 3D, direct frame buffer access is usually not available, and one has to rely on texture mapping to draw bitmaps onto the screen, while in the software rendering case, these bitmaps can be directly copied into the frame buffer.

The following two subsections explain how to optimally set up for hardware (on-screen) and software (off-screen) rendering. Since we assume that Direct3D Mobile will only be used for hardware-accelerated rendering, we restrict the discussion to how to set up OpenGL ES.

ON-SCREEN RENDERING

On-screen rendering is kind of the default and simpler case, since OpenGL ES contains comfortable EGL methods for setting up the render target (for more information about EGL methods, see www.khronos.org/egl).

All that is required is a call to the

```
EGLSurface eglCreateWindowSurface(EGLDisplay dpy,
      EGLConfig config, NativeWindowType win,
const EGLint *attrib list);
```

function. The only parameter that is different from the other `eglCreate` functions is `NativeWindowType`, which refers to a previously created window. On Windows (XP and Mobile) this type represents a standard window handle, while on Symbian it is a pointer to a `RWindow` object. In both cases the application developer has to create a native window beforehand, to which OpenGL ES then binds its render target.

A hardware-accelerated OpenGL ES driver is always specific to the device it is installed on and hence knows how to correctly bind its render target to a window, so this is guaranteed to work well. Unfortunately, this is not the case for software rendering: Due to bad display drivers on many current mobile phones, blitting the framebuffer into video memory can easily fail. OpenGL ES software implementations are typically not prepared to handle such cases, which is another reason to use off-screen rendering when no hardware acceleration is available.

OFF-SCREEN RENDERING

The EGL library provides two methods of off-screen rendering. The first method uses a PBuffer, which is allocated in non-visible graphics memory. Its main purpose is to support accelerated off-screen rendering, for example, for binding one render target as a texture to be use for rendering into a second render target. Similar to window surfaces, PBuffers do not provide direct access. Because of that we don't go into any more detail on PBuffers.

A PixMap represents a frame buffer that is always located in system memory, which means that it allows direct access to the stored pixel data. At the same time, this also means that hardware-accelerated OpenGL implementations do not support PixMap surfaces since they can only render into video memory.

Creating a PixMap render target works similarly to creating a window surface. Instead of creating a window beforehand, the application developer simply creates a native bitmap using OS functions, which is then passed to

```
EGLSurface eglCreatePixmapSurface(EGLDisplay dpy,
EGLConfig config, NativePixmapType pixmap, const EGLint *attrib list);
```

either as a handle (Windows XP or Mobile) or pointer (Symbian). Since the bitmap was created manually, one can use OS-specific functions to gain access to the internal pixel data, for example, for blitting a full-screen video background or drawing 2D GUI elements.

The main difference between PixMap and window surfaces lies in the fact that OpenGL ES does not feel responsible for presenting the PixMap render target on the screen. While one can simply call `eglSwapBuffers()` for the window surface, drawing PixMaps has to be done manually. On the other hand, this allows more advanced methods of bit blitting, such as using specialized libraries—e.g., PocketHAL (see www.droneship.com)—that support various methods of frame buffer blitting (DirectDraw, GDI, Gapi, raw video access, or even device-specific methods) to gain optimal performance as well as compliance. For this reason alone, PixMaps present the preferred method when using software rendering.

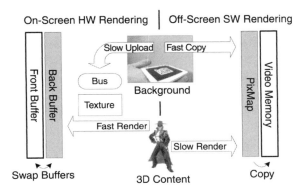

FIGURE 7.4.12   Software vs. hardware rendering in an AR application.

SCENE-GRAPH RENDERING

Although not so common in games, scene-graphs are omnipresent in graphics research. Their clear strength is flexibility. A scene-graph describes a hierarchical relationship between objects, which naturally models the real world: Most objects in close proximity are not somehow related to each other. Hence, objects can be grouped and parent-child relationships can be defined in a scene-graph. As an example, a hand can be modeled as the child object of the arm, which again is the child object of the character's body. When the body moves, both hand and arm move along. When the arm is lifted, the hand naturally shall be lifted too. The relationships are executed by traversing the scene-graph and applying transformations of an object to all its children, too.

Scene-graphs are typically implemented in object-oriented languages, such as C++. Two concepts are highly important for scene-graphs: reflection and fields. Reflection describes the ability of an object to report about its own state and structure.

In most scene-graphs every node reports its own type as well as all its attributes, typically called fields. This mechanism allows high-level concepts, such as modifying a node's attributes without knowing the node's type itself. This is important to make scene-graphs extendable: When a developer implements a new node type, other nodes can interact with the new node, even though the new node was not known at the compile time of the other nodes.

Reflection is important to implement the concept of fields. Rather than just simple data containers, fields are active objects that detect when their states are changed and can react accordingly. For example, a field might forward its state to another field. These "field connections" allow data flow other than just along parent-child relationships: Data can flow across or even into or out of the graph. Augmented reality applications typically use this concept to forward tracking information (the camera pose) directly into the related transform nodes. After the corresponding field connections have been set up, all parties communicate autonomously.

In C++, scene-graph reflection is typically implemented using class members: Static member variables contain class specific information. Unfortunately, writing to static data is not allowed on most Symbian devices. Even though newer OS versions allow this, it is still recommended that you not use it. Instead, a single instance, a scene-graph database, implemented as a singleton is recommended. At startup, each node registers its type and all reflection data at the database. A simple trick solves the problem of defining unique node type IDs: A pointer to a static class member (e.g., the node type name) is unique—even across multiple modules (DLLs). Hence, this also allows introducing new node types at runtime. While the type name of the node also provides a unique identifier, string comparisons are slow and therefore not recommended.

Not only scene-graph nodes, but also their fields require reflection. Since a single node typically contains several fields, their overall number quickly sums up. Hence, it is not appropriate that each field stores a complete copy of its reflection information (such as name, type, default value, etc.) since this would be an enormous waste of memory. For example, a single-integer field requires only 4 bytes of real data, but easily 10 times as much for reflection data. Instead, it is preferable to share type information among all fields of the same owner type (Figure 7.4.13). For example, all translation fields of transformation nodes can share a pointer to the very same field descriptor object that stores the data about all translation fields belonging to a transform node. Especially for large graphs, which use the same node types again and again, this can save a lot of memory.

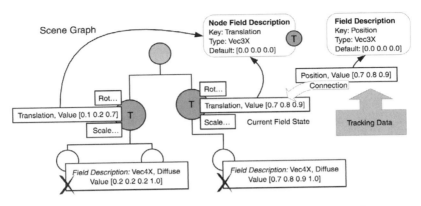

FIGURE 7.4.13   Field description sharing in a scene-graph.

VIDEO AND IMAGE PROCESSING

What makes graphics for augmented reality applications different from typical game-related graphics is the strong need for a live drawing camera feed as video background, which is then usually augmented with 3D renderings. Even more, the video feed is most often analyzed with computer vision techniques. This dual purpose puts different requirements on the video images; while computer vision algorithms are typically performed on grayscale images, rendering requires images in RGB format. On many phones, the video feed is delivered in neither of these formats, hence requiring conversion.

In AR applications images from the built-in phone camera have to be displayed on the screen and analyzed for pose tracking (determining the devices position in space) at a frame by frame basis. Since image data is large considering the low memory bandwidth and computational power of a mobile phone, only highly optimized approaches lead to satisfying results. Most cameras built into phones today already include simple processing units that allow outsourcing some of the processing tasks.

For example, most cameras in modern mobile phones perform lens undistortion internally. Every lens produces distortions to some extent. Typically, the lower the quality of the lens and the wider the field of view, the stronger radial distortions become. For accurate pose estimation results, these distortions have to be compensated, which can be computationally expensive. Yet since many camera phones already perform this step to some degree, the CPU is freed from doing it.

Furthermore, application programmers often have the choice between various video resolutions and sometimes even different pixel formats. This requires the programmer to decide which combination of parameters yields optimal results. To make things even more complicated, the choice is also influenced by the rendering system to find the video mode that best fits the screen's pixel format and resolution. Hence, it is ideal to perform a few benchmarks during the first application start-up.

The most common pixel formats delivered by today's mobile phone cameras are YUV (either 12 or 16 bits), RGB565, and RGB32. The last one is most well known on PCs. It stores the red, green, and blue channels interleaved in a double word, optionally using the fourth byte for storing an alpha channel. Since RGB32 requires 4 bytes per pixel, it is rather uncommon on mobile phones, which are low on memory size and bandwidth. The similar RGB24 format is uncommon on mobile phones, since an RGB24 pixel cannot be directly read into a single register, because ARM CPUs do not allow unaligned memory accesses. Instead 3-byte accesses plus merging would be required, which would tremendously slow down processing speed.

RGB565 is the dominant pixel format on mobile phones. It stores all three color channels in a single word (2 bytes, storing green at higher bit rate), thereby halving the memory usage compared to RGB32. YUV is different from the aforementioned pixel formats in that it is not based on the RGB color model, but uses a brightness (Y) and two chrominance (UV) channels instead. Since the human eye is more sensitive to brightness than colors, this allows saving bandwidth by storing the Y channel at higher data rates than U and V without loosing much quality. YUV appears in two main variants: YUV12, which stores pixels in three separate planes (Y at full resolution plus U and V at half resolution), and YUV16, which stores pixels interleaved in a YUYVYUYV… format.

Table 7.4.2 gives an overview of the strengths and weaknesses of the three aforementioned pixel formats. YUV can store images with a little as 12 bits per pixel. Since U and V are available at lower resolutions, they must be upsampled for displaying a color image. The format is highly suitable for computer vision (pose tracking) since the grayscale channel is directly accessible at full resolution. On the other hand, the format is unsuitable for rendering, since today's renderers mostly use RGB formats. RGB565 and RGB32 are both directly suitable for rendering. The actual renderer implementation determines which of the formats is optimally supported, while the other one is typically converted internally. RGB32 is suitable for computer vision tasks since conversion to grayscale is fast by summing up (either with or without weighting) the three channels. RGB565 requires first extracting the three color channels from the 16-bit word before they can be summed up. In practice, this is often speeded up using a lookup table.

TABLE 7.4.2 Suitability and Easiness of Format Conversion of Common Camera Pixel Formats

	Bits per Pixel	Suitability for Tracking	Suitability for Rendering	Conversion to Grayscale	Conversion to RGB
YUV	12 or 16	Very good	Not possible	Very fast	Slow
RGB565	16	Bad	Good	Slow	—
RGB32	32	Average	Good	Medium	—

FIXED POINT VS. FLOATING POINT

Any computationally intensive mobile phone application has to carefully select when to use floating point. Although some high-end mobile phones today include hardware floating-point units (FPUs), most deployed devices still have to emulate these operations in software. Instead, developers often use fixed point, which is based on native integer math extended a pretended fractional part. In general, the following observation for execution time holds for math operations on mobile phones:

```
32-bit fixed point < H/W floating point < 64-bit fixed point << S/W
floating point
```

Although the performance difference is small, fixed-point math using 32-bit integers is generally the fastest method, even if a hardware floating-point unit is available. This is because modern ARM CPUs can do most integer operations in a single clock circle. Even more due to the long tradition of using fixed-point math, these CPUs can do bit-shifting for free on most operations. As a result, fixed point is typically as fast as simple integer math, yet some modern ARM CPUs have vector floating-point (VFP) units that can run multiple operations in parallel. If code can be parallelized, this can yield a considerable speedup. In practice, manually created assembler code is required for good results.

In many cases 32-bit fixed point is not accurate enough or does not provide enough numeric range. Since software emulated floating point is much slower (typically 30–40 times slower than 32-bit fixed point), a good compromise is using 64-bit fixed point. Yet since today's mobile phones use 32-bit CPUs, fixed point based on 64-bit integers is generally three to four times slower.

Yet even if hardware floating-point units are available, specific operations such as square root and sine/cosine are sometimes still emulated and hence execute extremely slowly. If code is intensive on these operations, it can therefore be faster to use 64-bit fixed point even though an FPU is available.

CONCLUSION

This article covered a broad range of techniques that are important for creating games and other graphics-intensive applications to run on a large number of currently deployed phones. Special focus has been put on the specific requirements of augmented reality systems.

REFERENCES

[Atk06] Phil Atkin. High-performance 3D Graphics for Handheld Devices, www.khronos.org/developers/library/kmaf_cambridge_2006/High-performance-3D-for-handhelds_NVIDIA.pdf

[Bree96] D. E. Breen, R. T. Whitaker, E. Rose, M. Tuceryan. Interactive Occlusion and Automatic Object Placement for Augmented Reality, *Computer Graphics Forum*, 1996, 15(3), pp. 11–22

[Möl08] Thomas Akenine-Möller, Jacob Ström. Graphics Processing Units for Handhelds, *Proceedings of the IEEE*, 2008, 96 (5), pp. 779–789

[Pul05] Kari Pulli, Tomi Aarnio, Kimmo Roimela, Jani Vaarala. Designing Graphics Programming Interfaces for Mobile Devices, *Computer Graphics and Applications*, 2005, 25 (6), pp. 66–75

[Sch07] Dieter Schmalstieg, Daniel Wagner. Experiences with Handheld Augmented Reality, Sixth IEEE and ACM International Symposium on Mixed and Augmented Reality (ISMAR 2007), pp. 3–15

[Wag07] Daniel Wagner. PhD Thesis, http://studierstube.org/thesis/Wagner_PhDthesis_final.pdf

[Wen08] Mikey Wentzel. Shaders Gone Mobile: Porting from Direct3D 9.0 to OpenGL ES 2.0, *ShaderX⁶*, Charles River Media, pp. 415–434, 2008

Part VIII

3D Engine Design Overview

KENNETH HURLEY

ON THE DVD

ShaderX[7] has shaped up to be a great book. I was particular pleased with the 3D engine section, as the articles were very diverse and very educational. I was especially happy that we were able to include the Elemental Engine II on the DVD-ROM of the book. The engine is a free, open source engine and was released under a very liberal license similar to the MIT license. It is my hope that any future authors will use the engine to make demonstrations of the material presented. I have also written an article about the design and implementation of the engine, which is included in this section.

Two of my favorite articles are entitled "Designing a Renderer for Multiple Lights: The Light Pre-Pass Renderer" and "Using LUV Color Space with the Light Pre-Pass Renderer," which are related. Wolfgang Engel is of course the genius behind the light pre-pass renderer technique.

The other articles in this section all contain good-quality, highly valuable information for any good 3D engine. "Automatic Load-Balancing Shader Framework" uses PID control to balance shader usage. The "Game-Engine-Friendly Occlusion Culling" article is fantastic, and efficient culling is something every game engine needs. "Cross-Platform Rendering Thread: Design and Implementation" is of course of great importance to any 3D Engine for cross-platform capabilities. Finally, "Advanced GUI System for Games" is a good article on graphical user interfaces, which is also something all 3D engines need.

I would especially like to thank my beautiful wife for allowing me the time to edit and contribute to the *ShaderX* series of books. I would also like to thank Wolfgang Engel, a good friend and one of the smartest people I know.

8.1 Cross-Platform Rendering Thread: Design and Implementation

GUILLAUME BLANC

MOTIVATION

Despite the increased performance of processor cores, the CPU bottleneck is still difficult to overcome in modern games. GPU performance also increases from one hardware generation to the next, but getting the most out of it still requires more CPU power to feed the platform graphics API. Decoupling the rendering task with the help of a separate thread can alleviate the problem. On multi-core hardware architectures, this solution can theoretically allow frame time to be fully consumed by both the main game thread and the rendering thread, rather than shared.

The idea here is to abstract the low-level rendering API through large granularity rendering states and asynchronous commands. It does not deal with any scene graph or any high-level graphic engine optimization, which still remain good candidates for threading.

This article will demonstrate the relevance of the rendering thread concept, put forward a software design that also matches cross-platform development constraints, and finally get into some implementation details. Because it is not possible to explain every implementation detail, this article comes with a demo with full source code (see the DVD-ROM).

ON THE DVD

OVERVIEW

The two following sections introduce the design aspects this article focuses on: threading and abstraction.

THREADING DESIGN

The proposed design is close to the well-known client-server model used in network software architecture and low-level graphics APIs. The idea is to physically isolate two implementation layers and decouple execution as well as data. Execution decoupling is the principal aim of the rendering thread. Data isolation is essential in insuring thread safety. Figure 8.1.1 illustrates the software layers and introduces the command buffer concept.

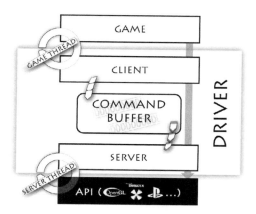

FIGURE 8.1.1   Driver software layers. A command buffer decouples the game and the server threads.

From the top to bottom of Figure 8.1.1:

- In its own thread, the game manages client objects and issues rendering calls to the client layer.

- According to internal state machine changes, the client pushes commands toward the server via the command buffer.

- From a separate thread, the server picks up commands from the command buffer. It finally translates those commands into equivalent platform graphics API objects and calls.

ABSTRACTION DESIGN

Abstraction enables platform-specific implementation to be hidden from the user. It also provides a simple yet exclusive programming model for every aspect of rendering, with respect to a few rules.

- The abstraction level should be low enough to give users the most freedom.
- The abstraction level should be high enough to surround each platform API granularity.
- Platform-specific code should be minimal, easily portable, and should permit any specific implementation.
- Platform-specific code should never be exposed to the game code.
- An abstracted client interface should be easily understandable and unambiguous.

The proposed design is close to standard graphics APIs. Basically, the client exposes a set of states that covers all the rendering pipeline stages as well as execution commands (draw, clear, swap, and so on). The requirement for guaranteeing the portability between platforms and allowing a lot of freedom in the implementation leads us to a one-to-many relationship between the client and the server states.

FUNDAMENTAL BLOCKS

Before diving headfirst into the implementation details, this article briefly introduces the fundamental design objects.

Command Objects

From the functional point of view, the command term represents the objects that are transferred through the command buffer. They are queued on the client side (usually by the game graphic engine code) as if they were functions to execute.

On the server side, command execution is separated into two phases. The build process (only executed each time a command has changed) translates the command to server-API-compatible objects. Once done, the dispatch process can be executed as many times as the command is queued, without the need for a new build.

Command Buffer

The command buffer's aim is to create a one-way bridge between the client and the server. This bridge decouples execution between the client and the server, running in its own thread. Commands are queued on the client side, and then processed in the same order from the other side. In conjunction with other algorithms, it also protects from concurrent multi-threaded accesses. Using a minimal locking mechanism, it should ensure that once a command is queued, every access from both the client and the server is secure.

State Machine and Macro State Objects

In the same way as OpenGL, DirectX, and almost all the other graphics APIs, the rendering pipeline is abstracted using a state machine, covering everything from the input layout to the blending stage via the rasterizer. This machine maintains the client rendering pipeline view, and also acts as a state cache in order to detect and avoid redundant state changes.

The one-to-many relationship between the client and the server states is achieved by the use of macro state objects, which are a relevant aggregation of atomic rendering states. Figure 8.1.2 illustrates such an aggregation through the example of a RenderTarget state.

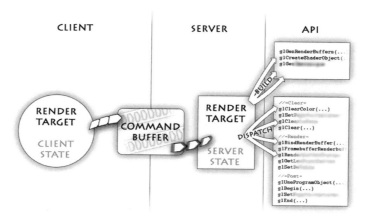

FIGURE 8.1.2 One-to-many relationship between the client and OpenGL server.

In this example, the RenderTarget state is a single object on the client side, which surrounds multiple domains.

- Clear information and operation (color, flags...)
- Render buffer characteristics (size, multisampling...)
- Post-effects parameters and execution (blur, bloom, tone map...)

On the server side, a macro state object breaks up into many API states and calls. The server build operation creates API objects that are preserved from one frame to the next, and the dispatch forwards everything to the API.

From a performance point of view, the macro object design reduces the number of states required to set up the client pipeline and, with the help of the state cache, reduces command buffer bandwidth usage.

DRIVER EXECUTION PROCESS

The driver execution process illustrated in Figure 8.1.3 describes the command and state objects' flow across software layers.

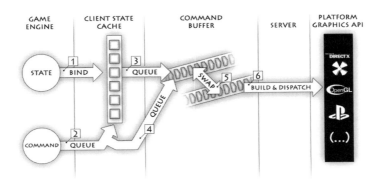

FIGURE 8.1.3   Driver execution process.

Process steps are as follows.

1. The game sets up the client state machine by binding state objects to the client state cache.

2. The game issues a command that validates the state machine and executes a rendering operation.

3. The state cache is flushed, and all outdated states (those modified since the previous flush) are queued into the command buffer.

4. The initiating command (step 2) is queued, and follows all the previously flushed states in the command buffer.

5. The game notifies the end of the frame, which signals to the client that buffers can be swapped.

6. The server picks up commands and states from the command buffer, and builds and dispatches platform API objects.

This diagram does not show server implementation details. Note that the server can also contain its own state cache in order to filter platform API redundant calls.

IMPLEMENTATION

DRIVER OBJECTS PATTERN

The design should address strong portability, performance, memory, and threading constraints. Although much used for abstraction purposes, the straightforward inheritance pattern, shown in Figure 8.1.4a, does not allow reaching these goals.

- It assumes that every platform has a similar solution to the same problem, that is, the same virtual functions to override. It is not a solution that different platforms can use to share a common code path.

- A lot of small virtual functions reduce performance.

- The virtual keyword is theoretically unnecessary, as only one implementation at a time exists for every object on a single platform.

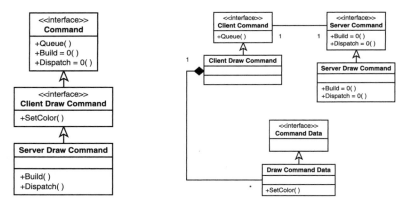

FIGURE 8.1.4 (a) Linear inheritance. (b) Preferred driver object pattern.

Figure 8.1.4b shows that from the abstraction point of view, client and server implementation are completely decoupled. This has several advantages compared to the previous solution in Figure 8.1.4a.

- Client code is not a one-to-one virtualized mapping of the server.

- The lifetimes of client and server objects are now separate.

- The physical separation of the code used on each thread reduces the risk of threading race conditions.

From the software point of view, the command is broken up into three objects.

- The client command exposes an interface, on the client side, for queuing and lifetime management purposes. It also hides threaded command data complexity.
- Command data tokenizes execution arguments, in other words, the data to be used for server code execution. Actually, they are the objects transferred through the command buffer.
- Server commands implement the platform graphics API–specific code. They are executed in parallel on the server side, and take as arguments (to the build and dispatch functions) the command data that was previously pushed to the command buffer.

Because the command data are real objects (rather than immediate values), they can contain any complex structures for which size do not matter, as only the command data pointer is referenced inside a command buffer packet. To illustrate this, one can imagine a deferred shade command, with command data that contains a complete spatial tree structure holding 100 lights.

Finally, state objects (which aren't part of Figures 8.1.4a and 8.1.4b) aggregate a client command object in order to take advantage of the command buffer queuing, and add state cache binding functions.

THREAD ISSUES

Synchronization: Command Buffer

Efficient and safe multi-threaded implementation is a must because a great many issues must be considered.

- Limit synchronization points. Minimize possible contentions and lock frequency.
- Write the clearest, simplest, and shortest possible code, such that complexity resides only in threading.

In the command buffer case, the double buffer technique allows the client to fill one buffer while the server empties the other.

There are only two possible synchronizations points. They can be efficiently implemented using a single `pthread`-like condition variable.

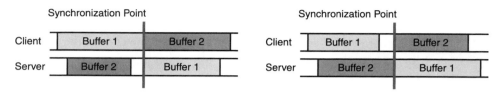

FIGURE 8.1.5 (a) Synchronize on client frame end. (b) Synchronize on server frame end.

- As shown in Figure 8.1.5a: the server is waiting for buffer 1 to be ready for dispatch. Buffer 2 has already been released on the server side.
- As show in Figure 8.1.5b: The client is waiting for the server to finish execution of buffer 2.

The situation illustrated in Figure 8.1.5b is less problematic, as the client thread (usually the main game thread) has lots of other things to execute during the frame. To fill the stall of the client as shown in Figure 8.1.5b, the client side function to release the buffer is separated from the acquisition one, such that synchronous operations can be interleaved between the two.

For each command queuing operation, the command buffer retains references to the server command object and the command data. These will both be used for the build and dispatch phases.

Thread Safety: Command Data Sharing Policy

Both the server thread and the game (through the client interface) need to access command data. For performance reasons, command data objects are not thread safe but instead are protected against concurrent accesses. This protection is in charge of the driver, which uses the following rule: A new command data object is created every time it needs to be modified while being accessed from another thread. That way only one thread can write to it at a time. Thus, if the driver is using a double buffer, the maximum number of command data objects at any one time is equal to the number of commands that were modified during the last two frames.

In practice, driver read and write access information is maintained inside the command data. This uses a counter that is incremented every time the driver acquires a reference to the command data and decremented afterward. If this counter value is zero, then the command data can be read or written freely from the client side. If the counter value is higher than zero, then it can be read, but the object needs to be duplicated in order to be written to. Note that a command cannot be locked twice for writing. As both threads use this reference counter, it is exclusively accessed and modified using atomic operations, similar to how the Windows interlocked API works.

Command data is considered as acquired by the driver as soon and as long as it is referenced by any driver component. In the case of a state object, the client state cache acquires the command data when the state is bound to an entry. Then any attempt to modify that state requires the creation of a new command data object. The same design applies to commands when they are queued in the command buffer, and therefore also applies to states when they are flushed from their cache (toward the command buffer). All command data references are released at the end of the frame while the command buffer is emptied. The command data again becomes available on the client side for any type of access.

This strategy results in a simple yet optimum wait-free and thread-safe concurrent sharing of command data.

Thread Safety: Command Locking Strategy

The data access strategy comes with another fundamental design rule: Nothing should maintain a reference to the command data outside the scope of a lock-unlock. Basically, if any access to the command data is contained within an explicit lock-unlock, then the driver is able to know how the data is accessed and can make a decision on how to handle the access.

This mechanism is also used internally, inside the client and the server stages, in order to maintain references to command data that, for example, were queued in the command buffer or bound to the state cache. This lock-unlock scheme implementation is based on the RAII design pattern, which takes advantage of the C++ deterministic construction-destruction scheme.

```
{
    // Create a raii object on the stack, which locks the command.
    sxCScopeLocker oLock(rCommand);

    // Get access to the Command Data acquired during the lock.
    sxCCommandData& rCommandData = oLock.GetData();

    // The following condition creates an inner function scope.
    if(TestSomething())
    {
        // The following return is inside oLock scope, so the
        // oLock destructor is called and rCommand unlocked.
        return;
    }
```

```
    // The following bracket marks the end of the scope so
    // oLock is destroyed and rCommand is unlocked.
}


// It is guaranteed that oLock is already destructed and that
// rCommand is not locked any more.
```

Beyond this example scope, the implementation differentiates the read and write locker object types. Associated with a strong const implementation, it permits at compilation time restriction of the code to the only suitable command data functions.

As this pattern is, by design, the only way to maintain access to the command data, the state cache and the command buffer entries inherit from the read locker object. In this way the command data is obtained at bind and queue times, and owned as long as referenced inside the driver.

Thread Safety: Server Deferred Destruction

Command object lifetime is managed by the game, which requires a lot of software flexibility to determine when it can be destroyed, as the game code should not be influenced by the server delayed execution and internal requirements.

Thanks to the command pattern in Figure 8.1.4b, which separates the client from the server part, the driver internally references only server objects and ignores client objects. Therefore, decoupling server object destruction from the client side is possible. The decision of whether an object should be destroyed or not is based on a reference count. Every server object embeds an atomic counter, which is incremented by a smart pointer every time the object is referenced in the driver, that is, within the command buffer, the state cache, or even deeper in the server code. As the client command also owns a reference count, this safely destroys the server object when its counter reaches zero, no matter which thread is releasing the reference last.

Command data objects also are in need of a similar mechanism, as server objects and implement the same solution.

Thread Safety: Platform Graphic API Calls

Most platform API calls are not thread safe, or if they are, have severe performance penalties when they are being called from more than one thread. The client-server design routes all concurrent platform API calls to the server thread (build and dispatch functions), except the destruction, which can happen from any thread.

To overcome this issue the smart pointer, in charge of maintaining the reference count, forwards the destruction to the server instead of directly executing it.

The server records these requests and executes the destruction in its thread, at the end of the rendering frame.

RESULTS

Figure 8.1.6 shows an Intel VTune Thread Profiler screenshot, running on an Intel Core 2 Duo, a NVIDIA GeForce 8800 GTS and built on the DirectX 9 graphic API.

In order to show implementation performance, the game code execution was deliberately simplified.

■ The main thread only contains the graphic engine rendering loop, but no game code.

■ The rendered scene is the simplest possible one, limiting server thread operations to direct platform API calls (no skinning, no post-effect…).

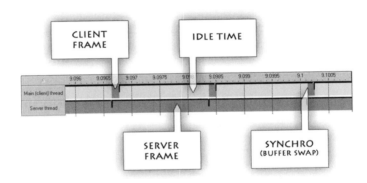

FIGURE 8.1.6   Intel VTune Thread Profiler double buffer screenshot.

The screenshot (Figure 8.1.6) demonstrates two important threading criteria that the implementation has solved.

■ As expected, the only synchronization point occurs on a buffer swap operation, in order for the two threads to exchange buffers once they both have finished.

■ Graphic rendering calls on the main thread, consisting of queuing commands and binding states, are done without any contention issue with the server thread, although some commands are locked and modified on the main thread.

The threading overhead can be deduced by comparing the frame time achieved in the non-threaded case (which does not use the command buffer) with the cumulated time of the two threads (in the double buffer case). This calculation gives an overhead of about 1% of the rendering frame time (game code is not considered), which attests that the command buffer cost is negligible and validates the threading design.

This same screenshot (Figure 8.1.6) also allows computing the "return of investment" of this threaded solution. Because the executed code is restricted to the queuing operations (on the main thread) and a straightforward DirectX dispatching (on the server), dividing server time by the active main thread time per frame gives an indication of how efficient the solution is. This computation gives a ratio of 16:1, meaning that the server thread is busy with DirectX calls for almost 100% of a frame and only requires 6% of the game thread. This ratio validates the performance of the abstraction design (using macro states), and confirms the validity of the rendering thread concept.

GOING FURTHER: ADD-ONS AND FEATURES

OPTIMIZATION: TRIPLE BUFFERING

As shown in Figure 8.1.7, the frame rate is limited by the longest of the two threads. The triple buffer scheme overcomes this issue.

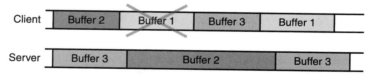

FIGURE 8.1.7 Triple buffer execution scheme.

As show in Figure 8.1.7, the triple buffer solution does not have any synchronization points at all. The policy is that whenever the client or the server threads notice that the three buffers are used, then the oldest buffer is discarded, which results in the following advantages:

- The client side never has to wait for a buffer to be released by the server; it frees the oldest buffer and reuses it immediately.
- The server always dispatches the newest buffer, that is, displays the newest image.

Furthermore, the client and the server threads are in this case also decoupled in terms of time: If the server is getting slow due to complex rendering, then the client can still loop at its own independent frame rate. Figure 8.1.8 demonstrates this behavior with a new Intel VTune Thread Profiler screenshot.

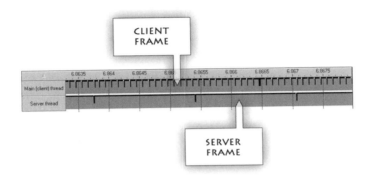

FIGURE 8.1.8   Intel VTune Thread Profiler triple buffer screenshot.

The drawback of triple buffering is the extra memory required to store the third buffer. Also, as any buffer can be discarded, it requires completely independent execution between every rendering frame.

OPTIMIZATION: MULTIPLE CLIENT AND SERVER THREADS

As is, this design suffers the same limitation as most of the current platform graphics APIs (except very-low-level console APIs); that is, only one thread at a time can queue to the command buffer, and only one thread can dispatch to the platform rendering API.

In order for the driver to support more than one queuing thread, the idea is essentially to create as many command buffers and state cache pairs as the number of concurrent threads. The pairs are ordered and chained such that they are treated in order on the server side. The tricky point is to reset the state cache at the beginning of each client queuing session, as pairs are completely independent from each other.

On the server side, if the platform API supports multiple concurrent rendering threads, then the idea is more or less the same. Threads are distributed along the command buffer, with the restriction that all the client states should be known at the starting point of the thread.

FEATURE: COMMAND BUFFER SERIALIZATION-BASED OPPORTUNITIES

For at least one frame, the command buffer keeps track of the whole rendering command sequence. Because it is based on self-contained objects, serializing part or all of it is easy and leads to interesting features.

- A problematic rendering sequence can be recorded on a console by a test team and replayed later on a console, or even on a PC for debugging (but would have to have some format conversion).

- Just like OpenGL display lists, part of the command buffer can be recorded during a frame in real time or as an offline process. Then it can be executed many times without the cost of command queuing and state binding.

- Serializing the command buffer into an XML-like format can also be a great help for debugging purposes.

CONCLUSION

This article proposes a wait-free rendering thread implementation, along with a consistent cross-platform abstraction policy.

The decoupling strategy is based on a client-server approach. The client code, which runs on the game thread, fills a command buffer with state and command objects. The server, running in its own thread, runs through the command buffer and translates it into platform-specific code and data.

The abstraction model is based on a one-to-many relationship between client and server states in order to minimize command buffer bandwidth usage. Dealing with multiple platforms, this macro object design allows any server-specific implementation while providing a simple yet solid interface on the client side.

The proposed solution matches modern hardware specifications and graphics APIs. For future threading needs, it will naturally scale and can be extended to support multiple client and server threads.

ACKNOWLEDGMENTS

I would like to thank every Libellule that helped me with this article, and especially Benjamin Segovia, François Jean, and Marc Dutriez, who gave me valuable help in their competence field.

8.2 Advanced GUI System for Games

PAWE ROHLEDER, INSTITUTE OF APPLIED INFORMATICS,
FACULTY OF COMPUTER SCIENCE AND MANAGEMENT
WROCAW UNIVERSITY OF TECHNOLOGY, WROCAW, POLAND

INTRODUCTION

Appropriate user interface design is one of the most essential elements in interaction with software. A graphical user interface (GUI) system, which consists of visual pointers, graphical icons, and other eye-candy widgets, is indispensable in every computer game.

This work proposes a very neat and robust way of managing and rendering GUI elements. The presented system architecture is based on individual screens (for example, game intro screen, main menu, options screen, etc.) called *layouts*. Each layout is a composition of primitive controls, labeled *widgets* (for example, buttons, checkboxes, edit boxes, combo boxes, sliders) (Figure 8.2.1). For the sake of simplicity and tidiness, the communication between application logic and controls is represented by refined template *callbacks* [Alexandrescu02], similar to *delegates* in C# [Microsoft08].

Additionally, this work emphasizes a layout rendering process to increase the attractiveness and variety of a GUI's visual appearance. Each layout with all its subordinate elements is rendered to a texture. Subsequently, the layout texture is drawn into the back-buffer with a specified post-processing filter (based on *DirectX effect files* [Microsoft07]). This approach allows the possibility of manipulating the layout rendering process (different layout style, or state visualizations, such as disabled, active, hovered, de-saturated, blurred, grayed, etc.) in a very elegant way.

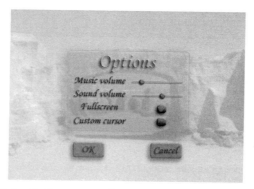

FIGURE 8.2.1 Options menu layout with several different widgets.

ARCHITECTURE

The most vital element in GUI system design is a flexible object-oriented architecture that allows defining controls in an easy and elegant way. We propose separating the GUI system into two parts: engine side and game side.

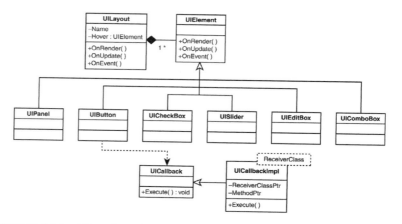

FIGURE 8.2.2 UML class diagram with GUI architecture on the engine side.

The engine side of a GUI system defines basic functionality as shown in Figure 8.2.2. the `UILayout` class specifies a single game menu screen and aggregates widgets inherited from the `UIElement` class. Each widget base class describes its basic behavior, such as handling input events from its parent layout (widgets can treat input events in a separate way). Events are handled by pointers to class member callbacks (see Listing 8.2.1), which allows the separation of the GUI code from game logic in a very elegant way.

Listing 8.2.1 General pointer to class method utility class

```
struct UICallback
{
    /// Execute callback
    virtual void Execute(UIElement* sender) {}
    /// Execute callback wrapper
    void operator () (UIElement* sender) { Execute(sender); }
};


template <class T> struct UICallbackImpl : public UICallback
{
    typedef void (T::*FnPtr)(UIElement* sender);
    /// Receiver class
    T*          Receiver;
    /// Functor
    FnPtr       Method;

    UICallbackImpl(T* receiver, FnPtr method): Receiver(receiver),
Method(method) {}
    void Execute(UIElement* sender) { (Receiver->*Method)(sender); }
};


/// Create UICallbackImpl macro
#define CREATE_UICALLBACK(rclass, rmethod, robj) new
UICallbackImpl<rclass>(robj, &rclass##::rmethod)
```

UILayout is responsible for widgets management, for example, updating and rendering owned controls, sending events to a hovered element, or even handling some additional functionality, such as modal dialog windows (i.e., message boxes).

Whereas the engine side of the GUI system ensures fundamental behavior, the game side specifies more detailed properties and functionality in accordance with game specifications. A specialized CCommonCtrl template class (see Listing 8.2.2) is proposed to define the common properties of all GUI elements for the given game (i.e., it contains a sprite object for 2D, or a mesh for 3D menu layout).

Listing 8.2.2 Widget classes (button, slider, static) on the game side

```
/// Common control class with general properties
template <class BASE> class CCommonCtrl : public BASE { /* Common
attributes/methods */ };


/// Button control class
class CButton : public CCommonCtrl<UIButton> { /* ... */ };
/// Slider control class
class CSlider : public CCommonCtrl<UISlider> { /* ... */ };
/// Animated static control class
class CAnimatedStatic : public CCommonCtrl<UIElement> { /* ... */ };
```

As shown in Figure 8.2.3, CCommonCtrl is used to define game-specific GUI controls with both engine-side basic functionality and game-side extension properties (see listing 8.2.2).

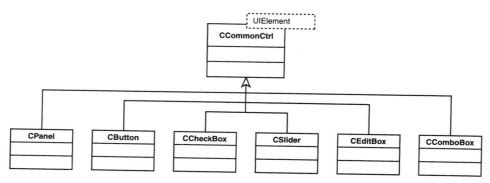

FIGURE 8.2.3 UML class diagram with GUI architecture on the game side.

RENDERING

Games use mostly 2D images or animations called *sprites* for different widgets' representation on the screen. When drawing sprites with hardware acceleration (Direct3D/OpenGL), we can run into performance problems when the number of rendered widgets is quite large. To address this issue we propose packing the GUI elements graphics into small numbers of bigger images [Scott].

The `UILayout` class is responsible for rendering each individual layout by calling the `OnRender` method for each owned child widget. The naive approach is to render each widget one by one directly into the screen. However, a more efficient way is to render all widgets into a screen-sized texture and then draw a single screen-sized quad with that generated texture. This process also allows applying post-processing filters to increase the visual appearance of the GUI rendering process. Post-processing can be used to diversify different layout states, such as hovered, non-active, or disabled states, by fragment shaders (i.e., blurring, de-saturating, graying, darkening).

CONCLUSION

This article demonstrated a flexible object-oriented GUI design system especially for (but not limited to) casual games. The proposed architecture allows the creation of a general toolset for GUI elements that can easily be extended according to game requirements. Pointers to method callbacks were used for handling input events to separate GUI code from game logic.

Additionally, post-processing effects were discussed to provide sophisticated rendering of GUI elements.

ACKNOWLEDGMENTS

Many thanks to Kenneth Hurley for proofreading and suggestions regarding this article.

REFERENCES

[Microsoft08] .NET Framework Developer Center, available online at http://msdn.microsoft.com/net-framework/.

[Microsoft07] "PostProcess," DirectX C++ Sample application, Microsoft DirectX SDK, September 2007.

[Alexandrescu02] Andrei Alexandrescu, *Modern C++ Design*, Addison-Wesley, 2002.

[Scott] Jim Scott, Packing lightmaps, tutorial available online at www.blackpawn.com/texts/lightmaps/default.html.

8.3 Automatic Load-Balancing Shader Framework

GABRIYEL WONG AND JIANLIANG WANG

INTRODUCTION

There have been many advancements in shading language technology since the introduction of programmable consumer graphics hardware earlier this decade. The primary driver of such innovation is the flexibility the hardware provides for graphics-related processes as well as other computing tasks. Shading languages have helped evolve the use of the hardware from just providing simple, limited hardware access to the use of elaborate and powerful constructs and semantics. As a result, there are more complex shader programs that handle larger content in applications such as scientific visualization, games, and virtual walkthroughs.

This article presents a novel approach by which shaders make use of automatic load control for interactive frame rates in real-time rendering applications. We introduce the concept of the proportional, integral, and derivative (PID) control principle in a shader application framework to regulate geometry load balancing for consistent rendering performance. The design of this framework is illustrated in Figure 8.3.1.

THE PROBLEMS

Many techniques have been developed over the years to control rendering loads for interactive applications. However, they usually offer little robustness, and they do not scale well with the complexity and variety of applications. We divide these techniques into *application-level* and *shader-level* mechanisms and provide a brief discussion of their weaknesses in addressing the bottleneck problems for interactive rendering.

- **Application-level mechanisms.** These include levels of detail (LODs) techniques [Luebke02] used on mainly varying geometry loads, visibility algorithms [Cohen03], image-based techniques [Shum00], and predictive scheduling methods [Luebke02].

- **Shader-level mechanisms.** Current shader compilers allow shader programs for various hardware profiles to be generated automatically, and they work with offline configuration processes to ensure the application runs properly. Procedural shader programs are another mechanism that provides configurability at runtime.

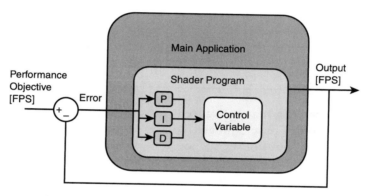

FIGURE 8.3.1   The shader application framework featuring proportional, integral, and derivative (PID) control components.

USER INCONVENIENCE

TIME-CONSUMING OFFLINE CONTENT PREPARATION

For discrete LOD selection systems, a range of 3D objects in various geometrical resolutions have to be generated offline. There are no universal rules for the LOD selection criteria for effective load balancing, and there is usually a requirement for iterative tweaking of the various LOD objects to ensure optimal visual quality.

Visibility algorithms for techniques such as occlusion culling, portals, and potentially visible sets (PVS) require preprocessing of the content before they are loaded into the application for effective rendering.

The previous approaches are time-consuming and usually increase quickly as application content and complexity increase.

PREPROCESS STEP BEFORE RUNTIME

Another common strategy to help with performance in rendering applications is through using a preprocess step based on different hardware capabilities. Shader programs are compiled for specific hardware profiles to ensure that they run efficiently. However, the support for a certain set of features does not guarantee any form of runtime performance at all. Hence, users may have to optimize the shader program by hand.

PERFORMANCE

CONSISTENT FRAME RATE GUARANTEE

Application-level techniques such as LOD techniques, visibility algorithms, and image-based rendering are known for providing only basic load balancing. They do not guarantee consistent frame rates. PVS and other algorithms that require offline processing are not typically suited for dynamically changing scenes. Predictive frame rate schedulers require an accurate model of the rendering process and its associated computation costs before acceptable performance is achieved.

EXPENSIVE COMPUTATION AND RESOURCE CONSUMPTION

The computation of the LOD selection process, if not carefully monitored, could be time-consuming and hence become ineffective for any application to undertake during runtime. In addition, techniques that require runtime reconstruction of scene data structure such as space partitions or PVS can degrade performance.

NON-GPU-CENTRIC EXECUTION

With frequent releases of increasingly powerful graphics hardware, the paradigm for developing an efficient interactive application is to push computation to the GPU. One drawback of applications doing the computations is that it consumes valuable CPU cycles. This may cause the GPU to be idle in some situations, which is undesirable for performance reasons.

THE APPROACH

This section introduces the concept and mathematical background of a PID controller before moving on to describe the deployment of such a mechanism in a shader program.

PROPORTION, INTEGRAL, AND DERIVATIVE (PID) CONTROL

This is an approach adopted in closed-loop feedback systems where the input variable (the control action) to a system (the plant) is continually adjusted by a controller to produce an output that follows a predefined set-point. Widely adopted in many real-world industrial processes, the PID control approach has been proven to be an effective and straightforward strategy for controlling complex systems that are nonlinear in nature [Baba02] [Petrov02]. Figure 8.3.2 illustrates the typical PID control system setup.

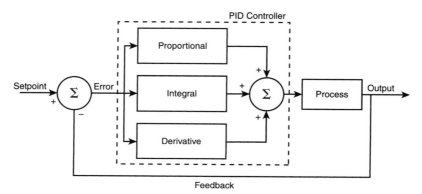

FIGURE 8.3.2   The PID controller interacts with the plant process through corrective actions spawned by the error between the feedback from the output and the reference set-point.

The proportional gain aims to directly rectify any difference between the reference set-point and the feedback signal by scaling the input signal. This usually results in a fast correction of the deviation of the output from the reference level. The integral gain removes any steady-state offsets from the reference level by taking into account the past errors. This prevents the process output from settling at a level that is different from the reference. Finally, when the output fluctuates greatly, the derivative gain measures the rate at which the error changes and moderates this value so that overall stability of the system can be improved. Equations 8.3.1, 8.3.2, and 8.3.3 describe the mathematical expressions of the proportional, integral, and derivative gains, respectively.

The proportional control signal, $p(t)$ is defined as

$$p(t) = K_p e(t)$$ **EQUATION 8.3.1**

where K_p is the proportional gain and $e(t)$ is the error signal.

Integral control depends on the summation of the error signals over time and is defined as

$$i(t) = \frac{1}{T_i} \int e(\tau)d\tau$$

EQUATION 8.3.2

where the integral time constant, T_i, is the adjustable controller parameter.

Since the derivative control action requires information on the rate of change in the error signal to perform its corrective action on the output, it is defined as

$$d(t) = T_d \frac{de(t)}{dt}$$

EQUATION 8.3.3

where T_d is the derivative time constant.

Therefore, a three-mode proportional-integral-derivative (PID) controller combines the strengths of each individual mode of control, and its output can be described mathematically by the summation of the expressions from Equations 8.3.1, 8.3.2, and 8.3.3 as

$$Y_c(t) = K_p e(t) + K_i \int_0^t e(\tau)d\tau + K_d \frac{de(t)}{dt}$$

EQUATION 8.3.4

where $K_p = K$, $K_i = K/T_i$, and $K_d = KT_d$.

ADOPTION OF PID COMPONENTS INTO A SHADER PROGRAM

Figure 8.3.3 illustrates how the main application communicates with the shader program that implements the PID load balancing. The implementation is not shader-language-specific, and it can be translated into another shader language with equivalent semantics.

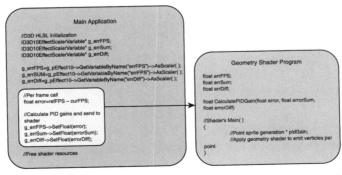

FIGURE 8.3.3   Shader application framework with PID control.

WORKFLOW

To utilize this shader application framework, the user has to first set a performance objective that in many instances is the frame rate. This parameter can be set easily in the main application via a variable and its value to direct the overall PID control action to keep the frame rate as close to the performance objective as possible. With reference to Figure 8.3.2, the frame rate error, which is the difference between the user-defined frame rate and the current frame rate, is used for the PID control gain computation. At every frame, this result will be sent to the shader so that the shader can integrate the PID gains and actuate the control action on the load that is to be controlled.

We adopted a sample application from Microsoft's DirectX 10 SDK in which a particle system was created solely with a geometry shader. The control variable in our test application is the particle sprite generator's numerical value. This provides a form of control of the total geometrical load of the application since the geometry shader emits primitives based on the total number of point sprites.

At this juncture, the individual PID control gain has to be evaluated by ad-hoc tests. However, once satisfactory gain values are found and set in the application, no further action is necessary to tweak the application to maintain its runtime performance. The corrective load control action is automatic.

DISCUSSION OF RESULTS

The shader application framework discussed in this article has many advantages over existing techniques. This section presents these strengths and discusses some of the technical considerations in implementing the framework.

USER CONVENIENCE

Easy-to-Use Shader Application Framework

As illustrated in Figure 8.3.3 the framework can be used for various types of shader applications. The code is simple and can be easily reused and adapted for different load-balancing variables.

Flexibility in Configuration

The usage of this shader application framework is not limited to the particle system example in this article. The noteworthy concept is the feedback information on the application's performance that can translate to control of load balancing or technique selection in the shader program.

PERFORMANCE

Coarse to Accurate Control

We conducted a test on the load-balancing performance by running the test application for approximately 2,000 frames and recording the frame rate for both the instance with PID control and the one without PID control. With reference to Figure 8.3.5, the instance without the PID control mechanism generated unstable frame rates that fluctuate widely across the user-defined level with a significant number of occasions when the application was running under the performance target. In contrast, the instance with the PID control was able to produce generally higher frame rates and consistently maintained frame rates above the user-defined level throughout the experiment. Since the PID gain was not tied directly to the triangle generation computation and since there is a time-dependent variable in the calculation, only a coarse level of control was possible. Nevertheless, the best results are obtained in instances where the PID gain can be directly applied to procedures related to load reduction such as geometry tessellation and mesh instancing.

Can Be Used for Multiple Objects and Purposes

Since a single interactive rendering application can make use of several shader programs, this implies that some form of global automatic load balancing may be achieved when using the same shader application template for different objects and even non-rendering tasks.

GPU REQUIREMENTS

The framework is reusable even as shader systems become more advanced. The setting of the performance objective and selection load control variable is independent of the shader program technology. There is no definite requirement for specific hardware support, and the shader application framework is certainly backward compatible.

CONCLUSION

We presented an automatic load-balancing shader application framework using the PID control principle in this article. This framework is easy to adopt and flexible for various types of shader programs. Based on industrially proven PID technology, this shader application framework eliminates the drawbacks of existing load-balancing techniques, which neither guarantee performance nor are easy to deploy due to the need to pre-process data. Finally, being GPU friendly, the shader framework presented is future proof.

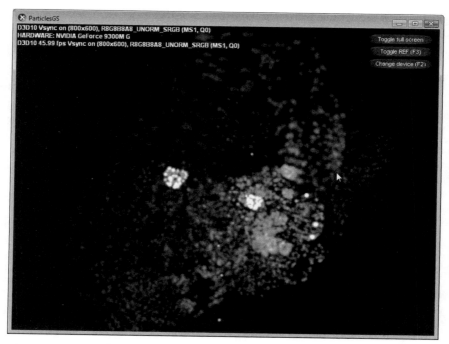

FIGURE 8.3.4   The test application from the DirectX 10 SDK that uses a geometry shader program to generate particles to mimic the visual effect of fireworks.

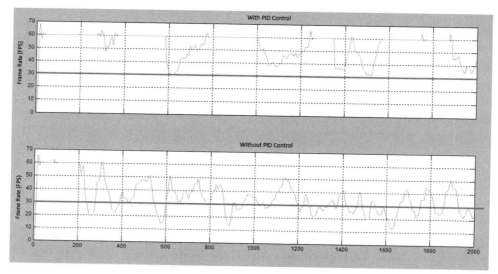

FIGURE 8.3.5   Experiment results.

ACKNOWLEDGMENTS

This work was made possible under the research and development support from the Defense Science Organization, Singapore, under grant DSOCL06184.

REFERENCES

[Luebke02] D. Luebke, M. Reddy, J.D. Cohen, A. Varshney, B. Watson, *Level of Detail for 3D Graphics*, Elsevier Science Inc, ISBN 1558608389, July 2002.

[Cohen03] D. Cohen-Or, Y. Chrysanthou, C.T. Silva, F. Durand, "A Survey of Visibility For Walkthrough Applications," *IEEE Transactions on Visualization and Computer Graphics*, vol. 9, no. 3, pp. 412–431, 2003.

[Shum00] H.-Y. Shum and S. B. Kang, "A Review of Image-based Rendering Techniques," *IEEE/SPIE Visual Communications and Image Processing* (VCIP) 2000, pp. 2–13, Perth, June 2000.

[Baba02] Y. Baba, T. Shigemasa, M. Yukitomo, F. Kojima, M. Takahashi, E. Sasamura, "A Model Driven PID Control System and its Application to Chemical Processes," SICE 2002. Proceedings of the 41st SICE Annual Conference, vol. 4, pp. 2656–2660, 5–7 Aug. 2002.

[Petrov02] M. Petrov, I. Ganchev, A. Taneva, "Fuzzy PID Control of Nonlinear Plants," Intelligent Systems, 2002. Proceedings. First International IEEE Symposium, pp. 30–35 vol.1, no.10–12, Sept. 2002.

8.4 Game-Engine-Friendly Occlusion Culling

Jiri Bittner, bittner@fel.cvut.cz,
Czech Technical University in Prague

Oliver Mattausch, matt@cg.tuwien.ac.at,
Vienna University of Technology

Michael Wimmer, wimmer@cg.tuwien.ac.at,
Vienna University of Technology

Introduction

Occlusion culling is an important technique to reduce the time for rendering complex scenes [1]. It saves CPU time, geometry processing time, and fragment processing time for objects that are occluded by other parts of scenes. The availability of so-called hardware occlusion queries has made occlusion culling easily available on commodity PCs [2,3,5]. Such a query returns the number of fragments that would be rasterized if an object (usually a bounding volume of a complex object) were rendered. Occlusion queries lead to significant speedups of rendering if many primitives are occluded, but they also come at a cost. Issuing an occlusion query takes some time, and it usually requires a change of rendering state. If we perform too many queries or there isn't a lot of occlusion in the scene, the overall rendering performance might even drop compared to pure view frustum culling. Another problem preventing the widespread usage of occlusion queries is the difficulty of integrating them into already optimized rendering loops of game engines.

This article presents a method that minimizes the overhead associated with occlusion queries. The method reduces the number of required state changes and should integrate easily with most game engines. The key ideas are batching of the queries and interfacing with the game engine using a dedicated render queue. We also present some additional optimizations that reduce the number of queries issued as well as the number of rendered primitives. The algorithm is based on the well-known coherent hierarchical culling algorithm, which we will briefly recap next.

COHERENT HIERARCHICAL CULLING

The coherent hierarchical culling (CHC) algorithm proposed by Wimmer and Bittner [5] aims at good utilization of the GPU by clever interleaving of occlusion queries and rendering. Note that CHC works on a spatial hierarchy such as bounding volume hierarchies (BVHs), kD-trees, or octrees. Using a spatial hierarchy has been shown to be a key for achieving reasonable gain of occlusion culling on complex scenes. CHC works well in many cases, but it also has several problems that we shall address in this article. First, let's recap how the CHC algorithm works.

THE CHC ALGORITHM

The CHC algorithm traverses a given hierarchy in a front-to-back order and issues queries only for previously visible leaf nodes of the hierarchy and nodes of the previously invisible boundary. Previously visible leaves are assumed to stay visible in the current frame, and hence they are rendered immediately. The result of the query for these nodes only updates their classification for the next frame. The invisible nodes are assumed to stay invisible, but the algorithm retrieves the query result in the current frame in order to discover visibility changes.

In more detail the algorithm works as follows: For previously invisible nodes it issues an occlusion query, which is then also stored in the *query queue*. For previously visible interior nodes it immediately recurses to its children. For previously visible leaves it issues an occlusion query and renders the associated geometry without waiting for the query result.

After each visited node the algorithm checks the front of the query queue. If the result of a query is available, the algorithm proceeds as follows: If the query result does not indicate a change in visibility, no additional work is required. Otherwise, if a previously invisible interior node becomes visible, its children are processed by putting them into the traversal queue (marked as previously invisible nodes). If a previously invisible leaf becomes visible, the associated geometry is rendered. If a previously visible leaf is found invisible, it is only marked as invisible (this change in visibility will be reflected in the next frame). The changes in visibility are propagated in the hierarchy by pushing visibility status up or down (see Figure 8.4.1). The pseudo code of the CHC algorithm is shown in Listing 8.4.1.

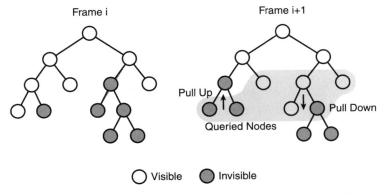

FIGURE 8.4.1 Visibility of hierarchy nodes determined by the CHC algorithm in two consecutive frames.

Listing 8.4.1 Pseudo code of the CHC algorithm

```
CHC begin
DistanceQueue.push(Root);
while !DistanceQueue.Empty() || !QueryQueue.Empty() do
     while !QueryQueue.Empty() &&
             (DistanceQueue.Empty() || FirstQueryFinished) do
                 while !FirstQueryFinished then wait;
                 N = QueryQueue.Dequeue();
                 HandleReturnedQuery(N);


     if !DistanceQueue.Empty() then
             N = DistanceQueue.DeQueue();
             N.IsVisible = false; // set invisible by default
             if InsideViewFrustum(N) then
                 if !WasVisible(N) then
                     QueryNode(N);  // query previously invisible node
             else
                 if N.IsLeaf then
                     QueryNode(N); // query only prev. visible leaves
                 TraverseNode(N);  // traverse previously visible node

End
```

```
HandleReturnedQuery(Q) begin
if Q.visiblePixels > threshold then
        if !WasVisible(N) then                // traverse previously
invisible node
                TraverseNode(N);              // which turned visible
        PullUpVisibility(N);                  // mark the node as visible
End


TraverseNode(N) begin
if IsLeaf(N) then
        Render(N);
else
        DistanceQueue.PushChildren(N);
End


PullUpVisibility(N) begin
while !N.IsVisible do                         // mark node as visible and propagate
        N.IsVisible = true;                   // this to its parents
        N = N.Parent;
End
```

PROBLEMS WITH CHC

The reduction of the number of queries (queries are not issued on previously visible interior nodes) and clever interleaving work very well for scenarios that have a lot of occlusion. However, for view points where much of the scene is visible, the method can become even slower than conventional view frustum culling, which is a result of numerous state changes and wasted queries. This problem is more pronounced on newer hardware, where rendering geometry becomes quite cheap compared to querying.

Another problem with CHC lies in the complicated integration of the method into the rendering loop of highly optimized game engines. CHC interleaves rendering and querying of individual nodes of the spatial hierarchy, which leads to a high number of engine API calls. Additionally, unless a dedicated depth-only pass is used, the method does not allow the engine to perform material sorting.

These two problems make the CHC algorithm less attractive for game developers, who call for an algorithm that is reliably faster than view frustum culling and is easy to integrate into the game engine. This article will provide several modifications to the CHC algorithm with the aim of solving its problems and delivering a game-engine-friendly occlusion culling method.

REDUCING STATE CHANGES

In the CHC algorithm a state change is required for every occlusion query. This state change involves disabling writing to color and depth buffers, which is then re-enabled after the query. Also, complex shaders should be disabled for the geometry rendered during the query.

On current GPU architectures state changes are still rather costly operations. It turns out that the state changes can cause an even larger overhead than the query itself. The overhead may be on the hardware side (e.g., flushing caches), on the driver side, or even on the application side. Thus, it is highly desirable to reduce the number of state changes to an acceptable amount. Game developers shoot for about 200 state changes per frame as an acceptable value on current hardware [6]. Our first step toward a game-engine-friendly algorithm is thus the reduction of state changes.

BATCHING QUERIES

A simple solution to avoid state changes for every occlusion query is to batch the queries instead of issuing them immediately. The rendering state is changed only once per batch, and thus the reduction of state changes directly corresponds to the size of the query batches we issue.

How do we batch the queries so that the batching does not harm the final visibility classification of hierarchy nodes? Our proposal is to use two additional queues for scheduling occlusion queries. These queues will be used to accumulate the queries for nodes of different visibility classifications, as we discuss in the next two sections.

BATCHING PREVIOUSLY INVISIBLE NODES

The previously invisible nodes to be queried are inserted into a queue that we call i-queue (i stands for previously invisible). When the number of nodes in the i-queue reaches a user-defined batch size b, we change the rendering state for querying and issue a query for each node in the i-queue.

As a result, for the batch of size b we perform approximately b times less state changes than the CHC algorithm. On the other hand, increasing the batch size delays the availability of the query results. This means that visibility changes could be detected later, and possible follow-up queries might introduce further latency, if there is not enough alternative work left (e.g., rendering visible nodes).

The optimal value of b depends on the scene geometry, the material shaders, and the capabilities of the rendering engine with respect to material sorting. Fortunately, we observed that precise tuning of this parameter is not necessary and that values between 20 and 80 give a largely sufficient reduction of state changes while not introducing additional latency to the method.

BATCHING PREVIOUSLY VISIBLE NODES

Recall that the CHC algorithm issues a query for a previously visible node and renders the geometry of the node without waiting for the result of the query. However, the result of the query is not critical for the current frame since it will only be used in the next frame. Therefore, we will not issue the queries immediately, but instead the corresponding nodes will be stored in a queue that we call v-queue. The nodes from the v-queue will then be used to fill up idle time: Whenever the traversal queue is empty and no outstanding query result is available, we process nodes from the v-queue.

As a result, we perform adaptive batching of queries for previously visible nodes driven by the latency of the outstanding queries. At the end of the frame, when all queries for previously invisible nodes have been processed, the method just applies a single large batch for all unprocessed nodes from the v-queue.

Note that before processing a node from the v-queue, we also check whether a render state change is required. It turns out that in the vast majority of cases there is no need to change the render state at all, as it was already changed by a previously issued query batch for invisible nodes. Therefore, we have practically eliminated state changes for previously visible nodes.

As a beneficial side effect, the v-queue reduces the effect of violations of the front-to-back ordering made by the original CHC algorithm. In particular, if a previously hidden node occludes a previously visible node in the current frame, this effect would have been captured only in the next frame, as the previously visible node would often be queried before the previously invisible node is rendered. This issue becomes apparent in situations where many visibility changes happen at the same time. Delaying the queries using the v-queue will make it more likely for such visibility changes to be detected. A visualization of state changes required by the described method is depicted in Figure 8.4.2.

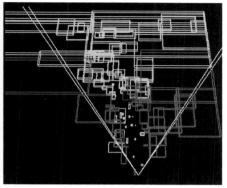

FIGURE 8.4.2   Visualization of state changes. (Left) View of a city scene. (Right) The culling algorithm introduces only two additional state changes (state change is depicted by changing the color of hierarchy nodes).

GAME ENGINE INTEGRATION

Integrating occlusion culling into game engines has received very little attention in the literature. Hence, we will have a look at how the described method can be integrated into the engine so that we can efficiently reuse the existing highly optimized rendering loops.

DEPTH-ONLY PASS

One possibility of integrating occlusion culling into a game engine is by using a dedicated depth-only pass for determining visibility, followed by shading passes for completing the picture. In the depth-only pass the content of the z-buffer is initialized, using occlusion culling, without writing to the color buffer. For subsequent shading passes we already know the visibility classification of all nodes in the hierarchy. We collect visible nodes and render them in an order that can be optimized by the engine (e.g., sorting by materials). For the shading passes we skip all invisible geometry at no cost. Additionally, invisible fragments of the geometry contained in visible nodes are culled early in the pipeline.

Using a depth-only pass we eliminate the problem of enforced front-to-back ordering due to occlusion culling for the shading passes, as we only have to maintain the front-to-back order for the depth-only pass. Since we do not use any materials or shaders in the depth-only pass, the enforced front-to-back order of geometry does not introduce any additional state changes. However, there might be a problem with engine API overhead if many rendering calls are issued. Additionally, the code for the depth-only pass and the shading passes might be shared in some engines, which might complicate the integration of occlusion culling into one of the passes.

Fortunately, there is a very simple workaround of this problem, which we describe next.

BATCHING THROUGH A RENDER QUEUE

We use the following idea to allow the game engine to perform its internal sorting optimizations: When our culling algorithm is going to render some geometry, we will not render it immediately. Instead we store the nodes to be rendered in a render queue. The render queue will accumulate all nodes scheduled for rendering. Note that many engines already contain a render queue that can be used for this purpose. If the engine API does not allow manipulating the render queue, we just add another queue to the method.

The contents of the render queue will be processed by the engine in a single API call just before a batch of occlusion queries is about to be issued. The engine can then apply its internal material and shader sorting and render the objects stored in the queue in the new order.

Note that the number of objects in the queue passed to the engine depends on the batch size of the i-queue, but it will also change during the frame. Typically, we will have large batches in the beginning of the frame and smaller batches later on. This follows from the fact that in the beginning of the frame we schedule rendering of many nearby visible nodes, while not processing many invisible nodes, which are being accumulated in the i-queue.

As an alternative, we can set a minimal number of primitives for issuing a render call. In this case the rendering API can be controlled independently from the query batch size. However, this approach can increase the number of rendered triangles, as some occlusion can be missed due to delayed rendering.

The overview of the different queues discussed so far is shown in Figure 8.4.3.

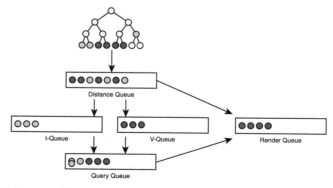

FIGURE 8.4.3   Different queues used by the algorithm. Darker gray nodes correspond to previously invisible nodes, and lighter gray nodes represent previously visible nodes. The overlapping previously invisible nodes in the query queue correspond to a multiquery that will be discussed later in the article.

SKIPPING TESTS FOR VISIBLE NODES

The CHC algorithm introduced an important optimization that reduces the number of queries on previously visible leaves. With this optimization a visible leaf is assumed to stay visible for n_{av} frames, and it will only be tested in the frame $n_{av} + 1$. As a result, the average number of queries for previously visible leaves is reduced by a factor of $n_{av} + 1$.

This simple method, however, has a problem that the queries get temporally aligned. The query alignment becomes problematic in situations when many nodes become visible in the same frame. For example, consider the case when the view point moves from the ground level above the roof level in a typical city scene. Many nodes become visible at once, and the queries of those nodes will be issued and then scheduled for the $n_{av} + 1$th frame. Thus, most of the queries will be aligned again. The average number of queries per frame will be reduced, but the alignment can cause observable frame rate drops.

The first solution that comes to mind is a randomization of n_{av} by a small random value. However, this does not solve the problem in a satisfying manner. If the randomization is small, the queries might still be very much aligned. On the other hand, if the randomization is large, some of the queries will be processed too late, and thus the change from visible to invisible state will be captured too late.

We propose a different solution. We will randomize only the first invocation of the occlusion query and then use regular sampling. After a node has turned visible, we use a random value $0 < r < n_{av}$ for determining the next frame when a query will be issued. Subsequently, if the node was already visible in the previous test, we would use a regular sampling interval given by n_{av} (see Figure 8.4.4).

The optimal value of n_{av} depends on the scene itself, visibility coherence, and hardware parameters as well as the rendering engine parameters. Fortunately, our results indicate that these dependencies are quite weak, and a value of 5–10 is a safe and robust choice in practice.

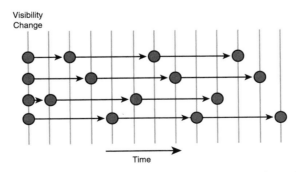

FIGURE 8.4.4 Scheduling of queries of visible nodes using randomization of the first invocation of the query.

FURTHER OPTIMIZATIONS

The previous sections described the core ideas of a game-engine-friendly occlusion culling algorithm. Here we present additional optimizations that further reduce the number of issued queries and the number of rendered primitives. Note that these optimizations are not critical for the game engine integration, but they further boost the performance by an additional 5–20%.

TIGHTER BOUNDING VOLUMES

Apart from the overhead introduced by occlusion queries, the success of a culling algorithm depends strongly on how tightly the bounding volumes of the spatial hierarchy approximate the contained geometry. If the fit is not tight enough, many nodes will be classified as visible even though the contained geometry is not. There are several techniques for obtaining tight bounding volumes, mostly by replacing axis-aligned bounding boxes by more complex shapes. These methods constitute an overhead of calculating and maintaining the bounding volumes, which can become costly, especially for dynamic scenes. Is there a solution that could provide tighter bounding volumes without the need for calculating more complex bounding shapes? The answer is yes, and it follows from the properties of current rendering architectures.

It turns out that when using up-to-date APIs for rendering the bounding volume geometry (e.g., OpenGL vertex buffer objects), a slightly more complex geometry for the occlusion query practically does not increase its overhead. A simple solution to our problem is thus to replace a single large bounding volume by several smaller ones. In the case of an internal node of the hierarchy, the tighter bounding volume can be obtained by collecting bounding volumes of its children at a particular depth (see Figure 8.4.5). For leaf nodes the tighter bounding volumes have to be constructed explicitly. Alternatively, we can construct a slightly deeper hierarchy and then mark interior nodes of the hierarchy containing less than a specified number of triangles as virtual leaves, that is, nodes that are considered as leaves during traversal. In this case the method of gathering child nodes can be used to establish a collection of tight bounding volumes also for the virtual leaves.

Increasing the number of bounding volumes provides a tighter fit to the geometry, but using too many small bounding volumes might be counterproductive due to either increased fill rate or transform rate. Therefore, when collecting the child nodes for the tight bounding volume, we limit the search to a specified maximal depth d_{max} from the node (transform rate constraint). Also, we test if the sum of surface areas of the bounding volumes of the children is not larger than s_{max} times the surface area of the parent node (fill rate constraint). The following values gave good results in our tests: $d_{max} = 3$, $s_{max} = 1.4$.

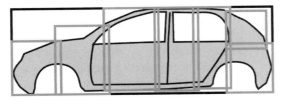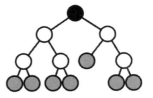

FIGURE 8.4.5   For a given node (in black) the tighter bounding volumes (in gray) are obtained by gathering several child nodes in the hierarchy.

Tight bounding volumes provide several benefits at almost no cost: (1) culling of leaves that would otherwise be classified as visible, which reduces the number of rendered primitives, (2) earlier culling of interior nodes of the hierarchy, which reduces the number of queries, (3) increased coherence of visibility classification of interior nodes, which avoids changes in visibility classification for interior nodes caused by repeated pull-up and pull-down of visibility.

MULTIQUERIES

Common occlusion culling techniques use one occlusion query per invisible primitive. However, if some invisible nodes remain invisible, a single occlusion query for all these nodes would be sufficient to verify their visibility status. Such a query would render all bounding boxes of the nodes, and return zero if all nodes remain occluded.

Assuming a certain coherence of visibility, we can group invisible nodes that are equally likely to remain invisible. A single occlusion query is issued for each such group, which we call a multiquery. If the multiquery returns zero, all nodes in the group remain invisible, and their status has been updated by the single query. Otherwise, the coherence was broken for this group and we issue individual queries for all nodes by reinserting them in the i-queue. Note that in the first case the number of queries is reduced by the number of nodes in the group minus 1. However, in the second case the multiquery for the batch was wasted, and we proceed by individual queries on the nodes.

To find suitable node groupings that minimize the effect of wasted batches, we use an adaptive mechanism based on a cost-benefit heuristics. Before we describe the actual heuristics, we first quantize the coherence of visibility in the scene, which will then be used as a major factor driving the cost model.

ESTIMATING VISIBILITY COHERENCE

In the vast majority of cases there is a strong coherence in visibility for most nodes in the hierarchy. Our aim is to quantify this coherence. In particular, knowing the visibility classification of a given node, we aim to estimate the probability that this node will keep its visibility classification in the next frame. There is a strong correlation of this value with the "history" of the node, that is, with the number of frames the node already kept the same visibility classification (we call this value visibility persistence).

Nodes that have been invisible for a very long time are likely to stay invisible. Such nodes could be the engine block of a car, for example, that will never be visible unless the camera moves inside the car engine. On the contrary, even in slow-moving scenarios, there are always some nodes on the visible border that frequently change their classification. Hence, there is a quite high chance for nodes that recently became invisible to become visible soon. We define the desired probability as a function of the visibility persistence i, and approximate it based on the history of previous queries:

$$P_{keep}(i) \approx \frac{n_i^{keep}}{n_i^{all}}$$

where n_i^{keep} is the number of already tested nodes that have been in the same state for i frames and keep their state in the I + 1th frame, and n_i^{all} is the total number of already tested nodes that have been in the same state for i frames.

The values n_i^{keep} and n_i^{all} are tabulated and constantly updated during the walk-through. In the first few frames there are not enough measurements for an accurate computation of $p_{keep}(i)$, especially for higher values of i. We solve this problem by piecewise constant propagation of the already computed values to the higher values of i.

As an alternative to the measured function, we suggest using an analytic formula that fits reasonably well with the measurements we did on several test scenes using typical navigation sequences:

$$P_{keep}(i) \approx 0.99 - 0.7e^{-1}$$

COST-BENEFIT HEURISTICS FOR MULTIQUERIES

To compile multiqueries we use a greedy algorithm that maximizes a benefit-cost ratio.

The cost is the expected number of queries issued per one multiquery, which is expressed as:

$$C(M) = 1 + p_{fail}(M) * |M|,$$

where $p_{fail}(M)$ is the probability that the multiquery fails (returns visible, in which case all nodes have to be tested individually), and $|M|$ is the number of nodes in the multiquery. Note that the constant 1 represents the cost of the multiquery itself, whereas $p_{fail}(M)^*|M|$ expresses the expected number of additionally issued queries for individual nodes. The probability p_{fail} is calculated from the visibility persistence values i_N of nodes in the multiquery as:

$$p_{fail}(M) = 1 - \prod_{\forall N \in M} p_{keep}(i_N),$$

The benefit of the multiquery is simply the number of nodes in the multiquery, that is, $B(M) = |M|$.

Given the nodes in the i-queue, the greedy optimization algorithm maximizes the benefit at the given cost. We first sort the nodes in descending order based on their probability of staying invisible, that is, $p_{keep}(i_N)$. Then, starting with the first node in the queue, we add the nodes to the multiquery, and at each step we evaluate the value V of the multiquery as a benefit-cost ratio $V(Mj) = B(Mj)/C(Mj)$. It turns out that V reaches a maximum for a particular M_j, and thus j corresponds to the optimal size of the multiquery for the nodes in the front of the i-queue.

Once we find this maximum, we issue the multiquery for the corresponding nodes and repeat the process until the i-queue is used up. As a result, we compile larger multiqueries for nodes with a high probability of staying invisible and small multiqueries for nodes that are likely to turn visible. An example of compiled multiqueries is depicted in Figure 8.4.6.

 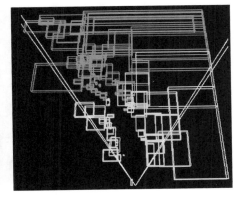

FIGURE 8.4.6   Visualization of multiqueries. (Left) A view of the city scene. (Right) (In)visibility of previously invisible nodes is successfully verified by only two multiqueries.

PUTTING IT ALL TOGETHER

When we combine all modifications to the CHC algorithm described in this article, we end up with a method that we call CHC++ [3]. CHC++ keeps the simplicity of the previous technique, but has several properties that make it more interesting for use in a game engine.

Let us summarize once more the main ideas of CHC++. The algorithm uses two new queues for scheduling queries (v-queue and i-queue). These two queues are the key for reduction of state changes. The i-queue accumulates processed nodes that have been invisible in the previous frames. When there are a sufficient number of nodes in the queue, we apply a batch of occlusion queries for nodes in the i-queue. Visible nodes scheduled for testing in the current frame are placed in the v-queue. The queries for nodes stored in the v-queue are used to fill up the idle time if it should occur. At the end of the frame the remaining nodes in the v-queue form a single batch of queries.

Visible geometry that is about to be rendered is accumulated in the render queue. The render queue is then processed by the rendering engine just before a batch of queries from the i-queue is about to be issued. The algorithm for scheduling the queries on previously visible nodes uses a temporally jittered sampling pattern to reduce the number of queries and to distribute them evenly over frames (Listing 8.4.2).

Listing 8.4.2 The pseudo code of the CHC++ algorithm

```
CHC++ begin

Collect


DistanceQueue.push(Root);
while !DistanceQueue.Empty() || !QueryQueue.Empty() do
      while !QueryQueue.Empty() &&
         (DistanceQueue.Empty() || FirstQueryFinished) do
               while !FirstQueryFinished && !v-queue.Empty() then
                     IssueQuery(v-queue.Dequeue()); // fill-up wait time
               N = QueryQueue.Dequeue();
               HandleReturnedQuery(N);
         else
```

```
        if !DistanceQueue.Empty() then
                N = DistanceQueue.DeQueue();
                N.IsVisible = false;                    // invisible by default
                if InsideViewFrustum(N) then
                        if !WasVisible(N) then
                                QueryPreviouslyInvisibleNode(N);
                        else
                                if N.IsLeaf
                                        if QueryReasonable(N) then
                                                v-queue.Push(N);
                                        else
                                                PullUpVisibility(N);
                                TraverseNode(N);
        if DistanceQueue.Empty() then           // no nodes to traverse
                IssueMultiQueries();            // issue multiqueries if any

while !v-queue.empty() do                       // issue batch of remaining
v-queries
        IssueQuery(v-queue.Dequeue());


.. .. // possible to do some other work


while !QueryQueue.Empty()                        // handle remaining v-queries
        N = QueryQueue.Dequeue();
        HandleReturnedQuery(N);


End CHC++



TraverseNode(N) begin
if IsLeaf(N) then
        Render(N);
else
```

```
        DistanceQueue.PushChildren(N);
        N.IsVisible = false;
End TraverseNode


PullUpVisibility(N) begin
while !N.IsVisible do
        N.IsVisible = true; N = N.Parent;
End PullUpVisibility


HandleReturnedQuery(Q) begin
if Q.visiblePixels > threshold then
        if Q.size() > 1 then
                QueryInvididualNodes(Q); // failed multiquery
        else
                if !WasVisible(N) then
                        TraverseNode(N);
                PullUpVisibility(N);
End HandleReturnedQuery


QueryPreviouslyInvisibleNode(N) begin
i-queue.Push(N) ;
if i-queue.Size() >= b then
        IssueMultiQueries();
End QueryPreviouslyInvisibleNode




IssueMultiQueries() begin
while !i-queue.Empty() do
        MQ = i-queue.GetNextMultiQuery();
        IssueQuery(MQ); i-queue.PopNodes(MQ);
End IssueMultiQueries
```

CONCLUSION

This article addressed issues of integrating occlusion culling into a game engine. We described several extensions to the previously published coherent hierarchical culling method in order to improve its efficiency and make its integration into optimized rendering loops of game engines easier. The core of the proposed algorithm remains simple and should be easy to implement in various frameworks. We also proposed several additional optimizations that provide a further increase of culling efficiency with reasonable implementation effort.

The described method provides more than an order of magnitude reduction of the number of state changes as well as the number of engine API calls. The number of queries is also significantly reduced. These savings should provide significant increases of frame rate; the actual speedup is largely dependent on the type of scene, the engine architecture, and the hardware used. The method copes well with the situation when the view point moves from a highly occluded region into a region with low occlusion when much of the scene becomes visible. In the scenes we tested, the new algorithm is typically between 1.5 and 3 times faster than CHC, while frame rates never dropped below standard view frustum culling.

ACKNOWLEDGMENTS

This work has been supported by the Ministry of Education, Youth and Sports of the Czech Republic under the research program LC-06008 (Center for Computer Graphics), the Aktion grant no. 48p11, and the EU under the FP6 project no. IST-014891-2 (Crossmod).

REFERENCES

[1] COHEN-OR D., CHRYSANTHOU Y., SILVA C., DURAND F.: A survey of visibility for walkthrough applications. *IEEE Transactions on Visualization and Computer Graphics.* (2002).

[2] GUTHE M., BALÁZS A., KLEIN R.: Near optimal hierarchical culling: Performance driven use of hardware occlusion queries. In Eurographics Symposium on Rendering 2006, (June 2006).

[3] MATTAUSCH O., BITTNER J., WIMMER M.: CHC++: Coherent Hierarchical Culling Revisited. Computer Graphics Forum, Proceedings of EUROGRAPHICS 2008.

[4] SEKULIC, D.: Efficient Occlusion Culling. *GPU Gems*, pp. 487–503. Addison-Wesley (2004).

[5] WIMMER M., BITTNER J.: Hardware occlusion queries made useful. *GPU Gems 2*, pp. 91–108. Addison-Wesley (2005).

[6] WLOKA, M.: Batch, Batch, Batch: What Does It Really Mean? Presentation at Game Developers Conference 2003.

8.5

Designing a Renderer for Multiple Lights: The Light Pre-Pass Renderer

WOLFGANG ENGEL, ROCKSTAR GAMES

R enderer design is like building a foundation for a house. The house might end up bigger or smaller than the foundation or too heavy. Knowing what will stand on the foundation up-front and doing some educated guessing about the soil and future extensions is a requirement to building a stable house.

In software design terms the foundation is the renderer design, and the house, size, and weight are the graphics requirement that is hopefully documented before the project starts. These requirement have a tendency to change during the project.

This article will focus on a renderer design that supports a huge number of lights. This design was implemented in games such as *GTA IV* and *Midnight Club Los Angeles*.

It will cover three different renderer design patterns that were used in the game development process in the last eight years to solve this problem: Z pre-pass renderer, deferred renderer, and light pre-pass renderer.

Z PRE-PASS RENDERER

The design pattern in this article that is labeled "Z pre-pass renderer" was used by John Carmack in *DOOM III*.

The idea is to construct a depth-only pass (Z pre-pass) first and therefore fill the Z buffer with depth data, and at the same time fill the Z culling. Then render the scene using this occlusion data to prevent pixel overdraw. This approach is used by hardware vendors in the design of their hardware and is very common today.

Rendering depth only can be done at two to eight times the speed compared to a combined color and depth write. Figure 8.5.1 shows the render passes.

655

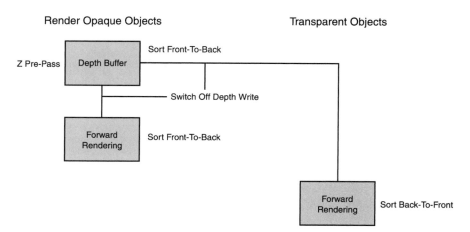

FIGURE 8.5.1   Render passes in a Z pre-pass renderer.

Figure 8.5.1 shows the opaque and transparent rendering passes in a Z pre-pass renderer.

After the opaque objects are drawn into the depth buffer, the depth writes to the depth buffer are switched off, and transparent objects are rendered front-to-back. This makes sure that the transparent objects do not write into the depth buffer at any time and are also not considered in the Z pre-pass.

A naïve multi-light solution that accompanies a Z pre-pass renderer design pattern would just render a limited number of lights in the pixel shader. Assuming that a pixel shader is written for up to eight point lights, this would mean that we can draw eight point lights per draw call, independent of whether the objects are opaque or transparent.

Although the shaders for opaque and transparent objects would remain similar, it would be necessary to split up geometry following the number of lights for certain game objects. This might be expensive because current graphics hardware has long pipelines, and it is very sensitive to the number of draw calls.

A more advanced approach stores light source properties such as position, light color, and other light properties in textures following a 2D grid that is laid out in the game world. An index texture would get the ID of the visible lights from the grid, and then the light properties of all those lights are fetched from the light property textures.

Because the texture fetch from the light property textures would depend on the result of a index texture fetch, current hardware will be slower with many texture fetches like this.

The advantage of this approach is that the rendering path regarding opaque and transparent objects would be quite similar.

The cost of using many lights with this approach led to the adoption of a render design pattern that is now called the deferred renderer.

DEFERRED RENDERER

The underlying idea of a deferred renderer is based on a paper from SIGGRAPH 1988 [Deering].

Similar to the Z pre-pass renderer, the deferred renderer pattern splits up rendering into two passes. While the Z pre-pass renderer only fills depth values to utilize the hardware depth and occlusion culling in the second pass, the deferred renderer renders all data necessary to render lights and shadows into render targets. This first pass is usually called the G-Buffer write or geometry pass. In the following second pass, called the lighting pass, each light is additively blended into the light buffer while solving the whole lighting equation each time. During each of these passes shadows are calculated.

A typical G-Buffer stores the data shown in Figure 8.5.2 [Valient].

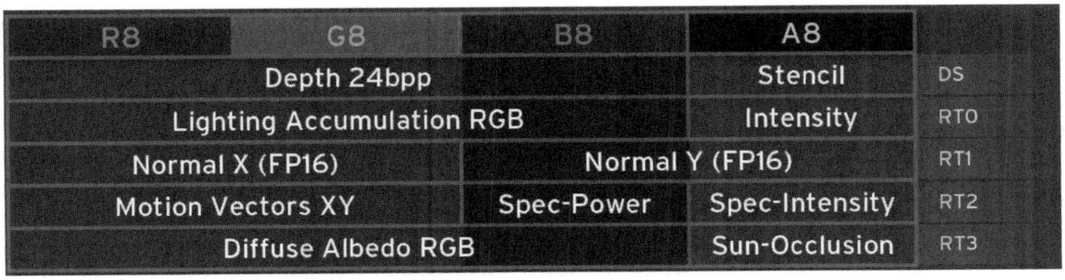

R8	G8	B8	A8	
Depth 24bpp			Stencil	DS
Lighting Accumulation RGB			Intensity	RT0
Normal X (FP16)		Normal Y (FP16)		RT1
Motion Vectors XY		Spec-Power	Spec-Intensity	RT2
Diffuse Albedo RGB			Sun-Occlusion	RT3

FIGURE 8.5.2   G-buffer layout (courtesy of Michal Valient).

Together with the transparent rendering path, a simple overview of the render passes is shown in Figure 8.5.3.

Using a G-Buffer is possible because data can be written at the same time into several render targets in a what are called multiple render targets (MRTs).

Killzone 2 uses all four render targets that belong to an MRT and one depth buffer in the first pass, the geometry pass. The render targets RT1, RT2, and RT3 and the depth buffer are filled in during this pass. Based on this data, the light buffer in RT0 is filled in during the lighting pass.

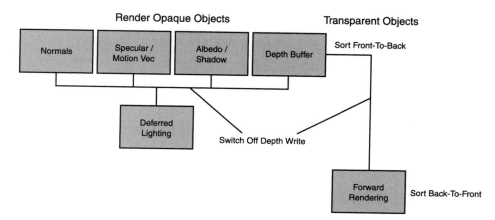

FIGURE 8.5.3 Render passes in a deferred renderer.

In general, the G-Buffer holds material data of all objects that are visible in the scene, motion blur vectors, depth data to reconstruct position, and stencil data. For all the objects, it holds the different specular properties, normals, and the different color values, so objects can differ in the way their specular reflection and albedo are calculated.

The main advantage of using a deferred renderer is the huge number of lights that can be additively blended into the light buffer independent of geometry restrictions or geometry draw calls. Additionally, it only requires rendering all opaque objects once for the main scene (apart from the scene rendering, geometry will need to be rendered several times for reflections, shadows, etc.).

Because transparent objects can't be rendered into the depth buffer, they need to be handled in a dedicated pass. In current games this pass is similar to what is described above for a Z pre-pass renderer. With the latest DirectX 10 hardware, newer techniques such as reverse depth peeling [Thibieroz07] or a stencil-routed K-buffer [Bavoil] can be used to catch several layers of depth, making it possible to render transparent objects like opaque objects.

There are several challenges with a deferred renderer. Reading and writing a G-Buffer consisting of four or five render targets substantially increases the hardware requirements. The hardware needs to support multiple render targets (MRTs) and needs to have support for a high amount of memory read bandwidth.

Because of the memory bandwidth requirements, several techniques were developed that are used to optimize memory bandwidth usage.

One simple way to optimize the bandwidth is by scissoring out the 3D bounding box volume of the light projected into a 2D rectangle [Placeres]. On recent NVIDIA hardware depth bounds can act as a 3D scissor that would scissor out in all three dimensions.

Another way to reduce the bandwidth usage is to render convex geometry and then use the depth buffer to reject rendering of non-lit pixels. For a point light this would be a sphere; for a spotlight it would be a spherical cone. When the camera is inside this volume, only the back faces of the volumes are rendered. Additionally, the back-facing pixels of this volume are only rendered when the depth buffer visibility test fails. This can be achieved by inverting the depth test when rendering the volumes (D3DCMP_GREATER instead of D3DCMP_LESSEQUAL) [Thibieroz04] (depending on the hardware platform, Z culling can rely on the direction of the depth test, and therefore changing this direction can decrease performance).

A more sophisticated way is to use the stencil test similar to the depth-fail stencil shadow volume technique. This requires rendering two passes. First, the bounding volumes are rendered into the stencil buffer, and then the light is blit into the light buffer.

When drawing the back-facing light volume geometry, the stencil test increments when the depth buffer test fails with D3DCMP_GREATER instead of D3DCMP_LESSEQUAL. When drawing front-facing light volumes, the depth test is set to D3DCMP_LESSEQUAL, and the stencil test decrements when the depth test fails. In the second pass, only lit pixels are rendered where the stencil value is greater than or equal to 1 [Hargreaves][Valient]. The stencil buffer is cleared to its default value during the blit. Hierarchical stencil support or stencil culling can additionally speed up the blit.

Hardware MSAA support is usually more complicated with a deferred renderer than with a Z pre-pass renderer because MSAA is encapsulated on the PC with DirectX in the runtime. On this platform programmers do not have much control over where and how the MSAA will happen.

On the Xbox 360 and PS3 platforms, hardware MSAA is possible but can be quite expensive because the whole G-Buffer needs to run in MSAA'ed resolution.

A different challenge with a deferred renderer is material variety. Because space in the G-Buffer is very limited, the variety of materials that can be used compared to a Z pre-pass renderer is quite small. Additionally, for all materials a very similar lighting equation needs to be used. Otherwise, pixel shader switching in the lighting stage would be too expensive.

The restricted material support and the huge amount of memory bandwidth required led to the idea of a light pre-pass renderer.

LIGHT PRE-PASS RENDERER

While a deferred renderer stores material properties in a G-Buffer, a light pre-pass renderer stores depth and normals in one or two render targets. In a second rendering pass, the light pre-pass renderer stores the light properties of all lights in a light buffer.

Because the light buffer only stores light properties and does not require rendering the whole lighting equation with shadows, reflections, and other effects, the cost per light can be lower compared to a deferred renderer.

Figure 8.5.4 shows the render passes of a light pre-pass renderer:

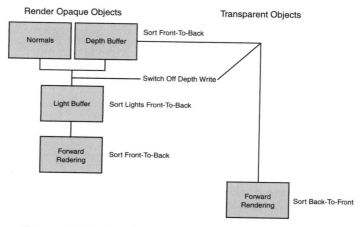

FIGURE 8.5.4 Render passes in a light pre-pass renderer.

For opaque objects there are three distinct rendering passes. The first pass fills up the depth buffer and the normal buffer.

Similar to all the other renderer design patterns, the light pre-pass renderer renders into the depth buffer first. Similar to a deferred renderer, it can also fill in a normal buffer in this render pass.

Normals in the normal buffer can be stored in view space [Placeres] or world space [Thibieroz04]. With an 8:8:8:8 render target, world space normals will be of better quality when they are stored in spherical coordinates.

Without support for MRT, the depth buffer and normal buffer would need to be filled in two render passes. Compared to a deferred renderer this allows a decrease of the minimum hardware requirements.

The light buffer stores light properties. These are all the properties that are used to differ light sources from each other.

In case of a Blinn-Phong lighting model, a simplified lighting equation for several point lights can look like this:

$$I = \text{Ambient} + \sum_i \text{Attenuation}_i (N.L_i * \text{Diffuse}_{\text{Color}} * \text{Diffuse}_{\text{Intensity}} + (N.H_i)^n * \text{Specular}_{\text{Intensity}})$$

EQUATION 8.5.1   All terms that hold the letter i as subscript need to be stored in the light buffer.

To save space in the light buffer, these light-dependent terms need to be stored by considering their locality in space by applying the diffuse term N.L and the attenuation factor to all of them. A typical light buffer might therefore hold the following terms:

Channel 1: $\sum_i N.L_i * \text{Diffuse}_{\text{Red}} * \text{Attenuation}_i$

Channel 2: $\sum_i N.L_i * \text{Diffuse}_{\text{Green}} * \text{Attenuation}_i$

Channel 3: $\sum_i N.L_i * \text{Diffuse}_{\text{Blue}} * \text{Attenuation}_i$

Channel 4: $\sum_i N.L_i * (N.H_i)^n * \text{Attenuation}_i$

EQUATION 8.5.2

Using the diffuse term N.L to restrict the specular term in channel 4 is done to restrict the specular reflection to the areas where diffuse lighting is visible. This is also necessary in case the normal and the light vector point in opposite directions; for example, in case the light vector is pointing toward the viewer and is occluded behind an object [Engel].

Having a light buffer set up like this packs the data tightly. Depending on the light overdraw and with the help of a scale value, an 8:8:8:8 render target should be sufficient to store all the lights.

The number of light properties that are stored in a light buffer like this should be enough to reconstruct the Blinn-Phong lighting model in a later rendering pass while using the light buffer as one light source as shown in Equation 8.5.3.

$$I = \text{Ambient} + (\text{LightBuffer}_{123} * \text{Diffuse}_{\text{Intensity}} + \text{LightBuffer}_4 * \text{Specular}_{\text{MaterialColor}} * \text{Specular}_{\text{Intensity}})$$

EQUATION 8.5.3

The approach covered so far limits the specular reflections to the shininess value of the light source but does not consider the material shininess.

If the specular term can be separated in a later rendering pass, a dedicated material shininess value can be applied as shown in Equation 8.5.4.

$$(\sum_i (N.H_i)^n)^{mn}$$ **EQUATION 8.5.4**

A specular term consisting of a light shininess and a material shininess property behaves differently than the specular term that is traditionally used in renderers. Adding up lights with a light shininess value and then applying the result to a material shininess value will show different results than having only one material shininess value that is added up in the light buffer. Because lights in the modern world can have very different specular characteristics, introducing a light shininess value should mimic reality better.

Applying a material shininess value to the specular reflection can be done in several ways.

1. Similar to a deferred renderer, a material specular shininess value can be stored in the normal or depth buffer (stencil area).
2. Moving into a different color space that reuses some of the ideas here to achieve a tighter packed render target.
3. A separate term can be stored to reconstruct the specular term in a later rendering pass.
4. The diffuse term stored in the first three channels of the light buffer can be converted to luminance and then used to reconstruct the specular reflection term.
5. The common rules for constructing a specular term can be bended by creating a new term that fits better into this renderer design.

While this article focuses on the third, fourth, and fifth approach, Pat Wilson's article [Wilson] shows how to use a LUV color space to store more light properties in one 8:8:8:8 render target and therefore keep the specular term separable as shown in Equation 8.5.4.

STORING AN ADDITIONAL DIFFUSE TERM

To reconstruct the specular term in the later rendering pass, an additional diffuse term can be stored. All the light properties that would need to be stored with the new term at the end of the list would look as shown in Equation 8.5.5.

Channel 1: $\sum_i N.L_i * Diffuse_{Red} * Attenuation_i$

Channel 2: $\sum_i N.L_i * Diffuse_{Green} * Attenuation_i$

Channel 3: $\sum_i N.L_i * Diffuse_{Blue} * Attenuation_i$

Channel 4: $\sum_i N.L_i * (N.H_i)^n * Attenuation_i$

Channel 5: $\sum_i N.L_i * Attenuation_i$ **EQUATION 8.5.5**

With the additional term we can reconstruct the specular term as shown in Equation 8.5.6.

$$(\sum_i N.L_i * (N.H_i)^n * Attenuation_i)/(\sum_i N.L_i * Attenuation_i)$$ **EQUATION 8.5.6**

The result of this equation can be used to apply a material shininess value as shown in Equation 8.5.4.

Because the diffuse and the specular terms are now separable in a later rendering pass, a wide range of different materials can be supported.

The disadvantage of this approach is that it requires an additional channel to store the fifth term, exceeding the number of channels of a four-channel render target and therefore requiring an additional render target for the light buffer.

CONVERTING THE DIFFUSE TERM TO LUMINANCE

Instead of storing a diffuse term in a separate render target as shown above to reconstruct the specular term in a later rendering pass, the diffuse term stored in channels 1–3 can be converted to luminance. This should be equal to an approximation of the value stored in channel 5 of Equation 8.5.5. It can be used like the diffuse term in Equation 8.5.6. Converting the diffuse term to luminance can be done by taking a dot product between the value triple [0.2126, 0.7152, 0.0722] [EngelPOSTFX] and the term stored in the fourth channel.

BENDING THE SPECULAR REFLECTION RULES

Another approach bends the rules about how to apply shininess. This can be done by applying the material shininess value to the term that is stored in the light buffer in the fourth channel as shown in Equation 8.5.7.

$$(\sum_i N \cdot L_i * (N \cdot H_i)^n * Attenuation_i)^{mn}$$ **EQUATION 8.5.7**

The main advantage of this solution is that all the light properties fit into four channels of a render target, and at the same time different material properties can be applied to surfaces. Equation 8.5.8 lists a few ideas on what can be done in the forward rendering path.

$$I = \text{Ambient} + \left\{ \begin{array}{l} \text{Minnaert+} \\ \text{Subsurface+} \\ \text{Reflections+} \end{array} \right\} (\text{LightBuffer}_{123} * \text{Diffuse}_{\text{Intensity}} + (\text{LightBuffer}_4)^{mn}\{\text{Fresnel}\} * \text{Specular}_{\text{MaterialColor}})$$

EQUATION 8.5.8

The terms in the curly brackets represent some of the material variety that is possible within the light pre-pass renderer (see the appendix at the end of this article for more information).

COMPARISON AND CONCLUSION

Compared to a deferred renderer, the light pre-pass renderer offers more flexibility regarding material implementations. Compared to a Z pre-pass renderer, it offers less flexibility but a flexible and fast multi-light solution.

The main disadvantage compared to a deferred renderer is the requirement to render all geometry for the main view twice, but this is what a Z pre-pass renderer requires as well, and compared to the amount of geometry that needs to be rendered in case there are, for example, four shadow maps and reflections, the proportional increase of vertex throughput for the additional geometry pass for opaque objects should be moderate.

Because the light pre-pass renderer only fetches two textures for each light, the read memory bandwidth is lower than for a deferred renderer.

Using MSAA in the light pre-pass renderer can be more efficient than with the deferred renderer. The depth buffer and the back buffer need to be MSAA'ed. Additionally, the normal buffer and the light buffer can be MSAA'ed too.

Because the light buffer only has to hold light properties, the cost of rendering one light source is lower than for a similar setup in a deferred renderer. For example, a directional light rendered with shadows, reflections, and all the other scene properties would take about 3.3 ms in a deferred renderer. With a light pre-pass the same light on the same hardware platform would take 0.7 ms to render into the light buffer, and probably the rest of the time would be spent in the later rendering pass. By increasing the number of directional lights, the cost per light will go down in the case of the light pre-pass renderer. Similar characteristics apply for point and spot lights.

The light pre-pass renderer is scalable on less powerful platforms. It does not require MRT support, and it consumes less read memory bandwidth compared to a deferred renderer. Therefore, it is suitable for platforms like the Wii or in general platforms that feature a DX8.1-capable graphics card.

ACKNOWLEDGMENTS

I would like to thank, in no particular, order Kenneth Hurley, Steve Reed, Thomas Johnstone, Raymond Kerr, Ray Tran, Christina Coffin, Simon Brown, Pat Wilson, Matthias Wloka, Michal Valient, Martin Mittring, Marco Salvi, and Michael Krehan for discussing various techniques described in this article with me. Many of those discussions have spiked new ideas or new thoughts that found their way into this article.

APPENDIX: APPLYING DIFFERENT MATERIALS WITH A LIGHT PRE-PASS RENDERER

Here is how the approximated skin model in the NVIDIA SDK 9.5 named lambSkinDusk [NVIDIA] can be used in a light pre-pass renderer. The original code is below.

```
float ldn = dot(L,N);

float diffComp = max(0,ldn);

Diffuse = float4((diffComp * DiffColor).xyz,1);

float subLamb = smoothstep(-RollOff,1.0,ldn) - smoothstep(0.0,1.0,ldn);

subLamb = max(0.0,subLamb);

Subsurface = subLamb * SubColor;
```

The code for the light pre-pass looks like this:

```
// convert the diffuse term in the first three channels
// of the Light Buffer to luminance
float Lum = dot(LightBuffer.rgb,float3(0.2126, 0.7152, 0.0722));


// the content of LightBuffer.rgb contains the same content
// as the Diffuse variable above
float subLamb = smoothstep(-RollOff, 1.0, Lum) - smoothstep(0.0, 1.0, Lum);
```

```
subLamb = max(0.0,subLamb);
Subsurface = subLamb * SubColor;
```

Using a Minnaert lighting model can be done like this [Hurley]:

```
// convert the diffuse term in the first three channels
// of the Light Buffer to luminance
float Lum = dot(LightBuffer.rgb,float3(0.2126, 0.7152, 0.0722));


// N.L^k * V.N^1-k
float Minnaert = pow(Lum, k) * pow(VN, 1-k);
Minnaert *= MaterialColor;
```

REFERENCES

[Bavoil] Louis Bavoil, Kevin Myers, "Deferred Rendering using a Stencil Routed K-Buffer," *ShaderX⁶*

[Deering] Michael Deering "The Triangle Processor and Normal Vector Shader: A VLSI System for High Performance Graphics," SIGGRAPH 1988

[Engel] Wolfgang Engel, *Programming Vertex and Pixel Shaders*, pp. 123–127, Charles River Media, 2004, ISBN 1-58450-349-1

[EngelPOSTFX] Wolfgang Engel, "Post-Processing Pipeline," www.coretechniques.info/index_2007.html

[Hargreaves] Shawn Hargreaves, "Deferred Shading," www.talula.demon.co.uk/DeferredShading.pdf

[Hurley] Kenneth Hurley, "Minnaert Shading," www.realistic3d.com/minnaert.htm

[NVIDIA] NVIDIA SDK 9.5, lambSkinDusk example on the following page: http://developer.download.nvidia.com/SDK/9.5/Samples/effects.html

[Placeres] Frank Puig Placeres, "Overcoming Deferred Shading Drawbacks," pp. 115–130, *ShaderX⁵*

[Thibieroz04] Nick Thibieroz, "Deferred Shading with Multiple-Render Targets," pp. 251–269, *ShaderX² – Shader Programming Tips & Tricks with DirectX9*

[Thibieroz07] Nick Thibieroz, "Robust Order-Independent Transparency via Reverse Depth Peeling in DirectX® 10," *ShaderX⁶*

[Valient] Michal Valient, "Deferred Rendering in Killzone 2," www.guerrilla-games.com/publications/dr_kz2_rsx_dev07.pdf

[Wilson] Pat Wilson, "Light Pre-Pass Renderer: Using a LUV Color Model," *ShaderX⁷*

8.6 Light Pre-Pass Renderer: Using the CIE Luv Color Space

INTRODUCTION

This technique describes the blending of colors in the CIE Luv color space, a method for accumulation without the use of alpha blending, and the integration of these features with the light pre-pass renderer [Engel08].

Traditionally, diffuse lighting is accumulated by adding RGB values together. The technique described here accumulates lighting data using the CIE Luv color space. This technique has advantages that expose more accurate data to the subsequent render passes, eliminate the saturation of light color in the light accumulation pass, and more closely model the human perception of light.

During RGB accumulation and scaling, the hue of a color can become distorted because the brightness of the color is tied to the chromaticity values. Chromaticity is the hue and saturation of a color, without taking into consideration the lightness. The RGB color space is not perceptually uniform, meaning that a shift in the color space does not equal the same shift in perceived color.

The additive blending of RGB colors is also limited by the range of the data type used to store each channel. This creates a problem for areas that are intensely lit by multiple lights, as the accumulated value of the diffuse term multiplied by the light color can quickly saturate. Changing the color space used for light accumulation to Luv allows any number of lights to blend together without distortion or saturation of color. It also allows for accumulation of the diffuse term without distortion from light color. This color space is uniquely suited for use in the light pre-pass renderer because of those advantages.

WHY CIE LUV?

The representation of a color in Luv color space contains two channels of chromaticity information (U, V) and one channel of lightness (L). Luv is a very attractive space for light accumulation because it allows for separate storage of lightness and chroma, avoiding the saturation issues that plague most lighting systems.

The Luv color space has been used to encode HDR images [Larson98] and has recently seen use for HDR render targets [Carucci08]. Accumulation of dynamic lighting data is one of the remaining areas where real-time rendering is still limited by the properties of the RGB color space. The ability to blend and accumulate lighting in Luv allows for the design of a deferred renderer where all data needed to generate a lit, textured fragment can be provided in a common HDR-friendly format.

WORKING WITH LUV COLORS

Conversion from RGB to Luv is performed by first converting from RGB to XYZ, and mapping the XYZ color into Luv through xyY.

$$R \in [0..1]$$
$$G \in [0..1]$$
$$B \in [0..1]$$

[M] is a RGB to XYZ conversion matrix

$$\begin{bmatrix} X \\ Y \\ Z \end{bmatrix} = [M] \begin{bmatrix} R \\ G \\ B \end{bmatrix}$$

$$x = \frac{X}{X + Y + Z}$$

$$y = \frac{Z}{X + Y + Z}$$

$$L = Y$$

$$u' = \frac{4x}{-2x + 12y + 3}$$

$$v' = \frac{9y}{-2x + 12y + 3}$$

$$L \in [0..1]$$
$$u' \in [0..0.62]$$
$$v' \in [0..0.62]$$

$$u_e = \frac{u'}{0.62}$$

$$v_e = \frac{v'}{0.62}$$

Converting back to RGB is done by converting Luv to xyY, XYZ, and then back to RGB.

$$u' = u_e * 0.62$$
$$v' = v_e * 0.62$$

$$x = \frac{9u'}{6u' - 16v' + 12}$$

$$y = \frac{4v'}{6u' - 16v' + 12}$$

$$X = \frac{Yx}{y}$$

$$Y = L$$

$$Z = \frac{Y(1 - x - y)}{y}$$

$$\begin{bmatrix} R \\ G \\ B \end{bmatrix} = [M^{-1}] \begin{bmatrix} X \\ Y \\ Z \end{bmatrix}$$

The exact value of the matrix [M] is dependent on the RGB working space, and can be adjusted for aesthetic reasons. The value of [M] for the sRGB working space is [Stokes96]:

$$\begin{bmatrix} 0.4124 & 0.3576 & 0.1805 \\ 0.2126 & 0.7152 & 0.0722 \\ 0.0193 & 0.1192 & 0.9505 \end{bmatrix}$$

The procedure for converting colors between RGB and Luv is a relatively lightweight computation for a GPU, and can be optimized by folding calculations into the linear transform. (See [Ericson07] for an in-depth discussion of optimized encoding and decoding of Luv on the GPU.)

Blending color values is accomplished by performing a linear interpolation between the destination, $U_{dest}V_{dest}$, and the source, $U_{src}V_{src}$. The equal mixing of two equally bright colors lies at the midpoint of the line formed between the two points, in a perceptually uniform color space. Mixing of colors with different lightness can be accomplished by using the relative lightness of the source and destination as an interpolation factor:

$$U_{final}V_{final} = \text{lerp}(\ U_{dest}V_{dest},\ U_{src}V_{src},\ \text{saturate}(\ 0.5 * L_{src} / L_{dest}\ )\ )$$

The results of this blend will always be in the range [0.0..0.62]. This ensures that any number of colors can be blended together without the result becoming clamped by the range of the data type used to store it.

When working with LUV accumulation, you may notice that blue lights appear much dimmer than they do when accumulating light color using RGB. This is because the color blue is perceptually much darker than green or red. The lightness of a color is determined by the center column of the matrix used to transform RGB to XYZ.

$$L = Y = 0.3576 * R + 0.7152 * G + 0.1192 * B$$

An example of the different results produced by light blending in RGB and light blending in LUV can easily be seen in a side-by-side comparison (see Figures 8.6.1 through 8.6.4).

FIGURE 8.6.1   Light blending in RGB.

FIGURE 8.6.2   Light blending in LUV.

FIGURE 8.6.3   Light blending in RGB.

FIGURE 8.6.4   Light blending in LUV.

LUV LIGHT BUFFER FORMAT

The format of the RGBA light accumulation buffer [Engel08] combines the blended light color with the diffuse term of the lighting equation by summing, over all pixels, the RGB light colors scaled by the diffuse lighting term of each light:

Channel 1: U_e

Channel 2: V_e

Channel 3: $\sum_i N \cdot L_i * \text{Attenuation}_i$

Channel 4: $\sum_i N \cdot L_i * (N \cdot H_i)^n * \text{Attenuation}_i$

Since only two channels are needed to store U_e and V_e, the blue channel can now be used to accumulate the diffuse term, which is the luminance value provided by the sum of all lights affecting the pixel.

Channel 1: U_e

Channel 2: V_e

Channel 3: $\sum_i N \cdot L_i * \text{Attenuation}_i$

Channel 4: $\sum_i N \cdot L_i * (N \cdot H_i)^n * \text{Attenuation}_i$

This technique can be used with an 8:8:8:8 buffer, as 8 bits is sufficient representation for U_e and U_e, but this will clamp the diffuse and specular accumulation. A 16:16:16:16 target can be used to get around this limitation. This technique does not make use of alpha blending, so it is compatible with graphics hardware that supports rendering to 64-bit targets, but not alpha blending to them.

GROUPING AND RENDERING LIGHTS

The functionality provided by alpha blending is not sufficient to blend the data now stored in the accumulation buffer. In order to have access to the data that each light needs to blend Luv colors, the applicable contents of the accumulation buffer need to be copied to an intermediate buffer.

```
for each_light as cur_light
{
    // Copy the contents of the accumulation buffer
    //to the intermediate buffer
    set_sampler_source( accumulation_target );
    set_render_target( intermediate_target );
    set_shaders( convex_copy_shader );
    draw_geometry( cur_light );

    // Use the intermediate buffer as the source for blending
    set_sampler_source( intermediate_target );
    set_render_target( accumulation_target );
    set_shaders( get_light_shader( cur_light ) );
    draw_geometry( cur_light );
}
```

Each light is drawn first to the intermediate target. The shader simply transforms the light geometry, and samples from the accumulation target by converting the screen-space position into a texture coordinate.

To minimize the number of render target switches, lights that do not overlap each other in world space should be sorted into bins. Since each light in a bin does not affect pixels lit by any other light in the same bin, all lights in a given bin can be accumulated without an intermediate copy step.

```
for each_light_bin as cur_bin
{
    // Copy the relevant contents of the accumulation
    // buffer to the intermediate buffer.

    set_sampler_source( accumulation_target );
    set_render_target( intermediate_target );
    set_shaders( convex_copy_shader );

    for each_light_in_cur_bin as cur_light
    {
        draw_convex_light_geometry( cur_light );
    }

    // Blend the lights into the accumulation buffer.
    set_sampler_source( intermediate_target );
    set_render_target( accumulation_target );

    for each_light_in_cur_bin as cur_light
    {
        set_shaders( get_light_shader( cur_light ) );
        draw_convex_light_geometry( cur_light );
    }
}
```

Light bins are based on world space overlap, and they save a significant number of target changes. Lights in a bin can overlap in screen-space without affecting the results of the blend, but will cause redundant copies to the intermediate buffer. The stencil buffer can be used to reduce the fill rate needed for each bin during the copy step.

As each light in a bin is drawn to the intermediate buffer, during the copy step, it only needs to copy areas of the screen that have not already been copied in this bin. One possible implementation is to use the current bin index as the stencil reference value, and as each light is drawn to the intermediate buffer, the value in the stencil buffer will be set to the reference value. The result is that a pixel is only copied if the value in the stencil buffer is less than the current bin index. (See Figures 8.6.5 through 8.6.7.)

```
// Copy the relevant contents of the accumulation
// buffer to the intermediate buffer.
set_sampler_source( accumulation_target );
set_render_target( intermediate_target );
set_shaders( convex_copy_shader );

set_stencil_cmp( greater );
set_stencil_ref( cur_bin_index + 1 );
set_stencil_pass_op( replace );

for each_light_in_cur_bin as cur_light
{
    draw_convex_light_geometry( cur_light );
}

set_stencil_cmp( equal );
set_stencil_pass_op( keep );

// Blend the lights into the accumulation buffer.
// ...
```

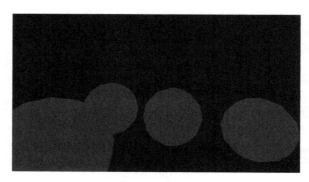

FIGURE 8.6.5

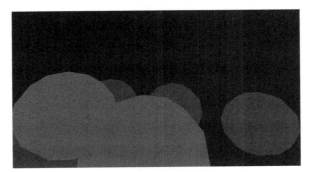

FIGURE 8.6.6

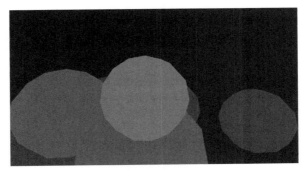

FIGURE 8.6.7

INTEGRATING LUV INTO LIGHT ACCUMULATION

During RGB accumulation, the luminance of the light color is multiplied into the diffuse term due to the nature of the RGB color space. To account for the luminance of the light color, the value of L can be substituted for the constant 1.0 in the attenuation calculation.

```
float attenuateLuminance( in float luminance,
                          in float3 attParams, in float dist )
{
    return saturate( luminance /
               dot( attParams, float3( 1.0, dist, dist * dist ) ) );
}
```

As each light is drawn, the blend interpolates between the destination U_{dest}, V_{dest} and the source U_{src}, V_{src}. If the intensity of the incoming light is equal to the intensity of the pixel represented in the current light buffer, than the resulting U, V is located at the midpoint of the line formed by (U_{dest}, V_{dest}), (U_{src}, V_{src}).

```
float2 outUV = lerp( destUV, sourceUV,
                    saturate( ( NL_Att_Src / NL_Att_Dest ) * 0.5 ) );
```

The HLSL code for blending light information:

```
float4 blendLightInfo( in float2 lightColorUV,
    in float NL_Att, in float RVn, in float4 accumCurrent )
{
    return float4( lerp( accumCurrent.rg, lightColorUV,
                    saturate( ( NL_Att / accumCurrent.b ) * 0.5 ),
                    accumCurrent.b + NL_Att,
                    accumCurrent.a + saturate( RVn * NL_Att ) );
}
```

CONCLUSION

Integration of these methods into the light pre-pass renderer [Engel08] produces a light buffer that more accurately represents the color and brightness of light as we perceive it. This technique provides a viable alternative to RGB accumulation and blending. The method used to blend Luv colors ensures that color information will not become saturated during accumulation. Accumulating the diffuse contributions of all lights affecting a fragment as its own term allows for proper blending of color based on relative brightness. The optimizations discussed help offset the performance impact of blending render target data without the use of an alpha blend.

The data exposed by this technique is in a common format that can be used for HDR source textures [Larson98] and in an HDR color target [Carcucci08], allowing for renderer designs that operate entirely in the CIE Luv color space.

ACKNOWLEDGMENTS

I would like to thank, in no order, Brian Richardson, Alex Scarborough, Wolfgang Engel, Clark Fagot, Tom Spilman, Ben Garney, and Justin DuJardin for all the help, encouragement, and brainstorming.

REFERENCES

[Larson98] Gregory Larson. "LogLuv Encoding for Full-Gamut, High-Dynamic Range Images," *Journal of Graphics Tools*, Volume 3, Issue 1, March '98, A.K. Peters. Ltd.

[Ericson07] Christer Ericson. "Converting RGB to LogLuv in a Fragment Shader," available online at http://realtimecollisiondetection.net/blog/?p=15

[Carcucci08] Francesco Carucci. "HDR Meets Black & White 2," Article 3.6, *ShaderX⁶: Advanced Rendering Techniques*, Wolfgang Engel, ed., 2008: pp. 199.

[Stokes96] Michael Stokes, Matthew Anderson, Srinivasan Chandrasekar, Ricardo Motta. "A Standard Default Color Space for the Internet - sRGB," available online at http://www.w3.org/Graphics/Color/sRGB

[Engel08] Wolfgang Engel. "The Light Pre-Pass Renderer," *ShaderX⁷: Advanced Rendering Techniques*, Wolfgang Engel, ed., 2009.

8.7 Elemental Engine II

KENNETH HURLEY

ON THE DVD

Elemental Engine II, which is included on the DVD-ROM, is an open source engine that was developed at Signature Devices, Inc. and was recently released for the benefit of the gaming community. The full source code to the engine and the MFC-based editor we call Graphics Development System, or GDS for short, is included on the DVD-ROM. It is our hope that future books will use this engine for demonstrations for articles. The system is not just a rendering engine, but a full-blown gaming system, including 3D renderer, physics, GUI, material system, exporter, animation system, culling system, sprites, particles, scene system, math library, input system, file I/O system, scripting, hierarchical state machines, shadow system, 3D sound system, font system, XML parsing, and more. GDS also includes editors for most of the systems.

Because we are big believers in design patterns, much of the engine and design philosophy is centered around the gang of four design patterns. We have developed a few design patterns of our own through the development of the Elemental Engine II. Several other coding guidelines were implemented to allow for flexibility and to easily swap out different modules. Before starting to write implementations of classes, we started out writing interfaces for the code modules. You will notice quite a few interface classes in the system.

Our system uses a "black box" approach in the design. The black box approach goes hand in hand with the philosophy of loose coupling as is the goal of design patterns. Essentially, each module that is developed should not know or care about the implementation of other modules outside of its scope. For instance, the rendering system should not have any knowledge of the physics system. In fact, the rendering system has an interface that allows other renderers to be written. This keeps the system renderer agnostic. Decoupling systems from each other is of the utmost importance for being able to easily swap out systems or completely disable systems without taking down the system. In most cases, you can simply remove a DLL from the system, and the Elemental Engine II will still function. The engine and the GDS editor uses a plug-in system following these principals.

Another approach we use is that we separate loading and saving from the system. This way we can use the same code for the editor and each game. In fact, the GDS editor uses the same loaders and savers that each of the games do. The loaders and savers also use the plug-in system.

The last approach that we use to provide loose coupling of code is a messaging system. The messaging system is used for communications between modules that we want to isolate from each other. For instance, the LUA scripting system uses messages to the animation system. The benefit of loose coupling becomes apparent when this system is used. For instance, if the animation system has not been updated, and the scripting system sends out a message that isn't recognized, the system simply logs that the message was not processed by any module into the log file, and the message is discarded. This essentially protects the system from crashing. From the very beginning we knew that we had to have a messaging system that does not use normal strings, as string compares are very slow in a system. We use a hash system for strings, and then we can quickly look up the message and the message handlers in the system.

The Component Object Module (COM) system developed by Microsoft is a great idea, but was a little unwieldy and not portable. We went with a similar approach, which we call COM light. Each module, that is, the rendering system, registers itself with the system. Macros are provided for each manager and message handlers to register themselves with the system. In sticking with the design pattern philosophy, most modules use a singleton pattern for managers that manage a set of objects. In fact, most objects are derived off of the IObject class. There are some complications with this system when we port our engine to consoles, in that most consoles don't use dynamically linked libraries. We solved this problem with a perl script that scans the source files and make sure that all libraries are linked. When modules are loosely coupled and designed so that they are not talking directly to each other through classes, the linker will remove the modules when linking release or retail builds, as the linker doesn't know that the modules are actually being used. This is an optimization of the linker. The perl script forces the inclusion of the correct modules for the system and the COM light system still functions as designed.

The GDS editor was developed using MFC for no other reason than that we had started developing the editor six years ago, and the .net framework or other GUI systems were not mature. GDS also follows the plug-in system and uses the same DLLs as the game system. Each individual editor in the system is also a plug-in into the main GDS application. GDS can be expanded very easily by adding a new plug-in. Each of the systems and editors in the GDS system is a plug-in.

A couple of other features worth mentioning that are built into the Elemental Engine II are the profiler and the unit test system. The profiler is a separate DLL and windowing system that allows the tracking of CPU usage for each of the modules. Each module decides what information can be tracked and sends the information to the profiler DLL with messages. The unit test system is a system that was used to test each of the systems as they were built or updated. They are simple hard-coded tests written in a simple MFC application to test interfaces to modules.

ON THE DVD

On the DVD-ROM you will also find just over 40 tutorials in video format on using Elemental Engine II and the GDS editor. There is a lot more to the system than these 40 tutorials cover, and we hope the development community will help build more tutorials. We have opened the engine to developers and hope that each developer will in return give back to the www.phatyaffle.com community that we have set up for gamers and game developers.

Part

IX

Beyond Pixels and Triangles

SEBASTIEN ST. LAURENT

With the increasing performance and parallelism of today's graphic processors, the appeal of transferring complex and CPU-hungry tasks to the GPU is becoming more appealing. This section focuses on techniques that go beyond the traditional pixel and triangle scope of the GPU and explores how other algorithms can take advantage of the GPU's hardware acceleration. This section includes the following articles.

In "Sliced Grid: A Memory and Computationally Efficient Data Structure for Particle-Based Simulation on the GPU," by Takahiro Harada, we explore a new data structure that allows the efficient storage of sparse data with current GPU architectures. Although the article focuses mainly on its uses within the scope of particle simulation, the method presented also applies to other algorithms that require sparse data storage.

In "Free-Viewpoint Video on the GPU," by Marcos Avilés, we take a look at how video looking at a scene from various viewpoints can be used to allow the scene to be reconstructed from an arbitrary viewpoint. Taking advantage of the GPU hardware, this article explores how the background information is extracted from the foreground. In addition, a novel approach to generate a mesh representation of the foreground information is used that allows a high detail of rendering for the reconstruction of the scene.

In "A Volume Shader for Quantum Voronoi Diagrams inside the 3D Bloch Ball," by Frank Nielsen, we take a look at how the power of the GPU can be harnessed to not only analyze but also display information in the advanced field of quantum computing. The article explores the analysis and display of quantum states through the use of Voronoi diagrams, with all computations being directly accelerated by the graphics hardware.

In "Packing Arbitrary Bit Fields into 16-Bit Floating-Point Render Targets in DirectX 10," by Nicolas Thibieroz, we explore a practical approach that allows you to take advantage of floating-point render targets to store arbitrary data. The article explores the data structure behind 16-bit floating-point textures and how they can be exploited to pack smaller values within the texture without data loss.

Finally, in "Interactive Image Morphing Using Thin-Plate Spline," by Xiaopei Liu, we take a look at a new approach to the classic problem of image morphing by taking advantage of GPU computing. This new approach makes use of thin-plate spines that can be easily accommodated to GPU computing and proves itself quite scalable in regard to the size of the images being morphed as well as the number of anchor points used.

9.1

Sliced Grid: A Memory and Computationally Efficient Data Structure for Particle-Based Simulation on the GPU

TAKAHIRO HARADA

INTRODUCTION

The importance of physics in real-time applications is increasing. Physics, although computationally expensive, brings natural motion and increases the realism of these applications. Modern GPUs have much higher parallelism and bandwidth than CPUs, making them an ideal processor for the implementation of real-time physics. There are several approaches to general-purpose GPU programming such as CUDA [NVIDIA07], but programming using direct shaders is still attractive for physics because it provides several benefits that are not available using other approaches.

Particle-based simulation is one of the methods used in physics simulation. It can be used to simulate fluids, elastic bodies, rigid bodies, and so on [Harada07]. It is especially well suited to the simulation of free surface fluids because it conserves mass and does not require additional computation for surface tracking, which is often a problem with grid-based simulations. Another advantage of this method includes the easy implementation of a unified solution for various materials, for example, where fluids and rigid bodies are coupled in a simulation framework. Although it has the advantages described above, it also has some disadvantages. Because of its Lagrangian nature, particles move freely within the computational domain. Therefore, the distribution of particles changes from frame to frame, and a search for neighboring particles must be done at each iteration, whereas connectivity between simulation elements is fixed in a grid-based simulation. This means that the computational burden will be higher in particle-based simulation, making processors with high computational power such as GPUs good candidates for particle-based simulation, especially for real-time applications.

Although most of the computation for a particle-based simulation can be implemented on the GPU, the search for neighboring elements cannot be implemented easily. There are several techniques that can be used to make the search efficient. Using a uniform grid is the simplest approach, in which a grid with cells of identical size is used and particle indices are stored in the grid cell [Harada07]. The neighbors are restricted to those whose indices are stored in the neighboring cells of the uniform grid. Although the uniform grid is easy to implement, it is not efficient from the perspective of memory consumption because it allocates memory for all cells whether they contain particles or not. This is a crucial concern when a large area is simulated, because the size of available memory is always limited. We can use a hierarchical grid to improve memory efficiency [Hernquist89]. However, accessing a leaf node in such a structure requires several memory reads, which is expensive on the GPU, and therefore a hierarchical grid is not the best choice when simulation speed is important.

This article presents a memory-efficient data structure called a sliced grid for particle-based simulation. The memory consumed by the sliced grid is much lower than that of a uniform grid, although it does not require as much memory access as a hierarchical grid. The sliced grid not only improves the efficiency of memory consumption, but also increases the computation speed compared to the uniform grid. The sliced grid is easy to implement and very efficient for particle-based simulations.

SLICED GRID

When we use a fixed uniform grid, a bounding box is defined to enclose the computational domain. The content of this bounding box is allocated whether or not a voxel is occupied by a particle as shown in Figure 9.1.1 (left). We can see that a large amount of memory is wasted. However, the sliced grid allocates memory as shown on the right of the figure. The procedure begins by determining the computational domain that is to be allocated in memory. Orthonormal basis vectors e^x, e^y, e^z and a uniform grid along the bases in the computational domain are prepared. The size of the grid is infinite, and the grid does not change the configuration of the space. Note that the grid is not allocated in the memory at this time. The first step is the computation of the number of voxels required to store the data and to allocate memory for them.

An axis is chosen from the basis, and the grid in the domain is divided into slices perpendicular to the axis. Each slice has the thickness of one voxel in the direction of the axis. Thus, the slices have one less dimension than the spatial dimension of the computation domain. If e^y is chosen as the axis, the slices are spread over the space of the bases e^x and e^z. The coordinate of a point $\mathbf{x} = (x, y, z)$ in

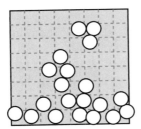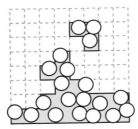

FIGURE 9.1.1 The area inside of the lines in the left figure shows voxels allocated in the memory when a uniform grid is used. The sliced grid allocates memory for the area inside of the lines in the right figure.

grid space is $(b^x, b^y, b^z) = (\mathbf{x}\, \mathbf{e}^x, \mathbf{x}\, \mathbf{e}^y, \mathbf{x}\, \mathbf{e}^z)$. After dividing the computational space into slices, the maximum and minimum voxel coordinates in the XZ plane $B^x_{i,max}, B^x_{i,min}, B^z_{i,max}, B^z_{i,min}$ for the ith slice are computed from all the coordinates of elements b^x_i, b^y_i, b^z_i in the slice as follows:

$$B^x_{i,max} = max_{j \in P_i}\{b^x_j\}$$
$$B^x_{i,min} = min_{j \in P_i}\{b^x_j\}$$
$$B^z_{i,max} = max_{j \in P_i}\{b^z_j\}$$
$$B^z_{i,min} = min_{j \in P_i}\{b^z_j\} \qquad \text{EQUATION 9.1.1}$$

where $P_i = \{j | b^y_j = i\}$.

With these values, the number of voxels in the X and Z plane n^x_i, n^z_i is computed as

$$n^x_i = \frac{B^x_{i,max} - B^x_{i,min}}{d} + 1 \qquad \text{EQUATION 9.1.2}$$

$$n^z_i = \frac{B^z_{i,max} - B^z_{i,min}}{d} + 1 \qquad \text{EQUATION 9.1.3}$$

where d is the side length of the voxels. Then, the number of voxels in slice i is calculated as $n_i = n^x_i n^z_i$. The sliced grid allocates memory for voxels inside the bounding box of a slice.

After a bounding box is defined, we can calculate the index of a voxel at (x, y, z) located in the bounding box i as follows,

$$v_i(x,y,z) = \left\lfloor \frac{x - B^x_{i,min}}{d} \right\rfloor + \left\lfloor \frac{z - B^z_{i,min}}{d} \right\rfloor n^x_i \qquad \text{EQUATION 9.1.4}$$

However, what we need is the global index of the voxel in the whole computational domain—that is, the index for all of the bounding boxes. The global index for the first voxel in the bounding box is computed because all of the global indices for the voxels within a bounding box can be calculated from the global index of the first voxel and the local index of the voxel within the bounding box.

Assuming that the computational region is divided into n slices, $\{S_0, S_1, S_2, ..., S_{n-1}\}$, the index of the first voxel in slice S_i is defined as the sum of the numbers of voxels in slice S_0 to slice S_{i-1};

$$p_i = \sum_{j<i} n_j$$

EQUATION 9.1.5

The index of the voxel to which a point (x,y,z) belongs is calculated in two steps. In the first step, the number of the slice in which the point is located is calculated using the minimum coordinate of voxels B^y_{min} in the Y direction as follows.

$$i = \left\lfloor \frac{b^y - B^y_{min}}{d} \right\rfloor$$

EQUATION 9.1.6

Then the index of the voxel $v(x,y,z)$ is calculated using the values that determine the bounding box in the slice.

$$v(x,y,z) = p_i + \left(\left\lfloor \frac{x - B^x_{i,min}}{d} \right\rfloor + \left\lfloor \frac{z - B^z_{i,min}}{d} \right\rfloor n^x_i \right)$$

EQUATION 9.1.7

From this equation, we can see that the values needed to identify the index of the voxel wherein a point is located are the values that define the bounding box of the slice $B^x_{i,min}, B^z_{i,min}, n^x_i$, the value used to determine the index of the slice B^y_{min}, the index of the first voxel within slice p_i, and the length of the side of a voxel d.

To construct the sliced grid, the bounding box of each slice is determined, and the index of the first voxel in each slice is calculated. After the values that are needed to identify the index of voxel are thus computed, values are stored in the voxels. To access the memory of a voxel, we calculate the global index of the voxel by Equation 9.1.7 with a few data reads. Unlike a hierarchical grid, which is a memory-efficient data structure, the sliced grid does not require a lot of memory access in order to obtain the index of a voxel.

IMPLEMENTING A SLICED GRID ON THE GPU

The sliced grid algorithm is useful for computation not only on the GPU, but also on the CPU. Although an implementation on the CPU is trivial, an implementation on the GPU requires the use of several shader techniques as presented in this section.

DATA STRUCTURE

If the sliced grid is computed on the CPU for use in a particle-based simulation running on the GPU, we cannot fully exploit the computation power of the GPU because we are required to deal with the consequence of the inefficient data transfer between the host and the device. Therefore, it is natural to implement the data structure on the GPU as well. The data required to calculate the global index of a voxel is the global index of the first voxel in each slice p_i and the values defining each bounding box—that is, $B^x_{i,min}, B^z_{i,min}, n^x_i$. The maximum voxel coordinates do not have to be stored because it is not used in Equation 9.1.7. Thus, a 1D texture with four color channels is prepared to store these four values for each slice. The texture has the same number of pixels as slices in our grid. In addition to this texture, a large 2D texture is prepared to store values of individual voxels. The 1D texture stores the keys, and the 2D texture stores the actual data.

COMPUTATION OF BOUNDING BOXES

First, we have to compute the bounding boxes of the slices. This means that the maximum and minimum voxel coordinates $B^x_{i,max}, B^x_{i,min}, B^z_{i,max}, B^z_{i,min}$ in the XZ plane have to be calculated for each slice. The computation is performed by a scattering operation using a vertex shader. The 1D texture is set as a render target, and a vertex is prepared for each particle. The vertex is rendered as a point primitive of size 1, and the index of the slice to which the particle is located is calculated from the position of the particle in Equation 9.1.6. Using the index of the slice, the vertex is rendered at the pixel corresponding to the slice. The following code is the vertex shader used to accomplish this operation.

```
void main(float3 texCrd:          POSITION,
       float3 inCrd:          TEXCOORD0,
       out float4 outPos:     POSITION,
       out float4 outCrd:     TEXCOORD0)
{
       float dd=2/(float)ONE_D_SIZE;
       //      Fetch particle position from texture
```

```
float4 inPos=tex2D(positionTex,texCrd.xy);

//        Compute Y grid coordinate (Eqn.6)
float yGCrd=floor((inPos.y-byMin)/d);

//        Output this vertex to the position
//        corresponding to Y grid coordinate
outPos=float4(0,0,0,1);
outPos.y=yGCrd*dd-1 + 0.5*dd;

//        Output XZ grid coordinates
//        (outCrd is written to color in fragment shader)
outCrd.xyzw=inPos.xxzz;

//        If particle is not alive
if(inPos.w < 0)
        outPos.xyz=OUT_OF_RANGE;
}
```

The fragment shader outputs the voxel coordinates (b^x, b^z) computed as a color. In this way, particles located on the same slice are rendered to the same pixel. What we have to do here is select the maximum and minimum coordinates. The operation is performed by using the alpha blending. The maximum and minimum coordinates are selected in one pass rendering by inverting minimum coordinates and using `glBlendEquation(GL_MAX)`.

Because the blending function is available on the GPU when it is used as a "graphics" processing unit, we can select the maximum values with ease. However, it is not available on other streaming processors. This means that it cannot be used when CUDA is selected to perform the computation on the GPU. If this algorithm is implemented with CUDA, several kernels will have to be developed in order to achieve the same result. The blending function eliminating the needs of these kernels can be seen as a function merging the computation results of all the threads in a kernel. The function may not be used often because of performance reasons, but it is very useful for many nongraphics applications. Not only the blending function, but also other raster operations, are useful because they can be used as functions merging all the threads as well.

COMPUTING THE INDICES OF THE FIRST VOXELS

The number of voxels n_i in each slice can be computed using the values defining the bounding box with $n_i = n_i^x, n_i^z$. The next thing we need to do is the computation of the index of the first voxel in each slice as defined by Equation 9.1.5 because the global index of a voxel in the bounding box is computed by using Equation 9.1.7. The evaluation of Equation 9.1.5 is prefixed by the sum of $\{n_0, n_1, ..., n_{m-1}\}$, where m is the total number of slices. If we evaluate the equation using a fragment shader by reading values from n_0 to n_{i-1}, the thread responsible for the last slice has to read $m - 1$ values from texture memory, whereas the thread handling the first slice has nothing to do. Although it is not much of a problem when the number of slices is small, it usually becomes inefficient because the number of slices is larger than a hundred for most simulations. Also, this is not efficient because the uneven distribution of the computational burden will cause some hardware threads to have to wait for other threads. Therefore, another strategy is employed to calculate the prefix sum [Harris07].

Instead of gathering n_j, whose index j is smaller than i, the value n_i is scattered over the elements for slices j. A 1D array in which a pixel is assigned to a slice is prepared and cleared with zero. The scattering operation on the GPU usually prepares a vertex for an element, but in this case a line is prepared for each element. As we have m slices, m lines are prepared. Line i is used to add n_i over the elements whose indexes are larger than i as shown in Figure 9.1.2. In the vertex shader, the two end points of the line are set to the pixel locations of slices $i + 1$ and m, respectively, but to the same color as shown in the following code.

```
void main(float2 inPos:              POSITION,
          float3 inCrd:              TEXCOORD0,
          out float4 outPos:         POSITION,
          out float4 outCrd:         TEXCOORD0,
          out float4 outColor:       COLOR0)
{
        float dd=2/(float)ONE_D_SIZE;
        float2 texCrd=float2(dd*0.5*0.5,(inPos.x+0.5)*dd*0.5);


        //      Read min and max
        //         minMax = float4(max.x,min.x,max.z,min.z);
        float4 minMax=      tex2D(MaxTex,      texCrd);
        minMax.yw=          -tex2D(MinTex,      texCrd).xz;
```

```
//          Compute nix and niz (Eqns. 9.1.2, 9.1.3)
float2 ni=float2((floor(minMax.x)-floor(minMax.y))/d+1,
                (floor(minMax.z)-floor(minMax.w))/d+1);


//          Output ni
outCrd=ni.x*ni.y;


//          Set position of vertex
outPos=float4(0,0,0,1);
outPos.y=floor(inPos.y)*dd-1 + dd;


if(noValueIsWritten(minMax))
        outCrd=0;
}
```

The fragment shader writes n_i to the color. In this way, n_i is written to the pixel for slices from $i + 1$ to m. The additive operation is performed via alpha blending. After rendering all the lines, we can obtain p_i for all the slices.

The other values $B_{i,min}^x, B_{i,min}^z$ and n_i^x are also necessary to compute the global index of a voxel besides p_i. Since we already have $B_{i,max}^x, B_{i,min}^x, B_{i,max}^z, B_{i,min}^z$, nothing has to be done for them. We compute Equation 9.1.2 in order to obtain n_i^x in another shader. Two rendering passes are necessary in this stage because the geometry rendered was lines in the computation of p_i, but points are used in the computation of n_i^x. At this point, all the values necessary to access to the memory as defined by Equation 9.1.7 have been computed.

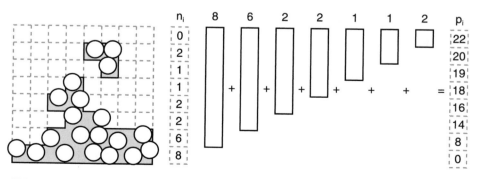

FIGURE 9.1.2 Indices of first voxels are computed by rendering a line for each slice.

Storing and Reading Values

Values required to compute the global index of a voxel have been computed. Thus, we can now access the memory associated with the voxel. At first, the slice index of a voxel is computed using Equation 9.1.6 with the projected position of the voxel to the axis $\mathbf{x} \, e^y$. Then the values $p^i, B^x_{i,min}, B^z_{i,min}, n^x_i$ for slice i are read, and the global index of the voxel is calculated with Equation 9.1.7. A value is stored to the grid by preparing a vertex and rendering it as a point primitive of size 1 to the corresponding pixel.

Results

Particle-Based Simulation

The sliced grid is introduced to several kinds of particle-based simulations—for example, the distinct element method (DEM) for granular materials [Mishra03] and smoothed particle hydrodynamics (SPH) for fluids [Harada07a]. For these simulations, particle indices are stored in the sliced grid before searching for the neighbors. We chose the side length of the grid equal to the diameter of particles and prepared memory to store four values per voxel. Values required to compute the global indices have to be calculated as described above before storing indices to the grid when the sliced grid is used. After computing these values, indices of particles are stored to the grid. Because the indices cannot be stored in the grid correctly by one pass rendering, when there is more than a particle in a voxel, we employed a multi-pass strategy as described in [Harada07a]. Boundary conditions are computed using a distance function.

Figure 9.1.3 shows a 3D DEM simulation using 65,536 particles. The particles are simulated in the cube indicated by the gray square. The simulated result is orthogonally projected to show the effect of the sliced grid clearly. If we used a uniform grid, all the space inside the cube would have to be allocated to memory, with a lot of empty space, but only the area indicated in gray in these figures has to be allocated when the sliced grid is used. The Y axis is selected as the axis in this simulation. The memory used by the sliced grid was at most only 7% of the memory used by the uniform grid. We can see that the sliced grid eliminates the empty space and increases the efficiency of the memory usage.

Figure 9.1.4 shows other DEM simulations using 100,000 particles and shows slices in three dimensions. Simulation conditions are the same except for the axis direction for the sliced grid. In the left, the X-axis is used as the direction, whereas the Y-axis is used in the right. As these figures show, we can choose an arbitrary axis to divide the space to the slices. The memory efficiency of the simulation depends on the choice of the axis.

FIGURE 9.1.3 A DEM simulation using 65,536 particles. The gray areas are the areas allocated in the memory when the sliced grid is used.

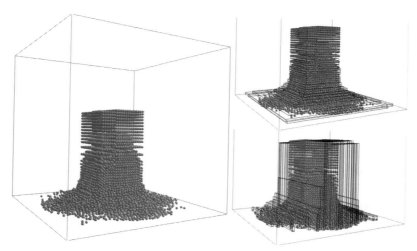

FIGURE 9.1.4 Different choices of the axis for the sliced grid.

The next example is the result of an SPH simulation. In Figure 9.1.5 a fluid is poured into a tank. The simulation used a particle of about 1M. To enclose the entire simulation region, we had to prepare 256×256×256 voxels, and hence 256 MB of memory was needed for a uniform grid. In contrast, the sliced grid only requires

15 MB at most. At the right of the figure is a screenshot of the simulation, and the left side shows the texture storing the grid. The color of the pixel indicates the number of indices stored in the voxel. We can see that the particle indices are stored very densely in the memory. Quantitative comparison to the uniform grid is also performed as shown in Table 9.1.1. We can see that simulations using the sliced grid are faster than ones using the uniform grid, although the sliced grid requires additional computation to store the data in the grid. Differences between them came from the neighboring search. Thus, we conclude that the speed up came from improvement of usage of the cache. For the sliced grid, more values that have to be read from the memory remain in the cache because the particle indices are stored very densely in the grid texture.

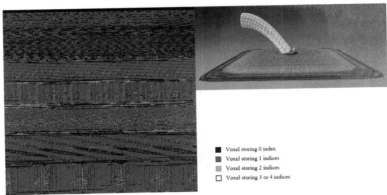

■ Voxel storing 0 index
■ Voxel storing 1 indices
■ Voxel storing 2 indices
□ Voxel storing 3 or 4 indices

FIGURE 9.1.5   Fluid simulation using SPH and the texture storing the voxel data.

TABLE 9.1.1 Comparison of the computation time between a simulation using a uniform grid and one using a sliced grid

Number of Particles	Uniform Grid	Sliced Grid
65536	60.9	53.1
262144	280.5	231.3
589824	685.9	567.9
1048576	1160.9	1070.3

Particle-based simulation that uses a uniform grid to perform a neighboring search has a restriction on the size of the computational domain because it requires a large amount of memory. The proposed method also removes the restriction on the size of the computational domain because we do not have to allocate memory for the bounding box covering the entire domain. Therefore, we can simulate a scene in a large area. Figure 9.1.6 shows the simulation result for a large area using about four million particles, and the size of the computational region is 700×700×256 voxels. When we use a fixed grid, about 2 GB of memory is needed just for the grid storing the particle indices. We could not simulate the scene using a fixed grid because the size is larger than the size of video memory available at the time of development. However, the sliced grid makes it possible to run the simulation with current hardware because the size of memory required by the sliced grid is about 150 MB.

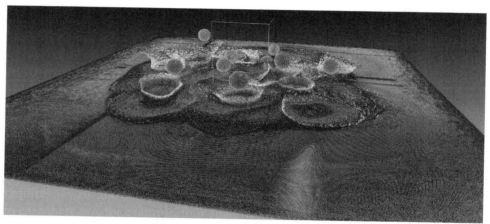

FIGURE 9.1.6   An SPH simulation in a large computational domain.

STORING THE DISTANCE FUNCTION

Our sliced grid is useful not only for particle-based simulations but also for many applications that use a grid. Another application of the sliced grid is for the efficient storage of a distance function that can be used to represent a boundary for our particle-based simulation. Although a uniform grid can be used to store the distance function, it is not efficient from the perspective of memory usage because only data in the narrow band is required for most cases. Here, a sliced grid can be introduced to increase the efficiency. The procedure used to store a distance function to a sliced grid is almost the same to store particle indices to the grid. The difference is that sampling points of a distance function are rendered as point primitives in order to obtain $B^x_{i,max}, B^x_{i,min}, B^z_{i,max}, B^z_{i,min}$ instead of rendering particles to compute slices. Figure 9.1.7 shows an example of storing a distance function on a sliced grid.

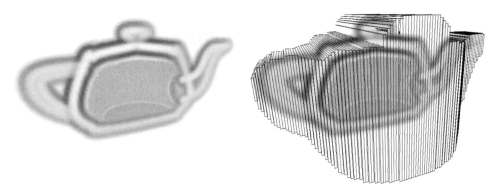

FIGURE 9.1.7   A distance function of a teapot stored in a sliced grid.

CONCLUSION

In this article, we presented the sliced grid, which can be used to store indices of particles efficiently, and its implementation on the GPU. When other programming environments on the GPU such as CUDA are used, several kernels have to be developed for the selection of the maximum and minimum coordinates for each slice. However, it can be performed easily by using graphics functions available when shaders are used for GPU programming. We showed that the introduction of the sliced grid for a particle-based simulation not only improves the memory efficiency, but also increases the performance of the simulation. The last example of storing a distance function to the sliced grid indicates that the sliced grid is also useful for other applications. Future work includes application for other particle-based simulation and dynamic selection of the best axis for the sliced grid.

REFERENCES

[Harada07] Takahiro Harada, "Real-Time Rigid Body Simulation on GPUs," *GPU Gems 3*, Addison-Wesley Pearson Education, 2007, pp. 611–632.

[Harada07a] Takahiro Harada, Seiichi Koshizuka, and Yoichiro Kawaguchi, "Smoothed Particle Hydrodynamics on GPUs," *Proc. of Computer Graphics International*, 2007, pp. 63–70.

[Harris07] Mark Harris, Shubhabrata Sengupta, and John D. Owens, "Parallel Prefix Sum (Scan) with CUDA," *GPU Gems 3*, Addison-Wesley Pearson Education, 2007, pp. 851–876.

[Hernquist89] Lars Hernquist and Neal Katz, "TREESPH-A Unification of SPH with the Hierarchical Tree Method," *The Astrophysical Journal Supplement Series* 70, 1989, pp. 419–446.

[Mishra03] B.K. Mishra, "A Review of Computer Simulation of Tumbling Mills by the Discrete Element Method: Part 1 Contact Mechanics," *International Journal of Mineral Processing*, 71(1), 2003, pp.73–93.

[NVIDIA07] NVIDIA, Compute Unified Device Architecture, 2007, www.nvidia.com/object/cuda_home.html

9.2 Free-Viewpoint Video on the GPU

Marcos Avilés and Francisco Morán

Introduction

Free-viewpoint video has become an active field of research in recent years. The goal is to provide the user with the possibility of freely navigating within dynamic real-world scenes by choosing arbitrary viewpoints even though the footage is recorded by just a small number of static cameras.

This article presents a novel technique, running entirely on the GPU, which realistically reconstructs the shape and appearance of an object from a set of images [Laurentini94][Franco03]. Although other hardware-accelerated algorithms have been proposed in the past [Li03], they all follow a strict image-based rendering approach, where the final image is obtained at display time by combining the information of the cameras and the viewer position. As there is no explicit geometric information about the 3D objects in the scene, the resulting images (and not shapes) can hardly "interact" with the rest of the scene, which means, for instance, that no shadows can be cast or occlusions taken into account. Our proposed algorithm not only reconstructs the actual geometry of the main target object, making it take part in the scene as any other virtual object does, but also applies a clever texture-mapping on the resulting mesh that also allows for significant visual improvement over previous approaches [Debevec98].

The system is composed of several stages, which are depicted in Figure 9.2.1. The starting point is a set of images taken from different cameras at exactly the same time. These cameras need to be calibrated; that is, their internal (field of view, skew, and principal point) and external (location and orientation) parameters must be known beforehand. This lets us project a 3D point in space into a pixel in the image, or back-project a pixel in the image to a ray in space, both of which conform to the basic tools of our algorithm. The foreground object (what we want to reconstruct) is then isolated in the images through a process of background extraction. The resulting set of silhouettes is input to the shape reconstruction module, which builds a volumetric approximation of the object. However, we are not really interested in the volume itself but only in its surface, as graphic cards are optimized to render triangles, not volumetric elements (voxels). A triangle mesh is then extracted from the volume and finally texture-mapped using the source images to provide it with the same appearance the real object had.

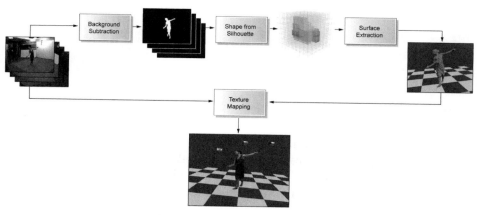

FIGURE 9.2.1 Stages and data flow of the reconstruction process. Note that, for illustrative purposes, the volumetric grid has been largely simplified.

BACKGROUND SUBTRACTION

Before proceeding with the volume reconstruction, the regions of interest—that is, the foreground object(s)—need to be isolated using a process of background subtraction. Background subtraction has been an active field of research in the past, and there are several techniques that cope with the problem. The basic scheme behind all of them is to subtract the current image from a reference image that models the background scene (see Figure 9.2.2). We will focus on the algorithm described in [Horprasert99], which is well suited for being implemented in the GPU and produces good results under reasonable settings. Nevertheless, a high-quality background subtraction can easily be achieved by using a dedicated environment like a blue screen.

FIGURE 9.2.2   Background subtraction. The foreground is isolated from the background and stored as a binary image.

BACKGROUND MODELING

During the process of background training, some parameters modeling the reference image are computed over a number of static background frames. Each of the pixels of the background is modeled statistically by a four-tuple $<E_i, s_i, a_i, b_i>$, where E_i is the expected color value, s_i is the standard deviation of color value, a_i is the variation of the brightness distortion, and b_i is the variation of the chromaticity distortion. More concretely:

$$E_i = [\mu_R(i)\ \mu_G(i)\ \mu_B(i)]$$

$$s_i = [\sigma_R(i)\ \sigma_G(i)\ \sigma_B(i)]$$

where $\mu_{R,G,B}(i)$ and $\sigma_{R,G,B}(i)$ are the red, green, and blue channels of the arithmetic mean and standard deviation of the ith pixel value, represented by $I_{R,G,B}(i)$, computed over N background frames. The remaining two parameters are defined as:

$$\alpha_i = \frac{\dfrac{I_R(i)\mu_R(i)}{\sigma_R^2(i)} + \dfrac{I_G(i)\mu_G(i)}{\sigma_G^2(i)} + \dfrac{I_B(i)\mu_B(i)}{\sigma_B^2(i)}}{\left(\dfrac{\mu_R(i)}{\sigma_R(i)}\right)^2 + \left(\dfrac{\mu_G(i)}{\sigma_G(i)}\right)^2 + \left(\dfrac{\mu_B(i)}{\sigma_B(i)}\right)^2}$$

$$\beta_i = \sqrt{\left(\frac{I_R(i) - \alpha_i\mu_R(i)}{\sigma_R(i)}\right)^2 + \left(\frac{I_G(i) - \alpha_i\mu_G(i)}{\sigma_G(i)}\right)^2 + \left(\frac{I_B(i) - \alpha_i\mu_B(i)}{\sigma_B(i)}\right)^2}$$

$$\alpha_i = \sqrt{\frac{\sum_{i=0}^{N} (\alpha_i - 1)^2}{N}}$$

$$b_i = \sqrt{\frac{\sum_{i=0}^{N} \beta_i^2}{N}}$$

All these values can be computed offline for each camera and stored locally, as they will be valid for all the reconstruction sessions as long as the camera positions and lighting conditions do not change.

PIXEL CLASSIFICATION

For each image being processed, we compute the difference both in brightness and chromaticity with the statistically modeled background. Pixels are thus classified as belonging to one of the following categories:

- **Background:** When both brightness and chromaticity are similar to those at the same location in the background image
- **Shaded background or shadow:** When they have similar chromaticity to the background pixels, but lower brightness
- **Highlighted background:** If they have similar chromaticity but higher brightness than the pixels in the background image
- **Foreground:** When the difference in chromaticity between them and the background image is high

By setting the appropriate thresholds to quantize these levels of similarity, we can easily classify each of the pixels. Note that, as different pixels yield different distributions of α_i and β_i, if we want to use a single threshold, we have to rescale their values accordingly:

$$\hat{\alpha}_i = \frac{\alpha_i - 1}{a_i} \qquad \hat{\beta}_i = \frac{\beta_i}{b_i}$$

IMPLEMENTATION

The implementation of this stage is fairly simple and straightforward. We render a "screen-aligned-and-sized" quad into an invisible texture buffer. By having this quad be the size of the output texture, we can have a pixel shader (PS) running for each output pixel. Both the current frame and the reference background image are set as textures, and the PS accesses their pixels through texture fetches. We use two RGBA floating-point textures to hold the eight values (three for E_i, another three for s_i, and one each for a_i and b_i) needed by the background image. For each pixel, we compute the normalized brightness and chromaticity distortion, $\hat{\alpha}_i$ and $\hat{\beta}_i$, and set the output color as either black or white depending on whether it belongs to the background or foreground (according to the thresholds described above).

SHAPE FROM SILHOUETTE

The idea behind our shape-from-silhouette algorithms is easy to understand. Each pixel in a silhouette image represents whether or not the visual ray from the optical center through that pixel intersects an object in the foreground of the scene. The union of these rays for all the points in the silhouette defines a generalized cone where the object must lie (although we have no information regarding depth). If we now consider the intersection of the generalized cones associated to a set of cameras, we can refine our spatial search and obtain a volume within which the object must be contained. This volume only approximates the true 3D shape, as it depends on the number of views, the positions of the viewpoints, and the complexity of the object. It is important to notice that, since concave areas are not observable in any silhouette, the silhouette-based reconstruction is only guaranteed to enclose the true volume. The best approximation, achievable in the limit by an infinite number of silhouettes captured from all the viewpoints outside the convex hull of the object, is called the *visual hull* [Laurentini94]. In practice, as only a finite number of silhouettes are combined to reconstruct the scene, the reconstructed volume is an approximation that includes the visual hull as well as other scene points. Figure 9.2.3 shows an example of a 2D scene reconstructed from three 1D silhouettes.

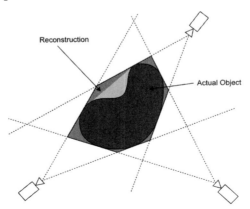

FIGURE 9.2.3   Intersection of the silhouette cones. Notice how the concave area in light gray will never be recovered, even if we increase the number of viewpoints.

Instead of trying to analytically compute the intersection of the viewing cones, which is not very GPU-friendly, we proceed in an alternative way. The whole volume of interest is discretized into $N \times N \times N$ equally sized voxels (N typically takes the values 128 or 256) and stored as a 3D texture in the GPU. Each voxel is then projected into all the silhouette images and tested for inclusion in the silhouette of the foreground objects. The final reconstruction will be composed of all voxels whose projection is included in all the silhouettes.

The size and position of the volume of interest are obtained by back-projecting the 2D bounding boxes of all views into 3D space and analyzing the resulting intersections in 3D space. This problem is solved by the CPU at initialization time through linear programming.

Instead of checking whether the whole projection of the voxel is included in a silhouette, we take a set of random samples in its interior and check their projections for inclusion. To perform the test for every voxel in the volume, we consider the 3D texture as an array of 2D textures. A PS covering each slice extent is run by rendering a quad from an orthogonal projection. Instancing can be used to render all the slices with only one call. In that case, the depth associated with each slice will be computed in the vertex shader (VS) through the INSTANCEID semantic.

Checking for the inclusion of the whole voxel projection can be an expensive operation, as it implies projecting its eight vertices and rasterizing the convex hull of their projections in the image. Nevertheless, if we consider that N is large enough (so the volume occupied by each voxel is relatively small) and that the image resolutions are the typical for standard video cameras, then the projection of a voxel at a medium distance covers only a few pixels in the image. Under these assumptions, checking just for the inclusion of the voxel center (which projects to only one pixel) seems to be a valid approximation.

The following code, written in Cg, shows a slightly simplified version, with only three silhouette images, of the PS:

```
void visualhull_fg(float3 voxelCenter : TEXCOORD0,
                   out unsigned int color : COLOR,
                   uniform float3x4 cameraProj[3],
                   uniform samplerRECT image0 : TEXUNIT0,
                   uniform samplerRECT image1 : TEXUNIT1,
                   uniform samplerRECT image2 : TEXUNIT2)
{
    // Put all the samplers in an array for easier access
    samplerRECT images[3] = { image0, image1, image2 };
```

```
float4 voxelCenterHom = float4(worldPos, 1.0);

bool inside = true;

for (int i = 0; i < 3 && inside; i++)
{
    // Project the voxel into the image
    float3 P = mul(cameraProj[i], voxelCenterHom);


    // Check whether its projection lies within the silhouette
    inside = texRECTproj(images[i], P).a > 0.0;
}


color = inside ? 1 : 0;
}
```

SURFACE EXTRACTION

Although we already have a 3D reconstruction of the object, it is described in terms of voxels, which is not the type of representation we are looking for. Since current graphic hardware is optimized for rendering triangle-based meshes, we need to extract the surface of our volume and convert it to a triangle mesh.

The well-known marching cubes algorithm [Lorensen87] was developed for extracting a polygon mesh from an isosurface defined in a 3D scalar field. Our volumetric reconstruction is indeed a scalar field, with the only particularity being that it is a binary one: Its values are restricted to 0 or 1, indicating whether the voxel is empty or occupied.

We sequentially analyze each of the voxels in the grid and, according to the value that the scalar field takes at each of its eight corners, determine the number and disposition of the triangles needed to represent the surface passing through that voxel. There is a total number of 256 configurations, which can be obtained from 15 unique cases through reflections and rotations (see Figure 9.2.4).

New vertices are placed in the middle of edges whose endpoints have different values. Thus, defining a convention for vertex and edge ordering, such as the one shown inFigure 9.2.5, we can easily store the triangle connectivity referred to these edges. As the maximum number of triangles that can be created for a single voxel is 5, and there are 12 edges, we only need to hold a maximum of 15 indices in the range [0..11] per configuration. These indices are then stored as columns of a 2D array with 256 rows. The special index −1 is used for configurations producing fewer than five triangles. For instance, a row like this

[0 10 1 0 8 10 8 11 10 -1 -1 -1 -1 -1 -1]

will result in three triangles with vertices at midpoints of edges (*e0*, *e10*, *e1*), (*e0*, *e8*, *e10*) and (*e8*, *e11*, *e10*).

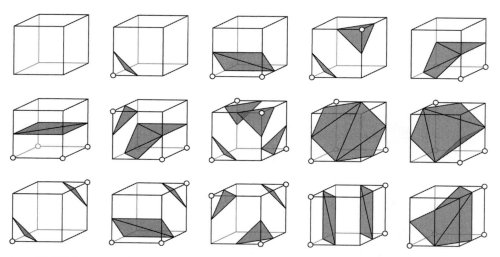

FIGURE 9.2.4 The 15 unique configurations of the marching cubes algorithm.

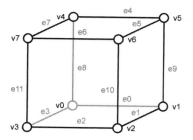

FIGURE 9.2.5 Convention for vertex and edge ordering.

To select the appropriate configuration, each of the eight voxel corners is tested in a particular order for having a non-zero value, and the resulting bit is logically appended through an OR operation to a byte-sized codeword, which uniquely identifies the exact configuration among the 256 ones described above.

This solves the problem of extracting a triangle mesh from our discretized visual hull, but geometry alone is still not enough: For rendering purposes, triangle—or, preferably, vertex—normals are extremely useful.

Vertex normals are typically computed as the average of the normals of the triangles sharing them, which implies determining the connectivity of the whole surface and, in the best of cases, an additional rendering pass. Instead, we calculate vertex normals directly from the 3D field by estimating the gradient (the partial derivative in the x, y, and z directions) at those points where the vertices are generated. The gradient is thus computed using central differencing on the corners of the four voxels adjacent to the edge where the vertex is inserted.

Depending on the direction of this edge and the direction along which we want to estimate the gradient, the volumetric function will be sampled on a different set of neighboring corners. Figure 9.2.6 shows which concrete corners are involved in the computation of the gradient of a vertex created along an edge parallel to the y-axis. Note that the remaining corner masks can be trivially obtained by rotation.

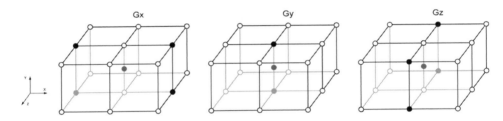

FIGURE 9.2.6   3D kernel for computing the gradient on a vertex generated along an edge parallel to the y-axis.

PUTTING IT ALL TOGETHER

A straightforward implementation of this part consists of a geometry shader (GS) that takes as input an array of points representing the location of the voxels in the grid. Additionally, two textures are passed as uniform variables: the 3D voxel occupancy function and the 256×15 triangle configuration table. The GS then processes each voxel and samples the volumetric texture at its eight corners to find out the configuration codeword. This codeword is now used to sample the triangle configuration texture. The corresponding row is read sequentially until index -1 is found, resulting in the generation of three vertices and one triangle per triplet of indices. The following block of code illustrates this.

```
// Find the codeword
int codeword = 0;
```

```
codeword |= tex3D(volumeTex, voxel + float3(0.0, 0.0, 0.0));
codeword |= tex3D(volumeTex, voxel + float3(  d, 0.0, 0.0));
...
codeword |= tex3D(volumeTex, voxel + float3(0.0,   d,   d));

// Create vertices
for (int i = 0; i < 5; i++)
{
    int3 edges = texRECT(triTable, float2(i, codeword)).rgb;
    if (edges.r < 0)
        break;

    createVertex(voxel, vertices.r,...)
    createVertex(voxel, vertices.g,...)
    createVertex(voxel, vertices.b,...)

    restartStrip();
}
```

The procedure createVertex takes both the voxel location and the edge index, and emits the vertex already transformed by the view-projection matrix. It also computes its normal as explained above.

The main drawback of this implementation is that all the heavy work (finding the configuration, generating vertices, estimating their normals) is done in the GS. Although the introduction of GSs in the programmable pipeline has provided quite a lot of flexibility, it has been at some cost, since their performance is substantially lower than that of VSs or PSs. Besides, the execution speed of GSs decreases as the maximum size of their output increases. In our case, the maximum output is 15 vertices, each consisting of 6 floats, for a total of 90 floats. Our target is then to try moving as much work as possible to other parts of the pipeline and to reduce the GS maximum output.

The former can be achieved by making using of the stream-out capabilities introduced in newer-generation cards. Instead of doing all the work in one pass, we split it into two passes. In the first pass, the GS outputs the location of the vertices, but no additional information, to a feedback buffer that is later employed as a vertex buffer in the second pass. As it is composed of triplets of vertices, each of them representing a triangle, a simple call to glDrawArrays will be enough to render them. The VS of the second pass will be then responsible of computing the vertex normals.

By moving the normal calculation to the VS, we have already reduced the maximum output of the GS to half its previous value. However, it can be further optimized by noticing that 32-bit floating-point precision is not really needed to encode the vertex coordinates. As the voxel grid is uniformly spaced (and the voxel dimensions are known beforehand), each voxel can be described using a triplet of (small) integer coordinates. Besides, we know that all the vertices on the surface are located in the midpoints of the edges in the grid; that is, we only need one additional bit to encode the fact that the vertex can be located half-way between two voxels. Even considering high-resolution grids of up to 512×512×512 voxels, only 9 + 1 bits are thus needed to encode each vertex coordinate. This means we can pack the three vertex coordinates in just one 32-bit integer instead of 3, reducing the GS maximum output to just 15 integers—that is, one-sixth of the initial amount!

Of course, this new strategy has the additional overhead of needing an extra pass, but even with that, its performance is considerably higher.

TEXTURE MAPPING

Now that the model geometry has been recovered, together with the vertex normals, the last step consists of endowing it with photometric information so that textures obtained from the source images can be mapped onto the object surface at rendering time. We analyze below the three alternatives we have considered.

VIEW-INDEPENDENT VERSUS VIEW-DEPENDENT TEXTURE MAPPING

Our first choice is to map the information coming from those cameras that are oriented perpendicularly to the surface, since the area to be mapped will be represented in the image with the lowest distortion (on the other hand, this same region will appear highly distorted on those images taken from cameras at a glancing edge). As in the unstructured lumigraph rendering algorithm detailed in [Buehler01], we let the influence of a single image in the final rendering be a smoothly varying function across the object geometry. More concretely, the contribution of each source image at a given 3D point on the object surface is proportional to the angle between the corresponding camera viewing direction and the normal at that point (see Figure 9.2.7a). We call this method *view-independent* texture mapping (VITM) because it does not depend on where the object is seen from, but only on its geometry (and of course the original camera setting). However, this implies that if the user, at rendering time, chooses a viewpoint matching any of the original ones, even exactly (i.e., same location, orientation, field of view…), the virtual view will not correspond to the original view, which is something that we might expect—but that we cannot achieve, as no other combination of cameras can describe the object better than the camera where the viewer is!

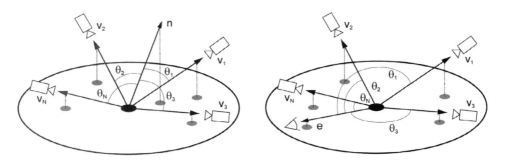

FIGURE 9.2.7 Weight calculation for view-independent (left) and view-dependent (right) texture mapping.

This leads us to consider *view-dependent* texturing mapping (VDTM) like the one described in [Debevec98], where the contribution of each camera is proportional to the angle between its viewing vector and the vector representing where the viewer is looking (see Figure 9.2.7b). With this approach, the virtual view will be mainly obtained from the set of cameras that is close (in orientation) to the user viewpoint.

AND THE WINNER IS... NONE OF THE ABOVE: HYBRID TEXTURE MAPPING!

In principle, VDTM sounds like "the" way to go, and it would indeed be… if the shape reconstruction were perfect! But it is not, for several reasons: The visual hull may have been overly "voxelized" (spatially sub-sampled), the binary decision of including or excluding a voxel is based on another sampling process, the marching cubes algorithm is not able to generate smooth shapes by itself, and so on. This is why the reconstructed 3D mesh, once projected in the frame buffer, has a many times bigger silhouette than it should. And, logically enough, a portion of the source image(s) corresponding to the background is erroneously texture-mapped onto the pixels lying in the "halo" between the real and reconstructed silhouettes. This artifact ranges from hardly noticeable to extremely annoying, when there is a large color difference between the background and the object (see Figure 9.2.8 (left). Besides, the regions of the object whose normal is almost perpendicular to the viewing direction will be covered by very distorted images.

The VITM approach described above does solve this problem, since all texture mapping assignments are intrinsic to the object (and to the placement of the cameras, but not to the viewpoint of the user), so each region is always textured with an optimal source image blend. However, as has been stated above, the marching cubes algorithm is unfortunately not known for generating smooth meshes, and distinctly faceted shapes are mishandled by VITM. Indeed, two object regions separated by a

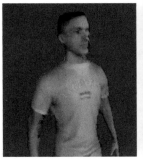

FIGURE 9.2.8 Comparison of different texture mapping schemes: view-dependent (left), view-independent (middle), and our proposed hybrid solution (right).

crease edge (set) will be textured with very different source image blends, and although in a mathematically perfect world the photometric information provided by two cameras for the same 3D point should be the same, in practice it is not. This causes another disturbing artifact, shown in Figure 9.2.8 (middle): texture mismatches in the borders of regions with different orientations.

The flaws of VDTM and VITM make us finally choose a hybrid texture mapping (HTM) scheme that avoids those flaws while combining the pros of both approaches (see Figure 9.2.8, right). First, the VITM coefficients that weight each camera contribution for a 3D point **P** are computed as the scalar product between the normal at **P** and the ray **R** looking at the optical center of the camera from **P**. Second, the VDTM coefficients are computed as the dot product between the user-chosen viewing direction and **R**. Both sets of coefficients are then added together, and the result is normalized so that they all sum up to 1 (to keep the lighting). The final color is thus obtained as the weighted combination (through the previously computed coefficients) of all the images, which are also applied through projective texture mapping.

The following code summarizes this stage:

```
// Weights for VITM
float alpha0 = max(dot(normal, normalize(pos.xyz - cameraPos[0])), 0);
float alpha1 = max(dot(normal, normalize(pos.xyz - cameraPos[1])), 0);
...


// Add the weights for VDTM
alpha0 += max(dot(viewDir.xyz, normalize(pos.xyz - cameraPos[0])), 0);
alpha1 += max(dot(viewDir.xyz, normalize(pos.xyz - cameraPos[1])), 0);
```

```
...


// Normalize the coefficients so that they all sum up to 1
float sumAlpha = alpha0 + alpha1 + ...
sumAlpha = sumAlpha > 0 ? 1 / sumAlpha : 1;
alpha0 *= sumAlpha;
alpha1 *= sumAlpha;

...


// Compute the (projective) texture coordinates for each camera
float3 texcoord0 = mul(cameraProj[0], pos);
float3 texcoord1 = mul(cameraProj[1], pos);

...


// Finally compute the output color as the weighted contribution
// of the cameras
float3 color = float3(0.0, 0.0, 0.0);
color += alpha0 * texRECT(image0, texcoord0.xy /texcoord0.z).rgb;
color += alpha1 * texRECT(image1, texcoord1.xy /texcoord1.z).rgb;

...
```

HANDLING VISIBILITY

Notice that something that deserves special care, regardless of the approach chosen from the three described above, is to avoid mapping on any triangle a portion of the image captured by a camera that was unable to see that triangle. Mapping the image from a camera to a triangle that is occluded by some other region of the objects would yield visually unacceptable results, as the portion of the texture that would get mapped corresponds to the occluding region.

These visibility tests can be performed using exactly the same machinery employed in shadowing (such as, for instance, shadow mapping), but computing the visibility with respect to a camera instead of doing it with respect to a light. Those cameras that are not seen from a given point will have their contribution weight set to zero.

CONCLUSION

We have presented a novel technique, running entirely on the GPU, for reconstructing the shape and appearance of a real 3D object from a set of images taken by real, calibrated cameras. A set of silhouettes resulting from a background extraction process is input to the shape reconstruction module of our system, which yields a set of voxels containing the visual hull of the object. The marching cubes algorithm is then run to obtain a triangle mesh onto which the adequate portions of the source images are mapped to have the virtual object look like the real one. The texture mapping module does not follow a completely view-independent approach, or a view-dependent one, but a hybrid scheme that combines the best assets of both. Both Figure 9.2.9 and Figure 9.2.10 illustrate the result by showing one time frame of two different sequences taken by eight cameras.

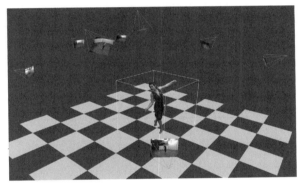

FIGURE 9.2.9   Screenshot from the "dance" sequence showing the reconstructed geometry and the location where the images were taken.

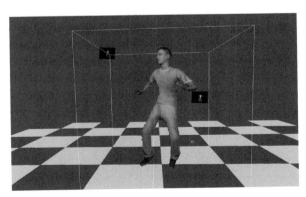

FIGURE 9.2.10   Screenshot from the "hip-hop" sequence.

Regarding performance, our probably-not-fully-optimized implementation runs at interactive rates over 25 fps on standard PCs equipped with NVIDIA GeForce 8800GTX cards for grid resolutions of 128×128×128 voxels and eight viewpoints. We have found, however, that the main bottleneck in our application is located (at least for small and medium-sized grids) on the texture uploading from the CPU to the GPU, as a whole set of images has to be moved from system to video memory every single frame. Using a compressed format for the textures such as DXTC could substantially alleviate this problem.

ACKNOWLEDGMENTS

The multiple-video "dance" sequence is taken from INRIA Rhône-Alpes multiple-camera platform Grimage and PERCEPTION research group [Perception06]. The 3D model used in the hip-hop sequence is courtesy of aXYZ design. The authors would also like to thank Wolfgang Van Raemdonck from IMEC for his generous help.

REFERENCES

[Buehler01] C. Buehler, M. Bosse, L. McMillan, S. J. Gortler and M. F. Cohen, "Unstructured Lumigraph Rendering," *Proceedings of ACM SIG¬GRAPH*, 425–432, August 2001.

[Debevec98] P. E. Debevec, G. Borshukov and Y. Yu, "Efficient View-Dependent Image-Based Rendering with Projective Texture-Mapping," *Proceedings of the Euro-graphics Rendering Workshop*, 105–116, June 1998.

[Franco03] J-S. Franco and E. Boyer, "Exact Polyhedral Visual Hulls," *Proceedings of the British Machine Vision Conference*, 329–338, September 2003.

[Horprasert99] T. Horprasert, D. Harwood, and L.S. Davis, "A Statistical Approach for Real-Time Robust Background Subtraction and Shadow Detection," *Proceedings of the IEEE International Conference on Computer Vision, Frame-Rate Workshop*, 1–19, September 1999.

[Laurentini94] A. Laurentini, "The Visual Hull Concept for Silhouette-Based Image Understanding," *IEEE Transactions on Pattern Analysis and Machine Intelligence*, **16**-2, 150–162, February 1994.

[Li03] M. Li, M. Magnor and H-P. Seidel, "Hardware-Accelerated Visual Hull Reconstruction and Rendering," *Proceedings of Graphics Interface*, 65–72, June 2003.

[Lorensen87] W. Lorensen and H. Cline, "Marching Cubes: A High Resolution 3D Surface Construction Algorithm," *Proceedings of ACM SIG¬GRAPH*, 163–169, July 1987.

[Perception06] The Multiple-Camera/Multiple-Video Database of the PERCEPTION group, INRIA Rhône-Alpes. https://charibdis.inrialpes.fr.

9.3 A Volume Shader for Quantum Voronoi Diagrams Inside the 3D Bloch Ball

FRANK NIELSEN (FRANK.NIELSEN@ACM.ORG)
ÉCOLE POLYTECHNIQUE (FRANCE)
SONY COMPUTER SCIENCE LABORATORIES, INC. (JAPAN)

INTRODUCTION AND PRELIMINARIES

In quantum information theory [NielsenChuang'00], particle state distributions are analyzed probabilistically by means of density matrices X.

A d-level system is characterized by a $d \times d$ square matrix with complex coefficients that satisfies the following three core properties:

1. X is equal to its conjugate transpose: $X = (X^*)^T$; that is, density matrix X is *Hermitian*. (The conjugate of a matrix is the matrix with all conjugate elements.)

2. X has *unit trace*, where the trace of a matrix is defined as the sum of its diagonal coefficients: $\text{trace}(X) = \sum_i X_{i,i} = 1$. This means that the trace of X has *no* imaginary part.

3. X is *semi-positive definite*. That is, we have for all d-dimensional vectors x, the following property: $x^T X x \geq 0$.

When studying systems representing statistically one quantum bit (or 1-qubit, for short), the above three conditions yield the following parameterized set of 2×2 density matrices:

$$X = \left\{ \frac{1}{2} \begin{bmatrix} 1+z & x-iy \\ x+iy & 1-z \end{bmatrix}, x^2 + y^2 + z^2 = 1 \right\}$$

where i denotes the imaginary complex number ($i^2 = -1$). Note that, unfortunately, there are no such simple equivalent representations of matrix densities for higher-level systems since the semi-positive definite property is much more delicate to handle in higher dimensions.

It follows that states of 1 qubit can be represented equivalently by a triplet of real numbers (x,y,z): a 3D point inside a unit ball centered at the origin.

In quantum theory, this unit ball is called the Bloch ball [NielsenChuang'00, Bloch], where a special parameterization proposed by physicist Felix Bloch is used to describe the quantum states [NielsenChuang'00]. Note that in classical information theory, the state of a bit is either true or false. For a quantum bit, its "state" is rather a superposition of states with respective probability given by the Hermitian density matrix.

Pure states X have degenerated matrices of rank 1 (that is, matrix X is not invertible). Pure states correspond to the density matrices parameterized by triplets lying on the surface of the Bloch ball: the Bloch sphere.

Mixed states have full rank 2: They correspond to triplets (x,y,z) falling strictly inside the Bloch sphere.

Von Neumann Quantum Entropy and Its Relative Entropy Divergence

In classical information theory [NielsenChuang'00], one uses the Shannon entropy on probability distributions p to define the following quantity that measures the degree of uncertainty of a distribution:

$$H(p) = \sum_i p_i \log \frac{1}{p_i} = -\sum_i p_i \log p_i$$

The distance between two statistical distributions p and q is then defined using the asymmetric Kullback-Leibler divergence:

$$KL(p\|q) = \sum_i p_i \log \frac{p_i}{q_i} \geq 0$$

Similarly, Von Neumann generalized this entropy measure and relative entropy distortion measure ("distance") to get, respectively, the quantum entropy and quantum divergence as:

$$H(X) = -Tr(X \log X)$$

and

$$I(P\|Q) = Tr(P(\log P - \log Q)) \geq 0$$

where the logarithm of a Hermitian matrix is defined from the matrix spectral decomposition.

Let the spectral decomposition of X be

$$
\text{Diag}(\lambda) = \begin{bmatrix}
\lambda_1 & 0 & \cdots & \cdots & 0 \\
0 & \lambda_2 & 0 & \cdots & \vdots \\
\vdots & 0 & \ddots & & \vdots \\
\vdots & & \ddots & \ddots & \vdots \\
0 & \cdots & \cdots & 0 & \lambda_d
\end{bmatrix}
$$

where $X = V \times \text{Diag}(\lambda) \times V^*$ is a diagonal matrix of d eigenvalues.

Then the logarithm matrix of X is defined as $X = V \times \text{Diag}(\log\lambda) \times V^*$.

A remarkable property between classic and quantum theory is given by the following inequality:

$$I(X\|X') \geq KL(\lambda,\lambda') \geq 0$$

where λ and λ' are the respective eigenvalues of matrix X and X'.

These information-theoretic divergences are not symmetric, nor do they satisfy the triangular inequality of metrics. Furthermore, the quantum divergence $I(.\|.)$ is not well-defined when right-side matrix X' is not full rank since the logarithm of the matrix cannot be properly computed (one of the eigenvalues is equal to zero).

QUANTUM VORONOI DIAGRAMS

Given a set of n density matrices $\{X_1,...,X_n\}$, called *sites* or *generators*, the *Voronoi diagram* of these quantum states defines a *partition* of the space into elementary *Voronoi cells*. The Voronoi cell of a given site is defined by the set of density matrices closer to that site than to any of the other sites. Since the divergence $I(P\|Q)$ is asymmetric, we consider the following three kinds of *Voronoi cells* as follows:

1. The right-side Voronoi cell: $\text{Vor}_R(X_i) = \{X_1 \mid I(X_i \| X) \leq I(X_j \| X)\}$

2. The left-side Voronoi cell: $\text{Vor}_L(X_i) = \{X \mid I(X \mid X_i) \leq I(X \| X_j)\}$

3. The symmetrized Voronoi cell obtained by symmetrizing the divergence:
   $\text{Vor}_S(X_i) = \{X \mid I(X \| X_i) + I(X_i \| X \mid) \leq I(X \| X_j) + I(X_j \| X)\}$

We are interested in interactively computing and visualizing these quantum Voronoi diagrams using GPU pixel shaders. Interactively exploring these structures proved to be very helpful for researchers to gain intuition. Indeed, interactive visualization helps in revealing structural properties, and may thus be useful in a number of settings including, for example, to get a visual feeling of the additivity property of Holevo's channel capacity [Holevo'04] that is conjectured to hold but not yet proved.

In the remainder, we distinguish two fundamental cases:

1. The quantum Voronoi diagrams of mixed density matrices
2. The quantum Voronoi diagram of pure density matrices

Figure 9.3.1 illustrates a cross-section of the Bloch ball showing the quantum Voronoi diagram of mixed density matrices on that cutting plane. The color figure is available from the web page indicated in the conclusion. The red lines depict the Voronoi affine separators (right-type), the blue lines show the dual curved Voronoi diagram, and the green lines show the symmetrized curved Voronoi diagram [NielsenBoissonnatNock'07]. For comparison, we also added the regular affine Euclidean Voronoi diagram in purple. A video showing an animation of the cross-section of the Bloch ball is available at the URL mentioned in the conclusion. The video allows one to observe the relationships of the internal quantum and Euclidean Voronoi diagrams.

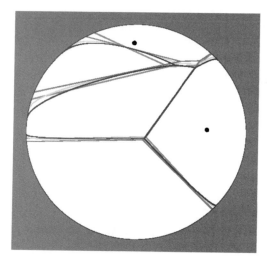

FIGURE 9.3.1   A cross-section of the Bloch ball showing the various quantum and Euclidean Voronoi diagrams. The Voronoi generators are rasterized using small-radii balls. Here, we see two of these "site balls" intersecting the cross-section plane.

Nielsen and Nock [NielsenNock'08] showed that the quantum Voronoi diagram is a kind of generic Bregman Voronoi diagram for the appropriate Bregman generator acting on Hermitian matrices. It follows that the right-side Voronoi diagram has affine bisectors and can be computed as a power diagram in disguise [NielsenBoissonnatNock'07]. The left-side Voronoi diagram can be computed from a right-side Voronoi diagram using a dual divergence defined by the Legendre convex conjugate [NielsenBoissonnatNock'07].

QUANTUM VORONOI DIAGRAMS FOR PURE STATES

Kato et al. [KatoImai'07] and Nielsen and Nock [NielsenNock'08] proved that the Voronoi diagram of pure density matrices lying on the Bloch sphere is equivalent to a spherical Voronoi diagram with respect to the geodesic distance (proportional to the angle defined by the pure states). Alternatively, this spherical Voronoi diagram can also be computed by intersecting the 3D Euclidean Voronoi diagram with the sphere (Figure 9.3.2).

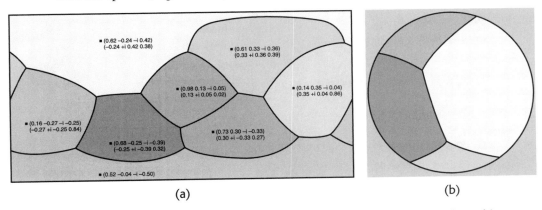

(a)   (b)

FIGURE 9.3.2   Using the GPU to visualize the quantum Voronoi diagram of 1-qubit pure states. Voronoi cells are (a) annotated with their corresponding density matrices on the latitude-longitude map, and (b) can be visualized on the Bloch sphere.

We compute this quantum Voronoi diagram on the Bloch sphere by choosing a latitude-longitude representation of the pure states (also called theta-phi representations using the 3D point spherical coordinates).

The GPU code for computing the quantum Voronoi diagram of pure states on the Bloch sphere consists of tracing the border of the Voronoi cells on this latitude-longitude environment map and using the texture mapping to wrap that environment texture onto the Bloch sphere.

The Cg per-pixel shader that allows the GPU to rasterize the Voronoi diagram onto the latitude-longitude map is given below. The shader proceeds as follows: It basically converts the 2D texture position pos passed as an argument into an equivalent 3D point lying on the sphere using a spherical to Cartesian conversion procedure. The shader calculates the distance between a given site and a point on the latitude-longitude texture map by first converting them into equivalent 3D points on the sphere using the function Spherical2Cartesian, and then calculating their distance on the sphere using the function DistanceSphere. For all pixels pos, the index of the closest Voronoi generator is found using the function Winner, and the color of the pixel is assigned according to the mapping function WinnerColor.

```
// Quantum Voronoi Diagram on the Bloch Sphere
// (c) 2007 2008 Frank Nielsen
// Density matrices: pure states
// (Quantum pure state Voronoi = Spherical Voronoi)


// Number & coordinates of Voronoi sites (pure 1-qubit systems)
#define MAXN 8
float2 position[MAXN];


// Bounding box of domain X
float minx,maxx,miny,maxy;


// Border thickness of Voronoi cells
float s=1.0/300.0;


// Max textures [0,1] coordinate to domain X: LERP rescaling
float2 ToDomain(float2 p)
{return float2(minx+(maxx-minx)*p[0],miny+(maxy-miny)*p[1]);}


// Convert latitude longitude to 3D xyz Cartesian coordinate
float3 Spherical2Cartesian(float2 tp)
{float3 xyz;
xyz[0]=cos(tp[1])*sin(tp[0]);
xyz[1]=sin(tp[1]);
xyz[2]=cos(tp[1])*cos(tp[0]);
```

```
return xyz;
}


float DistanceSphere(float2 tp, float2 tq)
{float3 P, Q;
float angle;
P=Spherical2Cartesian(tp);
Q=Spherical2Cartesian(tq);
angle=acos(P[0]*Q[0]+P[1]*Q[1]+P[2]*Q[2]);
return abs(angle);
}


// Reports the index of the closest point
int Winner(float2 p)
{
int i,winner;
float dist,mindist=1.0e5;

dist=DistanceSphere(p,position[0]);
mindist=dist;
for(i=1;i<MAXN;i++)
{
        dist=DistanceSphere(p,position[i]);
        if (dist<mindist)
                {mindist=dist;winner=i;}
}
return winner;
}


// A few colors
float3 c1=float3(0.575426,0.111484,0.979553);
float3 c2=float3(0.348125,0.875674,0.16422);
float3 c3=float3(0.88638,0.357219,0.288858);
```

```
float3 c4=float3(0.819391,0.31315,0.378887);
float3 c5=float3(0.859276,0.0589618,0.240242);
float3 c6=float3(0.382763,0.815882,0.287912);
float3 c7=float3(0.920255,0.955535,0.0535295);
float3 c8=float3(0.827662,0.193457,0.273507);


float3 WinnerColor(int p)
{float3 c;
if (p==0) c=c1; if (p==1) c=c2; if (p==2) c=c3;
if (p==3) c=c4; if (p==4) c=c5; if (p==5) c=c6;
if (p==6) c=c7; if (p==7) c=c8;
return c;
}


// Voronoi sphere on latitude longitude map
float3  VoronoiSphere(float2 pos: TEXCOORD0) : COLOR0
{
int index, indexx, indexy;
float2 posx,posy; // position of the shader pixel
float3 color;


// pos is in [0,1]
posx=ToDomain(pos+float2(s,0));
posy=ToDomain(pos+float2(0,s));
pos=ToDomain(pos);


index=Winner(pos); indexx=Winner(posx); indexy=Winner(posy);


if ((index!=indexx)||(index!=indexy))
      color=float3(0,0,0); // black
            else color=WinnerColor(index);
return color;
}
```

The C++ code and accompanying Visual C++ project is available in the program directory GPUQuantumVoronoiPure. A trackball user interface is provided for interactively exploring the Voronoi structures of these pure state density matrices.

QUANTUM VORONOI DIAGRAMS FOR MIXED STATES

The quantum Voronoi diagram of density matrices encoding mixed states is far more difficult to design since we need to visualize inside the Bloch ball structures using transparency. We design a volume shader that rasterizes the Bloch ball using RGB color and alpha channel attributes. This allows one not only to visualize the mixed state sites by transparency, but more importantly, allows us to display the various quantum right, left, and symmetrized Voronoi diagrams since they are all distinct for the case of mixed-state generators. To explain the basic programming principle, let us for now consider the regular Euclidean Voronoi diagram of 3D points. We design a pixel shader that, given a quad to texture, will rasterize the pixel by choosing a color according to the color assigned to its nearest generator. We can also clip this Euclidean Voronoi diagram to the unit sphere, and further choose to draw Voronoi bisectors (the borders of Voronoi cells) using simple tests to check whether neighborhood pixels have the same closest Voronoi generator or not. If not, the pixel belongs to the boundary of the Voronoi diagram: It is part of a Voronoi bisector. Figure 9.3.3 illustrates these software volume shaders using the traditional Euclidean distance to start with.

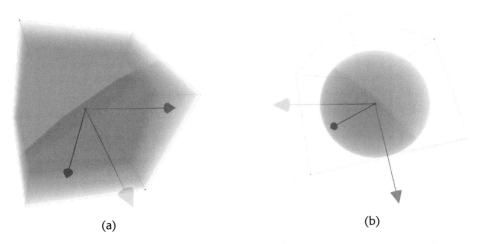

(a)   (b)

FIGURE 9.3.3   The left figure (a) visualizes the Euclidean Voronoi bisector of two antipodal generators. The right figure (b) similarly volumetrically renders these Voronoi cells delimited by the Euclidean bisector. These cells are all clipped with a unit sphere.

We can furthermore choose to color each cell of the Voronoi diagram with an attribute color and display the bisector "walls" using another specially chosen color.

Moreover, a target cell may be displayed with a different transparency attribute to emphasize its location and boundaries with respect to the other cells. Figure 9.3.4 illustrates the interactive visualization that modern GPUs offer.

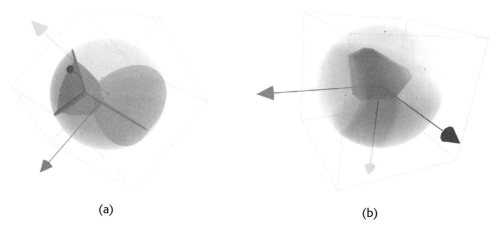

(a)   (b)

FIGURE 9.3.4   Using a pixel shader to render a volumetric Voronoi diagram with transparency attribute (a). The color of the Voronoi boundaries can be freely chosen to emphasize the boundaries of Voronoi cells. (b) A Euclidean 3D Voronoi diagram using a different transparency mode for the color of the target cell reveals the convex polyhedron structure of the internal Voronoi region.

The pixel shader fragment for performing these tasks is given below:

```
// (c) August 2008, Frank Nielsen
//
float radius=1.0;
float centerx=0.5, centery=0.5,  centerz=0.5;
float zzz; // slice level


float4 colorBloch=float4(0.0,0.0,0.0,0.00); // ambiance color


float4 colorRight=float4(0.5,0.0,0.0,0.01);
float4 colorLeft=float4(0.5,0.0,0.0,0.01);
float4 colorSymmetrized=float4(0.5,0.0,0.0,0.01);
```

```
float4 colorEuclidean=float4(1,0.0,0,1);
float4 colorBorder=float4(0.5, 0.5 ,0.5 ,1);

float4 colorWhite=float4(0,0.0,0,0);

#define  tt 0.01

float4 c0=float4(0.827662,0.193457,0.27350,tt);
float4 c1=float4(0.575426,0.111484,0.979553,tt);
float4 c2=float4(0.348125,0.875674,0.16422,tt);
float4 c3=float4(0.88638,0.357219,0.288858,tt);
float4 c4=float4(0.819391,0.31315,0.378887,tt);
float4 c5=float4(0.859276,0.0589618,0.240242,tt);
float4 c6=float4(0.382763,0.815882,0.287912,tt);
float4 c7=float4(0.920255,0.955535,0.0535295,tt);

float4 WinnerColor(int p)
{
float4 c;
if (p==0) c=c0; if (p==1) c=c1; if (p==2) c=c2;
if (p==3) c=c3; if (p==4) c=c4; if (p==5) c=c5;
if (p==6) c=c6; if (p==7) c=c7;
return c;
}

float s=0.01;
#define MAXN 8
float3 position[MAXN];

float SqrL2(float x1, float y1, float z1, float x2,float y2,float z2)
{return (x2-x1)*(x2-x1)+(y2-y1)*(y2-y1)+(z2-z1)*(z2-z1);}

double Distance(float3 p, float3 q)
```

```
{
double x1=p[0],y1=p[1],z1=p[2];
double x2=q[0],y2=q[1],z2=q[2];
return (x2-x1)*(x2-x1)+(y2-y1)*(y2-y1)+(z2-z1)*(z2-z1);
}


int Winner(float3 p)
{
int i,winner;
float dist,mindist=1.0e5;

dist=Distance(p,position[0]);
mindist=dist;
for(i=1;i<MAXN;i++)
{
        dist=Distance(p,position[i]);
        if (dist<mindist)
                {mindist=dist;winner=i;}
}
return winner;
}




float4  QuantumVoronoi(float2 pos: TEXCOORD0) : COLOR0
{
float rr=SqrL2(centerx,centery,centerz, pos.x,pos.y,zzz);
int index, indexx, indexy;
float3 npos, nposx,nposy; // position of the shader pixel

npos=float3(pos[0],pos[1],zzz);
index=Winner(npos);
```

```
if (rr<0.5*0.5)

{

        return WinnerColor(index);

}
else

        return colorWhite;

}
```

This shader is called whenever texturing 2D quads slicing the unit cube.

We render 200 z-slices for the above figures using the following OpenGL/Cg code:

```
// 200 slices
for(float l=1.0;l>=0.0;l-=0.005)

{

glEnable(GL_TEXTURE_2D);

cgGLEnableProfile(FProfile); CheckCgError();

cgGLBindProgram(FProgram); CheckCgError();

cgGLSetParameterArray3f(CGposition,0,MAXN,position);

cgGLSetParameter1f(CGzzz,l);

QuadZ(l);

cgGLDisableProfile(FProfile);

glDisable(GL_TEXTURE_2D);

}
```

For quantum Voronoi diagrams with mixed-state generators, we need to define explicitly in the shader the Von Neumann relative entropy between Hermitian matrix P and Hermitian matrix Q (encoded, respectively, by 3D points p and q strictly falling inside the Bloch ball). The formula is quite intricate but can be simplified by using the radii of p and q and their dot product $<p,q> = p_x q_x + p_y q_y + p_z q_z$. We calculate the divergence [KatoImai'07] as:

$$I(P||Q) = \frac{1+r_p}{2} \log \frac{1+r_p}{2} + \frac{1-r_p}{2} \log \frac{1-r_p}{2} - \frac{1}{2} \log \frac{1-r_q^2}{4} - \frac{<p,q>}{2r_q} \log \frac{1+r_q}{1-r_q}$$

Since the GPU shaders allow one to render at an interactive frame rate, we may also animate the generators by assigning them a velocity and observe that the quantum Voronoi diagrams of mixed states tend in the limit case of pure states to the regular Euclidean Voronoi diagram. The program QuantumVoronoiDiagramMixedStates.cpp provides a user interface for choosing and animating Voronoi generators.

QUANTUM CHANNEL AND HOLEVO'S CAPACITY

A quantum channel is modeled mathematically as a linear transform T. That is, a quantum channel is described by an affine map T that maps quantum states to other quantum states. The geometric effect of a channel is to map the Bloch ball to a deformed 3D ellipsoid by T, which is always strictly contained inside the Bloch ball. The Holevo capacity C(T) of this channel T is defined as the smallest radius of the ball enclosing the ellipsoid [NielsenNock'08] as follows:

$$C(T) = \inf_P \sup_Q I(T(Q) \| T(P)),$$

where I(.||.) denotes the quantum relative entropy.

Therefore, the Holevo capacity of a channel amounts to geometrically computing the smallest enclosing ball with respect to I(.||.) of the deformed Bloch ball. We provide several approximation algorithms in [NielsenNock'08].

Figure 9.3.5 shows such a relative entropy ball visualized using the same volume technique: slicing the unit bounding box and rasterizing using a pixel fragment shader.

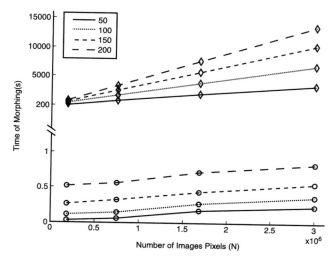

FIGURE 9.3.5 Visualizing the smallest ball enclosing the deformed Bloch ball using a software volume rendering based on a GPU pixel fragment.

CONCLUDING REMARKS

We have presented several pixel shaders for rendering the quantum Voronoi diagrams of 1-qubits represented by their density Hermitian matrices or equivalent 3D points in the Bloch ball. The quantum Voronoi diagram of pure-state sites amounts to computing a Voronoi diagram on the surface defined with respect to the geodesic arcs. This can be rasterized interactively on the GPU using a pixel shader that prepares a latitude longitude environment map that is then textured on the Bloch sphere. The quantum Voronoi diagram of mixed-state sites requires visualizing the inner structure using transparency. This is done by implementing a software volume renderer using Cg: We call a parameterized Cg pixel shader for every X,Y,Z quad plane that is rendered. This provides a nice volumetric visualization of the various quantum Voronoi diagrams that can then be interactively explored.

All materials including Cg/C++source codes and a video of a quantum Voronoi diagram sliced are available at the following web page:

www.lix.polytechnique.fr/Labo/Frank.Nielsen/QVD/

REFERENCES

[Bloch] Bloch Sphere, Wikipedia, retrieved August 2008/08/06 http://en.wikipedia.org/wiki/Bloch_sphere

[Holevo'04] Additivity of classical capacity and related problems, 2004. www.imaph.tu-bs.de/qi/problems/10.html

[KatoImai'07] Kimikazu Kato, Hiroshi Imai, and Keiko Imai, Error Analysis of a Numerical Calculation about One-Qubit Quantum Channel Capacity, 4th International Symposium on Voronoi Diagrams, pp. 265–269, 2007.

[NielsenBoissonnatNock'07] Frank Nielsen, Jean-Daniel Boissonnat, and Richard Nock, On Bregman Voronoi Diagrams, ACM-SIAM Symposium on Discrete Algorithms, SODA, 2007.

[NielsenChuang'00] Michael A. Nielsen and Isaac L. Chuang, *Quantum Computation and Quantum Information*, Cambridge University Press, ISBN 978-0521635035, 2000.

[NielsenNock'08] Frank Nielsen and Richard Nock, Quantum Voronoi Diagrams and Holevo Channel Capacity for 1-Qubit Quantum States, IEEE International Symposium on Information Theory (ISIT), 2008.

9.4

Packing Arbitrary Bit Fields into 16-Bit Floating-Point Render Targets in DirectX 10

NICOLAS THIBIEROZ, ADVANCED MICRO DEVICES, INC.

INTRODUCTION

Modern graphic accelerators enable the programmer to render 3D graphics into floating-point render targets. This capability is usually leveraged to benefit from the precision, flexibility, and increased range of floating-point formats compared to their integer counterparts. Modern GPUs are getting faster at writing and fetching 16-bit floating-point formats (e.g., DXGI_FORMAT_R16G16B16A16_FLOAT). However, there is usually a very significant performance impact from using 32-bit floating-point formats such as DXGI_FORMAT_R32G32B32A32_FLOAT. Furthermore, the installed base of 3D hardware supporting this format with useful operations such as filtering and blending is much lower than hardware supporting the more "common" 16-bit floating-point formats. It therefore makes sense to favor lower render target bit depths whenever possible.

It is often the case that rendering operations only need to store a selected number of values in floating-point precision (e.g., a normal vector); it is also common that additional outputs such as integer variables or bit fields also need to be written out. A typical example of this is deferred shading algorithms whereby render targets are used to store a variety of G-Buffer properties in different formats. While additional render targets or multiple passes can be used to store this extra data in a format matching the render target's, it is more economical (both from a memory and performance point of view) to try to utilize any spare channel that may exist in the multi-channel floating point render target(s) used.

Unfortunately, packing arbitrary data into 16-bit floating-point render targets is not as straightforward as it may at first seem. The main reason for this is due to the pixel shader output conversion process: floating-point (and integer) registers all operate in 32-bit precision inside the pixel shader, whereas output data is to be written into 16-bit floating-point render targets. This critical discrepancy requires the programmer to exert careful consideration when writing a pixel shader output that can be integrally represented in 16-bit floating-point format. This article shows how more than 15 bits of data can be arbitrarily packed and unpacked using a 16-bit floating-point render target channel without suffering from any loss of data resulting from pixel shader backend conversion and other special rules inherent to floating-point calculations.

16-BIT AND 32-BIT FLOATING-POINT FORMATS

The 16-bit (or *half-precision*) floating-point format used in common graphic accelerators has the following representation: 1 sign bit, 5 bits of exponent, and 10 bits of mantissa (also called the fractional part). The 32-bit (or *single-precision*) floating-point format uses 1 bit of sign, 8 bits of exponent, and 23 bits of mantissa [IEEE85]. Figure 9.4.1 shows bit arrangements for 16- and 32-bit floating point.

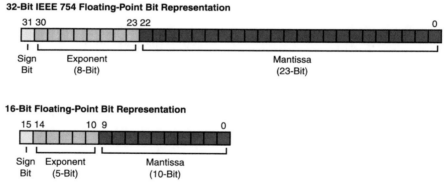

FIGURE 9.4.1   32-bit and 16-bit floating point bit representations.

Under DirectX 10 the precision of pixel shader registers is always single-precision (half-precision formats are only supported for legacy reasons and automatically get upgraded to 32-bit). In order to encode arbitrary bits into a 16-bit floating-point format, it is therefore essential that the 32-bit pixel shader output value can be integrally represented in half-precision. For instance, a pixel shader writing a floating-point output using more than 10 bits of mantissa for its meaningful data will see this value clamped when converted to half-precision, causing a loss of data in the process. This data loss is critical since we are using the floating-point representation to store arbitrary bit fields. Consider the following example: a 32-bit floating-point value of 1.2345678f corresponds to a 0x3f9e0651-bit representation. After writing this value out to a 16-bit floating-point channel of a render target, its bit representation becomes 0x3cf0. When the render target is read back, the half-precision will be converted to single-precision again (to match the internal pixel shader precision), and this value will become 1.2343750f, corresponding to a bit representation of 0x3f9e0000. Thus, any bits explicitly set in the least significant bits of our initial single-precision value are completely lost as a result of the conversion.

WRITING A VALID 32-BIT FLOATING-POINT OUTPUT

Shader Model 4.0 allows integer registers to be used as well as integer arithmetic and logical operations. These features allow the programmer to set or unset any selected bit, enabling the construction of bit fields at different "offsets" in the destination register. However, because the render target is 16-bit floating-point per channel, the pixel shader output type must be of the float type, and simply outputting an integer value will result in an integer-to-float conversion that will cause data loss. Fortunately, binary cast operations are also available. The Shader Model 4.0 asuint(x) and asfloat(x) functions simply output the binary representation of the input parameter into the desired type with no conversion. Those functions are equivalent to the following C++ code on a 32-bit platform:

```
DWORD asuint(float &f)

{

    return *(DWORD *)&f;

}


float asfloat(DWORD &d)

{

return *(float *)&d;

}
```

Using those functions it becomes possible to set the desired bits into a 32-bit unsigned integer register before outputting it as a float with no conversion.

CONVERTING BETWEEN SINGLE- AND HALF-PRECISION

Let us examine what happens when a 32-bit floating-point pixel shader output value gets stored into 16-bit floating point.

SIGN BIT

The sign bit is stored unchanged into bit 15 of the 16-bit floating-point output. The sign bit survives the conversion process and can therefore be used as storage for arbitrary data into bit 31 of our 32-bit floating-point representation.

MANTISSA BITS

32-bit floating-point values have 23 bits of mantissa, whereas 16-bit floating-point values have 10. Assuming the input fits into the half-precision range (which depends on the exponent value), the mantissa conversion will simply clamp (round-to-zero) the result to 10 bits, dropping the lowest 13 bits. The mantissa bits of 32-bit floating-point extend from bit 0 to bit 22. After dropping the lowest 13 bits, the mantissa configuration allowing the storage of arbitrary bits therefore extends from bit 13 to bit 22.

EXPONENT BITS

The conversion rule between half- and single-precision is a bit more involved when considering the exponent bits. Single-precision boasts 8 bits of exponent, while half-precision has 5. In both cases the exponent is biased, which means that a value is subtracted from it to make the real exponent. For single-precision floating-point the real exponent is equal to $(e - 127)$, while for half-precision it is $(e - 15)$. We need to take this bias into account when writing bits into the exponent bit field in order to ensure that the exponent value can be represented in half-precision. Failure to do so will lead to data loss, as too small or too large an exponent will result in the conversion to half-precision producing zero or $(+/-)$MAX_FLOAT, overwriting mantissa bits in the process.

To guarantee a value that can be represented in 16-bit floating-point, the (pre-biased) 8-bit exponent stored in the 32-bit floating-point register must fall between 112 and 143 inclusive, which leads to an exponent value between 0 and 31 that can be encoded in half-precision. However, there are still restrictions to work around due to special cases inherent to the IEEE 754 32-bit floating-point format specification. Those cases are triggered when the bits of the exponent are all set to zeros or ones. If all exponent bits are set, then the number represents either $+/-$infinity or a NaN (not a number), depending on the mantissa value. If all exponent bits are unset (zeros), then the number is denormalized and automatically gets flushed to zero as specified by the Direct3D 10 single-precision floating-point specifications. Both of those cases will lead to a loss of mantissa bits when converting from 32-bit to 16-bit floating-point. Those special exponent values must therefore be avoided to allow lossless conversions. Thus, the adjusted range of valid exponent values becomes 113 to 142 inclusive: A single precision exponent value of 113 results in a half-precision exponent of 1 (−14 after biasing), while 142 results in an exponent of 30 (15 after biasing).

The binary representation of the minimum and maximum exponent values is 01110001b (113) and 10001110b (142). The first four bits are either equal to 0111b or 1000b for any value within this range; we therefore have to set either encoding depending on the value requested for this particular bit. The remaining four bits of encoding are set in the four least significant bits (LSBs) as normal. As an example, if one wants to encode 10101b (21) into the 5-bit exponent of a 16-bit floating-point render target channel, then the data to write into the 8-bit exponent of the 32-bit floating-point output register is 10000101b. If the value to encode was 00101b (5), then the 8-bit exponent would become 01110101b.

Encoding arbitrary bits into the exponent field allows all five exponent bits of a 16-bit floating point render target channel to be utilized, albeit with the restriction that two values (00000b and 11111b) must never be used. For this reason it is a good idea to use the exponent to store mutually exclusive bit flags—for example, material flags, light types, shadow receivers, and so on. If the exponent bits are required to store linear integer values, then a bias will be required to ensure that the values 00000b and 11111b are never hit. For example, an integer value between 0 and 21 could be encoded by simply adding one to it, guaranteeing that 0 (and 31, since 21 + 1 is lower than 31) will never be set. Fixed or floating-point values may also require a scale factor to ensure that the maximum range of the 5-bit exponent is used. For example, an arbitrary value between 0.0 and 1.0 can be stored by scaling it with 29 and adding 1 to it, occupying the maximum encoding range available. Of course, the exponent field can be combined with the sign or mantissa bits of the 16-bit floating point value to allow more precise encoding of a particular number (as shown later on in this article).

Figure 9.4.2 illustrates how the bit representation of a 16-bit number should be stored into a 32-bit floating-point value so that it successfully converts to a 16-bit floating-point number at the pixel shader backend with no bit loss.

TOTAL RANGE AVAILABLE

Due to special floating-point values causing bit loss when converting between floating-point formats, the full range of bits available for encoding using 16-bit floating-point is not the full 16 bits. Both the sign and mantissa bits can be used with no precision loss, and thus $1 + 10 = 11$ bits are available for encoding (a total of $2^{11} = 2048$ different numbers). Out of the five exponent bits, all bit combinations but two are possible, corresponding to 30 different bit variations. Hence, the total number of different bit combinations that can be packed and unpacked with no bit loss using a half-precision number is $30 \times 2048 = 61{,}440$. This corresponds to 93.75% of the full range of an equivalent 16-bit integer.

16-Bit Floating-Point Bit Representation

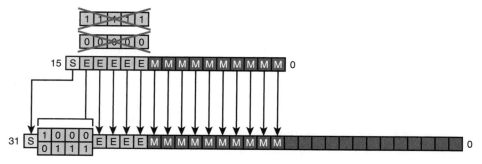

32-Bit IEEE 754 Floating-Point Bit Representation

FIGURE 9.4.2 Bit arrangements required for a lossless conversion of a 16-bit number into a 32-bit floating-point number prior to the pixel shader backend conversion to 16-bit floating-point.

PACKING AND UNPACKING CODE

The GPU shader unit generally executes integer operations such as bit shifts and type conversions at a slower rate than pure floating-point operations. For this reason it is important to design an efficient packing and unpacking mechanism that minimizes the occurrence of such operations.

The packing and unpacking code to use depends on the desired encoding configuration. Listing 9.4.1 is the raw HLSL conversion code, whereby the lowest 16 bits of an input integer variable are prepared as a 32-bit floating-point for lossless encoding into a 16-bit floating-point render target channel. It is important to remember the restrictions pointed out earlier in this article—namely, that bits 10 to 14 of the input variable must not all be set to 0 or 1 (otherwise, all bits will end up corrupted). As is often the case, the decoding process is simpler than the encoding.

Listing 9.4.1 Raw packing and unpacking code for 16 bits of arbitrary data

```
// Pack the lower 16-bit of input unsigned integer into a 32-bit
// floating-point number that will convert to a destination 16-bit
// floating-point render target with no bit loss.
// Bits 10 to 14 of the input unsigned integer MUST NOT be set to all
// zeros or ones.
```

```
float PackForFP16(uint u16BitsData)
{
    uint uValue;

    // Pack sign bit
    uValue = (u16BitsData & 0x00008000) << 16;

    // Pack exponent top bit
    uValue |= (u16BitsData & 0x00004000) ? 0x40000000 : 0x38000000;

    // Pack remaining 4 bits (0x00003C00) and mantissa (0x000003FF)
    uValue |= (u16BitsData & 0x00003FFF) << 13;

    // Return binary cast of value as a 32-bit float
    return asfloat(uValue);
}

// Unpack a 32-bit floating-point value (converted from a 16-bit
// floating-point render target) into the lower 16 bits of the
// unsigned integer originally input to the packing function
uint UnpackFromFP16(float fFloatFromFP16)
{
    uint uValue;

    // Binary cast of float value into unsigned integer
    uint uInputFloat = asuint(fFloatFromFP16);

    // Unpack sign and top exponent bit
    uValue = (uInputFloat & 0xC0000000) >> 16;

    // Unpack remaining 4 exponent bits and mantissa
    uValue |= (uInputFloat & 0x07FFE000) >> 13;

    // Return decoded value
    return uValue;
}
```

The lowest 16 bits of the input integer parameter are packed into a 32-bit floating-point number. This value will convert to a destination 16-bit floating-point render target with no bit loss, with the restriction that bits 10 to 14 of the input integer must not be set to all ones or zeros. If this condition is met, the unpacking from the 16-bit floating-point render target will restore the original integer parameter that was input to the packing function.

Listing 9.4.2 shows how to pack and unpack two arbitrary numbers between 0.0 and 1.0 within a 16-bit floating-point channel. The first number is packed with 8-bit fixed-point precision, while the second uses slightly less (around 7.91 bits) due to the exponent-encoding restrictions detailed in this article. Note that because of the initial quantization of the input floating-point numbers, it is expected that the unpacked floating-point outputs will not be an exact match of the inputs. Both packing and unpacking operations take about 7 ALU instructions on a Radeon HD48x0 graphic card, which equates to less than two clocks.

Listing 9.4.2 Packing and unpacking code allowing two positive normalized floating-point numbers to be packed and unpacked using a single channel of a 16-bit floating-point render target. The first number is encoded with 8-bit precision while the second number is encoded with about 7.91-bit precision.

```
// Pack two positive normalized numbers between 0.0 and 1.0 into a
// 32-bit floating-point number that will convert to a destination
// 16-bit floating-point render target with no bit loss.
// The first number is encoded with 8-bit fixed-point precision while
// the second number is encoded with ~7.91 fixed-point bit precision.
float Pack2PNForFP16(float a, float b)
{
    uint uValue;
    uint uEncodedb;

    // Number 'a' fits directly into FP16-representable mantissa (bit
    // 13 to 20)
    uValue = ( (uint)(a*255.0 + 0.5) ) << 13;

    // Number 'b' can only be represented with ~7.91 bit precision
    // which equates to 240 representable values. Hence multiply 'b'
```

```
    // with 239.0 to obtain a value between 0 and 239.
    uEncodedb = (uint)(b*239.0 + 0.5);

    // uEncodedb is encoded as: EEEEEMMSb
    // Because uEncodedb is a value between 0 and 239, the bit field
    // EEEEEb is never equal to 11111b. By adding 00001000b to the
    // encoded value we can also prevent the bit field EEEEEb to be
    // equal to 00000b.
    uEncodedb += 0x08;

    // Pack exponent top bit
    uValue |= (uEncodedb & 0x80) ? 0x40000000 : 0x38000000;

    // Pack remaining 4 exponent bits and 2 mantissa bits
    uint uTemp = (uEncodedb & 0x7E) << 20;

    // Pack sign bit
    uTemp |= (uEncodedb & 0x01) << 31;

    // Combine bit fields to make final value
    uValue |= uTemp;

    // Return binary cast of value as 32-bit float
    return asfloat(uValue);
}


// Unpack a 32-bit floating-point value into the two positive
// normalized numbers originally input to the Pack2PNForFP16 function
// Note that the initial quantization from floating-point inputs to
// 8 and ~7.91 fixed-point can result in loss of precision; thus the
// exact same floating-point input values may not be recovered.
uint Unpack2PNFromFP16(float fFloatFromFP16)
{
    float a, b;
    uint  uEncodedb;
```

```
// Binary cast of float value into unsigned integer
uint uInputFloat = asuint(fFloatFromFP16);


// Unpack 'a'
a = ( (uInputFloat >> 13) & 0xFF) / 255.0;


// Unpacking of 'b' is a bit more involved


// Unpack top exponent bit
uEncodedb = (uInputFloat & 0x40000000) >> 23;


// Unpack remaining 4 exponent bits and 2 mantissa bits
uEncodedb |= (uInputFloat & 0x07E00000) >> 20;


// Subtract 0x08 from exponent (no wrap around possible)
uEncodedb = uEncodedb - 0x08;


// Unpack sign bit
uEncodedb |= (uInputFloat & 0x80000000) >> 31;


// Calculate b
b = uEncodedb / 239.0;


// Return decoded values
return float2(a, b);
}
```

The two code listings shown here can be modified to accommodate the requirements of an application. For example, Listing 9.4.2 can easily be changed to store two normalized numbers between −1.0 and 1.0 (e.g., to store the two components of a normal vector with a known positive or negative Z component). Another example is to write a version of the code that packs and unpacks three positive normalized numbers under a 5/~5.91/5 bit arrangement. This could be useful to store color components not requiring a great deal of precision. As long as the rules explained in this article are followed, any encoding combination is possible.

PERFORMANCE CONSIDERATIONS

The performance cost of packing and unpacking numbers is quite negligible. The common trend in all graphic hardware is to boast more ALU power than other instruction types (e.g., texture fetches or branch instructions). Thus, sacrificing a few ALU instructions to reduce bandwidth or to avoid other costly solutions such as additional render targets or multi-passing is certainly a very reasonable choice to make. For example, a shader that is already bandwidth or texture fetch bound is unlikely to run any slower by adding packing or unpacking instructions to it.

CONCLUSION

This article showed how to safely pack and unpack arbitrary bit fields using 16-bit floating-point values, allowing maximum utilization of the storage capacity of the output surface. While an assumption was made that the packing recipient would be a render target, the same algorithms can be applied more generically onto other destination resources—for example, vertex or index buffers. The algorithms presented here can also be trivially adapted to the storing of arbitrary bit fields into 32-bit floating-point resources.

REFERENCE

[IEEE85] IEEE Computer Society (1985), IEEE Standard for Binary Floating-Point Arithmetic, IEEE Std 754-1985.

9.5 Interactive Image Morphing Using Thin-Plate Spline

Xiaopei Liu, The Chinese University of Hong Kong, xpliu@cuhk.edu.hk

Liang Wan, The Chinese University of Hong Kong,
City University of Hong Kong, liangwan@cityu.edu.hk

Xuemiao Xu, The Chinese University of Hong Kong,
xmxu@cse.cuhk.edu.hk

Tien-Tsin Wong, The Chinese University of Hong Kong,
ttwong@acm.org

Chi-Sing Leung, City University of Hong Kong,
eeleungc@cityu.edu.hk

INTRODUCTION

Image morphing has been widely used to create special effects in the entertainment industry. It consists of warping and blending, as blending the two images alone does not produce convincing transition results. In fact, warping is the most important component in image morphing. There are several warping techniques that can be used for image morphing, such as the mesh-based method [Lee94], the feature-based approach [Beier92], and using thin-plate spline (TPS) warping [Bookstein89]. TPS warping, due to the minimization property of bending energy, is a good choice among all the commonly used warping techniques. It introduces less distortion with consistent image content and thus usually produces high-quality morphing results. However, the high computational complexity of TPS usually leads to a slow warping process, even for medium-size images (e.g., images of resolution 600×400) with a small number of anchor points (e.g., 20–50 anchor points).

In this article, we describe a parallel technique for TPS warping using graphics hardware and apply it to achieve interactive image morphing. The accumulation of weighted TPS kernels is evaluated with pixel shaders, thus making the warping very fast even for large images with many anchor points. Figure 9.5.1 shows our image morphing results from using TPS warping on the GPU. The anchor points are scattered along the boundary of the foreground object to which image morphing is applied. The synthesis of one morphing frame only takes a very short time—for example, 0.038 second in Figure 9.5.1.

FIGURE 9.5.1 An example of our interactive TPS morphing on a GPU. The execution only requires 0.038 second for one frame in the morphing sequence, with an image resolution of 550×275 pixels and 52 user-specified anchor points.

THIN-PLATE SPLINE-BASED WARPING

Before we continue, we first review thin-plate spline (TPS) warping. Thin-plate spline, as an interpolation method, was introduced by Duchon [Duchon76] for geometric design. It models the physics of the bending of a thin metallic sheet. When TPS is applied to image warping, N pairs of corresponding anchor points in the source and the warped images should first be specified (Figure 9.5.2). This correspondence tells us where the anchor points (x_i, y_i) in the source image are moved during warping. Then, we can determine how a point (x, y) in the source image can be mapped to the position (x', y') in the in-between warped image, via the following equations:

$$x' = f_x(x,y) = a_0 + a_1 x + a_2 y + \sum_{i=1}^{N} \alpha_i \phi(\|(x,y) - (x_i,y_i)\|)$$

EQUATION 9.5.1

$$y' = f_y(x,y) = b_0 + b_1 x + b_2 y + \sum_{i=1}^{N} \beta_i \phi(\|(x,y) - (x_i,y_i)\|)$$

EQUATION 9.5.2

where (x,y) is a point in the source image, and (x',y') is the corresponding position in the warped image; a_0, a_1, a_2, and b_0, b_1, b_2 are the coefficients for affine motion; α_i and β_i are the coefficients for the ith pair of corresponding anchor points; (x_i, y_i) is one anchor point specified in the source image, and $\phi(\cdot)$ is the TPS kernel function that takes the following form:

$$\phi(r) = r^2 \log r \quad \text{EQUATION 9.5.3}$$

The polynomial terms, $(a_0 + a_1 x + a_2 y)$ and $(b_0 + b_1 x + b_2 y)$, in Equations 9.5.1 and 9.5.2 take account of affine motion, which introduces linear deformation. On the other hand, the summation terms in the equations account for nonlinear deformation. Since the TPS equations contain $2(N + 3)$ unknowns (a_0, a_1, a_2, b_0, b_1, b_2, α_i, and β_i), they must be determined before we warp the images. However, we have only N pairs of corresponding anchor points, and hence $2N$ equations. This yields an ill-posed linear system to solve. In order to solve it, two sets of extra constraints are enforced to the above equations:

$$\sum_{i=1}^{N} \alpha_i x_i = 0, \quad \sum_{i=1}^{N} \alpha_i y_i = 0, \quad \sum_{i=1}^{N} \alpha_i = 0 \quad \text{EQUATION 9.5.4}$$

$$\sum_{i=1}^{N} \beta_i x_i = 0, \quad \sum_{i=1}^{N} \beta_i y_i = 0, \quad \sum_{i=1}^{N} \beta_i = 0 \quad \text{EQUATION 9.5.5}$$

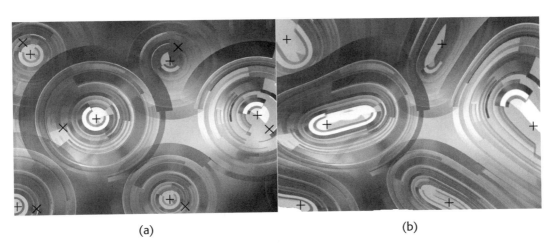

(a)   (b)

FIGURE 9.5.2   TPS warping with specified anchor points. In (a) the source anchor points "+" with corresponding warped anchor points "×" are specified. In (b) the image (a) is warped according to the correspondence, with the "+" indicating the warped anchor points.

Combining Equations 9.5.1, 9.5.2, 9.5.4, and 9.5.5, we are able to obtain two sets of linear equations, which form the following two linear systems:

$$P_x a = X' \quad \text{EQUATION 9.5.6}$$

$$P_y b = Y' \quad \text{EQUATION 9.5.7}$$

Equation 9.5.6 can be expanded to:

$$
\begin{bmatrix}
\phi_{11}, \phi_{12}, \cdots, \phi_{1n}, 1, x_1, y_1 \\
\phi_{21}, \phi_{22}, \cdots, \phi_{2n}, 1, x_2, y_2 \\
\ddots \qquad\qquad \vdots \\
\qquad \ddots \qquad\quad \vdots \\
\phi_{n1}, \phi_{n2}, \cdots, \phi_{nm}, 1, x_n, y_n \\
1, \quad 1, \quad \cdots, 1, \quad 0, 0, 0 \\
x_1, \quad x_2, \cdots, x_n, \quad 0, 0, 0 \\
y_1, \quad y_2, \cdots, y_n, \quad 0, 0, 0
\end{bmatrix}
\begin{bmatrix}
\alpha_1 \\
\alpha_1 \\
\vdots \\
\vdots \\
\alpha_n \\
a_0 \\
a_1 \\
a_2
\end{bmatrix}
=
\begin{bmatrix}
x'_1 \\
x'_2 \\
\vdots \\
\vdots \\
x'_n \\
0 \\
0 \\
0
\end{bmatrix}
$$

EQUATION 9.5.8

where ϕ_{ij} is the value of the kernel function taking the distance between the ith and the jth anchor points as parameter:

$$\phi_{ij} = \phi(r_{ij}) = r_{ij}{}^2 \log r_{ij}, \quad r_{ij} = \|(x_i, y_i) - (x_j, y_j)\| \quad \text{EQUATION 9.5.9}$$

The x'_i in the right-hand vector of Equation 9.5.8 is the x-coordinate of the ith anchor point. The linear system of Equation 9.5.7 can be expanded similarly for y-coordinates.

Equation 9.5.8 can be solved directly using Gaussian elimination. To improve the accuracy in solving the linear system, we perform QR decomposition on the coefficient matrix of Equation 9.5.8 before we solve the linear system with Gaussian elimination. Solving Equation 9.5.8 yields the values of $(N + 3)$ parameters for x-coordinates. The same solution process is applied to Equation 9.5.7 to obtain another $(N + 3)$ parameter values for y-coordinates.

Once the unknowns are determined, we can perform image warping. We can directly apply Equations 9.5.1 and 9.5.2 to each pixel in the source image to obtain the warped image. However, this forward mapping does not work since it usually leads to many holes in the warped result. In practice, we use a backward mapping approach to map each pixel position in the warped image to the source image and prevent holes.

$$x = f_x^{-1}(x', y'), \quad y = f_y^{-1}(x', y'), \quad \text{EQUATION 9.5.10}$$

f_x^{-1} and f_y^{-1} can be determined by interchanging (x,y) and (x',y') and using the warped anchor points (x_i',y_i') in the warped image instead of (x_i,y_i) in the source image as anchor points in Equations 9.5.1 and 9.5.2. Using this backward mapping, any pixel from the warped image can find its position in the source image, with the color determined from the corresponding pixel in the source image. Note that the positions mapped by Equation 9.5.10 can be located in sub-pixel in the source image, so bilinear interpolation of image color is performed here.

GPU IMPLEMENTATION OF TPS WARPING

The efficiency of TPS warping is quite dependent on both the image size and the number of anchor points. Referring to Equations 9.5.1 and 9.5.2, the TPS warping equation consists of two independent components: the affine term (the polynomial term in Equations 9.5.1 and 9.5.2) and the principle warp (the accumulated term in Equations 9.5.1 and 9.5.2). The affine term accounts for linear transform, which is very simple to compute, but the principle warp, which introduces nonlinear warping, is very time-consuming since it involves computation-intensive evaluation of the summation of kernel functions, which is dependent on the number of anchor points. However, these summations are independent of each other for every point because parameters and anchor points are fixed during the evaluation. Hence, the computation of different pixels can be fully parallelized. Therefore, we separately handle the principle warp and the affine term evaluations.

PRINCIPLE WARP

To evaluate the principle warp on the GPU, we pack the accumulated positions of pixels in an image into a floating-point texture, and use a pixel shader to evaluate the kernel functions. The texture has the same dimension as the input image. The accumulated position coordinate, which corresponds to (x',y') in Equations 9.5.1 and 9.5.2, is packed into each texel as the red and green components, leaving the two components unused. The pixel coordinate of the original image, which corresponds to (x,y) in Equations 9.5.1 and 9.5.2, is obtained by accessing the associated texture coordinates. We use `GL_TEXTURE_RECTANGLE_NV` as the texture target to store the texture so that the texture coordinates can be the same as the pixel coordinates.

Ideally, the principle warp is evaluated with one pass of the pixel shader. However, since the number of anchor points can be quite large and the number of available registers is limited, it is usually impractical to evaluate the principle warping function in one pass. Thus, multiple passes are required to finally compute the result of a warped position. To achieve this, we first divide the principle warp accumulation into different partial sums. Then we evaluate each partial sum with a shader pass and accumulate the sum to the result from the previous pass until all the partial sums are accumulated. The accumulation is achieved by using the standardized frame buffer object (FBO) in OpenGL. Listing 9.5.1 lists the shader code for the evaluation of principle warping within one pass.

Listing 9.5.1 Shader 1: Principle warp accumulation

```
#define ANCHOR_NUM 4

uniform sampler2DRect accumTex;

uniform vec4 rbfCoef[ANCHOR_NUM];

void main(void)
{
        float2 accumPos = texture2DRect(accumTex, gl_TexCoord[0].st);

        float r;

        for (int i=0; i< ANCHOR_NUM; i++)
        {
                r = distance(gl_TexCoord[0].st-0.5, rbfCoef[i].xy);

                accumPos += rbfCoef[i].zw * r*r*log(r+0.0000000001);

        }

        gl_FragColor = vec4(accumPos, 0, 0);

}
```

The macro `ANCHOR_NUM` defines the number of anchor points involved in the computation per pass. `accumTex` is the texture holding the accumulated values from principle warp computation. `rbfCoef` is an array containing the values of the TPS warping parameters. For each element in the array, the first two components (x and y) store the position of the anchor point (x_i, y_i), and the next two components (z and w) store the associated coefficients α_i and β_i. In the calculation of the TPS kernel function, a small value (e.g., `0.0000000001` in Listing 9.5.1) is introduced to avoid the overflow.

The choice of the number of partial sums, or equivalently the number of anchor points involved in each partial sum (`ANCHOR_NUM`), influences the execution speed of the entire accumulation. According to our experiments, we find that usually the execution reaches the optimal speed when `ANCHOR_NUM` is chosen to be 4. The influence on the execution speed for the number of anchor points involved in each partial sum is illustrated in Figure 9.5.3. In this experiment, we take a source image of resolution 500×375 and 50 anchor points in total.

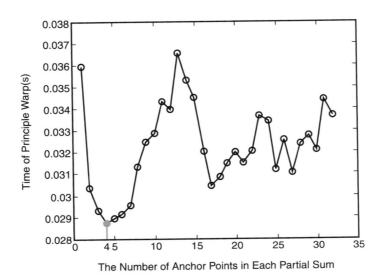

FIGURE 9.5.3   Influence on the execution speed based on the number of anchor points involved in each partial sum.

GPU WARPING

Once we obtain the accumulated principle warp, we can perform the image warping, which is accomplished by incorporating both the affine term evaluation and color interpolation. Since this process is also independent of image pixels, we use a GPU shader again and perform the image warping in parallel.

During warping, we input the evaluated principle warp as a texture. Then the warping is done by first adding the principle warp and the affine term, and then looking up the pixel color in the source image. Bilinear interpolation is automatically achieved by the graphics hardware during the texture lookup. Listing 9.5.2 is the shader code for image warping.

Listing 9.5.2   Shader 2: GPU warping

```
uniform sampler2DRect accumTex;
uniform sampler2DRect imageTex;
uniform vec4 affCoefX;
uniform vec4 affCoefY;
void main(void)
{
```

```
float2 accumPos = texture2DRect(accumTex, gl_TexCoord[0].st);
float2 curPos;
curPos.x=accumPos.x+affCoefX.x*(affCoefX.y+
        affCoefX.z*gl_TexCoord[0].s + affCoefX.w*gl_TexCoord[0].t);
curPos.y=accumPos.y+affCoefY.x*( affCoefY.y+
        affCoefY.z*gl_TexCoord[0].s+affCoefY.w*gl_TexCoord[0].t);
gl_FragColor = texture2DRect(imageTex, curPos);
}
```

To perform GPU-based TPS image warping, we first apply Shader 1 to compute the principle warp accumulation. Note that this accumulation may need multiple calls to Shader 1. Then, with the accumulated result, we call Shader 2 to incorporate the affine term and warp the source image to the desired destination. Figure 9.5.2b shows our GPU-based TPS image warping result from Figure 9.5.2a.

Interactive Image Morphing

Given the source and the destination images, we first specify a set of corresponding anchor points in the two images. Then we linearly interpolate with an interpolation parameter between the two sets of corresponding anchor points to obtain the interpolated anchor points. This forms two correspondences. One correspondence is between the interpolated anchor points and the anchor points in the source image. Another correspondence is between the interpolated anchor points and the anchor points in the destination image. The source and the destination images are both warped to the images determined by the interpolated anchor points to form two warped images. Finally, we blend the two warped images to get one frame in the morphing sequence. The blending ratio is equivalent to the interpolation parameter. As we sample the interpolation parameter, we can produce a smooth morphing sequence from the source image to the destination. Figure 9.5.4 demonstrates the TPS image morphing process.

The execution consists of three main steps: the solving of the TPS parameters, the evaluation of principle warp, and the final image interpolation with the affine term incorporated. As the solution of TPS parameters is performed only once, and the size of the matrix is normally not very large (because the user usually does not specify too many anchor points), it is possible to solve the matrix efficiently even on the CPU. In our experiments, it only takes tens of milliseconds for about 200 anchor points. If the number of anchor points is rather large—for example, 1000 or even larger—we may use the available GPU linear system solver to accelerate the solution process.

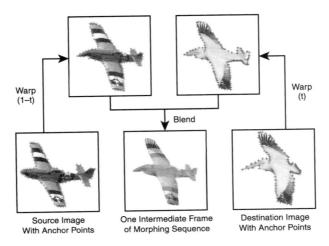

FIGURE 9.5.4   TPS image morphing process.

We make a comparison of CPU and GPU performance in Figure 9.5.5. All the statistics in Figure 9.5.5 are carried out on a computer equipped with an Intel Xeon 3.73GHz CPU (four cores) and an NVIDIA Geforce 8800 GTX GPU. In this experiment, we vary both the image resolution and the number of anchor points. As shown, the timing of CPU morphing is much longer than that of GPU morphing. More interestingly, the timing of CPU morphing increases more abruptly when the image resolution increases. For the number of anchor points (indicated in different line types), it is almost proportional to the timing of GPU morphing.

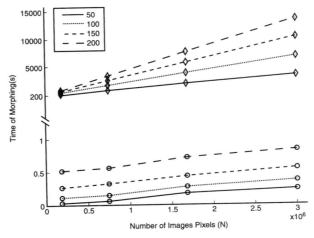

FIGURE 9.5.5   Comparison of GPU morphing to its CPU equivalent. Different line types indicate different numbers of anchor points. The lines with diamonds are for CPU morphing, while the lines with circles are for GPU morphing.

Note that the improvement in the execution speed is tremendous. This improvement is quite beneficial for people in the movie industry to interactively fine-tune the morphing result in order to produce high-quality special effects for different kinds of movies.

CONCLUSION

In this article, we presented a technique to achieve high-performance image morphing based on thin-plate spline (TPS). The proposed technique benefits the image morphing from the very fast execution speed. The TPS warping technique used in our image morphing minimizes the bending energy, which yields better visual effects compared to other commonly used warping techniques.

ACKNOWLEDGMENTS

This work is supported by the Research Grants Council of the Hong Kong Special Administrative Region, under RGC Earmarked Grants (Project No. CUHK 417107) and the Research Grants from the City University of Hong Kong (Project No. CityU 7002108)

REFERENCES

[Beier92] T. Beier and S. Neely. "Feature-Based Image Metamorphosis," *Computer Graphics* (Proc. SIGGRAPH '92), vol. 26, no. 2, pp. 35–42, 1992.

[Bookstein89] F. L. Bookstein, "Principal Warps: Thin-Plate Splines and the Decomposition of Deformations," *IEEE Trans. Pattern Analysis and Machine Intelligence*, vol. 11, no. 6, pp. 567–585, 1989.

[Duchon76] J. Duchon, "Splines Minimizing Rotation-Invariant Seminorms in Sobolev Spaces," *Constructive Theory of Functions of Several Variables*, Lecture Notes in Mathematics, vol. 571, pp. 85–100, 1977.

[Lee94] S.-Y. Lee, K.-Y. Chwa, J. Hahn, and S. Y. Shin. "Image Morphing Using Deformable Surfaces," in *Proceedings of Computer Animation* 1994, pp. 31–39, 1994.

Index

Numerics

1D blur, 546–547
2D blur, 547–548
2D interpolation, 126–127
3D engine design
    automatic load balancing, 627–634
        approach to, 629–631
        GPU requirements, 633
        performance, 629
        problems, 627–628
        results, 632–633
        user inconvenience, 628–629
        workflow, 632
    cross-platform rendering thread, 607–620
        abstraction design, 608–609
        command buffer, 609, 620
        command objects, 609
        driver execution process, 611
        implementation, 612–617
        macro state objects, 610
        multiple client and server threads, 619
        results, 617–618
        state machine, 610
        threading design, 608
        triple buffering, 618–619
    Elemental Engine II, 679–681
    GUIs for games, 621–625
    light pre-pass renderer, 655–676
        applying different materials with, 665–666
        bending specular reflection rules, 663–664
        CIE Luv color space, 667–676
        deferred renderer, 657–659
        diffuse term, 662–663
        overview, 660–662
        Z pre-pass renderer, 655–657
    occlusion culling, 637–653
        coherent, 638–641
        game engine integration, 643–644
        multiqueries, 647–649
        reducing state changes, 641–643
        skipping tests for visible nodes, 645
        tighter bounding volumes, 646–647
    overview, 605
3D Interpolation, 124–126
6DOF Pose, 578

A

abstraction, 515, 608–609
accumulation buffer, 227, 229–231
adaptive isosurface refinement, 18
adaptive re-meshing, 107–117
    demo, 116
    implementation of, 114–116
    LOD, 112–114
    results, 114
adaptive sampling, 474–475
adaptive tessellation mode, 43–44, 48–51, 75–78
afterlights, 202–205
alpha blending
    advanced GUIs, 551
    anti-aliased lines, 154
    OpenGL ES applications, 525–526, 529
    sliced grid, 690
    soft particles, 143
    SSAO, 416
    transparency, 218, *222f*
alpha channel, 135, 168, 221, 282
alpha compositing, 218
alpha testing, 522–523, 525–526

Note: Page numbers referencing figures are italicized and followed by an "*f.*" Page numbers referencing tables are italicized and followed by a "*t.*"

alpha-to-coverage, 219
ambient cubes, 465
ambient lighting, 176–177, 495–496
ambient occlusion (AO), 270–271, 425–427, 496.
    See also deferred ambient occlusion; image-
    space ambient occlusion; per-pixel ambient
    occlusion; screen-space ambient occlusion
ambient occlusion probes, 455–457
AMD GPUMeshMapper tool, 61, 69
amplification feature, 9
anchor points, *745f*
ANCHOR_NUM macro, 748
angle bias, 438
animated blur, 548
anti-aliased lines, 149–159
    abstract, 149
    method, 150
    shader code, 155–159
    texture creation, 150–152
    variations, 154–155
    vertex setup, 152–154
antipodal generators, *723f*
AO (ambient occlusion), 270–271, 425–427, 496.
    See also image–space ambient occlusion;
    deferred ambient occlusion; per-pixel ambient
    occlusion; SSAO
AoS (array of structs), 526
application-level mechanisms, 627–628
approximating subdivision process, 51, 68
AR. *See* augmented reality
array of structs (AoS), 526
arrays, 526–527
asfloat(x) function, 733
asuint(x) function, 733
ATI GPU tessellation library, 41, 47–48, 76
atomic counter, 616
attenuation function, *427f*, 434
attenuation parameter, *459f*
augmented reality (AR), 571–604
    developing
        main loop, 572–574
        occlusion between real and virtual objects,
            578–581
        off-axis projection camera, 574–576
        pose estimation, 576–578
    fixed point versus floating point, 603–604
    graphics API abstraction
        coordinate systems, 595–596
        geometry management, 589–590

geometry rendering, 591–595
        matrix stacks, 595–596
        overview, 586–588
        texture management, 589
    hardware versus software rendering, 596–599
    initializing, 583–586
    platform considerations, 581–583
    scene-graph rendering, 599–601
    video and image processing, 601–603
automatic load balancing, 627–634
    approach to, 629–631
    GPU requirements, 633
    overview, 627
    performance, 629
    problems, 627–628
    results, 632–633
    user inconvenience, 628–629
    workflow, 632

B
back-face culling, 203
background subtraction, 700–703
background texture, 552–553
bandwidth
    embedded platforms, 528
    limited, 516–517
    reducing, 545
    shadow systems, 364
    tessellation, 35, 62
    video stream extensions, *545f*
barycentric coordinates, 37–38, 485
base meshes, 107–110, 119–120, 562
batching
    previously invisible nodes, 641–642
    previously visible nodes, 642–643
    primitives, 520
    queries, 641
    through render queue, 644
battery life, 516
Battlezone game, 149
Bavoil, Louis, 411
benchmarking, 518–519
bias parameter, 458, *460f*
bidirectional reflection distribution function
    (BRDF), 175, 482, 490
bidirectional scattering surface reflectance
    distribution function (BSSRDF) model, 468
BIH (bounding interval hierarchy), 480, 483,
    487–489

bilateral filtering, 285–287, 291–295, 338
bilateral upsampling, 452
bilinear filtering, 200
bilinear interpolation, 135, 321
binary tree, 480
bit fields, 731–741
bit shifting, 244, 247–249
blended border objects, *552f*
Blinn-Phong model, 169–170, 176–177, 186, 661
Bloch spheres, 715–729
    Holevo's capacity, 728
    quantum channel, 728
    quantum Voronoi diagrams, 717–728
    Von Neumann quantum entropy, 716–717
bloom, 264
blurring. *See also* motion blur
    1D, 546–547
    2D, 547–548
    animated, 548
    edge-preserving, 419
    mipmap, 556–557
    naïve, *439f*
    post-processing, 553
    progressive, 548
    vertical, 224
Bookout, Dave, 411
bounding boxes, 686–690
bounding cubes, 446
bounding interval hierarchy (BIH), 480, 483, 487–489
bounding kd-tree, 480
bounding skd-tree, 480
bounding volumes, 646–647
box filtering, 493
BRDF (bidirectional reflection distribution function), 175, 482, 490
Bresenham interpolation, 125–126
Briney, Emmanuel, 411
BSSRDF (bidirectional scattering surface reflectance distribution function) model, 468
buffer copies, 528–530
buffer sharing, 255
build process, 609
burn transitions, 558–560

C
CAknApplication interface, 584
callbacks, 621

camera distance
    Crackdown graphics techniques, 201
    displacement mapping, 108, 112–113, *114f*
    real-time tessellation, 46, 48
    terrain rendering, 78
    weather effects, 377
camera image reading, 573
Cartesian coordinates, 62, 268, 347
cascaded shadow maps. *See* CSMs
CCommonCtrl template class, 623–624
CDF (cumulative distribution function), 261, 347–348
Ceitelis, Victor, 411
cells
    hydraulic erosion, 400, *401f*
    instant radiosity, 480
    Quick Noise, 133–134, 136, 138
    sliced grid, 686
central differences approximation, 93–103
central processing unit (CPU)
    accessing frame buffer from, 519–520
    LOD systems managed by, 74
    morphing based on, 562–563, *751f*
    motion blur work, 278
    sorting method, 244–246
centroid-based edge detection, 233–235
Cg per-pixel shader, 720
character rendering, 51–53, 61–68
CHC (coherent hierarchical culling), 638–641
child cells, 480
Cholesky factorization, 577
CIE Luv color space, 667–676
    colors, 668–671
    grouping and rendering lights, 672–675
    integrating into light accumulation, 675–676
    light buffer format, 671–672
    reasons for using, 668
circle of confusion, 266–268
class member callbacks, 622–623
closed form equations, 446
clouds, 190–192
clutter, 193–198
coherent hierarchical culling (CHC), 638–641
color buffer, 435–436
color quantization, 286, 301
color space conversion, 287
color transform, 555
COM (component object module) system, 680
command buffer, 608–609, 613–615, 619–620

command data objects, 609, 613–615
command data sharing policy, 614–615
command locking strategy, 615–616
compact varyings, 533
component object module (COM) system, 680
composition phase, 221–223
compression, 35–36, 62–66
continuous tessellation mode, 43–48
contour detection, *577f*
control mesh primitives
    OpenGL ES applications, 520
    real-time tessellation, 35–36, 38–40, 48, 53–54,
       59, 61
    terrain rendering, 81
Cook-Torrance model, 176–177, 186–187
coordinates
    augmented reality, 595–596
    barycentric, 37–38, 485
    Cartesian, 62, 268, 347
    parametric, 37–38, 122
    polar, 268
    spherical, 62
    texture, 40, 306, 317–321, 432, 533
    uv, 38, 40, 63, 353
Cornell box data set, 440
cosine-weighted distribution, 426
CPU. *See* central processing unit
Crackdown graphics techniques, 189–215
    clutter, 193–198
    deferred rendering, 201–205
    outlines, 198–201
    sky, 190–192
    texture map setup, 209–214
    vehicle reflections, 205–209
cracks, 68–70, *84f*, 120
crease shading algorithm, 428
CreateVertex procedure, 708
Crémoux, David, 411
cross-bilateral filter, 439
cross-platform rendering thread, 607–620
    abstraction design, 608–609
    command buffer, 609, 620
    command objects, 609
    driver execution process, 611
    implementation of
        driver objects pattern, 612–613
        safety, 614–617
        synchronization, 613–614
    macro state objects, 610

multiple client and server threads, 619
    results, 617–618
    state machine, 610
    threading design, 608
    triple buffering, 618–619
Crysis game, 413
CSMs (cascaded shadow maps), 305–329
    analytic method, 325–328
    approximated solution, 311–313
    exact solution, 309–311
    facetted shadow mapping, 365
    filtering across splits, 321–323
    flickering of shadow quality, 307–309
    non-optimized split selection, 315–317
    PSVSMS, 324–325
    storage strategy, 313–315
    texture coordinate computation, 317–321
cube maps, 313, *549f–550f*
cube tetrahedralization, 9–18
cubes. *See* hybrid cubes/tetrahedra extraction
cuboids, 449
CUDA, 690
culling
    back-face, 203
    horizon, 431
    occlusion, 637–653
        coherent hierarchical, 638–641
        game engine integration, 643–644
        multiqueries, 647–649
        reducing state changes, 641–643
        skipping tests for visible nodes, 645
        tighter bounding volumes, 646–647
    rough object, 520–522
    Z, 655, 659
cumulative distribution function (CDF), 261, 347–348
cylindrical projection, 405–408

D

D×d square matrix, 715
data isolation, 608
deferred ambient occlusion, 445–454
    from miscellaneous surfaces, 451
    optimization, 451–453
    from quads, 448–451
    from spheres, 447–448
    from triangles, 448–451
deferred lighting pass, 482
deferred renderer, 201–205, 657–659, 664

deferred rendering transparency, 217–224
  composition phase, 221–223
  future work, 224
  geometry phase, 221
  results, 221–224
deferred shading, 225–242
  implementation of, 231–240
  principles of, 226–227
  requirements for, 227–230
de-interlacing process, *220f,* 222, 224
delta value, 377
DEM (distinct element method), 693, *694f*
deposition, 396–399
depth buffer, 143–146, 272, 660
depth extents, 452
depth of field, 266–275, 282
depth range check, 418
derivatives, 322, 326
dest-alpha modulation, 202
de-swizzling, 451–452
DetectEdgePixel() function, 233
deterministic sampling, 474, 476
Difference-of-Gaussians (DoG), 285–286, 295–301
differential blending, 564
differential updating, 568
diffuse component, 181
diffuse lighting, 163–169, 176–179
diffuse shading, 453, *475f*
diffuse surfaces, 357
diffuse terms, 662–663
diffusion dipole, 163, 165
dipole method, 470
direct lighting, 496
Direct3D 10
  Gooch-like shading, 24–29
  isosurface extraction pass, 19–24
  shader for rendering into R2VB render target, 81–83
  tessellation, 60
  tetrahedralization, 11–18
Direct3D 11, 39–41
Direct3D Mobile, 585–586, 589, 591–592, 595
directed filtering, 285–302
  color quantization, 301
  color space conversion, 287
  flow field construction, 287–291
  orientation-aligned bilateral filter, 291–295
  separable flow-based DoG, 295–301
direction vectors, *180f*

directivity parameter, 458
dirty regions, 545
discard operations, 522–523, 525–526
disk-based approximation, *502f, 507f*
dispatch process, 609
displacement mapping
  adaptive re-meshing for, 107–117
    demo, 116
    implementation of, 114–116
    LOD, 112–114
    overview, 107–112
    results, 114
  terrain rendering, 74, 78–79, 83
  tessellation, 60–61, 68–70
display gamma, 182–184
dissolution, 396–399
distance attenuation, 418
distance impostor cube maps, 490
DistanceSphere function, 720
distinct element method (DEM), 693, *694f*
distribution factor, Cook-Torrance model, 176, *177f*
DivisionType variable, 112–114
DoG (difference-of-Gaussians), 285–286, 295–301
domain shader, 40, 53
double buffer technique, 613
Doug Jones demo, 162–164, 167, 169
draw calls
  adaptive tessellation, 49–51, 77
  continuous tessellation, 46
  Direct3D 10, 60
  rendering adaptively tessellated terrain, 89–90
  for rendering tessellated characters, 44–45
DrawAuto functionality, 18
driver execution process, 611
driver objects pattern, 612–613
dual art assets, 52
dueling frusta problems, 305, 364–365
DXT1-compression, 167
dynamic flow control, 537
dynamic geometry processing, 414
dynamic real-time shadows, 357–359

E

edge bleeding, *439f*
edge fins, 198
edge ordering, *706f*
edge pixel detection phase, 231–233
edge-preserving blur, 419

edges highlighting, *417f*
EGL library, 598
EglCreateWindowSurface function, 584
eigenvectors, 288–289, 298
Elemental Engine II, 679–681
embedded platforms, 528
energy conservation, 180
engine data set, *127f*
engine side, GUI system, 622
environment maps, 184, 346–349
environmental effects
    hydraulic erosion, 389–404
        boundaries, 400–401
        data structures, 390–392
        force-based, 394–398
        rendering, 401–402
        results, 402
        still water, 398–399
        terrain slippage, 399–400
        water movement, 392–394
    overview, 373
    sky representation, 405–409
    weather effects, 375–387
        artist-controlled weather, 384
        motion-blurred particles, 378–381
        occlusion, 382–383
        particle simulation, 376–378
Ericsson Texture Compression (ETC) format, 524
erosion. *See* hydraulic erosion
Euclidean Voronoi bisector, *723f*
evaluation shader, 38, 55–57
execution decoupling, 608
explicit surface representation, 4
exponent bits, 734–735
extrinsic parameters, 574
eye-space basis, 432–433
eye-space tangent vectors, 437–438

F

facetted shadow mapping, 363–371
    challenges, 363–364
    creating, 367–370
    existing approaches to, 364–365
    facetted approach, 365–366
    results, 370
facial animation, 561–569
    morphing
        CPU-based, 562–563

morph cache textures, 568–569
        morph target textures, 565–567
        overview, 562, 564–565
        vertex-shader-based, 563
    skinning, 562, 569
fading particles, 380–381
fake radiosity
    implementation, 464–465
    improvements, 465
    LIDR, 255
    light print, 463–464
    overview, 462–463
    SH coefficient blending, 464
fast fake global illumination, 455–466. *See also*
    global illumination effects
    ambient occlusion probes, 455–457
    fake radiosity, 462–465
    overview, 455
    screen-space radiosity, 462
    SSAO, 458–462
FBOs (frame buffer objects), 748
filtered importance sampling (FIS) algorithm, 346,
    358–359
filtered occlusion maps, 490
filtering
    adaptive geometry-sensitive box, 493
    bilateral, 285–287, 291–295, 338
    bilinear, 200
    box, 493
    CSMs across splits, 321–323
    directed, 285–302
        color quantization, 301
        color space conversion, 287
        flow field construction, 287–291
        orientation-aligned bilateral filter, 291–295
        separable flow-based DoG, 295–301
    GL_LINEAR mode, 546
    percentage closer, 314, 321–322
    prefiltering, 307, 321
    trilinear, 525
    visibility maps, 355–357
filters. *See also* Gaussian filter
    cross-bilateral, 439
    orientation-aligned bilateral, 291–295
    separable, 260
    Sobel, 287
    spatial-invariant, 259–262
    texture, 149, 151–152

fixed frame rate, 525
fixed-function tessellation unit, 40
fixed-point values, 603–604
flexible vertex format, 589
flickering shadow quality, 306–309
flipping, 556
floating-point render targets, 731–741
floating-point values
    Crackdown graphics techniques, 200
    extracting isosurfaces, 6
    OpenGL ES applications, 603–604
    real-time tessellation, 45, 48, 58
flow control, 536–537
flow field construction, 287–291
fmod function, 376–378
focal length, 266–267
fog, 377, 385
for loops, 122, 126
force-based erosion, 394–398
forward renderer, 226, 229, 243, 251
fragment shader
    directed filtering, 288–291, 294–295, 297–301
    importance sampling, 259, 262, 269
    OpenGL ES applications, 534
    sliced grid, 690, 692
frame buffer, 183–184, 402, 519–520, 568, 599
frame buffer objects (FBOs), 748
frame flipping, 574
frame rate, 544, 629
free-viewpoint video, 699–714
    background subtraction, 700–703
    shape-from-silhouette algorithms, 703–705
    surface extraction, 705–709
    texture mapping, 709–712
Fresnel reflectance, 169, 176, *177f*, 178–179, 184
front face method, 251–252
full-viewport quad, 491

G

gamma correction, 171
Gaussian blur, 546
Gaussian elimination, 746
Gaussian filter
    directed filtering, 288–289
    dynamic shadows, 355–356
    importance sampling, 259, 261–262, 264, 267–268
    interactive shadows, 338
Gaussian kernel, 548

Gauss-Newton optimizer, 578
G-buffer building phase, 219–221, 226, *227f*, 228–231
G-buffer writing phase, 228–229, 231, 233, 657–660
GDS (graphics development system), 679–681
generators (sites), 717
geometric factor, *461f*
geometric self-occlusion, 176, *177f*
geometry manipulation. *See also* terrain rendering
    adaptive re-meshing for displacement mapping,
        107–117
        demo, 116
        implementation of, 114–116
        LOD, 112–114
        results, 114
    isosurface extraction using geometry shaders, 3–32
        analysis, 29–32
        hybrid cubes/tetrahedra extraction, 7–29
        marching methods, 6–7
        results, 29–32
        scalar fields versus polygonal representation,
            3–6
    overview, 1–2
    quadrilateral patch tessellation, 119–129
        2D interpolation, 126–127
        3D interpolation, 124–126
        discussion, 128–129
        method, 120–123
        number of strips needed, 123
        results, 127
        strip locations, 124
        tessellating each strip, 124
    real-time GPU tessellation, 33–71
        accessing per-vertex data beyond input struc-
            ture declaration, 59
        adaptive tessellation mode, 48–51
        continuous tessellation mode, 45–48
        designing vertex evaluation shaders for, 53–58
        Direct3D 10, 60
        displacement map tips, 68–70
        lighting, 60–61
        pipeline, 37–41
        programming for, 41–45
        reducing surface cracks, 68–70
        rendering characters with, 51–53, 61–68
geometry phase, 221
geometry rendering
    with Direct3D Mobile, 591–592
    with OpenGL ES, 592–595

geometry shader (GS)
  free-viewpoint video, *707f*
  isosurface extraction using, 3–32
    analysis, 29–32
    hybrid cubes/tetrahedra extraction, 7–29
    marching methods, 6–7
    results, 29–32
    scalar fields versus polygonal representation,
      3–6
  per-pixel ambient occlusion using, 501–510
    algorithm, 502
    background, 502
    implementation of, 503–505
    results, 506–509
geometry texture, 490
ghost cells, 400, *401f*
ghosting, 528
GL_LINEAR filtering mode, 546
GlFrustum() function, 575
global illumination effects
  deferred ambient occlusion, 445–454
    from miscellaneous surfaces, 451
    optimization, 451–452
    from quads, 448–451
    from spheres, 447–448
    from triangles, 448–451
  fast fake, 455–466
    ambient occlusion probes, 455–457
    fake radiosity, 462–465
    screen-space radiosity, 462
    SSAO, 458–462
  image-space ambient occlusion, 425–444
    horizon culling, 431
    implementation of, 435–440
    input buffers for, 429
    with ray marching, 429–431
    reformulating, 431–435
    results, 440–442
    sampling hemisphere, 428
  instant radiosity, 479–494
    adaptive geometry-sensitive box filtering, 493
    algorithm, 481–482
    BIH traversal, 487–489
    deferring textures, 490
    distance impostor cube map, 490
    foundation of, 480–481
    light source sampling, 489
    lighting, 491–492
    performance, 493
    photon shooting, 489
    pyramidal occlusion maps, 490–491
    ray-triangle intersection, 484–487
    scene representation for ray tracing, 483–484
    VPL management, 490
  overview, 411–412
  per-pixel ambient occlusion, 501–510
    algorithm, 502
    background, 502
    implementation of, 503–505
    results, 506–509
  SSAO, 413–424
    approach to, 415–419
    future improvements, 423
    pixel shader, 420–423
    previous solutions, 414
    problems, 414
    results, 423–424
    variance methods for, 495–500
  subsurface-scatter maps, 467–478
    algorithm, 471–476
    creating, 471
    optimization, 474–476
    related work, 468
    rendering of translucent objects using, 471–474
    results, 476–477
    theory, 469–470
glossy surfaces, 358–359
glow, 263–265
glow effect data flow, *530f*
glow maps, 264
Gouraud shading, 321
GPUMeshMapper tool, 61, 69
gradient, 707–709
Grand Theft Auto IV (GTA4) game, 363–364, 370
graphical user interfaces. *See* GUIs
graphics development system (GDS), 679–681
Green's function, 136–137, 140
GS. *See* geometry shader
GTA4 (Grand Theft Auto IV) game, 363–364, 370
GUIs (graphical user interfaces), 543–560
  background, 552–553
  blending, 551
  blurs, 546–548
  for games, 621–625
  handheld requirements, 543–544
  lighting effects, 549–550
  mirroring, 550–551
  post-processing effects, 553–555

power consumption, 544–545
transitions, 555–560
vertex deforms, 551

H
halo fixing, 279–281
Halton series, 263
Hammersley series, 263
handheld devices
    augmented reality, 571–604
        developing, 572–581
        fixed point versus floating point, 603–604
        graphics API abstraction, 586–596
        hardware versus software rendering, 596–599
        initializing, 583–586
        platform considerations, 581–583
        scene-graph rendering, 599–601
        video and image processing, 601–603
    facial animation, 561–569
        morphing, 562–569
        skinning, 562, 569
    graphical user interfaces, 543–560
        background, 552–553
        blending, 551
        blurs, 546–548
        handheld requirements, 543–544
        lighting effects, 549–550
        mirroring, 550–551
        post-processing effects, 553–555
        power consumption, 544–545
        transitions, 555–560
        vertex deforms, 551
    OpenGL ES applications, 513–541
        fixed-function APIs, 531
        generic recommendations, 518–530
        Jadestone *Kodo Evolved*, 539–540
        mobile development, 514–518
        programmable APIs, 531–539
    overview, 511
hard outlines, *552f*
hard particles, 144
hardware AR rendering, 596–599
hardware occlusion queries, 637
HDR (high dynamic range) luminance values,
    263–264
HDR (high-dynamic-range) environment maps, 346
headlights, 201, 203–205
head-mounted displays (HMDs), 573

heads up display (HUD), 574
height fields, 205–206, 208–214, 429–430
height maps, 76, *93f*, 382–383
hemispherical projection, 405–408
Hermitian matrix, 717
hierarchical grid, 686
high dynamic range (HDR) luminance values, 263–264
high-dynamic-range (HDR) environment maps, 346
high-frequency noise, 418–419
highp modifier, 535, 537
HMD (head-mounted displays), 573
Holevo's capacity, 728
homogeneous media. *See* interactive shadows
horizon angles, *433f*
horizon culling, 431
horizon-based ambient occlusion. *See* image-space
    ambient occlusion
horizontal translation, 555
HTM (hybrid texture mapping), 710–712
HUD (heads up display), 574
hull shader, 40, 53
HWnd parameter, 586
hybrid cubes/tetrahedra extraction, 7–29
    adaptive isosurface refinement, 18
    cube tetrahedralization, 9–18
    marching tetrahedra, 18–29
    storing extraction results for re-use, 29
    voxelizing input domain, 8
hybrid texture mapping (HTM), 710–712
hydraulic erosion, 389–404
    boundaries, 400–401
    data structures, 390–392
    force-based, 394–398
    rendering, 401–402
    results, 402
    still water, 398–399
    terrain slippage, 399–400
    water movement, 392–394
hyperspace effect, 381

I
image abstraction. *See* directed filtering
image space algorithms, 257–302
    image abstraction by directed filtering, 285–302
        color quantization, 301
        color space conversion, 287
        flow field construction, 287–291
        orientation-aligned bilateral filter, 291–295
        separable flow-based DoG, 295–301

image space algorithms *(continued)*
  importance sampling, 259–276
    approach to, 260–263
    depth of field, 266–274
    glow, 263–265
    problem, 259–260
    tone mapping, 263–265
    versus uniform sampling, 275–276
  motion blur, 277–283
    CPU-side work, 278
    GPU-side work, 278–279
    halo fixing, 279–281
    hardware limitations, 282
    integration with post-processing pipeline, 282
  weather effects, 375
image-based lighting, 345–362
  algorithms, 346
  diffuse surfaces, 357
  environment map importance sampling, 346–349
  glossy surfaces, 358–359
  related work, 346
  results, 359–360
  visibility map generation, 349–357
image-space ambient occlusion, 425–444
  horizon culling, 431
  implementation of
    angle bias, 438
    combining with color buffer, 435–436
    cross-bilateral filter, 439
    eye-space tangent vectors, 437–438
    jittering, 436
    lower resolution, 440
    multisample antialiasing, 439
    per-pixel normals, 435
    variable step size, 437
  input buffers for
    depth image, 429
    normals, 429
  overview, 425–428
  with ray marching, 429–431
  reformulating, 431–435
  results, 440–442
  sampling hemisphere, 428
Imagination Technologies, 514, 529
implicit surface representation, 4
importance sampling, 259–276
  approach to, 260–263
  depth of field, 266–274

  filtered, 346, 358–359
  glow, 263–265
  overview, 259
  problem, 259–260
  tone mapping, 263–265
  versus uniform sampling, 275–276
incremental horizon angle, 433
indexed geometry, 532–533
indirect photon mapping. *See* **instant radiosity**
indirect shadows, *493f*
inline functions, 587
input buffers, 429
instanced geometry, 194
INSTANCEID semantic, 704
instant radiosity, 479–494
  adaptive geometry-sensitive box filtering, 493
  algorithm, 481–482
  BIH traversal, 487–489
  deferring textures, 490
  distance impostor cube map, 490
  foundation of, 480–481
  light source sampling, 489
  lighting, 491–492
  overview, 479
  performance, 493
  photon shooting, 489
  pyramidal occlusion maps, 490–491
  ray-triangle intersection, 484–487
  scene representation for ray tracing, 483–484
  VPL management, 490
Intel VTune Thread Profiler, 617–619
interactive shadows, 331–344
  hybrid approach to, 335–336
  implementation of, 338–342
  participating media, 332–334
  results, 342
  textured light sources, 336–338
interleaved attributes, 526–527
interleaved sampling, 273
interleaved strip-order geometry submission, 531
internal vertices, 126
interpolating subdivision, 51–52
interpolation
  2D, 126–127
  3D, 124–126
  bilinear, 135, 321
  Bresenham, 125–126
  linear, 669
  perspective, 319–320

interpolation parameter, 750
interpolative subdivision, 74–75
I-queue, 641, 644, 647, 650
irradiance volume technique, 463
isosurface extraction, 3–32. *See also* hybrid
    cubes/tetrahedra extraction
    analysis, 29–32
    marching methods, 6–7
    results, 29–32
    scalar fields versus polygonal representation, 3–6
isovalues, 4, 29

J

Jadestone *Kodo Evolved* game, *521f–522f*, 539–540
jaggy edges, 224
Java applications, 581–582
jittering, *357f*, 436, 474

K

Kajalin, Vladimir, 411
Kelemen-Szirmay-Kalos model, 169–170
KernelSize parameter, 458
keys, 264
Khronos API interfaces, 527. *See also* OpenGL ES
    applications
Ki, Hyunwoo, 411
Killzone 2 game, 657
Kodo Evolved game, *521f–522f*, 539–540

L

Laçador data set, *127f*
Lambertian reflectance, 181
Laplacian-of-Gaussian, 295–296
layer masks, 391–392
layouts, 621, *622f*
LDR (low dynamic range) luminance values, 263
least significant bits (LSBs), 735
levels of detail (LODs)
    adaptive re-meshing for displacement mapping,
      112–114
    quadrilateral patch tessellation for, 119–129
      2D interpolation to tessellate strips, 126–127
      3D interpolation to place triangle strips,
        124–126
      method, 120–123
      number of strips needed, 123
      results, 127

      strip locations, 124
      tessellating each strip, 124
    subsurface-scatter maps, 475–476
    vertex shaders, 524
LIDR. *See* light-indexed deferred rendering
light bins, 673–674
light blending, *670f–671f*
light index geometry lighting, 249–250
light index packing
    bit shifting, 247–249
    CPU sorting, 244–245
    multi-pass max blend equation, 245–246
light maps, 164, 166–169
light pre-pass renderer, 655–676
    applying different materials with, 665–666
    bending specular reflection rules, 663–664
    CIE Luv color space, 667–676
      colors, 668–671
      grouping and rendering lights, 672–675
      integrating into light accumulation, 675–676
      light buffer format, 671–672
      reasons for using, 668
    deferred renderer, 657–659
    diffuse term
      converting to luminance, 663
      storing additional, 662–663
    Z pre-pass renderer, 655–657
light print, 463–464
light source sampling, 489
light-indexed deferred rendering (LIDR), 243–256
    combining with other techniques, 250
    concept of, 243–244
    constraining lights to surfaces, 253–254
    future work, 255
    light index geometry lighting, 249–250
    light index packing, 245–249
    MSAA, 250–252
    multi-light type support, 254
    overview, 243
    shadows, 252–253
    technique comparison, 254–255
    transparency, 252
lighting. *See specific types of lighting by name*
lightning, 385
limit surface, 51
linear inheritance, *612f*
linear interpolation, 669
load-balancing. *See* automatic load-balancing
local illumination model, 175

local radiosity effect, 462
lock-unlock scheme, 615
LODs. *See* levels of detail
Lod parameter, 557
lookup tables, 7, 138, 183, 249
lossless conversion, *736f*
low dynamic range (LDR) luminance values, 263
low tessellated mesh, *438f*
low-discrepancy series, 263
lowp modifier, 536
LSBs (least significant bits), 735
Lua front-end rendering engine functionality, 9–10
Luv color space. *See* CIE Luv color space

M

macro state objects, 610
magic lens method, 573
mantissa bits, 734
maps. *See also* CSMs; displacement mapping;
    facetted shadow mapping; subsurface scatter-
    ing; subsurface-scatter maps; texture maps;
    visibility maps
    cube, 313, *549f–550f*
    distance impostor cube, 490
    environment, 184, 346–349
    filtered occlusion, 490
    glow, 264
    HDR environment, 346
    height, 76, *93f*, 382–383
    hybrid texture mapping, 710–712
    light, 164, 166–169
    parallel-split shadow, 305, 365
    parallel-split variance shadow, 323–325
    pyramidal depth impostor cube, *492f*
    pyramidal displacement, 481
    pyramidal occlusion, 490–491
    rich shadow, 468
    shadow, 253, 341–342, 364–365, 498
    specular, 170
    split shadow, 365
    tangent flow, 288–289
    tangent-space normal, 60–61
    tone mapping, 263–265
    variance, 498–499
    variance shadow, 341–342, 498
    view-dependent texture mapping, 709–710
    view-independent texture mapping, 709–710
    warped shadow, 364–365

marching cubes (MC) algorithm, 4–8
marching methods, 6–7
marching tetrahedra (MT) algorithm, 4–8, 18–29
marker pattern unprojection, 578
Marr and Hildreth edge detector, 295
massively parallel processing, 1, 3
math look-up textures, 533
MATLAB camera calibration toolbox, 574
matrix stacks, 595–596
MC (marching cubes) algorithm, 4–8
MCTs (morph cache textures), 568–569
mediump modifier, 535
mesh vertices, 39, 51, 107
meshes. *See also* adaptive re-meshing; control
    mesh primitives
    base, 107–110, 119–120, 562
    low tessellated, *438f*
    tetrahedral, 6, 8
    transforming using R2VB, 79–83
Microsoft Windows Mobile, 583–584
Microsoft Windows XP, 583–584
minification filter mode, 524
mipmap banding, 525
mipmap blur transitions, 556–557
mipmapping, 152, 321–322, 523–525
mirroring, 550–551
mobile phones, 581–582. *See also* handheld devices
Moltke crater, *96f*
Monte Carlo sampling, 430–431, 472
Moore-Penrose pseudo-inverse, 352–353
moria scene, *265f, 269f*
morph cache textures (MCTs), 568–569
morph target textures (MTTs), 565–567
morph targets, 562, 564
morphing
    CPU-based, 562–563
    MCT, 568–569
    MTTs, 565–567
    overview, 562, 564–565
    thin-plate spline, 743–752
        implementation of, 747–750
        interactive, 750–752
        TPS warping, 744–747
    vertex-shader-based, 563
motion blur, 277–283
    CPU-side work, 278
    GPU-side work, 278–279
    halo fixing, 279–281
    hardware limitations, 282

integration with post-processing pipeline, 282
weather effects, 378–381
movement transitions, 556
**MRTs (multiple render targets), 228–229, 657–658,
660**
MSAA. *See* **multisampling anti-aliasing**
MT (marching tetrahedra) algorithm, 4–8, 18–29
MTTs (morph target textures), 565–567
multi-light type support, 254
multi-pass max blend equation, 244–246
multi-pass rendering, 528–530
**multiple render targets (MRTs), 228–229, 657–658,
660**
multiple scattering, *476f*
multiqueries
cost-benefit heuristics for, 648–649
estimating visibility coherence, 648
overview, 647
multisampling anti-aliasing (MSAA)
deferred renderer, 659
deferred shading with, 225–242
implementation of, 231–240
principles of, 226–227
requirements for, 227–230
image-space horizon-based ambient occlusion,
439
LIDR, 250–252

N

naïve blur, *439f*
NativeWindowType parameter, 598
negation, 554–555
negative distance, 449
network receiving, 574
network sending, 573
non-edge pixels, 239
nonindexed rendering, 49
non-power-of-two (NPOT) textures, 523
nonuniform sampling, 262
non-virtual, non-inline methods, 587
normal-oriented hemisphere, *426f, 432f*
NPOT (non-power-of-two) textures, 523

O

obscurance, 270–274
occluder search, *492f*
occlusion, 415–416, 578–581
occlusion boxes, 382–383

occlusion culling, 637–653
batching, 641–643
coherent hierarchical culling, 638–641
game engine integration, 643–644
multiqueries, 647–649
skipping tests for visible nodes, 645
tighter bounding volumes, 646–647
off-axis projection camera, 574–576
offline content preparation, 628
off-screen AR rendering, 598–599
offset problem, 308–309
on-axis camera, *575f*
1D blur, 546–547
one-to-many relationship, 610
on-screen AR rendering, 597–598
OpenGL ES applications, 513–541
coordinate systems, 595
fixed-function APIs
interleaved strip-order geometry submission,
531
lighting model, 531
generic recommendations
alpha blending, 525–526
alpha testing, 522–523, 525–526
arrays, 526–527
batching primitives, 520
benchmarking, 518–519
buffer copies, 528–530
discard operations, 522–523, 525–526
fixed frame rate, 525
frame buffer, accessing from CPU, 519–520
interleaved attributes, 526–527
mid-scene texture updates, 527–528
mipmapping, 523–525
mixing 2D and 3D, 527
multi-pass, 528–530
opaque objects, 525–526
rough object culling, 520–522
texture compression, 523–525
geometry rendering
using vertex arrays, 592–593
using vertex buffer objects, 593–595
initializing, 584–585
Jadestone *Kodo Evolved*, 539–540
mobile development
battery life, 516
cross-platform, 514
limited bandwidth, 516–517
optimization utilities, 517–518

OpenGL ES applications *(continued)*
    variable graphics feature levels, 515
    variable performance levels, 515–516
    programmable APIs
        indexed geometry, 532–533
        optimizing shaders, 533–539
        per-vertex calculations, 531–532
        vertex buffer objects, 532–533
    vertex arrays, 590
    vertex buffer objects, 590
OpenVG interface, 527
optimization utilities, 517–518
orientation-aligned bilateral filter, 291–295
orthogonal projection, 438
outflows, 392–394, 399
outlines, 198–201
over-darkening, 447, 497, *506f*
over-tessellated geometry, 531–532

P
parallax shader, 198
parallel-split shadow maps (PSSMs), 305, 365
parallel-split variance shadow maps (PSVSMs),
    323–325
parametric coordinates, 37–38, 122
participating media, 331–334
particle-based simulation, 685–697
    results, 693–697
    sliced grid, 686–693
    weather effects, 375–378
partitioning, 210–211
PDFs (probability density functions), 469, 498
percentage closer filtering (PCF), 314, 321–322
per-edge tessellation factors, 38–39, 78, 85–92
Perlin noise, 133, 137–138
per-object motion blur, 277
per-pixel ambient occlusion
    image-space horizon-based, 428, 435
    using geometry shaders, 501–510
        algorithm, 502
        background, 502
        implementation of, 503–505
        overview, 501
        results, 506–509
per-pixel light comparison, *532f*
per-pixel normals, 435
per-pixel shading, 227, *241f*

per-sample shading, 227, 229–230, 236–239, *241f*
perspective projections, 438
perspective interpolation, 319–320
per-vertex data, 59, 531–532
per-vertex encoding range, *566f*
per-vertex light comparison, *532f*
per-vertex smoothed normals, 435
phantom objects, 580–581
photo UI transitions
    burn, 558–560
    mipmap blur, 556–557
    movement, 556
    swirl, 558
photon shooting, 489
photon tracing, 481
PID (proportional, integral, and derivative)
    control, *628f*, 629–633
pixel shader
    Crackdown graphics techniques, 204–205
    deferred rendering transparency, 219–222
    deferred shading, 227–239
    motion blur, 278, 280, 282
    multiplicative AO probes, 457
    real-time tessellation, 33–34
    selecting LOD level, 476
    shadows, 306, 315–317, 354–356
    soft particles, 145
    SSAO, 420–423
    weather effects, 383
pixelated blur transitions, 556–557
PixMap, 598
planar projection, 405–408
platform graphic API calls, 616–617
PMFs (probability mass functions), 347–348
polar coordinates, 268
polar effects, 553–554
polygonal patches, 74, 76
polygonal representation, 3–6
pose estimation, 573, 576–578
pose tracking, 601
positive distance, 449
post-blur step, *419f*
post-processing effects
    blurring, 553
    color transform, 555
    negation, 554–555
    swirl, 553–554
potentially visible sets (PVSes), 628–629

power consumption
    bandwidth-reducing algorithms, 545
    dirty regions, 545
    limiting frame rate, 544
    update on-demand, 544
POWERVR SGX, 534
POWERVR shell, 514
precipitation, 375–386
precomputed radiance transfer (PRT), 357, 465
prefiltering, 307, 321
preprocessing, 414, 629
pre-render actions, 573
pre-rendered glow texture overlay, *530f*
probability density functions (PDFs), 469, 498
probability mass functions (PMFs), 347–348
progressive blur, 548
Project Gotham Racing 4* game, 375, *376f
proportional, integral, and derivative (PID) control, *628f*, 629–633
PRT (precomputed radiance transfer), 357, 465
PSSMs (parallel-split shadow maps), 305, 365
PSVSMs (parallel-split variance shadow maps), 323–325
push-pull up sampling, 452
***PVRUniSCo* offline shader compiler, 534**
PVS (potentially visible sets), 628–629
pyramidal depth impostor cube maps, *492f*
pyramidal displacement maps, 481
pyramidal occlusion maps, 490–491

Q
quadrilateral patches, tessellation of, 119–129
    2D interpolation, 126–127
    3D interpolation, 124–126
    method, 120–123
    number of strips needed, 123
    results, 127
    strip locations, 124
    tessellating each strip, 124
quadrilaterals, 448–451, 577
quality scaling, *519f*
quantized SH coefficients, 465
quantum channel, 728
quantum Voronoi diagrams
    for mixed states, 723–728
    overview, 717–719
    for pure states, 719–723
query alignment, 645
query queue, 638, 641, *644f*

Quick Noise, 133–141
    background, 133–134
    future work, 140
    implementation of, 138–140
    limitations, 137
    math, 134–135
    real world application, 135–137
    results, 140
QuickNoiseSmall HLSL function, 136

R
R2VB extension, 49, 79–84
radiance transfer, 346
radiosity, 462. *See also* fake radiosity; instant radiosity
randomization, 645
randomly rotated kernel, 418–419
raw packing, 736–737
ray casting, 29, 69
ray marching, 205, 332, 335–338, 343, 429–431
ray tracing, 271, 416, 480–484
ray-triangle intersection, 484–487
RbfCoef array, 748
real-time GPU tessellation, 33–71
    accessing per-vertex data beyond input structure declaration, 59
    adaptive tessellation mode, 48–51
    character rendering with, 51–53, 61–68
    continuous tessellation mode, 45–48
    designing vertex evaluation shaders for, 53–58
    Direct3D 10, 60
    displacement map tips, 68–70
    lighting, 60–61
    pipeline for, 37–41
    programming for, 41–45
    reducing surface cracks, 68–70
    terrain rendering, 73–106
        per-edge tessellation factors, 83–92
        performance analysis, 103–105
        programming for, 76–79
        shading tessellated displaced surfaces, 93–103
        transforming meshes using R2VB, 79–83
real-time shading model, 175–187
    Blinn-Phong model, 176–177, 186
    Cook-Torrance model, 176–177, 186–187
    diffuse reflection of two-hemisphere, 185
    improvements, 179–180
    light-surface interaction, 178–179
    mathematical formulation, 180–185

reconstruction step, 109
recursive subdivision, 111, *112f*
refraction shader, 529
refractive index, 178
regolith, 391, 398–399
render queue, 644
rendering techniques, 131–257
  anti-aliased lines, 149–159
    abstract, 149
    method, 150
    shader code, 155–159
    texture creation, 150–152
    variations, 154–155
    vertex setup, 152–154
  Crackdown graphics techniques, 189–215
    clutter, 193–198
    deferred rendering, 201–205
    outlines, 198–201
    sky, 190–192
    texture map setup, 209–214
    vehicle reflections, 205–209
  deferred rendering transparency, 217–224
    composition phase, 221–223
    future work, 224
    geometry phase, 221
    results, 221–224
    transparency, 218–219
  deferred shading with MSAA, 225–242
    implementation of, 231–240
    principles of, 226–227
    requirements for, 227–230
  LIDR, 243–256
    combining with other techniques, 250
    concept of, 243–244
    constraining lights to surfaces, 253–254
    future work, 255
    light index geometry lighting, 249–250
    light index packing, 244–249
    multi-light type support, 254
    multi-sample anti-aliasing, 250–252
    shadows, 252–253
    technique comparison, 254–255
    transparency, 252
  Quick Noise for GPUs, 133–141
    background, 133–134
    future work, 140
    implementation of, 138–140
    limitations, 137

    math, 134–135
    real world application, 135–137
    results, 140
  real-time shading model, 175–187
    Blinn-Phong model, 176–177, 186
    Cook-Torrance model, 176–177, 186–187
    diffuse reflection of two-hemisphere, 185
    improvements, 179–180
    light-surface interaction, 178–179
    mathematical formulation, 180–185
  skin shading, 161–173
    background, 162–163
    data preparation, 171–172
    diffuse lighting, 163–169
    existing art, 162–163
    specular lighting, 169–170
    variation across face, 170–171
  soft particles, 143–147
    versus hard particles, 144
    implementation of, 145
    optimizing, 145–146
    results, 146
rendering thread. *See* **cross-platform rendering thread**
RenderTarget state, 610
render to texture, 548
RGB color space, 667–675
RGB24 pixel format, 602–603
RGB32 pixel format, 602–603
RGB565 pixel format, 602–603
RGBA light accumulation buffer, 671
rich shadow maps, 468
rigid-body transformations, 556
Roberto head, *167f, 170f*
rocky scene, *274f*
rough object culling, 520–522

S
SAH (surface area heuristics), 480
Sainz, Miguel, 411
sampling, 458, *459f–461f*
scalability, 35
scalar data sets, 5
scalar fields, 3–6
scene complexity, 414
scene-depth information, *579f*
scene-graph rendering, 599–601
screen-space indirect lighting solution (SSIL), 423

screen-space ambient occlusion (SSAO), 413–424
approach to, 415–419
fast fake global illumination, 458–462
future improvements, 423
instant radiosity, 481
overview, 427–428
pixel shader, 420–423
previous solutions, 414
problems, 414
results, 423–424
variance methods for, 495–500
screen-space radiosity (SSRad), 462
scrolling, 556
searchlights, 204
self-ambient occlusion, 455
semi-Lagrangian advection, 398
separable filters, 260
server deferred destruction, 616
SH (spherical harmonics), 350–351, 355, 357–358, 463–464
shader compilers, 534. *See also specific shaders by name*
shader-level mechanisms, 627–628
shading normals, storing, 487
shading passes, 235
shading tessellated displaced surfaces, 93–103
shadow maps, 253, 341–342, 364–365, 498. *See also* CSMs; facetted shadow mapping; subsurface scattering
shadow shafts, 332
shadow volumes, 253, 332–335, 341, 343
shadows, 303–371
combined, 252–253
CSMs, 305–329
analytic method, 325–328
approximated solution, 311–313
exact solution, 309–311
filtering across splits, 321–323
flickering of shadow quality, 307–309
non-optimized split selection, 315–317
PSVSMS, 324–325
storage strategy, 313–315
texture coordinate computation, 317–321
facetted shadow mapping, 363–371
challenges, 363–364
creating, 367–370
existing approaches to, 364–365
facetted approach, 365–366
results, 370

for image-based lighting, 345–362
algorithms, 346
diffuse surfaces, 357
environment map importance sampling, 346–349
glossy surfaces, 358–359
related work, 346
results, 359–360
visibility map generation, 349–357
interactive, 331–344
hybrid approach to, 335–336
implementation of, 338–342
participating media, 332–334
results, 342
textured light sources, 336–338
Shannon entropy, 716
shape-from-silhouette algorithms, 703–705
Sibenik Cathedral data set, 440
sign bit, 734
silhouette cones, intersection of, *703f*
SIMD (single-instruction, multiple-data) units, 6–7
single depth buffer, 416
single scattering, 467, *476f*, 477
single-channel discontinuity buffer, 453
single-instruction, multiple-data (SIMD) units, 6–7
singular value decomposition (SVD), 577
sites (generators), 717
6DOF pose, 578
skin shading, 161–173
background, 162–163
data preparation, 171–172
diffuse lighting, 163–169
existing art, 162–163
specular lighting, 169–170
variation across face, 170–171
skinning, 562, 569
sky representation, 190–192, 405–409
sliced grid, 686–693
bounding boxes, 689–690
data structure, 689
indices of first voxels, 691–692
storing and reading values, 693
smart pointer, 616
smoothed particle hydrodynamics (SPH), 693–696
SmoothStep function, 151
snapped directions, *436f*
SoA (struct of arrays), 526
Sobel filter, 287

soft particles, 143–147
    versus hard particles, 144
    implementation of, 145
    optimizing, 145–146
    results, 146
software AR rendering, 596–599
solid geometry, 416, *417f*
sound, weather effect, 386
space station scene, *274f*
space-filling curve approach, 565
spatial aliasing, 308
spatial hierarchy, 638, 646
spatial-invariant filters, 259–262
specular highlight, 182, 186, 549–550
specular lighting
    real-time shading, 176–178, 184, *185t*
    skin shading, 169–170
specular maps, 170
specular reflections, 661–664
SPH (smoothed particle hydrodynamics), 693–696
spheres, 447–448
spherical coordinates, 62
spherical harmonics (SH), 350–351, 355, 357–358,
    463–464
spherical projection, 405–408
Spherical2Cartesian function, 720
split indices, 324–325
split selection, 315–317
split shadow maps, 365
sprites, 624
SSAO. *See* **screen-space ambient occlusion**
SSIL (screen space indirect lighting solution), 423
SSMs. *See* **subsurface-scatter maps**
SSRad (screen-space radiosity), 462
stack-using kd-tree traversal technique, 487
standard deviation, 260, 262, 267
Stanford Dragon data set, 440
state changes, 641–643
state machine, 610
state objects, 615
static flow control, 537
static geometry processing, 414
stencil buffer, 278–279
stencil test, 227, 235–236, 238
step size, 437
still water erosion, 398–399
storing extraction results, 29
stream-out feature, 5, 39, 60
streetlights, 201, 203–204

struct of arrays (SoA), 526
structure tensor, 286, 288–289
subdivision surfaces, 52
subsurface scattering
    fast skin shading, 162, 164, 166, 168, 170–172
    real-time shading, 178
    using shadow maps, 467–478
        algorithm, 471–476
        overview, 467–468
        related work, 468
        results, 476–477
        theory, 469–470
subsurface-scatter maps (SSMs), 467–478
    algorithm, 471–476
    creating, 471
    optimization, 474–476
    related work, 468
    rendering of translucent objects using, 471–474
    results, 476–477
    theory, 469–470
superprimitives (superprims). *See* **control mesh**
    primitives
surface area heuristics (SAH), 480
surface extraction, 705–709
SVD (singular value decomposition), 577
swap interval, 525
swimming, 306
swirl effects, 553–554
swirl transitions, 558
Symbian application, 584
synchronization, 613–614
system values, 236
Szécsi, László, 412

T

tangent field, 288–289
tangent flow map (tfm), 288–289
tangent-binormal-normal (TBN) basis, 430
tangent-space normal maps (TSNMs), 60–61
TBDR (tile-based deferred rendering), 516
TBN (tangent-binormal-normal) basis, 430
terrain rendering, 73–106
    per-edge tessellation factors, 83–92
    performance analysis, 103–105
    programming for, 76–79
    shading tessellated displaced surfaces, 93–103
    transforming meshes using R2VB, 79–83
terrain slippage, 399–400

tessellation. *See also* **terrain rendering**
  on-the-fly, 119
  of quadrilateral patches, 119–129
    2D interpolation to tessellate strips, 126–127
    3D interpolation to place triangle strips, 124–126
    method, 120–123
    number of strips needed, 123
    overview, 119–120
    results, 127
    strip locations, 124
    tessellating each strip, 124
  querying for support, 41–43
  real-time GPU, 33–71
    accessing per-vertex data beyond input structure declaration, 59
    adaptive tessellation mode, 48–51
    character rendering with, 51–53, 61–68
    continuous tessellation mode, 45–48
    designing vertex evaluation shaders for, 53–58
    Direct3D 10, 60
    displacement map tips, 68–70
    lighting, 60–61
    pipeline for, 37–41
    programming for, 41–45
    reducing surface cracks, 68–70
tetrahedra, 6. *See also* **hybrid cubes/tetrahedra extraction**
texture arrays, 313
texture atlas, *314f*, 384
texture bombing, 198
texture compression, 523–525
texture coordinates
  correct computation of, 317–321
  CSMs, 306
  math lookup textures, 533
  snapping, 432
  tessellation pipeline, 40
texture fetch, 656
texture maps
  clutter, 194–195
  Crackdown, 209–214
  hybrid, 710–712
  view-independent versus view-dependent, 709–710
  visibility tests, 712
texture space, 110, 112
texture space diffusion, 162
texture twiddle, 545
Texture2DLod GLSL ES function, 524
textured light sources, 336–338

tfm (tangent flow map), 288–289
thick-layer approach, 586
thin-layer approach, 586
thin-plate spline (TPS) image morphing, 743–752
  implementation of, 747–750
  interactive, 750–752
  TPS warping, 744–747
3D engine design
  automatic load-balancing, 627–634
    approach to, 629–631
    GPU requirements, 633
    performance, 629
    problems, 627–628
    results, 632–633
    user inconvenience, 628–629
    workflow, 632
  cross-platform rendering thread, 607–620
    abstraction design, 608–609
    command buffer, 609, 620
    command objects, 609
    driver execution process, 611
    implementation, 612–617
    macro state objects, 610
    multiple client and server threads, 619
    results, 617–618
    state machine, 610
    threading design, 608
    triple buffering, 618–619
  Elemental Engine II, 679–681
  GUIs for games, 621–625
  light pre-pass renderer, 655–676
    applying different materials with, 665–666
    bending specular reflection rules, 663–664
    CIE Luv color space, 667–676
    deferred renderer, 657–659
    diffuse term, 662–663
    overview, 660–662
    Z pre-pass renderer, 655–657
  occlusion culling, 637–653
    coherent, 638–641
    game engine integration, 643–644
    multiqueries, 647–649
    reducing state changes, 641–643
    skipping tests for visible nodes, 645
    tighter bounding volumes, 646–647
  overview, 605
3D interpolation, 124–126
thresholding, 299, 559, *577f*
Tikhonov regularization, 353

tile-based deferred rendering (TBDR), 516
tiling, 201
T-junctions, 120
tone mapping, 263–265
torus topology, 400
TPS. *See* thin-plate spline image morphing
transitions, 555–560
translucency, 218, *476f*
transparency, 252. *See also* deferred rendering
    transparency
triangle strips, 121–126
triangle texture, 484
triangles, 448–451
trilinear filtering, 525
triple buffering, 618–619
TSNMs (tangent-space normal maps), 60–61
twiddled layout, 528
twirl effect, 553
2D blur, 547–548
2D interpolation, 126–127

U

UILayout class, 622–624
uniform grid, 686
uniform sampling, 275–276
uniform subdivision, 107–109
Unigine project, 305, *306f*
unpacking code, 736–737
unsharp masking, 497
update on-demand, 544
upsampling, 452–453
uv coordinates, 38, 40, 63, 353

V

variance maps, 498–499
variance shadow maps (VSMs), 341–342, 498
VBOs (vertex buffer objects), 532–533, 590
VDTM (view-dependent texture mapping), 709–710
vector floating point (VFP) units, 603
vehicle reflections, 205–209
velocity buffer, 277
vertex arrays, 590
vertex buffer, 194, 589
vertex buffer objects (VBOs), 532–533, 590
vertex deformations, 551, 555
vertex evaluation shaders, 53–58
vertex IDs, 9, 60, 62, 81, 84
vertex ordering, *706f*

vertex shader (VS)
    anti-aliased lines, 152–153, 155–159
    extracting isosurfaces, 5–6, 8–9
    rendering adaptively tessellated terrain, 90–93
    rendering to facets, 368
    for rendering with displacement mapping, 54–55
    shape-from-silhouette algorithms, 704
    sliced grid, 689
    tessellation, 37–38
    transforming mesh, 79
    visibility map generation, 354
    weather effects, 376, 379–380
vertex-shader-based morphing, 563
vertical blur, 224
very long instruction word (VLIW) hardware
    targets, 451
VFP (vector floating point) units, 603
video processing, 601–603. *See also* free-viewpoint
    video
video stream extensions, *545f*
view-dependent texture mapping (VDTM), 709–710
view-independent texture mapping (VITM), 709–710
virtual methods, 587
virtual point light (VPL) management, 490
virtual-pipe model, 392, 399
visibility coherence, 647–648
visibility function, 350–352
visibility maps, 349–357
    filtering, 355–357
    GPU implementation of, 353–355
    overview, 346
    spherical harmonics, 351
    theory, 352–353
visibility tests, 271, 502, 712
Visible Human Project data set, 29–30, *31f*
visual artifacts, 417
visual hull, 703
VITM (view-independent texture mapping),
    709–710
VLIW (very long instruction word) hardware
    targets, 451
volume rendering techniques, 4
volume shader, 715–729
    Holevo's capacity, 728
    quantum channel, 728
    quantum Voronoi diagrams, 717–728
    Von Neumann quantum entropy, 716–717
volumetric data sets, 4, 8
Von Neumann quantum entropy, 716–717

Voronoi bisectors, 723
Voronoi cells, 717
Voronoi diagrams, 717–728
voxelizing input domain, 8
VPL (virtual point light) management, 490
V-queue, 642, *644f*, 650
VS. *See* vertex shader
VSMs (variance shadow maps), 341–342, 498
VTune Thread Profiler, 617–619

W
warped shadow maps, 364–365
water movement, 392–394
water sinks, 390
weather effects, 375–387
    artist-controlled, 384
    motion-blurred particles, 378–381
    occlusion, 382–383
    particle simulation, 376–378
Wetzel, Mikey, 589
widgets, 621, *622f*
wind, 384–385
Window() method, 584
Windows Mobile, 583–584
Windows XP, 583–584
Winner function, 720
WinnerColor function, 720
world space, *377f*, 458
WorldMachine terrain modeling software, 93–103

X–Z
Xenon texture sampling mode, 208

YUV pixel formats, 602–603

Z culling, 655, 659
Z pre-pass, 420, 655–657
Z-buffer, 497, 580

License Agreement/Notice of Limited Warranty

By opening the sealed disc container in this book, you agree to the following terms and conditions. If, upon reading the following license agreement and notice of limited warranty, you cannot agree to the terms and conditions set forth, return the unused book with unopened disc to the place where you purchased it for a refund.

License:

The enclosed software is copyrighted by the copyright holder(s) indicated on the software disc. You are licensed to copy the software onto a single computer for use by a single user and to a backup disc. You may not reproduce, make copies, or distribute copies or rent or lease the software in whole or in part, except with written permission of the copyright holder(s). You may transfer the enclosed disc only together with this license, and only if you destroy all other copies of the software and the transferee agrees to the terms of the license. You may not decompile, reverse assemble, or reverse engineer the software.

Notice of Limited Warranty:

The enclosed disc is warranted by Course Technology to be free of physical defects in materials and workmanship for a period of sixty (60) days from end user's purchase of the book/disc combination. During the sixty-day term of the limited warranty, Course Technology will provide a replacement disc upon the return of a defective disc.

Limited Liability:

THE SOLE REMEDY FOR BREACH OF THIS LIMITED WARRANTY SHALL CONSIST ENTIRELY OF REPLACEMENT OF THE DEFECTIVE DISC. IN NO EVENT SHALL COURSE TECHNOLOGY OR THE AUTHOR BE LIABLE FOR ANY OTHER DAMAGES, INCLUDING LOSS OR CORRUPTION OF DATA, CHANGES IN THE FUNCTIONAL CHARACTERISTICS OF THE HARDWARE OR OPERATING SYSTEM, DELETERIOUS INTERACTION WITH OTHER SOFTWARE, OR ANY OTHER SPECIAL, INCIDENTAL, OR CONSEQUENTIAL DAMAGES THAT MAY ARISE, EVEN IF COURSE TECHNOLOGY AND/OR THE AUTHOR HAS PREVIOUSLY BEEN NOTIFIED THAT THE POSSIBILITY OF SUCH DAMAGES EXISTS.

Disclaimer of Warranties:

COURSE TECHNOLOGY AND THE AUTHOR SPECIFICALLY DISCLAIM ANY AND ALL OTHER WARRANTIES, EITHER EXPRESS OR IMPLIED, INCLUDING WARRANTIES OF MERCHANTABILITY, SUITABILITY TO A PARTICULAR TASK OR PURPOSE, OR FREEDOM FROM ERRORS. SOME STATES DO NOT ALLOW FOR EXCLUSION OF IMPLIED WARRANTIES OR LIMITATION OF INCIDENTAL OR CONSEQUENTIAL DAMAGES, SO THESE LIMITATIONS MIGHT NOT APPLY TO YOU.

Other:

This Agreement is governed by the laws of the State of Massachusetts without regard to choice of law principles. The United Convention of Contracts for the International Sale of Goods is specifically disclaimed. This Agreement constitutes the entire agreement between you and Course Technology regarding use of the software.